Social Knowledge in the Making

Social Knowledge in the Making

Edited by
CHARLES CAMIC,
NEIL GROSS, AND
MICHÈLE LAMONT

The University of Chicago Press
Chicago and London

Charles Camic is the John Evans Professor of Sociology at Northwestern
University and the author or editor of several volumes, including, most
recently, *Essential Writings of Thorstein Veblen*. Neil Gross is associate professor of sociology at the University of British Columbia and the author of
Richard Rorty: The Making of an American Philosopher. Michèle Lamont is the
Robert I. Goldman Professor of European Studies, professor of sociology, and
professor of African and African-American studies at Harvard University. Her
most recent book is *How Professors Think: Inside the Curious World of Academic
Judgment*.

The University of Chicago Press, Chicago 60637
The University of Chicago Press, Ltd., London
© 2011 by The University of Chicago
All rights reserved. Published 2011.
Printed in the United States of America

20 19 18 17 16 15 14 13 12 11   1 2 3 4 5

ISBN-13: 978-0-226-09208-9 (cloth)
ISBN-13: 978-0-226-09209-6 (paper)
ISBN-10: 0-226-09208-9 (cloth)
ISBN-10: 0-226-09209-7 (paper)

Library of Congress Cataloging-in-Publication Data
    Social Knowledge in the making / edited by Charles Camic, Neil Gross, and
Michèle Lamont.
        p.   cm.
    Includes bibliographical references and index.
    ISBN-13: 978-0-226-09208-9 (cloth : alk. paper)
    ISBN-10: 0-226-09208-9 (cloth : alk. paper)
    ISBN-13: 978-0-226-09209-6 (pbk. : alk. paper)
    ISBN-10: 0-226-09209-7 (pbk. : alk. paper)   1. Social sciences—Research.
2. Knowledge, Sociology of.   I. Camic, Charles.   II. Gross, Neil, 1971–
III. Lamont, Michèle, 1957–
    H62.S635 2011
    301.01—dc22   2011001799

To our students—past, present, and future

CONTENTS

This book concerns the thick underbrush of practices that are involved in the production, evaluation, and application of social knowledge, and in working on the project we have grown increasingly cognizant of the many knowledge practices that we ourselves engaged in along the way. Our computers at this point store thousands of emails sent back and forth among the three of us—and to and from dozens of others who have been associated with this volume in different capacities—as we formulated, rethought, and frequently recast our plans in view of an ever-changing web of intellectual and logistical challenges and opportunities.

The project originated in 2004 from a series of chance conversations that made us realize that we shared a sense of frustration. As sociologists, we had a common area of research interest: knowledge production and evaluation in the social sciences and the humanities. As we talked among ourselves, however, we were struck that one of the main sources of intellectual sustenance for each of us was the vibrant body of scholarship that dealt with knowledge production, assessment, and use in the natural sciences. Each of us, of course, had works that we greatly admired that addressed the development of knowledge in the social sciences and the humanities. Still, we felt that there was a marked disparity and that scholars in the field of science studies and related areas of contemporary research offered revealing insights into the production and evaluation of natural knowledge that had fewer counterparts in studies of social knowledge. For some time, we were unclear as to the reasons for this disparity and even less clear about what, if anything, might be done about it.

Eventually, we became convinced that at least part of the problem lay in the fact that the much-heralded "turn to practice" had, up to this time, penetrated the study of social knowledge in comparatively more limited ways.

We came to this realization not on our own but because of our growing awareness that, here and there in the social sciences and the humanities, scholars familiar with research in science studies but interested primarily in the development of social knowledge were definitely beginning to train their attention on knowledge practices outside the natural sciences. Even so, efforts of this kind seemed, at this point, relatively isolated from each other, spread across different disciplines and specialty areas and sometimes still overshadowed by work in the tradition of the sociology of knowledge. We thought that situating and organizing the more recent lines of research in relationship to one another could be beneficial and open up an agenda of new questions that, because they were as yet unanswered, might encourage more research in this vein—research that not only would eventually correct some of the existing imbalance between the study of natural knowledge and the study of social knowledge but (more importantly) would raise the general level of understanding of the processes by which different forms of social knowledge are produced, evaluated, and put to use. Our hope is that this volume takes a modest step in this direction.

In the course of this project, we have received substantial organizational support and collegial counsel, for which we are grateful. A grant from the Radcliffe Institute for Advanced Studies enabled us to conduct an exploratory seminar on "the social study of the social sciences and the humanities" in the spring of 2005 and to convene a superb group of scholars who helped us delineate and circumscribe our project. A few of them eventually became contributors to this volume. Others in that group included Mitchell Ash, Tom Bender, Homi Bhabha, Don Brenneis, Craig Calhoun, Marion Fourcade, Peter Galison, Howard Gardner, Joshua Guetzkow, John Guillory, Stanley Katz, Veronica Boix Mansilla, Ellen Messer-Davidow, Chandra Mukerji, Ted Porter, Steven Shapin, and Stephen Turner. This initial meeting led to a symposium in December 2007 hosted at the Russell Sage Foundation, where drafts of the chapters in this volume were first presented. These drafts benefited from the comments and suggestions of a sharp and diverse group of participants that included, in addition to our authors, Don Brenneis, Jamie Cohen-Cole, Marion Fourcade, Rakesh Khurana, Erin Leahey, and Diane Vaughan. For valuable advice on the manuscript that resulted from this symposium, we appreciate as well the reports of two anonymous reviewers from the University of Chicago Press.

Throughout this process, this project has also been generously supported by various units at our home institutions: Harvard University, Northwestern University, and the University of British Columbia. We thank those responsible for arranging this support and express our appreciation as well to

Adam Kissel, Phillis Strimling, Tracy Blanchard, Heather Latham, and Travis Clough for their able technical assistance. Finally, we warmly thank the authors of the chapters of this volume for joining us in this undertaking and accommodating our many requests along the way to its completion. The combined contributions of the authors, colleagues, administrators, editors, reviewers, staff assistants, and others with whom we had the pleasure of working kept us continually aware of what an irreducibly collective practice social knowledge making is.

INTRODUCTION

The Study of Social Knowledge Making

CHARLES CAMIC, NEIL GROSS, AND MICHÈLE LAMONT

In recent decades, scholars in various corners of the academy have lived through a major shift in knowledge culture. Beginning quietly around the time of the publication of Thomas Kuhn's *The Structure of Scientific Revolutions* (1962) and gathering momentum during the past quarter century, this shift has involved a growing awareness and appreciation on the part of humanists, social scientists, and scientists themselves of the ways in which mundane scientific practices enable and constrain the bodies of knowledge that scientists produce as well as the social worlds in which they work. This reflexive "turn to practice" has been fed by an explosion of sophisticated theory and research in the vibrant interdisciplinary field of "science studies," or "science and technology studies" (STS). Up to this point in its comparatively young history, however, the literature of STS has focused predominantly on the natural sciences, pure and applied, with a modest uptick of recent attention to the most conspicuously "scientific" of the social sciences. As leading scholars in the field now openly acknowledge, though, vast expanses of the dense forest in which the making of social knowledge occurs remain still to be illuminated from the perspective of the "turn to practice"—a telling lacuna in a historical era when social knowledge, academic and nonacademic, is of increasing salience and consequence in many areas of social life. This lacuna provides the point of departure for the present book, which is concerned with the practices by which a diverse range of social knowledge forms are produced, evaluated, and put to use.

We thank Steven Epstein and Scott Frickel for their detailed and extremely helpful comments on a previous draft of this introduction.

The volume contains thirteen original empirical studies of what we call *social knowledge practices*. As such, it is, we believe, the first collection of its kind, though (as we will elaborate) it descends intellectually from several existing traditions of scholarship in the social sciences and the humanities, most directly from the lineage of STS itself, as the chapters seek to focus some of the conceptual lenses of STS on a few of the many historical and contemporary locations of social knowledge production, evaluation, and use. In doing so, the hope of the contributors is that a vigorous flow of additional empirical studies will follow, leading to an accumulation of research and theory that trains the collective eye of scholars on the makeup and distribution of social knowledge practices, the processes through which they arise and change, their significance for the analysis and interpretation of the social worlds of their inhabitants, and their implications for an understanding of how these worlds both resemble and differ from those found in the natural sciences.

We divide this introduction into three sections. In the first, we attempt to clarify our terminology, indicating what we mean by social knowledge, practices, and so forth. As well, we offer a brief sketch of past scholarship on the making of social knowledge to furnish the context for the empirical chapters that follow. In the next section, we overview these chapters individually and situate them within the organization of the volume. In the last section, we consider what the thirteen chapters, taken as a whole, appear to suggest about social knowledge practices. On this basis, we also identify some of the previously unarticulated questions that the chapters open up as an agenda for future research on the topic.

I

Academic and popular writings frequently characterize the societies of the present epoch as "knowledge societies," "knowledge economies," or "knowledge cultures." Commentators use such expressions to describe the rapid acceleration, over the course of the last half century, of a trend that dates from the beginning of the Industrial Revolution: the massive influence of scientific research on everyday life, as demonstrated most recently by developments in the fields of biotechnology and information technology. This theme of the far-reaching practical effects of the contemporary natural sciences is consistent with scholarship on the pivotal role that the physical and chemical sciences played during the previous three hundred years in transforming methods of production and patterns of consumption, but the narrative generally occludes the place of multiple kinds of *social knowledge* in the knowledge societies of today.[1] A near cipher two centuries ago, social knowledge has subsequently become a ubiquitous feature of the societal landscape, buffeting those in our own time with urgent economic data, reports, and forecasts; reams of demographic information; statistics on crime, marriage, employment, housing, religiosity, and life satisfaction; polls and instant analyses of the state of the electorate and of national security conditions; as well as with social classificatory schemes, psychological evaluations, and educational test results—to say nothing of the literally hundreds of thousands of books, articles, and lectures that are produced annually both by academic social scientists and by journalists, jurists, pundits, personal advisers, and innumerable other creators and distributors of varieties of human knowledge that fall beyond the bounds of the natural sciences.

Our conception of social knowledge is an expansive one, and this volume examines only a small range of the many different forms of social knowledge. By "social knowledge" we mean, in the first instance, *descriptive information and analytical statements* about the actions, behaviors, subjective states, and capacities of human beings and/or about the properties and processes of the aggregate or collective units—the groups, networks, markets, organizations, and so on—where these human agents are situated. In some instances, social knowledge statements may contain significant "nonsocial" referents (as, e.g., in studies of the impact of climate changes on the welfare of the population of a certain region), but these referents constitute only one component of those statements. We omit from this definition fictional and fabricated material that might otherwise seem to fit our conception, reserving "social knowledge" for data and statements that seek to advance empirically based and empirically warrantable claims about the present, the past, or the future, though we include two further elements as well. These are (1) *normative statements* that draw on descriptive information to recommend or condemn certain courses of human conduct, programs for collective action, and so on; and (2) the *technologies and tools* of knowledge making—that is, the epistemic principles, cognitive schemata, theoretical models, conceptual artifacts, technical instruments, methodological procedures, tacit understandings, and material devices by which descriptive and normative statements about the social world are produced, assessed, represented, communicated, and preserved. We would emphasize, however, that we offer this definition solely for the purpose of orienting readers to

---

1. For valuable discussions of knowledge societies, see Gibbons et al. 1994; Knorr Cetina 2001; Moore et al. forthcoming; and Randel 2009.

the subject matter of this volume, not to impose hard-and-fast boundaries. The precise scope of social knowledge, we believe, differs across historical settings and varies significantly with the authority and ambitions of those who claim to speak on its behalf, as well as with the authority and ambitions of their opponents.

Because our language lacks an all-inclusive term for the women and men who participate in the production, evaluation, and use of what counts as social knowledge, throughout this volume different terms will appear in different contexts. When referring to those who specialize in producing, assessing, or applying social knowledge by virtue of faculty positions in higher educational institutions, we—and the other contributors—will use familiar expressions like "social scientists" and "scholars in the social sciences and the humanities," or we will speak more specifically of sociologists, anthropologists, historians, political philosophers, and so on. When we are discussing in addition (or instead) professional knowledge specialists located outside the academy, we will speak of social researchers, social policy experts, social knowledge makers, or social knowledge producers. Even the latter, most encompassing terms may mislead in certain instances, however, since (as several of the chapters make clear) some of the people involved in producing, evaluating, and applying social knowledge are not themselves specialized knowledge producers.

What any of these people *do* in the course of the production, evaluation, and application of the forms of social knowledge with which they deal is a topic that has, to this point in time, received relatively little empirical attention in the literature of the social sciences and the humanities. Many social scientists and humanists spend their entire professional lives creating social knowledge, but only sporadically have questions as to how this process occurs become the focus of systematic research in their own right. To be sure, all the disciplines that make up the social sciences and the humanities have a rich *prescriptive* literature on knowledge making, a vast storehouse of how-to manuals and other writings covering basic and advanced methods of research. Historically, however, none of these disciplines has placed social knowledge making among its primary subjects of empirical research.

In this circumstance, the topic of social knowledge making has for several generations led a fugitive and splintered existence on several disconnected islands of scholarship, whereupon a certain restrictive perspective on the subject has tended to hold sway. For easy reference, we call this perspective the "traditional approach to social knowledge" (TASK), recognizing that this viewpoint has existed more as a cluster of diffuse assumptions than as a formalized "approach" that scholars have branded as such. The locus classicus of TASK has been the literature of the history of ideas, specifically studies of the genesis of the ideas of individual social thinkers and intellectual movements, although the approach has also been common in work with the same focus in fields such as the history of philosophy, the history of political economy, the history of anthropology, and the history of psychology. Outside these historical specialty areas, TASK has figured more recently in research on the intellectual origins of a range of social policies as well as in various strands of scholarship in cultural studies.

Within our own discipline, too, TASK has been a major presence in the subfield known as the "sociology of knowledge"—a specialty area that serves conveniently to illustrate this common perspective on social knowledge making. By the "sociology of knowledge," we refer to the subspecialty with this name that took shape in Europe in the 1920s; bore fruit at mid-century in influential works by C. Wright Mills ([1941] 1966), Herbert Marcuse (1964), Lewis Coser (1965, 1971), and Alvin Gouldner (1965, 1970); and, following a fallow period, has recently experienced a vigorous revival with the appearance of detailed accounts of developments in philosophy (Bourdieu 1991; Bryant 1996; Collins 1998; Fabiani 1988; Gross 2008; Lamont 1987; Wuthnow 1989), psychology (Kusch 1995, 1999), economics (Yonay 1998), literature (Sapiro 1999), and sociology (Bourdieu 2004), as well as in the social sciences and the humanities at large (Steinmetz 2005).[2]

As this enumeration indicates, the sociology of knowledge deals in significant measure with instances of what we have called social knowl-

---

2. This revival of the sociology of knowledge has coincided with a growing interest in social knowledge on the part of scholars outside sociology. Among these, we would draw particular attention to work by philosophers (e.g., Fuller 1988; Hacking 1995; Taylor 1989), intellectual historians (e.g., Bender and Schorske 1998; Brick 2006; Daston 2000, 2004; Daston and Galison 2007; Hollinger 2006; Poovey 1998; Porter and Ross 2003; Ross 1991; Smith 1997), disciplinary historians (e.g., Capshew 1999; Mirowski 1989; Novick 1988), scholars concerned with disciplinarity and interdisciplinarity (Heintz and Origgi 2004; Messer-Davidow 2002), and social policy scholars (e.g., Babb 2001; Berman 1998; Blyth 2002; Campbell 2002; Goldstein and Keohane 1993; Hall 1989; O'Connor 2001; Rueschemeyer and Skocpol 1996; Somers and Block 2005). This listing is only illustrative, and many other contributions might easily be cited, including studies of applied knowledge contexts such as psychiatry, social work, and law (for further additions to this list, see below). Many authors in this volume have also contributed to this literature. We do not include their names here, however, because we wish to exempt their work from the statements about TASK that follow and to associate them with the alternative perspective that we will describe.

edge. This interest follows from the subfield's original mandate to open up all (or nearly all) of human thought to sociological examination, for the realm of social thought is one that calls out naturally as an avenue of investigation to sociologists who are on this mission—hence the longstanding concern on the part of sociologists of knowledge with the ideas (the doctrines, theories, propositions, etc.) of social and political thinkers, philosophers, economists, psychologists, and so forth. Of most relevance in the current context, though, is the fact that it is in studies where scholars have pursued this concern that the components of TASK stand out especially clearly. Although there are of course exceptions, studies in the sociology of knowledge typically take the following form: (1) focusing on a particular social thinker (or set of social thinkers), the researcher begins *post festum*, with the thinker's ideas already known, fixed in the canonical documents of his or her intellectual tradition or field (philosophy, economics, sociology, etc.); (2) working backward, the researcher then traces the "origins" of those known ideas to external social sources, generally conceptualized in terms of macrolevel economic, political, and ideological conditions, as well as the thinker's class- or group-based interests.[3] In this sense, the analytic approach of the sociology of knowledge has generally proceeded from an implicit input/output model, with societal macrofactors serving as inputs and finished ideas as outputs. This manner of treating the production of social knowledge is what we mean by TASK, and the contributions of the approach have in some ways been considerable. More explicitly than perhaps any other body of scholarship, research in this vein has linked social thinkers' abstract ideas to the material and cultural circumstances of the societies in which they live, while also identifying the connections between the social positions occupied by producers of social knowledge and the shape and content of their intellectual productions.[4]

Viewed in light of later developments, however, what TASK has widely neglected, in common with other input/output models, are the mediating terms—in this case, the day-to-day actions and processes through which the producers of social knowledge actually go about the on-the-ground

3. Mannheim 1936 provides the founding statement of this position. For later meta-analyses, see Merton 1945; Coser 1965; Camic 2001; and Camic and Gross 2001.

4. In this respect, the work of the sociology of knowledge has gone hand in hand with work in the allied subfield of the sociology of intellectuals, which, although less concerned with the production of social knowledge, has extensively treated the social position of intellectuals, especially in relation to social class and state structures. See, e.g., Brint 1994; Calhoun 1994; Eyal 2003; Eyal, Szelényi, and Townsley 1998; Eyerman 1994; Eyerman, Svensson, and Söderqvist 1987; Giesen 1998; Lin and Galikowski 1999; Suny and Kennedy 1999; and the valuable review by Kurzman and Owens 2002.

work of making, evaluating, and disseminating the kinds of social knowledge that they are involved in producing. In the current scholarly literature, the general term for actions and processes of this type is "practices," and we adopt this convention in this volume, hoping (as we stated above) to extend the contemporary "turn to practice" to the study of social knowledge in order not only to address a serious absence in the traditional approach to social knowledge but more importantly to foreground a set of empirical questions that TASK has thus far marginalized. In taking this step, we follow the lead of researchers in STS (as we will elaborate below) as well as the example of a diverse range of practice theorists throughout the social sciences and the humanities more broadly, including Margaret Archer, Pierre Bourdieu, Hubert Dreyfus, Michel Foucault, Harold Garfinkel, Anthony Giddens, Hans Joas, Sherry Ortner, William Sewell Jr., Quentin Skinner, Charles Taylor, and Charles Tilly, to name only a few.

In accord with this body of work, we define "practices" as the *ensembles of patterned activities*—the "modes of working and doing," in Amsterdamska's (2008, 206) words—by which human beings confront and structure the situated tasks with which they are engaged. These activities may be intentional or unintentional, interpersonally cooperative or antagonistic, but they are inherently multifaceted, woven of cognitive, emotional, semiotic, appreciative, normative, and material components, which carry different valences in different contexts. So understood, practices include *both* the "taken-for-granted routines" to which Swidler (2001, 75) calls attention and what Schatzki (2001, 7) refers to as "open sets of nonregularized actions." Still further, neither nonregularized nor routine modes of action are analytically reducible to the ideas and purposes of the agents undertaking them. That is so because, although some activities are highly sensitive to agents' objectives and beliefs, even in these instances purposive factors constitute—according to the writings of practice theorists—only one among the many heterogeneous contingencies that impinge upon and shape situated practices. As a rule, moreover, these contingencies fall neither on one or the other side of the hoary divide between "micro-" and "macro-" social forces, since practices—as several of the chapters in this volume will illustrate—generally enfold and meld together factors that nonpractice scholars have tended to assign to very different levels of the social world (see also note 21 below).[5]

Outside the ambit of TASK, the subject of social practices has gained sub-

---

5. In the account we have just given, we draw especially on Schatzki 1996; Schatzki, Knorr Cetina, and von Savigny 2001; and Turner 1994, 2002.

stantial traction among contemporary social scientists and humanists for a variety of reasons, some of them somewhat discrepant from others. The broadest point of consensus is that subjecting practices to analysis opens up the "black box" of social life: the intricate web of situated human experience which traditional conceptions of human action, social structure, and culture all elided. For some scholars, this move is motivated by *explanatory questions*, that is, by an interest in locating within practices the underlying causal processes or mechanisms by which certain social factors translate (or fail to translate) into various downstream consequences, as well as in identifying the upstream sources of those processes. For other scholars, *interpretive questions* have primacy, and comprehending agents' practices is essential for understanding the subjective meanings that they attach to what they say and do. For still other social scientists and humanists, practices are compelling objects of investigation on more *intrinsic grounds*; by examining them, researchers can either discover otherwise-concealed social regularities or (according to an inverse rationale) deconstruct the very notion of such regularities. Either way, scholars continue, analyzing social practices reinserts human conduct into its specific *historical contexts* and preserves its multidimensionality, thus not only challenging universalizing claims about the nature of action but encouraging *critical reflexivity* about this constitutive aspect of the social world on the part of researchers studying social practices—and, by extension, on the part of agents engaging in those practices.[6]

Because of its widespread neglect of the mundane actions and processes by which the makers of social knowledge carry out their work, TASK has necessarily sidelined this entire range of explanatory, interpretive, contextualizing, reflective, and intrinsic concerns. By so doing, moreover, not only has TASK left several major voids, but its very inattention to the daily routines of knowledge production, evaluation, and use has spawned the assumption, which runs deep in the sociology of knowledge, that the activities involved in social knowledge making are *monolithic and enclosed*. In civil engineering, a monolith is a structure, large or small, made up of simple and homogeneous elements combined into a single, solid block, and the metaphor fits the image of knowledge production latent in TASK.

6. In addition to their different justifications for studying social practices, practice scholars often differ in their conceptual and methodological approaches. Writing of researchers who study scientific practices, for example, Amsterdamska (2008, 209) has commented that they "do not share a common theory, or even a common definition of practice, but [simply] a family resemblance" with regard to the empirical problems they address. We would extend this remark to practice-oriented scholars in general, including the contributors to this volume.

Sociologists of knowledge do not, after all, deny that knowledge-making activities of a kind happen; rather, their studies recognize, at least implicitly, that social thinkers do read the literatures of their intellectual traditions and fields, do cogitate about weighty intellectual questions, and do write their thoughts down in words. Rarely, however, does TASK's conception of the everyday work of knowledge making go further than these unexamined (and unproblematized) activities of reading, thinking, and writing, each understood as joined to the others in a seamless bloc—and to characterize the production of social knowledge in this manner is, in effect, to depict it as a monolith (in miniature). Likewise, TASK has fostered an enclosed vision of the locational sites where the activities of knowledge making occur. Reading, thinking, writing—these are not actions that ordinarily have strong spatial associations. To the extent that sociologists of knowledge and other proponents of TASK have situated these activities at all, this has generally been within an imagined nexus that the sociologist constructs by overlaying the particular macrosocial forces that he or she wishes to emphasize onto the bounded space of the intellectual tradition, school, field, or academic unit to which the social thinker under study belongs. The circumscribed nexus that results is, by implication, the location of the thinker's cogitating, reading, and writing, as TASK overlooks other, more concrete sites of knowledge practices.

In our view, however, there is a promising alternative perspective, and it lies in the field of STS and in the example set by the ongoing efforts of STS researchers to open the black box of knowledge making in the natural sciences. A half century ago, something closely akin to TASK's monolithic and enclosed view of knowledge making was common among historians of science, who treated natural scientific knowledge mainly as "a system of propositions arranged into theories" formulated by scientists with tried-and-true methods that were "unproblematically associated with their specialties and disciplines" (Amsterdamska 2008, 205–6). No part of this image of the production of natural scientific knowledge has withstood subsequent scrutiny, however. For if the turn to practice that has rippled through the social sciences and the humanities in recent decades has had a radiating center, that center has been STS as the field has taken shape in the work of figures like Thomas Kuhn and (more explicitly thereafter) Barry Barnes, David Bloor, Michel Callon, Adele Clarke, Harry Collins, Lorraine Daston, Peter Galison, Donna Haraway, Karin Knorr Cetina, Sheila Jasanoff, Bruno Latour, Donald MacKenzie, Andrew Pickering, Trevor Pinch, and Steven Shapin, among many others, whose writings have, in different ways, shifted scholarly attention away from science as a finished product in the temple of human knowledge and toward the study of the multiple, multilayered, and multisited practices involved during the long hours when future kernels of scientific knowledge are still in the making.

This significant change in viewpoint has been much slower to reverberate outward to the study of social knowledge, however. Emerging as a critique of the historiography of the natural sciences, STS began with its focus riveted on the physical and biological sciences, and scholars in the area openly concede their long-running "bias toward studying the bigger and harder sciences" (Hackett et al. 2008, 6, quoting Ina Spiegel-Rosing, writing in 1977).[7] Not only did the physical and biological sciences stand out as the very prototype of Science; but as the privileged authorities on Nature, they also raised challenging questions that exerted a stronger pull within STS than the seemingly more transparent workings of the various "softer" sciences. More recently, though, STS has become more skeptical of that supposed transparency and more disposed to greater inclusiveness, as researchers have turned to the study of the computational and environmental sciences, medicine and engineering, and media and information technologies. Concurrent with this expansion, moreover, STS scholars have built the case that Nature cannot be privileged as a fixed, transhistorical category; that the boundary between Nature and Society is itself a social construction; that the knowledge-making practices of natural scientists are thoroughly configured by the social worlds that they inhabit; and that

7. We caution that we do not intend this sentence as a recap of the complex history of STS. The field's history is recounted elsewhere (see, e.g., Hess 1997; Sismondo 1997) and cannot be reviewed in this introduction. We would observe, however, that before STS crystallized in its current form, the social studies of science fell successively under the rubrics of the "sociology of science" and "the sociology of scientific knowledge," the former associated with the name of Robert Merton, the latter with that of Thomas Kuhn (among others). While both of these approaches predominately focused, like STS itself, on the natural sciences, both perspectives also spawned a modest amount of scholarship on the social sciences and the humanities. In particular, the Kuhnian era brought forth a number of studies that extended the Kuhnian concepts of "paradigm" and "scientific revolution" to developments in a range of disciplines that included economics, political science, sociology, anthropology, and linguistics (e.g., Bizzell 1979; Eckberg and Hill 1979; Friedrichs 1970; Lieberman 1989; Percival 1976; Ricci 1977; Ritzer 1980; Shedinger 2000; Stephens 1973; Worland 1972). For its part, the earlier Mertonian era called forth two lines of relevant work on social knowledge: first, research on the prestige rankings, mobility patterns, peer review processes, and citation patterns of social scientists, sociologists in particular (e.g., Bakanic, McPhail, and Simon 1987; Cole 1983; Cole and Cole 1973; Hargens 1988; Liebert 1976; Mullins 1973); second, studies of the academic institutionalization and professionalization of disciplines such as anthropology, economics, sociology, and history (e.g., Guillory 1993; Oleson and Voss 1979; Shumway 1994; Shils 1970). In recent years, scholars have reinvigorated research in the latter vein to address the development of newer academic fields like women's studies and African American studies (Messer-Davidow 2002; Rojas 2007; Small 1999).

those same practices have powerful spillover effects on the practices of social scientists.[8]

Despite all these salutary developments, however, STS itself has yet to investigate the practices involved in the making of social knowledge to anything approaching the extent that it has examined the practices in use in the physical and biological sciences (and in cognate fields) or to make social knowledge practices a core topic of empirical research.[9] By no means is this observation a criticism, since it would obviously be frivolous to fault STS scholars for investigating the very topics that constitute the agenda of their own field. Moreover, this is an agenda that STS researchers have pursued with great success, as is evident in the large, empirically detailed, and theoretically rich literature that they have produced, as well as in the light this literature has shed on some of the larger explanatory, interpretive, reflexive, and other concerns raised by practice theorists. Even so, researchers interested in social knowledge cannot miss the disparity. The authoritative (1,000 + page) third edition of *The Handbook of Science and Technology Studies* (Hackett et al. 2008), for example, lists literally thousands of studies of the natural sciences and related fields but scarcely any STS research dealing explicitly with the social sciences, let alone with humanistic and lay forms of social knowledge.

Despite its relatively thin past history in this regard, however, STS has recently shown signs of rising interest in a few "harder"—presumptively more "scientific"—types of social knowledge.[10] The first of these signs is a rapidly growing volume of research on the production and use of different kinds of economic knowledge, particularly financial knowledge—the one form of social knowledge that *The Handbook of Science and Technology Studies* singles out for discussion (see Preda 2008; more generally see Breslau 1997, 2003; Callon 1998; Callon, Méadel, and Rabeharisoa 2002; Evans 1997; Guala 2001; Guala and Salanti 2001; Knorr Cetina and Bruegger

---

8. The first three points that we mention here are currently commonplaces in the literature of STS. On the last point, see Bowker 2005; Epstein 2007; and Jasanoff 1995.

9. Tellingly, unlike the terms "scientific practices," "knowledge practices," and, of course, "practices"—used in reference to, for instance, physicists, chemists, biologists, physical anthropologists, medical researchers, and engineers—*there is not one mention* (to the best of our knowledge) of "social knowledge practices" in any article that has yet appeared in either of the two leading STS journals, *Social Studies of Science* and *Science, Technology, and Human Values*.

10. In addition to the three published indicators that we will now describe, we would mention a major workshop in 2005 sponsored by the Science Studies Program at the University of California, San Diego, entitled "Making Society, Knowing Society" (http://education.sdsc.edu/making_society/index.htm; accessed April 11, 2011). The STS Program at Cornell University has also occasionally offered a course called Social Studies of the Human Sciences.

2000, 2002; Knorr Cetina and Preda 2001, 2006; MacKenzie 2001a, 2001b, 2003, 2004, 2006; MacKenzie and Millo 2003; MacKenzie, Muniesa, and Siu 2007; Mirowski 1999, 2002, 2004; Morgan and Butter 2000; Pinch and Swedberg 2008; Power 1997; Preda 2006, 2009; Yonay 2000; cf. Ashmore, Mulkay, and Pinch 1989). A second development has been a modest flow of studies concerning the practices entailed in knowledge making in psychology[11] (Ashmore, Brown, and MacMillan 2005; Chamak 1999; Galison 2004; Osborne 1993; Shadish et al. 1995; Smith et al. 2000; Smyth 2001).[12] A third development has been a scattering of practice-oriented studies on some of the basic tools and technologies of social knowledge making:[13] focus groups (Lezaun 2007), survey interviews (Maynard and Schaeffer 2000), game-theoretic models (Swedberg 2001), and especially statistical methods (MacKenzie 1981; Porter 1986, 1995)—with work on this last topic shading over into a much larger literature on the history of quantification in the natural and social sciences (e.g., Camic and Xie 1994; Desrosières 1998; Hacking 1990; Marks 1997; Matthews 1995; Stigler 1986; Weintraub 1991, 2002).

Complementing STS's growing interest in these particular kinds of social knowledge practices, furthermore, have been four other relevant lines of research that are less immediately associated with STS: (1) studies of the history of social research methods (e.g., Calhoun 2007; Converse 2009; Igo 2007; Leahey 2004, 2005, 2006, 2008a, 2008b; Lemov 2005; Platt 1996); (2) work on the rhetoric of the social sciences and the humanities (e.g., Agger 2000; Bazerman and Paradis 1991; Green 1988; McCloskey 1998; Nelson, Megill, and McCloskey 1987); (3) scholarship on the organization of academic reference networks (e.g., Clemens et al. 1995; Hargens 2000; Pontille 2003; Whitley 1984) and of peer review and other evaluation processes in the social sciences and humanities (e.g., Brenneis 1994, 1999, 2006; Guetzkow, Lamont, and Mallard 2004; Lamont 2009; Mal-

11. We would also note Harry Collins's (1985) earlier study of parapsychology, as well as Joseph Ben-David and Randall Collins's (1966) classic (pre-STS) study of the institutionalization of the discipline of psychology. In the literature on the history of psychology, there have also been the seminal studies of Danziger (1990) and Hacking (1995) on knowledge-making practices.

12. Perhaps because of its more disputed credentials as a "science," sociology has received considerably less STS attention, though Lynch has examined the presentation of knowledge in sociological texts (see Lynch 1991; Lynch and Bogen 1997). In a different vein, Cole and Zuckerman (1975) have written about the development of the sociology of science, while Ashmore (1989) has done likewise for the sociology of scientific knowledge.

13. We would also call attention to STS-inspired work on the changing technologies of humanist scholarship (Mallard 2005; Ruhleder 1995).

lard, Lamont, and Guetzkow 2009; Strathern 2000); and (4) a burgeoning literature, mainly within cultural anthropology, on anthropologists'
knowledge-making practices.

Viewing these recent signs in tandem, an important trend in the study
of social knowledge seems to be under way. Indeed, if one groups together
and connects the several literatures to which we have just referred, we seem
to be witnessing the quiet passing of the traditional approach to social
knowledge and the overdue arrival of social knowledge practices as a central topic for empirical investigation. Nevertheless, so far as we are aware,
the scholars involved in these lines of research have yet to recognize this
point themselves or to inquire into the larger implications of their projects
for understanding the nature of social knowledge generally. To the contrary: the "connecting," "grouping together," and "viewing in tandem" that
we have just described represent our own integration of largely discrete
contemporary developments, not a concerted movement currently in progress either inside STS or outside it.

In this sense, the foregoing depiction of the rising tide of research on
social knowledge practices imposes upon the current situation a unity and
a teleology that it has yet to exhibit on it own. At the present time, for example, studies of economic and financial knowledge speak mainly to one
another and to work on the natural sciences and their technologies, not
to research on knowledge making in psychology, studies of focus groups
and survey interviews, work on the rhetoric of the social sciences and the
humanities, or scholarship on anthropological knowledge making—and
each of the converses holds as well. To be sure, the relative mutual isolation of these valuable bodies of work may feed the internal growth of each
of them; but their disconnection from one another nevertheless delays
wider recognition of social knowledge practices as objects of investigation in their own right. In our view, however, such recognition is essential. Until more researchers understand financial knowledge, psychological
knowledge, anthropological knowledge, survey knowledge, as well as the
many forms of social knowledge that have thus far gone unstudied, all as
branches of a larger species that is social knowledge, they will be diverted
from explicitly tracking and mapping the diverse members of this fertile
species, studying its branches *in relation to one another*, and examining the
similarities and differences in the practices by which the various branches
produce, evaluate, and apply the types of social knowledge with which they
deal. This angle of approach provides the starting point for the chapters
that follow.

II

Social knowledge, as we have said, is a ubiquitous phenomenon, as it has been, with ever increasing spread, since the middle decades of the nine-teenth century. To track it to sites along the full spectrum of its many his-torical and contemporary locations and adequately investigate its working in all those settings, however, is a task well beyond the scope of any single volume on social knowledge practices. That being the case, in planning this collection, we sought contributions that would consider social knowledge at some familiar and at some less familiar sites, treating practices of knowl-edge making not only within the established academic disciplines of the social sciences and the humanities but also in both interdisciplinary and nonacademic contexts. Likewise, we were concerned not to limit the range of knowledge-making practices to settings where knowledge production is central but also to include settings where processes of knowledge evalua-tion and knowledge application have priority.

This plan has resulted in the tripartite structure of the volume. The five chapters in part I, "Knowledge Production in the Disciplines," examine a few of the knowledge-making practices characteristic of some of the tradi-tional academic disciplines of the social sciences and the humanities. The three chapters in part II, "Knowledge Evaluation Sites," analyze a trio of in-terdisciplinary settings where practices of knowledge evaluation occur. Fi-nally, the five chapters in part III, "Social Knowledge beyond the Academy," consider several nonacademic institutions involved in the production and use of certain more contemporary forms of social knowledge.

The scholars who have written these chapters come from a range of aca-demic fields and do not represent a unitary professional group. Contribu-tors differ in their theoretical proclivities, the intellectual generations to which they belong, and the times and places that they treat in their chap-ters. As well, they differ in the research methods by which they carried out the studies that they here report. Several authors rely heavily on archival documents, supplemented with secondary sources; several others present results from interviews that they conducted with various social knowledge experts; still others make use of different kinds of ethnographic observa-tion; and one assembles and analyzes various quantitative data. Appropri-ately, a number of contributors combine these methods. As we will see, such methodological variety befits the different social knowledge prac-tices that these authors investigate. For all their differences, however, what unites the contributors is their departure from the traditional approach to social knowledge in favor of a careful analysis of some of the many situated activities by which producers of social knowledge actually go about their work.

In the five chapters of part I, "Knowledge Production in the Disciplines," social knowledge makers appear in the familiar guise of academic social scientists and humanists, and what each chapter does is to interrogate a neglected cluster of knowledge-making practices and probe its upstream sources and downstream effects. In the first three chapters, all concerned with turning points in the history of the social sciences and the humanities in the United States, the practices are those by which disciplinary specialists conceive and access the universe of documentary material from which they then build their own scholarship.

In chapter 1, Andrew Abbott focuses on researchers in the social sciences and the humanities who rely on library materials—books, periodicals, documents, archival records, and so on. Posing the question of how scholars in these fields acquire awareness of the existence of relevant library resources, sift and winnow those resources, and gain physical access to them at the particular institutions where they work, Abbott uncovers significant transformations, from the late nineteenth century to the present, in the technologies and accompanying practices involved in identifying and locating library materials. Propelled by a series of changes in the demography of American higher education, as well as by the interests of a supporting cast of librarians, commercial publishers, and representatives of professional organizations, these alterations in library research practice gradually transformed social scientists and humanists from scholars who had immediate physical access to the entire (but finite) literature of their disciplines into the specialists of recent decades who are increasingly overwhelmed by the quantity of publications and the proliferation of professional reference guides and, accordingly, have been deserting libraries and curtailing their reading. Still further, Abbott highlights how "access drove use": the direct connection between the materials that scholars had at their disposal, at different stages in the evolution of library practices, and the kinds of scholarship they were enabled to produce.

Chapter 2 concerns the discipline of history over the same period and furnishes an account convergent with Abbott's about major changes in knowledge-making practices. In the chapter, Anthony Grafton considers the day-to-day work that constitutes "historical work" and the two different "workplaces" that have defined it over time: the graduate seminar and the archive. Reminding those who view historical research as the study of collections of manuscripts in distant archives of the recency of this conception, Grafton emphasizes that from the 1880s to the 1950s most American historians worked chiefly with printed sources found at (or near) their local university. In doing so, they relied upon a standard package of techniques acquired in graduate research seminars, which were then hands-on apprenticeships in specially equipped rooms where, through recurrent technical exercises, historians-in-training became practiced in the critical examination of printed primary sources and other documents and in the construction (from these sources) of historical narratives on generally agreed-upon topics. As seminar graduates fanned out to different universities and pursed research careers according to this model, the result was a body of scholarship unified by the impress of the seminar, though subsequently "the relation between the discipline of historical research and that of the historical seminar has become less and less direct." Instead, as travel to remote archival collections (each distinctive and, ideally, never before excavated) became the sine qua non of historical practice—due to changes in the economics and demography of higher education—the seminar ceased to provide all-purpose instruction in the techniques of historical research. On Grafton's account, such developments have increasingly fragmented historical scholarship, causing it to splinter in accord with the diverse interests of the men and women entering the discipline.

In chapter 3, Rebecca Lemov examines a complementary aspect of social knowledge makers' use of available documentary material: the deliberate practices they sometimes undertake to configure stores of existing information into new forms. Lemov's case in point is the monumental effort of mid-twentieth-century anthropologists—and their allies in psychology, sociology, and psychoanalysis—to custom-build collections of relevant research materials by ransacking troves of cultural, social, and psychological data. Originating in a neoevolutionary project intended to facilitate the comprehensive and rapid comparison of all human cultures across a large number of commensurable categories, the construction of anthropological data banks, Lemov argues, acquired a life of its own as scores of university support personnel were employed to carve up printed texts, transfer the gleanings to index cards, and file the cards into predetermined categories—thereby giving rise to a new, more material and standardized notion of what constitutes a social scientific "fact." Almost immediately, however, this practice of fact making by data bank construction not only impugned the theory that spawned it (and several successor theories as well) but also negated its own claims to totality, as it encouraged other academic and lay users to build—often with funding from foundations and the U.S. government—ever bigger data banks that served, with each iteration, to enlarge the meaning of "fact," since a total data collection was never total enough for the practitioners involved.

The next two chapters shift attention to the present day and center on a different unit of analysis. Rather than focusing (like the historical chapters by Abbott, Grafton, and Lemov) on entire generations of social knowledge makers, both chapters take the intellectual career of a single knowledge producer as a lens onto a dimly understood knowledge practice. In chapter 4, Neil Gross and Crystal Fleming hone in on an everyday problem that is a counterpart to that observed by Abbott among contemporary researchers overwhelmed by vast quantities of relevant literature to read: the severe time-shortage problem that bedevils academics of today—and that Jacobs and Winslow (2004) have documented as growing worse in recent decades due to institutional changes inside and outside the academy. Faced with this and other impediments to carrying on with the production of new knowledge, different scholars inevitably respond differently, and Gross and Fleming report a case study of a contemporary American political philosopher whose means of "binding himself to the mast"—enmeshing himself in a thicket of interpersonal obligations that will necessitate progress on his work, though in small and easy steps—is the practice of presenting work in progress before audiences at multidisciplinary conferences likely to be lenient in their evaluations. Gross and Fleming argue for the knowledge-generating significance of this extremely widespread practice, viewing conference participation not only as an occasion for communicating mature ideas but as a mechanism that can cause humanists and social scientists to gravitate toward certain research topics, address them in particular ways, and then pursue or abandon their work on these topics depending on audience feedback.

In chapter 5, Johan Heilbron turns to an unusual but often highly influential type of social knowledge maker: the sociological "theorist" who develops general models and abstract concepts designed to have a wide range of empirical applications. Heilbron's example is the celebrated French sociologist Pierre Bourdieu, and his chapter builds the novel argument that the genesis of Bourdieu's own general theory was "not theoretical speculation or textual exegesis" (as proponents of TASK might have it) but rather "a distinctive research practice." Dissecting the features of this research practice, Heilbron brings to the fore Bourdieu's hands-on immersion in a long succession of empirical research projects that were carried out by collaborative, multidisciplinary research teams yet were focused on different social arenas—thus requiring Bourdieu to engage routinely in the further practices of "domain switching" and "boundary crossing." To these practices and several related "sociocognitive mechanisms," Heilbron traces Bourdieu's eventual move to formulate his sociology in a "generalizing mode" and to articulate the signature general concepts of his oeuvre.

Part II, "Knowledge Evaluation Sites," examines another important aspect of the process of social knowledge making. As we have just noted, Gross and Fleming describe multidisciplinary conferences as settings for the lenient informal evaluation of academic work in progress. Yet in the contemporary era, early-stage evaluation of academic projects often occurs as well in formal, often multidisciplinary settings where decisions are made that directly affect whether particular knowledge-making projects go forward, undergo revision, or reach termination. The practices by which three major sites of this type reach evaluative decisions, along with the sources and outcomes of those practices, form the subject of the next three chapters.

Chief among these sites of evaluation are peer review panels, which are the focus of chapter 6. Here Michèle Lamont and Katri Huutoniemi investigate peer review panels organized at the national level in the United States and Finland. Their analysis examines how the social scientists and humanists on these panels manage, even though they come from different disciplines and universities and convene only rarely, to reach agreement about the relative merits of project proposals when assessing a wide range of applications seeking research funding. Central to this process, Lamont and Huutoniemi show, is a set of informal, and sometimes inconsistent, procedural rules that the panelists tacitly co-construct and then adhere to in the course of their deliberations. This practice enables social scientists and humanists to bridge their disciplinary differences, to perceive panel decision making as fair and "objective" (i.e., as meritocratic rather than corrupted by academic politics and self-interest), and to achieve consensus about the relative intellectual quality of the projects under review. As Lamont and Huutoniemi observe further, however, these particular rule-making and rule-following practices are by no means inevitable. Rather, they develop most fully in multidisciplinary panels charged with ranking applications and making funding decisions, and they are attenuated in panels with different procedural mandates and composed of natural scientists (or scholars in only one discipline)—a finding clearly illustrating the effect of organizational structure and composition on evaluative practices.

In chapter 7, Laura Stark investigates another major venue for the evaluation of social knowledge in the United States. She considers state-mandated institutional review boards (IRBs) operating at the local university level, where they bring together diverse actors—drawn from various academic departments, the university administration, and the surrounding community—to determine whether university researchers seeking to study human subjects have designed their projects with adequate ethical protections for those subjects. In this case, the evaluative outcome at stake is not funding but authorization to undertake a research project. Even so, Stark raises a question that parallels that posed by Lamont and Huutoniemi: how do disparate evaluators reach collective agreement? She answers this by uncovering IRB members' practice of using the official minutes of their meetings—minutes that federal administrative law requires them to keep—not merely to report the outcome of their decisions retrospectively but also to negotiate among themselves the content of those decisions prospectively, thereby hammering out the specific project design requirements that social investigators thereafter have to satisfy to secure IRB approval for the research they want to conduct.

In chapter 8, Marilyn Strathern examines knowledge evaluation practices through a wide-ranging analysis of a contemporary institution of a newer but increasingly common type, the multidisciplinary research consortium: specifically, a "knowledge park," inclusive of both social and natural scientists, which formed after a group of university and university-affiliated researchers in the United Kingdom successfully submitted a proposal for government funding of the venture. At the core of the researchers' proposal, Strathern stresses, was "interdisciplinarity"—a notion that had recently become an element in the British government's policy strategy for creating knowledge that would be useful to the general public. Where the chapters by Lamont and Huutoniemi and by Stark consider situations where multidisciplinary panels provide an organizational means to evaluate the quality and adequacy of research proposals, in the instance that Strathern explores, multidisciplinarity expands into an explicit organizational objective and mandate and, thus, into a salient criterion, in and of itself, for knowledge evaluation. Entrenched in this way at the U.K. knowledge park, multidisciplinarity catalyzed knowledge-making practices that promised and privileged collaboration, partnership, and communication across disciplines in the high expectation that these various forms of synergy would bear fruit in the future and eventually bring forth useful results. Strathern demonstrates, however, how multidisciplinarity practiced in this future-oriented, teleological way not only unleashed rising and falling waves of confounding emotional energies among consortium members but also led to the devaluation and discard of those disciplines that consortium administrators could not easily reconcile with their teleology—or, in other words, to the paradoxical accomplishment of interdisciplinarity by the removal of the discipline of sociology itself.

Strathern situates the research consortium that she analyzes within a mixed academic and nonacademic milieu, and the five chapters in part III, "Social Knowledge beyond the Academy," continue this move outward from the traditional academic disciplines in the social sciences and the humanities to a range of less familiar, yet historically ever more prevalent extra-academic sites where social knowledge is made and put to diverse uses in the private and public sectors. Like the authors of the previous chapters, though, the contributors to this section seek to bring to light the knowledge practices constitutive of each site under investigation and to analyze their antecedents and consequences.

In chapter 9, Sarah Igo begins this set of inquiries by examining commercial survey research organizations in the United States in the 1930s and the origins of modern public opinion polling. In doing so, she focuses especially on the heavy public relations efforts of early pollsters, like George Gallup and Elmo Roper, to convince members of a skeptical citizenry not only to become willing research subjects and to respond to the queries of anonymous interviewers but to go further still and accept the results of small "representative" samples as legitimate indicators of the state of American opinion at large. Igo views these public relations efforts as part of a much larger battery of practices of persuasion on which social researchers depend to secure the consent and cooperation necessary, now as much as in the past, to get their subjects to answer questionnaires on intrusive topics, submit to experiments, and acknowledge that such knowledge-making activities are intellectually and socially worthwhile.

The next three chapters turn attention to different kinds of social policy knowledge. In the first of these, chapter 10, Sheila Jasanoff focuses on the knowledge practices of social policy makers in the area of regulation—by which she means regulation by governmental agencies of widening spheres of social life such as banking and trade, health and safely, and so forth. Taking, in particular, the example of policy specialists working to establish knowledge claims relevant to the management of the risks posed to population groups by various environmental hazards—claims that are a hybrid of social knowledge and natural knowledge—Jasanoff asks how knowledge of this kind "withstands partisan attacks and manages to keep the engines of policy humming." In answer, she emphasizes the importance to policy makers of wrapping their knowledge claims in the mantle of "objectivity." However, according to Jasanoff, "objectivity" actually carries different meanings in different Western democracies (and international organizations) and, in all contexts, becomes a robust property of policy knowledge only as a result of multiple knowledge practices dispersed over many institutions. With regard to the United States, Jasanoff emphasizes the role of knowledge evaluation processes that range from quantitative risk assessments, through peer review, to judicial oversight of the rules of regulatory agencies. She demonstrates how these evaluation practices have abetted U.S. policy experts' practices of public persuasion, enabling them to justify their knowledge claims as impartial, and also how these same practices have dovetailed with "specialized legal and political practices of reasoning" to cause the distinctively American view of objectivity to gain acceptance in global regulatory bodies like the World Trade Organization.

In chapter 11, Grégoire Mallard and Andrew Lakoff turn from regulatory policy to national security policy, contrasting two episodes involving U.S. security experts in the post–World War II period. Both cases point up the importance in this policy arena of knowledge-making practices that serve to envision a nation's future in ways that then affect deliberations about national security at the present time. Conceptualizing these practices as "techniques of prospection," Mallard and Lakoff examine their calculated use by security specialists to construct ambiguous events as security threats (or nonthreats) and thus to persuade political decision makers to act on the basis of these constructions. In the first episode, Mallard and Lakoff show how experts' application of econometric forecasting techniques to an issue that political leaders regarded as a vital strategic matter effectively removed the issue from policy controversy. Conversely, in the second episode, Mallard and Lakoff follow the process by which security experts transformed a perceived nonsecurity problem into one recognized to be of highest urgency through the technique of the scenario-based exercise, which enfolded the issue at stake into a carefully designed enactment of an emotionally charged national catastrophe. Both examples reveal security specialists as keenly skilled at crafting and mobilizing social knowledge to project national futures in ways that shape policy decisions in the present.

In discussing security experts as designers of societal scenarios, Mallard and Lakoff's second example highlights a feature of the practices of social knowledge making that has risen in consequence in recent decades and that the next chapter, chapter 12, considers in another context. Here, Daniel Breslau examines economists in their own role as designers—in this case, however, as designers not of future scenarios but of real-time markets in conjunction with current policy making in the area of energy regulation. Studying economic consultants who have been involved in filings to

U.S. federal regulatory agencies tasked with overseeing markets for wholesale electricity, Breslau analyzes the processes by which economic experts formulate blueprints for market redesign and characterizes their knowledge practices as a combination of "applied Platonism" and "mediation." Working to diagnose and address problems in existing electricity markets, economic consultants make constant appeal, according to Breslau, to the abstraction of the "competitive market" and then translate features of real markets into the language of this Platonic abstraction. By so doing, the experts produce a conceptualization of existing market flaws that guides them in crafting mechanisms (i.e., new sets of market rules) to compensate for market defects in ways that mediate between economic theory and noneconomic factors that consultants also seek to accommodate, including their own professional interests, the stakes their clients have in different markets rules, and the technology of electricity.

Significant as the kinds of social knowledge that Jasanoff, Mallard and Lakoff, and Breslau describe have been in the domains of social policy, however, new types of social knowledge have been no less consequential in the private sector, a point that is the motif of the volume's concluding chapter, chapter 13, where Karin Knorr Cetina carries economic knowledge out of the realm of U.S. regulatory policy and into the international world of high finance. As she does so, her object of investigation becomes social knowledge makers in their capacity as professional financial analysts who work on the trading floors of global banks and elsewhere, advising a diverse range of clients on investment decisions. Conceptualizing "financial analysis" as an enterprise concerned with the production and use of knowledge in the form of specialized *information*, Knorr Cetina examines how the practices that constitute the everyday work of professional analysts shape the character—the "epistemic features"—of this information and stamp upon it certain distinctive properties: namely, high temporal evanescence, strong emotional charge, and close dependence on proxy measures of the economic conditions with which financial research deals. Among these daily practices, Knorr Cetina stresses financial analysts' involvement in forecasting and promoting to their clients future scenarios to assuage present economic uncertainties, as well as analysts' entanglement—because they are advisers to actual investors—in the positive and negative emotional energies of their clients. A large army in present-day financial markets, financial analysts also represent, for Knorr Cetina, researchers from the still broader category of the "information knowledge sciences"—a category that scholars interested in social knowledge will seriously misunderstand, she suggests, if they restrict themselves to the template of the traditional academic sciences.

III

The knowledge sites examined in these chapters represent (as we have said) only some of the many locations of social knowledge production, evaluation, and application. Even if we limit attention to just these sites and view them in relation to one another, however, some instructive themes begin to emerge.

One of these themes is that *social knowledge practices are multiplex*, composed of many different aspects, elements, and features, which may or may not work in concert. Surveying the broad terrain mapped across the different chapters, we see, for example, the *transitory practices* of a short-lived research consortium as well as knowledge *practices that endure for generations* across many disciplines and institutions, such as techniques for accessing documentary materials, elaborate peer review processes, and various public relations techniques. We find *practices that anchor entire disciplines and professions*[14] (both academic and nonacademic, and for longer or shorter periods)—for example, the graduate research seminar in history, comprehensive data banks in cultural anthropology, persuasion tactics in survey research—and *practices constitutive of specialized forms of social knowledge*, such as those that underwrite the development of general sociological models. We witness *practices involving the construction of permanent storehouses of social knowledge* (historical scholarship, bibliographic guides, encyclopedia files) and *practices that conjure visions of the future that undergo constant replacement* amid the exigencies of the present (in national security and in different kinds of economic markets). And we observe knowledge *practices that confer "objectivity"* (to the deliberations of peer review panels and the

---

14. In speaking of practices that "anchor," we draw on Swidler's insight that "certain key practices anchor others and that these anchoring practices . . . play a key role in reproducing larger systems of discourse and practice" (2001, 90). However, where Swidler seems to argue for the necessity of anchoring practices, we would leave the issue open to empirical investigation, at least with regard to knowledge practices. To judge from the different cases treated in this volume, some knowledge institutions possess, while other knowledge institutions do not possess, anchoring practices, which (following Swidler) we understand as practices that are "pervasive" among the members of an institution, "enduring" over the course of the institution's history, and "influential in shaping" other practices within the institution (2001, 81). In our view, however, not only is each of these conditions a matter of degree, but even where all these conditions obtain to a significant degree, they may be interwoven with a variety of other knowledge practices that are relatively or fully autonomous.

claims of policy experts) and *practices tied to emotional waves* (whether of a small knowledge park or of the global economy). What is more, as revealed in the following chapters, these are only a few of the major axes along which social knowledge practices vary.[15]

Still further, such multiplicity obtains not only when different areas of social knowledge are contrasted but also when one looks inside single areas. As the chapters by Grafton, Lemov, and Knorr Cetina illustrate, the knowledge practices of individual disciplines and other knowledge-making institutions often change significantly from one time period to the next, for reasons that are part of the history of each entity. On top of this, there are the changes that occur inside individual disciplines and other knowledge institutions when higher-order transformations in the machinery of knowledge production (e.g., reduced physical proximity to library materials, the emergence of IRBs, refinements in quantitative risk assessment) diffuse outward to different sites.

Significant as they are, however, historical changes in knowledge practices scarcely capture the full complexity of the situation. This is so because—to judge from the preliminary evidence at hand—individual disciplines and other knowledge institutions also contain *a dense multiplicity of knowledge-making practices even in the context of a single historical period.* In our view, this is a point that especially merits attention. None of the practices described in the chapters of this volume are, after all, stand-alone activities, and few practices are entirely site specific. Variants and diverse combinations of many of them occur routinely. The typical social scientist or humanist of today, for example, engages not only in the knowledge practices that anchor his or her own discipline, and his or her specialty area(s) within the discipline, but in the practices involved in accessing documentary materials; participating in a wide range of conferences; seeking research funding from granting agencies and project approval from local IRBs; serving on multidisciplinary review panels and participating in interdisciplinary research consortia (including those that take social researchers deep into the domains of the natural sciences, both pure and applied); securing the cooperation of research subjects (or research institutions); es-

---

15. In addition to the several axes that we have just mentioned, the practices to be described also differ (inter alia) in (1) how explicitly practitioners verbalize them; (2) how uniformly executed they are; (3) how tightly supervised they are by institutional authorities; (4) how much latitude for improvisation they require or allow; (5) how much direct contact with living human subjects they entail; (6) how insulated they are from unexpected contingencies; and (7) how closely bundled together they are with other knowledge practices. The degree to which any of these dimensions (or any of those just suggested in the text) overlap with any other is an open empirical question for future research.

tablishing the objectivity of his or her knowledge claims; providing expert advice to government agencies or private organizations; and managing the interpersonal emotional energies that accompany these varied tasks. All this is to say nothing, moreover, of the concurrent practices (not explicitly treated in this volume) of assembling and analyzing data; collaborating with colleagues (close and distant) on research projects, administrative undertakings, and public policy initiatives; evaluating manuscripts for journal editors and book publishers; negotiating with editors and publishers on behalf of oneself and one's associates; teaching and mentoring; and crafting all the different types of written documents that these diverse situations call for. And the knowledge-making activities of social researchers and experts in nonacademic institutions are no less multiform, as the chapters by Igo, Jasanoff, Mallard and Lakoff, Breslau, and Knorr Cetina all make clear. At site after site, heterogeneous social knowledge practices occur in tandem, layered upon one another, looping around and through each another, interweaving and branching, sometimes pulling in the same directions, sometimes in contrary directions.[16]

That social knowledge practices possess this polymorphous character contradicts the monolithic view of knowledge making that the traditional approach to social knowledge assumed. As we observed above, from the vantage point of TASK, social knowledge production is a two-term equation consisting of external macrosocial factors, on the one side, and finished texts, on the other. Intervening practices are not included, aside from the implied activities of reading, thinking, and writing, as these automatically unfold at the will of the social thinkers under study. The ample evidence for the multiplexity of social knowledge practices that is presented in the following chapters, however, is at substantial variance with this familiar perspective and evocative, rather, of the intricate spider web of practices in which social scientists and humanists, as well as other social researchers and experts, routinely participate as they produce, evaluate, and use social knowledge.

We readily acknowledge that this picture is consistent with the literature of STS, as STS researchers have frequently drawn attention to the plurality of knowledge practices in use in the biological and physical sciences and in cognate fields (see Hackett et al. 2008). To observe this similarity, however, is by no means to suggest that social knowledge practices are variegated *in the same ways* that natural knowledge practices are variegated. At this stage of research on social knowledge, that conclusion would be prema-

---

16. We borrow some of our terminology here from Knorr Cetina 2001.

ture. An adequate appraisal of the similarities and differences between social knowledge–making practices and natural knowledge–making practices must—we would insist—await further studies of social knowledge making, a far more comprehensive survey of relevant research on natural knowledge practices than this introduction includes, plus systematic comparative studies of the two species of knowledge.[17]

That said, however, if we may allow ourselves a few impressionistic comments at this point, we notice several considerations that appear to heighten the complexity of social knowledge practices but seem less relevant with regard to natural knowledge.[18] These considerations include the work that social investigators must sometimes carry out to secure various kinds of subjective data from their research subjects and to persuade those same research subjects—skeptical human beings—to become study participants (Igo, Lemov, Stark); social researchers' deep enmeshment in the emotional lives of their subjects (Knorr Cetina); and the problems that social knowledge experts face in constructing future scenarios that involve human beings whose own actions in the present necessitate the continual reconstruction of those very scenarios (Knorr Cetina, Strathern, Mallard and Lakoff).

In addition, although natural scientists—at least as STS scholars have tended to portray them—are *not* ordinarily engaged in efforts to bring their research practices into conformity with the research practices of the social sciences and the humanities, natural science templates, real or imagined, often do impinge on social knowledge practices. Consider the following. Abbott recounts that humanists and social scientists have often looked upon libraries as "a crucial laboratory" for their research. Grafton discusses how nineteenth-century historians viewed their seminar rooms as equivalent to "the new laboratories that were founded in the same period" in the natural sciences. Lemov reports that the cultural anthropologists whom she examines regarded encyclopedia files as "a sort of laboratory on the

17. As we propose this comparison, we strongly caution against essentializing either the natural sciences, on the one side, or the social sciences and the humanities, on the other, and positing a fixed line of demarcation between them. As we have remarked, the domains of both natural knowledge and social knowledge, as well as the nature of the boundaries that separate them, are constituted historically and change over time.

18. This is not to raise the idle question as to which set of practices—those involved in social knowledge making or natural knowledge making—is *more* multiplex. Obviously, one could invert the statement we have just made in the text and identify considerations in natural knowledge production that are comparatively absent with regard to social knowledge. Our point is to recognize the plurality of both domains of practice but without thereby precluding examination of some of the different bases for their multiplicity.

basis of which social scientific research could be done" (quoting George Murdock). Heilbron points out that Pierre Bourdieu conceived his work as fundamentally similar to research in the natural sciences. Jasanoff observes that policy experts privilege objectivity in part because of its association with the neutrality of knowledge claims in the laboratory sciences. Breslau reports that energy market designers freely analogize their economic blueprints to the apolitical work of natural scientists. And Knorr Cetina describes how financial analysts, engulfed by the storms of global markets, nevertheless cast themselves as disinterested scientific researchers, conducting economic forecasting by careful scientific techniques. The frequency with which images of the "laboratory" and of other features of natural scientific research enter into the work of social knowledge makers—and this in the face of their contrasting views as to which attribute actually establishes conformity with the natural sciences (libraries? seminar rooms? data banks? objectivity?)—may well contribute to the multiplexity of social knowledge practices.

In challenging the accepted view that social knowledge practices are monolithic, the following chapters also throw into doubt the assumption that social knowledge practices transpire in enclosed spaces—that is, in what we described above as a nexus that consists of a social thinker's academic discipline or field as overlaid with a few select macrosocial factors. It is a further theme of the studies in this collection that *social knowledge practices occur in concrete social locations that are relatively porous*[19]—more loosely bounded and open to heterogeneous contingencies.[20]

The knowledge practices considered in parts II and III of this volume, for instance, take place not at all within traditional disciplinary enclosures but at specific sites that either adopt *multi*disciplinary academic structures (national funding panels, IRBs, a research consortium) or occur altogether outside the academy and exhibit a *non*disciplinary pattern (as with survey research organizations and teams of policy experts). Nor do any of these sites operate as self-contained intellectual fields or traditions. From first to last, the knowledge practices of survey researchers intertwine with members of the public at large, just as national security experts continually interface

19. By "relatively porous" we mean that sites of social knowledge making have boundaries that are selectively open to different factors in different times and places. In our view, it is likely that this differential permeability is patterned by various institutional processes and mechanisms (see point 7 below).

20. We see this point as consistent with the claim of practice theorists (see above) that practices are neither "micro" nor "macro" but are the arena where factors that sociologists ordinarily associate with different levels combine.

with political leaders, politicians, and the media. Even for the seemingly restricted purpose of establishing the objectivity of the claims of regulatory knowledge, specialists must (as Jasanoff shows) engage in highly dispersed practices that extend from federal agencies to the academy, the private sector, the courts, and back again to international regulatory bodies. Likewise, the informal norms that scholars develop inside the closed-door meetings of funding panels bear the strong impress of the procedures and mandates that organizational sponsors superimpose on the peer review process (as Lamont and Huutoniemi demonstrate), while the social knowledge practices of IRBs and research consortia unfold at a crossroad between formal requirements emanating from remote state bureaucracies, on the one side, and local negotiations among social scientists, natural scientists, lay administrators, and community members, on the other.

We acknowledge that these illustrations of the permeability of social knowledge practices describe sites where different genres of social knowledge are co-present from the start. However, the two chapters that deal exclusively with financial knowledge underscore this same attribute. Indeed, Breslau's market designers and Knorr Cetina's financial analysts produce knowledge by mediating between the economic principles and analytical techniques that they learn in the course of their educations, on the one hand, and client demands, professional interests, government regulations, and market forces, on the other. To be sure, when viewed according to the yardstick of traditional academic disciplines in the social sciences and the humanities, multidisciplinary research consortia, IRBs, commercial polling organizations, and the worlds of financial analysts, market designers, regulation specialists, and national security experts may all seem to be atypical sites of social knowledge production. Yet the porosity of knowledge practices in these "nontraditional" settings merely throws into relief the degree to which social knowledge practices are constituted (in part) from beyond the social spaces that they directly occupy even in the case of academic disciplines. Heilbron and Gross and Fleming examine scholars situated in two well-established disciplines (sociology, philosophy); but what proves central—indeed, foundational—to the work of both scholars are disciplinary practices in combination with the practices that they engage in beyond disciplinary boundaries, that is, in multidisciplinary collaborative projects and at interdisciplinary conferences.

This selective porosity is not simply an artifact of social knowledge making as it manifests itself in the contemporary era of avowed multidisciplinarity. Building encyclopedia data banks in the middle decades of the last century, cultural anthropologists mediated between the visions of ear-

lier anthropological writers, the material resources available for file building at their own universities, the data-gathering techniques then in vogue
among psychologists (and other specialists), and the priorities of private
foundations and (in wartime) of government agencies willing to finance
encyclopedic projects (Lemov). Producing historical scholarship over the
long course of the last century, historians likewise configured and reconfigured their knowledge-making activities in relation to local institutional resources (research materials, travel grants), alliances with other disciplines,
and the social composition of entrants into the discipline (Grafton). And,
for more than a century as well, the mundane library practices of humanists and social scientists, seeking merely to access books and periodicals,
have been intertwined with the institutional agendas of professional librarians; the local availability of funds to build collections of books, journals,
and documents; nationally centralized mechanisms for the distribution of
government publications; marketing decisions by the publishers of books,
journals, and reference sources; and the complex demography and ecology
of higher education (Abbott). Insofar as these examples, historical as well
as contemporary, furnish any indication, not enclosure but relative openness is among the core features of the spaces where the practices of social
knowledge production, evaluation, and use actually take place.[21]

Whether, to what extent, and with what effects the properties of social
knowledge practices emphasized in the following chapters operate at other
sites of social knowledge production, assessment, and application are issues for future research. Indeed, as the first set of empirical studies explicitly concerned with social knowledge practices, the chapters in this volume
open directly out onto a series of basic questions not previously raised in
a systematic way about the making of social knowledge. In our view, these
questions include the following.

1. *Range and distribution of social knowledge practices.* Of what does the
repertoire of social knowledge practices consist? In what ways does this repertoire resemble or differ from the repertoires of practices involved in the
making of natural scientific knowledge? What are the salient dimensions
along which social knowledge practices vary? (Above, we identify several
axes of analytic variation suggested by the studies in this volume, but that

21. This characterization, too, is consistent with the familiar claim of science studies scholars that natural knowledge is constituted through dispersed, heterogeneous networks that are
at once local and translocal (see, again, Hackett et al. 2008). Here also, though, we would leave
open the question as to why social knowledge and natural knowledge exhibit this apparent
similarity until there is more research on social knowledge practices and more systematic comparison of the results of this research with the findings of STS scholars.

listing is only preliminary.) At which sites are practices of different types found? Which practices are site specific, which widely dispersed? How does the range and distribution of practices vary by country and historical period? How has the growth of knowledge societies altered the composition and ecology of social knowledge practices? Do social knowledge practices in the present era exhibit a different (more future oriented) temporality than knowledge practices in earlier periods?[22]

2. *Components of social knowledge practices.* Insofar as social knowledge practices consist of cognitive, emotional, appreciative, and other components, how are these interwoven differently at different knowledge-making sites? How do social knowledge makers manage their emotions and selves in contexts of knowledge production, evaluation, and application? How are subjectivity and intellectual taste construed in these contexts and connected to the modes by which social knowledge is diffused and legitimated? How are they related to gendered and national cultures and to broader transnational referents in the world system of knowledge production? How do the emotive, cognitive, and other components of social knowledge practice affect interaction among knowledge makers, the ways in which they experience and negotiate controversies, and their processes of consensus formation? To what degree do these same components influence the representation of disciplines and interdisciplines?

3. *On-site interrelations.* To what extent are the multiple different social knowledge practices that are present at any one knowledge site coordinated with one another? To what degree does the heterogeneity of practices vary from site to site? Insofar as multiple knowledge practices are layered (as we propose above), by what processes are these (or other) modes of articulation and combination accomplished?

4. *Cross-site interrelations.* In circumstances (such as the multidisciplinary sites treated in part II of the volume) where social knowledge making brings together knowledge producers, evaluators, and users from different sites, to what extent and in what ways are the site-specific practices of each cluster of agents coordinated with those of the other agents? Insofar as there are common knowledge practices, dispersed across multiple sites (as in the case discussed in chapter 10), by what historical processes did these practices diffuse and attain the degree of legitimacy that they exhibit?

5. *Social knowledge makers.* Considered in terms of social class, gender, possession of cultural capital, and other social attributes, who engages in

---

22. This question is suggested by the contrast between the practices discussed in chapters 1–3, on the one hand, and those examined in chapters 8, 11, and 13, on the other.

social knowledge practices and how does the profile of social knowledge makers vary across time and space? To what degree are social knowledge makers specialists or laity, academics or nonacademics? By what mix of formal education, on-the-job learning, self-teaching, improvisation, and invention do different types of social knowledge makers become practiced in the practices that they use?

6. *Base and infrastructure.* On what cultural, political, economic, organizational, material, and other supports do different social knowledge practices rely? What cultural norms, political institutions, financial and organizational arrangements, cast of supporting personnel, and arsenal of technologies do different social knowledge practices presuppose?

7. *Antecedents.* Following social knowledge practices upstream, by what concatenation of processes and factors are different types of practices forged and maintained (for varying durations of time)? To what degree are social knowledge practices shaped directly at the point-of-practice itself as knowledge makers go about their everyday tasks (as in the instances considered in chapters 1–8, 12–13)? To what extent and in what ways are different social knowledge practices inflected as well by cultural, demographic, economic, political, and organizational factors located beyond the immediate point-of-practice? Insofar as the boundaries of knowledge sites are porous in regard to factors of the latter kind (as all thirteen chapters report), by what institutional processes and mechanisms are site boundaries constructed such that they are differentially permeable by different factors in different times and places?

8. *Contextual and interpretive implications.* Insofar as social knowledge practices form part of the immediate historical context where social knowledge makers are situated (as all the chapters show), in what respect does the inclusion of these practices into historical accounts of individual knowledge makers or of larger cohorts of knowledge makers facilitate hermeneutical scholarship in the humanities and the social sciences? In what ways does understanding that particular knowledge makers were involved in these (but not those) work routines, subject to the evaluation of their contemporaries according to these (but not those) processes, and so forth, deepen scholars' comprehension of the meanings that historical actors attached to their words and deeds, as well as scholars' ability to interpret those lines of conduct?

9a. *Explanatory implications: consequences for individual knowledge makers.* Following social knowledge practices downstream and taking individual knowledge makers as the primary unit of analysis (as in chapters 4–5), what social knowledge products—what descriptive and normative statements, lines of (academic or nonacademic) research and theorizing, sets of ideas, bodies of advice and instruction (to students, clients, policy makers), and so forth—do different bundles of social knowledge practices enable a knowledge maker to formulate? What career trajectories do these same practices facilitate or impede? Which practices do social knowledge makers mobilize to construct intellectual, professional, and political alliances with other knowledge makers and with diverse audiences and publics or otherwise to advance and legitimate their intellectual, professional, and political projects?

9b. *Explanatory implications: collective consequences.* Following social knowledge practices downstream and taking knowledge-making sites as the principal unit of analysis (as in chapters 1–3, 12–13), what ensembles of social knowledge products are enabled or constrained by the different repertoires of knowledge practices present within a discipline, profession, or other social knowledge–making institution at different times and places? By which processes or mechanisms do different practices exert such enablement or constraint? How does the repertoire of knowledge practices characteristic of a particular social knowledge-making site affect its social organization—for example, its hierarchical order, distribution of material and symbolic rewards, patterns of cooperation and conflict among its members, mode of recruiting new members?

10. *Reflexive implications.* To what degree does training an analytical lens on the day-to-day practices by which other social knowledge makers carry out their work raise critical self-awareness of one's own unexamined knowledge practices? In what ways can enlarged understanding of contemporary practices of social knowledge production, evaluation, and application lead to beneficial transformations in those practices?

To pursue, appropriately reformulate and elaborate, and eventually answer questions of these sorts will be the work of many more empirical studies of social knowledge making and—part and parcel with these studies—of the evolving practice of analyzing social knowledge practices. In an epoch when such practices are ubiquitous, research on the production, evaluation, and application of social knowledge should finally begin to keep pace.

References

Agger, Ben. 2000. *Public Sociology: From Social Facts to Literary Acts.* Lanham, MD: Rowman and Littlefield.

Amsterdamska, Olga. 2008. "Practices, People, and Places." In *The Handbook of Science* and Technology Studies, 3d ed., edited by E. J. Hackett, Olga Amsterdamska, Michael Lynch, and Judy Wajcman, 205-9. Cambridge, MA: MIT Press.

Ashmore, Malcolm. 1989. The Reflexive Thesis: Wrighting Sociology of Scientific Knowledge. Chicago: University of Chicago Press.

Ashmore, Malcolm, Steven D. Brown, and Katie MacMillan. 2005. "Lost in the Mall with Mesmer and Wundt: Demarcations and Demonstrations in the Psychologies." Science, Technology, and Human Values 30:76-110.

Ashmore, Malcolm, Michael Mulkay, and Trevor Pinch. 1989. Health and Efficiency: A Sociology of Health Economics. Philadelphia: Open University Press.

Babb, Sarah L. 2001. Managing Mexico: Economists from Nationalism to Neoliberalism. Princeton, NJ: Princeton University Press.

Bakanic, Von, Clark McPhail, and Rita J. Simon. 1987. "The Manuscript Review and Decision Making Process." American Sociological Review 52:631-42.

Bazerman, Charles, and James Paradis, eds. 1991. Textual Dynamics of the Professions: Historical and Contemporary Studies of Writing in Professional Communities. Madison: University of Wisconsin Press.

Ben-David, Joseph, and Randall Collins. 1966. "Social Factors in the Origins of a New Science: The Case of Psychology." American Sociological Review 31:451-65.

Bender, Thomas, and Carl E. Schorske, eds. 1998. American Academic Culture in Transformation. Princeton, NJ: Princeton University Press.

Berman, Sheri. 1998. The Social Democratic Moment: Ideas and Politics in the Making of Interwar Europe. Cambridge, MA: Harvard University Press.

Bizzell, Patricia. 1979. "Thomas Kuhn, Scientism, and English Studies." College English 40:764-71.

Blyth, Mark. 2002. Great Transformations: Economic Ideas and Institutional Change in the Twentieth Century. New York: Cambridge University Press.

Bourdieu, Pierre. 1991. The Political Ontology of Martin Heidegger. Translated by Peter Collier. Stanford, CA: Stanford University Press.

———. 2004. Science of Science and Reflexivity. Translated by Richard Nice. Chicago: University of Chicago Press.

Bowker, Geoffrey C. 2005. Memory Practices in the Sciences. Cambridge, MA: MIT Press.

Brenneis, Donald. 1994. "Discourse and Discipline at the National Research Council: A Bureaucratic Bildungsroman." Cultural Anthropology 9:23-36.

———. 1999. "New Lexicon, Old Language: Negotiating the 'Global' at the National Science Foundation." In Critical Anthropology Now: Unexpected Contexts, Shifting Constituencies, Changing Agendas, edited by George F. Marcus, 123-46. Santa Fe, NM: School of American Research Press.

———. 2006. "Reforming Promise." In Documents: Artifacts of Modern Knowledge, edited by Annelise Riles, 41-70. Ann Arbor: University of Michigan Press.

Breslau, Daniel. 1997. "Contract Shop Epistemology: Credibility and Problem Construction in Applied Social Science." Social Studies of Science 27:363-94.

———. 2003. "Economics Invents the Economy: Mathematics, Statistics, and Models in Work of Irving Fisher and Wesley Mitchell." Theory and Society 32:379-411.

Brick, Howard. 2006. Transcending Capitalism: Visions of a New Society in Modern American Thought. Ithaca, NY: Cornell University Press.

Brint, Steven. 1994. In an Age of Experts: The Changing Role of Professionals in Politics and Public Life. Princeton, NJ: Princeton University Press.

Bryant, Joseph. 1996. Moral Codes and Social Structure in Ancient Greece: A Sociology of Greek Ethics from Homer to the Epicureans and Stoics. Albany: State University of New York Press.

Calhoun, Craig. 1994. *Neither Gods nor Emperors: Students and the Struggle for Democracy in China*. Berkeley and Los Angeles: University of California Press.

——, ed. 2007. *Sociology in America: A History*. Chicago: University of Chicago Press.

Callon, Michel, ed. 1998. *The Laws of the Markets*. Malden, MA: Blackwell.

Callon, Michel, Cécile Méadel, and Vololona Rabeharisoa. 2002. "The Economy of Qualities." *Economy and Society* 31:194–217.

Camic, Charles. 2001. "Knowledge, the Sociology of." In *International Encyclopedia of the Social and Behavioral Sciences*, edited by Neil J. Smelser and Paul B. Baltes, 12:8143–48. London: Elsevier.

Camic, Charles, and Neil Gross. 2001. "The New Sociology of Ideas." In *The Blackwell Companion to Sociology*, edited by Judith R. Blau, 236–49. Malden, MA: Blackwell.

Camic, Charles, and Yu Xie. 1994. "The Statistical Turn in American Social Science: Columbia University, 1890 to 1915." *American Sociological Review* 59:773–805.

Campbell, John L. 2002. "Ideas, Politics, and Public Policy." *Annual Review of Sociology* 28:21–38.

Capshew, James H. 1999. *Psychologists on the March: Science, Practice, and Professional Identity in America, 1929–1969*. Cambridge: Cambridge University Press.

Chamak, Brigitte. 1999. "The Emergence of Cognitive Science in France: A Comparison with the USA." *Social Studies of Science* 29:643–84.

Clemens, Elisabeth S., Walter W. Powell, Kris McIlwaine, and Dina Okamoto. 1995. "Careers in Print: Books, Journals, and Scholarly Reputations." *American Journal of Sociology* 101:433–94.

Cole, Jonathan R., and Stephen Cole. 1973. *Social Stratification in Science*. Chicago: University of Chicago Press.

Cole, Jonathan R., and Harriet Zuckerman. 1975. "The Emergence of a Scientific Specialty: The Self-Exemplifying Case of the Sociology of Science." In *The Idea of Social Structure: Papers in Honor of Robert K. Merton*, edited by Lewis A. Coser, 139–74. New York: Harcourt Brace Jovanovich.

Cole, Stephen. 1983. "The Hierarchy of the Sciences?" *American Journal of Sociology* 89: 111–39.

Collins, H. M. 1985. *Changing Order: Replication and Induction in Scientific Practice*. London: Sage.

Collins, Randall. 1998. *The Sociology of Philosophies: A Global Theory of Intellectual Change*. Cambridge, MA: Harvard University Press.

Converse, Jean M. 2009. *Survey Research in the United States: Roots and Emergence, 1890–1960*. New Brunswick, NJ: Transaction.

Coser, Lewis A. 1965. *Men of Ideas: A Sociologist's View*. New York: Free Press.

——. 1971. *Masters of Sociological Thought: Ideas in Historical and Social Context*. New York: Harcourt Brace Jovanovich.

Danziger, Kurt. 1990. *Constructing the Subject: Historical Origins of Psychological Research*. Cambridge: Cambridge University Press.

Daston, Lorraine, ed. 2000. *Biographies of Scientific Objects*. Chicago: University of Chicago Press.

——, ed. 2004. *Things That Talk: Object Lessons from Art and Science*. New York: Zone Books.

Daston, Lorraine, and Peter Galison. 2007. *Objectivity*. New York: Zone Books.

Desrosières, Alain. 1998. *The Politics of Large Numbers: A History of Statistical Reasoning*. Translated by Camille Naish. Cambridge, MA: Harvard University Press.

Eckberg, Douglas Lee, and Lester Hill Jr. 1979. "The Paradigm Concept and Sociology: A Critical Review." *American Sociological Review* 44:925–37.

Epstein, Steven. 2007. *Inclusion: The Politics of Difference in Medical Research.* Chicago: University of Chicago Press.

Evans, Robert. 1997. "Soothsaying or Science? Falsification, Uncertainty and Social Change in Macroeconomic Modelling." *Social Studies of Science* 27:395–438.

Eyal, Gil. 2003. *The Origins of Postcommunist Elites: From Prague Spring to the Breakup of Czechoslovakia.* Minneapolis: University of Minnesota Press.

Eyal, Gil, Iván Szelényi, and Eleanor Townsley. 1998. *Making Capitalism without Capitalists: Class Formation and Elite Struggles in Post-Communist Central Europe.* London: Verso.

Eyerman, Ron. 1994. *Between Culture and Politics: Intellectuals in Modern Society.* Cambridge: Polity Press.

Eyerman, Ron, Lennart G. Svensson, and Thomas Söderqvist, eds. 1987. *Intellectuals, Universities, and the State in Western Modern Societies.* Berkeley and Los Angeles: University of California Press.

Fabiani, Jean-Louis. 1988. *Les philosophes de la République.* Paris: Editions de Minuit.

Friedrichs, Robert W. 1970. *A Sociology of Sociology.* New York: Free Press.

Fuller, Steve. 1988. *Social Epistemology.* Bloomington: Indiana University Press.

Galison, Peter. 2004. "Image of Self." In *Things That Talk: Object Lessons from Art and Science,* edited by Lorraine Daston, 257–96. New York: Zone Books.

Gibbons, Michael, Camille Limoges, Helga Nowotny, Simon Schwartzman, Peter Scott, and Martin Trow. 1994. *The New Production of Knowledge: The Dynamics of Science and Research in Contemporary Societies.* London: Sage.

Giesen, Bernhard. 1998. *Intellectuals and the German Nation: Collective Identity in a German Axial Age.* Translated by Nicholas Levis. Cambridge: Cambridge University Press.

Goldstein, Judith, and Robert O. Keohane, eds. 1993. *Ideas and Foreign Policy: Beliefs, Institutions, and Political Change.* Ithaca, NY: Cornell University Press.

Gouldner, Alvin W. 1965. *Enter Plato: Classical Greece and the Origins of Social Theory.* New York: Basic Books.

———. 1970. *The Coming Crisis of Western Sociology.* New York: Basic Books.

Green, Bryan. 1988. *Literary Methods and Sociological Theory.* Chicago: University of Chicago Press.

Gross, Neil. 2008. *Richard Rorty: The Making of an American Philosopher.* Chicago: University of Chicago Press.

Guala, Francesco. 2001. "Building Economic Machines: The FCC Auctions." *Studies in History and Philosophy of Science* 32:453–77.

Guala, Francesco, and Andrea Salanti. 2001. "Theory, Experiments, and Explanation in Economics." *Revue internationale de philosophie* 55:327–49.

Guetzkow, Joshua, Michèle Lamont, and Gregoire Mallard. 2004. "What Is Originality in the Social Sciences and the Humanities?" *American Sociological Review* 69:190–212.

Guillory, John. 1993. *Cultural Capital: The Problem of Literary Canon Formation.* Chicago: University of Chicago Press.

Hackett, Edward J., Olga Amsterdamska, Michael Lynch, and Judy Wajcman, eds. 2008. *The Handbook of Science and Technology Studies.* 3d ed. Cambridge, MA: MIT Press.

Hacking, Ian. 1990. *The Taming of Chance.* Cambridge: Cambridge University Press.

———. 1995. *Rewriting the Soul: Multiple Personality and the Sciences of Memory.* Princeton, NJ: Princeton University Press.

Hall, Peter A., ed. 1989. *The Political Power of Economic Ideas: Keynesianism across Nations.* Princeton, NJ: Princeton University Press.

Hargens, Lowell L. 1988. "Scholarly Consensus and Journal Rejection Rates." *American Sociological Review* 53:139–51.

———. 2000. "Using the Literature: Reference Networks, Reference Contexts, and the Social Structure of Scholarship." *American Sociological Review* 65:846–65.

Heintz, Christophe, and Gloria Origgi, eds. 2004. "Rethinking Interdisciplinarity: Emergent Issues." http://interdisciplines.org/medias/confs/archives/archive_3.pdf. Accessed April 11, 2011.

Hess, David J. 1997. *Science Studies: An Advanced Introduction.* New York: New York University Press.

Hollinger, David A., ed. 2006. *The Humanities and the Dynamics of Inclusion since World War II.* Baltimore, MD: Johns Hopkins University Press.

Igo, Sarah E. 2007. *The Averaged American: Surveys, Citizens, and the Making of a Mass Public.* Cambridge, MA: Harvard University Press.

Jacobs, Jerry A., and Sarah E. Winslow. 2004. "Overworked Faculty: Job Stresses and Family Demands." *Annals of the American Academy of Political and Social Science* 596:104–29.

Jasanoff, Sheila. 1995. *Science at the Bar: Law, Science, and Technology in America.* Cambridge, MA: Harvard University Press.

Knorr Cetina, Karin. 2001. "Objectual Practice." In *The Practice Turn in Contemporary Theory,* edited by Theodore R. Schatzki, Karin Knorr Cetina, and Eike von Savigny, 175–88. London: Routledge.

Knorr Cetina, Karin, and Urs Bruegger. 2000. "The Market as an Object of Attachment: Exploring Postsocial Relations in Financial Markets." *Canadian Journal of Sociology* 25:141–68.

———. 2002. "Global Microstructures: The Virtual Societies of Financial Markets." *American Journal of Sociology* 107:905–50.

Knorr Cetina, Karin, and Alex Preda. 2001. "The Epistemization of Economic Transactions." *Current Sociology* 49:27–44.

———, eds. 2006. *The Sociology of Financial Markets.* Oxford: Oxford University Press.

Kuhn, Thomas S. 1962. *The Structure of Scientific Revolutions.* Chicago: University of Chicago Press.

Kurzman, Charles, and Lynn Owens. 2002. "The Sociology of Intellectuals." *Annual Review of Sociology* 28:63–90.

Kusch, Martin. 1995. *Psychologism: A Case Study in the Sociology of Philosophical Knowledge.* London: Routledge.

———. 1999. *Psychological Knowledge: A Social History and Philosophy.* London: Routledge.

Lamont, Michèle. 1987. "How to Become a Dominant French Philosopher: The Case of Jacques Derrida." *American Journal of Sociology* 93:584–622.

———. 2009. *How Professors Think: Inside The Curious World of Academic Judgment.* Cambridge, MA: Harvard University Press.

Leahey, Erin. 2004. "The Role of Status in Evaluating Research: The Case of Data Editing." *Social Science Research* 33:521–37.

———. 2005. "Alphas and Asterisks: The Development of Statistical Significance Testing Standards in Sociology." *Social Forces* 84:1–24.

———. 2006. "Transmitting Tricks of the Trade: Mentors and the Development of Research Knowledge." *Teaching Sociology* 34:93–110.

———. 2008a. "Methodological Memes and Mores: Toward a Sociology of Social Research." *Annual Review of Sociology* 34:33–53.

———. 2008b. "Overseeing Research Practice: The Case of Data Editing." *Science, Technology, and Human Values* 33:605–30.

Lemov, Rebecca M. 2005. *World as Laboratory: Experiments with Mice, Mazes, and Men.* New York: Hill and Wang.

Lezaun, Javier. 2007. "A Market of Opinions: The Political Epistemology of Focus Groups." *Sociological Review* 55:130–51.

Lieberman, Leonard. 1989. "A Discipline Divided: Acceptance of Human Socio-biological Concepts in Anthropology." *Current Anthropology* 30:676–82.

Liebert, Roland J. 1976. "Productivity, Favor, and Grants among Scholars." *American Journal of Sociology* 82:664–73.

Lin, Min, with Maria Galikowski. 1999. *The Search for Modernity: Chinese Intellectuals and Cultural Discourse in the Post-Mao Era.* New York: St. Martin's.

Lynch, Michael. 1991. "Pictures of Nothing? Visual Construals in Social Theory." *Sociological Theory* 9:1–21.

Lynch, Michael, and David Bogen. 1997. "Sociology's Asociological 'Core': An Examination of Textbook Sociology in Light of the Sociology of Scientific Knowledge." *American Sociological Review* 62:481–93.

MacKenzie, Donald A. 1981. *Statistics in Britain, 1865–1930: The Social Construction of Scientific Knowledge.* Edinburgh: Edinburgh University Press.

———. 2001a. *Mechanizing Proof: Computing, Risk, and Trust.* Cambridge, MA: MIT Press.

———. 2001b. "Physics and Finance: S-Terms and Modern Finance as a Topic for Science Studies." *Science, Technology, and Human Values* 26:115–44.

———. 2003. "An Equation and Its Worlds: Bricolage, Exemplars, Disunity and Performativity in Financial Economics." *Social Studies of Science* 33:831–68.

———. 2004. "The Big, Bad Wolf and the Rational Market: Portfolio Insurance, the 1987 Crash and the Performativity of Economics." *Economy and Society* 33:303–34.

———. 2006. *An Engine, Not a Camera: How Financial Models Shape Markets.* Cambridge, MA: MIT Press.

MacKenzie, Donald A., and Yuval Millo. 2003. "Constructing a Market, Performing Theory: The Historical Sociology of a Financial Derivatives Exchange." *American Journal of Sociology* 109:107–45.

MacKenzie, Donald A., Fabian Muniesa, and Lucia Siu, eds. 2007. *Do Economists Make Markets? On the Performativity of Economics.* Princeton, NJ: Princeton University Press.

Mallard, Grégoire. 2005. "Interpreters of the Literary Canon and Their Technical Instruments: The Case of Balzac Criticism." *American Sociological Review* 70:992–1010.

Mallard, Grégoire, Michèle Lamont, and Joshua Guetzkow. 2009. "Fairness as Appropriateness: Negotiating Epistemological Differences in Peer Review." *Science, Technology and Human Values* 34:573–606.

Mannheim, Karl. 1936. *Ideology and Utopia.* New York: Harcourt Brace Jovanovich.

Marcuse, Herbert. 1964. *One-Dimensional Man: Studies in the Ideology of Advanced Industrial Society.* Boston: Beacon.

Marks, Harry M. 1997. *The Progress of Experiment: Science and Therapeutic Reform in the United States, 1900–1990.* New York: Cambridge University Press.

Matthews, J. Rosser. 1995. *Quantification and the Quest for Medical Certainty.* Princeton, NJ: Princeton University Press.

Maynard, Douglas W., and Nora Cate Schaeffer. 2000. "Toward a Sociology of Social Scientific Knowledge: Survey Research and Ethnomethodology's Asymmetric Alternates." *Social Studies of Science* 30:323–70.

McCloskey, Deirdre N. 1998. *The Rhetoric of Economics*. 2d ed. Madison: University of Wisconsin Press.

Merton, Robert K. 1945. "The Sociology of Knowledge." In *Twentieth Century Sociology*, edited by G. Gurvitch and W. E. Moore, 266–405. New York: Philosophical Library.

Messer-Davidow, Ellen. 2002. *Disciplining Feminism: From Social Activism to Academic Discourse*. Durham, NC: Duke University Press.

Mills, C. Wright. [1941] 1966. *Sociology and Pragmatism: The Higher Learning in America*. New York: Oxford University Press.

Mirowski, Philip. 1989. *More Heat than Light: Economics as Social Physics, Physics as Nature's Economics*. Cambridge: Cambridge University Press.

———. 1999. "Cyborg Agonistes: Economics Meets Operations Research in Mid-century." *Social Studies of Science* 29:685–718.

———. 2002. *Machine Dreams: Economics Becomes a Cyborg Science*. Cambridge: Cambridge University Press.

———. 2004. *The Effortless Economy of Science?* Durham, NC: Duke University Press.

Moore, Kelly, Daniel Kleinman, David Hess, and Scott Frickel. Forthcoming. "Science and Neoliberal Globalization: A Political Sociological Approach." *Theory and Society*.

Morgan, Mary S., and Frank A. G. den Butter, eds. 2000. *Empirical Models and Policy Making: Interaction and Institutions*. New York: Routledge.

Mullins, Nicholas C. 1973. *Theories and Theory Groups in Contemporary American Sociology*. New York: Harper and Row.

Nelson, John S., Allan Megill, and Donald N. McCloskey, eds. 1987. *The Rhetoric of the Human Sciences: Language and Argument in Scholarship and Public Affairs*. Madison: University of Wisconsin Press.

Novick, Peter. 1988. *That Noble Dream: The "Objectivity Question" and the American Historical Profession*. Cambridge: Cambridge University Press.

O'Connor, Alice. 2001. *Poverty Knowledge: Social Science, Social Policy, and the Poor in Twentieth-Century U.S. History*. Princeton, NJ: Princeton University Press.

Oleson, Alexandra, and John Voss, eds. 1979. *The Organization of Knowledge in Modern America, 1860–1980*. Baltimore, MD: Johns Hopkins University Press.

Osborne, Thomas. 1993. "Mobilizing Psychoanalysis: Michael Balint and the General Practitioners." *Social Studies of Science* 23:175–200.

Percival, W. Keith. 1976. "The Applicability of Kuhn's Paradigms to the History of Linguistics." *Language* 52:285–94.

Pinch, Trevor, and Richard Swedberg, eds. 2008. *Living in a Material World: Economic Sociology Meets Science and Technology Studies*. Cambridge, MA: MIT Press.

Platt, Jennifer. 1996. *A History of Sociological Research Methods in America, 1920–1960*. Cambridge: Cambridge University Press.

Pontille, David. 2003. "Authorship Practices and Institutional Contexts: Elements for a Comparison of the United States and France." *Science, Technology, and Human Values* 28:217–43.

Poovey, Mary. 1998. *A History of the Modern Fact: Problems of Knowledge in the Sciences of Wealth and Society*. Chicago: University of Chicago Press.

Porter, Theodore M. 1986. *The Rise of Statistical Thinking, 1820–1900*. Princeton, NJ: Princeton University Press.

———. 1995. *Trust in Numbers: The Pursuit of Objectivity in Science and Public Life*. Princeton, NJ: Princeton University Press.

Porter, Theodore M., and Dorothy Ross, eds. 2003. *The Cambridge History of Science*. Vol. 7, *The Modern Social Sciences*. Cambridge: Cambridge University Press.

Power, Michael. 1997. *The Audit Society: Rituals of Verification*. Oxford: Oxford University Press.

Preda, Alex. 2006. "Socio-technical Agency in Financial Markets: The Case of the Stock Ticker." *Social Studies of Science* 36:753–82.

———. 2008. "STS and Social Studies of Finance." In *The Handbook of Science and Technology Studies*, 3d ed., edited by Edward J. Hackett, Olga Amsterdamska, Michael Lynch, and Judy Wajcman, 901–20. Cambridge, MA: MIT Press.

———. 2009. *Framing Finance: The Boundaries of Markets and Modern Capitalism*. Chicago: University of Chicago Press.

Randel, Don Michael. 2009. "The Public Good: Knowledge as the Foundation for a Democratic Society." *Daedalus* 138 (Winter): 8–12.

Ricci, David. 1977. "Reading Thomas Kuhn in the Post-behavioral Era." *Western Political Quarterly* 30:7–34.

Ritzer, George. 1980. *Sociology: A Multiple Paradigm Science*. Boston, MA: Allyn and Bacon.

Rojas, Fabio. 2007. *From Black Power to Black Studies: How a Radical Social Movement Became an Academic Discipline*. Baltimore, MD: Johns Hopkins University Press.

Ross, Dorothy. 1991. *The Origins of American Social Science*. Cambridge: Cambridge University Press.

Rueschemeyer, Dietrich, and Theda Skocpol, eds. 1996. *States, Social Knowledge, and the Origins of Modern Social Policies*. Princeton, NJ: Princeton University Press.

Ruhleder, Karen. 1995. "Reconstructing Artifacts, Reconstructing Work: From Textual Edition to On-Line Databank." *Science, Technology, and Human Values* 20:39–64.

Sapiro, Gisèle. 1999. *La guerre des écrivains, 1940–1953*. Paris: Fayard.

Schatzki, Theodore R. 1996. *Social Practices: A Wittgensteinian Approach to Human Activity and the Social*. Cambridge: Cambridge University Press.

———. 2001. "Introduction: Practice Theory." In *The Practice Turn in Contemporary Theory*, edited by Theodore R. Schatzki, Karin Knorr Cetina, and Eike von Savigny, 1–14. London: Routledge.

Schatzki, Theodore R., Karin Knorr Cetina, and Eike von Savigny, eds. 2001. *The Practice Turn in Contemporary Theory*. London: Routledge.

Shadish, William R., Donna Tolliver, Maria Gray, and Sunil K. Sen Gupta. 1995. "Author Judgements about Works They Cite: Three Studies from Psychology Journals." *Social Studies of Science* 25:477–98.

Shedinger, Robert F. 2000. "Kuhnian Paradigms and Biblical Scholarship: Is Biblical Studies a Science?" *Journal of Biblical Literature* 119:453–71.

Shils, Edward. 1970. "Tradition, Ecology and Institution in the History of Sociology." *Daedalus* 99 (Fall): 760–825.

Shumway, David R. 1994. *Creating American Civilization: A Genealogy of American Literature as an Academic Discipline*. Minneapolis: University of Minnesota Press.

Sismondo, Sergio 1997. *An Introduction to Science and Technology Studies*. New York: John Wiley and Sons.

Small, Mario L. 1999. "Department Conditions and the Emergence of New Disciplines: Two Cases in the Legitimation of African-American Studies." *Theory and Society* 28: 659–707.

Smith, Laurence D., Lisa A. Best, D. Alan Stubbs, John Johnston, and Andrea Bastiani Archibald. 2000. "Scientific Graphs and the Hierarchy of the Sciences: A Latourian Survey of Inscription Practices." *Social Studies of Science* 30:73–94.

Smith, Roger. 1997. *The Norton History of the Human Sciences*. New York: W. W. Norton.

Smyth, Mary M. 2001. "Certainty and Uncertainty Sciences: Marking the Boundaries of Psychology in Introductory Textbooks." *Social Studies of Science* 31:389–416.

Somers, Margaret, and Fred Block. 2005. "From Poverty to Perversity: Ideas, Markets, and Institutions over 200 Years of Welfare Debate." *American Sociological Review* 70:260–87.

Steinmetz, George, ed. 2005. *The Politics of Method in the Human Sciences: Positivism and Its Epistemological Others*. Durham, NC: Duke University Press.

Stephens, Jerome. 1973. "The Kuhnian Paradigm and Political Inquiry." *American Journal of Political Science* 17:467–88.

Stigler, Stephen M. 1986. *The History of Statistics: The Measurement of Uncertainty before 1900*. Cambridge, MA: Belknap Press of Harvard University Press.

Strathern, Marilyn, ed. 2000. *Audit Cultures: Anthropological Studies in Accountability, Ethics and the Academy*. London: Routledge.

Suny, Ronald Grigor, and Michael D. Kennedy, eds. 1999. *Intellectuals and the Articulation of the Nation*. Ann Arbor: University of Michigan Press.

Swedberg, Richard. 2001. "Sociology and Game Theory: Contemporary and Historical Perspectives." *Theory and Society* 30:301–35.

Swidler, Ann. 2001. "What Anchors Cultural Practices." In *The Practice Turn in Contemporary Theory*, edited by Theodore R. Schatzki, Karin Knorr Cetina, and Eike von Savigny, 74–92. London: Routledge.

Taylor, Charles. 1989. *Sources of the Self: The Making of Modern Identity*. Cambridge, MA: Harvard University Press.

Turner, Stephen P. 1994. *The Social Theory of Practices: Tradition, Tacit Knowledge and Presuppositions*. Chicago: University of Chicago Press.

———. 2002. *Brains/Practices/Relativism: Social Theory after Cognitive Science*. Chicago: University of Chicago Press.

Weintraub, E. Roy. 1991. *Stabilizing Dynamics: Constructing Economic Knowledge*. Cambridge: Cambridge University Press.

———. 2002. *How Economics Became a Mathematical Science*. Durham, NC: Duke University Press.

Whitley, Richard. 1984. *The Intellectual and Social Organization of the Sciences*. Oxford: Oxford University Press.

Worland, Stephen T. 1972. "Radical Political Economy as a 'Scientific Revolution.'" *Southern Economic Journal* 39:274–84.

Wuthnow, Robert. 1989. *Communities of Discourse: Ideology and Social Structure in the Reformation, the Enlightenment, and European Socialism*. Cambridge, MA: Harvard University Press.

Yonay, Yuval P. 1998. *The Struggle over the Soul of Economics: Institutionalist and Neoclassical Economists in America between the Wars*. Princeton, NJ: Princeton University Press.

———. 2000. "An Ethnographer's Credo: Methodological Reflections following an Anthropological Journey among the Econ." *Journal of Economic Issues* 34:341–56.

PART ONE

Knowledge Production in the Disciplines

Library Research Infrastructure for Humanistic and Social Scientific Scholarship in the Twentieth Century

ANDREW ABBOTT

I have two major aims in this chapter. The first is empirical. I want to recover the practices, communities, and institutions of library researchers and their libraries in the twentieth century. There is at present almost no synthetic writing about this topic, and I aim to fill that gap. This empirical investigation points to a second, more theoretical one. There turns out to be a longstanding debate between librarians and disciplinary scholars over the proper means to create, store, and access the many forms of knowledge found in libraries. By tracing the evolution of this debate, I create a theoretical context for current debates about library research.

By library research I mean those academic disciplines that take as their data material which is recorded and deposited. Throughout the period here investigated, that deposit took place in libraries or archival repositories. In practice, the library research disciplines include the research branches of the humanities and a substantial portion of the social sciences: study of the various languages and literatures, philosophy, musicology, art history, classics, and history, as well as extensive parts of linguistics, anthropology, sociology, and political science. (In earlier years, economics would have been on this list as well.) It is work in these fields that I mean when referring to "library research" throughout this chapter. For convenience I sometimes denote these disciplines as HSS (for humanities and humanistic social sciences). I am not concerned with library use by nonexperts such as undergraduates, avocational readers, and the larger public, nor with library use by natural scientists, for whom the library is not, as it is for their HSS colleagues, a crucial laboratory.

Three major ruptures mark library research in the twentieth century: World Wars I and II and the academic market crash of the 1970s. World War I broke the German dominance of the academic system, paving the way for American leadership. World War II not only confirmed the hegemony of American scholarship (and of English as the language of scholarship) but also produced an explosion in American higher education. The end of this expansion in the 1970s produced a final rupture, resulting in the research system that is just passing away today.

The periods between these transitions can be thought of as research regimes, periods in which there was a more or less stable library research world. I shall call these the formative, interwar, postwar, and implosion periods, respectively. In this chapter I try to sketch the basic qualities of research in each of them: its demography, its library resources, its basic reference structure, and the habitus of scholarship that those three things implied. Since the absence of prior literature forces my work to be largely descriptive, I cannot here theorize these "research regimes" in any deep way. For the moment, they are simply periods in which library research took a recognizable, somewhat constant form.

Since estimating scholarly demography and library resources is most conveniently done across the whole century, however, I shall begin with general discussions of those themes. I then turn to the main analysis, which is by period.

Demography

One central determinant of a research regime is its demography, the number of active scholars at a given time. There is no obvious measure of this number, nor are there consistent records for the likely indirect indicators: faculty numbers, PhD numbers, and society members. Since faculty data are the least specifically tied to research, I shall here use the other two—PhD numbers and society membership data—to estimate the demography of library research.[1] For the major HSS disciplines, figure 1.1 shows rates of PhDs produced per year from the 1920s. The figure shows the five-year average for the period labeled, this being considerably more stable than year-to-year figures. I have not included data earlier than the 1920s, because disciplinary identities were quite unstable before that time. I have used a

1. Data from 1921 to 1970 come from the Bicentennial Edition of *Historical Statistics of the United States* (Bureau of the Census 1975, 1:388). Statistics since 1970 are taken from various numbers of the *Digest of Education Statistics*.

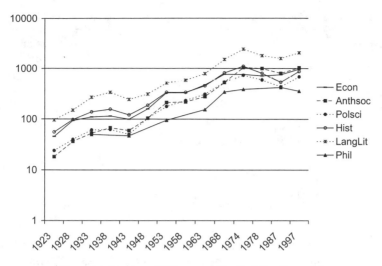

Figure 1.1. Number of PhDs granted by discipline (log scale)

logarithmic scale to show the short-term changes that would otherwise be overwhelmed by the long-term (through 1974) exponential growth.

Another view of PhD production comes from the full (1920–95) data series on PhDs in the Millennium Edition of the *Historical Statistics* (Carter et al. 2006), which presents PhD series for "Foreign Languages," "Letters" (presumably all humanities other than "Visual and Performing Arts"), and "Social Sciences and History." (Note that psychology is excluded.) Table 1.1 presents this sum for each decadal year in its second column. The other columns use a simple extrapolation to estimate the total number of PhD dissertations ever written in HSS up to a given date (the third column) and the proportion of the total of all dissertations written by 2007 that were written *after* the date shown (fourth column).[2] For example, 530 PhDs were conferred in 1930, and 5,502 dissertations had been written as of 1930 since the beginning of American academia, representing only 2 percent (100 percent − 98 percent) of the total of all dissertations available as of today. Roughly speaking, 5 percent of all American dissertations written by 2007 were written in the formative and interwar periods, about 20 percent during the postwar period, and the other 75 percent since 1970. By adding an initial founding generation (with European PhDs) to the ex-

2. I have linearly interpolated PhD production rates between a figure of 0 in 1890 and 140 (the first National Research Council number) in 1920. For the period after 1995, I have (conservatively) simply continued the 1995 figure to 2007.

Table 1.1   PhD production figures: Language, letters, and all social sciences

Year	PhDs total	PhDs to year	%	PhD holders alive and unretired after year	Age (years)
1920	140	2,100	99	2,467	37.7
1930	530	5,502	98	6,455	37
1940	825	12,535	96	13,222	38
1950	1,337	19,900	93	20,644	40.1
1960	1,845	36,201	87	35,197	40.4
1970	3,638	70,413	75	72,137	37.8
1980	5,268	134,962	52	126,227	39.6
1990	4,812	181,535	36	158,284	43
2000	~6,000	240,464	15	191,574	44.9

trapolation of the National Research Council data above, the 1920–95 data series can be used to estimate the number and age of people with doctorates alive and in academia at any given moment. These figures are shown in the final two columns of table 1.1.[3]

The size of professional societies provides a useful alternative measure of the size of the library research world (table 1.2). Like the PhD figures, however, society figures are somewhat elusive. The Carnegie Institution did a census of societies in 1908. The American Council of Learned Societies (ACLS) (in its *Bulletin*) kept consistent statistics for its constituent societies from 1920 to 1960. After that time, there is no single consistent listing. Regularly issued sources like *The World of Learning* (*WOL*) and *The Encyclopedia of Associations* are erratic in coverage. The former appears somewhat more accurate (because the figures change more often), so I have followed it here after 1960, designating the numbers from it Series B. (To make the transition clear, I have given both figures—from the ACLS and from *WOL*—for 1960. Note that *WOL* is often substantially below the ACLS totals for that year.) I have located exact data for two societies only (American Economic Association and American Sociological Association).

I have provided two sums to estimate the size of HSS academia as a whole. The first (libusersum) sums the memberships of the "library-user" societies (not all of them shown) among the ACLS constituent societies.

---

3. I have assumed a founding generation of 350 academics, distributed rectangularly across the ages from twenty-seven to sixty-two, 10 academics to each age-year. I have further assumed that all PhDs are conferred at age twenty-seven and that all scholars remain in the PhD pool for thirty-five years unless they die. I have estimated death with standard U.S. cohort life tables for the white (gender-pooled) population. The early years of the data are largely driven by these initial assumptions and so should not be taken seriously.

Table 1.2 Society memberships by year, 1908–2001

Series A[1]

	1908	1920	1925	1930	1935	1940	1945	1950	1955	1960
Am. Philological Assoc. (founded 1869)	594	656	1,007	1,100	1,057	1,050	1,020	1,112	1,193	1,400
Modern Language Assoc. (founded 1883)	650	1,650	2,795	3,642	3,810	4,412	3,900	6,128	8,289	11,000
Am. Historical Assoc. (founded 1884)	2,203	2,633	2,790	3,589	3,336	3,532	3,615	5,513	6,138	8,400
Am. Economic Assoc. (founded 1885)	751	2,335	3,547	2,710	2,506	2,966	3,961	6,631	10,411	14,018
Am. Political Science Assoc. (founded 1903)	308	1,300	1,521	1,747	1,834	2,637	3,299	5,140	6,084	7,000
Am. Sociological Assoc. (founded 1905)	100	800	1,193	1,530	1,300	999	1,242	2,673	4,584	6,638
Am. Philosophical Assoc. (founded 1900)	139	268	419	550	600	801	860	1,172	1,477	1,718
Am. Anthropological Assoc. (founded 1902)	269	—	—	936	925	1,101	1,108	2,937	3,265	4,200
Linguistic Society of Am. (founded 1924)				467	457	530	600	728	1,586	1,631
Ilbusersum	5,350	9,642	13,272	18,089	17,683	20,269	22,255	35,578	47,844	62,011
Weighted LUS	4,381	6,841	9,255	13,483	13,314	15,136	15,883	24,132	31,460	40,713
Growth		1.56	1.35	1.46	0.99	1.14	1.05	1.52	1.3	1.29

Series B

	1960	1965	1970	1975	1984	1991	2001
Am. Philological Assoc.	1,405	1,800	2,500	2,850	3,000	3,000	3,000
Modern Language Assoc.	10,700	20,000	30,000	30,000	30,000	28,000	32,000
Am. Historical Assoc.	8,500	12,000	16,000	18,500	14,000	14,000	16,000
Am. Economic Assoc.	10,159	13,025	18,908	18,348	20,162	21,578	27,000
Am. Political Science Assoc.	6,200	9,500	16,000	16,000	12,000	12,000	14,500
Am. Sociological Assoc.	5,200	7,789	13,485	14,654	11,600	12,841	13,000
Am. Philosophical Assoc.	1,703	2,267	2,900	5,500	6,200	8,000	10,000
Am. Anthropological Assoc.	2,062	2,600	6,000	7,114	10,000	10,000	10,000
Linguistic Society of Am.	1,800	—	4,500	4,500	6,000	7,000	7,000
Ilbusersum	51,029	72,365	111,793	123,966	120,162	123,619	140,100
Weighted LUS	35,263	52,002	76,120	87,293	82,741	84,015	95,100
Growth		1.47	1.46	1.15	0.95	1.02	1.13

[1] Series A data from the Carnegie Institution and the American Council of Learned Societies. Series B data from The World of Learning.

Table 1.3   Ratio of society members to PhD holders

Year	PhD holders	ACLS core	Ratio
1908	1,047	5,014	4.79
1920	2,467	9,642	3.91
1925	3,965	13,272	3.35
1930	6,455	15,804	2.45
1935	9,654	15,368	1.54
1940	13,222	17,498	1.32
1945	15,224	19,005	1.25
1950	22,108	31,306	1.42
1955	27,710	41,441	1.5
1960	35,197	54,374	1.54
1965	47,551	68,981	1.45
1970	72,137	105,793	1.47
1975	102,796	112,966	1.1
1984	139,305	106,962	0.77
1991	162,096	109,419	0.68
2001	195,506	125,500	0.64

The second sum ("weighted LUS") weights these societies by a rough esti-mate of their use of libraries.[4] This is a best estimate of the actual research group aiming to use the libraries. The "Growth" row gives the ratio of this second sum from period to period. Thus, the 1920 weighted LUS figure is 1.56 times that of 1908.

Combining the society data with the PhD data provides the interpretive key to this mass of information. Table 1.3 shows, for each year given, the ratio between the relevant societies figure—the total in the core ACLS so-cieties (American Philological Association, Modern Language Association, American Historical Association, American Economic Association, Ameri-can Political Science Association, American Sociological Association, and American Anthropological Association)—and the number of PhD hold-ers currently "available," in terms of the extrapolations discussed above. It is evident that the nonprofessionals were not immediately squeezed out of the "professional" societies but rather persisted in them almost up to World War II. Only around 1940 did the number of PhD holders in the system at a given time approach the number of society members.

A second important fact involves libraries more directly. The turnaround of this ratio after World War II reflects an increase in institutional member-

4. The humanists and historians count 1 per individual in this sum, the sociologists and political scientists count 0.5 per individual (also the linguists because so many of them are du-plicated in other societies), and the economists and anthropologists count 0.25 per individual. There undoubtedly remains some duplication in these data.

ships for the purpose of library subscriptions, reported in detailed ACLS data not shown. The postwar period thus saw much wider availability of core research periodicals via an upgrading of library holdings below the first- and second-tier facilities.

The third crucial fact in this table is of course the plunge of the society/ PhD ratio from 1970 on. A portion of this plunge, to be sure, reflects the emergence of PhDs in new fields outside the classical canon. But the majority of it probably reflects PhDs leaving academia. Indeed, by this estimate, from a quarter to a third of all PhDs in these fields were not to be found in the professional organizations, no doubt because they were not employed as academics.

Overall, these ratios imply that PhD numbers are the best guide to the size of library research academia before World War II, but that society membership numbers are the best guide afterward. The relatively slow growth of the societies in the interwar academic world (in table 1.2) conceals the rapid replacement of amateurs with professionals.

Libraries

This complex demography of research scholars inhabited a surprisingly small group of libraries, because graduate training—and to a considerable extent scholarship as a whole—was astonishingly concentrated for much of the twentieth century. As of 1925, one quarter of *all American PhDs ever conferred* had come from two institutions—Columbia and Chicago. Five institutions (those plus Harvard, Yale, and Hopkins) had conferred 50 percent, and ten institutions (those plus Cornell, Pennsylvania, Wisconsin, New York, and Illinois) had conferred 75 percent. Table 1.4 shows the equivalent statistics up through 1955. (Note that this is for all types of PhDs and hence includes education, speech, clinical psychology, etc.) As late as the early 1950s, fourteen institutions were responsible for half of all the PhDs

Table 1.4 Concentration of graduate education: All PhDs

Proportions of PhDs	Pre-1925	1926–37	1938–47	1948–55
One-fourth	2	3	5	5
One-half	5	9	11	14
Two-thirds	8	14	23	24
Three-fourths	10	19	29	33

Note: Figures are numbers of universities.

Table 1.5   Concentration by field, 1925–1935 and 1946–1955

	% of PhDs from top 5 departments		% of PhDs from top 20 departments	
	1925/26 to 1934/35	1946/47 to 1954/55	1925/26 to 1934/35	1946/47 to 1954/55
Psychology	45	31	80	54
Anthropology	88	71	96	83
Economics	42	45	82	69
History	37	39	73	64
Political science	42	41	80	70
Sociology	45	42	69	61
Fine arts	78	59	68	81
Classics	41	41	77	69
Philosophy	44	42	63	53
English	46	31	77	65
Other languages	45	—	82	—
All humanities	—	30	—	56
Total	38	25	74	50

Note: Figures are percents.

conferred in a given year.[5] For two decades in the interwar and postwar periods, respectively, table 1.5 shows the figures for the particular fields of interest here. These are typically higher than the table 1.4 figures, since universities tended to specialize (table 1.5 looks at the most prolific departments in each particular field, not the same five universities in all fields). Despite the declines, as of the mid-1950s it is still true that from 30 to 40 percent of PhDs in any given HSS field come from the five most prolific departments and that about two-thirds come from the twenty most prolific departments. Nor did the identity of the top five change much: California replaced Hopkins, but Harvard, Yale, Columbia, and Chicago remained in the top group. This means in turn that well into the postwar research period most library research dissertations were based in a small handful of libraries whose names are familiar to any seasoned library worker then or now: Widener, Sterling, Butler, Harper, Doe, and so on.

Throughout its long dominance, this handful of great university libraries was complemented by a handful of equally great nonuniversity libraries. Just as amateur scholars remained in the professional academic societies much later than we imagine, so too did the great public and specialty li-

5. All these data come from Irwin 1956, 67–79; and Marsh 1936, 76.

braries remain major research centers. The public libraries of Boston, New York, Philadelphia, Baltimore (Peabody Institute), and Chicago were great indeed; the New York Public Library trailed only the Library of Congress (LC) and Harvard in sheer size, while the Chicago Public Library was the only library with over a million volumes west of the Appalachians until the University of Chicago Library passed that level in 1931. There were great private libraries as well: Boston's Atheneum, with its notable rare books; Chicago's Newberry and Crerar Libraries, covering humanities and sciences, respectively; the great medical libraries of the New York Academy of Medicine and the Philadelphia College of Physicians. Washington had not only LC but also the immense collection of the Surgeon General. With few exceptions the great nonuniversity libraries were in Boston, New York, Philadelphia, Washington, and Chicago, as were the great PhD-producing universities other than Yale, which was, however, only a two-hour train ride from New York. The extraordinary preeminence of these "library cities" was well recognized at the time (see, e.g., Bishop 1926, 215).

For most scholars, however, the first recourse was their college or university library. The data available, although incomplete, show a number of things about these libraries.[6] First, all of them expanded rapidly during the twentieth century, in volumes, material expense, and, to a lesser extent, staff. Typically, the fifth-largest library at a given time point is about the size of the tenth-largest ten years later, and the tenth about the size of the twentieth ten years later. Second, libraries typically hired about one staff member per ten thousand volumes, a ratio that tended to fall somewhat, both at a given time and over time, as libraries grew larger. They thus probably had a fixed numerical core of workers—reference, cataloging, acquisitions, and other technical staff—who would simply handle more volumes as holdings expanded. These core workers were common to all libraries with research pretensions, but by the 1960s the elite research libraries (members of the Association of Research Libraries (ARL)—perhaps 1 percent of university libraries) had all passed beyond this technical core of library workers into a zone of purely optional hiring: area bibliographers and other such luxuries.

Third, within the elite libraries, however, there was considerable leveling both in volume numbers and in materials spending after World War II. This leveling was probably driven by government documents. The deposi-

6. Because of space constraints, I have removed here a detailed analysis of university library expansion based (up to 1961) on the twenty-four universities with complete data (Molyneux 1986) and (after 1961) on data from the Association of Research Libraries (various years of *Academic Library Statistics*). The conclusions presented in the text summarize this detailed analysis.

tory system sends every premier state institution the same mass of government documents, holdings that can be up to one-third of a collection. The apparent leveling in volumes thus conceals a great hidden difference in early monographic and serial holdings built up before World War II. These enduring differences remained crucial in disciplines like history, English literature, and German studies. It is thus not at all surprising that for the first half of the twentieth century, the roster of the top five university libraries in terms of sheer volumes coincides almost exactly with the roster of the five most prolific HSS PhD–producing universities: Harvard, Yale, Columbia, and Chicago were among the top five until 1961, when Chicago—then in financial rout—fell out.

Throughout the formative, interwar, and even into the postwar periods, then, library scholars were generally trained in first-rate libraries located in or near other first-rate libraries and then spent their careers in considerably less excellent libraries far away from this remarkable core. Because of this career pattern, it is not surprising that through all three periods the university librarians as well as the American Library Association (ALA) and the disciplinary societies emphasized investment in library infrastructure that would enable the location of distant resources by scholars who remembered fondly the libraries of Boston, New York, Washington, and Chicago. These located sources were then either borrowed via interlibrary loan or visited during holiday or sabbatical research trips.

By library infrastructure, I mean all those tools that enable scholars to conduct their research in libraries. To a certain extent, these are basic tools: bibliographies, indexes, and abstracts that identify sources in the three basic kinds of materials—periodicals, books, and archives/documents. But library research involves not only these core bibliographical tools but also highly organized guides to particular materials in particular areas. If one surveys the eleven editions of the ALA's *Guide to Reference Books*, the greatest increase is not in the core tools but in these reference works on "special subjects." These works took up a third of the pages of the first edition of the *Guide* (Kroeger 1902), half of the third (Mudge 1923), and two-thirds of the seventh (Winchell 1951). By contrast, core infrastructure remained about 12 percent of the pages in all three.

Core and specialized reference tools combined with trends in demography and library structure to produce a particular habitus of research, a way of doing library work in the scholarly environment of a particular moment. In what follows, I shall sketch for each period (research regime) how the demography, the libraries, and the tools combined to create a particular world of research practices. I apologize if the discussion is sometimes excessively detailed. These research worlds are old and unfamiliar; they can be re-created only by detailed description and analysis.

The Formative Era

Core Infrastructure

The formative era reference discussions in Kroeger (1902) and Mudge (1923) show that the most important scholarly reference sources were in French and German. The scholarly reference librarian—there were few of these—was expected to read those languages as well as English.

Periodical bibliography was surprisingly well served. There were numerous, if incomplete, German works, while in English there were the British Museum *Catalogue of Printed Journals* and Ayer's newspaper annual for American newspapers. Most important, *Poole's Index* gave a cumulated guide to the whole of nineteenth-century English-language periodical literature, the *Annual Literary Index* covered about 140 English and American periodicals from 1891 to 1910, and the *Reader's Guide to Periodical Literature* (an ongoing cumulative periodical author/title/subject index) began in 1900.

The brainchild of H. W. Wilson, the *Reader's Guide* was only one of the many ways in which this remarkable man transformed the face of American knowledge (on Wilson generally, see Lawler 1950). Wilson made two great discoveries. First, he realized that by locking the type on an entry but not on a page he could break up each monthly issue to be re-sorted into longer cumulations. Second, he cracked the collective-action problem that had plagued libraries for decades by charging *Guide* subscribers in proportion to the number of indexed periodicals to which they actually subscribed, charging, moreover, on a sliding scale that fell heavier on larger libraries. Despite the predictably anguished howls, Wilson's *Guide* became the progenitor of (and provider of seed money to) dozens of other indexes. Moreover, his pricing model facilitated most of the important bibliographical projects of the following decades, and his firm became the backbone of American librarianship. By 1907 Wilson had split off an academic version of the *Guide*, the *Supplement*, which in 1919 was renamed the *International Index* and absorbed the foreign-literature indexing consortium sponsored by the ALA. This would be the standard periodical bibliographic tool for smaller research libraries—and the first line of attack in the larger ones—until the Internet age.

Another bibliographic creation of the formative period was the ALA *Index to General Literature*, which indexed essays in books and which has survived in modified form (*Essay and General Literature Index*), although, unlike the *Reader's Guide*, it never spawned a scholarly version. Indexes came for newspapers as well: the *Times* index in 1906 and the *New York Times* index in 1913.

Book bibliography lagged. The various pieces of what is now *Books in Print* emerged in the 1890s from Wilson's predecessor and chief competitor R. R. Bowker. The British Museum *Subject Catalogue to Modern Books* started appearing in 1903, and the immense Courtney *Register of National Bibliography*—a bibliography of bibliographies—was published between 1905 and 1912. But there was no general subject index to books in print, and indeed, LC started selling its catalog cards—a major step toward national standardization in cataloging—only in 1901.

There were, of course, dozens of catalog classifications at this point; the Dewey decimal system was primus inter pares but clearly had difficulty with immense collections. Because many formative era research libraries had their own cataloging systems, scholars moving between research libraries had to master different systems. This was an onerous job, of course, but classified catalogs were themselves a recent innovation. Whereas most prior (before 1875) classifications had located books by acquisition number or some other irrelevance, Dewey's was "relative," permitting the insertion of new books in their (subject) position as they were acquired. As a result, only with the Dewey classification did shelf browsing become a viable research technique. It is striking in this regard that unlike Continental libraries, American university libraries appear to have been open stack for researchers from very early on.[7]

The situation was less auspicious with materials other than periodicals and books. Although lists of Continental dissertations were available, the American system had no centralized listing until 1933. The great indexes to British government documents were unmatched in the United States, although the *Checklist of Public Documents* went into its third edition in 1911, and subject indexes emerged for various sub-areas of government publications—from the Bureau of Labor Statistics, the U.S. Department of

7. For a historical discussion of one library's successive catalogs, see Weinheimer 1996. On open stacks, the ALA survey in the mid-1920s notes that of the larger U.S. college and university libraries, only the college libraries (ALA 1926, 2:167ff.) had open stacks for all students. University stacks were generally closed to undergraduates. See also Richardson 1908. For a shocked American reaction to Continental libraries, see Johnson 1943, 172, 181.

Agriculture, and even state governments. Government documents would be an enduring weak link in the American library chain.

Archival tools by contrast were strong. Particularly conspicuous were the Carnegie Corporation–sponsored guides to European archival materials relevant to the history of the United States. Spain, Russia, Germany, Paris, Rome, the British Museum, and the Public Record Office (PRO) eventually got separate volumes. Another important source was Johnston and Mudge's *Special Collections in Libraries in the United States* (1912), sponsored by the U.S. Bureau of Education, which reported on over two thousand libraries and included a chronological list of major imported collections and their acquirers.

Among general reference tools, an important body had to do with learned societies, which issued most journals. Here again, the German source (*Minerva*, which ceased publication in 1938, then reappeared in modified form after World War II as *World of Learning*) was the best. Both the Germans and the British had also produced massive national biographical dictionaries by the formative era, and *Who's Who in America* began in 1902.

Specialized Reference Tools

As for specialized areas, music is a good example, covered by multivolume bibliographical sources like Eitner's *Lexikon* and the British Museum *Catalogue of Printed Music*, as well as comprehensive multivolume reference sources like Grove's *Dictionary of Music* and multivolume surveys like the *Oxford History of Music*. Similarly vast bibliographies, reference works, and multivolume histories covered the various modern literatures, and *Notes and Queries*, an ongoing list of open research questions in literary fields, had been in existence since 1850. *Dramatic Index* began in 1909. (One of the few reference tools to disappear completely, it ceased publication in 1949).

In the social sciences were equally vast multivolume German bibliographies and handbooks, complemented by English-language equivalents— Palgrave's *Dictionary of Political Economy* in three volumes, for example. Statistical abstracts existed for most advanced economies, and Moody's, Poor's, and similar tools for business reference emerged in the 1910s. The discipline of history had numberless specialized reference works.

Across all disciplines, such specialized tools were most often multivolume works that assembled bibliography, substantive analysis, and ongoing

scholarly debate into a single source. Although usually aiming at completeness as of a given date, these in practice evolved steadily through ongoing
supplements and continuations.

The formative era scholarly researcher thus worked in a surprisingly
rich reference environment. Not only were these European and American
specialized works available, but the core infrastructure of ongoing indexing and bibliography for both books and periodicals was already under
construction. Document indexing was somewhat weaker, although still
substantial, and a few guides to important archives were available. On the
debit side, there was no comprehensive list of all the books in print, much
less a guide to where they might be, nor a single subject cataloging system
for them.

The Habitus of Scholarship

Research habitus is founded in demography. Table 1.1 suggests that in the
formative period there were about a thousand PhDs across all the social
sciences and humanities. Scholarly societies—at that time totaling about
four thousand members—were thus full of amateurs: do-gooders in the
American Sociological Association and American Economic Association;
adventurers, explorers, and museum staff in the American Anthropological
Association; antiquarians in the American Historical Association (AHA);
and so on. Thus, the center of research life at this point was often not the
university but rather a loosely public sphere of knowledge creation for
which we have no easy name and which vanished without a trace in the
triumph of the professors. Chances are that the university and professionalizing scholars were younger on average than the amateurs.

Given that scholarly societies typically had only a few hundred members, PhD scholars knew well their disciplinary colleagues, those colleagues'
work, and even their students' work, for journals published lists of doctoral
work in progress. Note, however, that many more persons than the PhD-
trained core taught in universities and colleges in this period: there were
36,000 faculty (of all types) in 951 schools in 1910 (Bureau of the Census
1975, 1:383). The expanding group of PhDs thus represented a serious upgrading of faculties as well as of societies.

Not only was graduate education concentrated in a few universities in
this period, but the books of those universities were to a considerable extent concentrated in departmental, rather than central, libraries. Such major
university collections as at Chicago, Hopkins, Illinois, and Indiana kept the
majority of their books in departmental libraries, and even Columbia and

Harvard had 200,000 and 350,000 departmental volumes, respectively, in the late formative era (Hanson 1917, 27). Such departmental libraries were typically small collections of core journals, indexes, and reference works, as well as a set of crucial monographs. These were often but by no means always duplicates of centrally held materials.

American departmental libraries derived from the German "seminary" library: the small teaching collection used by a professor and his students as a basis of intensive instruction and investigation, ideally in a location immediately adjacent to the main library stack (Adams 1887; for autobiographical accounts, see Burgess 1934, 198; Hicks 1968, 94; Larson 1939, 256). Harvard's Widener Library (1915) was designed on such a model, with rooms for seminar collections on its top floor and faculty research offices scattered throughout the building. Ideally, such departmental libraries were staffed by subject specialists; at Chicago, for example, these staff were the Fellows (the most senior graduate students) of the department involved (University of Chicago Library 1896, 6).

Departmental libraries meant that library research faculty had immediate, physical access to the principal tools of their trade: bibliographies, indexes, reference works, major periodicals. These were not in another building, much less across a large campus, but down a hallway or even next door. (For discussion, see Bishop 1926, 67). Moreover, the departmental library system meant that professors and their graduate students saw each other on a daily basis, giving graduate education an intensity evident in scholarly autobiographies of the period.

Not only were faculty and graduate students often running their own facilities, but faculty also played a substantial role in acquisitions. At Chicago, faculty acquisition requests might go directly to the trustees, bypassing the powerless superintendent of departmental libraries (sociologist W. I. Thomas). Indeed, a survey in 1917 found an extensive faculty role in acquisitions at most of the twenty-four major university libraries considered (Hanson 1917, 20ff.). This, too, reflected the German model, where seminary libraries began as the personal, home collections of particular professors (see, e.g., Sihler 1930, 62). A first-generation American academic like Columbia's John Burgess (1934, 217ff.) conceived of the university library as simply a larger version of the faculty-conceived specialty library.

The departmental library concept was, however, appropriate only to the great research institutions, whose librarians, even as late as the 1930s, were typically PhDs in disciplines (Zimmerman 1932, chap. 2). Most academic librarians detested departmental libraries on grounds of duplication, disarrangement, loss of books, loss of central control over cataloging and staff, and a host of other evils (Bishop 1901). Moreover, sheer library size was already raising the possibility of ending direct faculty access to books, either through a closed-stack system or by removal of books to a specialized stack building. Harvard's librarian William Lane made the case against such a centralized system with revealing vignettes of faculty research, which show that even at this early moment HSS library research practice already included extensive, unsystematic examination of myriads of materials "that would ordinarily be regarded as worthless" (Lane 1903, 14). Such trolling would never be recognized by most librarians as legitimate research practice, and even at the time the librarian colleagues discussing Lane's paper were already willing to send such little-used materials to nationally centralized depositories like LC, forestalling the possibility of such research altogether.

The divide between faculty and librarians over research practice was thus already evident in the formative era. Although the wide interests of faculty in the social sciences and modern languages were leading them to desire combining departmental libraries into larger units (Commission on the Future Policy of the University Libraries 1924, 55), they still wanted the convenience of concentrated reference resources as well as immediate access to large quantities of rarely used materials. By contrast, the librarians wanted centralization, administrative control over acquisitions, and—in some cases—even closed stacks, to which they believed systematic indexes would provide sufficient access.

Correlatively, librarians in the formative era were already beginning to demote faculty from their status as the dominant users of the library. Librarians' new rhetoric of "general education" emphasized general-periodical reading rooms, facilities for undergraduate education, and so on. This rhetoric portrayed librarians as defenders of liberal learning against "narrow" faculty specialism (Anonymous 1916; Bishop 1926, 219–22; Bliss 1912).[8] Faculty and graduate students, by contrast, found specialization both liberating and exciting.

Despite these harbingers of conflict, the relation between formative era faculty and their libraries was for the moment extremely close. Under the departmental library system, the small elite of true research faculty worked in close physical proximity to their local library resources and their gradu-

---

8. Librarians were not the only opponents of specialism. A substantial number of PhDs, particularly in literature, found graduate training in the German (i.e., philological) style to be pettifogging inanity. See, e.g., Canby 1947, 197ff., 212ff.; Johnson 1943, chap. 13; Leonard 1927, 224; Pattee 1953, 210; Perry 1935, 96ff.; Van Doren 1936, 95ff. Historians (e.g., Hicks 1968, 83ff.; Larson 1939, 256ff.) found seminars much more rewarding.

ate students. They controlled much of local library policy. Their reference infrastructure was surprisingly good and rapidly improving. Most of their librarians were either scholars themselves or had extensive training in bibliographical research (see, e.g., Richardson 1992). Concentrated in a few universities, library scholars also typically enjoyed conspicuously rich local holdings, to which their wealth of reference tools gave access, not to mention that most of the library resources of the United States were within a six- to eight-hour train ride of each other.[9]

The Interwar Era

Core Infrastructure

An important general change in the interwar era was the decline in reference tools written in foreign languages, from about half of Kroeger's (1902) core reference tools to a quarter or less in Mudge (1923). This was another divide between librarians and faculty, for most PhD programs required two foreign languages until well into the postwar period, and faculty remained heavy users of foreign source material.[10]

In periodical bibliography, Wilson's *International Index* continually expanded its coverage, steadily splitting off sub-areas as they became too large. Among the HSS spin-offs (which also took journals from the *Reader's Guide*) were the *Index to Legal Periodicals* in 1909, *Education Index* in 1928, and *Art Index* in 1931. In 1920 the *International Index* was indexing two hundred periodicals, seventy-four of them in foreign languages. In 1931 there were three hundred indexed, eighty-three of them in foreign languages.

Once a periodical reference was identified, however, one had to find a library with the periodical. The interwar era saw a great advance in this task: the 1928 *Union List of Serials in the United States and Canada*. The idea of "union lists"—lists of holdings across some set of libraries—was popular among librarians in the interwar period. At first regional, the movement aimed to provide scholars with comprehensive guides to local resources and to help avoid "costly duplication," a librarian obsession. Although early discussions about a periodical union list dated from 1912, not till the 1920s did an ALA committee, along with H. W. Wilson, achieve the goal

9. For example, W. E. Leonard's Columbia dissertation on Byron took him to "the libraries of Cambridge, Boston, Brown, as [well as] about New York" (Leonard 1927, 237).

10. I have no circulation evidence from the interwar period, but one can only assume that use of foreign sources was higher then than later, and, as of May 1956, 27 percent of faculty charges from the University of Chicago Libraries were in foreign languages (El-Sheniti 1960, 59).

by jawboning the necessary serial records out of over two hundred libraries and the necessary advance subscriptions out of forty (McHugh 1984).
By consulting the *Union List*, a scholar could locate the nearest of the 226
reporting libraries that possessed any particular volume of 75,000 periodicals (McHugh 1984, 2). To be sure, whole states were absent; a full 42 percent of the reporting libraries were in Washington, New York, Boston, Chicago, and Philadelphia. But the overall utility of the book was enormous
(McHugh 1984, 241–42).

Another type of serial resource proved a complete failure in this period, however. Although *Psychological Abstracts* (1927) produced some half-
hearted imitators, the abstracting concept made slow headway outside
medicine and the sciences (Manzer 1977, 134ff.). A *Social Science Abstracts*
journal ran from 1929 to 1933 and then failed. By contrast, *Chemical Abstracts* (1907) was already a longstanding success, providing an example
librarians would repeatedly tout (in vain) to HSS scholars.

The union list concept was occasionally applied to books. The 1919 *Census of 15th Century Books Owned in America* covered 13,200 copies of 6,640
titles, giving bibliographical information and location, thereby immensely
aiding scholarly access. Like many works in this era, it was produced by the
same distributed-processing model that had produced the *Oxford English
Dictionary*; scattered libraries and book owners contributed their own holdings or indexes to the larger enterprise, in this case run by the Bibliographic
Society of America.

But more general book bibliography lagged behind. The Library of
Congress had collected cards on an exchange basis since it first entered the
card business in 1901 (Lewis 1985, 19ff.). It sold copies of its in-house
cards to libraries wishing to save cataloging costs and exchanged cards with
the other great U.S. collections as a way of building up a single national
catalog, which came to be known as the National Union Catalog (NUC).[11]
By 1926 the collection had reached about two million cards, about one
quarter of the estimated eight million research works owned in America
(Schwegmann 1942, 230). A five-year Rockefeller gift (1927–32) built the
collection to 6.8 million cards. Partial copies of this newly complete card
catalog ("depository sets") were made available at about forty locations
throughout the United States from the early 1930s. For those near enough
to use them, these could shortcut postal requests through the LC clearing

11. The libraries whose exchange cards were amalgamated into the NUC are no surprise
(for a full list, see Winchell 1951, 35–36): among universities, Harvard, Princeton, Cornell, Illinois, Chicago, North Carolina, and Michigan; among public libraries, Boston, New York, and
Washington; among specialized libraries, the John Crerar and the Pan American Union.

house for interlibrary loans, which handled about ten thousand requests a year by the 1930s (Kletsch 1936).[12]

Exchange was necessary because despite the immense holdings of the major scholarly collections, overlap between them was surprisingly small (although to the more penurious librarians it seemed surprisingly large; see, e.g., Merritt 1942, 74). A 1942 sample study traced 2,442 randomly chosen NUC cards in the card catalogs of the forty-six ARL members (Merritt 1942, chap. 4). A scholar at Harvard would find 913 of those books and a reader at the New York Public Library 774. But only 244 were in both libraries. Most of the holdings of each library were thus unique with respect to the other even though they had a substantial common core. For a researcher, a good library would have extensive core and unique holdings, as did all the great university research libraries. But if even in the best libraries exchange could be important, for lesser libraries it was essential. And NUC provided the foundation for that exchange. Probably in part for this reason but also because of its easier expandability, major libraries were steadily drifting to the LC classification after 1920, by which time most LC classification schedules were available in print. This made scholarly life considerably simpler.[13]

The interwar situation for archives and manuscripts was complex. British historical manuscripts were located and to some extent indexed by the *Reports* of the Historical Manuscripts Commission, which began to appear in 1914. The huge holdings of the PRO were the subject of a two-volume

---

12. Chicago, Harvard, Michigan, the Boston Public, the John Crerar, and the U.S. Department of Agriculture were other libraries loaning more than a thousand volumes a year in this period; ALA 1926, 2:221–22.

13. On this change generally, see Tauber 1940, 191ff.; Tauber 1941. Reclassification was a time-consuming process that got in the way of scholarship. See various entries in the ALA *Catalogers' and Classifiers' Yearbook*, e.g., 1:67ff., 113ff. (1933), 5:65ff. (1936), and 8:104 (1939), the last noting the transition of the Boston Public Library into the LC fold. Tauber (1941, 32) finds a median of eleven years to reclassify a college or university library. Jacobs and Spencer (1933) chronicle the saga of reclassifying about forty thousand titles in the University of Rochester Library "after considerable prayer and some correspondence, but without much light from either source" (64). For an unflattering portrait of library life in a peripheral state university library in the late interwar period, see Wilson et al. 1939. A similar unevenness is shown in Tauber 1941, chap. 7. Tauber found that most faculty did not care much about classification, whereas librarians assumed that scholars would prefer classifications that "suggested" new materials. Faculty were uninterested in librarians' thoughts about what they ought to read, viewing the librarians purely as technocrats who should restrict themselves to guaranteeing the location of works whose identification as important was faculty prerogative. This was yet another sign of scholars' early disinterest in general-purpose indexing. Tauber (1941, 230, 238) found that although about 70 percent of faculty surveyed were in the stacks at least once a week, less than 40 percent of them looked in the catalog before going into the stacks.

guide in 1923–24. In the United States, the LC Manuscript Division started circularizing repositories in the 1910s and issued a *Check List of Collections of Personal Papers* in 1918, covering 56 replying libraries (out of 232 circularized). A 1924 edition brought coverage to 131 repositories. Although not quite as concentrated as other library resources, archival sources also tended to be on the East Coast.

More generally, American public documents, from 1895 to 1940, were collected and indexed in the *Document Catalog* issued at the end of each congressional session. Other government bibliographies were numerous but haphazard (Smith 1947). The historical documents situation improved suddenly when Congress, after decades of lobbying, finally created the National Archives in 1934. The Depression provided another unexpected boon for library researchers when Harry Hopkins put unemployed scholars to work preparing inventories and bibliographies of public and private document holdings (the Works Progress Administration's Historical Records Survey; Kidder 1943).

General reference tools also made some advances in the interwar era. The *Encyclopaedia Britannica* produced an important new edition (the fourteenth), the *Oxford English Dictionary* was completed (1928), the *Dictionary of American Biography* (1943) brought American biography onto a par with its British and Continental cousins, and White's *Conspectus of American Biography* (1937) finally provided an index to the haphazard *National Cyclopedia*. The *Times Atlas* appeared in 1920, and the first edition of the *Atlas Mira* in 1937.

Specialized Reference Tools

While the core infrastructure made major gains in the interwar era, in specialty areas the harvest was yet richer. *Granger's Index* to poetry dates from 1918, and we find in Mudge (1923) author dictionaries (giving use of words, indexes of subjects, and lists of characters) for writers from Homer and Dante to Balzac and Hawthorne. Literary students also had the MLA's *American Bibliography* from 1921, a general index to all writings by Americans on the modern literatures. The British equivalent, the *Annual Bibliography of English Language and Literature*, first appeared in 1921 as well, as did *The Year's Work in English Studies*, an annotated annual review. The monumental *Encyclopédie des sciences religieuses* had reached dozens of volumes by the mid-1920s, and an eight-volume *Bibliographie bouddhique* appeared in 1930–37.

As for the social sciences, in 1915 a consortium of special librarians launched the Public Affairs Information Service (PAIS)—a comprehensive guide to current affairs and related periodicals that was issued weekly and cumulated annually. Unlike the *International Index*, PAIS included government documents and other nonjournal sources. Moreover, it was selective and anchored in the research environment, being produced in the New York Public Library's Economics Section. Other important social science tools emerged as well. The first *Encyclopedia of Social Sciences* (fifteen volumes) appeared in 1935, and the enormous cumulative *London Bibliography of the Social Sciences* appeared in four volumes and two supplements from 1931 to 1937. The League of Nations, the International Labor Office, and other international organizations spawned a host of annuals, bibliographies, and reviews throughout the period. For the more data hungry, the *Dictionary of Occupational Titles* saw publication from 1939 to 1944. Finally, history saw a number of major reference works in this period: the *International Bibliography of the Historical Sciences* (beginning in 1926), the ALA-AHA *Guide to Historical Literature* (1932), the *Encyclopedia of World History* (1940), and, for the current period, *Facts on File* (1940).

This explosion of reference works—mostly generated by specialists themselves, although sometimes in alliance with special librarians—meant a quantum leap in the ability of library scholars to find and use what they actually had in their own libraries. All the same, reference tools could help only if a library owned them. Even so large a library as Cornell—the ninth largest academic library in the United States at the time—possessed by the end of the interwar period only 55 percent of the titles in Mudge and indeed only 41 percent of the Mudge titles in social science (Wilson, Downs, and Tauber 1947, 138).

The Habitus of Scholarship

The explosion of specialized reference works led to changes in the practice of scholarship in the interwar period; library researchers drifted away from the general infrastructural tools of the librarians toward the specialized ones created by their colleagues. Indeed, it is not clear that they ever left the specialist universe.

Again, demography sets the stage. Although library-based academia nearly tripled in size in the 1910s and 1920s, it remained a small world—probably about ten to fifteen thousand total. Journals continued to list doctoral dissertations under way, suggesting that disciplinary scholars kept up on all ongoing or new doctoral work. Academia got a little younger as the new PhDs came to dominate and as PhD production expanded, but average age began to rise again as PhD production slowed. Disciplinary professionalization gradually drove the amateurs out of the scholarly societies, which consequently grew only slowly. Typically, they had from 1500 to 2000 members. To the individual academic researcher, this replacement of dilettantes by experts meant better colleagues without a large increase in quantity. At the same time, faculties (as opposed to societies) still included many non-PhDs. Total faculty numbered 48,615 in 1920 and 82,936 in 1930, while the HSS research group numbered about 10,000 and 18,000, respectively. The ratio did not change substantially.

Much of the scholarly habitus of the formative period carried over into the postwar period (see, e.g., Hicks 1968, 138). The departmental library system continued, and in many cases departments still controlled the purchase of books for their own libraries. An ALA survey in the mid-1920s found that departmental libraries in the twenty universities reporting typically contained about a quarter of a university's collection (although some universities included law or medical school libraries as "departmental" libraries). Yale, for example, had thirty-four different departmental libraries (ALA 1926, 2:182), containing 17 percent of the total collection.

That immediate physical access to books was regarded as necessary to first-class scholarship is evident from a 1924 University of Chicago report: "For the humanistic departments and schools the provision of library facilities which will in reality facilitate and encourage discovery means, in practical terms, the provision of a study immediately adjacent to the stacks for every senior member of the Faculties and an individual working space in the stacks for every junior member of the Faculties and every active regular graduate student" (Commission on the Future Policy of the University Libraries 1924, 4). Not surprisingly, scholars in this period were extremely active library users. In a survey of faculty in two large universities, Tauber (1941, 230) found that around 25 percent of faculty entered the library stacks daily and another 40 percent at least weekly. For humanists in particular the equivalent figures were 44 percent and 32 percent, respectively. Even allowing for response bias, these are extraordinary figures.

But the days of the departmental system were numbered. The great centralized research libraries all date from the late formative and interwar periods: Harper (Chicago) in 1910, Doe (Berkeley) in 1911/17, Widener (Harvard) in 1915, Gilman (Johns Hopkins) in 1916, Stanford (unnamed) in 1919, Michigan (unnamed) in 1920, Walter (Minnesota) in 1924, Illinois (unnamed) in 1926, Sterling (Yale) in 1931, and Butler (Columbia) in 1934 (Kaser 1997, 87–101). And if most of these newly centralized libraries followed Widener's lead in containing departmental or seminar facilities, they nonetheless removed those facilities from the faculty's home space. Faculty now had to leave their main classroom buildings to do graduate training and library research.[14]

With centralization came administrative control, particularly of acquisitions, which were running forty thousand or more items per year at the major research collections by the end of the interwar period (Molyneux 1986). A Special Libraries Association study of departmental libraries found fully 10 percent of staff time devoted to "watching for and acquiring new materials" (Hausdorfer 1938, 22). Although faculty no doubt ceded quickly on this burdensome issue, faculty involvement remained intense. So large an institution as Penn was still able in 1940 to obtain detailed analyses by more than fifty faculty of the adequacy of its holdings in their research areas (Bibliographical Planning Committee of Philadelphia 1940).

For their part, some librarians also resisted the drift toward centralization and generalism. The combination of specific subject expertise with library training had been implicit in the role of graduate fellows in departmental libraries, and such "research librarians" became standard in the new industrial libraries. The Carnegie Foundation briefly invested in a similar idea for academic libraries (Henkle 1938). The issue of specialized knowledge was related to the larger debate on the proper duties of reference librarians. Reference librarians prepared bibliographies on demand in many research libraries (Rothstein 1954, 105ff.). The Missionary Research Library's staff, for example, would prepare annotated bibliographies, make copies of excerpts, and follow bibliographical trails for patrons (Hering 1931). But despite some gestures toward subject specialization, centralization inevitably combined with financial pressures to guarantee that a minimalist theory of reference service came to dominate most university libraries in the interwar period (Rothstein 1954). The researcher was left to his own devices, and another wedge appeared between faculty and librarians.[15]

14. There is some indication (Works 1927, 66) that support for departmental libraries was strongest in the sciences, which were relatively more able to retain those libraries near laboratories and faculty offices. Humanists appear to have wanted ready reference materials near the stacks and hence often went along with centralization. The Works study shows, however, that "helpers" in departmental libraries in this period were often appointed and paid by the department, not the library (Works 1927, 131). For a balanced view of centralization—unusual at the time—see Branscomb 1940, chap. 7. On graduate teaching in the (Harvard) library in this period, see Perry 1935, 242ff. On the defeat of a plan to site the Yale Graduate School adjacent to Sterling Library, see Cross 1943, 183.

15. It was in the interwar period that librarians first began to do research on "scholarly needs for information." All this work (which dates from the 1930s) concerned the natural sciences or medicine (see Stevens 1951, 13ff.).

Beyond the individual library, the demographics of the system drove other important changes. Rapid expansion of the PhD pool decentralized graduate education. Inevitably, there was a rise in locally based dissertations, a change evident in the shift to newspaper sources in history dissertations (McAnally 1951, 40) and reported in autobiographies as well (e.g., Hicks 1968, 161ff.). Thus, while the professional associations and the librarians collaborated to build resources for research on the traditional canon (a joint effort that would bear fruit after World War II in things like the publication of the Adams family papers), young scholars were professionalizing local history as a way of finding their primary materials locally. There were, to be sure, strategies for overcoming local scarcities. Hicks (1968, 140) reports taking summer teaching jobs at places like Harvard, George Washington, and Northwestern as a way to visit the great library cities and get paid for it. But in general, access drove use: scholars who could not access certain kinds of materials simply shifted their practices and indeed the topics of their scholarship.

All the same, the interwar period saw considerable leveling of the library playing field, largely through increased spending and the inevitable leveling in terms of deposited government documents. This effect was especially pronounced in the social sciences, dependent as they tended to be on more recent material. The great collections maintained and even increased their lead in materials spending, but workers in second-tier libraries could now count on core staffs, reference collections, and a much stronger interlibrary infrastructure to identify and locate materials unavailable locally. Second-tier cities began to develop their own union lists to mimic the astounding richness of the library scenes in Boston, New York, and Chicago.

A facilitator of this new leveling was the proliferation of reproduction technologies. Here too there was extensive collaboration—in securing copies of canonical sources from Europe, for example—although there was also a good deal of local photostating and copying (Putnam 1929, 697). At the close of the interwar period came microfilm, which, although it did not quite initiate the revolution expected, did enable the exchange of large amounts of material over great distances at relatively small price.

Although embedded in all these rich resources, the library scholar of the interwar era nonetheless still faced a finite literature. Reporting on scholarly publishing for the year 1927, Donald Bean found 352 new scholarly books (excluding texts) in the humanities and 428 in the social sciences. There were about twenty-five to thirty scholarly periodicals in big fields like history, literature, and economics, about fifteen to twenty in smaller fields like sociology, political science, and anthropology, and about five in tiny fields like archeology and philosophy.[16] One can calculate from his figures (1929, 11–12) that in most HSS fields a scholar could read everything published in his entire field by reading about five hundred to seven hundred pages a week. In reality, reading rates were no doubt lower, but a complete command of most or all of the ongoing research in his subfield was easily within the reach of any active scholar in this period.

The Postwar Era

Core Infrastructure

The core infrastructure continued its evolution and consolidation in the postwar era. The *International Index* (*II*) remained a major source for periodical bibliography, and in the mid-1950s Wilson accepted the academicization of America and moved the disciplinary flagship journals like the *American Historical Review* and the *Journal of Political Economy* out of the *Reader's Guide* and into the *II*. Nonetheless, although by this time the *II* was indexing about 175 journals, many established disciplinary journals were beneath the *II* radar screen. In practice, the PAIS *Bulletin* was a more effective index for the social sciences (Advisory Committee 1950; Quinn 1951, 48). And fields as important as musicology and philosophy received ongoing specialized periodical indexes only in 1949 and 1967, respectively. Moreover, as Europe recovered from war, there was a broader universe to be indexed; UNESCO's *International Bibliography* series engaged sociology (1951), economics (1952), history of religions (1952), political science (1953), and anthropology (1955), covering a wide variety of work in multiple languages.

In the postwar period abstracting and review essays finally spread to library research fields. *Sociological Abstracts* began in 1952, although lack of cumulation hampered its utility for many decades. *Historical Abstracts* began in 1955, with American history splitting off in 1964, and the twentieth century becoming a separate tool in 1971. Economics possessed abstracting journals fitfully in the 1950s before the *Journal of Economic Literature*

---

16. See also Stock 1928. Comparing his own figures on scholarly society membership with publishing data, Bean found that the various humanities and social sciences typically have one journal per 100–150 members. There was a new scholarly book for every 20–30 members across the various fields. Both figures are within the order of magnitude of current figures. For example, the American Sociological Association has about 13,000 members and the Institute for Scientific Information counts ninety-three sociology journals in its data base, one per 140 members.

emerged in 1969 as a permanent bibliographical tool. Anthropology had a *Biennial Review* from 1959 to 1971. *International Political Science Abstracts* dates from 1951. Equivalent humanistic tools were less forthcoming. To be sure, the MLA's *American Bibliography* internationalized into the far more comprehensive *MLA International Bibliography of Books and Articles on the Modern Languages and Literatures* in the mid-1950s. But although *Abstracts in English Studies* appeared from 1958, it abstracted only articles on literature, from about 190 periodicals, and lacked both cumulation and good indexing. *Philosophic Abstracts* ran from 1939 to 1954 and folded. An *Index to Religious Periodical Literature* finally began in the early 1950s, and a *Religious and Theological Abstracts* in 1958.

Abstracts were to some extent a sign that the periodical literature had begun to seem overwhelming, even if the number of journals indexed in *II* stayed close to Bean's listing of 154. Moreover, not only were there more articles to read, but they were also now much easier to find. Postwar library researchers basked in a vastly expanded edition of the *Union List* (1943), containing the records of about 115,000 titles in 620 libraries. Every state was now represented, thirty-two states by five or more contributing libraries and eighteen by ten or more. To be sure, one-third of the contributing libraries were in eight major cities, but the periodical system was far more effectively national. From 1953 onward, there was a running union list of new titles (*New Serial Titles*).

The 1943 edition of the *Union List of Serials* was complemented by three other union lists, all produced on the same model (and by ALA-Wilson cooperation) toward the end of the interwar period: the *List of Serial Publications of Foreign Governments, 1815–1931* (1932), *American Newspapers, 1821–1936* (1937), and *International Congresses and Conferences* (1938) (see Zubatsky 1982, chap. 6). Other important tools of general bibliography dating from the end of the interwar era were Ulrich's periodicals directory (1932), the *Deutsche Gesamtkatalog* (fourteen volumes by 1939), Wilson's *Bibliographic Index* (1938), and Besterman's monumental *World Bibliography of Bibliographies* (1939), which grew to 65,000 entries in 1949 and 117,000 in 1966. All in all, the core bibliographical tools of the postwar era could find for a scholar far more work than he could possibly read and evaluate.

The postwar period also saw a revolution in book bibliography. The Bowker firm's *Publishers Trade List Annual* (*PTLA*), an annual, bound collection of publishers' catalogs, which began publication in the nineteenth century, was simplified into the author-title *Books in Print* (1948), which in 1957 finally got a subject index. The British equivalent, *British National Bibliography* (*BNB*), emerged in 1950. These meant far more effective subject access to current materials than had been available before, an important tool for scholars.

But retrospective bibliography also saw a revolution. By the end of the interwar period, the forty scattered LC depository catalogs, although fairly heavily used (by library staff, not faculty—see Munson 1946, 44), were increasingly expensive both in space and in maintenance. Moreover, smaller libraries had no access to them. Yet the NUC was crucial to scholarship: about 14 percent of NUC holdings were not in LC (Lewis 1985, 33), which meant that LC itself could not serve as a default "library with everything." The result was the printing, completed in 1946, of the 167-volume *Catalog of Books Represented by Library of Congress Printed Cards* (*CBR*), containing a little under two million cards, essentially a copy of the most complete (LC) depository catalog. The *CBR* sold widely: 216 educational institutions bought a copy, including not only the major research libraries but also small colleges, state colleges, and lesser universities (Lewis 1985, 142). The *CBR* contained very little locational information, but it brought an enormous portion of national bibliography within the reach of a much larger group of faculties than had previously had access to it.[17]

The *CBR* also had a huge demonstration effect. Its publication format of multiple slightly reduced cards printed in columns on a page proved enticing, and in the late 1950s the G. K. Hall firm embarked on a profitable career of publishing the catalogs (usually author-title but sometimes subjects as well) of dozens of important libraries and specialized collections. Among the early takers were great special collections like the New York Public Library's Oriental (1960) and Jewish (1960) collections, as well as the American Geographical Society (1962). Hall also published specialized tools like the New York Public Library's subject headings (five volumes, 1959) and the Chicago Art Institute's *Index to Art Periodicals* (eleven volumes, 1962). The 1960s would bring much larger catalogs, running to dozens of volumes, often from libraries outside the university orbit: the Peabody Museum (fifty-three volumes, 1963), London's celebrated School of Oriental and African Studies (twenty-eight volumes, 1963), the U.S. Geo-

17. The *Union List of Serials* symbolized a much wider movement for union lists of all kinds. By 1942 there were regional union catalogs for states like California and New Jersey, for regions like the Chapel Hill and the Philadelphia metropolitan areas, for subject areas (*The Howard University Union Catalog of Titles by and about the Negro*), for area-subject combinations (*The Boston Medical Library Union List of Medical Literature in Massachusetts Libraries*), and so on. In addition to these were the forty distributed copies of the *Library of Congress Depository Catalog*. Every major university library in the United States (and such smaller schools as Bowdoin and Dartmouth) had such a catalog, which would have been the anchor of its interlibrary loan system.

logical Survey (twenty-five volumes, 1964), the U.S. Department of Health, Education, and Welfare (twenty-nine volumes, 1965), the John Crerar Library (seventy-seven volumes, 1967), and the New York Academy of Medicine (seventy-seven volumes, 1969). (For a complete bibliography, see Nelson 1982.) These were truly astounding tools for scholarship.

The *CBR* also indirectly helped researchers by reinforcing the continuing drift of major research libraries to the LC classification system (see Tauber and Feinberg 1974). This process had been steadily under way since the mid-1930s, following the demonstrated success of early adopters like Chicago and Michigan. By the mid-1970s, a survey found that 90 percent of American and Canadian university libraries that contained over 500,000 volumes used the LC system (Michael 1976).

Archives also became steadily more locatable through the postwar period. The Historical Records Survey had done a vast amount of work at the end of the interwar period, producing the dozens of volumes of the *Inventory of Federal Archives in the States*. On such a basis, tools like Billington's "Guides to American History Manuscript Collections in Libraries of the United States" (1952) became possible. Then in 1959 came the first volume of the *National Union Catalogue of Manuscript Collections*, which had been planned since the 1930s by committees of the AHA, the Society of American Archivists, and the American Association for State and Local History (see Billington 1952). The first volume described 7,300 manuscript collections in 400 repositories. Annual volumes (occasionally cumulated over longer intervals) brought this total to 29,350 collections in 850 repositories by the end of 1971. Such tools were heavily used by scholars. Government documents, by contrast, limped along through the postwar era with the awkward *Monthly Catalog* and its occasional cumulations.

As for other materials, *Doctoral Dissertations Accepted by American Universities* dates from the late interwar period (1933). *Microfilm Abstracts*, the ancestor of *Dissertation Abstracts* (1952) and University Microfilms, began in 1938. Although *Dissertation Abstracts* increased its coverage steadily, a fatal weakness remained: of the five midcentury doctoral giants, Berkeley, Chicago, and Harvard remained outside *Dissertation Abstracts* as of 1960. More disturbing, careful citation surveys of social scientific work in the 1950s show that dissertations were seldom cited in published work, constituting only 1 percent of all citations in political science and sociology and considerably less than that in economics.[18] A JSTOR search of all *PMLA* article

18. The studies involved are Livesay 1953; Mark 1956; Martin 1952; McAnally 1951; Meier 1951; Quinn 1951. Jesse Shera, then professor in the University of Chicago Library School,

texts finds the word "dissertation" in 14 percent of all articles in the two decades 1901–20, 11 percent in 1921–40, 8 percent in 1941–60, and 6 percent in 1961–80. To be sure, almost 10 percent of all interlibrary loan requests in the late postwar period were for dissertations and theses, running to perhaps 100,000 requests per year (Palmour et al. 1972, 44; Thomson 1970, 26). But this was nothing compared to the vast use of monographs and serials nationwide. A 1956 census of all materials circulated to faculty at Chicago, where library copies of dissertations circulated routinely, found that dissertations were only 0.9 percent of circulation in the humanities division and 3.8 percent in the social sciences division (El-Sheniti 1960, 62). The rapidly improving tool was thus serving a vanishing market; scholars seemed to be assuming that all work of quality and importance would be published (see McAnally 1951, 50).

Specialized Reference Tools

In the postwar era, specialized reference tools continued their rise and domination of library research practice. Already in 1944 an exacting study of sources for library materials in dissertations in English literature showed the overwhelming advantage of specialist-created research tools like the *Cambridge Bibliography of English Literature* over the catalog and general subject classification systems: "The process of bibliography is more purposeful and realistic than that of cataloging and classification. The bibliographer . . . begins with a subject and asks what books are related to it. The cataloger begins with a book and asks what subjects are related to it" (Swank 1945, 67). The strength of these specialist-created tools lay in their highly focused nature. *Current Sociology* (from 1952) devoted each whole issue to a monograph and bibliography of some specific area within sociology, written by a specialist. In the early 1950s there were three separate ongoing bibliographies covering parts of philosophy. In literature, the Tannenbaum *Elizabethan Bibliographies* series (1937–47) covered each minor figure with fifty pages of bibliography and each major figure with many more; individual plays of Shakespeare could command one hundred or more pages. Indeed, in Sheehy's 1976 ninth edition of the *Guide to Reference Works*, the whole category of "Guides" to particular minor authors was cut because these had become so plentiful during the postwar era (Sheehy 1976, 334). By 1964, specialist reference sources in the social sciences were so extensive that they

---

supervised these studies as part of a project to decide whether to store part of the Chicago collection.

required a five-hundred-page guide of their own (White 1964). It seems, in summary, that the postwar period saw an extraordinary flowering of highly specialized reference tools.

The Habitus of Scholarship

This immense flowering of specialist tools was part of a great sea change in academia. After the war, five years' worth of pent-up demand for graduate education—aided by GI Bill funding and powered by anticipation of jobs teaching other former GIs—transformed the academic world. As table 1.3 shows, the library-based scholarly societies grew from about 15,000 members in 1945 to over 72,000 in 1970.[19] The high PhD "birthrate" balanced with falling mortality rates to keep the age of the researcher pool stable at around forty years (thirteen years post-PhD), until the 1960s bubble finally pushed it down to thirty-seven around 1970 (see table 1.1). And in this period the PhD finally became the modal degree for the university system, although expansion of the state college and related systems kept HSS PhDs from increasing their total proportion of all faculty in higher education.

Centralization of graduate education finally began to decline in the postwar era. So also did the geographical centralization of certain kinds of library resources, particularly government documents and core research periodicals; such resources were now available at many more universities. However, library staff sizes per volume tended also to decline; there were more materials but to some extent less help with them.

For the scholars themselves, the postwar era was a new world: on the one hand, a world of high expectations, maintained by a buoyant job market; on the other, a world of relentless specialization, of proliferating sections within associations and indeed of separate subsocieties. Broad knowledge of dissertation work in progress was impossible; only via specialization could one retain a grasp of new doctoral work. To the extent that fields had delimited objects of study, dissertation topics were exhausted at a heroic pace. An implication of this overload was that disciplines lost contact not only across the broad range of their subfields but also with their own pasts. On the one hand, a rhetoric of progress entailed ignoring the past;

19. As many dissertations were written between 1945 and 1956 as had been written from 1890 to 1945, and as many were written between 1956 and 1968 as had been written to 1956. Note, however, that while postwar expansion was sudden, the *rate* of expansion steadily slowed in the postwar period until the search for military deferments created the PhD bubble of the 1960s. The slowing expansion may indicate that PhDs were already being driven out of academia by oversupply in the 1960s.

on the other, exponential growth meant that most of the work available to be read was in fact recent work. By the mid-1970s, with most disciplines producing more than four hundred PhDs per year, even first-order specialization was not really an option. Complete command even of a subfield was impossible.

To be sure, it appears that the total amount published remained proportional to the number of scholars. Following the procedures of Stock (1928), Bowker (1945) found 238 journals at the beginning of the period, again very close to the one journal per 100–150 scholars observed both by Bean (1929) and at present. But given the heroically increased numbers, even constant output rates produced a flood of material. It is therefore no surprise that there began to be complaints about scholarly overload and the loss of knowledge through sheer welter.

This was in part a structurally induced complaint, since the librarians thought that the answer to the problem was "better access" or "more effective bibliographical control." Better access tools—which inevitably made scholars happier, particularly at peripheral universities—in practice just meant access to more material, which in turn increased the problem of welter. Surprisingly, selective tools did not in general flourish. Specialty journals carried many book reviews, but a well-funded national attempt at a selective cross-disciplinary book review journal failed in the mid-1950s after a ten-year run (*United States Quarterly Book List*, 1944–56; the nonscholarly literature had had Wilson's *Book Review Digest* since 1905).

In this period scholars came to rely almost completely on specialist resources—both specialized reference works and the specialty scholarly literature itself—for their basic bibliography. They used the librarians' core infrastructure only in case of a failure somewhere along a chain of references or when searching for the rarest of materials (see Kraeling 1951, 111–14). Otherwise, they ignored the "view from nowhere" subject indexing of the librarians, however detailed it might be (Hazen 1952; Altick 1954).

The evidence for this change is overwhelming. A 1946 Chicago study found social science graduate students relying for bibliography on reading lists and article reference lists but only occasionally on periodical indexes (Brown 1946). A 1952 study of patron bibliographical sources at the John Crerar Library found that standardized indexes provided only 20 percent of the references and that those with MAs or higher degrees found over half of their references in the footnotes of periodicals or books (Williams 1952). The 1956 ALA Catalog Use study found indexing and abstracting journals almost never cited as bibliographical sources by faculty or graduate students: footnote or chapter bibliographies and hearsay dominated, although graduate students did admit to using professors' bibliographies (Jackson 1958, 26). A detailed Johns Hopkins survey in 1962 showed that even when HSS faculty and graduate students were engaged in known-item search, they pursued it only half the time through an author-title catalog but fully a quarter of the time through simple stack browsing. Subject catalogs and subject searches—for librarians their key contribution to knowledge access—were almost never used.[20] In a 1961 Chicago study, 169 people in the stacks—90 percent of them faculty or graduate students—reported the use of five hundred books total, of which fewer than a third were identified by call numbers ahead of time. A quarter were picked "because I was looking for a book of this general nature," and almost 20 percent through casual or systematic browsing. Of the books said to be "of some or great value," fully 43 percent were found by browsing of one sort or another (Bowen 1961). An item-based study by Chicago's librarians (Fussler and Simon 1961, chap. 8) was clearly embarrassed by the levels of browsing use found and in fact systematically misinterpreted its results to favor the librarians' preferred strategy of storage of "unused materials," on the ground of "what every good scholar knows [sic]: browsing alone cannot serve as a satisfactory basis for a serious literature search" (Fussler and Simon 1961, 205).

The didacticism of this last remark pervades the library literature of the period, in which the unwillingness of faculty to consult librarians' subject indexes became a standing joke (Hitchcock 1962, 10). Librarians in this period dreamed of the ultimate subject index, in part because they believed such an index would justify their relegating rarely used materials to storage.[21] In this, librarians of the postwar period were heavily influenced by indexing and abstracting in the natural sciences, both because of their apparent success in serving need and because the rapid obsolescence of scientific collections made storage an obvious and acceptable strategy for space problems. (See, e.g., the essays of Shera, Tauber, Henkle, and Fussler in Shera and Egan 1951.)

In their unscientific way, library researchers continued to spend much

20. I recalculated these figures from the raw data in Johns Hopkins University Research Library 1963, 89–91.

21. The belief that accurate subject indexing would overcome the scholarly problems created by storage drove the wonderfully detailed Chicago citation studies. The otherwise inexplicable focus on whether or not citations gave actual page numbers reflected Jesse Shera's desire to ascertain the minimal indexing unit. That that unit proved smaller than the article spelled disaster for the storage project, because such indexing was unaffordable. Library research scholars' desertion of the core bibliographical apparatus has been rediscovered in the information science literature since 1970, condemned by its own ignorance of history to imagine this an important new discovery. See, e.g., Stone 1982 and Watson-Boone 1994.

time in the library, although not as much as before the war. A Michigan survey in 1961 found that 40 percent of nonpsychology social scientists and 50 percent of English faculty reported using the library more than once a week. But at the same time, 50 percent of the faculty in social sciences and 40 percent of the English faculty said that their book and journal needs were completely or to a great extent satisfied by sources other than the university library, chiefly by their own or colleagues' personal collections (Survey Research Center 1951, 8–11). A crucial factor here was the sudden expansion of paperback publishing both in the trade world (Doubleday Anchor [1953], Knopf-Vintage [1954], Viking Paperbound [1955], Oxford Galaxy [1956]) and in the university press world (Cornell Great Seal [1955], Chicago Phoenix [1956], California [1956]). In many cases these were backlist titles, but new material was published as well (Schick 1958). As professors' own holdings expanded, the library became more than ever of importance to them precisely for its rarely used materials, even as librarians became increasingly interested in sending those very materials to storage.

The center of the dispute—recognized by only a few at the time—was historical research. The only scholars who needed truly gargantuan libraries were those—whatever their discipline—for whose work library material had historical, as opposed to substantive, value. Obsolescent research, ephemera, worthless screeds: librarians would happily throw them all away to make room for new material. But the historians often wanted just that material. "There is only one type of research—historical research—for which the flood of print does constitute a problem, not because it uses all of recorded knowledge but because it never knows what part of such records it may have to use" (Taube 1942, 247–48). Indeed, it is likely that the gradual leveling of academic libraries—in government documents, core periodicals, and materials expenditures—exacerbated this fact. All these forces meant that current holdings were much more uniform systemwide, which in turn made many of the social scientists and even a considerable number of humanists satisfied with the libraries they found as they scattered out of the elite library cities.[22] But for historical researchers, the sheer volume of

22. Another sign of equalization was the fact that librarians had given up on cooperation in acquisitions. This had been a major librarian theme in the interwar era (e.g., Bishop 1926, 223–25; Works 1927, chap. 3), along with the correlative idea that libraries and indeed research faculties should specialize. In the postwar era, librarians, like everyone else, expected all universities—and their libraries—to be excellent in all areas. The postwar period also saw a rapid decline in the importance of the nonuniversity libraries, with the conspicuous exceptions of LC and the New York Public Library. In 1958 a quarter of the business at the John Crerar Library was fulfilling photocopy orders sent in from elsewhere—essentially a depository function (McGeever 1958, 21).

resources remained crucial. A careful study in the postwar era showed that historical dissertations were extreme on every dimension by comparison with "textual" or "experimental" ones: by an order of magnitude, they used more library material, more library material that no one else had used, and more material not in the local library.[23]

The Implosion Era

Demography

Since the implosion period is defined by a demographic transition, we must start with demography. In the mid-1970s, market saturation and fiscal crisis halted the founding of new colleges and universities. Existing universities stopped hiring. The academic job market consequently died just as a flood of Vietnam War–induced PhDs finished graduate school. In the resulting catastrophe, as many as a third of new PhDs could not find academic jobs. Social science PhD production fell by nearly one-third, as did PhDs in language and letters (fig. 1.1). The crisis in PhD birthrates produced an eerie stability: the number of library-based academics remained around 80,000 until the mid-1990s finally brought new growth (table 1.3). Consequently, the average age of researchers rose steadily throughout this period, to nearly forty-five by 1996, the last year for which there is fully comparable data (table 1.1). The demographically dynamic academia of the postwar period was thus replaced by an almost immobile one during the implosion years.

A hidden consequence of the aging of academia seems to have been a decline in reading. The heaviest readers for academic work are graduate students and young faculty. Older faculty have disciplinary, professional, and administrative obligations that command much of their time. When academia ages rapidly, then, the proportion of all scholars who are active readers declines sharply. This seems to have happened in the implosion period.[24]

23. Surveying one hundred dissertations across three institutions and five fields (history, classics, education, botany, and psychology), Stevens (1951, 1953) divided them into historical, textual, and experimental. Historical dissertations typically cited a hundred or more titles uncited by any other dissertation in this list and over sixty titles not in the local library. Experimental dissertations, by contrast, typically cited only seventeen unique items and four nonlocal ones.

24. Reading in academics is in many ways a Ponzi scheme; young scholars read the work of their advisers, the work of those who influenced their advisers, and so on back to the "classics." "Reading the work of someone" is thus strictly analogous to sending five dollars to the list of

An empirical indication of this sharp change is the end of specific citation. Today's HSS journals contain very few citations to particular pages
within cited items, even when those items are large books. But detailed
citation studies from the early 1950s show that at that time typically a third
or more of all citations involved unique pages, and two-thirds involved at
least some specific page range of the cited text. The decline of such specific
citation must have reflected at least in part a decline in direct engagement
with particular sources, whether this meant less careful initial reading or
unwillingness to return to a source after writing to specify the exact location of one's dependence on it.[25]

The implosion period's buyer's market enabled a rapid rise in academic
standards outside elite institutions. This upgrading put a new premium on
publication. To be sure, the ratio of journals to discipline numbers was
roughly the same in the late 1970s as in the figures of Bean and Stock in
the 1920s and of Bowker in the 1940s.[26] But the absolute numbers were
much greater and the sheer welter of material was mind-numbing. In the
quantitative sciences, meta-analysis emerged as a statistical technique for
reducing dozens of incommensurable studies to a comprehensible set of
findings. There was no equivalent for the library researchers.

Core Infrastructure

Ironically, now that the core infrastructure was less central to research,
it reached its apogee. In periodicals bibliography, the implosion period
brought at last the long-heralded indexes to everything. The year 1965 saw
the publication of the final (third) edition of the *Union List of Serials*, covering all periodicals published prior to 1949 and detailing the holdings of
156,000 titles in about a thousand libraries. Eight years later, *New Serial
Titles* was cumulated for the period 1950–70, bringing comprehensive peri-

---

people on a chain letter. When demographic forces raised the average age of scholars by ten
years during the implosion era, the Ponzi scheme collapsed.

25. For the citation data, see the studies cited at note 18. An indication of how seriously
scholars took getting their facts right is the existence of professional citation checkers. For an
autobiography of one such person, see Rowe 1939.

26. This calculation assumes that ISI reached as deep into the pool of possibilities as did its
predecessor: that is, the existence of journals is measured by their being indexed in the ISI. On
that assumption (and using the table 1.3 figures) the numbers of scholars per journal for the
(Bean) social sciences (in 1975) are 124 for anthropology, 99 for sociology, 131 for political
science, and 155 for economics. In the (Bean) humanities (for 1980, in order to let the coverage stabilize) the figures are 63 for philosophy, 85 for history, and 128 for literature. Machlup
and Leeson's (1978, 22) numbers of journals (for 1973) are considerably lower (and the ratios
correspondingly higher), but they involve only American journals, unlike ISI.

odical bibliography and location to within three years of the then present. Finally and most important, the Institute for Scientific Information (ISI) transferred its decade-old "citation index" format from the natural sciences to the social sciences (Social Science Citation Index [SSCI]—1973) and to the arts and humanities (Arts and Humanities Citation Index [AHCI]—1978). Although mainly touted for their power to follow bibliographical chains through citation links, these two tools introduced en passant a new, pared-down version of periodical indexing to compete with the longstanding Wilson tools, which by now had split into *Humanities Index* and *Social Sciences Index*. ISI called its system Permuterm Indexing, for it consisted of a listing of every pair of substantives in every title of the source articles. (The standard name for it was Keyword-in-Context-Indexing [KWIC].) The low cost of the ISI format meant that its coverage could be wide and easily expanded. In 1975/76, *Humanities Index* was indexing 257 journals while AHCI was indexing 963. The comparable figures for *Social Sciences Index* and SSCI were 272 and 1,517.[27]

The revolution came in books as well. The 685-volume *National Union Catalogue, Pre-1956 Imprints* was completed in 1980, after twelve years. Unlike its predecessor, the *CBR*, the *NUC Pre-1956* contained all the locational information on the NUC cards; many items were located to dozens of libraries. Librarians could realize at last their dream of ultimate democracy: everybody would have rapid access to everything. At the same time, the interlibrary loan burden on the major collections would be lightened.

Even government documents and archives reached new levels. A cumulative index to the *Monthly Catalog* appeared in 1973–75, and the Congressional Information Service released through the 1980s a set of massive historical indexes of the entire Serial Set. (Still outside, unfortunately, were the millions of documents not in the Serial Set; astonishingly, sources like Poore's *Descriptive Catalogue* [1885], Ames's *Comprehensive Index* [1905], and the *Document Catalog* [1893–1940] remained important indexes well into the implosion era.) Even archives got into the act. The *National Union Catalogue of Manuscript Collections* got a cumulative personal-name index in 1988.

But these tools, while supremely powerful, were in fact only rarely relevant to the research process. Library researchers utilized them in extremis,

27. Stevens 1974 is a good review of the indexing situation at the time. Despite a great deal of computing advance, we are more or less in the same place today, having the same debates. KWIC/KWOC indexing has largely triumphed over controlled vocabulary indexing, no doubt on cost grounds. For a history of KWIC indexing, see Fischer 1966. Like several other important librarian innovations, it saw its first major use in chemistry.

having long since turned for their everyday work to more focused, special-ty-produced reference tools. Indeed, even the librarians succumbed to specialization. The eleventh edition of the ALA *Guide to Reference Works* gave up at last on the notion of a single editor; fifty subject specialty librarians contributed individual sections, while Editor Robert Balay was merely a collator. Most of these individual sections were larger than the entire first edition of the *Guide to Reference Works*.

The Habitus of Scholarship

I have already underscored the demographic conditions of the implosion period. Academia was large. Single disciplines had as many or more re-searchers than all of academia had in the interwar period. Publication rates were as high or perhaps even higher per researcher than they had been throughout the century, with a resulting flood of material. The central fact of the research habitus of this period was thus overload. In 1970 there were fifty-three university libraries bigger than the Harvard library in 1914. Inter-library loan in the 1970s ran to over a million items, and that was only the number of fulfilled requests: items requested were probably double that figure (Palmour et al. 1972, 52). Annual acquisitions in large ARL libraries typically ran about 200,000 items, roughly three times what they had been twenty years before.

What this meant within disciplines can be easily imagined. The *American Sociological Review* reviewed one hundred books in 1950. By 1972 the sociologists had a separate book review journal (*Contemporary Sociology*), which was reviewing over three times as many books. In its first year (1952/53) *Sociological Abstracts* produced 586 abstracts from 17 fully covered and 24 partially covered journals. Twenty years later (1972) it was producing 7,317 abstracts (5,050 of English-language materials), from 129 full-indexed journals, several hundreds of partially or occasionally indexed journals, and dozens of society meetings. Sociology produced an average of 161 PhDs per year during the 1950s but 654 PhDs per year between 1971 and 1976.

In every discipline the facts were the same. During the postwar period, specialization seems to have been the chief means of dealing with over-load. Disciplines kept some semblance of unity by retaining a somewhat arbitrary core of canonical works. It was in this epoch, for example, that sociology began to treat Max Weber and Emile Durkheim as if they rep-resented the entire corpus of European social theory. That this was not in the least true did not lessen the utility of having a few core texts to bind together an exploding and fragmenting discipline.

The canon/specialization means of integrating disciplines was, however, exhausted by the beginning of the implosion era, because in the last analysis most of the forms of HSS knowledge do not take well to specialization. What seem to have replaced specialization (even beyond the library-based areas of HSS) were what I have elsewhere (Abbott 2001, 25ff., 148ff.) called "generational paradigms": groups of scholars who created their own conventional subcanons, allied themselves to certain methodologies, and attacked somewhat conventionalized problems. These paradigms would evolve for twenty years or so before being replaced by other paradigms with other subcanons, methodologies, and conventionalized problems.

With respect to library research, generational paradigms solved the problem of welter by means of conventional choices of important sources. But while this helped to some extent, other aspects of the library research habitus seem in this period to have headed toward breakdown. For example, the number of citations in a given article multiplied by an order of magnitude, most of the change coming in the 1970s. This change was likely driven by technology (the citation indexes provided a much larger range of potential material to cite, and word processors made it easy to copy references from older papers), by double-blind reviewing (which encouraged the citation of any possible reviewer), and by the need to signal membership in generational paradigms and other disciplinary subcommunities.[28] In terms of library research practice, this multiplication of references must have had important effects, because as we have seen, library research scholars get most of their bibliography from other people's reference lists. The newly padded reference lists made bibliographical work harder because they suppressed quality selection. The fifty-page "Bibliographical Essays" that completed many new historical monographs were the equivalent in books.

It is also true that in the library system earlier in the twentieth century, availability—at least for secondary materials—had in fact been a proxy for quality. The books and journals unavailable in a given field in a given library were of lower average quality than those that were available. To a cer-

---

28. The ballooning of reference lists is so familiar as to need no data. See, e.g., Abbott 1999, 167. For an example, the fifty articles in the *American Journal of Sociology* in 1960 had a median of fifteen references; the thirty articles in 2005 had a median of seventy-four references. Double-blind reviewing—which no doubt drove much of this—began in the mid-postwar era in sociology and other social sciences (Abbott 1999, 144–47). It started in humanities journals somewhat later.

tain extent, this was, of course, a self-fulfilling prophecy, but the incentives of authors, subscribers, librarians, editors, and publishers all dovetailed to make it true a priori. Other factors intervened, to be sure. But certainly for the English-language literature, breadth of availability correlated fairly strongly with quality. As a result, increased access usually meant not only more material to evaluate but also a disproportionately greater need for selectivity.

All these factors suggest that in the implosion period, the library research system lurched into breakdown. Many of the traditional mechanisms for dealing with overload were incapable of handling the vast mass of material. Even subspecialties were large and faceless. PhD production was decentralized and uneven. Reading and other detailed engagements with texts seemed in decline. Meanwhile, the core research infrastructure was more inclusive and less selective than ever. General availability weakened a longstanding proxy for quality. And even specialized practices like pillaging colleagues' reference lists had become substantially less effective. There was more and more stuff and less and less way to make sense of it. Indeed, the very notions of knowledge quality and progressive cumulation seemed to need recasting in the context of the implosion era library research system.

Conclusion

In summary, the library research system that evolved in twentieth-century America contained a powerful and differentiated set of tools and practices. To a considerable extent, librarians and scholars collaborated to build a system that was extraordinarily effective at identifying and finding material locally, as well as at finding material elsewhere if need be. But despite their collaboration, the librarians and the scholars drifted steadily apart; two very different visions of knowledge emerged.

The first was that of the librarians. Librarians saw the researchers as only one among their clienteles. While that clientele was obviously the chief reason for immense library budgets, librarians also served undergraduates, who seemed a more needy—and certainly more numerous—group of users. Moreover, librarians saw themselves as the voice of centralized good sense against the irrationally self-serving demands of particular researcher communities. They thus pursued a vision of universal knowledge, knowledge without specialization, knowledge potentially available to everyone.

With respect to research users in particular, librarians' goal from the 1920s onward was a democratic, universal system in which any scholar would have some kind of access to everything in the library research system nationwide. There were three parts to this project: identification, location, and physical access itself. For identification, librarians proposed the universal index. Subject indexing, within controlled vocabularies like the LC or Wilson headings, would identify needed materials. Since librarian ideology prevented selectivity, in practice such indexes steadily extended their coverage and detail, factors that combined with the steady expansion of academia itself to make them enormous and ultimately less useful. For location, librarians produced local card catalogs of varying quality and a large collection of union lists, archive indexes, and other locational tools, relying in the last analysis on LC. It is clear that the interuniversity aspect of this system was an immense success throughout the century. Library scholarship was inconceivable without it.

As for the third issue, physical access, the librarians shaped both local and interuniversity access decisively. Locally, they centralized all materials early in the century, destroying the original library research habitus and unwittingly fueling the explosion of specialized reference and bibliographical tools. Between libraries, they created a jury-rigged access system that relied on interlibrary loans, microfilm, and other forms of duplication. Funding this system was a problem, because the weight of it fell overwhelmingly on a few great collections. At times it did not work very well, and it broke down completely under the immense pressures of the implosion period.

Scholars pursued a quite different project. Their aim was the actual creation of knowledge, but unlike the librarians this was particular and actual knowledge, not generic and potential knowledge. They too were concerned with identification, location, and physical access. But their identification practices were always rooted in each other's work. They dropped out of the "universal index" project almost at the start, preferring to identify their materials through the work of other specialists. They built and staffed specialty-internal tools from the 1920s onward. Moreover, they did a surprising amount of their identification by random search: browsing in the stacks, brute-force trolling in ranges of documentary materials, and so on. By contrast with this reliance on specialty tools and trolling for identification, however, for *location* they were much more reliant on the librarians' system.

In terms of physical access, the scholars again dissented from the librarian system. For one thing, they often let physical access drive use. That is, they often started with access rather than with identification. This was the origin of the new social history with its roots in local archives. Moreover, they often bypassed the interlibrary loan system, preferring to take themselves to sources located elsewhere (partly in order to browse or troll them) rather than calling the materials to their local library. Like the scholars' identification practices, these were designed to optimize the productivity of the research hour rather than to embody, as did the librarians' approach, an abstract model of the process of scholarship.

The scholars also remodeled their social structures to deal with the problem of welter. They dealt with quantity by creating disciplines, then specialized subdisciplines, then generational paradigms. All of these constituted somewhat arbitrary limitations on the kinds of things researchers had to know in order to conduct their work, reducing the task of identification to a feasible size.

The story of twentieth-century library research infrastructure is thus the story of the failure of a universalist approach to knowledge, the failure of a knowledge-from-nowhere. Successful forms of library-based knowledge were built on somewhat arbitrary limitations (what the librarians called "narrow specialism") that permitted the creation of highly specified and selective identification tools, which in turn allowed the purposive scanning of extremely sparse primary sources that would otherwise have yielded nothing. The librarians' much-vaunted universalist project turned out to be appropriate only for neophytes. Real knowledge could be produced only by communities that took a view "from somewhere," that embraced what seemed like forms of bias and even systematic blindness in order to permit exploration of the immense record of human endeavor. Like Odin, the researchers gave up an eye in exchange for the ability to see clearly.

References

Abbott, Andrew. 1999. *Department and Discipline*. Chicago: University of Chicago Press.

———. 2001. *Chaos of Disciplines*. Chicago: University of Chicago Press.

Adams, Herbert Baxter. 1887. "Seminary Libraries and University Extension." *Johns Hopkins University Studies in Historical and Political Science* 5:439–64.

Advisory Committee. 1950. "Bibliographical Services in the Social Sciences." *Library Quarterly* 20:79–99.

Altick, Richard D. 1954. "The Scholar's Paradise." *College and Research Libraries* 15:375–82.

American Library Association. 1926. *A Survey of Libraries in the United States*. 4 vols. Chicago: American Library Association.

Anonymous. 1916. "The Professor versus the Library." *Pedagogical Seminary* 23:262–68.

Bean, Donald P. 1929. "American Scholarly Publishing." Report to the General Education Board. Mimeo.

Bibliographical Planning Committee of Philadelphia. 1940. *A Faculty Survey of the University of Pennsylvania Libraries*. Philadelphia: University of Pennsylvania Press.

Billington, Ray Allen. 1952. "Guides to American History Manuscript Collections in Libraries of the United States." *Mississippi Valley Historical Review* 38:467–96.

Bishop, William Warner. 1901. "The Problem of the Departmental System in University Libraries." *Library Journal* 26:14–18.

———. 1926. *The Backs of Books*. Baltimore, MD: Williams and Wilkins.

Bliss, Henry E. 1912. "Departmental Libraries in Universities and Colleges." *Educational Review* 43:387–409.

Bowen, Alice. 1961. "Non-recorded Use of Books and Browsing in the Stacks of a Research Library." MLS thesis, University of Chicago.

Bowker, John W. 1945. "A List of American Learned Journals Devoted to Humanistic and Social Studies." *Bulletin—American Council of Learned Societies* 37:1–70.

Branscomb, Bennett Harvie. 1940. *Teaching with Books*. Chicago: Association of American Colleges and American Library Association.

Brown, Margaret Cornelia. 1946. "The Use Made of the Subject Catalog by Graduate Students in the Social Sciences." MLS thesis, University of Chicago.

Bureau of the Census. 1975. *Historical Statistics of the United States*. 2 vols. Washington, DC: Government Printing Office.

Burgess, John William. 1934. *Reminiscences of an American Scholar*. New York: Columbia University Press.

Canby, Henry Seidel. 1947. *American Memoir*. Boston: Houghton Mifflin.

Carter, Susan B., Scott Sigmund Gartner, Michael R. Haines, Alan L. Omstead, Richard Sutch, and Gavin Wright, eds. 2006. *Historical Statistics of the United States*. 5 vols. New York: Cambridge University Press.

Commission on the Future Policy of the University Libraries. 1924. *Tentative Report*. Chicago: University of Chicago Press.

Cross, Willbur Lucius. 1943. *Connecticut Yankee*. New Haven, CT: Yale University Press.

Downs, Robert Bingham, ed. 1942. *Union Catalogs in the United States*. Chicago: American Library Association.

El-Sheniti, El-Sayed Mahmoud. 1960. "The University Library and the Scholar." PhD diss., University of Chicago.

Fischer, Marguerite. 1966. "The KWIC Index Concept." *American Documentation* 17:57–70.

Fussler, Herman Howe, and Julian Simon. 1961. *Patterns in the Use of Books in Large Research Libraries*. Chicago: University of Chicago Library.

Hanson, James C. M. 1917. *Report of the Committee Appointed in November 1914 to Investigate the Relations of Departmental Libraries in the University of Chicago*. Chicago: University of Chicago Press.

Hausdorfer, Walter. 1938. "Professional School and Departmental Libraries Survey." Mimeo. New York: School of Business Library, Columbia University.

Hazen, Allan T. 1952. "Reflections and Observations on Subject Analysis: The Research User." In *The Subject Analysis of Library Materials*, edited by M. F. Tauber, 191–95. New York: School of Library Service, Columbia University.

Henkle, Herman H. 1938. "An Interpretation of Research Librarianship." *School and Society* 47:494–99.

Hering, Hollis W. 1931. "The Research Library and the Research Librarian." *Special Libraries* 22:7–11.

Hicks, John Donald. 1968. *My Life with History*. Lincoln: University of Nebraska Press.

Hitchcock, Jennette E. 1962. "Objective Subjectivity." *College and Research Libraries* 20:9–14.

Irwin, Mary. 1956. *American Universities and Colleges*. 7th ed. Washington, DC: American Council on Education.

Jackson, Sidney L. 1958. *Catalog Use Study*. Chicago: American Library Association.

Jacobs Elizabeth P., and Robinson Spencer. 1933. "What Price Reclassification?" *Catalogers' and Classifiers' Yearbook* 3:64–78.

Johns Hopkins University Research Library. 1963. "Progress Report on an Operations Research and Systems Engineering Study." Mimeo. Baltimore, MD.

Johnson, Henry. 1943. *The Other Side of Main Street*. New York: Columbia University Press.

Kaser, David. 1997. *The Evolution of the American Academic Library Building*. Lanham, MD: Scarecrow Press.

Kidder, Robert Wilson. 1943. "The Historical Records Survey." *Library Quarterly* 13:136–49.

Kletsch, Ernest. 1936. "The Union Catalogue of the Library of Congress." Washington, DC.

Kraeling, Carl H. 1951. "The Humanities." In *Bibliographic Organization*, edited by J. H. Shera and M. Egan, 109–26. Chicago: University of Chicago Press.

Kroeger, Alice Bertha. 1902. *Guide to the Study and Use of Reference Books*. Boston: Houghton Mifflin.

Lane, William Coolidge. 1903. "The Treatment of Books according to Their Use." *Library Journal* 28:9–16.

Larson, Laurence Marcellus. 1939. *The Log Book of a Young Immigrant*. Northfield, MN: Norwegian-American Historical Association.

Lawler, John Lawrence. 1950. *The H. W. Wilson Company*. Minneapolis: University of Minnesota Press.

Leonard, William Ellery. 1927. *The Locomotive-God*. New York: Century.

Lewis, Robert Meriweather. 1985. "From Card to Book." MLS thesis, University of Chicago.

Livesay, Martha J. 1953. "Characteristics of the Literature Used by Authors of Books in the Field of Economics." MLS thesis, University of Chicago.

Machlup, Fritz, and Kenneth Leeson. 1978. *Information through the Printed Word*. Vol. 2, *Journals*. New York: Praeger.

Manzer, Bruce M. 1977. *The Abstract Journal*. Metuchen, NJ: Scarecrow.

Mark, Francis Munz. 1956. "Characteristics of the Literature Used by Contributors to American and English Economics Journals." MLS thesis, University of Chicago.

Marsh, Clarence Stephen. 1936. *American Universities and Colleges*. 3d ed. Washington, DC: American Council on Education.

Martin, Gordon Pershing. 1952. "Characteristics of the Literature Used by Authors of Books on Political Topics." MLS thesis, University of Chicago.

McAnally, Arthur M. 1951. "Characteristics of Materials Used in Research in United States History." PhD diss., University of Chicago.

McGeever, Emmett Bernard. 1958. "A Study of the Use of a Classified Catalog." MLS thesis, University of Chicago.

McHugh, William A. 1984. "The Publication of the First Edition of the Union List of Serials." MLS thesis, University of Chicago.

Meier, Elizabeth L. 1951. "Characteristics of the Literature Used by Contributors to American Sociological Journals." MLS thesis, University of Chicago.

Merritt, Leroy C. 1942. "The Administrative, Fiscal, and Quantitative Aspects of the Regional Union Catalog." In *Union Catalogs in the United States*, edited by R. B. Downs, 3–125. Chicago: American Library Association.

Michael, Mary Ellen. 1976. "Summary of a Survey of the Use of the Dewey Decimal Classification in the United States and Canada." In *Major Classification Systems*, edited by

K. L. Henderson, 47–58. Urbana: University of Illinois Graduate School of Library Science.

Molyneux, Robert E. 1986. *The Gerould Statistics*. Washington, DC: Association for Research Libraries.

Mudge, Isadore Gilbert. 1923. *New Guide to Reference Books*. Chicago: American Library Association.

Munson, Frances L. 1946. "The Use of the Depository Catalog in a University Library." MLS thesis, Columbia University.

Nelson, Bonnie R. 1982. *A Guide to Published Library Catalogs*. Metuchen, NJ: Scarecrow.

Palmour, Vernon E., Edward C. Bryant, Nancy W. Caldwell, and Lucy M. Gray. 1972. *A Study of the Characteristics, Costs, and Magnitude of Interlibrary Loans in Academic Libraries*. Westport, CT: Greenwood.

Pattee, Fred Lewis. 1953. *Penn State Yankee*. State College: Pennsylvania State College.

Perry, Bliss. 1935. *And Gladly Teach*. Boston: Houghton Mifflin.

Putnam, Herbert. 1929. "American Libraries in Relation to Study and Research." *Library Journal* 54:693–98.

Quinn, Edward W. 1951. "Characteristics of the Literature Used by Authors of Books in the Field of Sociology." MLS thesis, University of Chicago.

Randall, William M., and Francis L. D. Goodrich. 1936. *Principles of College Library Administration*. Chicago: American Library Association and University of Chicago Press.

Richardson, Ernest Cushing. 1908. "Open Shelves for University Libraries." *American Library Association Bulletin* 2:323–27.

Richardson, John V. 1992. *The Gospel of Scholarship*. Metuchen, NJ: Scarecrow.

Rothstein, Samuel. 1954. "The Development of Reference Services in American Research Libraries." PhD diss., University of Illinois.

Rowe, Addie Frances. 1939. *An Autobiographical Sketch*. Cambridge, MA: Harvard University Press.

Schick, Franklin Leopold. 1958. *The Paperbound Book in America*. New York: Bowker.

Schwegmann, George A. 1942. "The National Union Catalog in the Library of Congress." In *Union Catalogs in the United States*, edited by R. B. Downs, 229–63. Chicago: American Library Association.

Sheehy, Eugene P. 1976. *Guide to Reference Books*. Chicago: American Library Association.

Shera, Jesse H., and Margaret E. Egan, eds. 1951. *Bibliographic Organization*. Chicago: University of Chicago Press.

Sihler, Ernest G. 1930. *From Maumee to Thames and Tiber*. New York: New York University Press.

Smith, Sidney Butler. 1947. "The United States Government as Bibliographer." PhD diss., University of Chicago.

Stevens, Rolland E. 1951. *The Use of Library Materials in Doctoral Research*. PhD diss., University of Illinois.

———. 1953. "The Use of Library Materials in Doctoral Research." *Library Quarterly* 23:33–41.

Stevens, Mary Elizabeth. 1974. "Strategies for Organizing and Searching." In *Changing Patterns in Information Retrieval*, edited by C. Fenichel, 47–79. Washington, DC: ASIS.

Stock, Leo Francis. 1928. "List of American Journals Devoted to the Humanistic and Social Sciences." *Bulletin—American Council of Learned Societies* 8:16–55.

Stone, Sue. 1982. "Humanities Scholars." *Journal of Documentation* 38:292–313.

Survey Research Center. 1951. *Faculty Appraisal of a University Library*. Ann Arbor: University Library, University of Michigan.

Swank, Raynard. 1945. "The Organization of Library Materials for Research in English Literature." *Library Quarterly* 15:49–74.

Taube, Mortimer. 1942. "The Realities of Library Specialization." *Library Quarterly* 12: 246–56.

Tauber, Maurice F. 1940. "Reclassification and Recataloging." In *The Acquisition and Cataloging of Books*, edited by W. M. Randall, 187–219. Chicago: University of Chicago Press.

———. 1941. "Reclassification and Recataloging in College and University Libraries." PhD diss., University of Chicago.

———, ed. 1952. *The Subject Analysis of Library Materials*. New York: School of Library Service, Columbia University.

Tauber, Maurice F., and Hilda Feinberg. 1974. "The Dewey Decimal and Library of Congress Classifications." *Drexel Library Quarterly* 10:56–74.

Thomson, Sarah Katherine. 1970. *Interlibrary Loan Involving Academic Libraries*. Chicago: American Library Association.

University of Chicago Library. 1896. *The Library Manual*. Chicago: University of Chicago Press.

Van Doren, Carl. 1936. *Three Worlds*. New York: Harper.

Watson-Boone, Rebecca. 1994. "The Information Needs and Habits of Humanities Scholars." *RQ* 34:203–16.

Weinheimer, James. 1996. "Finding Calasio." *Princeton University Library Chronicle* 58:32–56.

White, Carl Milton. 1964. *Sources of Information in the Social Sciences*. Totowa, NJ: Bedminster Press.

Williams, Gordon R. 1952. "A Study of the Bibliographic Sources Used by Library Patrons." MLS thesis, University of Chicago.

Wilson, Louis R., Harvie Branscomb, Ralph M. Dunbar, and Guy R. Lyle. 1939. "A Survey of the University of Georgia Library." Mimeo: Chicago: American Library Association.

Wilson, Louis R., Robert Bingham Downs, and Maurice F. Tauber. 1947. *Report of a Survey of the Libraries of Cornell University*. Ithaca, NY: Cornell University.

Winchell, Constance M. 1951. *Guide to Reference Books*. Chicago: American Library Association.

Works, George A. 1927. *College and University Library Problems*. Chicago: American Library Association.

Zimmerman, Lee Franklin. 1932. "The Academic and Professional Education of College and University Librarians." MA thesis, University of Illinois.

Zubatsky, David Samuel. 1982. "No Book Should Be out of Reach." PhD diss., University of Illinois.

TWO

In Clio's American Atelier

ANTHONY T. GRAFTON

Experienced ornithologists of scholarship see historians as unusually dull birds. Recognizable at a distance by their L. L. Bean clothing, easy to pick out in crowded forests by the simplicity of their calls, they lack both the striking plumage worn by leading figures in humanities departments, where a star system operates, and the vast hierarchies of dependents that surround established colleagues in the social sciences. Yet they too create knowledge in a wide variety of ways. Some historians—Jared Diamond and Niall Ferguson, to take two very different, very successful cases in point—devise comprehensive theories and frame helpful analogies designed to make the past explain the present and generate policies for the immediate future. Others—for example, Jonathan Spence and Laurel Thatcher Ulrich—drill into quaint and curious volumes of forgotten sources and spin the materials they find into fascinating stories that reach an equally wide public. Still others use new sources and modes of research to reconfigure established subjects like the Holocaust and World War II. Historians in France have generally abandoned the thousand-page dissertations that proved the scholarly bona fides of an earlier generation. Historians in Germany continue to write them, complete with pulverizingly detailed overviews of the older and newer secondary literature. In both countries professional historians enjoy a presence in elite media that Americans can only envy, but they are still surpassed by the British telly-dons parodied by Alan Bennett in *The History Boys*. The present chapter offers a provisional survey of only one province in the republic of historical letters, as it stands in 2011: the professional practice of history in the United States. It argues that many of

Warm thanks to the editors for organizing the Russell Sage Foundation symposium and for their comments on the first draft of this paper.

the dilemmas with which historians have wrestled for the last century and more are in fact the results of the discipline's difficult rebirth in the late nineteenth century, when players replaced gentlemen on the pitch, and an artistic form of writing once cultivated by and for members of a social and political elite was reconfigured by the anxious, underconfident hand of upwardly mobile professional scholars.

Clio's Rebirth

Professional history in America came into being in the late nineteenth century under the zodiacal sign of Leopold von Ranke. True, Ranke served Americans more as a celestial deity to be invoked by the members of a cult than as an effective instructor in the real intricacies of historical work. By the time Americans actually started coming to study in Berlin, Ranke was so old, his voice so weak, and his accent so strong that they could make out little of what he actually said (Berg 1968). And the American version of scientific history, with its refusal to contemplate any form of philosophy, amounted to a savage form of reductionism rather than a real transplantation of German *Geschichtswissenschaft*. Still, the new history took shape with remarkable speed in the years between 1884 (when only twenty professors and assistant professors held posts formally devoted to history) and 1895 (the year of the founding of the *American Historical Review*). By then, a hundred university teachers, almost half of them veterans of a stay at a German university, were designated as historians, and more posts were being created (Hamerow 1987, 49). Clio, in these years, seemed a German muse, captivated by the great research universities and academies where German scholars like Ranke and Theodor Mommsen, surrounded by teams of disciples, practiced a new kind of coordinated, industrial scholarship.

No wonder then that the new American professional historians set out to make their students master the new methods of archival scholarship and source criticism that Ranke had devised. They established what they called seminars, or seminaries: not classes, originally, but rooms equipped with catalogs, collections of primary sources, and journals. Over time, the seminary has metamorphosed into the seminar, a two- or three-hour class for graduate students, and its inhabitants have come to include women and people of color. Yet for all the transformations that history has undergone in the intervening century, the dilemmas that emerged in the first seminars have remained with us ever since. We begin our inquiry into how historians make knowledge in the present with a study of how they made it in the past.

Clio's American Ateliers

The early seminary was an austere and masculine space, designed to enable students to master the tools of their trade and use them to compose reports, which they then read aloud to their teachers and colleagues. The Johns Hopkins seminar—which became a model—was lined with and crisscrossed by shelves of dark wood. Marshaled in battalions and companies, uniformly bound series of catalogs, journals, primary sources, and monographs surrounded the young historians, who took notes while sitting on hard, wooden chairs at long tables.

It is not hard to read the message that this setting conveyed to its inhabitants: they were entering a workplace. As its organizer noted, "As you enter the seminary-library, which occupies a room fifty-one by twenty-nine feet, the most noticeable object is the long library-table around which students are seated, every man in his own place, with his own drawer for writing materials." To become a historian, one had to master the sources on the shelves—a process that involved fiercely concentrated reading, pen in hand, and the making of formal excerpts. A standard exercise for early members of the seminar required them to summarize issues of the new European historical journals for their comrades. All worked together, cutting out and organizing articles from newspapers and periodicals, which they then filed for future reference. More advanced students were distinguished from the rest: they sat in alcoves at "tables for special work." Great historians and political thinkers, or at least portraits and busts of them placed high in the room, presided over the efforts of the young who hoped to emulate their careers. History, in this space, was above all a practice, to be learned by doing what was revealingly called "historical work"—a practice as precisely defined, densely technical, and physically and spiritually demanding as those developed in the new laboratories that were founded in the same period (Adams 1884, 106).

Yet it was never absolutely clear what historical work comprised. In one sense, the seminar opened up the whole past to those who entered it: it gave them access to a vast range of sources, themes, and problems. A single student at Hopkins might investigate, through primary sources, subjects that ranged from the Greek city through medieval constitutional history to the administration of a nineteenth-century president. The seminar's catholic interests were vividly embodied in its "Historical Museum," a collection of objects that included not only Greek weapons but also "axes, spear-heads, knives, spindle-whorls, ornaments representing the stone and bronze ages of Switzerland" and another stone axe that was "a relic of the Maryland aborigines," as well as Etruscan pottery and Roman coins (Adams 1884, 125–26).

At the same time, however, the seminar also defined professional history in a way that narrowed its compass and excluded a great deal. The famous slogan painted on the Hopkins seminar wall, a quotation from the distinguished British historian E. A. Freeman, blazoned this point forth: "History is past politics, politics is present history" (Adams 1884, 119).

History, in other words, dealt with the state and its life. The new professional historians at Hopkins and elsewhere devised elaborate, powerful courses, organized around clear theses, to drive this point home and show what it meant in practice. History traced the origins of American freedom—which it generally took as an unmitigated good—to the traditions of self-government nourished deep in the Germanic forests or, a little later, to the geographical openness and rich resources of the North American continent (Adams 1884, 97–107).

Seen from this point of view, history was an improving narrative, to be savored and replicated. In its double form, the new professional history attracted many young men and a smaller but substantial number of young women. Its products filled the history departments that gradually took shape at the end of the nineteenth century. As an elective system replaced the uniform curriculum of the old colleges, history won independence from political science and economics, and a historical epic of the winning of freedoms—rooted in the Magna Carta, institutionalized with the rise of the British House of Commons, and triumphant at the American Revolution—became a central curriculum subject. In America's first age of reform and expertise, in other words, history established itself as professional in two senses. To gain a doctorate, which became the license to work in an ambitious university or college, young historians had to master the new practice with all its refinements. To win students, find publishers, and attract readers, they had to develop their version of the new narrative and present it effectively in the classroom and in synthetic textbooks (Higham [1963] 1983).

It soon became clear—it became so, in fact, at the very origins of professional history—that the double form of historians' work posed problems. The linked careers of Herbert Baxter Adams, who created the Hopkins seminar in 1880, and John Franklin Jameson, who in 1882 received the first PhD there and taught at Hopkins until he moved to Brown in 1888, exemplify these vividly. Both men did pioneer work. They played vital roles in the development of the American Historical Association and in the imposition of professional standards of research.[1] In the end, moreover, both men succeeded brilliantly. The products of Adams's Hopkins seminar became the first and dominant professional historians in the United States. When William Rainey Harper offered Adams the chair at Chicago, Adams hurled all his metaphors into one basket, using the period languages of industrial capitalism and imperialism to reply in the negative: "I have the best department of history and politics in this country. It is at once the largest and the strongest. It has a wide-spread colonial system and a very loyal body of graduate students. . . . My track is laid. My machine is built. Steam is up and, although we are still on the up grade, there is a certain momentum in a moving train like the Johns Hopkins University" (Adams 1938, 155). Adams did not exaggerate: at the last convocation, Hopkins had awarded doctorates to Charles Homer Haskins and Frederick Jackson Turner—two of the very few historians from this era whose work remains challenging and continues to be read, as Adams's own writing does not (Benson, Constable, and Dunham 1982; Billington 1973; Bogue 1998). Ten years later, Jameson actually took the job that Harper had offered Adams. He too is still remembered, above all as a great organizer of sources and bibliographies, the organizer of the Library of Congress manuscript collection, and the creator of the National Archives.

Yet the two men's relations were complex and often difficult—and not merely because Jameson, like any ambitious graduate student before or since, fiercely resented the power that Adams held over his future. Adams was more than a promoter. He developed a highly personal version of history—one that located in Germany the ancestor not only of American scholarship but also of America itself. In his courses—and his lectures at other institutions—he traced a direct line from ancient German forest clearings to the modern New England town meeting. With a casual flair for anecdote, Adams cited as evidence not documents but stories that he had picked up in summer vacations in the Neckartal or on Cape Cod and Cape Ann. He leapt to conclusions—and connected communities across time and space—with the ease of a historical Nijinsky. On May 9, 1881, Adams told the Harvard Historical Society:

> The student has only to cross the river Neckar from Heidelberg to find himself in the Odenwald, or forest of Wodan, the most classic as well as the most

1. A rich body of sources—including Jameson's enormous diary and both men's letters, as well as many publications—gives us a privileged view of their collaboration. For Adams, see Adams 1938. For Jameson, see Donnan and Stock 1956; Rothberg and Goggin 1993–2001.

primitive region in all Germany. The student has only to travel a few hours southward from the Odenwald and the Bergstrasse to reach the heart of the Black Forest. In either of these parts of Germany he can discover surviving features of the ancient village community system as described by Tacitus. With the *Germania* for a guide-book, let us follow the student through a Teutonic village. . . . Tacitus probably saw what every stranger sees to this day on visiting the country villages of South Germany, namely, compact settlements, but with separate buildings and home lots, exactly like those of a New England farming town.

Without ever citing anything so precise as an actual document, Adams cheerfully traced what he liked to call "Aryan institutions . . . advancing westward" and offered his own work as a model for eager students across the "Aryan" United States. He argued that it was not even necessary for Hopkins to teach modern English and French history, since "the Middle Age was the formative period" (Adams 1882). Thanks to his one-sided admiration for Germanic freedom, even within the medieval period Adams exaggerated the importance of "the local institutions under the Anglo-Saxons" and played down the role of Norman and Angevin innovations.

These irresponsible generalizations reduced Jameson—committed as he was to professional history—to gibbering fury (another and milder-tempered Adams student, Haskins, devoted part of his career, in later years, to quietly proving that the Normans had played a major role in British and Continental history) (Haskins 1909, 1959). When Adams discussed the origins of internationalism in a lecture, Jameson commented, typically: "This one, after a very rambling introduction, discussed the rather remotely prefatory subject of the origin of the family. It was a cheap and superficial performance, intended to amuse an audience of young women with nothing to do. I'd be ashamed to work so hard for popularity and reputation among those whose opinion is valueless" (Rothberg and Goggin 1993–2001, 1:52).

In Jameson's jaundiced but not inaccurate view, Adams exaggerated wildly when he claimed that he had introduced the German form of seminar teaching and scholarship at Hopkins—the very innovations, that is, that had made Adams and his school famous.[2] And he had no excuse for

2. Jameson, diary entry, September 29 (30), 1882. "I don't like the way things are evidently going to go on. Adams has a lot of half-educated young fellows, or not educated at all, sets them to work ambitiously at high-sounding subjects neither they nor he are half fit to treat, and then, when the crude performance is done, it is to be printed and published with a lot of others, and the seminary is to resolve itself into a mutual admiration society over 'our series' and 'our scientific work.' It makes me vexed" (Crothberg and Goggin 1993–2004, 1:64–65).

doing so. A graduate of Exeter and Amherst, Adams had studied history and public law at Heidelberg, where he received his doctorate summa cum laude—a rare triumph for an American—in 1880. He knew the German methods from personal experience and liked to describe his experiences at Heidelberg and Berlin (Cunningham 1981). In the second volume of the Johns Hopkins Studies in Historical and Political Science, which Adams founded, he published a long article, entitled "New Methods of Study in History Instruction." Here he presented his field as a science, in Baconian, rather than German, terms: "A story is told of the introduction of biology to a class in an American college by a young professor, who, when asked by the college president if he did not intend to begin his classwork with a study of great principles, replied, 'No, we shall begin with a bucket of clams.' If there is any guiding principle in the study of historical as well as of natural science, it is 'The way to that which is general is through that which is special'" (Adams 1884, 25). Adams described to his readers in detail the rigorous training he had undergone in the German seminar system:

> Instead of meeting as a class in one of the university lecture-rooms, the historical seminary, composed of only six men, met once a week in a familiar way in the Professor's own house, in his private study. The evening's exercise of two hours consisted in the critical exposition of the Latin text of a medieval historian, the *Gesta Frederici Imperatoris*, by Otto, Bishop of Freising, who is the chief original authority upon the life and times of Federic Barbarossa. . . . Each man had before him a copy of the octavo edition of Bishop Otto's text, and the conductor of the seminary translated it into German, with a running comment upon the subject matter, which he criticized or explained in the light of parallel citations from other authors belonging to Bishop Otto's time, to be found in the folio edition of Pertz's *Monumenta Germaniae Historica*. (Adams 1884, 66)

At Hopkins, Adams suggested, the historical seminary also concentrated on forming skilled practitioners through technical exercises. It met first in the Peabody Library and later in its purpose-built set of rooms, in the new library at Hopkins. The material presence of the printed documents, Adams stressed, played a vital role in teaching the new scientific history: "All the sources of information, used or mentioned by members of the seminary, were exhibited upon the long table, and were passed around for purposes of illustration. The advantage of seeing and handling the books mentioned in a lecture or bibliography, is very great, compared with the simple transcription of catalogue-titles into a note-book—a method prevailing in German lecture-courses. The Baltimore seminaries are laboratories where books are treated like mineralogical specimens, passed about from hand to hand, examined, and tested" (Adams 1884, 103). Everyone who entered the seminary, Adams claimed, learned what to do with that vital bucket of clams.

In fact, though, the seminary, as Jameson experienced it, departed radically from its supposed German models. Adams himself noted one chief difference. The German seminaries were noted for their rigor, even ferocity. The Göttingen-trained medievalist Charles Gross explained that when a student presented a "thesis" or paper at a historical seminar: "One or two critics (*Referenten*) are appointed for each thesis, who comment upon the production after it has been read. A free discussion of the subject then follows, the professor and students doing all in their power to show the utter lack of *Wissenschaft* in the author's method" (Adams 1884, 71). Mommsen and Droysen, the greatest of the Berlin historians, refused to admit foreign visitors to their seminars. The criticism directed by members at one another, they explained, was so "pitiless and severe" that it had to be kept confined within a circle of intimates.

At Hopkins, by comparison, though the décor—which included a stand of antique arms—suggested that combat might take place, kindness reigned. Adams evoked the happy spirit of collaboration: "A word is passed here, a hint is given there; a new fact or reference, casually discovered by one man, is communicated to another to whom it is of more special interest. . . . The Baltimore seminary is individually ambitious, but it hails with delight the rise of similar associations elsewhere" (Adams 1884, 108–9). In fact, as Jameson recorded over and over again, discussion at the Hopkins seminar resembled the legendary collaboration of Freeman and his favorite Oxford colleague: "All the best butter from all the best tubs; Stubbs butters Freeman, and Freeman butters Stubbs." A diary entry from October 1882 is typical: "I paid close attention and made notes for criticism; which, however, Adams rather shut off, very dexterously, he no doubt thought. In theory he last year approved of the practice of general criticism; but in practice he prefers to keep men encouraged to productiveness by refraining from criticism of poor work, and talking in a vaguer way of the general excellence of this sort of work" (Rothberg and Goggin 1993–2001, 1:65). At many sessions of the Hopkins seminary Adams invited visiting firemen or retread politicians to speak, and many of the Hopkins students, as Jameson bitterly complained, showed no engagement with the sources when they read their papers. What should have been a self-criticism session of Maoist savagery and precision degenerated into a mutual admiration society. Or—to put it differently—when the seminar's two spirits came into conflict, the need for unity, coherence, and interesting presentations took precedence over the grinding, meticulous pursuit of exact knowledge.

For all Adams's flaws, the young Jameson emerges as the less attractive of the two figures. It is hard to sympathize with the knowingness and self-righteousness of his conduct in the seminary, as he himself described it:

> I had made a few notes, but Adams gave no chance to criticise, and when a few minutes of other talk had intervened, I concluded it had grown cold, and I'd better say nothing. But just as we were about to break up, Rose put a question which was really a criticism. That bringing the matter up, I felt I ought to pitch in, and did so. I had selected some six or eight errors, notable and easily disproved, and made points of those. Well, I was rather insistent about them, and might perhaps have been a little calmer and more deferential, but I had been bored to death, like all the rest, by his tediousness, and in addition vexed beyond measure, as none of the rest of them seemed to be, by the pretentious ignorance of the [speaker]. (Rothberg and Goggin 1993–2001, 1:79)

Of one class that Jameson taught, he wrote, "It isn't going to be so hard to run this class, if there are only to be two men in it, but I should rather it were not these two Jews. I don't like Jews; they are almost never gentlemen, and they have no soul or sympathetic qualities." A year before, by contrast, Adams had sent to Andrew Dickson White of Cornell a remarkably warm and perceptive letter about Charles Gross: "The man will have a success as a lecturer and as an original investigator; but I fancy it will be very difficult for him to get a start as a regular instructor in an American College, on account of his Jewish connections. A University position must be created for him in some way, for he is really too brilliant and too well-trained for any subordinate kind of work" (Rothberg and Goggin 1993–2001, 1:70).

For all Jameson's criticisms, too, Adams, his pupils, and his fellow German-trained scholars played a central part in creating the conditions for real graduate work around the United States. Michigan, for example, which became a center of historical teaching earlier than its rivals, lacked the systematic collections of historical sources and monographs and the seminar system that Adams introduced. Edward Channing's Harvard PhD thesis "consisted of seventy-eight (badly) handwritten pages, compiled within a year and a half of getting his B.A." (Novick 1988, 48).

By contrast, Adams's pupils created real research seminars and harassed administrators to give them the necessary infrastructure—Jameson at Brown and then at Chicago, Turner and Haskins at Wisconsin. Even those who landed at less likely places did their best, as George Howard wrote to Adams from Lincoln, Nebraska, in May 1883, to emulate Adams's effort to "develop among us the habit of drinking at the Quellen and of fruitful study so peculiar to academic life in Germany." Though Howard taught between eighteen and twenty-five hours a week, he still hoped to open "a seminar for advanced students and graduate students" (Adams 1938, 64–67). George Lincoln Burr, who built up the historical collections at Cornell until they were, for a time, the best in the United States and supported the superb graduate program that turned out R. R. Palmer and many other greats, was not a Hopkins man but, like Adams, had studied in Europe, at Leipzig.[3]

Still, it seems clear that, from the start, professional history in America has had conflicting goals, ideals, and methods encoded in its DNA. Adams and Jameson, in their years together, embodied many of these. History—as Adams practiced it—sought to provide narratives and information that would be of interest and use to undergraduates and other intelligent general readers, including, ideally, the possessors of political office and power. When Adams described history as a school of politics, he meant that he saw it as an ideal preparation for many forms of public life. He took pride in the fact that some members of the Hopkins seminary took advantage of its rich collection of newspapers and journals to become journalists: "Without professing to be a school of journalism, the seminary has furnished writers for each of the prominent papers in the city of Baltimore and for some at a distance, while several of its members have secured editorial positions" (Adams 1938, 118).[4] The American Historical Association still reflects this commitment in its public charter and in its efforts to create a history center in Washington; in its early years it enlisted Theodore Roosevelt as a member, and other public men served as its presidents. Frederick Jackson Turner, who became famous for a synthetic thesis about the role of the frontier in American history, and Woodrow Wilson, who took the lessons of history into a career that spanned both university and national politics, were faithful in their way to the Hopkins historical seminary, where both had taken their doctorates. The same ideals were espoused by other highly influential professional scholars: one example is Allan Nevins, who never received a PhD and worked as a journalist for a decade and a half—and then moved into teaching history, first at Cornell and then at Columbia,

3. See the monumental account—cut in half from an unimaginably detailed dissertation—of Gabriele Lingelbach 2003.

4. For institutional developments at a number of universities, see Lingelbach 2003, 227–64; for the course of professionalization and the dominance of successive institutions, see 331–73.

where he devoted himself to grand-scale biographies and an eight-volume history of the Civil War, and continued to practice broadcast journalism for many years.

Yet Jameson took another set of messages and practices away from Baltimore—even if he internalized them mostly by holding Adams's professions of scholarship against their author. History, for Adams, needed to find a niche in a highly competitive environment and could achieve that only by continual, compulsive self-advertisement. History, for Jameson, needed to turn inward, to create a collegial body of inquirers, a community of the competent, and write for them. And Jameson was not the only one to learn these lessons. Haskins, another early Hopkins product, pursued a brilliant career in medieval history at Wisconsin and Harvard, where he became dean of America's greatest graduate school. He devoted his career to writing work on medieval science, education, and institutional history, much of it based on study of the original sources in European libraries, that remains of interest.

Haskins's career, however, is suggestive in another respect as well. By concentrating on Adams and Jameson, I have tried to suggest that formal training in history has conflicting impulses at its core. But it is equally important to note that many, perhaps most, influential historians in America have built their careers around efforts, if not to resolve these conflicts fully or transcend them, at least to respond to them creatively, without denying the need for either precise research or broad synthesis. Haskins, for example, composed not only erudite studies in medieval science but also eloquent lectures on the rise of the universities and the Renaissance of the twelfth century, in which he used his matchless knowledge of recondite primary sources to give general arguments color and dimensions. He fully appreciated the need to support research and worried when young scholars from Harvard found themselves at small colleges that refused to give them funds for research trips or even to pay for interlibrary loans.[5] But he also admired works of synthesis, like the historian Michael Rostovtzeff's "popular volume on Rome," which he praised for its clarity of exposition and for setting "a new standard in the use of . . . illustrative material in close

---

5. See Samuel Flagg Bemis to Charles Homer Haskins, Colorado Springs, November 8, 1919; Haskins papers, Princeton University Library; and Haskins to Bemis, November 20, 1919. Haskins assured the younger man, who had complained that "to buy a pair of shoes is a serious possibility to be closely figured over and is the subject of a family conference of no mean importance," that "the purchase of a pair of shoes is as serious a family question in Cambridge as at Colorado Springs!" But he also helped Bemis obtain the position at Yale where he in turn became a famous teacher.

connection with your text," and he looked for ways to widen the horizons of medieval historians.[6]

In Jameson's early years as a professor, he became the country's most articulate defender of the historian's technical craft. In a brilliant lecture at Chicago, where Jameson taught until 1905, he explained that the wheel of culture had turned, in ways that made it impossible for him and his students to produce historical narratives that showed the range and flair of a Parkman:

> If in times of literary transition, it is difficult to say what is cause and what is effect, at least we can perceive that certain phenomena arrive together. The rise of professional or professorial history-writing coincided with the rise of realism in fiction. We may fairly maintain that both had the same cause, a discontent with rhetorical and imaginative presentations of human life, bred in the minds of a generation to which Darwin and his fellows had taught the cogency and the pervasiveness of scientific laws. Since Darwin, it has been no more possible for the age to produce a crop of Macaulays and Michelets than it is possible for those who picture running horses to expel from their minds what they have learned from Mr. Muybridge's photographs of animal locomotion. (Rothberg and Goggin, 1993–2001, 1:270)

For one who believed as devoutly as Jameson in the hallucinatory vividness and analytical precision of the stop-action detail, the unique value of the hard nugget of new fact, the most important feature of the historical landscape in America was its lack of scholarly libraries and archives to match the great European national and university collections. Until the growth of travel grants and cheaper transport that followed World War II, historians did their research mostly in their own institutions—a condition that meant that a master's dissertation written at Stanford rested on a very different base of sources than it would have if the author had stayed at Cornell, where she would have had access to the historical library developed by Burr (Kammen 1973, 125).[7] As Jameson explained, historians found their books "in the general libraries into which they have been gathered somewhat incidentally," and their documents "either in the offices of government business into which they have flowed in the course of that business, and in which by our national carelessness about archives they have

6. Haskins to Rostovtzeff, December 8, 1927, Haskins papers, Princeton University Library.

7. "The Cornell library would have provided you with a lot of pamphlets and newspapers which you have not had" (Kammen 1973, 125).

mostly been left, or else, in the case of the correspondence of public men, in the hands of more or less careful descendants" (Jameson 1923, 30). No wonder, then, that he devoted much of his life to the cataloging of materials for American history in the better-organized European libraries, to the organization of the manuscript collection at the Library of Congress, and to the creation of the American National Archives.

Yet by 1923 even Jameson believed that this trend had gone far enough. At the celebrations for the opening of Michigan's Clements Library of Americana in 1923, he celebrated the rise of systematic historical collections. But he also admitted that "the work of the last sixty years has consisted in the accumulation of materials, work of the pick and spade, work of the quarryman and mason rather than of the architect." And he predicted that "the natural next development is into an age of generalization, of synthesis, of history more largely governed and informed by general ideas" (Jameson 1923, 39–41). In 1925, moreover, Jameson suited his storytelling action to his word, offering a brilliant set of revisionist lectures on the social history of the American Revolution at Princeton (Jameson 1926). Jameson, the high priest of erudition, thus joined the larger movement of historical revisionism more generally associated with writers like Charles Beard, Mary Beard, and Carl Becker. Though none of the others shared Jameson's passion for the material evidence, all of them insisted that the explicit statements and professions of the leaders of the revolution did not reveal all their true motives and interests.

Unexpected outcomes of this kind continue to make the development of historical research unpredictable, and hence predictably exciting. The expansion in the source base and the effort to improve access to it continue today. A hundred years ago Burr wrote eloquently of his adventures in European bookshops in the 1870s, compiling the vast Cornell collection of manuscripts and books connected to witchcraft: "lectures over or library closed, there were always the book-shops. . . . now locked from morn till eve in the back-street warehouse where a Bologna bookseller keeps his reserves, now haggling with the Neapolitan huckster who knows his volumes only by their shape. . . . Oh, the joys of those *Wanderjahre!*" ([1902] 1943, 296). Fifty years after Burr, the Harvard historian Archibald Cary Coolidge worked with similar expertise and enthusiasm, and on a far larger scale, to create in the Widener Library the world's fullest and richest collection of the printed sources for history—in many cases, for histories in which no one would specialize until the second half of the twentieth century (Bentinck-Smith 1976). And in the decades around 2000, Roy Rosenzweig and many others set to work to create digital data bases far larger in scale than anything that had preceded them—and to make them accessible to anyone with a computer and access to the World Wide Web (Cohen and Rosenzweig 2005). The task of creating and re-creating history's technical base never ends, and never will.

Neither, of course, does that of crafting the narratives needed by a larger society. Conservative critics often decry the decline of traditional forms of political and military history—as if Adams, or some historian of a later generation, set permanent limits for what merited inclusion in a national story. Historians, however, have not abandoned telling the stories of revolution and civil war, industrialization and twentieth-century American hegemony, or their counterparts in other histories. Rather, they have widened them to include the women and the people of color and the slaves and servants, whose experiences always formed part of the past even when they played no part in professional historians' versions of it, and whose lineal descendants are the students and readers for whom historians now write. Like the process of expanding technical knowledge, that of crafting stories about the past is one that has no natural stopping place. And, of course, the two processes regularly intersect, as newly available sources stimulate new investigations, and new questions reveal the existence of sources of unsuspected interest.

Learning to do historical work, in other words, involves, and will involve for the foreseeable future, as it has since history became a profession, two very different pursuits. On the one hand, the apprentice historian must find a set of documents (verbal or visual, textual or material)—ideally ones that have not been exploited before—and show that they can yield new knowledge: ideally, information that has not been previously tapped by other historians. On the other hand, the same apprentice historian must devise a set of questions to answer and locate a set of methods to apply—questions and methods that will locate his or her work in a significant position on the fragmented mental topography of the historical discipline. If all goes well, finally—and it often does not—the sources chosen for mining will respond instructively to the questions and methods chosen for refining the results, and the results will include both a first book that reaches a reasonable number of professional readers and a form of instruction accessible and attractive to a fair number of students. Recruitment, training, and professional development of historians are all meant to make this complex process of searching, matching, and production as brief, efficient, and rewarding as possible.

Yet this apparently simple process had often proved extremely bumpy and difficult in practice. Even those historians who are admired by most of their colleagues for their success at both of these enterprises often feel they have failed. Nevins, the great Columbia historian of American history, was convinced, by the last years of his career, that he was a loner and that no other history department would have hired him. The great Columbia Europeanist Garrett Mattingly, a generation later, found no way to reveal the vast erudite foundations on which his brilliant studies of Renaissance politics and law rested without making his books so unappealing that only university presses would publish them: "To him the university press was the very symbol of the withdrawal of history into the academic citadel which he deplored and distrusted" (Hexter 1966, 16). Yet no one formed more successful professional scholars than Nevins and Mattingly. And the difficulties, both practical and emotional, have only expanded as history itself, in the period since World War II, has expanded its methodology to include forms of inquiry developed in the social sciences, political philosophy, and literary criticism.

Who Joins Clio's Workforce, and Why?

Recruitment of historians into graduate study has changed strikingly over the last few decades. From the 1930s through the expansion years of the 1950s, most historians came from relatively modest circumstances. John Snell, the chief author of an early study of the training and recruitment of historians, found that of the ten institutions that produced the most undergraduates who went on to earn doctorates in history, four were public institutions in the once-normal sense, supported chiefly by state budgets and accessible to anyone who could work his or her way through: Berkeley, City College of New York, Michigan, and Wisconsin (Perkins and Snell 1962). Most of their subjects raised their social position by choosing academic careers—a fact already noted by contemporary observers at Yale and Brown, who complained that the profession attracted too few gentlemen and too many recent immigrants (Bridenbaugh 1963). Many, perhaps most, saw the ethnic and cultural diversity of the stream of young people entering the discipline as a disadvantage, as city-raised scholars unacquainted with the traditions of small-town, rural America became the dominant transmitters of its traditions. And even a firm liberal like Carl Becker, who was on the closest of terms with Jewish students like Leo Gershoy and Louis Gottschalk, had to discuss their ethnicity in the letters with which he tried to find them positions (Kammen 1973).

By contrast, in recent years the stream of young people becoming historians has included large numbers of not only male Jews and Catholics, the chief scourges of traditionalists in the older generation, but also women and members of a number of self-conscious minority groups. An American Historical Association study of the recruitment of graduate students in the period from 1989 to 2002 found that three public institutions—Berkeley, Michigan, and UCLA—remained among the ten top producers of undergraduates who took PhDs in history. But CCNY had vanished from the top ten. The three that remained took a larger proportion of their students from the economic elite than they had in the past, and it was their size rather than the intensity of their instruction that made them produce many professional historians. They sent far smaller percentages of their undergraduate history students on to graduate work than their counterparts in the private sector. The Ivy League actually plays a larger role now in the recruitment of young historians to elite doctoral programs than it did two generations ago—even though it produces a considerably smaller percentage of PhDs than it used to (Bender et al. 2004). As the prestige of the program where a historian is trained does much to predict his or her professional success—more so than in a number of other disciplines—it seems clear that even as history has become more varied in sex and gender, race and ethnicity, the social and cultural origins of future historians have narrowed somewhat (Burris 2004).

For current purposes, however, another aspect of these statistics matters more. Normally, between 4 and 5 percent of the graduates of elite private research universities attend academic graduate programs: more in mathematics and the sciences, fewer in the social sciences and humanities. In history, however, the numbers play out very differently. Harvard and Yale produce far more historians with doctorates than UCLA or Michigan, both far larger institutions with excellent history departments. Some 9 percent of those who take BAs in history at Harvard and Yale go on to earn PhDs (vs. 2 percent of majors at UCLA and 5 percent at Michigan). At Princeton, 7 percent of history BAs earn PhDs; at Chicago and Wesleyan, as many as 16 percent.

It seems unlikely that public recognition of the power and brilliance of current historiography lures so many elite undergraduates into choosing graduate study. Journalists and freelance writers win the Pulitzer Prizes for History as often as professional historians (see Hamerow 1987). Book critics complain regularly that few of the professionals, whatever their interests, can write in a style accessible to a large public.[8] Conservative critics

8. For one ha'penny's worth of example from an intolerable deal of possibilities, see Scott Stossel, review of Sarah Igo, *The Averaged American*, *New York Times*, January 21, 2007: "Here's a tip. When deciding whether to buy an academic book marketed to a general audience, flip to the acknowledgments to look for tell-tale phrases like this one: So-and-so 'deserves special

insist that recent fashions in the choice of subjects and methods have made history irrelevant to large debates about politics and society (see, e.g., Himmelfarb 1987). An alternative historical association with its own periodical has come into being, dedicated to, among other causes, bringing history back into the literary and curricular public square: "The Historical Society invites you to participate in an effort to revitalize the study and teaching of history by reorienting the historical profession toward an accessible, integrated history free from fragmentation and over-specialization."[9] A look at any airport bookshop confirms that those who actually read history for pleasure are often consuming the work of journalists, or even of scholars, like Jared Diamond, who have come to history from another discipline.

What elite universities have in common, however, is a pedagogical exercise. At the departments whose graduates now dominate the graduate schools, all students, or at least all candidates for honors, write senior theses. Sometimes supported by substantial research grants that make archival trips possible, sometimes based on local documents or printed materials held by the research universities' great libraries, and—in the last few years—sustained by newly digitized primary sources, these exercises give every able student at certain universities a chance to do firsthand research, usually under the guidance of a professor or graduate student. Senior theses in history, moreover—unlike theses in many humanistic fields, which rarely have the theoretical sophistication required of professionals—approximate the work done by graduate students and professionals, well enough that some of them achieve publication in whole or in part.[10] A century after Jameson, it seems, the quintessentially centrifugal experience of research (of "historical work") is still what pulls students into the discipline as a whole—even as distinguished practitioners complain, as Jameson himself eventually did, that much historical writing is too narrow, too technical, and too esoteric.

---

mention for his indispensable advice and counsel as I turned my dissertation into a book.' Beware! Vestigial Dissertation Syndrome alert! Common symptoms include turgid prose and microscopic narrowness of topic. So after finding that tip-off in the acknowledgments of 'The Averaged American,' by Sarah Igo, I braced myself for a slog." This prefatory invocation of a commonplace is all the more striking since Stossel went on to review the book itself very favorably, describing it as "briskly written, forcefully argued and broad in scope."

9. The Web page of the Historical Society can be found at http://www.bu.edu/historic/about.html (accessed April 11, 2001).

10. This has been true for a long time. When Joseph Kennedy insisted on arranging the publication of John F. Kennedy's Harvard senior thesis, Arthur Schlesinger Jr. advised against the plan, on the grounds that at any good university at least a hundred seniors produced work of the same level every year.

Clio's Toolbox

The ways in which historians learn their craft and do their "work," examined over time, show a mixture of continuities and changes that are still, in large part, determined by the original structures of the profession. The structure of historical education, to begin with, is still largely determined by the two contrasting drives that ruled the Johns Hopkins seminar a century and a quarter ago—and has been so for decades. In some ways, to be sure, the continuities are harder to detect than they used to be. Professional history—as we saw at the outset—was defined at its origins as a site-specific practice. For decades, American historians—even those who planned to focus their research and writing on the United States—worked at desks surrounded by the products of European scholarship. Most American historians, moreover, were more or less required to master certain traditional core subjects that were seen as central to undergraduate education, such as English constitutional history—a story studied, as in Britain, at least through World War II, by analysis of Stubbs's *Charters*, a canonical anthology of primary sources. As late as the 1930s, when Carl Schorske studied at the Harvard history department, students still banded together to study current trends in historiography around the world—and a student like Schorske, dedicated to the study of modern Europe, might still dedicate much of his time as a beginning student to a comprehensive study of ancient Athens, which provided him with a model for the global but rigorous study of a single culture (Schorske 1987). To that extent, the Hopkins seminar with its canon of primary sources and its bristling ranks of European journals still seemed the appropriate place for any historian to be formed in his or her craft.

Over time, however, the relation between the discipline of historical research and that of the historical seminar has become less and less direct. Even before the great expansion of the 1960s, some of the most promising historians mastered the tools of historical research before they arrived at graduate school. When John Hope Franklin began graduate work at Harvard in 1935, for example, he had already benefited from an advanced training in research, thanks to the teaching of Theodore Currier at Fisk University:

> I felt secure academically, financially, and socially. At Fisk I had even taken
> two modern foreign languages in order to meet Harvard's requirement, and
> in Currier's seminars I had learned how to write a research paper. Since I was
> secretary to the librarian at Fisk for four years, I had learned how to make the

best use of reference materials, bibliographical aids, and manuscripts. Even when I met my advisor, Professor A. M. Schlesinger, Sr., I did not feel intimidated, and I was very much at ease with him while discussing my schedule and my plans. (Franklin 1988, 9–10)

C. Vann Woodward—later Franklin's close friend—studied literature and philosophy as an undergraduate at Emory. But he too came to graduate school—in his case, the University of North Carolina—steeped in the experience of primary research, since he had chased the papers of Populists around the back roads of the South for years and had already gained access to what would become the principal source of his first book, the private papers of Tom Watson (see Roper 1987). A decade later Natalie Zemon Davis began "to read primary sources, following the French Revolution day by day through *Le Moniteur*, which seemed to me even more fascinating than Marcel Proust's *À la recherche du temps perdu*," in Leona Gabel's undergraduate seminar at Smith (Davis 1997, 9). The move from reading of secondary sources to excavation of primary sources has become even more typical of undergraduate history in recent years.

In the same time, as historical literature multiplied and the fields of historical research gradually fragmented, graduate instruction came to focus less than ever on technical instruction in historical scholarship (actual documentary editing, collective examination of primary sources in the original, and the like) and more and more on providing some acquaintanceship with the wider world of historical writing, normally divided into "fields," three or more of which each graduate student had to master. Research seminars in fields with a relatively restricted base of sources and a fairly uniform set of language requirements—such as ancient and medieval European history—continued to emphasize the direct, collaborative study of primary sources that Jameson had hoped to find at Johns Hopkins. In some fields—such as intellectual history—courses still focus on the reading of primary sources, but if these were not originally written in English, they are almost always studied in translation.

For the most part, graduate education in history takes a single, and often a painful, form: a week-by-week tour of large areas conducted on the classical model of the American tour of Europe: "If this is Tuesday, we must be in Belgium." Like the tour, this process demands, at least in theory, speed, energy, and a great willingness to assimilate new information: each week, students cursorily examine several large works of scholarship, learning to identify the high points of their arguments and the peculiarities of their methods and gaining a general acquaintance with the periods and places

covered. Like a tour, this process can provide sound and useful information. Over time, if all goes well, students develop personal charts and time
lines of both the history and the historiography of their fields, which in
turn prove fundamental when they develop their own courses. Yet like a
tour as well, this process can also lead to massive feelings of indigestion,
discomfort, and futility. Once settled at Harvard, Franklin found that he
could not wait to leave, since he felt he had little to learn there about either
historical method or his subject, the history of African Americans. Once established at North Carolina, Woodward almost failed his general examina-
tions, since the broad reading they required seemed so much less rewarding than the filling out of file cards with material from primary sources.

Nowadays, accordingly, as for many years in the past, the imposing
journals, reference works, and primary sources that line some historical
seminars and study rooms function at chiefly the level of gesture and décor.
They signal something about the nature of the enterprise of graduate study.
But the precise and accessible messages that they beamed out to new students like Jameson ("Master us and become a historian"; "No documents,
no history") have decayed—or, to put it better, their signal has been lost
in the vast noise of multiple sources, fields, and methods that every new
historian has to receive. "Books do furnish a room": nowadays, that is the
main function of what were once the canonical sources of history.

Two forms of exercise still impose a certain unity on history as practice. On the one hand, history departments offer courses for beginning
students—courses designed to bring together all new students and give
them a sense of unity and common enterprise. But these too take highly
varied forms. When an American Historical Association committee investigated how graduate students responded to these courses, they found nothing resembling consensus:

> While students like the idea of an introductory course, they are often dissat-
> isfied with the courses in practice. Indeed, the Committee heard students at
> different institutions complain that the courses were too focused on theoret-
> ical issues (such as postcolonialism or gender studies), not focused enough
> on theoretical issues, too concerned (or not concerned enough) with the his-
> torical development of the discipline, incoherent, idiosyncratic (depending
> on the instructor's own research interests), or simply irrelevant to the stu-
> dent's already (prematurely?) defined interests. (Bender et al. 2004, 59)

The discipline of history as a whole, in other words, and most of its individual departments, have reached nothing like a consensus about the proper

content of an introduction to the discipline, and history departments cannot offer anything like the basic methods courses available in neighboring departments in the social sciences.

The other—and much more powerful—unifying experience takes the form of archival research—an exercise engaged in, nowadays, not only by social and political historians but also by most intellectual historians, even when their central interest lies in the interpretation of printed texts. But archival research remains site specific in its form and demands. In recent years, moreover, the sites have multiplied, and the price of entering each of them has become higher and more tightly defined, in ways that exacerbate the fragmentation of historical practice. The seminar was always an ordered approximation of a wider, unbounded world of sources—one that, in the course of the nineteenth and early twentieth centuries, became accessible in public and private archives around the world. Even Adams insisted that his seminar had a double existence: its members had a local habitation in Baltimore, but the virtual community expanded each summer to include the archives where they hunted unpublished documents. Through the 1950s, historians often contented themselves with studying printed sources. Jerome Blum, for example, revolutionized the social history of Russia with a book drawn entirely from printed sources in the Library of Congress, while Robert Palmer told his students that they could go to Europe after they had exhausted the contents of Princeton's Firestone Library. Over time, however, the price and difficulty of travel decreased, grants became more widely available, and historians arrived at a new consensus about the source basis on which their books should rest. The experience of archival work—of doing firsthand research not in a university's collection of printed sources in California or Massachusetts, however rich, but in collections of manuscripts and documents around the nation and the world—has come to define professional history.[11]

Natalie Zemon Davis, whose teachers had not worked in European archives or told her what to expect when she arrived at Lyon, vividly conveys what firsthand research felt like:

> My first days under the dim lamps at the Municipal Archives were traumatic.
> I had done my inventory searching well and knew all my call numbers, but
> my teachers had not warned me about the difficult handwriting of sixteenth-

---

11. In practice, of course, the forms of site-specific learning vary widely. Compare Peter Brown's (2003) account of a very different but equally distinctive one, the Lower Reading Room of the Bodleian Library in Oxford.

century notaries. They had never used such materials themselves. As David Pinckney has reminded us, before World War II most American historians of France worked from printed sources. John Mundy, sifting through the archives in Toulouse right after the war, was part of a new generation of researchers, as was I a few years later. The Lyonnais were pretty surprised to see me, too: "Why aren't you studying your own history?" they asked. Meanwhile, a kind archivist came to my aid with an introduction to sixteenth-century paleography. (1997, 13)

Davis and her contemporaries—like the great Florentine historian Gene Brucker and their colleagues in other fields—spread the taste for original documents to their students. Immersion in the particular flavors and textures of the original sources became the historian's ritual bath, and memories of the archive became their madeleines. Most historians, whatever their specialty, enjoy a version of Davis's experience, though few could describe it so well:

> When it came time to pack up my 100s of 3 × 5 cards, I realized that I had a powerful memory association with the Lyon archives, one that I would have many times again whenever I worked in a local archival setting. The room itself became closely identified with the traces of the past I was examining: the smell of its old wood, the shape of its windows, the sounds from the cobblestone streets or running stream. The room was a threshold in which I would meet papers that had once been handled and written on by the people of the past. The room was like Alice's mirror, the Narnia wardrobe, or—to give the Huron metaphor—the mysterious hole under the roots of a tree through which one falls for a time into another world. (1997, 13–14)

The taste for archives and the tactics needed to wheedle information about uncataloged documents from their apparently obdurate keepers—to gain access to more than a canonical three documents at a time, or just to get a good seat in particular collections—have become core experiences for historians (see Farge 1989).

Yet archives can separate as well as unite. For American historians now work in archives around the world, and the attendant practical demands have ratcheted up the need for specialized knowledge. The linguistic skills that a historian of China needs to muster—including not only greater fluency in Chinese than older generations attained but also extensive competence in Japanese—differ radically from the personal, intellectual, and linguistic competences that historians of Soviet Russia have had to obtain, so that both groups have penetrated document collections unknown to previous Western scholars. All historians know the sensory overload of the archive; nowadays, moreover, many historians bring large parts of their archives home, in the form of digital photographs, or access privileged parts of them from their home computers. Yet the problems they struggle with, from the primal ones of decipherment to deeper questions of relevance and interpretation, remain worlds apart. It now takes systematic effort to keep the majority of students in a given department engaged with one another's work. The generally shared experience of archive diving no doubt helps to underpin the relatively high level of comity and the generally shared standards that outside observers have noted in historians coming from very different fields. In some ways, though, it does even more to set subdisciplinary communities apart than to unite them.

Clio's Neighbors: A Third Strand in the Weave?

Many historians believe that one radical shift did take place in the nature of history as intellectual work. In the 1950s and 1960s, external and internal pressures coincided to change historical practice. The practitioners of renewed and newly confident social sciences—above all, highly quantitative forms of economics and demography—settled and cultivated vast spaces on the mental map of disciplines that matters so much to deans, foundation officials, and the other high sheriffs who stand watch over research funds. At the same time, well-informed historians came to think that the economic history and historical demography practiced in Britain and the more exciting histories based on serial records produced in France offered a kind of knowledge about the past at once more rigorous and more exciting than anything that traditional techniques could yield. Quantify the revenues and expenses of the Spanish Crown in the sixteenth and seventeenth centuries and you could work out whether its imports of silver had in fact tripped a price revolution. Quantify the harvests of farmers in early-modern France and you could prove that they had scrabbled hopelessly, trying to feed themselves and their children inside a Malthusian trap. Quantify the births and deaths recorded in the magnificent Florentine *catasto*, or property tax returns, of 1427, and contextualize the results, and you could reconstruct and explain that most private and unreachable of domains, the sexual conduct of the past. Quantify the work done by antebellum slaves, the goods they possessed, and the treatment given them and you could rigorously test divergent theories about the Northern and Southern economies. Or just tabulate the lengths of voyages across the Mediterranean world and set them on a map—as Fernand Braudel famously had—and you could express the experience of space and time in terms that would have meant much to period actors. So, at least, it seemed in that day when to be young and counting things was very heaven.

The votaries of the new quantitative method argued that their work amounted to a second historical revolution—one parallel in rigor, depth, and impact to the one that the single name Ranke had symbolized for earlier American scholars (Fogel 1996). Yet cliometrics, as one of its creators, Robert Fogel, recalled with some puzzlement, was often greeted, not as a new way to obtain new forms of that exact knowledge of the past that historians had long sought, but as a final barbarization of the historical tradition. Critics denounced the expenditure of vast resources on the collective projects often necessary for quantification, while traditional, individualistic forms of research went begging; the corruption of the historian's immaculate prose by graphs, tables, and technical terms; and the extraordinarily heavy-handed, uninsightful way in which some quantitative historians used literary and documentary sources. Many quantifiers limited their demands to modest proportions, arguing only that historians needed to take account of the computer and the new methods it made possible. Yet even moderate claims often acted like oil on a fire, especially when interjected into a discussion made already heated by the claims of Fogel and other leaders in the field. Who had the right to turn historians into "scientists" and to transmute their works from traditional prose into the graph- and table-ridden language of science?

No wonder, then, that Fogel's own chief work on slavery—which he and his partner Stanley Engerman had tried to make more palatable to readers by separating analysis from narrative—provoked some of the most savage public anatomies ever inflicted on a historical corpus (see Woodward 1974; Haskell 1975; Gutman 1975). No wonder either that by the mid- to late 1970s, influential historians—some of whom, like Emmanuel Le Roy Ladurie and Lawrence Stone, had promoted quantification in their early work—had turned away from rigorous analysis of large data sets to case studies of individuals, based on newer, softer methods drawn from anthropology (see Stone 1979).

History's romance with hard social science seemed to many to represent a radical change in the way historians worked. Never before had historians drawn so heavily, it was argued, on the ungainly professional jargon of other fields; never before had they subjugated their precious documents and data to hypotheses drawn from other disciplines, times, and places. The turn that many eminent scholars made in the 1970s and 1980s to a different form of social science—an ethnographic form, which yielded histories more recognizable in literary form, if not in subject matter—reassured some observers that anyone who came like a conqueror, planning to transform history by the application of a new and rigorous method drawn from the outside, would end up humbled, offering nothing more than one new color that would find a modest space on Clio's palette.

But other observers, even moderate ones, argued that the new cultural history, like the serial, quantitative history its proponents rejected, took the discipline in new and problematic directions—toward the study of marginal cases, outcast groups, and collectivities, away from the study of leaders, decision makers, and influential thinkers. This view has been partly confirmed—but also partly refuted—by the development of specialties in recent years. The data record a decline in the number of diplomatic, economic, and intellectual historians and an increase in the number of historians of culture and gender—but they also show little significant change in the number of political and military historians and a modest rise in historians of science and religion (see, e.g., Hamerow 1987). Yet the larger sense that history may be metamorphosing into new and partly unrecognizable forms has been confirmed, in a different way, by the rise of another set of new approaches, also drawing on other disciplines, that have shocked traditionalists in recent years at least as much as quantification did in the 1960s and 1970s: postcolonial studies, for example, and the group of interpretive methods often identified as "the linguistic turn" (see Toews 1987).

In the end, the changes in history's ways of working that have been brought about by new alliances with other fields do not amount to a transformation, much less a revolution. The main reason that cliometrics and its successor movements seemed so radical is that historians' memories are very short where their own discipline is concerned. Everyone knows that the *Annales* enriched history by the introduction of methods from economics and social science. But historians have largely forgotten that though Adams defined history as past politics, he defined past politics as an interdisciplinary study. He himself had mastered public law, political economy, and art history, as well as history, in Germany. His seminar trained not only historians but also political scientists and economists—as its departmental name long announced. Though Adams himself did not introduce the methods of comparative politics into his seminar, he was first tolerant and then enthusiastic when his pupil Woodrow Wilson did so. He encouraged Jameson to study and lecture on "phys.-geog.-hist."—physical geography and its relation to history. Jameson did so, though with a characteristic "feeling of depression and disgust" (Rothberg and Goggin 1993–2001, 1:103).

Adams himself took a strong interest, in later years, in a moderate form of the social gospel and enthusiastically studied the economic historian Arnold Toynbee's work on the East End of London. By the 1890s, he was making clear in public addresses on various occasions that history, as he envisioned it, embraced a number of the social sciences (Cunningham 1976; Ross 1991). No wonder then that his pupils, direct and indirect, included the economist Richard Ely, the sociologist Albion Small, and the political scientist Jesse Macy, as well as Wilson. To a considerable extent, the social sciences in America budded off from the tree that Adams planted (Ross 1991).

Subsequent announcements of the need to expand history's toolbox have usually been accompanied by clangs of rhetoric more militant than that of Adams. A hundred years ago, "new historians" like James Harvey Robinson and Charles Beard proclaimed the need for history to draw on the new methods and perspectives of the social sciences—which had only just emerged from the dominance of history to develop methods of their own. Fifty years ago, William Langer, editor of the Langer Series of fact-packed and fairly traditional textbooks on European history, told his fellow historians that the application of psychoanalytic perspectives to historical actors was "the next assignment," and Richard Hofstadter acquainted his students not with the archival sources he himself generally shunned but with the new insights of sociology and anthropology—a method that led some of them, at least temporarily, into professional disaster (Langer 1958). In recent years, some of the most distinguished historians in the United States have proclaimed the need for history to ally itself with new fields from molecular biology and genetics to cognitive science. In each case, defenders of tradition howled. In each case, however, the reformers had come not to subvert Clio but to enlarge her toolbox. Few of them have seriously demanded that historians jettison their traditional equipment or abandon their traditional standards. In fact, one could argue that the need to form alliances with new disciplines, every generation or so, is plotted as solidly into history's ways of working as the need to plunge into the sources and to weave compelling stories from them.

Clio's Work

The rise of subspecialties with their own methods and technical languages is, in the end, simply part of the process of specialization that began in the new seminars more than a hundred years ago. Often, in fact, the application of new approaches has gone hand in hand with the realization that once-neglected sources—from Florentine tax returns to the interrogations of the German Reserve Police Battalion 101—could yield historically vital information. Even the complaints that the new forms of historical writing have engendered belong to an ancient tradition, founded by such critics of Rankification as Theodore Roosevelt, who argued that the new, specialized historians, who concentrated on details and addressed one another rather than a wide public, "have done much real harm in preventing the development of students who might have a large grasp of what history should really be" (Hamerow 1987, 55).

At the outset of the twenty-first century, the making of historical knowledge remains a complex and precarious enterprise—one made endlessly difficult by the contrasting pressures exerted by the historian's life, and more difficult, perhaps, than it was a century ago, by the endless fragmentation of specialties and publications. History's failure to develop a consensus on the methods that every student needs has run counter to the professed desires of many innovators, who have claimed that they wanted to change the discipline as a whole. But it has also made it possible for the members of many history departments to pursue an eclectic range of approaches and genres. More important still, individual historians have found in history's chaos, down to the present, the freedom that enables them to adopt new approaches and to enter new fields simply by reading their way into new literatures, an approach that historians find rich and rewarding, though the victims of their depredations often disagree. Jameson and Adams would no doubt find much to deplore—as well as something to praise—in the seminars mounted by contemporary departments. More remarkable—and, perhaps, distinctive—is the fact that they would recognize so many of the methods used and the goals pursued by the very different scholars who inhabit the world these men created. Perhaps the ornithologists are right after all.

References

Adams, Herbert Baxter. 1882. *The Germanic Origin of New England Towns, read before the Harvard Historical Society, May 9, 1881 . . . with the Notes on Co-Operation in University Work*. Baltimore, MD: Murray.

———. 1884. *Methods of Historical Study*. Baltimore, MD: Murray.

———. 1938. *Historical Scholarship in the United States, 1876–1901: As Revealed in the Correspondence of Herbert B. Adams*. Edited by W. Stull Holt. Baltimore, MD: Johns Hopkins Press.

Bender, Thomas, Colin Palmer, Philip Katz, and the Committee on Graduate Education of the American Historical Association. 2004. *The Education of Historians for the Twenty-first Century*. Urbana: University of Illinois Press, 2004.

Benson, Robert, Giles Constable, and Carol Lanham, eds. 1982. *Renaissance and Renewal in the Twelfth Century*. Cambridge, MA: Harvard University Press.

Bentinck-Smith, William. 1976. *Building a Great Library: The Coolidge Years at Harvard*. Cambridge, MA: Harvard University Library.

Berg, Günter. 1968. *Leopold von Ranke als akademischer Lehrer: Studien zu seinen Vorlesungen und seinem Geschichtsdenken*. Göttingen: Vandenhoeck und Ruprecht.

Billington, Ray Allan. 1973. *Frederick Jackson Turner: Historian, Scholar, Teacher*. New York: Oxford University Press.

Bogue, Allan. 1998. *Frederick Jackson Turner: Strange Roads Going Down*. Norman: University of Oklahoma Press.

Bridenbaugh, Carl. 1963. "The Great Mutation." *American Historical Review* 68:339–40.

Brown, David. 2006. *Richard Hofstadter: An Intellectual Biography*. Chicago: University of Chicago Press.

Brown, Peter. 2003. *Life of Learning*. ACLS Occasional Papers, vol. 55. New York: American Council of Learned Societies.

Burr, George Lincoln. [1902] 1943. "A Witch-Hunter in the Book-Shops." In *George Lincoln Burr: His Life by Roland H. Bainton, Selections from His Writings*, edited by Lois Oliphant Gibbons. Ithaca, NY: Cornell University Press.

Burris, Val. 2004. "The Academic Caste System: Prestige Hierarchies in PhD Exchange Networks." *American Sociological Review* 69:239–64.

Cohen, Daniel, and Roy Rosenzweig. 2005. *Digital History: A Guide to Gathering, Preserving, and Presenting the Past on the Web*. Philadelphia: University of Pennsylvania Press.

Cunningham, Raymond. 1976. "Is History Past Politics? Herbert Baxter Adams as Precursor of the 'New History.'" *History Teacher* 9:244–57.

———. 1981. "The German Historical World of Herbert Baxter Adams: 1874–1876." *Journal of American History* 68:261–75.

Davis, Natalie Zemon. 1997. *A Life of Learning*. ACLS Occasional Papers, vol. 39. New York: American Council of Learned Societies.

Donnan, Elizabeth, and Leo F. Stock, eds. 1956. *An Historian's World: Selections from the Correspondence of John Franklin Jameson*. Philadelphia: American Philosophical Society.

Farge, Arlette. 1989. *Le goût de l'archive*. Paris: Le Seuil.

Fogel, Robert. 1996. *A Life of Learning*. ACLS Occasional Papers, vol. 34. New York: American Council of Learned Societies.

Franklin, John Hope. 1988. *A Life of Learning*. ACLS Occasional Papers, vol. 4. New York: American Council of Learned Societies.

Gutman, Herbert. 1975. *Slavery and the Numbers Game: A Critique of "Time on the Cross."* Urbana: University of Illinois Press.

Hamerow, Theodore. 1987. *Reflections on History and Historians*. Madison: University of Wisconsin Press.

Haskell, Thomas. 1975. "The True and Tragical History of *Time on the Cross*." *New York Review of Books*, October 2.

Haskins, Charles Homer. 1909. *The Administration of Normandy under Henry I*. London: Spottiswoode.

———. 1959. *The Normans in European History*. New York: Ungar.

Herlihy, David. 1981. "Quantification in the 1980s: Numerical and Formal Analysis in European History." *Journal of Interdisciplinary History* 12:115–53.

Hexter, J. H. 1966. "Garrett Mattingly, Historian." In *From the Renaissance to the Counter-*

Reformation: Essays in Honour of Garrett Mattingly, edited by Charles Carter, 13–28. London: Cape.

Higham, John. [1963] 1983. *History: Professional Scholarship in America.* Reprint, Baltimore, MD: Johns Hopkins University Press.

Himmelfarb, Gertrude. 1987. *The New History and the Old.* Cambridge, MA: Harvard University Press.

Jameson, John Franklin. 1923. *The American Historian's Raw Materials.* Ann Arbor: University of Michigan.

———. 1926. *The American Revolution Considered as a Social Movement.* Princeton, NJ: Princeton University Press.

Kammen, Michael, ed. 1973. *"What Is the Good of History?" Selected Letters of Carl L. Becker, 1900–1945.* Ithaca, NY: Cornell University Press.

Langer, William. 1958. "The Next Assignment." *American Historical Review* 63:283–304.

Lingelbach, Gabriele. 2003. *Klio macht Karriere: Die Institutionalisierung der Geschichtswissenschaft in Frankreich und den USA in der zweiten Hälfte des 19. Jahrhunderts.* Göttingen: Vandenhoeck und Ruprecht.

Novick, Peter. 1988. *That Noble Dream: The "Objectivity Question" and the American Historical Profession.* Cambridge: Cambridge University Press.

Perkins, Dexter, and John Snell. 1962. *The Education of Historians in the United States.* New York: McGraw-Hill.

Roper, John Herbert. 1987. *C. Vann Woodward, Southerner.* Athens: University of Georgia Press.

Ross, Dorothy. 1991. *The Origins of American Social Science.* Cambridge: Cambridge University Press.

Rothberg, Morey, and Jacqueline Goggin, eds. 1993–2001. *John Franklin Jameson and the Development of Humanistic Scholarship in America.* 3 vols. Athens: University of Georgia Press.

Schorske, Carl. 1987. *A Life of Learning.* ACLS Occasional Papers, vol. 1. New York: American Council of Learned Societies.

Stone, Lawrence. 1979. "The Revival of Narrative: Reflections on a New Old History." *Past and Present* 85:3–24.

Toews, John. 1987. "Intellectual History after the Linguistic Turn: The Autonomy of Meaning and the Irreducibility of Experience." *American Historical Review* 92:879–907.

Townsend, Robert. 2005a. "Privileging History: Trends in the Undergraduate Origins of History PhDs." *American Historical Association Perspectives* 43:14–20.

———. 2005b. "What's in a Label? Changing Patterns of Faculty Specialization since 1975." *American Historical Association Perspectives* 43:21–26.

Woodward, C. Vann. 1974. "The Jolly Institution." *New York Review of Books,* May 2, 1974.

THREE

Filing the Total Human

Anthropological Archives from 1928 to 1963

REBECCA LEMOV

By this method anyone can find in a few moments all existing material on every vital subject.

—George P. Dudley, describing the Cross-Cultural Survey (1942)

In the summer of 1947 a Harvard graduate student named Bert Kaplan set out from Cambridge to the New Mexico desert to study a Navaho tribe living near the small farming town of Ramah. He was undertaking something different from the typical anthropological approach to fieldwork, which generally involved living with a family, cultivating long-term personal relationships, absorbing the language, observing sacred ceremonies, and attending to incidental events of daily life, then writing a synthetic monographic account. Instead, his task was to gather social knowledge in a new way. He went to the field to do just one thing: to give tests of several kinds to people of a variety of types and then gather the results in a compendium of data. Although he focused with particular intensity on veterans of the recent war, as well as young Navaho children, he also attempted to gather a representative set of test results spanning the whole population. What kind of tests? Kaplan had in hand four projective psychological measures: the Rorschach inkblot test; the Thematic Apperception Test, a picture-based test he administered in two standard varieties; and a sentence completion test.[1]

1. At the time of Kaplan's data-gathering trip, the Navaho were the largest and probably most studied of all extant American Indian groups. Organized anthropological research on the Navaho extended back to the late nineteenth century, and publications on many facets of life were, by summer 1947, extensive. Among all the Navaho, the Ramah Navaho (population four hundred in 1940) became by the mid-twentieth century arguably the most intensively researched, or were well on their way to becoming so by means of the larger project with which Kaplan was to be affiliated. And in fact the Ramah Navaho had undergone psychological test-

Driving a late-model Buick from hogan to hogan spread out across miles of countryside, Kaplan sought out people willing to take his tests, paid them a modest sum, and assured them that they were thereby helping to improve the plight of their people, as well as contributing to the progress of scientific understanding in general. Accompanied by his interpreter, a Navaho man named Dave Skeet who was practiced in explaining the purpose of the tests to people in a less academic manner, Kaplan went wherever potential subjects were to be found. Occasionally, they were out in the fields, as the psychologist recalled in the introduction to his published data set:

> Although the majority of the tests were given at the Hogan of the subject, frequently with the entire family looking on, some were obtained at my own cabin in Ramah, while a fair number of others were given at various odd places which happened to be convenient. For example, Dave Skeet and I, while driving along, might meet some likely subject riding on horseback. We would stop, Dave would explain our mission and we would sit down on the ground next to the car and proceed with the test. Another time the subject we were looking for was out herding sheep and we hunted him up and gave the test out in front of the herd of sheep. (Kaplan 1956, 5)

In this manner the two duly gathered psychological results and "in no case did a subject resist taking the test." (Sometimes, though, the test taker responded by interjecting a memory of having taken it in the past: a nineteen-year-old Navaho veteran recalled that a Radcliffe student had given him the same test some years before and that he did not know what to say.)[2] Although such plein-air testing situations admittedly "diverge

---

ing previously, in 1939–42, as part of the Ramah Project under the auspices of anthropologist Clyde Kluckhohn and the psychiatrist husband-and-wife team of Alexander and Dorothea Leighton. See Lamphere 1979, 19. In coming years, at least five additional tests were added to the four Kaplan brought with him in 1947, including the Goodenough Draw-a-Person test, the Stewart Moral-Ideological Test, and the Sentence Completion Test. These amounted to what field-workers called the "Battery," which increasingly formed a standard methodological toolkit for gathering "subjective materials" from non-Western cultural groups around the world.

2. The Radcliffe student mentioned was Helen Bradley, doing summer anthropology research under the auspices of the Ramah Project. Another Navaho man, a loquacious thirty-one-year-old who took the Thematic Apperception Test on August 24, 1947, remarked, on being shown one evocative picture in the series, "I told Róheim that was a whore house" (Kaplan 1956). Geza Róheim, the Hungarian-born Freudian psychoanalyst and anthropologist, was taken by Harvard anthropological colleagues on occasional visits to work in Ramah and given the chance to administer some psychological tests experimentally (c. the early 1940s). My point in mentioning these apparently irrelevant asides is to suggest that data gathered from the tests also provided insight into the *process of being studied*, the subjects' experience of being used as sources of knowledge, and not simply the stated goal of accessing the untutored subjective life.

widely from the standard situation in which the Rorschach is given," this difference might prove an advantage, Kaplan argued, for people were more spontaneous outside doctor-patient settings, and their lack of understanding of the "personal implications of the test" would tend to render their performances more revealing (Kaplan 1956, 5).

This impromptu approach to administering what were portrayed as advanced, accurate tests that would reveal the inner states and deep-seated personality structures of their takers augured a new way of doing social science. Increasingly prevalent after World War II, the large-scale giving of projective tests to American Indian, South Pacific, Nepalese, Pathan (Pakistani), Melanesian, Chinese, Irish, and many other subjects from around the world stemmed from an imperative to capture the workings of subjectivity by deploying to best advantage the latest in high-end techniques pulled from the era's bevy of methodological innovation. Projects such as Kaplan's flourished in "a highly developed methodological culture and sensibility" then taking hold in American social science, especially within large swathes of anthropology, sociology, and psychology (on the highly developed methodological culture and sensibility in American sociology, see Platt 1993, 27; cf. Danziger 2000, 343–45). Grounds-clearing statements and strong assertions flourished about the nature of the research situation and the kinds of knowledge it could generate. Tests were an important part of this methodological revolution: they allowed researchers to make rigorous comparisons of personality structures—kinds of selves—across cultures and among social structures. In fieldwork settings, high-tech tools confronted seemingly low-tech people, and the assertively modern met the purportedly traditional. Large sets of data began to stack up.

Here it is useful to note that Kaplan was training in the Department of Social Relations at Harvard, key members of which would soon, beginning in 1949 and extending through 1956, designate the area of Ramah as a de facto social science laboratory. The eminent Alfred Kroeber then hailed it as "an ongoing field laboratory, conceived, developed, and operating as such," while Harvard's Committee of Overseers upgraded it to a more ambitious type of laboratory: as they put it, the cultures converging at Ramah "make up, in their small farming and grazing area, an ideal laboratory" (Kroeber 1948; on the Ramah project, see Powers 1999, 2000). Ideal, that is, for an effectively controlled study of a fortuitous circumstance according to which five separate cultures—Zuni, Navaho, Texan homesteader, Mormon, and Spanish American—lived in close proximity to one another and shared a single environment. With the environment's effects held constant by accidents of history, differences in how each of the five groups instructed its inhabitants to live their lives would come into clear view. In turn, this off-site lab would be a spot to maximize the amount and quality of empirical materials with which to build a unified social science, one that not only was properly scientific but also integrated anthropological, sociological, and psychological approaches.

Kaplan's experiment in data gathering took place on another level as well: the encyclopedic. That summer's worth of records of Navaho subjects extracted in field, road, and hogan not only fed the work of several other Harvard researchers but eventually joined the records of over ninety contributing field-workers who had effectively spanned the globe. Within the decade, Kaplan merged his results with the results of others to amass an archive—"micropublished," each page condensed to tiny, thumbnail size, and legible only by a specialized microprint reader—of many thousands of pages of data (by my estimate, 30,000). Records of the inner lives, random stories, test results, and dreams of people from a variety of cultures, the result constituted, in Kaplan's words, "a rich resource of primary data in anthropology and in psychology, which otherwise might be lost or destroyed, and which might be of research significance in the future" (CPR 1956a). Call it a data base of consciousness, a repository of humankind's most elusive human qualities, or an anthropological archive: assembled between 1955 and 1963, it remains today in the Library of Congress and several other research libraries across the country in micropublished form. In this way, a veritable sluice of social knowledge flowed from seemingly unlikely encounters.

The Factual Sensibility and the Anthropological Bank of Knowledge

In beginning in this way—in media res, with Kaplan in Ramah—I am making a case for attending to the practices of knowledge making among social scientists, however untoward they may seem, however unexamined they may have been.[3] In particular I want to ask how the practices of anthropologists, psychoanalysts, sociologists, psychologists, and allied social and natural scientists here treated can bring into relief new problems for scholars of science very broadly conceived (including, for example, "science, technology, and society," the sociology of knowledge, and the history

---

3. "The field" has been little looked at by historians of science and intellectual historians of anthropology but rather is often taken as a given. Instead, as two historians of anthropology recently argued, scholars should "work toward a historical understanding of the *process of ethnographic knowledge production* itself" (Bashkow and Dobrin 2007, 14, emphasis in original).

of science and ideas). A "focus on practice [means] not just what scientists think or write but also what they do and the materials they work with," as a felicitous recent phrasing has it (Landecker 2007, 24). What, then, did mid-twentieth-century, data-hungry social scientists do? What materials did they work with?

In this chapter I show that the history of producing anthropological and psychological knowledge is instructive when looked at "on the ground," step by step, as it were, even if that ground gives onto, for example, a quite unexpected meeting between sheepherders and test givers. Practices of fact collecting changed how theorists used and understood those facts. This understanding, in turn, altered collecting and archiving practices. This feedback loop of influence—of theory on fact and fact on theory—relates directly to the topic at hand in this volume. Data set by data set, encounter by encounter, group by group, and subject by subject, the building of anthropological archives forms a chapter of a larger history important today, at a moment when social knowledge has never been a more pressing concern both for researchers and, frankly, for anyone with a computer and an Internet connection, for it reveals a great deal about knowledge-making projects, the imperatives of which have only grown.[4]

A primary aim in this chapter is to mark the arrival of certain kinds of facts that had not existed before. I do this by describing efforts before, during, and after World War II to create storage systems for social, cultural, and personal facts. Large anthropological archives have generally been portrayed as the products of the 1950s and later; standard scholarship rarely refers to earlier experiments in large-scale data collection. The entry in the *International Encyclopedia of the Social and Behavioral Sciences* for "Databases:

---

4. The collecting of specifically social knowledge has accelerated since the mid-twentieth century. Formerly only a select few—innovators in social data gathering, mainly social scientists—encountered the kinds of problems that arise when gathering such knowledge. Today, for academic researchers, students, and professionals of various stripes, their problems are run-of-the-mill headaches. A telling example of the spread of imperatives from specialists to "citizen social scientists" is the growth of self-tracking tools and programs to gather and pool data about activities, moods, social life, sleep, wake-up time, breakfast cereal (type consumed), music (songs listened to), and even ideas (had). See especially the Quantified Self movement: http://www.quantifiedself.com/. That a founder of the movement, Gary Wolf, had a *New York Times Magazine* cover article recently is an index of the spread of this approach and attendant concerns: "The daily habits of millions of people [are] starting to edge uncannily close to the experiments of the most extreme experimenters" (Wolf 2010). In retrospect, social scientific data gatherers can be seen to have paved the way for this form of experimentation. See also http://daytum.com/, which "helps you collect, categorize and communicate your everyday data." An iPhone application, "Mr. Counter," will allow the user to track and store any data she wants. See iTunes download link: http://itunes.apple.com/in/app/mr-counter/id306574255?mt=8 (accessed April 11, 2011).

International" locates the origin of modern data bases of social knowledge decidedly after the war (Rockwell 2001). A later entry devoted to the Human Relations Area Files (penned by the president of HRAF) neglects to mention that its own data collection activities began a good two decades before 1949 (Ember 2001). Counter to this tendency toward selective historicization, the following history of a series of American anthropological data banks shows that the later, more comprehensive projects relied on, indeed could not have existed without, their prewar prototypes.

In naming these *"anthropological* data banks" I do not mean to say they were exclusively the products of anthropologists, for they were not. Yet they were animated by an anthropological sensibility, even as they incorporated the methods and data of psychologists, sociologists, and even historians, ethologists, and other experts (on a distinctive anthropological sensibility, see Clifford 1988). Nor do I mean to equate them precisely with late-model data bases as they are commonly known circa the early twenty-first century, for these earlier apparatuses were not primarily electronic and emerged at the very cusp of what is now widely known as the Information Age. More accurate are specific actors' terms for the containers used (such as "Microcard Publications," "the Files," and "banks of knowledge"), as well as for the contents held (such as "human documents," "personal-verbal data in anthropology," or, more generally, "subjective materials").[5] In the process of aspiring to collect a complete set of sociocultural knowledge in a given area—comprehensive cultural, social, and personality data filling out requisite taxonomic categories—and render it in a form accessible to any qualified user at any moment, it was necessary to make use of and even promote the most advanced technological aids; at the same time, older, less glamorous methods of fact collection persisted and intermingled with new devices. Such Rube-Goldberg-like concatenations emerge in several episodes below.

As the editors of this volume have aptly characterized developments in recent decades, social scientific knowledge initially slipped through the cracks of historiographical and scholarly approaches devoted to scrutinizing the processes involved in the *making* of knowledge. Even as the much-vaunted turn to practice reanimated a drifting discipline of history of science in the mid-1980s and jump-started an emerging cross-disciplinary enterprise, science studies, in the late 1980s and early 1990s, it oddly but almost entirely neglected the role of knowledge-gathering practices, tools,

---

5. "Personal-verbal data in anthropology" was Clyde Kluckhohn's term. Other such terminology included "personal documents" and "human documents" (Robert Redfield, Gordon Allport, respectively). These terminological usages are found in Gottschalk, Kluckhohn, and Angell 1945, vii, 79; see also Allport 1942.

and techniques in the social and human sciences. The most obvious reason for this failure to address social knowledge making in the turn to practice was the persistence of a marked and not illogical tendency to gravitate to the "harder" and more prestigious, more bounded, more monied, and altogether "realer" sciences, roughly reduplicating the Comtean scale of positive sciences. The physical sciences were the limiting and most distinctive cases of the positive sciences, which were notable for their embodiment of "the distinctively scientific form of rationality" (Daston 1981, 280).[6] In their turn to the study of practices, sociologists and historians of science gave new importance to the place of experiment—focusing especially on experimental craft and laboratory life, including spaces for experiment, in the physical and biological sciences. (Key science studies texts that foregrounded experiment are Buchwald 1995; Gooding, Pinch, and Schaffer 1989; and Shapin and Schaffer 1985; a useful overview is Isaac 2009.)

Much as science was seen by its own practitioners as more authoritatively scientific to the extent that it qualified as a physical or natural science, so did sociologists and historians adopt this view implicitly, even as they began a slow-boiling critique of purely internalist approaches to the study of science. Retrospectively reviewing the classic mid-1950s consensus-style volume *Critical Problems in the History of Science*, practice-oriented reformer Martin Rudwick concluded that most contributors shared a "conception of science not only as natural knowledge, but also as knowledge that is hard, concrete, objective, and impersonal, in implicit contrast to any other realm of knowing" (Rudwick 1981, 269). Oddly enough, in attempting to gain credence for newly practice-oriented approaches, innovators persisted in these assumptions, initially relegating experimental psychology, cultural anthropology, psychoanalysis, and sociology (and economics and ethnology as well) to a dim corner. With them went the bulk of social knowledge, save for the beachhead case of probability and statistics, which, not surprisingly, formed the concern of such practice-oriented scholars as Porter, Daston, Morgan, and others, the forward guard of an attempt to study the turn to practice in the social sciences (Gigerenzer et al. 1990; Hacking 1975; Porter 1988). A related concern with postural practices of reading, note-

6. That the Comtean hierarchy of positive science is still powerfully felt is testified to in popular writing, where this sort of scaled assumption remains common; see, for example, a 2010 David Brooks op-ed in the *New York Times*, which critiques the scientific standing of economics as a field and urges its exemption from the expectation that it will provide positive, predictive, and "actionable" knowledge in the light of its failure to do so in the calamitous downturn of 2008–9. Brooks wonders, along with other commentators he cites, "why economics is even considered a science. Real sciences make progress." The social sciences are constantly threatening to fall off the bandwagon of science entirely.

taking approaches, and book-making techniques arose alongside these developments, highlighting humanistic knowledge-making practices (e.g., Blair 1992, 2004; Daston 2004). Illuminating the empirical processes of knowledge making in the full range of social sciences lay ahead.

A way station in expanding the turn to practice was marked by a renewed interest in collecting and classification among scholars in diverse fields—anthropology, communications, intellectual history, and science studies. To sort things out, to arrange them logically, and to pigeonhole ideas, concepts, and forms could be seen as meaning-making practices in themselves.[7] Knowledge-organizing devices such as the early-modern curiosity cabinet (*Wunderkammer*), the physic garden, alchemical collection, memory theater, and "theater of knowledge" (*theatra sapientia*) grew in interest for historians of science as more than simply the eccentric, pseudo-scientific ancestors of up-to-date systematics. (A limited list of the voluminous relevant literature includes Blair 1997; Bredekamp 1995; Eco 1997; Findlen 1996; for an overview, see Pearce 1995.) The very strangeness of these compendious protoencyclopedic devices raised important questions about scientific practice itself. In Amsterdam, Oxford, Venice, Paris, Augsburg, and Uppsala, the cosmopolitan traveler could view collections of ephemera and exotica brought together from around the world: stuffed dodos, Roman jars, Inuit costumes, pairings such as "a flying squirrel" and "another squirrel like a fish," Turkish and other foreign shoes and boots, a grouping of things changed into stone (including a piece of human flesh, gourds, olives, and an ape's head) and, hanging from the ceiling, the inevitable crocodile, all this assembled according to an order seemingly painstaking yet inscrutable (at least to the modern viewer). Physical display and written catalog might differ, suggesting dueling ordering systems. Repositories for "any thing that Is Strang," in the words of the Duke of Buckingham, inspire a reaction in the retrospective onlooker akin to Michel Foucault's on learning of a "certain unknown (or apocryphal) Chinese encyclopedist" who elaborated a taxonomy of all living animals, including an entire

---

7. Sociological and anthropological studies of classification systems in non-Western cultures have a long lineage. The American approach to cross-cultural taxonomy inspired Claude Lévi-Strauss's *The Savage Mind* (1966), which was preceded and succeeded by a vigorous literature of ethnobotany and ethnozoology. In the French tradition, the sociology of classification began with Emile Durkheim and Marcel Mauss's 1903 essay in *Année sociologique*, "De quelques formes primitives de classification," published as *Primitive Classification*; this essay continues to inspire reassessment and reexamination—e.g., in Bloor 1982 and Coser 1988. Intellectual and social historians turned to the history of encyclopedic devices, as well; see, e.g., Darnton 1985. For an important sociology of scientific knowledge (SSK) contribution to studies of classification, see Star and Bowker 1999.

category dedicated to "those who have just knocked over the water jug" (or flower jar)—laughter and amazement (Foucault [1966] 1994, xv; Duke of Buckingham quotation in Daston 1988, 456).

Historians of science in the 1980s and 1990s found curiosity cabinets significant not merely as precursors to modern museums and their uber-rational ordering systems. Rather, they added the twist that such cabinets in the very scrutability of their ordering systems had something to teach about the processes by which real science makes itself real, serious science makes itself serious, and rational enterprises of all kinds make themselves rational. In an overview, Daston painted a picture of curiosity cabinets newly seen not as freakish jumbles of oddities but as "compilations of counterexamples" that inspired the development of a new "factual sensibility" in the work of Bacon and others. In natural philosophy writings before curiosity cabinets, the empirical and the factual were not the same, Daston argued: "Their works were empirical but not factual: observation of nature occurred aplenty, but they were firmly lodged in the context of confirmation or instruction." Galileo's dialogues maintained this older tradition: "Although observations about ships, statues, fire, the moon, and so forth, overflow the pages, all are mustered in support of theoretical or at least explanatory points. Objects and events do not dangle; 'facts,' in the sense of nuggets of experience detached from theory, are absent" (1988, 465). The proliferating juxtapositions of *Wunderkammer* constituents and the contrapuntal displays of other ordering devices spurred the emergence of a sense that facts were detachable, arrangeable "nuggets."[8] Also in the 1980s and 1990s, an emerging post-Foucauldian literature (i.e., the Foucault of *The Order of Things*) on the history of nineteenth-century classification made a parallel point: classifying practices are of interest not because they reveal a top-down imposition of order on the blooming buzz of nature but because they allow a glimpse into the processes involved in the making and unmaking of positive knowledge itself—its coming-into-form. (For a reexamination of nineteenth-century classificatory practices, especially zoological, see Burnett 2007, 7–9; also Ritvo 1997 and Larson 1994.) Anxieties and hopes attend.

My discussion takes anthropological data banks as just such collections, but of modern rather than early-modern facts. In them, the carving up of texts and raw research documents (including psychological test pro-

---

8. Along with the factual sensibility, the seventeenth-century educated person and philosopher of science witnessed the triumph of the "associated ideas of crucial experiment and a neutral observation language" (Daston 1988, 467).

tocols) resulted not simply in millions upon millions of discrete units of fact but, more generally, in the advent of *specific kinds of facts*: facts that aspired to taxonomic totality, facts extracted assembly-line style from books or from field reports, facts typed on 5" × 8" cards, facts filed and Xeroxed, facts stored, facts shrunk down to microcard size, facts circulated in new ways. Having been carved out, these facts can be seen not only to have detached themselves from their original theoretical remit but also to have taken on a significant kind of solidity: these facts became things. They were neutral (this was important) and fairly sterile: free of context and partiality. They were theory free yet part of a universalist creed (on the understudied topic of the search for totality in knowledge-collecting projects, see Galison 2008; Poovey 2004). Therefore, as we will see in the discussion of the Human Relations Area Files' and other data banks' many constituent facts, they could be deployed in countless ways, for war and peace.

Prewar

In the mid- to late 1920s a little-known professor in Yale University's anthropology department, George Peter Murdock, spent long hours hatching a plan to collect and suitably arrange all the cultural data of at least two thousand different primitive tribes. Originally envisaged as a one-man, midnight-oil-burning effort to absorb a lifetime's worth of scholarly vim, the project over time took the form of a team-based, cross-disciplinary enterprise—with money from American military, government, and philanthropic foundation sources alike—to assemble a set of files that was occasionally known as, and may indeed have been, the biggest filing cabinet in the world. In the course of several iterations, first as a private project involving ambitious bibliographical research (initially mentioned in 1928), next as the multiplex Cross-Cultural Survey (named in 1931), and finally as the networked Human Relations Area Files (incorporated in 1948), the files constituted themselves at the forefront of a dynamic transformation in twentieth-century social knowledge–making practices and, in particular, the factual sensibility, as discussed above.

On the one hand, the files were rather traditionally encyclopedic. Overall, their aim and scope, as one of its founders described their filing system, was "to permit the ordering of information on man's various environments—including climate, geography and topography, flora and fauna, as well as the physical, social, and behavioral characteristics of a people, their beliefs, value systems, religion, and philosophy" (Ford 1971,

176). Their office was to amass, with scientific steadiness and bureaucratic efficiency in equal measure, this range of data for all then-existing or ever-existing worlds, beginning with "a representative ten percent sample of all the cultures known to history, sociology, and ethnography" (Murdock 1949, viii). On the other hand, the files' relationship to their constituent information was less traditional, for the method of standard "processing" that eventually solidified in the mid-1930s entailed, in addition to taxonomically exact marking practices, a veritable disassembly line of texts. Even as culture in general was broken down into constituent parts according to a codebook of over seven hundred categories (described below), each relevant book or article was read, coded accordingly, typed in duplicate, stored on file cards, and maintained in systematic fashion so that the resultant data could be recombined or extracted or processed at will. All this immense labor proceeded without the aid of computer or electronic data base, relying on human clerk-processors and typing pools. Speed and ease of access were of the essence. The files' innovation lay in the area of not only what but *how to* file.

The story of Murdock's background and place in contemporary anthropological debates will allow his files, which appear inevitable only with hindsight, to come into relief. As Dorothy Ross has argued, it was first an elite segment of American society that consolidated the different domains of social science during the 1870s: "Generally the sons of native Protestant families, they had been taught in college that they constituted an elite of learning and virtue whose leadership American society should follow. They regarded themselves, often quite explicitly, as a natural aristocracy generated by and in some ways identified with the 'people,' but yet a class apart" (1979, 112). At this time the fields were not yet professional but retained their orientation in a genteel tradition. Within a generation, these gentlemanly few found themselves displaced by men whom Ross describes as "militant" and "heterodox," scholars from the middle and arriviste classes who were interested in making their respective fields into professions, for reasons both of career security and of prestige their bloodlines could not lend them. By the 1920s, such aggressive professionalizing—with its stern emphasis on being scientific in method and functionalist in theory—had won out in most fields of the social sciences, but as Ross suggests, cycles of genteel traditionalism and upstart revolt continued to recur through the 1920s. Fitting Murdock into this pattern, we can see him as an old–New England type from impeccable circumstances who found himself pulled into the heterodox realms of the Yale Institute of Human Relations, itself suspect at Yale among scholars of the older disciplines.

Murdock was a transitional figure. Old-guard without the civic note or political urge, he expressed his love of republic less in public reckoning than in national service. Although raised an old-stock Connecticut Yankee (his great-great-great-great-grandfather Peter Murdock immigrated around 1690 from Scotland to Long Island; his son John and all other ancestors later settled on the outskirts of Meriden, Connecticut), his life began at the tail end of the nineteenth century in the patrician and agrarian setting of his father's farm. His primary-school education took place in a one-room schoolhouse a short walk from there. It seems most likely to have ended in or near a library: as a professor he was renowned for his encyclopedic knowledge, gained by spending nights from 5 p.m. to 8 a.m. in the library in addition to his regular teaching duties. An obituary by one of his colleagues noted, "In the course of his research, Murdock acquired a more exhaustive knowledge of world ethnography than any anthropologist I have ever known" (Spoehr 1985, 309). In between farm and library, however, military events took him to Mexico in 1916 as a National Guardsman under Pershing to quell Pancho Villa's uprising, to World War I campaigns as an artillery lieutenant, and to Okinawa in World War II as a lieutenant colonel doing anthropology and police work. Throughout his life, his armchair regimen was interrupted by more regimental activities.

Accounts of Murdock often mention a fateful meeting in 1922 with Franz Boas, the eminent American anthropologist, during which Murdock, then a twenty-five-year-old law school dropout fresh from voyaging around the world with the help of a family inheritance, attempted to gain entry to Boas's fold in Columbia University's PhD program, only to be denied with the pronouncement that he was "nothing but a dilettante." What these accounts fail to mention is that it was Murdock himself who told this story, in 1965, having recently departed Yale after thirty-two years of involvement in and eight years of heading its anthropology department, and his attitude was evidently that Boas's words had by then been revealed as false prognostication. In the intervening years, Murdock pursued a course resolute against and often hostile to the work of Boas and certain of his students.

This opposition seems to have been partly temperamental: Boas, or "Papa Franz," as he was fondly known in certain circles, tended to attract a more humanistically inclined student. Among his most influential later students were Ruth Benedict, Margaret Mead, Paul Radin, and Edward Sapir, all of whom were self-consciously artistic, wrote novels or poetry for the "little magazines" in their off-hours, defined themselves as adherents of Randolph Bourne's cosmopolitanism, and identified profoundly and personally with society's outsiders. For example, Benedict's discussions of the abnormal or the deviant were made with the aim of making deviations from expected standards acceptable, and if in the end her formulation in major works such as *Patterns of Culture* (1934) would seem to force normality upon what was different by the act of placing it on a scale of analyzability, as Christopher Shannon has convincingly argued, still her impulse was to accommodate differences rather than eradicate them (e.g., Benedict 1934, 76; see also Shannon 1995). On the other hand, Murdock and his (eventual) flock of students, tended to model themselves as impartial scientists, devoting little attention to making their writing popular or accessible and identifying personally with the societal norm itself, thereby transforming it into the ideal it constituted in their work.[9]

The Boasian-Murdockian conflict played itself out in terms of not only temperament but theoretical orientation as well. After Boas rejected him, Murdock went back to Yale to study under sociologists A. G. Keller and W. G. Sumner in what was then a joint anthropology and sociology department. His earliest intellectual influence stemmed from these two perpetuators of the nineteenth-century evolutionist tradition, against whose work Boas so vehemently argued as inadequately inductive and therefore inadequately scientific. German-born Boas's own historical-diffusionist method set itself up in direct opposition to this earlier comparative method. Counter to intuition, as Boas argued, the act of making anthropological comparisons while invoking the comparative method—an invocation popular at least until the 1960s in anthropology and in some cases longer—was not a simple commonsense procedure but a maneuver based on an unwarranted theory. Pioneered by E. B. Tylor in *Primitive Culture* (1877), the comparative method proceeded from the assumption that currently existing cultures could be used as evidence of cultures that no longer existed. As a result, it was felt that scrutiny of the current array of cultural forms yielded proof of an evolutionary march: successive stages of savagery, barbarism,

---

9. To put it bluntly, Murdock was a WASP who attracted many students of like background. Favored Murdock student John Whiting described this dynamic gracefully in recalling that Murdock frequently expressed pride in having been raised on a working farm and knowing how to use equipment such as flails, scythes, cradles, and stone boats. Having been raised on a similar gentlemanly "diversified" farm, Whiting recalled easily passing Murdock's wonted "informal oral exam," in which he quizzed graduate students regarding matters of ox husbandry and the building of stone walls (Whiting 1986, 683). On the other hand, David Schneider, also a graduate student under Murdock at Yale but from a Jewish middle-class background, recalled not feeling quite accepted and wrestling with the question of whether to adopt Murdock's classification system while in the field in 1948 on the island of Yap. (He did.) See Bashkow 1991. For a discussion of how Murdock organized his magnum opus, *Social Structure* (1949), as a sort of scientific paean to the "Connecticut Yankee" as both ideal and norm for human conduct, see Lemov 2005, chap. 8.

and civilization revealed themselves. According to Boas, such unilinear evolutionary schemes, in their eagerness to force the evidence to fit their too-perfect design, did not allow for the myriad particulars of culture and, as another of his students, Alfred Kroeber, showed, for the ways these particulars spread among "culture areas." With Boas and the Boasians, then, the word "culture" took on its modern anthropological meaning: one no longer referred to stages on the road to true culture but to *cultures* themselves as holistic entities (Stocking 1968, 203).

Murdock's first vision for his files, as mentioned, was a neoencyclopedic undertaking in the form of a comprehensive bibliography of works on all known cultures, which, in fact, he had begun compiling in his free time. It was characteristic of the man that when Murdock gave voice to something new, it was not via hazily expressed visions of a future Shangri La of knowledge but, instead, fulsome lists. This early accounting endeavor was a harbinger of a life devoted to thoroughness in fact gathering. By 1931, Murdock's bibliography had taken a more pointed form. The annual progress report of the Yale Institute, with which Murdock was then only loosely affiliated, buttonholed his project as "a comprehensive study of the cultural traits in 2000 primitive tribes [intended] to test the various theories of social evolution by statistical techniques."[10] Note that even at the outset of the project there was a connection between a "comprehensive" collection of facts ("cultural traits") and a range of tests (statistical, comparative, or otherwise) which then became possible.

Things of this sort had been tried before. Pre-Murdock there had been several failed attempts to file something like the totality of cultures: a Dutch sociologist, F. Steinmetz, had set out in 1898 to file the vital elements of 1500 cultures but lacked the technological means and clerical assistance, having only one or two "lady helpers" (Harris 1968, 608). Then too, E. B. Tylor had made a similar attempt to classify all existing marriage and descent institutions in his 1889 article "On a Method of Investigating the Development of Institutions," but kinship was after all only one of many parts making up a culture. Herbert Spencer in his *Descriptive Sociology* (seventeen volumes published between 1873 and 1934) and later Sumner and his students in *The Science of Society* (1927) had tried to draw up a full outline of the totality of culture but had not been able or inclined to file each

10. Plans to mention Murdock's project in the Institute of Human Relations report are referred to in a letter that the head of the institute wrote to Murdock asking if his description fit Murdock's project, to which Murdock responded that it was "sufficiently correct" but that the files were only in their preliminary stages, with completion years off (May 1931; Murdock 1931).

bit of cultural data underneath it. These efforts, incomplete as they were, fortified Murdock in his goal of building a massive repository of information from all known cultures—what he later called a "sample of the world's cultures"—in order to be able to test hypotheses about large questions.

Within the decade, between 1928 and 1938, Murdock transformed his files into a comprehensive system and a collaborative project. Even as he rose within Yale's anthropology department, gaining its chair at the end of that period, Murdock assembled a committee of six key members— graduate students and junior professors in anthropology and sociology—to undertake the task of cataloging all of cultural variety in all its forms, starting with four hundred ethnic groups. The six approached as a team their initial job of carving up all the component bits that make up culture and publishing them in the first of what would eventually be many editions of the *Outline of Cultural Materials*, or *OCM*. The team's second job was to carve up the world into its geographical parts and to publish this scheme, correspondingly, as the *Outline of World Cultures*, or *OWC* (Murdock et al. 1938; Murdock et al. 1954). They hired two strata of data "processors"—a team of graduate students and their wives to go through texts and mark the targeted information—and an auxiliary team of typists and office workers to do the clerical work of typing and filing. The result was a streamlined process to take apart a text. Some drew up the *OCM* (by a process described below), some marked the essential information according to its dictates, others carved it out and cataloged it, and myriad typists typed it on 5″ × 8″ index cards. Entire texts became coded parts. Out of "any and all available sources" (namely, books, journals, periodicals, magazines, recorded conversations, etc.), the systematic extraction of data proceeded (Dudley 1942).

The task of filing "all aspects of human existence" among each of four hundred ethnic groups—a starting point, figured as approximately 10 percent of all known cultures—loomed large, and its magnitude did not escape the original filers, who debated the finer and less fine epistemological issues their work raised. The world's cultures were relatively easy to carve up and designate, for each world area could be assigned to a set of drawers, beginning with Asia in the upper left-hand corner, so that Iroquois became "NM9 Iroquois," the Admiralty Islands "OM6 Manus." The other part of the task, "cultural materials," constituted more of a challenge. Although participants were aware of predecessors' attempts at such schemes, none of these was felt to be standardized enough. Instead, they would start from scratch, assigning to each member of the group several "large blocks" of culture, such as Kinship, Magic, Politics, the Reproductive Cycle, or Material Culture and Technology, each of which he would break down in the most logical possible way. In the *OCM*, two-digit numbers from 10 to 88 marked each major heading, and a third or fourth digit marked each sub-division thereof, thus communicating with that numerical coding a confidence in the impartiality and neutrality of the divisions provided. The three-digit *OCM* numbers 471, 472, 473, 474, 475, 476, 477, and 478, for example, acted as subcategories of 47, "Reproduction," and corresponded, respectively, to "Theory of Reproduction," "Menstruation," "Conception," "Pregnancy," "Abortion, Infanticide, and Illegitimacy," "Childbirth," "Unusual Births," and "Postnatal Care." Four-digit sub-subcategories also could be designated. Each subtopic included component elements and could be broken into further parts: 4741, 4742, 4743, etc. Those remnants that were not anyone's "specialty" were divvied up or went to Murdock. After experimenting with different divisions, each scholar reported back with his conclusions on the most seemly breakdown as it appeared to him.

Because of the decision to retain a numerically and alphabetically coded, text-based form of the data rather than convert it to, say, zeroes and ones, the file builders used "certain other marking conventions" to regulate the reader's passage through them, in the manner of musical notation, indicating what was to be emphasized and what was to be ignored. These included the two-digit, decimal, bracketed, asterisked, zeroed, and superscript markings. Each addressed a shortcoming in the filing or indexing system. Two-digit codes, for example, appeared instead of the preferred three-digit codes when a textual passage contained information pertaining to two or more categories, such as a description of women ritually preparing themselves, which fit categories 301 Ornament, 302 Toilet, and 305 Beauty Specialists. In this instance, it was easier and more efficient to file the passage under the more encompassing 30 Adornment. On the other hand, decimals allowed the two- and three-digit categories to be combined to permit refinement of focus (a practice that was ultimately discontinued "due to the technical difficulties in filing and processing" [Ford 1970, 6]). Brackets indicated that the category referred to was only a brief mention within the page, or that the category did not carry over to the following page. Asterisks functioned as cross-references. Zeroes (000) beside a paragraph marked irrelevant material within the excerpt—that is, anything that did not fit into a preordained category.

As momentum gathered for the files, Murdock began to be dissatisfied with the evolutionary framework he had once embraced. An index of his questioning is found in the 1934 book *Our Primitive Contemporaries*, which gave overviews of eighteen different cultures (seventeen drawn from Murdock's nascent files and selected to be "geographically representative," one from a summer's fieldwork among the Haida). Sacrificing analytical depth for a kind of pointillist assemblage of detail about everything from mode of subsistence to political organization, from preferred games to religious organization, and at last attitudes toward death, he intended, he explained, to avoid unnecessary theorizing and stick to presenting "only facts." Yet elsewhere in the same text, Murdock bemoaned the limitations of what he called "mere . . . facts" ("mere systematic groupings of facts from the whole world") in communicating the full, lived experience of a culture and the importance of anthropological work (1934, v–vii). Caught in a push-and-pull between the appealing yet constricting nature of facts, Murdock was engaged in a redefinition of exactly what constituted a fact in anthropology and the social sciences more generally during this time. Was it enough to work with discrete, processed, and (in effect) mass-produced facts that, while tremendously productive, also tended to restrict the possibilities of what they could convey?

Paradoxically, mass-produced facts offered their own set of possibilities that were different from those of old-style scholarship. They may have been restricted—for example, in the limited context they provided, in their abstraction from their original sources, in their ability to be unplugged and replugged into any argument—but this sturdy, all-purpose quality might also be a strength. As a behaviorist program promoting a vision of social engineering took hold at the Yale Institute of Human Relations in the mid-1930s, Murdock signed on with vigor. He in effect unplugged his project from its previous theoretical mainstay. The institute needed Murdock (his emphatically non-Boasian anthropology would replace that of Boas-favorite Edward Sapir, who had moved to Yale during these years only to be found untenable), and Murdock needed the institute (its authoritative and frankly fashionable theory could highlight and justify his fact-based program). As he recalled some years later, "I was asked what could be done to present a program of anthropological research which would fit into the Institute's program of unified social science research" (Murdock 1942). In a series of discussions at weekly Monday Night Groups with key sociologists and experimental psychologists there, he jettisoned the evolutionary framework and reformulated his files' task as one that took as central the anthropologist's role as provider and storehouse of facts. A pivotal series of conversations with the hard-to-resist sociologist-cum-psychologist John Dollard completed the conversion. Together the two proposed sometime around April 1936 that the files could be reenvisioned as "an orderly way [to deal] with fundamental scientific issues." The files would not simply be a collection of lumpish materials awaiting a theory but a direct way of studying how culture works to train the deepest impulses of the individual and bring order to social life. As they wrote: "The assumption is that, over a period of time, a culture tends to maintain only such restrictions against [the] drive life as are necessary. All culture is therefore functional, with the exception of a few unimportant odds and ends. The restrictions which cultures find it necessary to place on individuals indicate at the same time counter pressures from the organic side against the culture on the part of these individuals" (Dollard and Murdock 1936).

As Dollard soon reported, "Pete Murdock has taken a new and warm interest in our work, which is very helpful since we do not get much from the anthropologists directly" (Dollard 1936). The files were now neither Kellerian nor Boasian but, increasingly, Murdockian, as influenced by his new associates at the institute. The process of amassing cultural facts on a new scale and in a newly systematic manner, it seems, had changed their collectors' theoretical orientation itself.[11] Did the files likewise help transform the institute's theorizers' theories? Perhaps, at this stage, less so, but I would suggest that when Murdock and his archiving apparatus entered their inner circle, the reigning sense there of what constituted properly "integrated social science" (Murdock 1939a) altered to include a data-driven style of anthropology.

According to the literary scholar Mary Poovey, "an unresolvable antinomy" characterized the long history of the universal knowledge projects of Western modernity. "This antinomy, which sets up an uneasy relation between empirical data and universal or abstract theories, informs even the most basic epistemological unit of modern knowledge projects, . . . the modern fact" (Poovey 2004, 183–84). In setting out to compile long lists and large files of custom-made "modern facts" and develop a standard method to process such facts, Murdock was weighing in on this "antinomy." He amassed facts first in relation to one universal theory (evolution) and next in relation to another (behavioral laws governing human action). In doing so, he and his facts in turn changed the theories under the auspices of which they had been gathered. Murdock showed his project to be adaptable: his vision was of anthropology as a repository that could adapt to new theories and test any hypothesis about the social and human order of things. Once constituted as facts, facts were no longer simply vehicles of programs. They could be engines.

11. As a member of the Murdockian team subsequently pointed out, Murdock was sui generis: in the 1930s he "initiated the Murdockian cross-cultural approach to ethnology. This was quite different from the speculative unilineal stage theories of the early evolutionists or the particularistic approach of the historical school" (Whiting 1986, 683).

War

By 1940 Murdock's team, the Cross-Cultural Survey, had "processed" almost one hundred cultures and filed the resulting cache of index cards. Enthusiasm ran high and Murdock reported around that time that the files were "going great guns this summer" (Murdock 1939b). A sense of mission in which anthropology, in ordering itself, would contribute to a unified social science, pervaded the project: "Field work, instead of being dissipated in random investigations, [will] be focused on the gathering of materials essential to the development of an integrated social science," he reported (Murdock 1939a). The timing of the initial filing was perfect, as if perfectly designed for the outbreak of war, and with the spread of the war after Pearl Harbor to little known areas of the world, "the files . . . acquired a practical value which had not been anticipated," as a wartime publication was soon to note (Cross-Cultural Survey 1943a).

It is a commonplace to observe that World War II was an engine of transformation in military technology, in human relations, in propaganda techniques, in code making and breaking, and indeed in the project of "governing the soul" (Rose 1999; see also Herman 1995). The Yale files are perhaps a surprising place at which to glimpse thoroughgoing transformation, embedded as they were in the dogged pursuit of rendering facts in material form. What one finds during the war, however, is less a change in content than in form. As a result, the current idea about the purpose of gathering "all" data, or "complete" knowledge, was altered. Facts in their very materiality, their very ability to be collected, were increasingly connected to political and strategic problems. There was some struggle, and some debate, over this change.

Yet again, the files proved plastic things. As the war drew the anthropologist, his team, and his files ever deeper into its prosecution, Murdock could be heard in boardrooms and at strategic meetings framing the apparatus in a new and bold way. An auxiliary set, the Strategic Index of Latin America, was to help identify native labor supply for the rubber plantations and potential insurgents or traitors in Brazil and other unstable nations. The files realized their full capacity only when used. Merely to use them, furthermore, made of them *"a sort of laboratory* on the basis of which social scientific research could be done" (SILA 1942, emphasis added). Note that this model—of the files-as-laboratory—was rarely made explicit in the prewar days, when they often figured as helpful if auxiliary data banks that supported the experimental work of the Yale sociologists and psychologists with whom Murdock had been working. Now, it seems, the idea of the files as *a de facto laboratory in themselves* was part of the essential vision of their functioning as (in effect) modular testing sites: the encyclopedic project was building files and gathering data, so the new logic went, in order to conduct experimental research in a productive scientific environment. The experiment was not elsewhere but here, *in* the facts and the way they were assembled, juxtaposed, and manipulated. Experiments need not be anchored in actual, physical laboratories—indeed, in anthropology they could not be. The facts of the files themselves constituted a replacement lab. Now, a dedicated team for Latin America imported "standard procedure" from the original files to take books replete with Latin American data "from the library shelf to the end of processing."[12]

For Murdock and other stalwarts, the files (in this case, the strategic index focusing on Latin America) justified themselves precisely in their ability to orient themselves instantly around problems that had not yet arisen. It was their universal panoply that allowed their mission potentially to become quite specific—in the snap of fingers, in the blink of an eye, one could get the information necessary, and the harried scientist or scholar who hitherto had been forced to "ransack" the literature, Murdock wrote around this time, now could "secure his information in a mere fraction of the time required to [consult] the sources for himself" (Murdock 1942, 362).

Advocates of the files working with Nelson Rockefeller at the Office of Inter-American Affairs agreed: Willard Z. Park argued that they were useful in their ability to pull together information on problems as they arose: "Our interest in developing the Strategic Index of Latin America was to make it possible for us to assemble information on a given area or on some topic given us by the Coordinator's office in the quickest time" (SILA 1942). The files themselves could be adapted to any demand, and in this flexibility—rather than in special expertise, honed focus, or in-depth analytical capabilities—lay their strategic utility. Murdock went further, asserting potential weakness to be a strength: facts themselves, as collected and

12. Adapted for wartime purposes, "standard procedure" for processing a text was as follows: "The book is first analyzed by Mr. Keen who assigned it the appropriate area designation. [Each political area of Latin America received a special designation.] It is given a bibliography slip in quadruplicate. It then goes to a marker, to one who perhaps may have some personal interest in the particular area which the book covers. The most important process is that of marking the book. The marker uses two guides, the mimeographed 'SILA Outline' and the printed *Outline of Cultural Materials.* The marker does four things: (1) marks the passages to be taken out and given appropriate numbers, (2) makes out cross-reference slips, (3) makes photography slips, (4) writes an evaluation." Maintaining a supply of typists, fortunately plentiful in a university town, was also discussed. Selection of books to process was also critical, as the government issued "directives" indicating which areas were of primary importance (SILA 1942).

"made" by his standardized process, linked instantly to practical problem solving, and this link was bound to strengthen as more facts piled up. "At first anyone wishing information on some specific problem may find only about 10% of the data in the files and the rest in the Library of Congress or elsewhere, but as the file grows, 50% and then 75% will be found there" (SILA 1942). An ever-growing file containing ever-more-comprehensive data on all cultural materials in all parts of the world: this was the Murdockian vision.

Marking the rise of this approach to data, and its authors' newfound sense of on-the-ground purpose, Yale Institute of Human Relations director Mark May turned over fourteen offices on its top floor, formerly the home of some of Robert Yerkes' gorillas, to an expanded filing team. Processing and filing, with the aid of an ever-increasing corps of abstractors, file clerks, secretaries, typists—and, too, a photographer, a draftsman, a bibliographer, two full-time bookkeepers, and a newly hired corps of translators—could now press on at peak levels. By November 1942, Murdock announced, workers had filed a total of 30,467 pages on Latin America, with more to come. A year later, the navy financed additional processors to move operations along at a faster clip and address other geographical areas. Taking over more space at Yale, the newly designated Naval Research Unit No. 1 focused on gathering strategic facts about Oceania and the Far East and processing them according to Murdockian principles.

Within the year, naval strategic experts declared Murdock's fact-gathering work "of immediate military value" (CCS 1943b). In March 1943 Murdock accepted a commission as a naval lieutenant commander, while two of his protégés, John Whiting and Clellan Ford, joined on as lieutenants (junior grade). All three sailed with the Pacific fleet, providing anthropological expertise and performing "police work" on small islands of the Marianas, the Carolines, the Marshalls, and Okinawa, which lay like stepping stones between Hawai'i and Japan.

Postwar

Wartime data-gathering experiences of social scientists paved the way for what could be called a more total totality. Certainly a vision of plenitude had been part of anthropological archiving all along. The makers of the Yale files had designed their system from the outset to be systematic, had standardized the processing procedures, and above all had aimed at filing "all aspects of human experience." Yet in the years following the war, many new filing systems arose that at once drew directly from the

Yale files but modified them in important, and varying, ways, with the aim—overall—of making a total filing system more complete than had existed before.

The decade immediately following the end of the war, in particular, saw the proliferation of devices to collect—or, in the phrase of one prominent researcher, to "nail down"—a full range of anthropological and psychological data, beyond the earlier taxonomy, in usable form.[13] Expansive definitions of possible ranges of facts allowed more inclusive filing systems to emerge. Three changes followed. First, many new filing devices aimed to collect not only the processed bits of previously published materials but data in its unprocessed form: field notes, raw test results, firsthand accounts not yet subjected to analysis. Murdock himself acknowledged this shortcoming of his original approach and spoke of the desperate need to assess the amount and quality of unpublished materials and then to annex them. Every anthropologist had unpublished observations, every department had stockpiles of MA and PhD theses, and if one toted up the travelers' accounts, administrative records, and bulging bureaucratic memoranda from all over the world, one had a towering mass of nearly completely inaccessible data. As Murdock wrote, "Of this enormous body of descriptive data, only an infinitesimal fraction is accessible to any individual scholar, even if he makes every effort and utilizes the most modern of reproducing techniques. Short of a large-scale program for the systematic location, reproduction, and distribution of such materials," the data are effectively unavailable (1953, 483).

Second, postwar fact-gathering enterprises defined themselves against their precursors: somewhat snippily, as we will see, they aimed to "fill in the gaps" left by earlier universalist projects and by insufficiently full repositories of data—in particular, the Yale files. A new generation, in short, saw new gaps. It is my contention that those new gaps opened up in a range of challenging areas. What could be called a sort of inner-space race seized hold of the social sciences, and this led scientists to grab for materials that earlier had been ignored. In particular, there was growing concern with values, subjective states, and something that could more generally be called the "innerness" of human experience.

The third change that threads through these postwar projects, in consequence, is a quality of vaulting ambition. It grew in two respects. Many social scientists, viewing the war as a Rubicon crossed, asserted nothing less

13. Psychologist Robert Sears at Harvard's Laboratory of Social Development, who participated in the Five Cultures Project (described below) spoke of overhauling Murdock's more materialistic schema so as to "nail down a very substantial body of facts and set of principles" on values (Sears 1951).

than their own indispensability to the affairs of state. As one of Murdock's protégés put it, the U.S. government "could scarcely afford not to support an organization that could supply it with accurate, critically evaluated, usefully organized, basic information on peoples of the world" (Ford 1970, 13). For other fact gatherers, their ambitions had less to do with their status in Washington than with their ability to collect materials that had never been successfully captured before. A new-dawn élan coupled with the growth of new data-processing technologies lent momentum even to endeavors such as Kaplan's, with which this chapter began.

Clearly, Murdock's Cross-Cultural Survey—restructured as a data-sharing network across many universities, with installments of file cards (baptized the Human Relations Area Files, Inc. in 1948) sent out monthly to member institutions—aspired to categorize and collect *all* the data that made up human experience in a representative sample of societies and cultures known to history and ethnography. Equally clearly, it did not do this, and as certain diplomatically phrased but occasionally pointed aspersions from the postwar cohort of data collectors were soon to suggest, the files were weak on data that went beyond designated slots of institutionalized rituals, myths, material-culture artifacts, and "systematic beliefs" that they subsumed under the two-, three-, or four-digit categories. Although designed to be impartial and complete, the filing schematization still emphasized certain parts of culture and society over others. (Its tilt could not be more clearly symbolized than in the title of the master schema, the *Outline of Cultural Materials*—emphasis on the *material* rather than the psychological—which during the period examined in this chapter underwent four painstaking rounds of revision, in 1938, 1945, 1950, and 1961.) Taking a veiled swipe at Yale's filing system under Murdock, Harvard's Clyde Kluckhohn, head of the ambitious Five Cultures Project, assured his funders that "we are doing something besides the Sears Roebuck type of inventory" (1951). New types of inventories for new concerns: in the postwar years, Freudian, neo-Freudian, and post-Freudian theories guided practices. Researchers singled out facts freshly made out of muddy domains such as impulses, motivational forces, and psychic drives.

A bellwether of a more general unease came in 1955 when the Murdockian *Outline* received criticism from an otherwise staunch ally, the psychological anthropologist A. Irving Hallowell, for having built a place in its taxonomy for the "soul concept" but not the "self-concept." And by soul, Hallowell complained, Murdock and his researchers meant, unavoidably, the soul as construed by and through religion "rather than in a psychological frame of reference, relevant to the generic fact of man's self-awareness on the one hand, and the content of a culturally constituted self-image, on the other" (1955, 77). In short, the files' pigeonholes had left out the whole domain of psychology, of self. It was within psychology's province (constituted of phenomena such as awareness of self, image of self, cultural influences on individual personality formation, and general psychological ways of knowing) that postwar file builders would attempt to focus, not by jettisoning Murdock's existing file system but by augmenting, altering, expanding, and jury-rigging it.

So it was that an array of postwar anthropological archives arose to capture masses of social and personal knowledge not only from inside cultures (via fieldwork and the processing of resulting monographs and articles) but also within psyches (via testing and the production of raw, uninterpreted protocols). Here are a few examples:

The University of Chicago Committee on Human Development embarked on its 1942–47 collection of data on Indian life histories and psychological makeup, which included securing Rorschach and Thematic Apperception Test (TAT) results from the members of five different tribes spread over the continental United States. The Harvard Social Relations Department's Five Cultures "Values Project" collected, coded, and filed records of values and beliefs in its designated "field laboratory" at Ramah from 1949 to 1953 (some of its researchers drew on Kaplan's collected Rorschach and TAT results; others contributed new data; still others brought additional psychological tests into the field to add to the project's files). In a further effort to collect reams of intimate, personal data, the Harvard Laboratory of Human Development's Six Cultures Study of Socialization, conducted from 1954 to 1963 with generous Ford Foundation support, amassed multiple filing cabinets' worth of records of children's play and cultural beliefs from a sampling of six cultures that spanned the globe. (Initially, the project's planners hoped to extract data from a world sample of a hundred societies, but they had to narrow their sights to six due to practical difficulties; see Whiting 1994.) Likewise, the Coordinated Investigation of Micronesian Anthropology, under Murdock's direction, took forty-seven field-workers in 1947 to the Occupied Area of the western Pacific to gather subjective materials as well as more run-of-the mill ethnographic observations, in what the navy described as the most complete study ever attempted of a given place and its peoples.[14]

Not to be outdone, Margaret Mead in 1944 began a systematic study that extended through the 1950s and that extracted data (housed at Columbia

14. Organizers called it "the largest cooperative research enterprise in the history of anthropology" (Murdock et al. 1947).

University) from literature, film, informant interviews, focus groups, and projective techniques about cultures as various as China, Thailand, Italy, Syria, France, Germany, Russia, Romania, and Great Britain. In 1952 the Cornell University Program on Culture and Applied Social Sciences implemented intensive cross-disciplinary studies, including the giving of projective tests to whole populations of several world regions (Bang Chan, Thailand; Senapur, India; among the Inuit of Canada; and among the Navaho of the American Southwest). A 43,750-acre Peruvian village called Vicos, purchased by the university, was a site for intensive data gathering and an experiment in "participant intervention," led by one of Murdock's students. And in Britain, the Mass-Observation Project—motto: "The Science of Ourselves"—instigated a collaboration among an anthropologist, a poet, a surrealist filmmaker, and many sociologically inclined participants to collect, starting in 1938, all kinds of data in a single bank, including even dreams and trivia, as well as diary accounts of daily life. (Of the latter, the memorably titled *Among You Taking Notes* serves as a paradigmatic example [Mitchison 1985].)

In the course of these intensive data-gathering projects, researchers built special devices out of a congeries of available pre-electronic or quasi-electronic technology. They extended and modified rather than rejected the original files' undergirding logic, stretching the earlier system in different ways to accommodate psychodynamic, life-history, and projective-test-generated facts. (An exception is the case of the Mass-Observation Project, which was not linked to the Murdockian project, save loosely through the figure of Bronislaw Malinowski.) Postwar data banks did not dismiss so much as bolster and, despite widespread criticism, strengthen the claims to adequacy of knowledge embedded within the earlier files. And as with Murdock's in the 1930s, these new compendia of data—although they tailored themselves initially to top-down theoretical concerns—ended up reflecting the exigencies of facts themselves. From the bottom up, by the mid-1950s, the challenges of data, its future, its past, its difficulties, its mass, and its sheer overwhelmingness became matters of debate among some social scientists.

Here, it should be said that Murdock himself displayed little interest personally in adding "subjective" or psychological categories to his files, although some of his students became keen culture-and-personality investigators, and although he authorized (with certain caveats) such alterations to classificatory systems designed on the Yale model as were necessary to accommodate the more elusive phenomena of the subjective life. Murdock himself continued to pursue the dream of a total data set and a complete tally of existing cultures: a list of every known culture appeared in 1954 in Murdock's *Outline of World Cultures*. A cross-cultural data set saw publication in 1957 in the *World Ethnographic Sample*, consisting of 565 cultures coded for 30 variables. Anyone could generate a hypothesis about how social groups work and test it almost instantly with the help of the sample. An eventually even larger data set, appearing in installments in the journal *Ethnology* between 1962 and 1967 as the "Ethnographic Atlas," contained almost 1,200 cultures coded for over 100 variables. The aim was to be able to conduct de facto experiments with a secure, reliable, and properly distributed sample of the world's different cultures (Murdock and White 1966; Murdock 1967).

Leaving Murdock to his sample, which occupied him to the end of his career (emeritus at Yale, he set up shop at the University of Pittsburgh caching data sets and calibrating ethnographic samples), I invite you to return to the figure with whom this chapter began, Bert Kaplan, collecting data intensively in Ramah. Kaplan had started out as a graduate student in the summer of 1947 giving psychological tests en masse to support his Harvard friends and colleagues in building a repository of subjective "stuff" useful in their own research. Within the next half decade, the ambit of the project grew: the brainchild of Kaplan, it was to be a clearing house for "personality materials" gathered from cultures "other than our own" (CPR 1956a). Kaplan combined his test results with those of others into a remarkable compendium, the *Microcard Publications of Primary Records in Culture and Personality*, published in four volumes from 1956 to 1962. By then, dozens of ethnographers, psychologists, and sociologists had contributed their unpublished fieldwork records and results for the benefit of others. They were creating a high-tech research network.[15]

Although guided at first by the drive to collect such "inner" materials and share them, Kaplan and his gathered team increasingly espoused an entrepreneurial approach to data. They spent more time in meetings discussing micropublishing options (microcard vs. microfiche or other alternatives), expense of storage per unit of data, and the pros and cons of having data available only via portable data-reading devices. Within ten years

15. With funding from the National Institute of Mental Health and the National Research Council, under the aegis of the National Academy of Sciences, Kaplan and his cohort of anthropologists, psychologists, and micropublishers built an experimental data bank to hold thousands of pages of "rich personality materials from over 70 cultures which have been collected by means of projective tests, life histories, dreams and interviews" (CPR 1956b). Their vision was to have every research library in the United States carry two copies, constantly updated and readable via the appropriate Readex microprint machine.

of Ramah residents taking their tests, the knowledge produced there—including "49 Rorschachs, 6 Modified TATs, 12 Murray TATs and 7 Sentence Completion Tests of Zuni Young Men," "Rorschachs of 60 Navaho Adults and Children, and Modified TATs, Murray TATs and Sentence Completion Tests of 14 Navaho Young Men, TATs of 13 Hopi Young Men and Women," and "Rorschachs of 24 Spanish-American Young Men" (Kaplan 1956)—fed a cache of data that would revolutionize, via an imminent information storage revolution, scholarship itself. The data-gathering imperative took on a life of its own, and Kaplan et al. increasingly focused their efforts on the need to protect data against its inherent fragility. In an odd twist, a project designed to maintain fragile materials such as dreams and Rorschach results ended up aiming its preservation efforts at information itself, newly understood as threatened.

Scary as the prospect of disappearing data was, its flip side was the hope for a data-rich future. Kaplan saw it clearly:

> If we look a decade or two into the future, we can predict the availability of the great systems of information storage and retrieval, such as the Minicard system of Eastman Kodak, which are now under development. These systems will combine an almost infinitely great storage capacity with astonishingly quick and sophisticated powers of search and retrieval. The practical import of such systems will be to give quick access to any information within the realm of psychology. (Kaplan 1958, 53)

True enough, Kaplan's experiment in networking information failed—for only four of a projected several dozen volumes were ever produced, only a few libraries continue to carry this massive data set (deeply archived), and fewer still have the necessary Readex machines to read the data—but it was a productive kind of failure. It both epitomized and furthered the drive to archive *all* of human culture and experience and to make that *all* available to any qualified investigator at just about any library in the land. Quick access to any relevant information was a goal common to all the projects discussed here, more and more explicitly envisioned in the last.

The Craft of Knowing

How does understanding the "precise practice and craftsmanship of knowing," a goal science studies scholars have long pursued (Latour 1986, 3), enrich the study of social sciences? Do anthropological archives offer special opportunities for doing so? A purpose of this chapter is to argue that they do. The large trajectory traced here has been from early-modern to modern facts, all collected in custom-built devices. From *Wunderkammern* and their ilk to anthropological archives in their variety, they are Borgesian examples of "limited catalogues of endless things" (for Borges quotation, see Zamora 2002, 69).

Of course, early-modern facts differ from the kinds of facts that emerged in early- to mid-twentieth-century social science research. Looking at the fact-collecting practices employed provides some clues about precisely *how* they differ. I have suggested above, following Daston, that curiosity cabinets marked a pivotal moment in the emergence of the "factual sensibility," of facts as given *things*, things that have a materiality of their own. What we see in the curious modern cabinets of innovators such as Murdock and Kaplan is a further evolution of what a fact can be, particularly in its relationship to ideas. If prewar data collectors mobilized their facts to support their theories, only to have the fluidity of their theories revealed, and if wartime data collectors began to use their files as laboratories for working out practical problems on the ground, then postwar data collectors continued to pursue this transformation. They turned their collections into de facto factories for facts. To marshal data became an end in itself. And that data became significant in its sheer possibility.

Finally, data were no longer just data, playing a supporting role to evolutionary, behaviorist, or neo-Freudian theory. As Murdock augured during World War II, data sets became sites akin to labs for hypothesis creating and testing. Files of facts were not only materials, they were generative, iterative. They extended into the inner life ("subjective materials") in the postwar period and allowed this new frontier to become, itself, a realm of intervention and experiment (via, e.g., the burgeoning fields of social psychology, sociometry, coercive interrogation, and culture and personality; on the rise of experiment in social psychology, see Danziger 2000; on the growth of scientific interview techniques as interventions, see Lemov 2010). "Facts themselves" were, as they continue to be, in flux.

References

Allport, Gordon. 1942. *The Use of Personal Documents in Psychological Science*. New York: Social Science Research Council.
Bashkow, Ira. 1991. "The Dynamics of Rapport in a Colonial Situation: David Schneider's Fieldwork on the Islands of Yap." In *Colonial Situations: Essays on the Contextualization of Ethnographic Knowledge*, edited by George Stocking, 170–242. Madison: University of Wisconsin Press.

Bashkow, Ira, and Lise M. Dobrin. 2007. "The Historical Study of Ethnographic Field-work: Margaret Mead and Reo Fortune among the Mountain Arapesh." *History of Anthropology Newsletter* 34:3–14.

Benedict, Ruth. 1934. "Anthropology and the Abnormal." *Journal of General Psychology* 10:59–82.

Blair, Ann. 1992. "Humanist Methods in Natural Philosophy: The Commonplace Book." *Journal of the History of Ideas* 53:541–51.

———. 1997. *The Theater of Nature: Jean Bodin and Renaissance Science.* Princeton, NJ: Princeton University Press.

———. 2004. "Note-Taking as an Art of Transmission." *Critical Inquiry* 31:85–107.

Bloor, David. 1982. "Durkheim and Mauss Revisited: Classification and the Sociology of Knowledge." *Studies in History and Philosophy of Science* 13:267–97.

Bredekamp, Horst. 1995. *The Lure of Antiquity and the Cult of the Machine: The Kunstkammer and the Evolution of Nature, Art and Technology.* Princeton, NJ: Markus Wiener Publishers.

Brooks, David. 2010. "The Return of History." *New York Times,* March 26.

Buchwald, Jed, ed. 1995. *Scientific Practice: Theories and Stories of Doing Physics.* Chicago: University of Chicago Press.

Burnett, D. Graham. 2007. *Trying Leviathan: The Nineteenth-Century New York Court Case That Put the Whale on Trial and Challenged the Order of Nature,* 1–18. Princeton, NJ: Princeton University Press.

Clifford, James. 1988. *The Predicament of Culture: Twentieth-Century Ethnography, Literature and Art.* Cambridge, MA: Harvard University Press.

CPR (Committee on Primary Records). 1956a. Minutes of meeting of Committee on Primary Records on January 19, 1956. Division of Anthropology and Psychology, A&P: Committee on Primary Records: Meetings: 1956. National Research Council–National Academy of Sciences Archives.

———. [1956b]. "Notice" of formation of Committee on Primary Records in Anthropology and Psychology. Division of Anthropology and Psychology, A&P: Committee on Primary Records: Meetings: 1956. National Research Council–National Academy of Sciences Archives.

Coser, Lewis A. 1988. "Primitive Classification Revisited." *Sociological Theory* 6:85–90.

Cross-Cultural Survey. 1943a. "The Cross-Cultural Survey." Introduction to "Strategic Bulletins of Oceania," nos. 1–8, compiled by the Cross-Cultural Survey. IHR, Yale University, Restricted. National Archives.

———. 1943b. Memorandum from MacLean to Pence re CCS. May 18, 1943. National Archives, R.G. 38, stack 370, row 12, compartment 8, shelf 4, box 9.

Danziger, Kurt. 2000. "Making Social Psychology Experiential: A Conceptual History, 1920–1970." *Journal of the History of the Behavioral Sciences* 36:329–47.

Darnton, Robert. 1985. *The Great Cat Massacre and Other Episodes in French Cultural History.* New York: Vintage.

Daston, Lorraine. 1981. "Critical Problems in the History of Science." Retrospective Review. *Isis* 72:262–83.

———. 1988. "The Factual Sensibility." *Isis* 79:452–70.

———. 2004. "Taking Note(s)." *Isis* 95:443–48.

Dollard, John. 1936. Letter to Margaret Mead. November 23, 1936. Margaret Mead Papers, Library of Congress.

Dollard, John, and George P. Murdock. 1936. "Memorandum to Dr. Mark A. May concerning a Research Job That Needs to Be Done." [April 1936?] Yale University Archives, YRG 37-V IHR, series II, box 11.

Dudley, George A. 1942. Assistant to the Assistant Coordinator, Office of the Coordinator of Inter-American Affairs. "Project Authorization [of Strategic Index of Latin America]." April 1, 1942. National Archives, R.G. 229, entry 1, stack 350, row 76, compartment 2, shelf 4, box 134.

Durkheim, Emile, and Marcel Mauss. [1903] 1967. *Primitive Classification.* Translated by Rodney Needham. Chicago: University of Chicago Press.

Eco, Umberto. 1997. *The Search for the Perfect Language.* London: Blackwell.

Ember, Melvin. 2001. "Databases: Core: Anthropology and the Human Relations Area Files (HRAF)." In *International Encyclopedia of the Social and Behavioral Sciences,* edited by Neil Smelser et al., 3238–40. New York: Elsevier Publishing.

Findlen, Paula. 1996. *Possessing Nature: Museums, Collecting, and Scientific Culture in Early Modern Italy.* Berkeley and Los Angeles: University of California Press.

Ford, Clellan S. 1970. "HRAF, 1949–1969: A Twenty Year Report." *Behavior Science Notes* 5:1–64.

———. 1971. "The Development of the *Outline of Cultural Materials.*" *Behavioral Science Notes* 3:173–85.

Foucault, Michel. [1966] 1994. *The Order of Things: An Archeology of the Human Sciences.* New York: Vintage.

Galison, Peter. 2008. "Ten Problems in History and Philosophy of Science." *Isis* 99: 11–124.

Gigerenzer, Gerd, et al. 1990. *The Empire of Chance: How Probability Changed Science and Everyday Life.* Cambridge: Cambridge University Press.

Gooding, David, Trevor Pinch, and Simon Schaffer, eds. 1989. *The Uses of Experiment: Studies in the Natural Sciences.* Cambridge: Cambridge University Press.

Gottschalk, Louis, Clyde Kluckhohn, and Robert Angell, eds. 1945. *The Use of Personal Documents in History, Anthropology and Sociology.* New York: Social Science Research Council.

Hacking, Ian. 1975. *The Emergence of Probability: A Philosophical Study of Early Ideas about Probability, Induction and Statistical Inference.* Cambridge: Cambridge University Press.

Hallowell, A. Irving. 1955. *Culture and Experience.* Philadelphia: University of Pennsylvania Press.

Harris, Marvin. 1968. *The Rise of Anthropological Theory: A History of Theories of Culture.* New York: Columbia University Press.

Herman, Ellen. 1995. *The Romance of American Psychology: Political Culture in the Age of Experts.* Berkeley and Los Angeles: University of California Press.

Isaac, Joel. 2009. "Tangled Loops: Theory, History and the Human Sciences in Modern America." *Modern Intellectual History* 6:397–424.

Kaplan, Bert. 1956. "Rorschachs of Sixty Navaho Adults and Children and Modified TATs, Murray TATs and Sentence Completion Tests of Fourteen Navaho Young Men." In *Microcard Publications of Primary Records in Culture and Personality,* edited by B. Kaplan. LaCrosse, WI: Microcard Foundation.

———. 1958. "Dissemination of Primary Research Data in Psychology." *American Psychologist* 13:53–55.

Kluckhohn, Clyde. 1951. Letter to the Rockefeller Foundation concerning the Five Cultures Project. January 8, 1951. Rockefeller Archive Center, RF: R.G. 1.2, series 200, box 510, folder 4365.

Kroeber, Alfred. 1948. Letter to Samuel Stouffer evaluating Five Cultures Project. May 24, 1948. Harvard Archives, UAV 801.2010.

Lamphere, Louise. 1979. "The Long-Term Study among the Navajo." In *Long-Term Field*

Research in Social Anthropology, edited by George M. Foster et al., 19–44. New York: Academic Press.

Landecker, Hannah. 2007. *Culturing Life: How Cells Became Technologies.* Cambridge, MA: Harvard University Press.

Larson, James L. 1994. *Interpreting Nature: The Science of Living Form from Linnaeus to Kant.* Baltimore, MD: Johns Hopkins University Press.

Latour, Bruno. 1986. "Visualization and Cognition: Drawing Things Together." *Knowledge and Society* 6:1–40.

Lemov, Rebecca. 2005. *World as Laboratory: Experiments with Mice, Mazes, and Men.* New York: Hill and Wang.

———. 2010. "'Hypothetical Machines': The Science-Fiction Dreams of Postwar Social Science." *Isis* 101:401–11.

May, Mark. 1931. Letter to George Peter Murdock. January 20, 1931. Yale University Archives, YRG 37-V, IHR, series II, box 11, file 11–95.

Mitchison, Naomi. 1985. *Among You Taking Notes: The Wartime Diary of Naomi Mitchison, 1939–1945.* London: Gollanz.

Murdock, George Peter. 1931. Letter to Mark May. January 22, 1931. Yale University Archives, YRG 37-V, IHR, series II, box 11, file 11–95.

———. 1934. *Our Primitive Contemporaries.* New York: Macmillan.

———. 1939a. "Proposed Program for Anthropological Research under the Direction of the IHR as part of a Coordinated Program of Research Aimed at the Achievement of an Integrated Social Science." Memorandum. August 1939. Yale University Archives, YRG 37-V, IHR, series II, box 11, folder 11–95.

———. 1939b. Letter to Director Mark May. August 12, 1939. Yale University Archives, YRG 37-V, IHR, series II, box 11.

———. 1940. "The Cross-Cultural Survey." *American Sociological Review* 5:361–70.

———. 1942. Meeting of Advisory Board of Strategic Index of Latin America. August 29, 1942. National Archives, State Department, R.G. 229, entry 1, stack 350, row 76, compartment 2, shelf 4, box 134.

———. 1949. *Social Structure.* London, Macmillan.

———. 1953. "The Processing of Anthropological Materials." In *Anthropology Today: An Encyclopedic Inventory*, edited by Alfred Kroeber, 476–87. Chicago: University of Chicago Press.

———. 1967. "Ethnographic Atlas: A Summary." *Ethnology* 6:109–236.

Murdock, George Peter, and Douglas White. 1966. "Standard Cross-Cultural Sample." *Ethnology* 9:329–69.

Murdock, George Peter, et al. 1938. *Outline of Cultural Materials.* New Haven, CT: Institute of Human Relations.

Murdock, George Peter, et al. 1947. Bulletin re Coordinated Investigation of Micronesian Anthropology Project. May 13, 1947. National Academy of Sciences–National Research Council Archives, ADM, EX Bd., Pacific Science Board, CIMA.

Murdock, George Peter, et al. 1954. *Outline of World Cultures.* New Haven, CT: Human Relations Area Files.

Pearce, Susan. 1995. *On Collecting: An Investigation into Collecting in the European Tradition.* London: Routledge.

Platt, Jennifer. 1993. *A History of Sociological Research Methods in America, 1920–1960.* Cambridge: Cambridge University Press.

Poovey, Mary. 2004. "The Limits of the Universal Knowledge Project: British India and the East Indiamen." *Critical Inquiry* 31:183–202.

Porter, Theodore. 1988. *The Rise of Statistical Thinking, 1820–1890*. Princeton, NJ: Princeton University Press.

Powers, Willow Roberts. 1999. "The Harvard Study of Values: Mirror for Postwar Anthropology." PhD diss., University of New Mexico.

———. 2000. "The Harvard Study of Values: Mirror for Postwar Anthropology." *Journal of the History of the Behavioral Sciences* 36:15–29.

Ritvo, Harriet. 1997. *The Platypus and the Mermaid, and Other Figments of the Classifying Imagination*. Cambridge, MA: Harvard University Press.

Rockwell, R. C. 2001. "Databases: International." In *International Encyclopedia of the Social and Behavioral Sciences*, edited by N. Smelser et al., 3225–30. New York: Elsevier Publishing.

Rose, Nikolas. 1999. *Governing the Soul: The Shaping of the Private Self*. New York: Free Association Books.

Ross, Dorothy. 1979. "The Development of the Social Sciences." In *The Organization of Knowledge in Modern America, 1860–1920*, edited by Alexandra Oleson and John Voss, 107–38. Baltimore, MD: Johns Hopkins University Press.

Rudwick, Martin. 1981. "Critical Problems in the History of Science." Retrospective Review. *Isis* 72:262–83.

Sears, Robert. 1951. Letter to Evon Vogt with Proposal. March 12, 1951. Harvard Archives, UAV 801.2010.

Shannon, Christopher. 1995. "A World Made Safe for Differences: Ruth Benedict's *The Chrysanthemum and the Sword*." *American Quarterly* 47:459–680.

Shapin, Steven, and Simon Schaffer. 1985. *Leviathan and the Air-Pump: Hobbes, Boyle, and the Experimental Life*. Princeton, NJ: Princeton University Press.

SILA (Strategic Index of Latin America). 1942. Meeting of Advisory Board of Strategic Index of Latin America. August 29, 1942. National Archives, State Department, R.G. 229, entry 1, stack 350, row 76, compartment 2, shelf 4, box 134.

Spoehr, Alexander. 1985. "George Peter Murdock, 1897–1985." *Ethnology* 24:307–17.

Star, Leigh, and Geoffrey Bowker. 1999. *Sorting Things Out: Classification and Its Consequences*. Cambridge, MA: MIT Press.

Stocking, George W., Jr. 1968. *Race, Culture, and Evolution: Essays on the History of Anthropolgy*. Chicago: University of Chicago Press.

Whiting, John W. M. 1986. "George P. Murdock, 1897–1985." *American Anthropologist* 88:682–86.

———. 1994. "Fifty Years as a Behavioral Scientist: Autobiographical Notes." In *Culture and Human Development: The Selected Papers of John Whiting*, edited by E. H. Chasdi, 14–44. New York: Cambridge University Press.

Wolf, Gary. 2010. "The Data-Driven Life." *New York Times Magazine*, April 26.

Zamora, Lois Parkinson. 2002. "Borges' Monsters: Unnatural Wholes and the Transformation of Genres." In *Literary Philosophers: Borges, Calvino, Eco*, edited by Jorge Gracia et al., 47–84. New York: Routledge.

FOUR

Academic Conferences and the Making of Philosophical Knowledge

NEIL GROSS AND CRYSTAL FLEMING

It was Friday night and Mike Johnson, a political philosopher at a major midwestern research university, was feeling panicked.[1] He and his wife had flown into Paris on Thursday. They had spent Friday strolling the boulevards and going to see an exhibit at the Pompidou and had capped the day off with a dinner at a restaurant in the Marais. Eight months earlier, Mike had submitted a paper proposal to an international scholarly organization that was holding its annual conference in Paris. In the months since learning that his proposal had been accepted, Mike had done quite a bit of thinking about the topic of the paper—a new one for him, though not far from longstanding concerns—but he had landed at Charles de Gaulle Airport with little more than a rough outline and some reading notes. His talk was Saturday at noon. His plan had been to get up early Saturday morning and spend a few hours pulling together his presentation, but when he and his wife returned from dinner at midnight, he started worrying that he might do poorly the next day, particularly given that most of the other panelists did not work in political theory and might not exactly get what he was up to. So he buckled down and worked until 4:30 a.m. transforming his notes into a more coherent, if still incomplete, paper draft that framed his contribution for an interdisciplinary audience. His talk the next day went reasonably well, he told us during an interview several weeks later. He

---

1. We have given the subject of this chapter a pseudonym and altered our discussion of the case to conceal his identity. Given his professional stature, and the fact that American academic philosophy is a relatively small field whose major players are easily identifiable, concealing Johnson's identity required that we describe him as working on topics different from those on which he actually works. Where we have made alterations to the case, we have tried to do so in ways that preserve its essential sociological features. Johnson has read and commented on the chapter, and we have used his feedback to help ensure that the empirical materials remain true to life.

had not been the star of the panel, but neither had his performance been embarrassingly bad.

The incident just described is likely to be familiar, in broad outline, to nearly every producer of social knowledge. Galling as it may be to critics of academe who charge it with wastefulness, in the globalized world of the early twenty-first century there is nothing unusual about an elite professor using his research account to finance a trip to a conference in an appealing destination; the right to do so with minimal administrative oversight is one of the perquisites of the job. Nor is scholarly procrastination rare. Despite how routine conference-going is, however, we argue that close analysis of Johnson's presentation in Paris, and of the circumstances leading up to it, illuminates an important and typically overlooked social practice by which scholars bring knowledge into being: the use of conference presentations as vehicles for moving projects forward from the state of conception toward execution and completion. To be sure, not every published article or book has early incarnation as a paper given at an academic conference. Nor are all conferences, or types of conference presentations, equally important in this regard. But we theorize that for many producers of social knowledge today conference attendance is not simply about traveling the world, seeing old friends, keeping up with the latest academic gossip, or staying abreast of recent intellectual developments. It is also about forcing oneself, at the risk of considerable embarrassment if one does not do so in time, to transform an abstract idea or plan for a paper into a more concrete text that can be presented orally, and whose argumentative power—and potential to make a significant contribution—can be gauged on the basis of audience reaction. The in-depth case study we develop in this chapter thus suggests that conferences can be key sites for the social orchestration of academic knowledge and for the intrusion of sociality into forms of social knowledge production, like political theory, that might at first glance seem to take place entirely within practitioners' heads. Before recounting the history of Johnson's presentation in Paris, we discuss how sociologists of knowledge have typically theorized the social functions of academic conferences. We then provide evidence from the Johnson case to show how preparing for and giving conference presentations constitute an important practice of knowledge production.

The Social Functions of Academic Conferences

While scholars at elite schools, like Johnson, attend many more conferences than others, conference-going is a standard feature of contemporary academic life. Worldwide, there are more than seventeen thousand scientific associations and scholarly societies (Opitz 2002). In the American humanities and social sciences alone, nearly seventy major scholarly associations are constituent members of the American Council of Learned Societies, while hundreds of other, smaller organizations—some regional, some topical, some political—also dot the academic landscape. In the United States, on whose academicians we focus in this chapter, there are, in addition, more than 4,200 institutions of higher education. On the assumption that most major scholarly associations, and many smaller ones, too, hold yearly conferences, that nearly all doctorate-granting universities play home each year to many dozens of conferences, large and small, and that many schools that grant master's and bachelor's degrees do so as well, then it is likely the case that not a day goes by—except perhaps for major holidays—without a large number of American[2] professors trudging to the airport, surreptitiously eating fast food, and jetting off to conferences to talk with colleagues about ideas.

In light of this level of activity, it is surprising that sociologists of ideas have had relatively little to say about academic conferences. To our knowledge, no book has ever been written on the subject. Historians of science have written about particular conferences (e.g., Abir-Am 1987), about conference series (e.g., Daemmrich, Gray, and Shaper, 2006), and about specific periods in the history of the conference as a social form (e.g., Everett-Lane 2004). But when sociologists have turned their attention to academic conferences, they have usually done so only in passing. What work has been done clusters around four key functions that conferences are hypothesized to serve: intellectual communication, professional socialization, the reproduction of academic status hierarchies, and the legitimation of new subfields or paradigms. We refer to these as functions because much of what sociologists have had to say about conferences comes out of an older, functionalist tradition in the sociology of science associated with the work of Robert K. Merton.

A classic theme in the sociology of knowledge was that intellectuals who are isolated from one another tend to be less productive and creative than those in frequent contact with their peers. Coser expressed this view in *Men of Ideas*, where he argued that intellectualism is dependent upon thinkers having "an audience, a circle of people to whom they can address

2. Our chapter focuses on the American academic context. Whether the practices of conference-going we describe are common among producers of social knowledge in other national settings, and how they intersect with other practices enacted in those settings, remain open empirical questions.

themselves and who can bestow recognition," as well as "regular contact with their fellow intellectuals," which offers them "communication" by means of which "they can evolve common standards of method and excellence, common norms to guide their conduct" (1965, 3). French salons and eighteenth-century British coffee houses were among the "settings for intellectual life" that Coser examined, but the Royal Society, a key institution in the Scientific Revolution whose meetings might be considered precursors to the contemporary academic conference, was another. Precisely because most participants in Royal Society meetings were amateurs, the communication among them made possible by the meetings was crucial, "instill[ing] in individual scientists a sense of membership in a community of like-minded men" and "dr[awing] the man of science from the isolation of private laboratories and libraries into the public world, where he encountered others similarly devoted to their calling" (34).

The importance of scientific meetings to the development of science was also suggested by Merton, whose work inspired Coser's chapter on the Royal Society. Merton argued that the activities of the Royal Society received not simply legitimation but also cultural shading from the broader sociohistorical context—in particular, from the rise of ascetic Protestantism in England, which valorized natural philosophy over scholasticism. To the extent this was so, the Royal Society and the forms of communication it encouraged among its members provided a specific pathway by which science might be shaped by the prevailing "social order."[3] Merton also famously conceived of "communism," or "common ownership of goods," as a key aspect of the "normative structure of science" (Merton 1973, 273) and argued that science can only realize itself to the extent that scientists freely share their findings with one another—an activity facilitated by conferences and other types of meetings.

The idea that science and intellectual life rest on a bedrock of communication and interaction was extended by later sociologists of science working in the Mertonian tradition, some of whom attended to the special significance of conferences in this regard. Hagstrom (1965), for example, embracing Merton's emphasis on scientific norms but paying more attention to the institutional means by which deviation from them is discouraged, urged that science be thought of as a communications system in which scientists make "gifts" to the scientific community in the form of research findings and receive professional recognition in return. Although he devoted only a few pages to conferences, Hagstrom suggested that con-

---

3. For a more elaborated discussion of this point, see Shapin 1996.

ferences figured in this system not so much because they are venues where scientific information gets exchanged—in his view this was more the case for smaller, more exclusive meetings, which might alone approximate, in the efficiency of their information-exchange function, the role of journal publication—but because "the meetings of scientific societies serve as forums in which . . . recognition [is] awarded" (29). At meetings and conferences, scientists who have done good work receive both formal and informal recognition from their peers, which encourages them to continue conforming to scientific ideals. In a similar vein, Crane (1972) argued that one of the most significant practical problems faced by any knowledge producer is to obtain sufficient understanding of what is happening in her field that she may make relevant contributions and not be preempted in her findings by others. Research areas capable of developing forms of social organization that allow researchers to solve this communication problem will tend to grow more quickly, and among such forms are dense social networks comprising "invisible colleges" of scholars, as well as settings, ranging from specialized university departments to conferences, where invisible college members can come together to share ideas, display solidarity, and coordinate their knowledge production for maximal scientific gain (see Mullins 1973).

More recently, the notion that conferences serve a communicative function has animated several small-scale empirical studies. Soderqvist and Silverstein (1994), for example, use data on attendance at academic meetings and conferences to trace the emergence of the field of immunology, reasoning that those who attend many such meetings make up the core of the field and use conferences as an opportunity to exchange ideas. Likewise, in their analysis of the European Regional Science Association meetings, Van Dijk and Maier find that "the material presented at conferences is usually more closely related to the current work of researchers than any journal publication, and being in the same location at the same time allows for more immediate communication and discussion than any other scientific institution" (2006, 485).

Related to this communicative function is the role that conferences may play in sustaining patterns of stratification in the scientific community. At least since the work of Cole and Cole, sociologists have paid theoretical attention to the fact that intellectual communities allocate more status and prestige to some of their members than to others. Not all would agree with Cole and Cole's functionalist claim that "a substantial part of the efficient operation of science depends upon the way in which it allocates positions to individuals, divides up rewards and prizes it offers for outstanding performance, and structures opportunities for those who hold extraordinary talent" (1973, 15), but no approach to the social study of science or intellectual life that failed to recognize the stratified nature of the scientific/ intellectual enterprise would have much value.

Cole and Cole examined the ways in which the different institutional positions scientists may occupy, as well as some of their individual characteristics such as gender and race, affect the reception of their ideas. They wrote little about conferences per se, but their exploration of some of the social mechanisms behind the "Matthew effect" that Merton identified— the tendency for already-successful scientists to receive greater recognition than less-successful ones for work of similar quality—suggests that conferences may help to reproduce inequality in science in two ways. First, consistent with the argument of Hagstrom, conferences are sites where scientific societies confer awards to prominent researchers, consecrating their elite status. Second, as venues where intense scientific communication takes place, conferences and scientific meetings, though often open in principle to all members of the scientific community, are in fact locales where those in favored social positions can actualize their communicative and social network advantages: meeting with high-status colleagues to exchange ideas, discussing their work in progress, planning future projects, and so on. Pursuing these ideas in an empirical study, Fender, Taylor, and Burke (2005) find that, with other factors held constant, economists who present their papers at major conferences are more likely to have those papers eventually published in elite economics journals. Taking a different tack, Blumen and Bar-Gal analyze meetings of the Israeli Geographical Society, pointing out that though female geographers are overrepresented in terms of conference attendance, they are underrepresented when it comes to carrying out the more prestigious task of chairing a session—a pattern they see as helping to reproduce gender hierarchies in the field, such that though conferences represent "meeting place[s] where people present and receive knowledge," they must also be seen as "site[s] where power relations are exercised" (2006, 341). The insight that conferences help to reproduce patterns of intellectual inequality also informs Collins's (1998) work on the sociology of philosophy. For him, success in intellectual life depends not just on holding a privileged position in intellectual networks but also on thinkers receiving the bursts of emotional energy that come from recognition by other high-status intellectuals, specifically in face-to-face settings. In Collins's view, conferences and other scientific meetings represent one such setting.

Two other social functions that conferences serve have also received attention. Participation in academic life requires a long training and apprenticeship during the course of which bodies of knowledge are passed along to novices, who are also socialized into their fields' norms, values, knowledge-making practices, and epistemic cultures. Conferences may be important sites for professional socialization—or so argues Ergi in a study of conferences in the field of management studies. Recognizing the Durkheimian point that "the academic conference" might "be viewed as a ceremonial" (1992, 91) that celebrates the values of its sponsoring organization, Ergi insists that "the function of academic conferences as vehicles for socializing participants within the academic profession" must not be overlooked. "At the observable surface level," she notes, "conference participants learn from the conference program what types of knowledge and means of gaining such knowledge [are] valued by the academic profession. . . . On a less observable level, conference participants learn what are the valued attitudes and behaviors within the academic profession's culture" (92). Dolan et al. make the same point in a study of doctoral candidates in the field of political science: "Attending conferences is . . . a part of becoming socialized into the political science profession" (1997, 754).[4] Related ideas may be found in work on academic professionalization (e.g., Haskell [1977] 2000), which treats the emergence of national disciplinary societies as essential to professionalization projects not simply because such societies can coordinate and regulate the activities of their members and represent their collective interests to external constituencies but also because societies' annual meetings help to establish and reinforce collective identities within disciplinary fields.

A final view of the social function of conferences, though they would recoil at the term "function," is offered by some science studies scholars. From the standpoint of an analysis of the internal politics of science, mounting a high-profile conference can be a way to assert and establish the legitimacy of a new subfield, theory, or approach, while those within the scientific community, or outside it, who wish to contest dominant paradigms or ways of proceeding may come to view conferences as strategic targets for attack and/or places where they can attempt to enlist others in their efforts at intellectual or institutional change.[5]

4. Dolan et al. (1997) find that nearly all PhD students in political science in the United States attend at least one academic conference during the course of their graduate education, that 64 percent present at least one paper, and that the main determinant of whether students present a paper is not rank of department but faculty encouragement and the provision of funds for conference travel.

5. For example, see Epstein's (1996) discussion of how disruption of conference activities featured in efforts by activists to change the pace and direction of AIDS research.

Although a great deal more empirical research could and should be done to flesh out these ideas, we think they are essentially sound; conferences do indeed serve each of these functions. As we became more fully immersed in the Mike Johnson case, however, for reasons we describe below, it seemed to us that no existing sociological work on conferences adequately described what he was doing in the lead-up to (or aftermath of) his trip to Paris. An important practice involved with the production of social knowledge was being ignored.

A Paper Takes Shape

We first became aware of Johnson's plan to write the paper he would present in Paris in December 2006. Five months earlier, one of the authors of this chapter (Gross), in thinking about what contribution he might make to a volume on knowledge-making practices, formulated the idea of following a paper in political theory from conception to execution, interviewing the author at multiple points along the way and observing the knowledge-making process in real time. There was no plan to focus on conferences specifically. Instead, since there had been so little study to date of the practices by which more humanistic producers of social knowledge, in particular, ply their trade and bring knowledge into being, the idea was to take an inductive approach, observing a paper in development and documenting the entire spectrum of social practices—the socially embedded ways of thinking and doing—that made it possible. After initial negotiations with a more senior political theorist fell through, contact was made with Johnson. It was decided that Fleming should coauthor the chapter, and Johnson, who has some interest in the social sciences and thought the project interesting, agreed to be interviewed by us multiple times, share copies of all communications relating to the paper he was writing, and provide us with drafts showing its progression. The condition was that we conceal his identity.

As mentioned previously, Johnson works in the area of political philosophy and sees himself as a contributor to the broader enterprise of political theory. For those unfamiliar with it, political theory is an interdisciplinary field located at the intersection of the humanities and social sciences; most of its major players hail from philosophy and political science. In the American context, the field traces its origins to the mid-twentieth century,[6]

---

6. The classic sociological account of the emergence of hybrid fields around philosophy is Ben-David and Collins 1966.

when two important intellectual developments occurred. The first was the marginalization of social and political concerns within academic philosophy under the influence of the logical positivists, who saw philosophy's primary goal to be that of clarifying the nature of science so as to establish firmer foundations for it. The second development was the behavioralist revolution in political science, which created a split in that discipline between scholars pursuing normative concerns and interested in the history of political thought, who soon found themselves in the minority, and those who sought to develop a value-free and universalistic science of political behavior (Gunnell 1988). These developments, which had as their common denominator a new emphasis on rigor throughout the human sciences that was linked to major structural changes in the American university sector (Gross 2008), had the effect of orienting political theorists in both disciplines toward one another and away from their respective disciplinary mainstreams. In the 1970s, political philosophy experienced something of a renaissance within philosophy itself as high-status philosophers like John Rawls found ways to work in the field that raised no quality objections from their more philosophy of science and language-minded colleagues, and as the program of the logical positivists gasped its last breath.[7] In political science, growing epistemological skepticism similarly opened up space for political-theoretic interests, at least until rational-choice theory burst onto the scene. Meanwhile, leading European intellectuals located in other disciplines, from Jürgen Habermas to Michel Foucault, could be found insisting that descriptive and normative social analysis are inseparable, an insistence that further broadened the multidisciplinary span of political theory. By the 1980s, political theory had emerged as a relatively small but stable niche that scholars in a number of disciplines could aim to occupy, competing for space in high-profile journals like *Ethics* or *Philosophy and Public Affairs* and for book contracts with leading presses in the area like Princeton, MIT, and Cambridge.

During our first interview, we probed Johnson's entry into this intellectual field. His path to becoming a successful philosopher is not typical in a discipline whose ranks, especially at the highest levels, are filled by those from the upper middle class. Johnson, who is of mixed Irish and Native American descent, grew up in the Pacific Northwest, the oldest of six children in a working-class family. His parents, he told us, recognized that education was the key to a more prosperous life for their children, but they did

---

7. We discuss briefly below how the demise of logical positivism led not to the abandonment but simply to transformation in the larger intellectual project of analytic philosophy.

not keep many books around the house for him and his siblings to read or do much else to facilitate their educational pursuits. Following the lead of the friends he made growing up, in high school Johnson was "a jock, I ran track, played basketball, so I didn't really concern myself with studies." He did not let his involvement in athletics wreck his grades, though. During his senior year, he decided to apply to college but, lacking any know-how about the admissions process, ended up submitting applications only after a high school guidance counselor encouraged him to do so, and too late for consideration by many schools. Luckily, a nearby university, a second-tier state school, was accepting second-round applications and was eager to admit a qualified Native American applicant.

As a first-generation college student, Johnson initially sought an academic experience that would maximize his prospects on the labor market after graduation, and so he declared a business major. But he found his business courses stultifying. He says that then, as now, his "biggest fear" occupationally was that of being "bored," and when he "started thinking about four or five years" of studying business, he realized that "that's not going to work for me. So I just started taking courses all around." He found himself intrigued by his courses in religion and sociology, but his religion professors, keying into his probing cognitive style, encouraged him to undertake some coursework in philosophy, a subject he had "never even heard of." Soon after taking his first philosophy class, he was hooked. The subfield that most captured his attention was political philosophy, the fourth-largest research area in the discipline.

Although Johnson is modest, he told us that his instructors were impressed with his quick mind, verbal facility, affable nature, and the fact that he seemed so committed to his studies. Indeed, having realized early on in college that he was academically underprepared, he threw himself into his schoolwork, reading widely and immersing himself in informal social networks composed of other academically motivated and intellectually savvy students. He ended up becoming close with several of his philosophy professors, and they were the ones to suggest that he consider graduate school. His parents certainly had not pushed him in this direction, but neither did they oppose his newfound aspiration. The fact that, as a promising minority applicant, he was likely to receive fellowship support made graduate school a realistic possibility given his financial constraints. Johnson also became intellectually radicalized in college through exposure to Marxism, making the prospect of a career in academe—one of the few occupations in American society where political radicalism is openly accepted—all the more appealing.

Johnson says that as an undergraduate he was barely aware of the split in the American philosophy profession between those who take an "analytic" approach and those more closely associated with "Continental" philosophy and allied intellectual traditions. Where work in the former vein proceeds from the assumption that "one cannot make a judicious assessment of any proposed thesis until one understands its constituent concepts" (Stroll 2000, 8) and aims stylistically for clarity and logical rigor in argumentation, work in the Continental tradition tends to be more engaged with the history of philosophy and written in a more abstruse style. Throughout the second half of the twentieth century, analytic philosophy, initially tied to the program of the logical positivists, has dominated the American philosophical scene, though the tradition has undergone significant change over time (Leiter 2004).

Fortunately, Johnson managed to secure access to good career advice early on despite attending a lesser-ranked undergraduate institution. At the urging of his undergraduate mentors, he applied to the top doctoral programs, all analytic in orientation, and was accepted into several of them. Johnson credits affirmative-action policies with helping to open up these opportunities. His teachers had their views about which graduate program it would be best for him to attend, but now it was a professor at one of the schools to which he had been admitted who stepped forward to say, as Johnson recalls, "You know, I never tell students this. This is really their decision but I'm telling you, you need to come here. You don't have anyone to really tell you how things work so I'm going to tell you.'" "That was really, really wonderful advice," Johnson says. "So I went there."

In graduate school, Johnson retained his interest in Marx—an interest that fit well with his "intellectual self-concept" (Gross 2008)[8] as a philosopher both from and of the working class, which was more salient to him at that time than his ethnic identity. Few of his professors were Marxists—in fact, his adviser was a libertarian—but he says he was not discouraged from writing about Marx. The lesson he absorbed instead was that it was fine to write about a figure in the history of philosophy so long as one does so with the goal, not of exegesis, but of advancing a clear and convincing argument concerning some philosophical question of interest to the contemporary analytic community. "I . . . felt free to write about Continental

8. Intellectual self-concept refers to the type of thinker a scholar understands herself to be, an understanding embedded in her more or less stable narratives of selfhood. Gross (2008) argues, against Bourdieu ([1984] 1988) and Collins (1988), that intellectual self-concepts may be highly influential in shaping the intellectual choices thinkers make at various junctures in their careers.

figures if I wanted to," Johnson told us, "but it was just going to be in a certain idiom." The questions Johnson took up in his dissertation moved beyond political philosophy and into the domain of the philosophy of the social sciences: is historical materialism an intrinsically functionalist social theory, and if so, can its explanatory logic be salvaged?

But while such questions were fair game for his professors, Johnson quickly discovered when he went on the job market that there was much less interest in Marx in the American philosophical community than he might have hoped. The collapse of the communist bloc did not spell the end of Marxism in American academe, but in disciplines like philosophy where it was never a very popular intellectual orientation or object of study to begin with, Marxism came to seem, after 1989, something of an antiquated concern. Johnson had expected to do well on the job market. "People kept telling me, they were like, 'Look, you know, [a Native American] philosopher coming from [a top graduate program], everybody thinks you're great. We're going to write you some strong letters. There's no question that you're going to have your pick of jobs.' . . . I sort of half believed it." He applied for positions in many of the major departments but was offered only one interview and did not get the job. It soon became clear to him that his focus on Marx was marginalizing him professionally. "I knew that there was a problem when I went on the market. . . . I was really naïve, I think. . . . Nobody ever said maybe you shouldn't rely on Marx to get a job. . . . What I was doing was interesting and [I] just didn't think anything of it." Eventually he was offered a post-doc at a second-tier institution, one that would roll over into a tenure-track assistant professorship. In his new job Johnson's work on Marx continued to be problematic for him: he recalls being frustrated by his inability to get what he thought were excellent papers on Marxism published in the main journals of the discipline.

Johnson told us that he would have been perfectly happy to remain in his first position, but at other points in our interview it became clear that he was disappointed by his experience on the job market. It is commonplace for young academicians to experience downward mobility after completing their PhDs—after all, only a small percentage of graduates of top programs can be immediately hired as assistant professors at equivalently ranked institutions—and this can pose significant challenges for self-esteem for those who take academic status structures, and their own positions in them, seriously, as Johnson had come to do. Johnson recalls being frustrated during this time not only by his inability to publish but also by the fact that "I wasn't getting opportunities to give talks. No one was inviting me to give a talk or anything and I wanted an opportunity to present my work." It was in this sociobiographical context that his intellectual trajectory was first affected by his experiences at an academic conference.

One day he saw an announcement for an interdisciplinary conference on the property rights of indigenous peoples. This is not a high-prestige topic in political philosophy, but a growing body of work by anthropologists, historians, philosophers, and others examines from both an empirical and a normative angle the struggles of native peoples worldwide to retain or regain control over cultural objects, artifacts, and symbols that were long ago appropriated by colonizers. The topic held some interest for Johnson: as an undergraduate he had had the idea for a paper that would address some of the normative issues involved with special reference to the Native American context. Since then he had been well trained in the analytic tradition and now imagined that this training might allow him to make real headway with the paper, exploring some of the concerns over restitution and property rights regimes with a level of clarity and philosophical rigor that he realized, if only from a distance, was atypical in an area of research that takes many of its cues from abstruse postcolonial theory. Looking to branch out into new philosophical territory, Johnson wrote the idea for his proposed paper as an abstract and submitted it to the conference organizers. His proposal was accepted, which meant that he would have to spend the summer hammering out a draft of the paper so as to have something to present. Although few prominent philosophers would be attending the conference, a number of intellectuals from other fields whose work Johnson admired would be there, so he felt special pressure to make the paper a good one. After a summer's worth of work, he told us: "[I] gave a short, like twenty-five-minute version of [the paper] and it got a really strong reaction. Both positive and negative in the sense that people were really on board or they were really opposed. . . . But they weren't dismissive and I thought, 'I have something.'" In large part because of this feedback, Johnson vowed to continue working on the paper and see where it led him. Where it led him was back into the arms of the disciplinary elite.

Later that year, he saw an advertisement for a junior-level position at a major midwestern research institution in an ethnic studies department; the position was open to scholars in a variety of fields. A prominent professor in the program had heard about Johnson's new research and was intrigued and encouraged him to apply for the job. Despite his work in the interdisciplinary field of political theory, Johnson closely identified himself with the discipline of philosophy. He had never before considered taking a position in an ethnic studies program but realized this might be his best opportunity to move up to a more prestigious institutional locale where the level of intellectual engagement would be higher. He decided to apply. Having learned the lesson from his first job market experience that what you study matters, in his application he forefronted his work on indigenous property rights. To his surprise, he was offered the job—an offer he thinks had to do not just with the quality of his work but as well with the prestige value to the program of hiring a philosopher of Native American descent writing about highly topical indigenous issues. Over the next few years, he reworked his property rights paper, publishing it in a prominent journal, wrote several other papers on related topics, and eventually turned the project into a book manuscript that he published with a major university press. The papers and book were very well received. Johnson was granted tenure.

It was at this point in his career—not long after the publication of his book and after having received word of his promotion, when he was in something of a lull in terms of productivity and was casting about for a next project—that he formulated the plan to write the paper he would present at the Paris conference. One of the insights gleaned from intensive study of the case of Richard Rorty (Gross 2008) is that although concerns over career strategy may be important for present-day American academics throughout their lifetimes, they are especially important in shaping the choices thinkers make in the early stages of their careers as they seek out good academic jobs and then tenure. Once tenure is secure, academicians may still be much concerned with their standing in the intellectual field, but they risk no complete loss of income, benefits, or professional standing if they end up doing work that flies in the face of their colleagues' expectations. For this reason, at this point in the intellectual life course, pressures for "intellectual self-concept coherence" and authenticity mount. Such a transition, from a career stage where status concerns are central to one where self-concept concerns are, is very much evident in the Johnson case. Ascending into the upper echelons of academe required that he reinvent himself as a philosopher focused on Native American issues, but he still retained, if only latently, the self-concept of a thinker with working-class roots. With tenure secure, he felt a burgeoning freedom to do work that would be consistent with this self-concept, whatever its consequences for his professional standing. Marxism per se no longer compelled him, but as he started looking around for a post-tenure project, he found himself returning again and again to questions of class inequality. How might one's legal and ethical responsibilities change amid the growing inequalities that characterize today's capitalist democracies?

What are the ethical limits to resistance to class oppression? In graduate school, Johnson had encountered the writings of John Steinbeck. He had wondered whether Steinbeck's work might be understood as a literary exploration of some of the philosophical questions about class that interested him and whether writing about Steinbeck might give him a useful way into such questions. This idea, unelaborated and undeveloped, had been in the back of his mind for some time, but he had shelved it while working on his indigenous property rights project, not least because few analytic philosophers write about literary texts—a fact that made him worried that doing so prior to receiving tenure might tarnish his reputation. As a tenured professor, however, he felt free to explore the possibility of writing about Steinbeck.

As Johnson explained it, the first step was to find a conference at which he could speak on the topic. This would force him to write up a paper, and he could use the feedback he received not only as an indication of the viability of the project but possibly as the basis for a revision. As Johnson put it when we first interviewed him, "I usually give papers before I publish them. I give them to sort of really figure out, 'Is something there?'" He saw an online announcement for the Paris conference—the yearly meeting of an interdisciplinary scholarly association that brings together humanists and social scientists to discuss class and class inequality. The organization and its meetings are not especially prestigious, but this was exactly what Johnson was looking for, as it meant that the conference was a relatively "low-stakes" venue in which he could "do something experimental"—namely, write philosophically about literature. One of the panels seemed relevant, so in September he emailed the panel organizers directly, sending a copy of the note to the president of the association, whom he knew from prior interactions. "Please consider my proposal below (and attached) for the upcoming . . . conference. . . . I think my proposed presentation would fit naturally into [one of the panels], though I'm happy to be placed in any workshop that the committee thinks appropriate." Johnson's email signature, which listed his institutional affiliation, had not yet been updated to reflect the fact that he was now tenured (his promotion would not be effective until the following fall), but the institutional affiliation itself signaled his professional status. Whether this led his abstract to be evaluated more favorably cannot be known, but the president of the association as well as the panel organizers, all at lower-tier institutions, wrote back separately the next day to thank Johnson for his submission. Two months later, he found out that his proposal had been accepted. It was now time for him to elaborate his ideas.

Academic Conference-Going and "Idea Concretization"

As we poured over the transcript of our interviews with Johnson and thought about the trajectory of his career and paper, a number of interesting social practices stood out. For example, seeking to make up in college for a lack of inherited cultural and intellectual capital, Johnson purposely sought out friends with higher levels of capital endowment, using his interactions with them as an opportunity to learn and grow. Likewise, when the professor in the graduate program Johnson eventually decided to attend took the unusual step of reaching out and explaining to him why, given the logic of the field, the only strategic thing to do was to go there, she was engaging in a practice of active mentoring. Mentoring is a topic that sociologists of ideas have barely begun to explore, despite the recognized importance of teacher-student ties in the work of Collins (1998) and others and growing interest in mentoring among sociologists concerned with educational inequalities (e.g., Erickson, McDonald, and Elder 2009). Important as these and other practices appeared to be, however, we were more struck by the central role that conference-going played—twice—in the autobiographical narrative Johnson unfolded for us. At two key turning points in his career, one as he launched the project that would catapult him into the disciplinary elite, the other as he set out to carve a post-tenure reputation, Johnson used conferences to test and develop his ideas and push them forward. On reflection, this was something we had both ourselves done on numerous occasions. But the fact that the practice is so familiar does not eliminate the need for a detailed account of it. Ultimately, we decided that the provision of such an account represented a better use of the Johnson data than did documenting all the activities involved in the production of his paper.

The starting point is this: an analytically neglected feature of social knowledge production—indeed, of all knowledge production—is that it is, quite simply, hard work. Identifying promising topics for research, generating and thinking through hypotheses, gathering and analyzing data, and writing up the results, and doing these things again and again, year after year, can be utterly exhausting, especially because they represent only one part of an academic's job. More humanistically oriented scholars involved with the production of social knowledge confront a different set of work tasks, but careful archival or library research and the crafting of long, detailed articles or books require no less energy and drive. There are no doubt academicians who bound out of bed in the morning eager to write all that they can that day, whether out of intrinsic interest in the subject matter or a desire to be recognized by their peers. For many others, however—and even for self-starters when it comes to projects about which they may not have as much enthusiasm—in light of the difficulty of doing good work, procrastination and avoidance are every bit as common.

The fact that scholarship requires energy has not gone completely unrecognized by sociologists. For example, sociologists of science in the Mertonian tradition have considered some of the factors associated with scientific productivity and have found the most important category of these to be the resources differentially available to scholars at different types of institutions; among other things, resource availability such as staff support and graduate research assistants affects the amount of time and energy scientists have left over for research. Likewise, Collins (1998) puts the notion of emotional energy front and center in his network-structural theory of intellectual life, arguing that intellectual stars are able to maintain high levels of productivity because they are emotionally charged up by positive attention.[9] What such work, insensitive to questions of practice, does not take up—cannot take up because of its paradigmatic commitments—is the range of techniques, habits, recipes for action, and tricks of the trade that scholars use, in different ways depending on their structural positions, to overcome tendencies toward inertia and keep themselves energized and productive.

One of the most common of these techniques, it seems to us, is for scholars to obligate themselves to others by promising the completion of a text by a given deadline, often in connection with collective intellectual endeavors. Working with collaborators or agreeing to write a chapter for an edited volume are not simply ways of organizing research or getting into print: they are also means by which scholars bind themselves to the mast, to use Jon Elster's (1977) evocative image from Greek mythology,[10] forcing

9. More generally, however, sociologists of ideas have been inattentive to the fact that intellectual work is a form of labor involving corporeal activity and inevitably raising issues of motivation and control. Other sociologists have been better at recognizing the point. Joseph Hermanowicz, studying physicists in the sociology of careers tradition of Everett Hughes, notes that "although autonomy in science (and in the academy more generally) has been popularly depicted as a luxury, it is also a curse. No organizational imperatives tell the scientist, unlike the lawyer or the doctor, that he or she has to get up each morning to work. And after each day of effort, the scientist is left not completely knowing what those efforts will bring" (1998, 19). Neo-Marxist higher-education scholars (e.g., Slaughter and Rhoades 2004) also treat academic work as labor, as do other Marxists writing about intellectual life (e.g., Wright 1978).

10. In *The Odyssey*, Ulysses instructs his shipmates to bind him to the mast of his ship so that he will not be lured by the song of the Sirens. Elster develops this into a theory of "imperfect rationality." At its core is the idea that it is commonplace for actors "to carry out a certain decision at time t1 in order to increase the probability of another decision being carried out at time t2" (1977, 470). Schelling analyzes the same phenomenon in his paper "Enforcing

themselves to buckle down and actually produce research and/or writing lest they be seen as breaking their promises, disappointing colleagues, and violating professional norms. In the midst of the deadline pressures that follow from these self-initiated commitments, academics can frequently be heard saying things like "Why did I ever agree to this?"—but the reason they did, we contend, is because they realize, at the level of practical reasoning, that if they did not, many papers they might have liked to have written would never be completed.

Promising to write an original paper for an academic conference, as Johnson did, is a special case of the more general practice of binding oneself to the mast. Two features distinguish conference presentations from other commitments. First, because conference presentations require a high degree of spatiotemporal coordination with other actors (e.g., discussants, other panelists, and audience members) as well as public staging, academic talks involve unique scheduling constraints (Winship 2009): unlike self-imposed deadlines (or even deadlines imposed by editors or colleagues), which can be fudged or moved, conference presentations, much like class lectures or the speaking appearances familiar to public intellectuals, are fixed, scheduled events. One is either there ready to give a talk, or one is not. Skipping a conference presentation can and does happen, but doing so carries with it significant social costs, because real people, who have displaced themselves to be in a particular place at a particular time, are counting on hearing a paper. An academic's evaluation of the costs involved in withdrawing from a promised conference presentation is one of the factors determining whether the promise can function as an impetus for completing the necessary intellectual work.

The second distinguishing feature of conference presentations is that while they force knowledge producers to come up with something to say in time, in other respects such presentations are relatively low-stakes affairs. Any time an academician promises to deliver a future piece of work, there are risks. If the intellectual product assembled turns out to be shoddy, there may be repercussions for one's intellectual reputation, a much-valued resource. In some settings for which professors tie themselves to the mast, such as edited volumes or colloquium talks in leading departments, expectations are very high. Because this is so, papers written for volumes or given as colloquium talks, at least by savvy professors, tend to be derived

---

Rules on Oneself" and gives academic conferences as one of his examples, discussing normative "rules" that arise "about writing a conference paper in plenty of time to revise it before the event and to get it into the hands of discussants at a decent interval before they are to discuss it" (1985, 359).

from mature intellectual projects—ones scholars have been working on for some time and around which their thinking is already highly developed. By contrast, while some conference presentations, such as those taking place in "plenary" sessions, are high profile, most are not. Audiences are usually not large, restrictions on presentation length are such that no one expects a perfectly fleshed out contribution, and there is a general expectation among conference-goers that some papers may be experimental and that their authors should be afforded evaluative leniency. For most academics who agree to give original papers at conferences, therefore, the aim in binding themselves to the mast by doing so is not to force the production of a ready-to-publish draft but simply to move a project forward from a state of lesser to greater completion. This may be understood in terms of the process of "idea concretization."

Among producers of social knowledge, there seem to be some who form crystal-clear pictures in their heads of the papers and books they want to write next. Others have only vague, diffuse notions about the arguments they intend to craft. For scholars in the latter category, the process of writing a paper or book is one of progressive idea concretization in which, over time, vague and abstract plans, formulations, insights, communicative urges, and hypotheses come to be transformed, pinned down, and given concrete argumentative form. Writing original papers for conferences is a vehicle for idea concretization in three senses: (1) it forces one to finally write up one's thoughts enough to stage a coherent oral performance; (2) the encouragement or discouragement that one receives from fellow panelists, commentators, and audience members helps one determine whether a newly minted project is worth following through to completion; and (3) beyond mere encouragement or discouragement, the *specific* feedback an intellectual receives about her work in a conference setting may influence the future direction of that work, depending on a variety of factors, including the nature of the social relationship between the intellectual and the person providing the feedback, the kinds of professional exigencies the intellectual is facing at the time, and the cultural lens through which that feedback is interpreted.[11] Social interaction is crucial to each of these aspects

---

11. It is worth noting that the feedback received at conferences differs in key respects from that received in other ways. Unlike informal comments on papers that one receives from friends and colleagues, conference feedback is not always respectful, and the relative intellectual heterogeneity of most conferences means that one may receive comments from scholars who are not part of one's intellectual circle and who disagree as to paradigmatic matters. Unlike peer review, the identity of a commentator is not concealed at a conference, and conference-based comments contain both verbal and nonverbal elements that must be deciphered.

of idea concretization, such that papers initially presented at conferences, no matter how isolated the other work practices of their authors or how far removed from immediate social or political concerns their topics, forever bear the mark of the social. That Johnson was using the Paris conference as a vehicle for idea concretization, and that this had a significant effect on the knowledge production process as it played out in his case, became all the more clear to us as the date for his trip approached.

A Deadline Looms

With his conference proposal accepted, Johnson made plans to get started on his paper. Shortly after he heard back from the conference organizers, he reread several Steinbeck texts and wrote up a Word document of his notes. For each text he made a list of the main characters and summarized the plot, presumably so that he would have these details at hand later on and would not have to rely exclusively on his memory. More importantly, for each text he also wrote out a paragraph or two of his own observations on the way that Steinbeck seemed to be grappling with philosophical themes to do with class oppression and resistance. These observations flowed from and were organized in terms of a one-page list Johnson also made of the core philosophical questions he wished to address. Johnson's plan was to add textual material to these notes in the coming months and then reorganize them so that they would come to resemble a finished paper.

Like most elite academicians, however, Johnson works on multiple projects simultaneously. When we first interviewed him, not long after he had heard that his paper proposal had been accepted, he told us that during that semester he was also committed to finishing a chapter for an edited volume on an entirely different topic, one that would require a good deal of research. He hoped to find time to work on both projects. This proved difficult. Johnson was juggling a full teaching load and administrative responsibilities and had recently received job offers from several other schools, which had required visits to the campuses and embroiled him in lengthy negotiations. Also, his wife was pregnant. Come mid-March, about five weeks before the conference, Johnson still had made little progress with his Steinbeck paper. He emailed us one day to say that he had carved out an afternoon to read more of Steinbeck's work, along with a couple of articles about him. He had updated his notes to reflect the additional reading, but they still looked nothing like a paper.

A month later, now about a week before the conference, Johnson came down with a bad cold but under the gun managed to make some revisions to his notes, transforming his summaries of several of the texts, which had been schematic in previous versions, into more coherent sentences and paragraphs that advanced an interpretive argument rather than merely summarizing plots. Was this going to be enough? Later that week, with his departure for Paris looming, he realized he was in trouble. He emailed us to report, "I have a few more note[s] and ideas but not a real presentation. Attached is what I'll leave with tomorrow. My panel is not until Saturday, so I'll have a chance to work on it in [Paris.]"

When producers of social knowledge write papers to give at conferences, they may or may not feel compelled to tailor them for the occasion. Generally speaking, and in line with classic work on expectation states theory (Berger, Rosenholtz, and Zelditch 1980), the higher profile the conference or panel, and the lower the speaker's academic status relative to other speakers, commentators, or likely audience members, the more tailoring will occur. In this case, given Johnson's higher status than that of the panel organizers and the fact that the conference itself was not terribly prestigious—which had increased its appeal for Johnson—alongside the fact that the panel he was on was something of a catch-all rather than a venue where the organizers had a coherent intellectual agenda, he felt little pressure to make his presentation conform substantively to organizer or audience expectations. Even in such a context, however, the setting imposed constraints upon his work. At the very least, producers of social knowledge, much like those in the physical and biological sciences, want the knowledge claims they advance to be seen as "credible" (Latour and Woolgar 1979) and typically write their conference papers to achieve this effect.

Putting on a credible presentation in Paris required that Johnson attend to two interrelated concerns. First, he had to make sure that his presentation would be not just logically coherent but rhetorically elegant. Philosophy, especially in the analytic style, puts less emphasis on writerly flourishes than other humanities fields, but no humanist will get very far with his ideas unless he knows how to turn a phrase and command some rhetorical force. Johnson described to us his concerns in this regard under the heading of "craft." In an interview after the conference, he told us that he had spent a lot of time in the days leading up to the presentation "thinking" about "how to cast" the paper. "I have a kind of. . . . obsession with craft," he said. "I want the thing to hang together in a certain way, to have a certain kind of elegance." He rehearsed in his head several possible openings as well as different structures for the talk. Second, Johnson had to manage the interdisciplinarity of the conference setting. He had learned ahead of time who else would be on his panel and discovered that he had been paired, not with other philosophers or political theorists, but with scholars from other disciplines who were experts on Steinbeck. This meant that he could not assume that other panelists or audience members would share his paradigmatic assumptions—which he would either have to bracket or make clear at the outset of his talk—and also that he would have to work especially hard to convince the Steinbeck experts that his interpretation, constructed without the benefit of any formal literary training, deserved to be taken seriously. Johnson wanted his conference paper to be seen as credible, not just to avoid embarrassment, but more importantly so that the paper could do the job of serving as a test balloon for the ideas that it embodied and not engender a false reaction.

Right before he left for Paris, Johnson came up with what he thought might be a good opening for his talk, one that would help him solve the credibility problem. He remembered having once read an essay published shortly after the *Grapes of Wrath* had appeared. The essay offered an inter-pretation of the book that Johnson thought had become popular and with which he disagreed. Not the least benefit of starting with a quotation from it would be that doing so would demonstrate his own familiarity with twentieth-century American literature—that he knew more than Steinbeck alone and hence had some literary authority. He "grabbed" the essay "to take with me and read on the plane. [I] thought about it a little bit more and thought, 'Well, I see an angle here.' So that gave me an entry point." He was still unsure, however, about a structure for the rest of the talk. How should he organize his ideas? Besides *Grapes of Wrath*, which Steinbeck texts should he cover? During the plane ride, and in Paris the next day, he talked over some of the issues with his wife, who is not a philosopher but knows a lot about philosophy. They discussed the merits of including certain texts rather than others. The plots of some seemed too complex to present in the twenty-five minutes Johnson had allotted to him, while others seemed too distant from his philosophical concerns. His wife also offered some useful suggestions for how he might frame the philosophical issues in ways that would grab the attention of an interdisciplinary audience.

When Johnson and his wife returned from dinner Friday night, he had a better sense for how he was going to proceed but worried that he did not have much down on paper. "I didn't have anything, really," he told us. "I mean I had some ideas, but it was nothing that I could present. And you never know. [At] these conferences . . . the quality of the papers varies considerably. Sometimes there are very good papers and then there are re-ally bad ones. . . . You don't want to be on a panel where there are a bunch of good papers and your paper is really terrible. . . . I was a little nervous about that." So, after his wife went to bed, he sat down and wrote out an introduction. After starting with the quotation from the other writer whose book he had brought with him on the plane, the introduction stated that his goal in the presentation was to analyze Steinbeck's work as "philosophical fiction." The introduction went on to describe what Johnson meant by this term and what philosophical commitments he saw as present in Steinbeck's writings. By 4:30 a.m., he had written out fifteen hundred words of prose—enough to take up about fifteen of his allotted twenty-five minutes. He still could not decide which of two additional Steinbeck works to focus on, so before he went to bed he appended his now revised reading notes for both to the introduction he had just drafted. In his talk the next day, he opened by reading the introduction verbatim and then spoke extemporaneously from his notes for the remainder of the time. As a newly tenured professor, Johnson knew that his entire reputation was not riding on the talk, but he also described feeling some of the same pressures he had experienced as a junior faculty member:

> Every public appearance you feel like you've got to bring your A game . . . because you don't know who is in the audience. . . . So I usually feel like I have to come with my best stuff. But [this time] I told myself, I was like, "Okay, you have tenure, you've got. . . . a body of work and a reputation and it's not going to really be harmed by any one conference or paper or whatever." So I was trying to tell myself that. But of course the old sense of how you go at it is kicking in. . . . I have a . . . strong sense of professionalism, so you know, I did want to do a good job.

The talk did not go terribly, but neither was it a smashing success. Certainly he did not receive the same kind of reaction, positive or negative, that he had received several years earlier at the indigenous property rights conference. Most of the people in the audience directed their questions toward the other panelists. One of the panel organizers, a historian, did ask Johnson a question—about whether Steinbeck could legitimately be seen as doing what Johnson was suggesting—but Johnson interpreted the query, a challenge, as overlain by paradigmatic and epistemological differences. As he put it to us, "I've come to believe that in terms of interdisciplinary enmity, historians and philosophers may be. . . . natural enemies" in the sense that historians "focus on the particular, the local, the contingent, you know—context," in contrast to the philosophical focus on the "universal, the transcendent." He had interpreted Steinbeck as participating in a larger conversation about social justice that stretched across the ages, whereas the historian saw him as more bound up with his time and place. Johnson responded politely but forcefully to the criticism but more generally found that no one was jumping out of her seat to tell him how interesting or important the paper was. He was not terribly upset by this reaction at the time—part of his reason for attending the conference *had* simply been to take a nice trip with his wife. Yet, significantly, Johnson's work on the paper slowed to a standstill in the months that followed. While there are other possible explanations for his lack of progress on the project (including the imminent arrival of his first child, his other commitments, or even our monitoring of his work), we suspect that the lack of positive feedback at the conference also played an important role. By the end of that summer, Johnson had hired a research assistant to help familiarize him more with the secondary literature on Steinbeck, perhaps reflecting his sense, not least resulting from his conference experience, that if he was going to write about a literary figure, even for the purposes of advancing a philosophical argument, he had better be able to do so in a manner that would be persuasive to a literary studies audience. But he had done no additional writing on the paper, and by the end of that fall it was no further along.

Only in the semester following was Johnson able to make some headway with the piece. As a newly prominent figure in his field, he had been asked to give the keynote address at a midsized academic conference in March focused on questions of philosophy and oppression. He decided to present his new work on Steinbeck, which meant that he would now have to write up a full draft of the paper. As this was to be a formal address with strict time limitations, the document he wrote was only 6,500 words and was written in the clear, jargon-free style for which Johnson had become known. As his earlier version had done, the paper made a case for interpreting Steinbeck as a writer of "philosophical fiction" addressing questions of how people ought to live amid class inequality, and it glossed this interpretation as running contrary to conventional wisdom, which held Steinbeck to be a writer of "protest fiction." To help foreclose criticism of this interpretation by Steinbeck experts (of the kind he had been subject to in Paris), he inserted a paragraph in which he claimed that Steinbeck's philosophical musings about class followed in a long tradition of such work in "American letters"; here he appeared to be drawing on some of the secondary literature his research assistant had pulled for him. This rhetorical move, despite the fact that it was accompanied by Johnson's insistence that he would "not take this opportunity" to "defend his placement" of Steinbeck "in this tradition of thought" in any detail, not only served to bolster Johnson's literary authority, as a philosopher who was familiar enough with the history of American literature to speak confidently about its traditions, but also made his interpretive claim seem less radical and more plausible: he was not claiming that Steinbeck had invented some heretofore-unrecognized literary tradition but merely suggesting that he be seen as belonging to a somewhat different literary camp than was commonly understood. After marshaling evidence from Steinbeck's writings to support this interpretation, the paper went on to consider the philosophical lessons these writings contained, using Steinbeck's ideas as a jumping-off point for an elaboration of Johnson's own philosophical views.

We did not attend the conference, but that summer Johnson reported to us in an email that the talk "was well received, with lots of interesting questions from the participants and audience." His ideas had now been sufficiently elaborated, honed, made credible, and protected against obvious criticism as to generate positive audience response. The comments of audience members may not have been "particularly probing," as Johnson went on to tell us, so that he had no plans to "change anything in the paper in response to their feedback," but the fact that the talk had gone well gave new energy to the project. Had it not gone well—had this been the second time his paper on Steinbeck failed to win over an audience—it seems likely the project would have been abandoned and that Johnson would have cut his losses.

In Johnson's view, though, the paper still had some way to go before it would be ready for publication, and to move it toward completion he made plans to give versions of it in several colloquium talks in the coming year in top philosophy departments, where the criticism would presumably be more intense, forcing him to hone it even more. He also learned that a major conference on Steinbeck was to be held the following summer in London, and he made plans to attend.

Conclusion

The goal of this volume is to begin the process of identifying and documenting the wide variety of social practices involved with the production, dissemination, and evaluation of social knowledge in diverse intellectual, institutional, and temporal settings. If the history of science and technology studies serves as any guide, attention to social practices should position sociologists of ideas and others to formulate more robust and realistic accounts of the origins of social knowledge and of its circulation and effects. In this chapter our aim was to explore, by means of an in-depth case study, one such social practice: the presentation of original papers at academic conferences as a means for moving intellectual projects forward. Although not all published books or articles begin as conference presentations, we theorized, on the basis of the experiences of a political philosopher, that agreeing to give a paper at a conference is a way of "binding oneself to the mast"—of forcing oneself, at the risk of shame and embarrassment, to work through the practical difficulties of intellectual labor in order to show up at a conference prepared to make a coherent and credible presentation. Under certain conditions, we argued, conferences can also serve as test balloons for new projects, allowing presenters to gain valuable feedback about their ideas that may spur them on, lead them to make course corrections, or abandon projects and ideas to which peers react negatively.

Case studies are extraordinarily useful for building and illustrating empirically grounded theories, but they have obvious limitations. Among the many questions raised by our chapter that our methodology does not permit us to answer are the following: How common is the practice of conference-going enacted by Johnson? How does its enactment vary depending on an academician's career stage, disciplinary location, and institutional status? What are the major dimensions along which academic conferences vary, besides the obvious ones of size, prestige, and recurrent or one-shot status, and are there different practices of conference-going and conference paper presenting associated with each? In what proportion of cases do scholars actually modify or abandon projects that are poorly received at conferences? What are the "cultural pragmatics" (Alexander, Giesen, and Mast 2006) of a successful conference presentation? How does tying oneself to the mast by agreeing to give an original paper at a conference intersect with other habits, routines, and tricks of the trade that producers of social knowledge may deploy? And, not least important, when did the practice come into being? On this last point, while the history of academic conferences in general remains unwritten, our hunch is that the specific use Johnson made of the Paris conference became a stable component of academic repertoires only in the second half of the twentieth century as participation in national and regional scholarly associations soared and as it became easier and cheaper to travel great distances to participate in academic gatherings. Time pressures on academics (Jacobs and Winslow 2004) may also have been a factor here, as professors, trying to maintain their productivity against the onslaught of other demands on their time, sought more opportunities to tie themselves to the mast. Future research should attempt to establish whether this historical dating is correct, as well as provide answers to the other questions we have outlined.

Before drawing the chapter to a close, there is a final issue worth considering. Our discussion of the Mike Johnson case has been geared around individual-level concerns: the role that giving papers at academic conferences plays in the production of knowledge by single academics. Yet one of us (Gross 2009) has argued previously that, conceived of as more or less habitual ways of solving problems that arise for actors in the course of life, practices also form the basis for causal relationships in the social world that stretch across micro-, meso-, and macrolevels of analysis; and that identification of practices and the circumstances in which they are enacted provides the key to a richer causal social science. What, if any, are the implications of the practice we have focalized for broader causal relationships and patterns in the production of knowledge? We would offer the following preliminary hypotheses. (1) Given how important the presentation of original papers at conferences seems to be for moving projects forward, there should be a direct relationship between, on the one side, levels of conference-going and the resource endowments necessary to support it for individuals, for scholars situated at particular types of institutions, and for scholars in specific national contexts and, on the other side, levels of academic productivity—and not simply for reasons to do with communication given by neo-Mertonian sociologists of science. (2) Following from point 1, globalization and the increase in academic travel associated with it should be implicated in the aggregate increases in scholarly productivity registered in recent decades. Finally, we believe that the capacity of a producer of social knowledge to give a successful oral performance of her or his conference paper—which is partially but not exclusively a function of the content of the ideas—may have a significant bearing on the long-term trajectory of that paper. Although the Mike Johnson case is an exception, we see such a capacity as often linked to levels of parental cultural and intellectual capital: on average, academics from "cultured" backgrounds will be seen as better, more stylish presenters. To the extent this is so, (3) academic performances in conference settings should be important sites for the intergenerational reproduction of the cultural and intellectual elite, independent of the role that conferences may play in sustaining internal academic status hierarchies. (Gross's notion of intellectual self-concept, though developed as a critique of Bourdieu, was never meant to deny that class reproductive processes thread through academic life.) These hypotheses, of course, must be subjected to empirical scrutiny. But at the very least our case study suggests that conference-going—a routine activity for contemporary producers of social knowledge—deserves more attention from sociologists of ideas.

References

Abir-Am, Pnina. 1987. "The Biotheoretical Gathering, Trans-disciplinary Authority and the Incipient Legitimation of Molecular Biology in the 1930s: New Perspective on the Historical Sociology of Science." *History of Science* 25:1–70.

Alexander, Jeffrey C., Bernhard Giesen, and Jason Mast, eds. 2006. *Social Performance: Symbolic Action, Cultural Pragmatics, and Ritual*. New York: Cambridge University Press.

Ben-David, Joseph, and Randall Collins. 1966. "Social Factors in the Origins of a New Science: The Case of Psychology." *American Sociological Review* 31:451–65.

Berger, Joseph, Susan Rosenholtz, and Morris Zelditch. 1980. "Status Organizing Processes." *Annual Review of Sociology* 6:479–508.

Blumen, Orna, and Yoram Bar-Gal. 2006. "The Academic Conference and the Status of Women: The Annual Meetings of the Israeli Geographical Society." *Professional Geographer* 58:341–55.

Bourdieu, Pierre. [1984] 1988. *Homo Academicus*. Translated by Peter Collier. Stanford, CA: Stanford University Press.

Cole, Jonathan, and Stephen Cole. 1973. *Social Stratification in Science*. Chicago: University of Chicago Press.

Collins, Randall. 1998. *The Sociology of Philosophies: A Global Theory of Intellectual Change*. Cambridge, MA: Harvard University Press.

Coser, Lewis. 1965. *Men of Ideas: A Sociologist's View*. New York: Free Press.

Crane, Diana. 1972. *Invisible Colleges: Diffusion of Knowledge in Scientific Communities*. Chicago: University of Chicago Press.

Daemmrich, Arthur A., Nancy Ryan Gray, and Leah Shaper, eds. 2006. *Reflections from the Frontiers, Explorations for the Future: Gordon Research Conferences, 1931–2006*. Philadelphia: Chemical Heritage Press.

Dolan, Julie, Martha Kropf, Karen O'Connor, and Marni Ezra. 1997. "The Future of Our Discipline: The Status of Doctoral Students in Political Science." *PS: Political Science and Politics* 30:751–56.

Elster, Jon. 1977. "Ulysses and the Sirens: A Theory of Imperfect Rationality." *Social Science Information* 16:469–526.

Epstein, Steven. 1996. *Impure Science: AIDS, Activism, and the Politics of Knowledge*. Berkeley and Los Angeles: University of California Press.

Ergi, Carolyn. 1992. "Academic Conferences as Ceremonials: Opportunities for Organizational Integration and Socialization." *Journal of Management Education* 16:90–115.

Erickson, Lance D., Steve McDonald, and Glen H. Elder, Jr. 2009. "Informal Mentors and Education: Complementary or Compensatory Resources?" *Sociology of Education* 82:344–67.

Everett-Lane, Debra. 2004. "International Scientific Congresses, 1878–1913: Community and Conflict in the Pursuit of Knowledge." PhD diss., Columbia University.

Fender, Blakely, Susan Taylor, and Kimberly Burke. 2005. "Making the Big Leagues: Factors Contributing to Publication in Elite Economics Journals." *Atlantic Economic Journal* 33:93–103.

Gross, Neil. 2008. *Richard Rorty: The Making of an American Philosopher*. Chicago: University of Chicago Press.

———. 2009. "A Pragmatist Theory of Social Mechanisms." *American Sociological Review* 74:358–79.

Gunnell, John. 1988. "American Political Science, Liberalism, and the Invention of Political Theory." *American Political Science Review* 82:71–87.

Hagstrom, Warren. 1965. *The Scientific Community*. New York: Basic Books.

Haskell, Thomas L. [1977] 2000. *The Emergence of Professional Social Science: The American Social Science Association and the Nineteenth-Century Crisis of Authority*. Baltimore, MD: Johns Hopkins University Press.

Hermanowicz, Joseph C. 1998. *The Stars Are Not Enough: Scientists—Their Passions and Professions*. Chicago: University of Chicago Press.

Jacobs, Jerry, and Sarah E. Winslow. 2004. "The Academic Life Course, Time Pressures, and Gender Inequality." *Community, Work, and Family* 7:143–61.

Latour, Bruno, and Steve Woolgar. 1979. *Laboratory Life: The Social Construction of Scientific Facts*. Beverly Hills, CA: Sage.

Leiter, Brian, ed. 2004. *The Future for Philosophy*. New York: Oxford University Press.

Merton, Robert K. 1973. *The Sociology of Science: Theoretical and Empirical Investigations*. Chicago: University of Chicago Press.

Mullins, Nicholas. 1973. *Theories and Theory Groups in Contemporary American Sociology*. New York: Harper and Row.

Opitz, Helmut, ed. 2002. *World Guide to Scientific Associations and Learned Societies*. New York: Saur.

Schelling, Thomas. 1985. "Enforcing Rules on Oneself." *Journal of Law, Economics, and Organization* 1:357–74.

Shapin, Steven. 1996. *The Scientific Revolution*. Chicago: University of Chicago Press.

Slaughter, Sheila, and Gary Rhoades. 2004. *Academic Capitalism and the New Economy: Markets, State, and Higher Education*. Baltimore, MD: Johns Hopkins University Press.

Soderqvist, Thomas, and Arthur Silverstein. 1994. "Participation in Scientific Meetings: A New Prosopographical Approach to the Disciplinary History of Science—the Case of Immunology, 1951–72." *Social Studies of Science* 24:513–48.

Stroll, Avrum. 2000. *Twentieth-Century Analytic Philosophy*. New York: Columbia University Press.

Van Dijk, Jouke, and Gunthur Maier. 2006. "ERSA Conference Participation: Does Location Matter?" *Papers in Regional Science* 83:483–504.

Winship, Christopher. 2009. "Time and Scheduling." In *The Oxford Handbook of Analytical Sociology*, edited by Peter Hedström and Peter Bearman, 498–520. New York: Oxford University Press.

Wright, Erik. 1978. "Intellectuals and the Class Structure of Capitalist Societies." In *Between Labor and Capital*, edited by Pat Walker, 191–212. Boston: South End Press.

FIVE

Practical Foundations of Theorizing in Sociology

The Case of Pierre Bourdieu

JOHAN HEILBRON

Defined neither by a well-circumscribed subject matter and a corresponding form of professional expertise, like psychology and economics, nor by a shared point of view like history and perhaps philosophy, sociology has traditionally aspired to be a general social science. Since notions such as "human society" or "social processes" that are commonly used to characterize the sociological perspective do not provide more than a terminological minimum, the actual practice of sociologists is best understood in its context, that is, first and foremost, in relation to other disciplines and subdisciplines. Sociology may thus be understood as belonging to a "third culture," one that is uneasily situated between the humanities and the natural sciences and within which humanistic and scientific orientations coexist and collide (Lepenies 1988). A similar observation holds for sociology in relation to the other social sciences. For institutional reasons, French sociologists have predominantly defined themselves in relation to philosophy, the "crowning discipline" (Fabiani 1988) in the Faculty of Letters. Depending on the local and the national context, other sociologists have allied themselves with history, anthropology, or economics. Sociology's claim of being a general social science is thus inseparable from its varied relations to other disciplines and domains of knowledge.

As a consequence of this peculiar position in the division of academic labor, sociology has been a discipline with a high degree of plasticity. What sociologists collectively produce tends to have a low level of cognitive and professional codification, a high degree of pluralism, dispersion, and context dependency, and a rather volatile intellectual status. Sociology has historically fluctuated from being among the most prestigious intellectual pursuits to constituting little more than a specialty of "leftovers," as pioneering American sociologist Albion Small famously commented. In addition to the more general reasons that apply to all disciplines, even the most autonomous ones, there is thus a specific reason, based on this peculiar position in the intellectual division of labor, why knowledge-making practices in sociology depend strongly on the conditions under which they are exercised. An appropriate means, therefore, to understand the production of sociological knowledge is to examine the way sociologists have operated within and across the division of intellectual work. Sociologists have broadly followed one of two strategies: either they have tried to become recognized specialists in a certain domain and have there confronted other knowledge specialists, or they have ventured to construct a perspective that claims some sort of general validity. Since the dynamics of specialization are relatively well known and hardly specific to sociology, it is perhaps more interesting to consider sociologists who have been involved in mobilizing concepts and ideas across different domains of knowledge in order to propose a general understanding of the social world. The French sociologist Pierre Bourdieu (1930–2002) is an illuminating case in this respect. Recognized as one of the most eminent sociologists of the second half of the twentieth century, Bourdieu's work has provoked numerous interpretations, comments, and debates. So far, however, there have been few—if any—attempts to reconstruct how Bourdieu actually produced his central insights and, in particular, how these were rooted in his particular research practice.

Sociological Inquiry in a Generalizing Mode

In proposing to grasp central aspects of Bourdieu's sociological practice, the aim of this chapter is to show how he constructed the general sociological model that underlies all of his mature work since the publication of *Distinction* ([1979] 1984) and *The Logic of Practice* ([1980] 1990). If one were to condense this model into a sort of analytical formula, however artificial that may be, one might say that Bourdieu conceptualized sociology as a science of *social practices*—that is, as a science concerned with structured regularities, which are neither completely systemic nor entirely random and the logic of which is fundamentally at odds with the dominant paradigms in the social sciences, whether centered on human action, rational choice, or social systems. To account for these practices, they need to be understood as located in relatively autonomous social spaces (fields), which are defined by struggles over specific stakes between agents that are characterized by the volume and composition of their resources (capital) and by the dispositions by which they are inclined to use these resources (habitus). The indicated terms (practice, field, capital, habitus) are not the only concepts of Bourdieu's approach; there are several others (domination, symbolic violence, *illusio*, *doxa*, strategy, homology, reproduction), but these can, at least provisionally, be seen as refinements of the basic model.

In analyzing the genesis of this sociological model, I will argue that it can be understood as the outcome of a distinctive research practice. It was the immersion in a plurality of open-ended collaborative research endeavors, and not theoretical speculation or textual exegesis, that eventually produced Bourdieu's mode of sociological analysis. From his early studies on Algeria to the last full-fledged monograph he published during his lifetime, *The Social Structures of the Economy* ([2000] 2005), Bourdieu's major books are all based on uncommonly diverse empirical work. Since Bourdieu's central concepts can be shown to have emerged in various research undertakings, I will first argue that his particular research practice originated in the context of his Algerian experiences and was then transposed to metropolitan France. After examining this distinctive mode of conducting and organizing inquiries, I will reconstruct the emergence of his basic concepts within specific research projects and indicate how they gradually received a more general meaning and, finally, how they were put together, resulting in the general model I briefly summarized above (a schematic visual overview is presented in figure 5.1). In the last section, I suggest a conceptualization of the principles that seem to underlie the process of knowledge making in Bourdieu's case and that will probably have some significance beyond the single case I am concerned with here.[1]

Sociogenesis of a Research Practice

Understanding research practices implies studying how, under specific conditions, researchers do their work. In the domain of science studies there are, broadly speaking, two distinct ways of achieving this. Structural approaches emphasize the way in which research practices are embedded in larger academic and other structures and consider how the outcome of the

1. This chapter is based on the totality of Bourdieu's publications (for a bibliography, see Delsaut and Rivière 2002), secondary literature, especially the volumes that contain testimonies of his students and collaborators (Bouveresse and Roche 2004; Dubois, Durand, and Winkin 2005; Encrevé and Lagrave 2003; Mauger 2005; Pinto, Sapiro, and Champagne 2004), and my own observations and experiences dating to when I first met Bourdieu as a foreign student in Paris in 1979.

research process is produced by the way research groups maneuver within this larger set of constraints and opportunities. Another type of approach, following the example of laboratory studies, tends to focus on patterns of interaction in microsettings as the best way to account for the results of the research process. Since the two do not necessarily exclude one another, I will in this chapter combine them, first, by briefly indicating some of the structural conditions under which Bourdieu's inquiries evolved and, then, by focusing on the particular way Bourdieu—given these general conditions—developed a distinctive research practice of his own.[2]

One of the structural features of research practices is that the specific skills and dispositions of researchers that feed into the research process tend to be all the more important if the research has a low level of institutionalization, when, in other words, a variety of possible roles exists and much of the required work is not strictly predefined. That was the situation of French social science when Bourdieu started his work. Since he entered, not a well-structured universe, but a field that was in the process of emerging, the position he constructed inevitably reflected the particular dispositions that guided his choices. In reconstructing the genesis of Bourdieu's research practice I will, therefore, start by briefly recalling the circumstances in which he worked in Algeria and France as well as his social trajectory and the dispositional characteristics that are associated with it.

When he began the research for his first publications, Pierre Bourdieu was a promising and somewhat rebellious young philosopher. Raised in a remote mountain village in the southwest of France, where his father had become a postal employee, the young Bourdieu made it all the way up to the Parisian Ecole normale supérieure, the selective training school of the French intellectual elite. In his self-analysis, he identified the contrast between his provincial and popular upbringing and the long years of "scholastic confinement" in boarding schools in Pau and Paris, from his eleventh to his twenty-fourth year, as the formative tension of his career. This dual experience was at the root of ambiguities toward the world of Parisian intellectuals and academics and constituted, more generally, what he called his "cleft habitus" (Bourdieu [2004] 2007, 100): his inclination to play the intellectual game at a high level and his persistent revolt against its pretentiousness, its illusions, and its lack of realism and responsibility.

Studying philosophy in Paris at the end of the 1940s and the beginning

---

2. My analysis in this respect complements Bourdieu's own account (Bourdieu 2008), which concentrates on field dynamics.

of the 1950s, Bourdieu's intellectual universe was marked by the towering figure of Jean-Paul Sartre and the existentialism and phenomenology that dominated both the intellectual field and the more restricted sphere of academic philosophy. Like Michel Foucault (who was not much older) and a few others, Bourdieu was most tempted by the other pole of the philosophical spectrum.[3] Although interested in the more scientifically oriented forms of phenomenology, especially in the work of Merleau-Ponty and Husserl, Bourdieu was more fundamentally attracted to the philosophers who worked on conceptual questions in the history of science and philosophy, to the scrupulous historical epistemology of Georges Canguilhem, who was also a well-known *résistant*, and to the rigorous history of philosophy (Martial Guéroult, Jules Vuillemin). While planning to write his PhD on "the temporal structures of affective life," which was to be supervised by Canguilhem, his Algerian experiences profoundly changed the course of his life. Bourdieu was sent to Algeria in 1955 for his military service; in 1960, following an intervention by Raymond Aron, he was urgently flown back to France because his name had appeared on the "red list," implying that he was in danger.

Upon arriving in the French colony, which had been in a state of emergency since 1955, Bourdieu was sent to an air force unit to execute administrative tasks.[4] About a year later, he was assigned to the information and documentation service of the General Government in Algiers, which had one of the best-stocked libraries and was a meeting place for all those with a scholarly interest in the country (archivists, missionaries, ethnographers, journalists, colonial administrators). Here the young philosopher met visiting specialists, was drawn into scholarly, informed debates about the country at war, and did most of the reading for *The Algerians* ([1958] 1962). His first book offered a sober and synthetic overview of the country, its different groups of inhabitants (Kabyles, Shawia, Mozabites, Arabic-speaking peoples), and colonial politics and society. *The Algerians* was written at a moment in time when the war for national liberation was spreading from the countryside to the urban centers, simultaneously becoming a cause among French intellectuals. In Bourdieu's perception many intellectuals were ill-informed, ignoring the complexities of the situation,

3. For Bourdieu's own account of his trajectory, see especially "Fieldwork in Philosophy" (in Bourdieu [1986] 1990) and his self-analysis (Bourdieu [2004] 2007). For a comparison of the trajectories of three well-known *normalien* philosophers (Bourdieu, Derrida, Foucault), see Pinto 2004.

4. For information about his Algerian years, see especially Sayad 2002; Yacine 2003, 2004, 2008; Wacquant 2004; and the special issue of *Ethnography* 5, no. 4 (2004).

and some of them, particularly Sartre and Fanon, held unrealistic and "irresponsible" views.[5]

After finishing his military service and shortly after the "battle of Algiers" (1957), Bourdieu joined the University of Algiers, teaching philosophy and sociology and initiating fieldwork with the help of students, while in his spare time continuing to work on his PhD. A major part of his field research was undertaken within the framework of a research association, the Association pour la recherche démographique, économique et sociale (ARDES), which provided the funding and lent the inquiries its social, as well as its scientific, legitimacy. Out of this collaborative work came his first articles and two additional books. Realized with a team of Algerian researchers and coauthored with three young statisticians from the Algerian office of the French bureau of statistics (INSEE), Bourdieu produced the nearly six-hundred-page *Travail et travailleurs en Algérie* (Work and Workers in Algeria; Bourdieu et al. 1963), a detailed inquiry into the functioning of the urban economy. With his former student Abdelmalek Sayad, and again with the help of several other Algerian students, he also studied the resettlement camps that the French military had imposed on more than two million Algerian peasants and that are analyzed in *Le déracinement* (The Uprooting; Bourdieu and Sayad 1964). The ethnological work on Kabyle ritual and kinship probably started slightly earlier, in 1958, and was related to the rising figure of Claude Lévi-Strauss and the promise of structural anthropology.

Although it has proven difficult to reconstruct how Bourdieu's Algerian work was actually carried out, its first distinctive characteristic was the intense fieldwork itself. Bourdieu was one of the few intellectuals who considered that his presence in Algeria and his political sympathies had to imply a serious scholarly effort. He was not content with "reading left-wing newspapers or signing petitions; I had to do something as a scientist" (Bourdieu [1986] 1990, 39). This commitment through research distinguished Bourdieu from most of his schoolmates and fellow academics, both in Algeria and in France. Some of them, like his future companion Jean-Claude Passeron, who was also in Algeria, considered that research into the complexities of Algerian society ran the risk of troubling the struggle for independence (Passeron 2004, 25).

Undertaken in unusually difficult circumstances, Bourdieu's research did not resemble the sedentary existence of academic life to which he was ac-

5. See especially the texts republished in Bourdieu 2002c; for Bourdieu's position in relation to other French intellectuals, see Le Sueur 2001; Rioux and Sirinelli 1991.

customed. Developed through a heterogeneous network of collaborations, the inquiries were the product of a peculiar set of social dynamics. Included in his diverse collaborative network were his students, who were his first informants and some of whom became research associates and collaborators (Abdelmalek Sayad), a few independent scholars (like the left-wing Catholic director of the library of the General Government, Emile Dermenghem, or the young historian André Nouschi), various Algerian intellectuals who started out as novelists, journalists, or teachers (Mouloud Feraoun, Malek Ouary, Mouloud Mammeri), members of the Social Secretariat who were under the authority of the bishop of Algiers and who in 1959 and 1960 published his first articles and chapters (Bourdieu 2008), as well as the already-mentioned statisticians of the Algerian office of the INSEE. There were, on the other hand, very few connections to the academic experts of the University of Algiers, many of whom were conservative orientalists, who did not do any fieldwork and were isolated from anthropological and sociological debates and most of whom favored a French Algeria.[6]

Analytically the research dealt with questions about the unity and diversity of traditional Algerian society, the consequences of colonialism, the transition from a precapitalist to a capitalist market economy, and the social and economic conditions for organized political action. Such a brief enumeration, however, pertains more to the outcome of the research than to the research process itself. From the point of view of understanding Bourdieu's research practice, its predominant characteristic was that nothing of it was self-evident, since none of the intellectual routines applied, neither Bourdieu's own working habits as a philosopher nor the standard procedures of social science research. The war and the "clash of civilizations," as he called it, made philosophical issues and procedures seem irrelevant, while applying standard methods of anthropological fieldwork or statistical research was highly problematic. Bourdieu's collaborators seem, at least in part, to have shared this experience. The statisticians of the INSEE, for example, quickly found out that the categories they intended to use for their survey of the labor market were inadequate. To have "a job" or to be "unemployed" designated something quite different in Algeria at war than in metropolitan France. Even within the Algerian context the variation was striking: the Kabyles, for example, tended to define periods of "unemployment" quite differently from other groups.

The researchers were thus forced to confront questions for which there were no standard answers. If Bourdieu was eager to collaborate with the

6. For Bourdieu's perception of this intellectual universe, see Bourdieu 2003a.

statisticians because he was searching to enlarge his knowledge and was tempted to use any insights he could, the statisticians and economists of the INSEE, for their part, were glad to complement their skills with Bourdieu's intellectual training and his sociological and anthropological knowledge. The collaboration led to a rethinking of both the design and the way of organizing the research (Seibel 2004). Classical anthropological fieldwork was also far from self-evident. It was suspect in the eyes of many Algerian intellectuals, including Sayad and Mammeri, because it was bound up with colonial rule and because issues of myth, ritual, and kinship seemed irrelevant for the political struggle. More broadly conceived ethnographic studies were perhaps more appropriate, but they raised scientific problems that the statisticians were all too familiar with, problems of selection bias and generalization (i.e., how to generalize on the basis of qualitative case studies).

Not much is known in detail about how the collaborative research experiment actually came about, but in *Travail et travailleurs en Algérie* (Bourdieu et al. 1963), Bourdieu explicitly addresses some of the major issues. He does so in a critical analysis of the predominant "ideologies of science," as he calls them, which he considers to be obstacles for an effective and realistic research practice. In the general introduction, Bourdieu discusses the "conflict of methods," especially of statistical and ethnographic methods, which he interprets in sociological terms as being rooted in the separation of scientific and literary training and in the status anxieties of its practitioners. Instead of ignoring or denying the competence of one another, Bourdieu argues that the reality of the situation imposes the "collaboration of methods." Various arguments are given why the reciprocal relationship between statistical and interpretive procedures, and the permanent *va-et-vient* between the two, should be considered a vital necessity: "Statistical regularities have sociological value only if they can be comprehended. And, the other way around, subjectively comprehensible relations constitute sociological models of real processes only if they can be observed empirically with a significant degree of confidence" (Bourdieu et al. 1963, 11). In the actual fieldwork different methods were thus combined: observations and interviews went along with distributing standardized questionnaires, which, once filled out, allowed quantification and statistical treatment. Transcending the cleavage between ethnographic fieldwork and survey research was—and would remain—the hallmark of Bourdieu's research work.

In the preface to the second part of *Travail et travailleurs*, Bourdieu takes up a number of other themes as well. Discussing an article by Michel Leiris in which Leiris contends that studies conducted under colonial conditions would be objectionable, Bourdieu explains the choices that were made and describes the way the research was conceived and conducted. His presentation ironizes grand proclamations and moralizing judgments, recalling with Parmenides that no object, however reprehensible politically or morally, is unworthy of scientific scrutiny. While vigorously defending scientific inquiry, he does not claim any scientific neutrality: "What one may demand in all rigor of the anthropologist is that he strives to restore to other people the meaning of their behaviors, of which the colonial system has, among other things, dispossessed them" (Bourdieu et al. 1963, 259). Significantly, Bourdieu discusses several aspects of the research process that he considers crucial but that are absent from the standard discussions of research methodology, such as the importance of the composition of research teams (paying attention to the particular role of women in the research process and insisting on the necessity of having a mixed Algerian-French research team) and the effect of the social origin of the interviewer on the social interaction and the results of the interview (Bourdieu et al. 1963, 257–67).

This practical reflexivity (although that was not yet the term used), which is at odds with the routinized compartmentalization of academic tasks, had its origins in the research collaboration that emerged in the exceptional circumstances in Algeria. The separation of methods, the divorce between scholarly questions and political issues, and the lack of reflexive awareness that all tend to characterize academic work were radically called into question. The young Bourdieu responded to these challenges by conceiving research as a collective effort, guided by the need of orchestrating a plurality of researchers, methods of inquiry (observations, interviews, statistical analysis), and scholarly resources (dissolving the boundaries between anthropology, sociology, and labor economics), and by reflexively facing the problems that came up instead of following standard rules and established precepts. This style, which became typical of all Bourdieu's research undertakings, also provided him with a fundamental theoretical problem: how can the knowledge of objective structures, indicated by statistical frequencies or structures of myth and ritual, be reconciled with the knowledge of the lived experience of the actors? How do objectivist modes of knowledge relate to subjective understandings? Whereas this question pervades his early research, it is elaborated theoretically for the first time in the introduction to the book on photography (Bourdieu et al. [1965] 1990) and more fully in his first major theoretical statement, *Esquisse d'une théorie de la pratique* ([1972] 2000). Bourdieu's research experiences in Algeria were, in short, not merely the beginning of his oeuvre but its very foundation.

Transposing and Multiplying the Algerian Model

The conceptual innovations with which Bourdieu's work is commonly associated can be seen in a variety of research projects that he finished or undertook after returning to France. When he came back in March 1960, the conditions for the social sciences in France were favorable. Since the establishment in 1958 of an autonomous *licence* (bachelor) degree in sociology, sociology, like other social science disciplines, was expanding rapidly: the number of students was growing, faculty positions were opening up, there was a strong growth of research funding, and a host of new social science journals were launched—*Sociologie du travail* (1959), *Archives européennes de sociologie* (1960), *Revue française de sociologie* (1960), *Études rurales* (1960), *Communications* (1962), *L'homme* (1961). Lévi-Strauss, whose seminar Bourdieu attended, had become the challenger of Sartre, and with the emerging fascination with structuralism, intellectual attention shifted from humanistic disciplines to more scientific versions of the humanities (linguistics, semiology) and the social sciences. In these circumstances, Bourdieu's research experience, combined with his educational credentials, gave him an advantage over other aspiring sociologists. Starting as Raymond Aron's assistant at the Sorbonne, Bourdieu taught in Lille (1961–64), gave the first sociology course at the national school of statistics (ENSAE, from 1964), and conducted a seminar at the Ecole normale supérieure (1964–84). His main position was in the Sixth Section of the Ecole pratique des hautes études (EPHE), a graduate school and research institution. The Sixth Section was directed by Fernand Braudel and was the locus of the most advanced social science research in France. It was here that in 1962 he became general secretary of Aron's Centre de sociologie européenne (1959) and was elected director of studies (1964–2001).

Being part of an institution that gave its members a large degree of freedom in defining their pedagogical and research tasks, under conditions of rapid institutional expansion and a growing public interest in the social sciences, Bourdieu was in a favorable position to capitalize on his Algerian experiences. The new research projects he undertook continued the dynamics of his Algerian inquiries. Organized as a collective enterprise, in an unbureaucratic, partly improvised, and open-ended manner, they typically combined ethnographic and survey methods, focusing on critical issues of social transformation. Theoretical aspirations were present as well. Weberian ideas on legitimacy and ideal types were interwoven with Marxian notions of class and Durkheimian reflections on social morphology and symbolic classifications. The work of Bourdieu's emerging research group was conceived, not in terms of any particular theory, specific method, or distinct research specialty, but in a language that was borrowed from the French epistemological tradition. This tradition, represented especially by Bachelard and Canguilhem, had redefined philosophy as an epistemological reflection on scientific work. In *The Craft of Sociology* ([1968] 1991), Bourdieu, Chamboredon, and Passeron used this epistemological tradition to state their view on social science research. Extending ideas from his Algerian work, Bourdieu and his companions defined social science research as a rigorous scientific endeavor that did not fundamentally differ from research in the natural sciences and that was critical and unorthodox precisely because it was rigorously scientific (breaking with "common sense," "ideologies," and other "preconceived notions" of the social world). This conception allowed the integration of different research methods as well as of concepts that belonged to rival theoretical traditions (Marx, Weber, Durkheim). In the context of French social science at the time, this research style simultaneously opposed the "empty theories" of general theorists like Georges Gurvitch, the empiricism that had been prevalent in the previous generation of French sociologists, and the more recent conceptions of quantitative "methodology" (represented by Paul Lazarsfeld and Raymond Boudon).

Bourdieu's first research project in France was a study of his native village in the Béarn region. It was related to his Algerian experiences, which had reactivated memories of the peasant community of his youth. In talking to Kabyle peasants about "honor," he often wondered what peasants from own region would have told him and how he would have understood their stories. The detailed inquiry into the social transformation of his native village and the crisis that peasant families went through was conceived as a complement to his Algerian investigations, a kind of *Tristes tropiques* in reverse, as he called it, a way to confront the insights and working method he had obtained in Algeria with the universe with which he was intimately familiar.[7] Using the same combination of research methods and a similar

---

7. The project apparently also led to a reconciliation with the world he had left behind when he was still a boy, that is, with his parents and old acquaintances and friends. It affirmed that scrupulous research matters, that it can "restore to people the meaning of their actions" (Bourdieu [1962] 2002b, 128), and that it can similarly affect the researcher. In the introduction to the reedition of his book-length article on celibacy, Bourdieu recalls "the emotional atmosphere" in which the research was undertaken. As he experienced an unanticipated mobility, a self-inflicted "degradation" from the sovereign heights of Parisian philosophy to the lowest lows of rural sociology, his research on celibacy in the Béarn was accompanied by the "confused dream" of reintegration into the world in which he was born (2002a, 10; [2004] 2007, 60). By interviewing older peasants with the help of his father, taking pictures of his home

exploratory and collaborative style, the Béarn research proved that it was possible to transfer his Algerian experiences to the French context and that it was possible to become a full-fledged social scientist, instead of pursuing his PhD with Canguilhem and looking for a job in philosophy. If the Algerian experience had marked his *initiation* into a new intellectual life, his study on marriage patterns in the Béarn produced a vital *confirmation* of his existence as a social scientist.

After the Béarn project, from 1961 onward, a whole series of intensive research projects followed on photography (Bourdieu et al. [1965] 1990), banks and their clientele (Bourdieu et al. 1963), the public of European art museums (Bourdieu and Darbel [1966] 1990), and a whole range of university faculties and elite schools. The study on the social uses of photography exemplifies the research carried out. It concerned an apparently minor topic that hardly existed as an object of scholarly inquiry and that carried little cultural prestige. But it allowed the raising of fundamental questions about cultural practices, because there were few economic or technical obstacles to photography, and because the practitioners who were interviewed expressed their views and cultural preferences far more frankly than when they were asked about legitimate high culture (painting, classical music). The organization of the research was typical as well. The final book, of which Bourdieu is the editor and main author, was based on twenty different research operations over a period of four years. Starting in Aron's seminar on the role of images in industrial society and partly financed by Kodak, the project included exploratory studies, ethnographic fieldwork, surveys, and case studies, involving some twenty people in various capacities (students, aspiring sociologists, occasional collaborators, colleagues). The numerous projects on higher education had a similar dynamic. *Les héritiers* (The Inheritors; [1964b] 1979), written with Passeron, was likewise based on observations (some carried out by Bourdieu's students in Lille), several case studies, and a questionnaire that was distributed through personal connections to university colleagues in various French cities. Just as Claude Seibel, one of the statisticians who had coauthored *Travail et travailleurs en Algérie* (Bourdieu et al. 1963), contributed to the research on the Béarn, Alain Darbel, another statistician with whom Bourdieu had worked in Algeria, contributed to *Les héritiers*.[8] Not only was the type of research

---

town, and talking to old school friends, a "part of myself was given back to me" ([2004] 2007, 62). The passage from philosophy to sociology thus turned out to be unexpectedly rewarding.

8. For discussion of the empirical material on which *Les héritiers* is based, see Bourdieu and Passeron [1964b] 1979; Bourdieu, Passeron, and de Saint-Martin 1965. On the context, see

similar to what Bourdieu had done in Algeria, but several of the people involved were the same as well.

Sociological Research as an *Ars Inveniendi*

These varied and intensive collaborative projects constituted the primary activity of Bourdieu's research group during the 1960s and much of the 1970s. It was in the course of these projects that Bourdieu's central notions appeared. The first concepts were related to understanding the complexities of social behavior. In his Algerian work he had used phenomenological themes and ideas while resisting notions that were associated with the philosophy of a free and consciously choosing subject (Sapiro 2004). For reasons similar to those that had ignited his critical reaction to Sartre's philosophy of freedom, Bourdieu opposed the misguided universalism of *homo economicus*, a concept that, he argued, ignored the historical and social conditions for the rational pursuit of economic interests. Given the "clash of civilizations" and the contradictions between the traditional peasant economy and the logic of market exchange, Bourdieu's analysis focused on differences in economic ethos and diverging attitudes toward time and the future.

In the research on celibacy in the Béarn, he encountered a similar problem. There, the traditional mode of inheritance and reproduction was in crisis as well, as was apparent at the yearly village Christmas ball, where city folk were dancing with the local girls while bachelor peasants looked on. How could these men, who inherited the land and the houses, have become "unmarriageable"? The notion of habitus that Bourdieu introduced in this research project referred to the bodily dispositions that disqualified the peasants in comparison with the increasingly present city-dwellers. Similar to Mauss in his essay on body techniques, Bourdieu used the term *habitus* or *hexis* for the set of acquired characteristics that have become a second nature, designating inclinations that are beyond the reach of conscious decisions (Bourdieu [1958] 1962, 115). In *Le déracinement* Bourdieu used the notion in a more general manner, not only for bodily postures but as a "permanent and general disposition with regard to the world and the others" (Bourdieu and Sayad 1964, 102). A more elaborate and systematic use of the term appears in the postscript to two essays by Erwin Panofsky,

Masson 2001 and various chapters (especially those by Yvette Delsaut and Jean-Claude Passeron) in Chapoulie et al. 2005.

which Bourdieu brought together and translated (Bourdieu 1967). Panof-sky comments on the similarities between Gothic architecture and scho-lastic treatises. Both seem to derive from the same construction principles, and Panofsky explains the similarity by observing that architects and theo-logians went to the same school, thus acquiring the same mental habits. The concept of habitus (in fact, Panofsky spoke only of a "habit-forming force") is here used in a more active sense, as a principle of invention, a way of handling and organizing very different material, rooted in the so-cialization of the producers. Bourdieu presents this explanation as having a very general meaning, at odds with other explanatory strategies: with the cult of the individual genius, with unspecified references to the Zeitgeist, as well as with the structuralist analysis à la Lévi-Strauss, Althusser, or Fou-cault, all of whom radically eliminated the actors and abstracted from a theory of action.

By its subsequent use in different research projects, first in the study on celibacy, then in Le déracinement, finally in the epilogue to Panofsky's essays, the habitus notion emerged as a general concept for a theory of action. The progressive conceptualization draws on various research experiences and is achieved primarily by combining the earlier interest in economic behavior with the more recent work on the pivotal role of the school system. In all of these senses, the concept emerged as a generalization: it is produced nei-ther by sudden intuition nor by an exercise of theoretical exegesis but, first and foremost, as a conceptual account of successive research experiences. Informed by his theoretical training and driven by his propensity to find an alternative for subjectivist theories of action and objectivist accounts of structures, Bourdieu characterizes habitus as a "generative grammar" of action (borrowing Chomsky's expression) that explains similarities across different practices resulting from the interiorization of external conditions. Habitus is thus a mediating structure between objective conditions and actual conduct and in that sense analytically comparable to notions like "ethos" or "attitude" that Bourdieu also used and that had been essential for understanding the mismatch between the dispositions of traditional peasants (both in Algeria and in the Béarn) and the new conditions under which they were forced to live.

The research projects on the school system and educational inequalities apparently raised quite different questions. In The Inheritors ([1964b] 1979), Bourdieu and Passeron argued that to explain the unequal access to higher education, cultural inequalities are a crucial yet largely unacknowledged selection mechanism. The knowledge of, the taste for, and the "attitudes" toward culture were the most important hidden factors in the process of removing pupils from the working classes. The "rational pedagogy" the authors advocated at the end of their study could therefore be based only on a sociology of cultural inequalities. The more general issue of whether in a period of ongoing economic growth inequalities were disappearing or would remain significant was the theme of a workshop that Bourdieu and Alain Darbel organized in 1965. Bringing together members of the Centre de sociologie européenne with statisticians and economists from the INSEE, the workshop was a direct continuation of the project on the Algerian labor market, with all four authors of *Travail et travailleurs en Algérie* being present. The idea was to mobilize various disciplines and competencies (including several laypeople who wrote reports based on their professional experiences) to analyze the social and economic transformation of French society. Instead of the monodisciplinary and large-scale congress organized at the same time by the French sociological society, Bourdieu and Darbel typically preferred a small-scale, multidisciplinary workshop, uniting what they considered to be the most advanced social science disciplines (economics, sociology, anthropology, statistics). Since there was "no accepted general theory" of society, each specialist could succeed in raising new questions only if he knew and recognized "the limits of his own concepts and assumptions" (DARRAS 1966, 426).

In the context of this renewed dialogue with statisticians and economists, Bourdieu reformulated his analysis of educational inequalities by proposing the concept of "cultural capital." Referring to the unequal chances of access to higher education, he presented a general model that was sure to provoke discussion with the economists: "Each family transmits to its children, more in an indirect than in a direct manner, a certain cultural capital and a certain ethos, a system of implicit and profoundly interiorized values, which contributes to define, among other things, the attitudes toward cultural capital and toward the school system. The cultural heritage that under these two aspects differs by social class is responsible for the initial inequality of children before the school selection and thus, to a large degree, for their unequal rates of success" (Bourdieu 1966b, 388).

In the context of the mid-1960s the introduction of the notion of cultural capital had a double significance. It was, first, an attempt to enlarge, differentiate, and correct standard economic analysis, arguing that educational inequalities are primarily a matter of differences in, not income or wealth, but cultural resources. This cultural capital, furthermore, is handled, not following a rational-choice logic, but rather on the basis of a certain ethos that is the result of the socialization of the actors. This enlarged and revised "economic" analysis simultaneously represented a way of importing economic notions into the disinterested realm of culture and education. In that sense it represented the refusal of a basic dichotomy of thought as well as a constructive way to transcend it. Many of Bourdieu's conceptualizations display this paradoxical dialectic of thinking with and against, with economic concepts against standard economics, with structural analysis against structuralism. Considering "culture" as "capital" implied bridging an irreducible and irreconcilable opposition and is an apt illustration of Bourdieu's propensity to move beyond the dominant divisions—*dépasser* is one of his favorite verbs—not by theoretical synthesis, but by a research-driven conceptualization in a multidisciplinary context. To understand this dynamic, the conventional history of ideas and the erudite search for "influences" are of little use, because they do not inform us about the inclinations that are at work in using, borrowing, or proposing certain concepts, and because they ignore the context in which specific parts of the intellectual tradition are selected and (re)activated while most others are not.

The idea of cultural capital would rapidly obtain a more general significance. Just as culture functioned as capital, "prestige" and "honor" could be conceived as symbolic capital. They thus became ingredients in the critical theory of culture that Bourdieu intended to develop, while simultaneously giving rise to a new issue. In the introduction to the photography book, Bourdieu states that sociologists should not leave "anthropological questions" (in the original, not in the disciplinary, sense of the term) to speculative philosophy. Since a proper theory of human action should include both the objective chances and the lived experience of the agents, it was necessary to leave the "fictitious opposition" of objectivism and subjectivism to philosophers and to recognize that the analysis of objective probabilities, subjective experiences, and their intermediary mechanisms are "inseparable moments" of scientific analysis (Bourdieu, Passeron, and de Saint-Martin 1965). In this early, programmatic statement, Bourdieu does not mention the concepts of habitus and capital. The same is true of his book with Darbel *The Love of Art* ([1966] 1990). In the first editions of both studies, Bourdieu still uses more or less equivalent terms such as "ethos," "dispositions," or "attitudes." It is only in the years after 1966 or 1967 that Bourdieu moves toward a more unified approach, combining his notions of habitus and capital in relation to specific practices, a process that culminates in *Esquisse d'une théorie de la pratique* ([1972] 2000), his first, albeit provisional, theoretical synthesis.

Although the word "practice" is used in a factual sense, in expressions such as "cultural practices" it obtains a theoretical significance as well. In trying to overcome the opposition between "objectivism" and "subjectiv-ism," Bourdieu considered these theoretical approaches as different "mo-ments" of analysis or as different types of knowledge. Transcending or com-bining the two, as he had already done in various research projects, thus required a reflection on the status of the old as well as of the new theory. In a little-known article of this period, Bourdieu thus calls for a "theory of sociological theory" (Bourdieu 1968). This metatheoretical reflection was required not only for an adequate understanding of objectivist and subjec-tivist theories but also for defining an alternative theoretical program. In consciously addressing the issue, Bourdieu displays a form of reflexivity, which was undoubtedly rooted in the fact that he was unwilling to take the theoretical game for granted, just as he had not taken empirical research for granted. Instead of elaborating some kind of academic synthesis, Bour-dieu typically stepped back and first reflected on the act of theorizing and on the very notion of theory.

Out of this reflection came his project for a "theory of practice," a proj-ect that was the result not so much of his wish to overcome the "dichotomy of objectivism and subjectivism" but more specifically of his sociological understanding of "objectivism" and "subjectivism" as particular modes of relating to the world. In some articles during these years, Bourdieu explic-itly advocates a "sociology of sociology" (Bourdieu and Passeron 1967) or, more generally, a sociological understanding of theorizing. In dissecting the production of "theory," Bourdieu observes that objectivist theories are theories produced from the perspective of the outside observer, describing actual behavior as the result of following "rules" or as the "realization" of laws. In his research on kinship, however, Bourdieu found that what anthropologists consider to be widespread rules of matrimonial exchange were actually obeyed very infrequently. Instead of uniform rules that peo-ple would "obey," actual practices are the result of the strategic uses of probabilities attached to social positions. Although the subjectivist mode of knowledge produces an opposite distortion by understanding behavior as the outcome of conscious intentions or rational choices, it is equally rooted in an intellectualist understanding of human behavior. Both the structuralist and the subjectivist mode of understanding suffer from a simi-lar ethnocentric bias.

After sociologically interpreting subjectivism and objectivism as forms of intellectual ethnocentrism, Bourdieu calls the "third type" of knowledge he intends to develop: "praxeological." Initially he defines it as a distinc-tive type of theory that dialectically combines the objectivist or structural mode of knowledge with the phenomenological mode of understanding

(Bourdieu [1972] 2000, 162–63). The general ambition of this new type of theory, outlined in *Esquisse d'une théorie de la pratique* ([1972] 2000), is best expressed on the cover of the first edition. The theory of practice is characterized succinctly as a contribution to the "unification of the human sciences by destroying all the false alternatives that it suspends or interdicts, such as the opposition between objectivism and subjectivism." It is added that the theory of practice includes a "theory of theory," because it cannot ignore the effects of theorizing on the objects it tries to apprehend. Unlike other theories, the theory of practice tries to account for the cognitive effects of the various theoretical postures on the objects they try to understand. Although the expression "reflexive theory" is not yet used, that is clearly what was intended.

Esquisse d'une théorie de la pratique ([1972] 2000), Bourdieu's first theoretical synthesis for the "anthropology" he had announced earlier, is thus also a contribution to the rethinking of theorizing. It contains a theoretical account of the social world that is based on the notions of habitus and different forms of capital (economic, cultural, symbolic, and social capital) and is conceived as a "generalized economy of practices." And it is simultaneously a reflection on theorizing as a particular relationship to the world, a relationship that engenders biases and distortions that represent fundamental obstacles for an adequate understanding of social practices. Bourdieu systematically elaborated this view in subsequent work on "scholastic biases," primarily in *The Logic of Practice* ([1980] 1990) and *Pascalian Meditations* ([1997] 1999). This dual character of the *Esquisse*, presenting a theory of social action as well as a theory of theorizing about the social world, was related to the reflexive inclination that was already present in Bourdieu's work on Algeria, as well as to the institutional and political changes occurring around 1970. The student revolt and political mass movements had disrupted the political and economic confidence of the 1960s and had politicized the universities. On a microlevel, they led to a break between Aron and Bourdieu; Aron and a few of his collaborators quit the Centre de sociologie européenne, thus leaving Bourdieu in charge and giving him greater liberty to develop his own program. One of the changes at the Centre de sociologie européenne in this period was that the collaborative project with Chamboredon and Passeron to publish a three-volume collection to be entitled *The Craft of Sociology* was discontinued. The first volume had been published in 1968, but the subsequent volumes never appeared, in all likelihood because Bourdieu had come to the conclusion that the theory of practice he was working on had implications for the teaching of sociology that no longer corresponded with the initial project. Specialists in epistemology and methodology, Bourdieu wrote, are "necessarily condemned to consider the *opus operatum* rather than the *modus operandi*, which besides a certain delay implies a systematic bias" (Bourdieu [1972] 2000, 221). From the point of view of his theory of practice, *The Craft of Sociology* suffered from scholastic fallacies; it was too "professorial" in its epistemological preliminaries and ran the risk of becoming a set of "routinized precepts of a new methodology" or, "worse still, a new theoretical tradition" (Bourdieu, Chamboredon, and Passeron 1972, 6).

There is, finally, one other concept in need of a brief comment, not to analyze its genesis and gradual elaboration, but simply to recall that its trajectory displays the same dynamic as that of Bourdieu's other conceptualizations. Emerging in a particular line of research, parallel to other endeavors, the field concept obtained a more general meaning in and through other research projects and was elaborated theoretically in a reflection "with and against" Max Weber before it was finally integrated into his general approach. The notion first appeared in his 1966 article on the intellectual and cultural field, in which it is argued that "creative projects" can be understood only when situated in the specific set of social relations in which they emerge (Bourdieu 1966a). The title of the article, "Intellectual Field and Creative Project," expresses the programmatic intention of bridging the opposition between structural analysis of intellectual production and a quasi-Sartrean understanding of creative acts. One of the central ideas was to use Weber's analysis of religious specialists and its differentiation between priests, prophets, and magicians to understand the cultural and intellectual field. Two years later, Bourdieu characterized Weber's analysis as a paradigmatic example of a relational approach to the social world, and argued that this relational mode of thinking is the most significant property of structural analysis (Bourdieu 1968, 697). In redefining structuralism in this manner, Bourdieu rendered it compatible with a theory of action, and the field concept thus obtained a more general significance than in the original 1966 article. Somewhat later again, Bourdieu returned to the issue more systematically. By rethinking Weber's sociology of religion, he proposed the first systematic formulation of his field theory (Bourdieu 1971c). The notion of field allows analysis of the structural similarities of different social universes, and for reflection on such analogies Weber's sociology of the religious field provides a model. In the course of the 1970s, the concept was applied to the religious field (1971b), the field of power (1971a), and the scientific field (Bourdieu 1976); it was then, in a second movement of synthesis, combined with the "anthropological" approach outlined in the *Esquisse* ([1972] 2000), in which the field concept had not appeared systematically. Replacing the term "system," which had been used in the work on education—for example, in *La reproduction* (Bourdieu and Passeron 1970)—the field concept served the purpose of contextualizing the analysis of social practices presented in the *Esquisse*.

Sociocognitive Principles of a Theoretically Oriented Research Practice

If we reconsider Bourdieu's sociological practice from a more theoretical point of view, it seems to display several sociocognitive mechanisms that in all likelihood have a significance beyond his particular case. Perhaps the most general characteristic of Bourdieu's working habits is that they were embedded in a highly distinctive type of research practice, which owed its characteristics to his Algerian experiences. Much could be said about how Bourdieu's familiarity with phenomenology or other theoretical traditions shaped his work, but the actual uses he made of these modes of thinking were consistently rooted in the specific dynamics of his research enterprise.

These *research-based conceptualizations* obtained a more general meaning by *domain switching*—that is, by their use in a research project in which the concepts were to account for different issues that, seen from a more general point of view, could be treated as similar. Instead of the more common strategy of increasing specialization, the multiple domains Bourdieu explored allowed him to transfer insights and experiences from one domain to the other, thus favoring empirically grounded generalizations. *Crossing disciplinary and institutional boundaries* worked in a similar manner. Instead of a predominantly monodisciplinary and intra-academic orientation, Bourdieu's collaborative research style included a plurality of social knowledge makers, thus stimulating the mobilization of ideas and points of view from a variety of disciplines (philosophy, anthropology, sociology, economics, linguistics, art history), research practices (statistics, ethnography), and professional and social backgrounds. If innovation results from "new combinations," as Schumpeter held, it requires a variety that Bourdieu not merely encountered but consciously sought and organized. In this sense, his case illustrates some of the insights of recent studies of creativity and innovation (Collins 1998; Uzzi and Spiro 2005).

What has not received sufficient attention in the literature on creativity and innovation, however, is that the variety that allows for new combinations and that can result from domain switching and boundary crossing merely leads to fragmentation or eclecticism—unless there are mechanisms to keep them in check. Bourdieu's case is interesting in this respect as well, because his research practice displayed three such countervailing mechanisms. The first one was the presence of a general scientific ambition, a common style of work, and a shared conception of research among members of his research group. The sense of a common purpose that defines a "circle" or a "school" stimulates exchange and collaboration among its members (Farrell 2001), discourages fragmentation, and promotes what may be called *focused variation*. On the cognitive level this had the effect of pooling resources, stimulating comparisons, and thinking by analogy, all in order to achieve higher levels of coherence and generality. *The Craft of Sociology* explicitly advocates collective research and the construction of "analogical models" (in opposition to "mimetic models"). For Bourdieu himself, as for several other French social scientists, this general ambition was rooted in his original training in philosophy and, in particular, in the French tradition of historical epistemology.

A second mechanism for dealing with the variety that was present in all his endeavors is the *reflexivity* that Bourdieu acquired in the exceptional circumstances in Algeria and that he was probably inclined to elaborate because of his atypical life trajectory. Since he was not spontaneously at ease in the Parisian intellectual world into which his school success had brought him, he could not take its mode of operation for granted. The reflexive mode of working he developed was a way of coping with this situation, allowing him to rethink and reframe the problems he faced and leading him to move beyond major oppositions and dichotomies. The most crucial result of this reflexive posture was probably his theory of practice itself, which he conceived as a fundamental break with the various forms of intellectualism that tend to distort scholarly accounts of the social world.

A third and final device that mitigated the potentially centrifugal effects of the research variety was the habit of regularly returning to his initial objects of study to exploit newly won insights for rethinking previous work and deepening his grasp on the issues at stake. *Le bal des célibataires* (2002a) characteristically contains three successive analyses of celibacy in the Béarn. While the initial text (1962) was analytically centered on observable bodily dispositions, the second text, ten years later, focused more broadly on the way peasant families manage the stock of their economic and symbolic capital, whereas the last text, published in 1989, adds yet another dimension, the one captured by field analysis, namely the fact that local marriage patterns had become increasingly embedded in a unified national social space, which had the effect of devaluing local resources. The notions of habitus and capital thus came to function within a well-circumscribed field transformation. A similar movement or progression can be documented in his work on higher education and in his studies of symbolic goods and cultural production fields. As a consequence of his practice of reflexively monitored domain switching and boundary crossing, which he combined with an "eternal return" to his previous objects of study (Bourdieu in Delsaut and Rivière 2002, 193), Bourdieu fell on neither side of the frequent partition between sociological generalists and specialists but combined the qualities of the hedgehog and the fox as he articulated his distinctive approach to sociological theory.

Figure 5.1. Simplified Scheme of the Genesis of Pierre Bourdieu's Conceptual Model

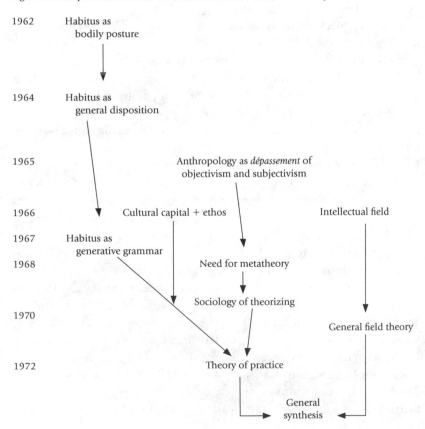

References

Bourdieu, Pierre. [1958] 1962. *The Algerians*. Boston: Beacon Press.

———. 1963. *La banque et sa clièntele: Eléments d'une sociologie du crédit*. 2 vols. Paris: Centre de sociologie européenne.

———. 1966a. "Champ intellectuel et projet créateur." *Les temps modernes* 22:865–906.

———. 1966b. "La transmission de l'héritage culturel." In *Le partage des bénéfices: Expansion et inégalités en France*, edited by DARRAS, 384–420. Paris: Minuit.

———. 1967. "Postface." In *Architecture gothique et pensée scolastique*, by E. Panofsky, 135–67. Paris: Minuit.

———. 1968. "Structuralism and the Theory of Sociological Knowledge." *Social Research* 35, no. 4: 681–706.

———. 1971a. "Champ du pouvoir, champ intellectuel, habitus de classe." *Scolies: Cahiers de recherche de l'Ecole normale supérieure* 1:7–26.

———. 1971b. "Genèse et structure du champ religieux." *Revue française de sociologie* 12: 295–334.

———. 1971c. "Une interprétation de la théorie de la religion selon Max Weber." *Archives européennes de sociologie* 12:3 21.

———. 1976. "Le champ scientifique." *Actes de la recherche en sciences sociales* 2–3: 88–104.

———. [1979] 1984. *Distinction: A Social Critique of the Judgment of Taste*. Cambridge, MA: Harvard University Press.

———. [1980] 1990. *The Logic of Practice*. Cambridge: Polity Press.

———. [1986] 1990. *In Other Words: Essays towards a Reflexive Sociology*. Cambridge: Polity Press.

———. [1989] 1996. *The State Nobility: Elite Schools in the Field of Power*. Cambridge: Polity Press.

———. [1997] 1999. *Pascalian Meditations*. Cambridge: Polity Press.

———. [1972] 2000. *Esquisse d'une théorie de la pratique*. 2d ed. Paris: Seuil.

———. 2002a. *Le bal des célibataires: Crise de la société paysanne en Béarn*. Paris: Seuil.

———. [1962] 2002b. "Célibat et condition paysanne." In *Le bal des célibataires: Crise de la société paysanne en Béarn*, 17–165. Paris: Seuil.

———. 2002c. *Interventions, 1961–2001: Science sociale et action politique*. Textes choisis et présentés par Franck Poupeau et Thierry Discepolo. Marseille: Agone.

———. [1997] 2002d. "Retour sur l'expérience algérienne." In *Interventions, 1961–2001: Science sociale et action politique*, textes choisis et présentés par Franck Poupeau et Thierry Discepolo, 37–42. Marseille: Agone.

———. 2003a. *Images d'Algérie: Une affinité élective*. Ouvrage conçu par Franz Schultheis et Christine Frisinghelli. Arles: Actes Sud.

———. 2003b. "Participant Objectivation." *Journal of the Royal Anthropological Institute* 9: 281–94.

———. [2000] 2005. *The Social Structures of the Economy*. Cambridge: Polity Press.

———. [2004] 2007. *Sketch for a Self-Analysis*. Cambridge: Polity Press.

———. 2008. *Esquisses algériennes*. Paris: Seuil.

Bourdieu, Pierre, Jean-Claude Chamboredon, and Jean-Claude Passeron. 1972. *Le métier de sociologue*. 2d ed. Paris and La Haye: Mouton.

Bourdieu, Pierre, and Alain Darbel. [1966] 1990. *The Love of Art: European Art Museums and Their Public*. Cambridge: Polity Press.

Bourdieu, Pierre, Alain Darbel, Jean-Paul Rivet, and Claude Seibel. 1963. *Travail et travailleurs en Algérie*. Paris and La Haye: Mouton.

Bourdieu, Pierre, and Jean-Claude Passeron. 1964a. *Les étudiants et leurs études*. Paris: Centre de sociologie européenne.

———. 1967. "Sociology and Philosophy in France since 1945: Death and Resurrection of a Philosophy without Subject." *Social Research* 34:162–212.

———. 1970. *La reproduction: Eléments pour une théorie du système d'enseignement*. Paris: Minuit.

———. [1964b] 1979. *The Inheritors: French Students and Their Relation to Culture*. Chicago: University of Chicago Press.

Bourdieu, Pierre, Jean-Claude Passeron, and Monique de Saint-Martin. 1965. *Rapport pédagogique et communication*. Paris: Centre de sociologie européenne.

Bourdieu, Pierre, and Abdelmalek Sayad. 1964. *Le déracinement: La crise de l'agriculture traditionnelle en Algérie*. Paris: Minuit.

Bourdieu, Pierre, and Loïc Wacquant. 1992. *Invitation to Reflexive Sociology*. Cambridge: Polity Press.

Bourdieu, Pierre, et al. [1965] 1990. *Photography: A Middle-Brow Art*. Cambridge: Polity Press.

Bouveresse, Jacques, and Daniel Roche, eds. 2004. *La liberté par la connaissance: Pierre Bourdieu (1930–2002)*. Paris: Odile Jacob.

Calhoun, Craig, Edward LiPuma, and Moishe Postone, eds. 1993. *Bourdieu: Critical Perspectives*. Cambridge: Polity Press.

Chapoulie, Jean-Michel, Olivier Kourchid, Jean-Louis Robert, and Anne-Marie Sohn. 2005. *Sociologues et sociologies: La France des années 60*. Paris: L'Harmattan.

Collins, Randall. 1998. *The Sociology of Philosophies*. Cambridge, MA: Belknap Press of Harvard University Press.

DARRAS. 1966. *Le partage des bénéfices: Expansion et inégalités en France*. Paris: Minuit.

Delsaut, Yvette, and Marie-Christine Rivière. 2002. *Bibliographie des travaux de Pierre Bourdieu*. Pantin: Le Temps des Cerises.

Dubois, Jacques, Pascal Durand, and Yves Winkin, eds. 2005. *Le symbolique et le social: La réception internationale de la pensée de Pierre Bourdieu*. Liège: Editions de l'Université de Liège.

Encrevé, Pierre, and Rose-Marie Lagrave, eds. 2003. *Travailler avec Bourdieu*. Paris: Flammarion.

Fabiani, Jean-Louis. 1988. *Les philosophes de la République*. Paris: Editions de Minuit.

Farrell, Michael. 2001. *Collaborative Circles: Friendship Dynamics and Creative Work*. Chicago: University of Chicago Press.

Gingras, Yves. 2004. "Réflexivité et sociologie de la connaissance scientifique." In *Pierre Bourdieu, sociologue*, edited by Louis Pinto, Gisèle Sapiro, and Patrick Champagne, 337–47. Paris: Fayard.

Lepenies, Wolf. 1988. *Between Literature and Science: The Rise of Sociology*. Cambridge: Cambridge University Press.

Le Sueur, James. 2001. *Uncivil War: Intellectuals and Identity Politics during the Decolonization of Algeria*. Philadelphia: University of Pennsylvania Press.

Masson, Philippe. 2001. "La fabrication des Héritiers." *Revue française de sociologie* 42: 477–507.

Mauger, Gérard, ed. 2005. *Rencontres avec Pierre Bourdieu*. Broissieux: Editions du Croquant.

Nouschi, André. 2003. "Autour de sociologie de l'Algérie." *Awal: Cahiers d'études berbères*, nos. 29–35.

Passeron, Jean-Claude. 2004. "La sociologie en politique et vice versa: Enquêtes sociologiques et réformes pédagogiques dans les années 1960." In *La liberté par la connaissance: Pierre Bourdieu (1930–2002)*, edited by Jacques Bouveresse and Daniel Roche, 15–104. Paris: Odile Jacob.

Pinto, Louis. 2004. "Volontés de savoir: Bourdieu, Derrida, Foucault." In *Pierre Bourdieu, sociologue*, edited by Louis Pinto, Gisèle Sapiro, and Patrick Champagne, 19–48. Paris: Fayard.

Pinto, Louis, Gisèle Sapiro, and Patrick Champagne, eds. 2004. *Pierre Bourdieu, sociologue*. Paris: Fayard.

Rioux, Jean-Pierre, and Jean-François Sirinelli. 1991. *La guerre d'Algérie et les intellectuels français*. Brussels: Editions Complexe.

Sapiro, Gisèle. 2004. "Une liberté contrainte: La formation de la théorie de l'habitus." In *Pierre Bourdieu, sociologue*, edited by Louis Pinto, Gisèle Sapiro, and Patrick Champagne, 49–91. Paris: Fayard.

Sayad, Abdelmalek. 2002. *Histoire et recherche identitaire*. Saint-Denis: Editions Bouchene.

Seibel, Claude. 2004. "Les liens entre Pierre Bourdieu et les statisticiens à partir de son expérience algérienne." In *La liberté par la connaissance: Pierre Bourdieu (1930–2002)*, edited by Jacques Bouveresse and Daniel Roche, 105–19. Paris: Odile Jacob.

Uzzi, Brian, and Jarrett Spiro. 2005. "Collaboration and Creativity: The Small World Problem." *American Journal of Sociology* 111:447–504.

Wacquant, Loïc. 2004. "Following Pierre Bourdieu into the Field." *Ethnography* 5: 387–414.

Yacine, Tassadit, ed. 2003. "L'autre Bourdieu." *Awal: Cahiers d'études berbères*, nos. 27–28.

———. 2004. "Pierre Bourdieu in Algeria at War." *Ethnography* 5, no. 4: 487–509.

———. 2008. "Aux origines d'une ethnosociologie singulière." In *Esquisses algériennes*, by Pierre Bourdieu, 23–53. Paris: Seuil.

PART TWO

Knowledge Evaluation Sites

SIX

Comparing Customary Rules of Fairness

Evaluative Practices in Various Types of Peer Review Panels

MICHÈLE LAMONT AND KATRI HUUTONIEMI

Introduction

In this chapter we offer an analysis of intersubjective understandings concerning how to identify quality in the evaluation of scholarship. We focus on peer review, the practice by which the worth of research is evaluated by those with demonstrated competence to make a judgment. We analyze aspects of epistemic cultures, defined by Karin Knorr Cetina (1999) as machineries of knowledge—what we understand to be the social and cultural structures that channel, constrain, define, and enable the production and evaluation of knowledge. Of all forms of academic evaluation, peer review is the most widely used. While other methods of evaluation (such as bibliometric measures) are gaining in popularity, they indirectly rely on peer evaluations and are typically considered less credible than peer review, especially in the humanities and the social sciences.

Evaluation is a major aspect of the knowledge-making process. It has the function of gatekeeping, filtering, and legitimating knowledge. It is also a process where standards of excellence are set and maintained, contested, and reshaped. Evaluations are used not only for separating the qualified from the less qualified but also for distinguishing between competing types of high-quality research. Evaluation practices in general, and the practices of peer review panels in particular, are both informative of how standards are intersubjectively constructed and determinant of what is prized in research. Through various conventions, peer review panels enable certain types of knowledge while constraining others. Better understanding of these conventions is thus crucial for gaining insight into one particular link between practices and politics in knowledge production.

Most of the research on research assessment has focused on issues raised by Robert K. Merton's influential work in the sociology of knowledge:

consensus in science; issues of universalistic and particularistic criteria of evaluation relating to the ethos of science; and the variously construed "Matthew" and "Halo" effects of reputation and prestige (Cole 1992; Cole and Cole 1981; Cole, Rubin, and Cole 1979; Liebert 1976; Merton 1996; Mulkay 1991). The question for most researchers is whether judgments about "irrelevant," particularistic characteristics, like the age and reputation of the author, affect the evaluation of his or her work. Other studies (Bell 1992; GAO 1994; Roy 1985) are also concerned with the fairness of the peer review process. The questions posed by these researchers imply that a unified and fair process of evaluating knowledge can be put in place once particularistic considerations are eliminated. The empirical literature on the topic largely confirms these normative assumptions by showing that peer evaluations are not highly correlated with factors other than scientific "quality," as measured by different quantitative indicators. Nevertheless, we contest the notion that one can separate cognitive from noncognitive aspects of evaluation, as we understand the evaluative process as deeply interactional, emotional, and cognitive and as mobilizing the self-concept of evaluators as much as their expertise (Lamont 2009).

More recent studies have revealed various "intrinsic biases" in peer review such as "cognitive particularism" (Travis and Collins 1991), "favoritism for the familiar" (Porter and Rossini 1985), and "peer bias" (Chubin and Hackett 1990; Fuller 2002). These effects show that peer review is not a socially disembedded quality-assessing process in which a set of objective criteria is applied consistently by various reviewers. In fact, the particular cognitive and professional lenses through which evaluators understand proposals shape evaluation. It is in this context that the informal rules that peer reviewers follow become important, as do the lenses through which they understand proposals and the emotions they invest in particular topics and research styles. Thus, instead of contrasting "biased" and "unbiased" evaluation, we aim to capture how evaluation unfolds, as it is carried out and understood by emotional, cognitive, and social beings who necessarily interact with the world through specific frames, narratives, and conventions, but who nevertheless develop expert views concerning what defines legitimate and illegitimate assessments, as well as excellent and less stellar research.

We are interested in how scholars serving on peer review panels construct the customary rules they follow in making funding decisions. More specifically, we aim to analyze the social conditions that lead panelists to an understanding of their choices as fair and legitimate and to a belief that they are able to identify the best and the less good proposals. As in Lamont (2009; see also Guetzkow, Lamont, and Mallard 2004; Lamont, Mallard, and Guetzkow 2006; and Mallard, Lamont, and Guetzkow 2009), our analysis puts much more emphasis on meaning in the evaluation process, including evaluation criteria, than did earlier studies. We interviewed individuals serving on various types of peer review panels that evaluate fellowship or grant proposals. We found that almost without exception, these individuals consider their deliberations fair and believe that meritocracy guides the process of selection—that is, that they are able to identify the top proposals. Their investment in a "culture of academic excellence" precludes them from framing the outcome of the deliberations as an expression of cronyism.[1]

The distinctive focus of this chapter is on comparing conditions for legitimacy across various types of evaluation settings. In the emerging literature on evaluation practices, there has been too little comparative work on *meaning making* and evaluation, leaving a gap in our understanding of variations in evaluation processes across national, organizational, and scholarly contexts (for a comparison of evaluation, dependency, and risk, see Whitley 1984). It is our aim to start filling this gap. We expect evaluative practices qua practices to vary to some extent across settings. This is so for at least two reasons. First, there are discipline-specific practices that researchers are socialized into early on (e.g., as we will see, a mode of evaluation that appears to be modeled more on deliberative democracy for humanists/social scientists versus one that is modeled on a "court of law" for natural scientists). Second, practices emerge from the dynamics and exigencies of particular intersubjective contexts (e.g., whether a panel happens to be uni- or multidisciplinary). In other words, definitions of scientific worth are interaction and context dependent. This is the case even if these practices are (1) grounded in connoisseurship, expertise, and knowledge that are largely stabilized (i.e., no longer controversial) and (2) part of much broader academic evaluation cultures that are institutionalized (to a varying extent at the national and international levels).

The analysis is based on two parallel but interconnected empirical studies, conducted in the United States and in Finland. In the United States, we

---

1. The conditions for their belief in the fairness of their evaluation include but are not limited to the customary rules of evaluation. Other factors include the process of selection and recruitment of evaluators: whether funding organizations construe this selection as determined by the expertise and status of reviewers, the habitual participation of the latter in elite academic circles, their academic training and professional status, etc. The Social Science and Humanities Research Council of Canada has gathered data on academics who do not typically apply for research funds or serve on selection committees. These data will soon allow social scientists to better understand how such academics perceive the legitimacy of evaluative mechanisms.

studied five different multidisciplinary funding panels in the social sciences and the humanities. This study was concerned, not with differences across panels, but with documenting the customary rules that panelists use.[2] We also studied four panels organized by the Academy of Finland. From the outset this study was explicitly concerned with the effects of the mix of expertise on panels and on how customary rules were enacted. The idea was to compare panels with varying degrees of specialization (unidisciplinary panels and multidisciplinary panels) and with different kinds of expertise (specialist experts and generalists). However, in the course of comparing results from the two studies, other points of comparison beyond expert composition emerged: whether panelists rate or rank proposals, have an advisory or decisional role, come from the social sciences and humanities fields or from more scientific fields, and so on. Our exploratory analysis points to important similarities and differences in the internal dynamics of evaluative practices that have gone unnoticed to date and that shed light on how evaluative settings enable and constrain various types of evaluative conventions. Note that we are not concerned with national differences in cultures of evaluation (e.g., with contrasting how the American and Finnish "cultures" would enable and constrain different customary rules of evaluation). This topic will be taken up in future research.

In the United States, we studied five different multidisciplinary funding competitions: those of the Social Science Research Council (SSRC), the American Council of Learned Societies (ACLS), the Woodrow Wilson National Fellowship Foundation (WWNFF), a Society of Fellows at a top research university, and an anonymous foundation in the social sciences. As is often the case in American grant peer review (except in federal agencies such as the National Institute of Health and the National Science Foundation), evaluators involved in these competitions ranked proposals and made funding decisions (although in some cases their decisions had to be formally approved by the research board of the funding institution). In Finland, we studied four evaluation panels organized by the Academy of Finland. We considered panels in the areas of the social sciences; environment and society; environmental sciences; and environmental ecology. Unlike the American competitions under consideration, the Finnish evaluation procedure decouples peer review and funding decisions. A similar procedure has been adopted by a consortium of fifteen national research councils that have joined forces to fund research in the social sciences in

---

2. Not focusing on organizations themselves was a condition for gaining access to these panels.

Europe (see www.norface.org). It includes countries with large and smaller research communities, such as France, Germany, and the United Kingdom, on the one hand, and Austria, Denmark, Iceland, and Slovenia, on the other. Thus, our comparison contrasts two significant and widely used models of peer review.

Among the most salient customary rules of evaluation, deferring to expertise and respecting disciplinary sovereignty manifest themselves differently based on the degree of specialization of panel members: we find that there is less deference in unidisciplinary panels where the specialties of panelists more often overlap. There is also less respect of disciplinary sovereignty in panels concerned with topics such as "the environment and society" that are of interest to wider audiences. And there is more explicit reference to the role of intuition in grounding decision making in less specialized panels. While there is a rule against the conspicuous display of alliances across all panels, strategic voting and so-called "horse trading" appear to be less frequent in panels that "rate," as opposed to "rank," proposals and in those that have an advisory, as opposed to a decisional, role. Moreover, the customary rules of methodological pluralism and cognitive contextualism (evaluating proposals according to the standards of the discipline of the applicant) are more salient in the humanities and social science panels than they are in the pure and applied science panels, where disciplinary identities may be unified around the notion of scientific consensus, including the definition of shared indicators of quality. Finally, while the analogy of democratic deliberation appears to describe well the work of the American panels, the Finnish science panels may be best described as functioning as a court of justice, where panel members present a case to a jury.

Our argument unfolds through a description of the *customary rules* followed by panelists in the United States and Finland. These are intersubjective rules that guide panel deliberations without being formally spelled out. Panelists cannot always articulate these rules, as they often take them for granted. However, they make them apparent when they describe the appropriate and inappropriate behaviors of fellow panelists, as their praise and criticisms articulate the rules that are to be respected.[3] Academics are never formally taught these rules but learn them throughout their professional socialization, so that these rules inform how they go about shaping and presenting their work. Interviews suggest that by adhering to such rules,

---

3. Our analysis is inspired by the ethnomethodological approach to examining the rules of social order. See in particular Garfinkel 1967.

evaluators are able to bridge their epistemological differences and perform the task of evaluating while maintaining their belief that their evaluation is legitimate (Mallard, Lamont, and Guetzkow 2009). Customary rules are thus the social conditions that lead panelists to build consensus with other evaluators and to perceive the process as fair.

In our analysis, the term "fairness" refers to the collective outcome of following the rules—that is, to the shared belief among panelists that meritocracy guides the process, while corrupting forces, self-interest, and, in particular, politics are kept at bay. Fairness is crucial for producing *legitimacy* in peer evaluations (Lamont 2009). As argued elsewhere (Lamont, Mallard, and Guetzkow 2006), the rules for legitimacy that we have identified are in line with Max Weber's analysis of the role of expertise in providing legal-rational legitimacy (Weber [1956] 1978, 99–100)—it requires the use of impersonal, abstract, and consistent rules.

Methods

In the United States, we studied five different multidisciplinary funding competitions over a two-year period, for a total of twelve panels. Each of the American competitions under consideration has a different focus: the SSRC competition funds social science dissertations that require qualitative research abroad; the ACLS competition targets all the humanities as well as the interpretive social sciences and funds faculty members at all ranks; the WWNFF competition supports graduate dissertations in gender studies; the Society of Fellows supports postdoctoral scholars across the social sciences and the humanities; and the anonymous foundation funds various types of social science research. Panelists for these competitions evaluate and rank proposals and make collective funding decisions.

We conducted a total of eighty-one open-ended, semistructured interviews with individuals involved in the final deliberations of these competitions, including fifteen interviews with program officers. The interviewees selected originated from a wide range of disciplines—anthropology, economics, English, history, philosophy, political science, sociology, and so forth—reflecting the multidisciplinary nature of the competitions under study. These panelists typically teach at American research universities and do not know one another prior to deliberations.

Again, we also studied four evaluation panels organized by the Academy of Finland. Their evaluation procedure is as follows. Program officers put together expert panels organized loosely around disciplines or themes, defined by the range of submitted applications in a given round. International experts mostly from Europe are invited to serve. They meet in person to collectively rate proposals (from 1 to 5) and write consensus reviews of them. Each panel focuses on a subset of proposals concerned with a topic or research area. Before the meeting, each proposal is reviewed by two panel members who draft reviews and are charged with presenting the case to the rest of the panel. All the members of the panel can consult these preliminary reviews, as well as the applications, online prior to the deliberations. After the meeting, the collective ratings and written evaluations produced by the panel are forwarded to one of the four Research Councils of the Academy of Finland, which make funding decisions for all proposals under consideration. The Research Councils are composed of Finnish scholars who are nominated for a three-year period by the Finnish government. Our study was not concerned with how the councils make funding decisions but focused solely on the workings of evaluation panels.

Data collection involved phone interviews with eighteen (out of twenty-seven) panel members who served on the selected four panels. We also conducted face-to-face interviews with ten funding officers. The selection of panels was determined in conversation with the academy, with a view to including panels with varying degrees of specialization in the research fields we are familiar with. The Social Sciences panel was multidisciplinary, considering proposals from sociology, social psychology, social policy, social theory, social work, and cultural studies. It was composed of experts from these various fields. The Environment and Society panel was also multidisciplinary, but differently so: the panelists were not specialists in one discipline but often had degrees in multiple disciplines and were knowledgeable about a wide range of interdisciplinary topics. They typically considered interdisciplinary proposals that dealt with environmental issues or with social-environmental interactions from a social, political, economic, technological, or other perspective outside the sphere of the natural sciences. The Environmental Sciences panel evaluated proposals that dealt with natural processes in various environments, including forests, soils, peatlands, and vegetation. This panel was also multidisciplinary, since both the proposals and the experts spanned across fields. The Environmental Ecology panel was unidisciplinary. It operated with a thematically and epistemologically coherent set of proposals emanating from one field, the ecology of aquatic environments. All the panelists were ecologists of some sort. Table 6.1 illustrates how the Finnish panels differ from each other and from the American panels (which all have a similar composition).

Table 6.1 Comparison of the evaluative settings of the American and the Finnish panels

	American panels	Finnish panels			
		Social Sciences	Environment and Society	Environmental Sciences	Environmental Ecology
Specialization of the panel	Multidisciplinary	Multidisciplinary	Multidisciplinary	Multidisciplinary	Unidisciplinary
Specialization of panelists	Experts	Experts	Generalists* and interdisciplinary experts	Experts	Experts
Technology of evaluation	Ranking	Rating	Rating	Rating	Rating
Role in decision-making process	Distribute awards	Inform award-making process	Inform award-making process	Inform award-making process	Inform award-making process
Field of research	Social sciences and humanities	Social sciences	Interdisciplinary	Applied science	Pure science

*Our term "generalist" refers to a person whose expertise is characterized by broad knowledge beyond any one academic field. While we sometimes use the term "expert" as the opposite of "generalist," we acknowledge that a "generalist" is a kind of expert, too. Generalists have special expertise precisely because they have a broader view than most other experts.

In both studies, we interviewed panelists shortly after the panel deliberations. During the interviews, panelists were asked to describe the arguments
they made about a range of proposals, to contrast their arguments with
those of other panelists, to discuss their general conception of academic
excellence, and other related topics. In the case of American panels, we had
access to the ranking of applicants produced before deliberations by panelists and to the list of awards given. In the case of the Finnish panels, we had
access to ratings and preliminary reviews produced before and after deliberations. We asked evaluators to explain what happened in each case, what
arguments were made to produce the end results, why each "winner" was
selected, and what arguments had been made by whom against and in favor of each applicant. Throughout the interviews, we asked panelists to put
themselves in the role of privileged informer and to explain to us how the
process of peer review works. They were encouraged to take on the role of
the native describing to the observer the rules of the universe in which they
operate. It is in this context that we take their description to provide us with
information not only on the frame they use to make sense of the evaluative context but also on its operation—for instance, concerning the type of
behavior that tends to be penalized by panelists. In addition to interviews,
we were able to observe three sessions of panel deliberation in the United
States. These inform the analysis but are not at the center of the study.

Customary Rules of Fairness:
How They Operate and Under Which Conditions

Deferring to Expertise and Respecting Disciplinary Sovereignty

Our observations of the American panels suggest that one of the basic assumptions guiding peer review is that each member of a panel must be
able to engage in full, equal, and free exchange of opinion through deliberation—that they follow rules not unlike those of deliberative democracy.
However, the reality of committee composition puts limitations on these
ideal conditions of equality: panel members vary in age, race, and gender,
and they represent institutions of uneven prestige. More importantly, each
of the panelists claims expertise on a specific subset of topics covered by
the proposals—thus, the importance of deferring to expertise and respecting disciplinary sovereignty.

For many proposals, alternative framings are possible. Is a proposal well
written or glib? Is it broad and daring or dilettantish? Is it current or trendy?
Painstakingly focused or disappointingly obscure? Panelists formulate in-

terpretive frames and attempt to convince one another that theirs is the most adequate. It is this context that gives rise to "deferring to expertise," a foundational rule for sustaining collective belief in the fairness of peer review.

When panelists want to advocate a position regarding a proposal, they invest energy in staking their rightful claim to evaluate it. That is, they mark their territory. In other cases, they draw on previously established proofs of competence. In this context panelists give more weight to the opinion of experts: this is essential when panelists are comparing proposals that speak to a wide range of unfamiliar topics. A historian noted that a proposal "looks good until somebody says there's a whole literature that you cannot reasonably be expected to know." Particularly when listening to someone who "comes in extremely expert and careful and [is] a person I respect a lot," this historian finds it prudent to defer. "[If this expert] says, '. . . this is really a fairly banal proposal,' then I just sort of say that must be true."

The most common form of deference involves what we call the customary rule of "respecting disciplinary sovereignty." Panelists' opinions generally are accorded more weight with regard to proposals emanating from "their" field. Violating this rule creates major conflicts, as panelists often feel slighted if their competence is not respected.

Unsurprisingly, we find that this rule is more widely respected in the American panels, which are all multidisciplinary, than in the one Finnish panel that can be defined as unidisciplinary, the Environmental Ecology panel. Overlapping expertise makes it more difficult for any one panelist to convince others of the value of a proposal when opinions differ; insisting on sovereignty would result in intense conflict for scientific authority. While distance lends authority to the view of others, the toughest rivals are those who are closest—this was anticipated by Emile Durkheim, who, in *The Division of Labor in Society*, pointed out that "the closer the functions are to one another, the more points of contact there are between them, and as a result, the more they are in conflict."[4] And indeed, in the Environmental Ecology panel we observed that panelists working within the same field or on closely related topics tended to have the strongest disagreements.[5] This is acknowledged by the panelists themselves. As one of them put it: "When it was clear that the first person was a real expert on this particular field which the second person hasn't known, obviously they deferred to

4. To continue the quotation: "The Magistrate is never in competition with the industrialist. But the brewer and the winegrower, the draper and the maker of silks, the poet and the musician often attempt to mutually supplant each other" (Durkheim [1893] 1984, 267).

5. See Langfeldt 2004 for similar findings.

the first person's opinion. . . . But it changes the climate of the discussion if you're both huge experts on this field; then you can argue about it."

The rule of deferring to expertise also appears to play out differently depending on the substantive issues with which the panel is concerned. Indeed, we found that less weight was put on specialized expertise and more was put on general arguments having to do with the common good in the panel Environment and Society, which concerns the social aspects of environmental changes—a topic that is broadly debated by the wider public, the media, and activists who claim the right of nonexperts to participate in decision making about issues that affect their lives.[6] In the eyes of one evaluator serving on this panel, the combination of expert opinion and broader considerations is essential for reaching optimal decisions:[7]

> I think you need to have the experts in the field to comment, particularly if there's a proper methodology and if there's a proper question, because only they really know the literature. However, I do think we need a wider group to ask bigger questions, like: "Is this particular research of sufficient interest for public funding?" Also I think often nonexperts can ask sort of idiot questions like "Why do you do this?" which can often be a shock to a specialist.

We also find that the relevance of the customary rule of deferring to expertise varies with the co-presence of generalists and experts on a panel. This was particularly evident again in the Finnish panel Environment and Society, which had a mixed membership. Individuals serving on this panel tended to consider all proposals "fair game" and viewed them as located in a disciplinary no-man's-land. Since the legitimacy of the process was not entirely based on the use of specialized expertise, consensus was more often reached through mutual learning, compromising, or simply by relying on panelists' integrity or intuition. As one of the panelists described the situation: "You could put your hands on your heart and then say to each other, 'Do you really, honestly, think that it is a "good" proposal, or an "excellent" proposal? What do you think, really?'" The persuasiveness of a colleague was often enough to convince other panel members, even in the absence of expertise or warranted arguments.

In the two Finnish panels that were composed of experts from different disciplines (the Environmental Sciences and the Social Sciences), the

---

6. On scientific and lay expertise, see Collins and Evans 2007. On this topic, see also Stark 2006.

7. On the complementarity of expert and nonexpert opinion, see Collins and Evans 2007.

panelists followed the same pattern as the American panels and deferred to expertise. A member of the Social Sciences panel, for example, recalled a discussion on a cultural policy proposal, which she rated high until she was persuaded by an expert on the topic to lower her grade:

> I ranked it very high because I saw it was doing something new, particularly in the way that it was intersecting with cultural theory. But I've never worked in cultural policy—it's not really my area of expertise—and [another panelist] had worked in cultural policy, and she kind of convinced me that this wasn't anything particularly new and that it actually had some kind of methodological errors. So that was an instance where . . . the decision on a ranking was about respecting someone's expertise, so in the end I said, "Okay, fine, right, you've convinced me; actually, you've convinced me!"

Pragmatic Use of Alliances and Strategic Voting

Many interviewees in the American panels reported that they aligned themselves with different panelists at different times and that others seemed to do the same, thus suggesting that the process is not "political" or that people do not engage in quid pro quo, which would unfairly privilege some less meritorious proposals. When they did recognize affinities with some other panelists, panelists often took pains to stress that these were not "corrupting" influences.

Despite this desire for neutrality, many panelists also believed that strategic voting and horse trading were to some extent unavoidable. Strategic voting refers to the practice of giving a low rank to some proposals ("lowballing") in order to increase the likelihood that other proposals will win. It may also mean boosting the ranking of a mediocre or controversial proposal to improve its chances for funding. Horse trading means enabling the realization of other panelists' objectives in the hope that they will reciprocate. Some construed this as nonmeritocratic, because the "horses" being traded are not necessarily equivalent, and one of them may "win" because of "politics" as opposed to intrinsic strength.

The role of strategic voting and horse trading varied across the panels, depending on whether evaluators were charged with rating or ranking and on whether evaluators made the final decisions or served in an advisory role. The American panels ranked proposals in relation to one another and made decisions concerning awards. In contrast, the Finnish panels rated each proposal on a 1-to-5 scale, and the ratings were then forwarded to a research council that made the funding decisions based on the ratings.[8] In this latter case, the directions from the funding agency to panelists explicitly encourage them to evaluate the intrinsic strengths and weaknesses of each proposal instead of comparing and ranking. Strategic voting does not play as much of a role in such a context since each proposal under consideration could, in principle, receive the highest score. Because the proposals are not explicitly pitted against one another, there is less of a sense that one should engage in quid pro quo to ensure that one's favorite will "win."

However, there is evidence that evaluative contexts in which proposals are rated rather than ranked do not necessarily discourage strategic behavior. Some panelists were skeptical about the value of "abstract" (as opposed to comparative) rating, since in any case only top-ranked proposals have a chance of receiving funding. Whereas some perceived the process as fair because they "judge the proposals on their own merit," others viewed the process as "meaningless." As one of the most critical panelists explained:

> There's a problem that we are not ranking the proposals, although we know the proposals very well. . . . If you [analyze] our grades, it will be a kind of normal distribution: there are lots of number three, which are useless, and very few fives and fours, I guess. And I don't think we assigned any ones, and just a few twos. So the Finnish committee that will take over after us, they are not very much helped by our statements or grading. . . . They will have to do everything again by themselves, and do the ranking by their own criteria. I think this is kind of meaningless.

Critical voices tacitly advocated in favor of more strategic behavior, including comparative ranking, but they were deterred by the explicit instructions of the funding agency. This illustrates how the evaluative technique imposed by the funding agency influences the behavior of panelists. However, it does not determine it entirely, as the evaluators are also guided by the evaluative practices that they have developed elsewhere. The peer review culture that is part of the larger academic world is also likely to influence their behavior.

---

8. Fuller (2002, 237) distinguishes between one-chamber and two-chamber representation of peers by analogy with legislative bodies and notes that each type has its own special functions and problems. However, he presents no empirical observations to elaborate those findings.

Promoting the Principles of Methodological Pluralism and Cognitive Contextualism

Observations of and accounts concerning the multidisciplinary American panels suggest that these are not a forum for challenging other methodological or disciplinary traditions. Panelists abide by the rule of methodological pluralism. They are encouraged to evaluate proposals according to the epistemological and methodological standards that prevail in the discipline of the applicant—and are personally committed to doing so. This principle, which we have dubbed "cognitive contextualization" (Mallard, Lamont, and Guetzkow 2009), was summarized by an evaluator as he described the dynamics of his panel:

> [There are] differences between people who work with large data sets and do quantitative research. And then the very polar opposite, I suppose, folks who are doing community-level studies in anthropology. There are such different methodologies that it's hard to say that there's a generalizable standard that applies to both of them. We were all, I think, willing and able to understand the projects in their own terms, fortunately, and not try to impose a more general standard, because it would have been extremely difficult. . . . I wouldn't hold a candidate in political science responsible for what seemed to me to be having overly instrumental or diagrammatic ways of understanding what they're going to do, because they have to have those. They have to have certain clarity; they have to have a certain scientism.

The premium put on "cognitive contextualization" pushes panelists to downplay their personal preferences and to assess proposals through the lenses that are distinctive to the applicant's field.

Maintaining consistency in criteria for judging qualitative and quantitative proposals is crucial to panel legitimacy, and it is complicated by the fact that panelists compare different subsets of proposals (defined by shared topics, comparable relative ranking, or proximity in the alphabet) at different times. The characteristics that are shared by any one batch of proposals vary and may make different criteria of evaluation more salient, as a historian pointed out:

> It does sometimes happen that we get some that are very close to each other, and I always go back again and look at the ones that I thought were really the best and really the worst and see if they're really all that much differ-

ent. It's like working yourself through any batch of applications or papers or whatever: your standards kind of evolve as you go through it. I don't sort mechanically. . . . Until I've read the whole batch, I don't even know exactly what the standards are going to be.

While the respect of disciplinary differences is salient in most kinds of panels, the principles of methodological pluralism and cognitive contextualization appear to be most supported by the epistemology of the social sciences and especially that of the humanities. Indeed, a close examination of the Academy of Finland panels reveals that the members of the Social Sciences panel were indistinguishable from their American counterparts with respect to these rules. Their discussion of the appropriate criteria for evaluating some business school proposals illustrates the salience of cognitive contextualization. The panelists noticed that there was no expert on that field among themselves, which made them worry about imposing sociological criteria on those proposals. A sociologist pondered:

Obviously we could use a general social science expertise to evaluate the proposals, but . . . it was quite difficult for us to place them, as it were, academically, because we don't know what the norms and values of the business school kind of proposal might be. So, for instance, from a sociological point of view, we found them lacking in many ways, but it could be that within that kind of business and critical management studies those kinds of proposals are actually great some time, but we didn't have anyone with that exact area or expertise to, kind of, give us the kind of key markers.

In contrast, the more strictly scientific panels appeared to be more committed to using consistent standards for evaluating all proposals, as opposed to adjusting their judgment to what counts as "good work" across fields. This goes hand in hand with an epistemological culture where controversies between what is defined as true and false tend to be less open-ended, as scientific and other types of evidence may more strongly constrain debates and the "blackboxing" process (as described by Latour 1987). Moreover, consensus formation may be more central to the identity (and, possibly, evaluative cultures) of scientific disciplines. This concern for consistency is illustrated by an ecologist who recalled many occasions where the panelists worried about inconsistency: "Sometimes we went back to previous applications and said: 'If we evaluated that in this and this way, then we have to use the same criteria when we are looking at this one.' . . . If we say that a person hasn't been abroad means that and that, we will have to use the same criteria for another application. I think we tried to be fair."

An important means of producing coherent evaluations among environmental scientists was a harmonization of rating scales. At the start of the meeting, these panelists had discussed "in what journals we would have outstanding, excellent, and very good papers, in this sequence, or only good papers." Whenever panelists hesitated about giving a 5 (the highest ranking) to a proposal, they reported having discussed: "Can it, if we are lucky, [lead to findings that could] be published in *Science* or *Nature*?" Thus, they attempted to agree on shared matrixes through indirect indicators of quality, which streamlined evaluation. They perceived consistency as crucial for fairness, since panelists were convinced that scientific quality could best be detected by the use of given criteria. The chair of a panel demonstrated the legitimacy of the evaluation he presided over by arguing: "The grade 'five' proposals would have received a similar grading in any of the national or international panels on which I have sat." The concern for consistency was low in the American and Finnish humanities and social science panels because most experts serving on these panels believed that evaluators played a crucial role in defining the lenses through which quality can be recognized.

The comparison of different panels also reveals that the generalists in the panel of Environment and Society did not share the same concern for cognitive contextualization that we found among more specialized experts in both the American and the Finnish panels. In spite of their social science orientation and background, these panelists prided themselves on their detachment from disciplinary traditions and on their ability to locate seemingly disparate proposals within a broad matrix of evaluation. This may be because they are simultaneously involved in several different epistemic communities, which often requires an ability to see beyond particular criteria and to compare relatively smoothly proposals emanating from a range of disciplines, that is, proposals that could easily be viewed as incommensurable. Thus, they did not argue in favor of methodological pluralism. Instead, they typically favored general criteria of quality that are shared across the social and environmental sciences. As one of them put it:

> What we [were] looking [for] was not particularly disciplinary attributes of the applications. We were looking at things like research design, is it going to produce useful results, would the results be useful for policy makers? These sorts of methodology [concerns.] Is it well-explained and good . . . ? They were more generic questions rather than is it good sociology or good economics or good this or good that? And I think we all really took that view.

The Environment and Society panelists thus encouraged each other to downplay epistemological differences between disciplines and strengthen what was shared in their conceptions of quality. However, this process was sometimes costly and required thorough discussions on methodological questions. This became evident in a series of disagreements between two panel members, whose opinions on several proposals strongly differed. Both were experts in case study methodology, but their theoretical backgrounds diverged. During a private discussion at breakfast, they came to an agreement concerning where their criteria of evaluation could overlap. One panelist explained: "I had not been as critical on [particular methodological choices], because I've read [the proposals] in the context that I worked from, and I didn't have as much problem with these methodological decisions. But I concurred with his concerns when he went through them in some detail."

The panelists came to an agreement on a new set of similar criteria about how to evaluate case study applications. Such negotiations of meaning were essential to allow panelists to "save face" and sustain the conditions necessary for continuing the work of the panel. At the same time, the emerging understanding between the two parties renewed the panelists' belief in the legitimacy of their decisions.

Limiting Idiosyncratic Tastes and Self-Reproduction

Rational legitimacy, Weber reminds us, comes from the application of impersonal and consistent rules ([1956] 1978, 212–71). Thus, by trying to bracket their idiosyncratic tastes, panel members help sustain collective belief in the fairness of deliberations. An English professor serving on one of the American funding panels advocated distinguishing between one's personal preferences and criteria of competence, and privileging the latter when the two are in conflict. In subordinating personal preferences to more neutral standards, this scholar explicitly protects the legitimacy of the process, but he also recognizes the role of individual subjectivities in evaluation. But this panelist is more scrupulous than many. Most reviewers uphold the legitimacy of the process when they seamlessly fold their idiosyncratic preferences and tastes into the formal criteria of evaluation. So, for example, they tend to define originality in ways that are in line with the type of originality that their own work exhibits. As one interviewee acknowledged, evaluators tend to like what speaks to their own interests: "I see scholarly excellence and excitement in this one project on food, possibly because I see resonance with my own life, my own interests, who I am, and other people clearly don't. And that's always a bit of a problem, that excellence is in some ways what looks most like you."

During interviews with the American panelists, multiple examples of how panelists' idiosyncratic interests shape their votes emerged. Apparently, equating "what looks most like you" with "excellence" is so pervasive as to go unnoticed by some. Moreover, panelists cannot spell out what defines an "interesting" proposal in the abstract, irrespective of the kinds of problems that captivate them personally. Most behave as if they have no alternative but to use their own personal understanding of what constitutes a fascinating problem in order to do the work that is expected of them.

A close examination of the two more scientific panels of the Academy of Finland suggests that natural scientists may be more explicit in their efforts to bracket idiosyncratic tastes and avoid self-reproduction than are the social scientists in the two national settings we studied. This is suggested by evidence revealing how scientists on these panels (Environmental Sciences and Environmental Ecology) attempt to cancel out idiosyncrasies by relying even more on collective judgments. The role of the group was perceived as crucial for "judging the arguments and viewpoints" of individual experts, "trying to find balance in the discussion," and "discussing the general principles."

Whereas we argued at the outset that the American panels in the social sciences and the humanities followed principles analogous to those of deliberative democracies, the more appropriate analogy for the natural science panels may be that of a court of justice. Scientists are more concerned with consistency in evaluation and maintaining impersonal criteria than they are with sustaining full, equal, and free exchange of opinion. Accounts by panelists indicate that the reviewers in charge of presenting a proposal played the role of an expert witness, and the rest of the panel acted as a critical jury. Thus, panelists found it important that experts discussed each proposal "in front of the evaluators." The panel on Environmental Ecology had even set up a routine of assigning the task of drafting each evaluation statement to a panelist who was "a little further removed from the field of the applicant" so that the given proposal was "not so close with his personal emotions." This panelist acted "as a kind of independent judge, [who] could look more at the formal aspects, keep things equal, and judge across different cases."

The belief in the value of calibration was also present among the social scientists, but to a lesser degree and it took a somewhat different form. In the American panels and the two Finnish panels consisting of social scientists (Social Sciences and Environment and Society), the experts acknowledged personal standpoints as inevitable components of evaluation. Rather than trying to cancel out the biases that each panelist brought to the evaluation process, as was done by environmental scientists and ecologists, social scientists tended to believe that free exchange of opinion helped them become aware of their personal mind-sets and made them more open to rethinking their evaluation. A Finnish social scientist explained this social process as follows:

> The panel would have to be explicit about how it understood the criteria, in relation to the application, and those discussions would be explicit and substantive. One could then detect different perspectives around the criteria. . . . I think where positions were very different, I would say, "This is my take on it, this is how I saw it, but"—you know—"okay, having heard what you said, and looked at some of the other applications, where we had some similar discussions, I can see that I was possibly underestimating the importance of x, y, and z."

This quotation indicates that relativism in judgment, or awareness of how worldviews affect evaluation, is part of the social science culture of evaluation. More comparative data will be needed before we can fully ascertain whether and how scientists understand the place of tastes and "individual perspectives" in evaluation.

Conclusion

This chapter has discussed the customary rules of evaluation that panelists typically follow in making decisions and analyzed the specific applicability of those rules to panels that work in various evaluation settings. We consider our customary rules to be part of "epistemic cultures" and essential to the process of collective attribution of significance. In this context, considering reasons offered for disagreement, how disagreements are negotiated, and how panelists interpret agreement is essential to capturing fairness as a collective accomplishment.

Our interpretive analysis posits that evaluative practices are shaped and constrained by the context in which they occur, including intersubjective agreements concerning the conditions for fair and optimal evaluation. Instead of contrasting "biased" and "unbiased" evaluation, we examine how panelists construe the evaluation process, including the role played by intersubjectivity in assessment (Lamont 2009). Contrary to what is suggested by the classical approach to peer evaluation (e.g., Cole and Cole

1981), extracognitive factors do not corrupt the evaluation process but are intrinsic to it. Moreover, the fairness of the process is not undermined by nonrational features (cf. Longino 2000) but is created through intersubjective rules that evaluators follow to distinguish between legitimate and illegitimate behavior.

Our primary objective was to illuminate how the structure and composition of panels can influence customary rules. Table 6.2 highlights our main findings. The rules of deferring to expertise and respecting disciplinary sovereignty vary in importance, being less important in unidisciplinary panels and panels that deal with topics that interest broad audiences. The customary rules of methodological pluralism and cognitive contextualism are more salient in the humanities and social science panels than they are in the science panels. Finally, a concern for the use of consistent criteria and a bracketing of idiosyncratic taste is more salient in the sciences than in the social sciences and the humanities, due in part to the fact that in the latter disciplines evaluators may be more aware of the role played by intersubjectivity in the evaluation process.

More evidence will be needed before we can draw definite links between the features of panels and customary rules. Larger samples and a broader range of panels will have to be considered before we begin tracing processes with a finer brush and before we can start generalizing about trends and causal processes. For example, rating and ranking could have a different impact on customary rules depending on whether one is considering science panels or panels in the social sciences and the humanities. Moreover, other factors are likely to influence whether panelists engage in strategic behavior—for example, the availability of resources systemwide, the degree of competitiveness for these resources, how they are distributed, and so on. Social psychological theories and methods could be especially helpful in drawing causal conclusions about judgment and decision making in different panels (Olbrecht and Bornmann 2010). At the same time, classical social psychological approaches typically do not factor in the place of meaning making in the interpretation of criteria and how evaluative cultures vary among nations.

Future research could also consider variations across a range of national settings and types of panels. It should analyze specifically how national academic cultures and the internal characteristics of national research and higher-education systems (including their size, spatial dispersion, diversity, steepness of institutional hierarchies, dependency on the state and nonprofit funding sources, etc.) influence the functioning of panels, evaluative cultures and practices, and customary rules of evaluation more broadly

Table 6.2 Conditions affecting and modifications of selected customary rules of fairness

Customary rules	Conditions favorable	Conditions unfavorable	Modifications of the rule
Deferring to expertise and respecting disciplinary sovereignty	· Panels composed of experts from multiple fields	· Unidisciplinary panels · Panels that consider topics of interest to nonacademic audiences · Panels composed of generalists	· Argumentation of alternative perspectives · Taking account of both expert opinion and broader considerations · All proposals are "fair game"; use of mutual learning and intuition
Pragmatic use of alliances and strategic voting	· Panels that rank proposals and make final decisions	· Panels that rate proposals and have an advisory role	· Evaluating the intrinsic strengths and weaknesses of each proposal
Methodological pluralism and cognitive contextualism	· Social sciences and humanities panels composed of experts	· Natural sciences panels · Panels composed of generalists	· Concern for consistency of criteria across cases · Use of a general matrix for comparison to assess "incommensurable" proposals
Limiting idiosyncratic tastes and self-reproduction	· Social sciences and humanities panels · Natural sciences panels		· Democratic deliberation · Court of law

(including faith in the general legitimacy of the system; for an analysis of the evaluation crisis in the French higher-education system, see Cousin and Lamont 2009).

While in this chapter we have stressed differences between the humanities and social sciences, on the one hand, and the sciences, on the other, there exist parallels that should be examined more closely. Calibration may be valued across all fields as a way to limit differences in standards due to professional affiliations and other factors. Also, while the natural scientists did not promote methodological pluralism or cognitive contextualism as such, they clearly avoided challenging each others' standpoints explicitly. Compromises were thus created through a balance between competing criteria or by drawing on a majority opinion, rather than by imposing particular standards. We may explore whether, in fact, evaluative practices across fields have started converging. It is quite possible that in the context of an increasingly present audit culture in higher education and research (Strathern 2000), evaluative practices are becoming standardized and widely institutionalized (nationally and internationally) while disciplinary differences are declining to various extents (with economics leading the pack and the interpretive social sciences defending national distinctiveness). This in itself defines an important path for future research on the evaluative cultures of the social sciences.

Our study opens a new window through which to look at some contested effects in the peer review of research proposals. Numerous scholars have pointed out both potential and observed risks in the peer review system. It is argued that the system is conservative and suppresses innovative research. Effects such as nepotism and old-boyism in peer review are seen to hinder pioneering research (Chubin and Hackett 1990; Roy 1985), while "cognitive particularism" and "favoritism for the familiar" function to support the kind of research the reviewers themselves are conducting (see, e.g., Porter and Rossini 1985; Travis and Collins 1991). At the same time, scholars working with the organization of evaluation panels have found that evaluation by groups is less problematic than evaluation by individuals, while other flaws may arise due to group dynamics (Grigg 1999; Langfeldt 2001, 2004; Laudel 2006). Our findings on customary rules point in the same direction. But they also suggest that some of the perverse effects of peer review, such as cronyism, the pursuit of self-interest, and cognitive particularism, may be influenced by the way panels are set up. Much more work is needed on this topic before we can reach definite conclusions.

It is sometimes claimed that funding officers can manipulate the peer review system to deliver the recommendations they prefer by shrewdly choosing reviewers (Roy 1985). These claims do not pay attention to the complexities that the social dimension brings about in evaluation panels. However, it is an interesting question whether a proper understanding of the impact of various social conditions on the workings of panels would improve the evaluation process. While specific decisions are hardly predictable, it is possible that a better understanding of the impact of various types of set-ups would lead program officers to put in place optimal processes of deliberation. We believe that the question should be of interest for policy makers and for the larger academic community. Consensual standards in academic evaluation may influence what kind of research gets supported and may thus have long-term consequences for the cognitive development of the social sciences.

References

Bell, Robert. 1992. *Impure Science: Fraud, Compromise and Political Influence in Scientific Research*. New York: John Wiley.

Chubin, Daryl, and Edward Hackett. 1990. *Peerless Science: Peer Review and U.S. Science Policy*. Albany: State University of New York Press.

Cole, Jonathan, and Stephen Cole. 1981. *Peer Review in the National Science Foundation: Phase Two of a Study*. Washington, DC: National Academy Press.

Cole, Stephen. 1992. *Making Science: Between Nature and Society*. Cambridge, MA: Harvard University Press.

Cole, Stephen, Leonard Rubin, and Jonathan Cole. 1979. *Peer Review in the National Science Foundation: Phase One of a Study*. Washington, DC: National Academy Press.

Collins, Harry, and Robert Evans. 2007. *Rethinking Expertise*. Chicago: University of Chicago Press.

Cousin, Bruno, and Michèle Lamont. 2009. "Les conditions de l'évaluation universitaire: Quelques réflexions à partir du cas américain." *Revue mouvements* 60:113–17.

Durkheim, Emile. [1893] 1984. *The Division of Labor in Society*. New York: Free Press.

Fuller, Steve. 2002. *Knowledge Management Foundations*. Boston: Butterworth-Heinemann.

GAO (General Accounting Office). 1994. *Peer Review Reforms Needed to Ensure Fairness in Federal Agency Grant Selection*. Report to the Chairman, Committee on Governmental Activities, U.S. Senate. Washington, DC: General Accounting Office.

Garfinkel, Harold. 1967. *Studies in Ethnomethodology*. Englewood Cliffs, NJ: Prentice-Hall.

Grigg, Lyn. 1999. "Cross-disciplinary Research." Discussion Paper. Commissioned Report no. 61. Australian Research Council.

Guetzkow, Joshua, Michèle Lamont, and Grégoire Mallard. 2004. "What Is Originality in the Humanities and the Social Sciences?" *American Sociological Review* 69, no. 2: 190–212.

Knorr Cetina, Karin. 1999. *Epistemic Cultures: How the Sciences Make Knowledge*. Cambridge, MA: Harvard University Press.

Lamont, Michèle. 2009. *How Professors Think: Inside the Curious World of Academic Judgment*. Cambridge, MA: Harvard University Press.

Lamont, Michèle, Grégoire Mallard, and Joshua Guetzkow. 2006. "Beyond Blind Faith:

Overcoming the Obstacles to Interdisciplinary Evaluation." *Research Evaluation* 15: 43–55.

Langfeldt, Liv. 2001. "The Decision-Making Constraints and Processes of Grant Peer Review, and Their Effects on the Review Outcome." *Social Studies of Science* 31:820–41.

———. 2004. "Expert Panels Evaluating Research: Decision-Making and Sources of Bias." *Research Evaluation* 13:51–62.

Latour, Bruno. 1987. *Science in Action.* Cambridge, MA: Harvard University Press.

Laudel, Grit. 2006. "Conclave in the Tower of Babel: How Peers Review Interdisciplinary Research Proposals." *Research Evaluation* 15:57–68.

Liebert, Roland. 1976. *Disintegration and Political Action: The Changing Functions of City Governments in America.* New York: Academic Press.

Longino, Helen E. 2000. *The Fate of Knowledge.* Princeton, NJ: Princeton University Press.

Mallard, Grégoire, Michèle Lamont, and Joshua Guetzkow. 2009. "Fairness as Appropriateness: Epistemological Pluralism and Peer Review in the Social Sciences and the Humanities." *Science, Technology, and Human Values* 34:573–606.

Merton, Robert K., ed. 1996. *On Social Structure and Science.* Chicago: University of Chicago Press.

Mulkay, Michael. 1991. *Sociology of Science: A Sociological Pilgrimage.* Philadelphia: Open University Press.

Olbrecht, Meike, and Lutz Bornmann. 2010. "Panel Peer Review of Grant Applications: What Do We Know from Research in Social Psychology on Judgment and Decision Making in Groups?" *Research Evaluation* 19:293–304.

Porter, Alan L., and Frederick A. Rossini. 1985. "Peer Review of Interdisciplinary Research Proposals." *Science, Technology, and Human Values* 10:33–38.

Roy, Rustum. 1985. "Funding Science: The Real Defects of Peer Review and an Alternative to It." *Science, Technology, and Human Values* 10:73–81.

Stark, Laura. 2006. "Morality in Science: How Research Is Evaluated in the Age of Human Subjects Regulation." PhD diss., Princeton University.

Strathern, Marilyn. 2000. *Audit Cultures: Anthropological Studies in Accountability, Ethics and the Academy.* London: Routledge.

Travis, G. D. L., and Harry M. Collins. 1991. "New Light on Old Boys: Cognitive and Institutional Particularism in the Peer Review System." *Science, Technology, and Human Values* 16:322–41.

Weber, Max. [1956] 1978. *Economy and Society.* 2 vols. Berkeley and Los Angeles: University of California Press.

Whitley, Richard. 1984. *The Intellectual and Social Organization of the Sciences.* Oxford: Clarendon Press.

SEVEN

Meetings by the Minute(s)

How Documents Create Decisions for Institutional Review Boards

LAURA STARK

Knowledge Evaluation as Statecraft

Institutional review boards (IRBs) regulate interactions between research-ers and the people they study if researchers work for an organization that gets money from the U.S. federal government. Today, most universities, hospitals, and scholarly institutes do get public money in some form. Be-cause research review is required at the *sites* of knowledge production, IRBs end up overseeing researchers who earn their pay not only as biomedical scientists but also as social scientists and humanists in the United States and, increasingly, abroad (Hedgecoe 2010; Heimer and Petty 2010). This has been the case since 1966, but IRBs have been more fastidious and con-servative in enforcing regulations that attempt to protect human subjects since 2000. As a result, more social research has been pulled into regula-tory purview (Bledsoe et al. 2007; Schrag 2009; Stark 2007).

The ideas in this chapter are part of a larger study of IRBs as examples of what I call "declarative bodies," expert groups that are empowered by governments to make decisions without consulting citizens, for example, through public referenda (Stark, forthcoming). I am interested in how, through the process of evaluation, experts who make up declarative bod-ies—such as IRBs, data- and safety-monitoring boards, funding panels, editorial boards, and film-rating committees—have a hand in creating the products of art and science that they are reviewing. Part of the work of declarative bodies involves creating and then sustaining the image that members have reached a legitimate decision. Bureaucratic documents are central to this task, and I open up this phenomenon in the current chapter.

When researchers look beyond the administrative burden of IRBs, they find that IRBs are consequential because they affect how researchers go about creating knowledge—and, as a result, the kinds of things that are knowable. IRBs rarely endorse or reject research proposals in their entirety on their first encounter with a potential study. Instead, IRB members suggest (read: require) changes that a researcher could make to the proposal that would result in the board's approval. IRBs might suggest changes to researchers' site selection, sample size, recruiting methods, or interview questions, for example. This coercive power to change research is quite effective since getting approval is the ultimate goal for researchers who submit protocols. Today, IRBs are powerful, pervasive, and deeply unpopular among researchers. And yet, we comply.

Max Weber might attribute this miracle of begrudging obedience to the coercive authority of the modern administrative state. As this volume highlights, the processes by which social knowledge is made, judged, and used today are inseparable from the demands of the state. Particularly since the middle of the twentieth century, the work of social scientists has been indebted to governments, either directly through sponsorship of their own research or indirectly through funding of the places in which most researchers are now employed (Steinmetz 2009). Public money has come with strings attached, however. In the case of IRBs, government administrators anticipated expensive lawsuits from human subjects who started to identify themselves as members of a group with specific legal rights starting in the late 1960s (Stark, forthcoming). The government required research review boards (initially, as a matter of federal policy and later as a matter of federal law) to deflect liability away from government funders and to redirect lawsuits toward the research organizations that the state funded. The case of research review corresponds more generally to changes in patronage of scholarship in the twentieth century (toward the state) and to changes in the place of scholarly work (within institutions funded at least in part with public money). Human-subjects regulations exemplify how the state—particularly through administrative law—began to guide research as a vocation in ways that Weber was beginning to anticipate at the close of World War I (Shapin 2008; Thorpe 2006; Weber 1920).

This chapter complements its companions in part II of the volume by showing how sites of research evaluation are multilayered settings. The conference rooms in which research evaluations take place are simultaneously academic settings structured by disciplinary standards of evaluation and state settings beholden to the rule of law. On the one hand, scholars have shown that academic evaluations occurring in group settings—by admissions committees, funding panels, editorial boards, and IRBs, for example—depend on interpersonal power dynamics, disciplinary definitions of worth, disparities in rhetorical skill, and happenstance (Lamont 2009; Waddell 1989; Brenneis 1994; Tsay et al. 2003; Guetzkow, Lamont, and Mallard 2004; Stark, forthcoming; Stevens 2007). On the other hand, the settings in which evaluations take place are also constrained by the state, and this fact shapes how evaluators, including IRB members, judge research. Administrative laws set nuts-and-bolts requirements, for example, about who can serve as an evaluator on government-mandated panels that judge ethics protocols, grant proposals, tenure and promotion cases, and data veracity. Of consequence for this chapter is that administrative laws also set requirements for how decisions should be recorded. For the state to achieve legal authority, as Weber aptly described, "administrative acts, decisions, and rules are formulated and recorded in writing, even in cases where oral discussion is the rule or is even mandatory" (1978, 219). True to kind, in the case of IRBs, the Code of Federal Regulations (CFR) instructs boards to produce meeting minutes that record "attendance at the meetings; actions taken by the IRB; the vote on these actions including the number of members voting for, against, and abstaining; the basis for requiring changes in or disapproving research; and a written summary of the discussion of controverted issues and their resolution" (45 CFR 46.115). I focus on knowledge evaluation as a process structured by the state and explore how the men and women who evaluate social knowledge use administrative documents as instruments for decision making.

This chapter highlights the material life of knowledge evaluation and explains why documents are indispensable technologies of evaluation in modern social research. Documents serve to recast a collection of individuals gathered around a conference table as "the IRB," which is the only actor empowered to make decisions in the name of the state according to 45 CFR 46. This observation fits within a broader literature, described below, on how documents create new social actors. The novel claim of this chapter is that documents also change the evaluations that reviewers make. In the case of IRB meetings, the fact that individual opinions can be presented as the view of "the IRB" erases personal accountability. And in creating the social actor known as "the IRB," documents liberate individual evaluators to make what they consider to be extreme judgments—judgments with which researchers legally must comply.

How to Do Things with Documents: Two Perspectives

A remarkable feature of research evaluation is the imperative toward consensus, despite the fact that consensus is not formally required for most evaluative groups. They are more often required to vote, and yet they work toward consensus nonetheless. Group members act *as if* they should each agree on a shared judgment that they all can get behind, and they develop informal rules about how to reach a common view, as Lamont and Huutoniemi showed in the case of funding panels (see chap. 6, this volume). In the year that I spent observing IRB meetings, members always voted on protocols as required by regulation, and yet I saw only one "no" vote (from a disillusioned member who soon quit the board). In most reviews, group members typically disagreed with each other at the beginning of meetings and gradually moved toward unanimity. The most defiant act of protest was to abstain from voting—in other words, to remove oneself from participating in the vote altogether, an example of which I explore in the next section.

Evaluative groups work toward consensus because individual evaluators, generally speaking, have no power on their own. Members of IRBs and other similar groups have legal authority from the state (however tentative and contested) only to the extent that they can act as a unit. There are barriers to collective agreement, however. Group members have competing interests, different standards of evaluation, and unfamiliar habits for justifying opinions. When individual group members differ in their views—or recoil at their colleagues' styles of presenting their views—it poses a problem for the group as a whole.

Enter the administrative document. Philosopher J. L. Austin, in his now-classic lectures *How to Do Things with Words* (1962), argued that people who are authorized to act on behalf of the state (e.g., by performing marriages) can invent new social realities with their say-so. As if by magic, they can create the new consensual realities that their voices had merely described. Austin, who was exploring language as an action, focused on the spoken word and did not explore how this magical power might depend on material artifacts (Law 2008; MacKenzie, Muniesa, and Siu 2007). Words on paper, however, bolster the authority of spoken words. And, as I suggest in this chapter, words on paper also change what power holders are willing to say. Often the practice of recording people's views will temper more extreme opinions, but in the case of closed settings such as IRB meetings, documents can also encourage people to accentuate their more extreme views.

Formal administrative documents (such as social surveys, patient his-tories, consent forms, and prison intake records) help to constitute new types of people (Americans, the diseased, subjects, and deviants), espe-cially as objects of the state (Foucault [1977] 1995; Hacking 2002; Heimer 2001; Igo 2007; Rose 1998; Shore and Wright 2000; Timmermans and Berg 2003). This "constitutive perspective," as I call it, explains how adminis-trative documents force people to identify as a given type—often as part of an effort by scientists and government administrators to compare and accumulate information about people and events across time and location as part of modern statecraft (Orloff 2005, 198–99). As a result, documents subtly encourage us to adopt the terms provided by science and the state when we think about ourselves and others. New social actors are brought into being through the identities, roles, and assessments provided to peo-ple through administrative documents. As I will show, IRB meeting min-utes, which are required by the state, invent "the IRB" as a unitary social actor.

When social actors are constituted in administrative documents, they are also placed in a story line. Documents give an official account of events that puts all relevant readers and relationships on the same page, both liter-ally and figuratively. It is curious to observe that, in practice, administrative documents tend not to be particularly effective in fulfilling their purported purpose of organizing and keeping track of people. Records and forms are often incomplete or haphazard, but this should not be understood only as errors in documentation. Omissions and open-endedness in formal records are part of a narrative in which the relationships are ongoing between vari-ous social actors bound by administrative documents (such as researchers and IRB members). In his influential study of patients' clinical records at the UCLA Medical Center, sociologist Harold Garfinkel described the docu-ments as bad enough to make one wonder "why 'poor records' as poor as these should nevertheless be so assiduously kept" (1967, 200). Garfinkel eventually argued that "bad" records were actually tools that helped their readers understand the past and potential future of a clinician's relation-ship with a patient, in his words, "a reconstructable record of transactions between patients and clinical personnel" (197). Formal documents always provide an idiosyncratic version of past events and of potential future ac-tions despite the deceptively objective, authorless style of most official re-cords (Reed 2006; Smith 2006).

I want to add to this "constitutive perspective" what I describe as an "anticipatory perspective" on documents. Using the case of IRB meetings, I will argue that members of evaluative groups use their knowledge of how their deliberations will be recorded to alter their deliberations as they are under way—and thus to shape the very decisions that the documents eventually record. IRB members, for example, invoke the meeting minutes of their current deliberation—before the minutes have been written. One consequence of using a document *in potentia* as a discursive tool, I show, is that it prompts IRB members to pursue different courses of action and, consequently, reach different decisions than they would if their deliberation were documented in a different way. In the case of IRBs, documents like meeting minutes do not just chronicle decisions. The decisions are, in part, the product of how the evaluation process is documented.

Comparing Deliberations and Documents

It goes without saying that the documents I study here, IRB meeting minutes, give simplified versions of complicated events. Yet meeting minutes do not merely give abridgments; they give accounts of events that have been abridged in particular ways. This section explores what is lost and what is gained in the process of translating between deliberations and documents.

To do so, I compare two accounts of IRB meetings: one account that is given in the meeting minutes and another that is offered in transcripts of IRB deliberations. The transcripts are drawn from my ethnography of IRB meetings at two large research universities (which I call "Greenly" and "Sander State") over the course of one year in the mid-2000s.[1] In the current chapter, I follow the ethics review of two studies, one from each board, in which the researchers planned to gather evidence for their studies either by watching or by talking to people. Thus, I examine "IRB meetings by the minutes" in two senses: as the evaluations took place over time and as evaluations were represented in documents.

All IRBs are structured in the same basic way according to federal regu-

---

1. To protect my own research subjects and the institutions that granted me generous access, I will be vague about my research sites where specificity would serve only to enrich my appearance of scholarly credibility, not readers' understanding of the context or my argument. Also, I should note that many of my ideas presented in this chapter grow out of additional research that I conducted (but that I do not cite here): interviews with members at the two IRBs, observations and interviews at one medical school IRB for five months, interviews with a national sample of IRB chairs at Research 1 universities (according to the Carnegie Classification of Institutions of Higher Education), and extensive archival research on ethics review practices within the National Institutes of Health from 1952 through 1974. For more information about the broader project and my methodologies, see Stark, forthcoming.

lation.[2] As a result, the boards that I describe in this chapter are by definition quite typical. All IRBs must have at least five members, some may have as many as twenty, and the boards I observed had around ten. Most university board members are on the faculty, so they are reported to the federal government as "experts" in the topic, method, or population that they study. Nonetheless, the task of these experts is to judge others—namely, other researchers and faculty members, who also claim rare and special knowledge in a given area. This regulatory requirement sets up within IRB meetings the persistent puzzles of research evaluation in general: namely, who counts as having relevant expertise and how do you know?

Federal regulations also require specific types of members who are nonexperts, bureaucratically speaking. These include, for example, "community" members who in theory provide a counterpoint to the formal experts, and prisoner representatives who advocate for research participants who are incarcerated. In addition, some of the greatest power holders in ethics review are IRB administrators, who attend meetings and participate in deliberations with clarifying questions, regulatory insight, and, on occasion, personal opinion. Although they do not vote, board administrators do type the meeting minutes, which then serve as the template for the formal letters that are sent to researchers detailing any changes the board requires.

Despite their otherwise typical structure, both boards that I will describe used one uncommon practice (Taylor, Currie, and Kass 2008): the researchers under review were invited to IRB meetings, and in some instances, reviews were scheduled only if the researcher could attend the meeting. Four decades ago as the current human-subjects review system crystallized within the National Institutes of Health, researchers were increasingly removed from ethics deliberations because they came to be seen as contaminants, rather than aids, to sound moral evaluation (Stark, forthcoming). Although the IRBs I observed were unusual in inviting researchers to meetings, this practice makes the Sander State and Greenly IRBs all the more useful to study: if any ethics review process could seem "transparent" and inclusive, it would be those carried out by boards that made a concerted effort to involve the researchers themselves.

The meetings of the Sander State and Greenly IRBs had a steady routine: the researchers sat outside the meeting room until the administrators

2. Despite structural similarities, IRBs tend to reach divergent conclusions about how a researcher would need to change a given study before it can be approved. The regulations setting out the organization of IRBs are 45 CFR 46.

collected them at the preset time. The researchers then fielded questions from the IRB members, after which they left so that board members could further discuss the studies. The meaty issues were brought up and resolved in the boards' deliberation and final discussion stages, after the researcher left and before the vote. Although administrators did tally yeas and nays, voting was largely a symbolic exercise. In short, votes brought no surprises because by the end of the review, a consensus was set by definition. After the meeting, board administrators typed their handwritten notes into meeting minutes that were kept on file, and they then sent formal letters to the researchers based on the meeting minutes. These minutes and letters described what, if anything, the researcher would need to change before the board would grant approval.

The Greenly IRB: A Successful Attempt to Change a Study

The review of a planned study at Greenly called Teaching Children to Manage Emotions seemed from the outset as if it would be "pretty straightforward," in the words of the board chair (transcript 1, line 631). A professor of education near the end of a long and distinguished career at the university was leading a study of preschool children at a local day care facility for low-income families. Her aim was to assess whether children would better temper their frustrations and enthusiasms after they had taken an expert-designed behavior-training course. The point of the course was to prepare children behaviorally for school, and the goal of the investigators was to promote the course nationwide if it proved effective. To control for any effects that the children's family background might have on their behavior, the parents who consented to the study would be observed with their children, and these parents would be given several psychological tests via interviews. Prior to the meeting, three IRB members had pre-reviewed the study: a professor of exercise physiology and a young clergyman had recommended approval without revision; a physician asked the investigator to tone down the tantalizing language about parents' compensation and raised three points of clarification about how the study would be run. The "primary investigator," named Dorothy, came to the IRB meeting at her appointed review time and brought along her junior faculty co-investigator, who described the project, fielded many questions about the study, and occasionally amplified board members' comments by repeating them into Dorothy's ear. Compared with other reviews, the discussion with these researchers ran somewhat long, but when they left they seemed to have satisfied the physician's pre-review criticisms by agreeing to a few changes and to have placated other board members who had raised concerns during the discussion. The board chair told the researchers before they pushed back from the conference table, "I think you responded to all the questions that I know of" (857). This was the last face-to-face exchange between Dorothy and her colleague and the board members.

Despite the positive signs, however, the review of this project was not as straightforward as the board chair had anticipated. The board eventually approved a revised version of the study, but the go-ahead came several months after the researchers' visit. Board members discussed the study for the first time immediately following their visit, after which the board asked for revisions. Board members then discussed the revised study at the next month's meeting and agreed to approve a future version of the study once the researchers submitted another round of revisions. The design of the study was not the enduring problem; rather, the way in which the researchers wanted to explain the study to parents was the crux of the issue.

The minutes of both of the meetings in which the study was discussed stated that the IRB's problem rested specifically with the consent form for parents. The meeting minutes also made plain that researchers were being asked to revise several word choices in the consent form. I am going to focus on one requested revision in particular, which is the last bulleted point in the minutes from the day the study was first discussed. This account of the deliberations explains that "the Board tabled any decision" until the researchers provided it with a revised consent form that included "a brief description, in lay language, of each of the measures" that researchers would be taking of parents and children.

How does this account of actors and events compare with the account offered in meeting transcripts? In the rest of this section, I will examine board members' deliberations as seen through the transcripts, and then I will return to the meeting minutes to take a second look at the deliberations as seen from the formal record. My goal is not to reveal "the true story" of this review but instead to offer insight into what is lost and gained through the process of translation on which both of these accounts depended.

Immediately after the researchers left the first meeting, a thread of discussion began that stretched across several board meetings. A psychologist on the board, Kevin, outlined for board members what he took to be a dire ethics problem that he had not directly raised with the researchers. According to him, what the researchers were pitching to board members and to parents as a measure of vocabulary was, in fact, an IQ test. When a straight-shooting kinesiologist on the board, Ted, paraphrased Kevin's point, "So, you're saying that she's misrepresenting what the tests are actually measuring?" Kevin replied that she was "not misrepresenting; just not stating" (865–66).

Recent criticisms of IRBs tend to portray boards' requests to change words as petty caviling: requesting small word changes is a way that boards exercise symbolic power, the argument goes. This position overlooks, however, how word changes can imply fundamental changes in study research practices and, thus, potential findings. Words that appear in or disappear from state-mandated documents, such as meeting minutes, affect what is knowable and how the social world can be known. The board members at Greenly, for example, discussed in the meeting that making Dorothy change the description of her vocabulary measure was not simply semantic but would have practical consequences such as decreasing study enrollment, delaying the start of research, creating additional work for the researchers, and provoking ill will toward the board. What could compel board members to force what they regarded as a consequential change to study procedure?

The "modifications" that board members require to any given study are the products of their evaluations not only of the content of the study but also of each other's credibility in advocating certain types of changes (Stark, forthcoming). During closed-door deliberations, IRB members tended to justify their views in three main ways: by invoking either their professional experience (such as having researched a similar group of people), their private experience (such as having cared for their own sick child), or publicly available matters-of-fact (such as knowing the most recent demographics of a neighborhood). Board members tended to find warrants based on professional experience most persuasive because it is, by definition, both uncommon and expert knowledge and thus difficult to contest.

During the deliberations over Teaching Children to Manage Emotions, Kevin told board members about his own professional experience of having developed the very instrument that the researchers planned to use in the study, suggesting that he understood the nature and implications of the test better than anyone on the board. Using the technical term for the measure of a person's so-called general intelligence, Kevin explained that what the researchers claimed was a vocabulary test for the parents was "the best G estimate of intelligence from one subtest from [the Standard Intelligence Scale]. And that's what she's giving. She's getting IQ on the parent" (906). Kevin explained that vocabulary qua IQ was "an important piece of informa-

tion about an individual" and "almost as serious" as getting genetic information using "a blood stick that no one's told you about" (953). Although
he felt the researchers had good intentions, Kevin reiterated throughout the
meeting that the measure was "intrusive," "too intrusive," and "very intrusive." He encouraged board members to make the researchers give parents
a fuller description of each of the psychological tests, which would include
the contested vocabulary-IQ measure, and to provide parents with sample
questions so their consent could be better informed (872).

The view of the Greenly IRB as recorded in the meeting minutes should
be seen as Kevin's opinion harnessed to the authority both accorded to and
required by IRB members in federal regulation. My aim is not to rule on
whether Kevin's understanding of the test is accurate or his description fair.
Instead, I want to demonstrate how warrants, like Kevin's story about his
professional experience, serve as language strategies that speakers can use
to try to persuade listeners to agree with their points of view by describing why they should agree and by demonstrating that they have authority
in such matters. Importantly, Kevin's view was not the only viable position among board members. A more sympathetic view of the study came
from Nancy, the IRB administrator, who often commented on education
research that came to the IRB based on her personal experience sending her
own children through various local programs. In this case, Nancy volunteered that "I understand [Dorothy's research program] is very good" (878)
in terms of the positive effects that the courses had on children. Nancy also
suggested why Dorothy's research team might describe the tests to parents
rather loosely: "I know from her previous experience with a lot of this, she
doesn't want to frighten people" (970). As listeners, other IRB members
played an essential role in authorizing or rejecting their colleagues' claims
to have special insight into a study on the basis of which an investigator
must change research plans.

In this case, most board members at Greenly treated Kevin's claim to
professional experience as most credible, and in so doing they solidified
his views as the most authoritative in the evaluation of this study. It is important that Nancy, Kevin's detractor, also joined the growing consensus of
board members, and so there was no trace of her alternative view in the
eventual meeting minutes. After Kevin reiterated his position that the researchers should describe the vocabulary measure to parents as an IQ test,
Ted responded, "I think that's right. She has consent for vocabulary but not
for IQ," (906–13), and the board chair told Kevin, "I can see your point. . . .
I looked at these [test] names and I didn't think about that [IQ]" (879–87).

Yet even as Kevin advocated his view, spelled out recommendations, and warranted his credibility to speak on the matter, he often pulled back—not in his certitude that the investigators were collecting data on IQ but in his willingness to demand changes to the study, or as he put it, his willingness "to throw a monkey wrench into this (study)."[3] The board chair responded to this vacillation:

CHAIR: It sounds like at a minimum she needs to better explain what the testing is and potentially what it entails, whether that's IQ or depression and so forth, so that people at least understand. Now the question is whether they will know which test is which. They're not going to because, I mean, [IQ Test Name] doesn't mean anything to anybody, except you.

KEVIN: That's right.

CHAIR: I mean, I shouldn't say that. Maybe it means something to somebody else here.

GROUP: [Laughter]

CHARLIE (PHYSICIAN): It means something to all of us, we just don't know what! [Laughs]

GROUP: [Laughter]

CHAIR: That's because our IQ isn't high enough to know this! [Laughs] (895–902)

This exchange marks a tension caused by the fact that, in order to evaluate research, IRB members necessarily claim knowledge of some sort about an area in which the investigator also claims expertise. The result at Greenly was that Kevin interspersed his critiques of the study with encouragement that it should nonetheless go on as planned. He was reluctant to force changes to the study because he felt certain that Dorothy, a senior researcher, would know that he, a junior faculty member, was responsible for demanding the labor-intensive changes that would affect study enrollment. "My gut impression is that we don't necessarily want to stop this," he explained, "because I'm the one who gets identified on this and I'm dead meat on this campus, just to let you know. And I know there'd be repercussions because with her—her chair calls my chair, et cetera, et cetera, et cetera. It's because I'm the only one here who can identify this" (951).

In this situation, the meeting minutes served as a remarkably useful tool

---

3. According to my transcription conventions, parentheses indicate an inaudible phrase or word that has been paraphrased based on field notes.

to manage the relationship between Kevin, his colleagues on the board, and the researchers. Kevin had successfully persuaded his fellow IRB members that the researchers were measuring IQ, that IQ was a sensitive piece of information, and that changes to the study were imperative. Yet he simultaneously insisted that the researchers should not be asked to change study procedures because it might jeopardize his professional standing outside the IRB. Kevin was not appeased until Nancy, abandoning her appeals to his sense of duty to protect study participants, reminded Kevin that "the minutes don't record you personally" (987–92). The meeting minutes, as board members discussed, could describe changes general enough to conceal Kevin's pointed concern but specific enough to ensure that the researchers would have to elaborate on the test as he recommended.

The meeting minutes for this review were entirely typical in form and therefore very useful for board members in managing accountability in the review. The meeting minutes gave the title of the study and named the two researchers, which focused responsibility for the study on them. On the flip side, however, the meeting minutes invoked "The Board" as the single social actor involved in the decision (specifically, in this case, "The Board tabled any decision on this protocol . . ."). According to the meeting minutes, The Board was the united, uniform agent that acted in reviews: the minutes explained that The Board "discussed" and at times The Board "approved." To deal with this potentially awkward linguistic form, in which one organizational actor requested changes from two individual researchers, requests for study changes were written as commands in the meeting minutes: for example, "Provide an attachment which gives a brief description . . ."

The transcript of the deliberation, by contrast, offers an account of the study review that could be thought of as an exchange between Kevin, Dorothy, and her co-investigator, with an audience of university colleagues backing and rejecting competing claims to expertise. In the meeting minutes, however, Kevin's acute sense of personal responsibility during the deliberation was obscured, and the story line of what happened during the meeting most likely did not fit with researchers' experiences of the event because the key debate developed after they had left. When compared with the deliberation transcript, the meeting minutes provided a distinctive, unintuitive account of the social actors who were linked and the events that transpired during the study review. Board members' discussion of how Kevin's opinion might be recorded in the minutes was instrumental in getting his opinion into print and into the study design as the research went forward.

The Sander State IRB: A Failed Attempt to Change a Study

A proposed pilot study at Sander State, called Home Environment and Life Outlook, provides a vivid example of how one board member's strongly felt but ultimately unpersuasive views were translated into and managed through the meeting minutes. In the study, the researchers, who were from the Department of Human Ecology, planned to compare whether features of assisted-living group homes affected residents' perceived quality of life. The researchers intended to interview residents, all of whom had mild dementia, and to observe their homes and how they used them—for example, to see whether there were plants that they watered, small pets that they fed, or yards in which they walked. The study was given a conditional approval on the day it was reviewed, which meant that the researchers did not have to submit a revised study, against the protest of one board member.

The section of the meeting minutes that I explore is a statement that asked the researchers: "Please note that IRB discussion indicated concern over co-morbidity factors influencing methodology." This statement is revealing in what it includes: the suggestion, with the use of the words "IRB discussion," that board members had an internal disagreement. This statement is also curious in what it excludes—most consequentially, a formal demand that researchers change their study design. Finally, it is worth noting that this statement accompanied one of the few votes of resistance from a board member (an abstention on principle) that I saw during my year observing deliberations.

During the study review, board members asked the researchers to fix a number of inconsistencies between the project description and the consent form, requests that were easily agreed to. Two board members lingered on the issue of how, precisely, researchers would establish that the people with dementia were cognizant enough to give informed consent to participate in the study. Then Henry, a middle-aged board member, started the line of inquiry that would eventually prompt him to refuse to vote on this study. Henry pointed out that there are many different health problems that cause people to have dementia, and he asked the researchers, "Are you interested at all about causations [of dementia]? Do they have any relevance? Or would they have any relevance to your assessment of whether or not [residents] like this place versus this place?" In an exchange that lasted two or three minutes, the junior member of the study team, who was leading the research in practice but not on paper, repeated that their focus was on residents' perceived quality of life, not on the underlying causes of dementia per se.

Eventually, the IRB chair looked to the other board members and asked, "Anything else?" This was a strategy that the chair used both to exhaust all the possible questions that board members might have while the researchers were present and also, as in this instance, to truncate seemingly inappropriate discussion. The board chair's question did not follow from a resolved debate, in other words. Rather, the question imposed an end to the discussion of whether disease etiology mattered in this study.

Henry resisted this attempt to close discussion. "I just had a concern that the categories that you're drawing would make causation (important for understanding) cognitive impairment," he began again. "And it would appear to me, just on the surface, and obviously I'm not a learned individual in this area, so (I'm trying to sort this out). It seems to me, there may be some bias introduced if one person's impairment is due to A causation versus B causation. There may be some bias in there" (transcript 1, line 246). Consider how Henry presented himself and his credibility in voicing this critique. Henry's official status on the board was as a community member because he was not employed by the university. Yet he had graduate training in biochemistry and had worked as a bench scientist, so board members often relied on his judgment (along with that of physicians on the board) when they reviewed clinical trials. At this moment, though, Henry did not warrant his credibility but instead deferred to the researchers' expertise by claiming that he was "not a learned individual in this area." With this further questioning, the junior researcher, rather than claim as before that the cause of dementia was irrelevant to the study, instead explained that the medical records of participants were too difficult to access because of privacy regulations for health information. The IRB chair then directly called on a different board member and effectively gave the floor to another person and topic. The researchers soon left.

The IRB chair at Sander State also used a technique that made it easy to follow the creation of a formal account of the meeting. After researchers left meetings, he read back to the board members his notes on what had been decided in the researchers' presence, which the administrator would type verbatim as the meeting minutes and use in an official letter to the researchers that told them what "action" the board members had taken. Often, the board members had a common sense of what changes they had requested, and a vote followed smoothly. In this case, the board chair read back his minutes-in-the-making, and two board members motioned to approve the study with the listed changes. As they were about to vote, however, Henry intervened. Noting that his concerns had been left out of the list of modifications, Henry explained why it was essential that board members agree to include his recommended changes.

This time, Henry made the same critique of the study, but he warranted his view differently: he justified his opinion with his professional experience. "It's my own personal belief that the criterion for this population that she's working with is critical," he began. "And etiology is associated with causation of dementia. To my mind, from my experience working in this area, it can have an effect on how you look at life." His fellow board members were not persuaded:

HENRY: Multiple sclerosis patients who have dementia, (they can't go anywhere) and they know that it's progressive and that their brains are shrinking. Their ventricles are getting larger, the substance of the brain is wasting away. Versus a (diabetic) patient who has had diabetes and over the years is starting to get diabetic dementia. Those two people have different outlooks on life. Whether/[4]

NIGEL (LINGUIST): She's not interested in the cause; she's interested in the result, it seems to me. They're interested in the result.

SAM (PHYSICIAN): I don't think it makes a difference to her study.

HENRY: I think it does, because she's looking at: How do environmental effects within this environment in which they are housed affect their outlook? How does that affect them? How does that make them feel? I think if you have a disease that changes your outlook on life, and how you feel day-to-day, your outlook on how that environment affects you, positively or negatively, is (a factor) . . . Your disease changes your perception of your environment. It does. (606–15)

Board members continued to emphasize the investigators' expertise in this study area over Henry's expertise. His claim to "experience working in this area" did not appear to be compelling to board members for an interview-based study in human ecology. One social scientist on the board rebuffed Henry for "commenting on methodology," although board members often required changes in study design on the logic that researchers, at a minimum, are obligated to produce useful data to justify involving people in research at all. In this case, however, in response to Henry's assertion that the researchers would not get "useful" data, another board member defended the researchers. This former dairy scientist defended the investigators' pre-

4. The slash indicates that the speaker was interrupted.

rogative to define their standards of research according to their discipline rather than by Henry's competing ideals:

> Doesn't the usefulness of the data depend on the type of knowledge that you're talking about? You might interpret the results of this research as being "Well, it's useless because I don't believe that they screened out this and this and this." And so your interpretation as a result might be quite different from someone else's. But it strikes me that with the methodology that they're using, it really doesn't matter too much as far as they're concerned. (620)

At the same time, the Sander State board members were quite conciliatory toward Henry. As Donald Brenneis (1994) has observed, review boards tend to be remarkably collegial groups because members are often selected (out of any number of experts in their fields) for their ability to be civil during an activity defined by disagreement. One board member at Sander State told Henry that he could "understand your concern" but at the same time reminded board members that getting health information was not "practical" in this study and that the project was only a pilot study.

In a similar spirit of mollification, another board member suggested: "Our board report could also just have an addendum that says 'Discussion indicates that we are concerned about the multi-disease (problem), and we discussed those as being influential on your study.' We could just say we're concerned" (630). A third board member then asked that everyone vote and move on. In the end, the meeting minutes reproduced these final conciliatory words: "Please note that IRB discussion indicated concern over co-morbidity factors influencing methodology." The researchers would not have to change anything about their study after reading this sentence. They were not its only readers, though. This phrasing was a note to Henry as well as a point of information for the researchers. Henry and the other board members would also read and endorse the minutes at their subsequent meeting. Thus, the minutes served to manage relationships among board members in this case.

It is revealing, in addition, that in six months of meeting minutes that I collected, this was the only statement that constituted the Sander State IRB as anything but a single, unified social actor. In other minutes, readers would learn: "The IRB expresses concern . . ." (71); "The IRB suggests . . ." (342–43); in the future, "The IRB would like to discuss . . ."; and even

"The IRB commends [researchers] for a well-prepared set of responses and well-thought-out rationale." The exception in the case of Henry's critique highlights the rule that when board members endorse an individual's viewpoint, their unity is implicit in their self-description as "The IRB."

Conclusion: Two Perspectives Revisited

At most American universities, IRBs are the groups charged with the task of evaluating whether researchers plan to treat properly the people whom they intend to study. What has piqued my interest in this chapter is not how scholars feel about ethics review. (The consensus is that we feel frustrated; see Stark 2007.) I have been interested, rather, in exploring interactions between the practices and the products of evaluation. Studying evaluation as a social process offers an opportunity also to explore the practice of statecraft and to consider its effects on knowledge production.

A central instrument in the exercise of coercive power is the administrative document. In this chapter, I followed two studies from their first moments of airtime in IRB meetings until they were written into meeting minutes. These studies exemplified general processes that I observed from the inside, so to speak, of human-subjects review. During IRB deliberations, individual board members offered opinions and then warranted their views; they failed or succeeded in persuading colleagues of their credibility to judge the research and thus build members' consensus around it. At Greenly, for example, Kevin warranted his opinion that researchers should change their description of psychological measures by reciting his professional experience with the very test that researchers planned to use. Meanwhile, at Sander State, Henry failed to persuade other board members that he had special insight that would justify making researchers take into account the causes of participants' dementia in an interview-based study.

Meeting minutes were written in a way that portrayed IRBs as unitary social actors who evaluated studies. That is to say, individuals' successful attempts to build consensus during board deliberations were presented in the meeting minutes as the actions and opinions of "The Board" or "The IRB." As the constitutive perspective to studying documents would suggest, actors who figure prominently in state administration—whether patients, deviants, or IRBs—are most firmly endowed with social reality when they become fixed in administrative documents.

As a result, the ethics review process, which is intended to make scholars ethically accountable for their studies by producing managerial records of their planned activities and required behavior, in turn obscures the agency (and, thus, the accountability) of the individual actors who make up the boards. In saying that these members "make up" the IRB, I want to point out that individuals not only compose the boards but also do the inventive work of harnessing their opinions to the collective authority derived from administrative law (Hacking 2002). Practices of accountability (Strathern 2000) produce the accountability of individual researchers and of The IRB as an organizational unit. Simultaneously (and somewhat ironically), this process erases the accountability of individual board members.

As I described them, the opinions that were eventually adopted as those of The IRB were outcomes of a process of consensus building. But individual board members' efforts to consolidate support for their positions (both failed and successful) were left out of the meeting minutes. If members' justifications had been recorded for public inspection, one practical implication might be that readers of the minutes could contest the legitimacy of these justifications and the changes required based on them. The seeming objectivity of a claim can become "stronger" or "weaker"—that is, it can be contested and settled to a greater or lesser extent—depending on who makes the claim and whether it is documented in a way that enables the claim to stand outside any one person or context (Latour 1987; Shapin 1994). One aim of formal records, however, is to invent impersonal, rational stories of how events transpired and authoritative instructions for how events should play out in the future.

In sum, meeting minutes give an account of deliberations that are distinctive in systematic ways: with different actors and different actions than appear during deliberations. It is tempting, as a result, to think of the relationship between deliberations and documents as exclusively one-directional, with people's actions being followed by records that are followed by further actions and so on forward through time.

As I have shown, however, the process of translation between deliberation and document in ethics review actually moves in both directions. Recall Kevin's predicament at Greenly. Despite his initial reluctance to become professional "dead meat" at the hands of a powerful researcher, he became willing to allow a substantial change to her study precisely because, as the board administrator reminded him, the minutes would not record him personally. The erasure of Kevin's agency that would occur in the process of creating meeting minutes was explicit during the deliberation, and this in turn fueled his critique of the protocol, which was ultimately consequential for the researchers. Likewise, at Sander State, board members used the future minutes of their current meeting overtly to manage relationships as the deliberation was still under way. In this case, Henry had failed to persuade other members that they should adopt his opinion despite his deep and enduring conviction that the researchers should be made to gather additional health data on study participants. To finally close deliberation in the face of Henry's persistent reopening of debate, a fellow board member suggested that a nonbinding comment (ostensibly written to the researchers) be included in the minutes. It is worth noting that this board member phrased her suggestion during the deliberation in the form of meeting minutes, a so-called hybrid utterance (a version of which was indeed written into the minutes). Specifically, she offered that board members could "just have an addendum that says 'Discussion indicates that we are concerned about the multi-disease (problem), and we discussed those as being influential on your study'." Intentionally composed in such a way that researchers did not actually have to alter their study plan, the meeting minutes were used in the deliberation to make a show of collective dissatisfaction—purportedly for the researchers' edification but practically to manage Henry and to manage board members' ongoing colleagueship with him. IRB members' cognizance of the stylistic conventions that would be used later to write the meeting minutes informed the changes that board members ultimately asked researchers to make.

Board members not only were aware that their decisions would subsequently be documented but also were alert to how the constraints of meeting minutes could be useful during deliberations. Exploring what I have called an "anticipatory perspective" to studying documents, I argued that board members' sense of how the minutes of their current discussion would be written served as a social resource that they used to manage relationships—between each other and between themselves and researchers. As I have described it, the process of evaluation in ethics review was simultaneously a process of translation between the languages of deliberation and documentation. And like other translations, the process worked in both directions. Not only did meeting minutes record decisions and reproduce the categories, standards, and narratives of evaluation that had been used in ethics review, but the unwritten minutes also steered the course of deliberation as it was still under way.

Thus, the outcomes of knowledge evaluation not only change the landscape of research by making some studies possible and others wholly unworkable. Evaluative groups, such as funding panels and editorial boards, encourage researchers to "revise and resubmit" their work based on reviewers' comments, which is akin to the works-in-process phenomenon that

Gross and Fleming explore in chapter 4. Similarly, universities shift their research foci or hiring priorities to make their work commensurate with assessment standards, as Strathern has demonstrated in her recent work (chapter 8, this volume; Strathern 2000; see also Espeland and Sauder 2007). Likewise, IRBs change research practices by requesting "modifications" to social research before they approve it. Members of ethics committees, funding panels, editorial boards, conference committees, and assessment exercises actively reshape how researchers do their work—and thus what they come to know—through the process of evaluation.

Administrative documents are often thought of as records of these eventual decisions. But documents are not only artifacts of evaluations. They are also actively used tools that evaluators deploy to help them make decisions. Before documents become buried treasures in administrative files for scholars to unearth as artifacts, they are imagined objects, which evaluators use in the practice of research evaluation to enable their work to move forward. In this way, the end products of evaluation alter the dynamic process of evaluation itself.

References

Austin, J. L. 1962. *How to Do Things with Words*. Oxford: Clarendon Press.

Bledsoe, Caroline, Bruce Sherin, Adam Galinsky, Nathalia Headley, Carol Heimer, Erik Kjeldgaard, James Lindgren, Jon Miller, Michael Roloff, and David Uttal. 2007. "Regulating Creativity: Research and Survival in the IRB Iron Cage." *Northwestern University School of Law* 101:593–642.

Brenneis, Donald. 1994. "Discourse and Discipline at the National Research Council: A Bureaucratic Bildungsroman." *Cultural Anthropology* 9:23–36.

Carson, John. 2007. *The Measure of Merit: Talents, Intelligence, and Inequality in the French and American Republics, 1750–1940*. Princeton, NJ: Princeton University Press.

Espeland, Wendy Nelson, and Michael Sauder. 2007. "Rankings and Reactivity: How Public Measures Recreate Social Worlds." *American Journal of Sociology* 113:1–40.

Foucault, Michel. [1977] 1995. *Discipline and Punish: The Birth of the Prison*. Translated by A. Sheridan. New York: Vintage, Random House.

Garfinkel, Harold. 1967. *Studies in Ethnomethodology*. Englewood Cliffs, NJ: Prentice-Hall.

Guetzkow, Joshua, Michèle Lamont, and Grégoire Mallard. 2004. "What Is Originality in the Humanities and the Social Sciences?" *American Sociological Review* 69:190–212.

Hacking, Ian. 2002. *Historical Ontology*. Cambridge, MA: Harvard University Press.

Hedgecoe, Adam. 2010. "Research Ethics Review and the Sociological Research Relationship." *Sociology* 42:873–86.

Heimer, Carol. 2001. "Cases and Biographies: An Essay on Routinization and the Nature of Comparison." *Annual Review of Sociology* 27:47–76.

Heimer, Carol, and JuLeigh Petty. 2010. "Bureaucratic Ethics: IRBs and the Legal Regulation of Human Subjects Research." *Annual Review of Law and Social Science* 6:601–26.

Igo, Sarah E. 2007. *The Averaged American: Surveys, Citizens, and the Making of a Mass Public*. Cambridge, MA: Harvard University Press.

Lamont, Michèle. 2009. *How Professors Think: Inside the Curious World of Academic Judgment*. Cambridge, MA: Harvard University Press.

Latour, Bruno. 1987. *Science in Action: How to Follow Scientists and Engineers through Society*. Cambridge, MA: Harvard University Press.

Law, John. 2008. "On STS and Sociology." *Sociological Review* 56, no. 4: 623–49.

MacKenzie, Donald A., Fabian Muniesa, and Lucia Siu, eds. 2007. *Do Economists Make Markets? On the Performativity of Economics*. Princeton, NJ: Princeton University Press.

Orloff, Ann Shola. 2005. "Social Provision and Regulation." In *Remaking Modernity*, edited by Julia Adams, Elisabeth S. Clemens, and Ann Shola Orloff, 190–224. Durham, NC: Duke University Press.

Reed, Adam. 2006. "Documents Unfolding." In *Documents: Artifacts of Modern Knowledge*, edited by A. Riles, 158–77. Ann Arbor: University of Michigan Press.

Rose, Nikolas. 1998. *Inventing Our Selves: Psychology, Power, and Personhood*. Cambridge: Cambridge University Press.

Schrag, Zachary M. 2009. "How Talking Became Human Subjects Research: The Federal Regulation of the Social Sciences, 1965–1991." *Journal of Policy History* 21:3–37.

Shapin, Steven. 1994. *A Social History of Truth: Civility and Science in Seventeenth-Century England*. Chicago: University of Chicago Press.

———. 2008. *The Scientific Life*. Chicago: University of Chicago Press.

Shore, Cris, and Susan Wright. 2000. "Coercive Accountability." In *Audit Cultures: Anthropological Studies in Accountability, Ethics and the Academy*, edited by Marilyn Strathern, 57–89. London: Routledge.

Smith, Dorothy E. 2006. "Incorporating Texts into Ethnographic Practice." In *Institutional Ethnography as Practice*, edited by D. E. Smith, 65–88. New York: Rowman and Littlefield.

Stark, Laura. 2007. "Victims in Our Own Minds? IRBs in Myth and Practice." *Law and Society Review* 41:777–86.

———. Forthcoming. *Behind Closed Doors: IRBs and the Making of Ethical Research*. Chicago: University of Chicago Press.

Steinmetz, George. 2009. "Neo-Bourdieusian Theory and the Question of Scientific Autonomy: German Sociologists and Empire, 1890s–1940s." *Political Power and Social Theory* 20:71–131.

Stevens, Mitchell L. 2007. *Creating a Class: College Admissions and the Education of Elites*. Chicago: University of Chicago Press.

Strathern, Marilyn. 2000. "New Accountabilities: Anthropological Studies in Audit, Ethics, and the Academy." In *Audit Cultures: Anthropological Studies in Accountability, Ethics and the Academy*, edited by Marilyn Strathern, 1–18. London: Routledge.

Suchman, Mark. 2003. "The Contract as Social Artifact." *Law and Society Review* 37: 91–141.

Taylor, Holly A., Peter Currie, and Nancy E. Kass. 2008. "A Study to Evaluate the Effect of Investigator Attendance on the Efficiency of IRB Review." *IRB: Ethics and Human Research* 30:1–5.

Thorpe, Charles. 2006. *Oppenheimer: The Tragic Intellect*. Chicago: University of Chicago Press.

Timmermans, Stefan, and Marc Berg. 2003. *The Gold Standard: The Challenge of Evidence-Based Medicine and Standardization in Health Care*. Philadelphia: Temple University Press.

Tsay, Angela, Michèle Lamont, Andrew Abbott, and Joshua Guetzkow. 2003. "From Character to Intellect: Changing Conceptions of Merit in the Social Sciences and Humanities, 1951–1971." *Poetics* 31:23–49.

Waddell, Craig. 1989. "Reasonableness versus Rationality in the Construction and Justification of Science Policy Decisions: The Case of the Cambridge Experimentation Review Board." *Science, Technology, and Human Values* 14:7–25.

Weber, Max. 1920. *The Vocation Lectures*. Indianapolis: Hackett Publishing Group.

———. 1978. *Economy and Society*. Vol. 2. Edited by Guenther Roth and Claus Wittich. Berkeley and Los Angeles: University of California Press.

EIGHT

An Experiment in Interdisciplinarity

Proposals and Promises

MARILYN STRATHERN

The grant proposal has become a focus for a certain kind of interdisciplinary practice in academia, at least in the United Kingdom, and at least as far as research councils and their interpretation of government policy are concerned. The body known as Research Councils UK, for example, actively invites explicitly interdisciplinary applications. More than that, interdisciplinarity has become a new sign and measure of good practice. However, across the social sciences, as well as the arts and humanities, the fact that some subject areas are seen as interdisciplinary by their very nature does not mean they are necessarily more attractive to funders than are conventional disciplines. On the contrary, the Research Councils' mandate (it is almost that) has come with an evangelical fervor most obviously addressed to *disciplines as such*, for it is designed to promote new forms of synergy and creativity by converting conventional disciplines away from an inward-looking to an outward-looking orientation. In this way, "interdisciplinarity" signals to funders a specific academic virtue.

This chapter was originally presented under the title "Interdisciplinarity in Judgment: New Modes of Evaluative Practice." I thank the conveners of the Russell Sage conference that formed the foundation for this volume for asking an unusual question and for their subsequent editorial commentaries. The comments of colleagues at the conference are also much appreciated.

The substance of this chapter draws on a research project carried out with colleagues to whom I am particularly in debt. Our project, Interdisciplinarity and Society: A Critical Comparative Study, was funded by the U.K. Economic and Social Research Council (ESRC) (RES-151-25-0042-A) as part of a Science in Society program under the direction of Steven Rayner, 2004–6; I warmly thank co-investigators Andrew Barry and Georgina Born, as well as Gisa Weszkalnys and above all Lena Khlinovskaya Rockhill, from whom I have learned so much. Other teachers include Jeanette Edwards, Sarah Franklin, and Monica Konrad. Dr. Ron Zimmern could not have been a more welcoming host to the anthropological study of the Genetics Knowledge Park in 2004–5.

From the standpoint of Research Councils, however, it often turns out not to be enough for grant applicants to flag exploratory intentions or to make forays into other territories. Indeed, in the social sciences, ventures of the latter kind may be actually frowned upon, since an academic research proposal[1] can be criticized if the lead discipline appears to stray into domains beyond its conventional subject matter when it should, instead, be enlisting experts from these other domains. So, for example, social-cultural anthropology's claims to being a comparative endeavor may appear as a quite inadequate substitute for seeking out different sources of expertise by enrolling others—that is, nonanthropologists—in the proposal. There is, then, associated with the first virtue (interdisciplinarity) a second sought-after virtue: collaboration or partnership. Collaboration is most powerfully enacted where the sources of expertise remain disciplinarily distinctive. As displayed in proposals, the rhetoric of collaboration has then various, intertwined effects. One is found in the issue of accountability, as the question constantly looms as to how—by what means—the creative effects of collaboration can be evaluated. In the case of social science, the chapters in the present volume raise the further question of how concerns about evaluation may affect working practices in knowledge making. The related phenomenon explored in the present chapter, however, is less how social science is evaluated in interdisciplinary contexts than how interdisciplinary contexts create an atmosphere of evaluative expectations in which certain kinds of judgments about social science are anticipated.

That interdisciplinarity and collaboration appear to Research Councils as virtues, as I call them, points to a habit of thinking about disciplines that springs from the aspirations of funding bodies and impinges on knowledge practices. These aspirations inform the specific historical and local site of the present chapter. The United Kingdom is not an isolated example in Europe, but it is perhaps closest to the United States in the extent to which academic disciplines are given an institutional (university) base. Conversely, the U.K. example perhaps has some comparative purchase for a U.S. readership interested in knowledge practices because of the way in which so much university-based research is tied to national research councils, each of which must put a financial case to the government for resources. Alongside defending "blue skies" research, it is expected that research councils will also argue for "usefulness" and "relevance," that is, for what society will get back from expenditures from the public purse. Unsurprisingly, this

---

1. On the possibilities of analyzing the research proposal as artifact or text, see Brenneis 2006; Riles 2006.

same ethos also governs research sponsored by government departments. Making a *visible* contribution to social ends joins a third virtue—the ability to communicate—to those of interdisciplinarity and collaboration. Scholars and researchers who demonstrate the latter two attributes thereby give evidence of communicating (as distinct from trespassing) beyond the borders of their disciplines, putting themselves halfway toward the goal of being useful and relevant in their ability to reach a wide audience. Especially if that audience is the general public, the third virtue imagines availability (accessibility) as an end point of research.

This manner of thinking reflects an ambivalent approach toward disciplines in U.K. research policy. On the one hand, expertise is understood as located within distinctively demarcated areas. On the other hand, disciplines by themselves are frequently regarded both as insufficient for many of the research tasks that emerge in the form of problems in the real world and as requiring, in consequence, supplementation. Much of the serious, as well as popular, media manage to imply that disciplines per se, like universities, are somehow ivory tower constructions that, left to their own devices, will produce knowledge of use only to themselves. To impact the real world, they must be able to communicate.

This outlook speaks to one of the distinctive features of social knowledge: its potential to contribute to or be part of what is being studied. Only in a rather circumscribed sense does one say that historians make history or that literary critics contribute to the genres with which they are engaged. In contrast, academically created social knowledge may be put on a par with other kinds of knowledge that a society generates about itself, more often than not with the assumption that this knowledge can be used. If the social sciences offer primary sites for collecting social knowledge, however, there are also many satellite locations where others cull this knowledge and in turn pass it on. Indeed, semiacademic or nonacademic institutions sometimes take it on themselves to filter and disseminate social, as well as natural, knowledge that has been produced in academia, acting as brokers for a public audience. Especially when brokering for the public knowledge originating in the natural sciences, satellite institutions of this type produce what we might regard as little-recognized forms of social knowledge. How they do so, however, is necessarily affected by the nature of these institutions. Like other social organizations with a vision of the ordering of the social world, such institutions have their own agendas, producing social knowledge through the efforts of interested persons enrolled in an ongoing social enterprise. Alongside such institutional effects, moreover, are the effects of the wider milieu of contemporary trends, including debates and values in higher education, research, and government policy—examples of the porosity of social knowledge practices mentioned in the introduction of this volume.

This chapter examines a research-oriented project that ran in the United Kingdom from 2002 to 2007 to illustrate the workings of both these institutional and milieu effects. The project crossed university and public sector lines and is of interest as an experiment in social knowledge making. Its aims were to create explicitly "social" knowledge—as well as ethical, legal, and other forms of knowledge—and its short history also offers insight into the way knowledge indeed can be "socially" made.

The experiment took the form of an interdisciplinary consortium. The consortium's original proposal to its funders, in this case two government departments, delineated an enterprise that would bring together genetics research, clinical applications, and ethical reflection, along with social science understandings—and would do so in ways accessible to and communicable to a wider public. The project was part of a vision for the future that sought to shore up the reputation of science—which at the time (2000–2001) was somewhat in the doldrums (following a succession of badly managed health scares)—by bringing science "into society." In these years, interdisciplinarity was becoming increasingly embedded in the Research Councils' policy and coming to lie at the heart of U.K. government research strategy (Barry, Born, and Weszkalnys 2008, 22; see also Wilsdon and Willis 2004). At periodic moments in the past, the possibility of interdisciplinary collaborations had attracted the attention of scientific and social reformers (for the United States, see Abbott 2001, 131–33); the post–World War II program for unified knowledge was one such moment (see Cohen-Cole 2003), and the start of the new millennium seemed another.[2] In any event, the consortium in question took as foundational an explicitly interdisciplinary remit. Within it, several different disciplines across the natural and social sciences had distinct roles to play. What is more, the premise of interdisciplinarity would decisively affect the fate within the larger enterprise of particular social sciences. As we shall see, the original grant proposal played a consequential role in constituting this fate.

2. Although as an object of inquiry interdisciplinarity is relatively understudied, Barry, Born, and Weszkalnys (2008, 42) point to a small number of empirical studies of contemporary interdisciplinary research (there are five "recent examples"). Their own research, which lays out three modes of interaction and three logics of performance, is a major statement on working practices. It is pertinent to the present account insofar as it puts my one case into a much wider context of interdisciplinary possibilities.

In considering this case, I shall use a representational device sometimes employed in social anthropology, though not particularly typical of it. In lieu of generalizing from the case (i.e., using the case to give evidence regarding a more general social or cultural form), I offer the reader an invitation to recognize (or not) that he or she is—herein—in a familiar world characterized by features that may otherwise pass unnoticed. To this end, my technique will be, as I briefly describe the case at hand, to draw in circumstances beyond the case itself by eliciting the assumed knowledge of the imagined reader.[3] This device is not meant to displace reportage and empirical investigation; it simply exploits the possibility of shared understanding. As well, the device carries ethical freight, in that it allows writer and reader alike to acknowledge their proximity to the social life being described. When the writer's subject matter concerns practices of which he or she is very much part—as is true of the general research practices that lie behind the specific case discussed in this chapter—there must also be much shared social knowledge in the background. At the same time, the reader's recognition of this background is not always instant; and the writer's job may be not only to foreground but also to uncover what is not at first apparent. One way of signaling features of knowledge-making practices about which a writer expects the reader to have a flash of recognition is, as below, via the strategy of false distancing through irony. This strategy can be especially apposite in cases where critical commentary may be the more forceful if it is indirectly rather than directly stated.

This chapter is in four parts. The first section provides a brief description of the institutional context of the experiment in interdisciplinarity at hand in the hope that the reader will recognize—find familiar—aspects of the social knowledge–making project that informed it. The second section argues that the particular case responds to and endorses wider contemporary trends in the way disciplines have come to be evaluated and, prompted by this discussion, uncovers from the material of the specific case a process of the prospective negative evaluation of social scientific knowledge. Reflecting on this not-immediately-apparent process, the third section considers some of the logical and epistemological difficulties that social science may encounter in interdisciplinary contexts. The fourth section concludes with a brief discussion of the kinds of social knowledge that the practices found at the institution in question might have created.

---

3. Sometimes the familiarity has to be built up, through ethnographic description, say; sometimes the writer can make assumptions about what that world might be.

The Institutional Context: A Knowledge Park

Begun in 2002, the interdisciplinary consortium had the title of a Genetics Knowledge Park (one of six such ventures set up by the then U.K. Departments of Health and Trade and Industry and by the Welsh Assembly) and was designed to address issues arising from a number of technological innovations in the area of human genetics. "Science and Society" was the project's generic flag. The hope was that a multipronged approach would simultaneously enhance genetic knowledge and expose it to ethical, legal, and social scrutiny in order to allay public fears. The need for the project arose from a mixture of positive and negative views, at once overoptimistic and fearful, about the new genetics. The idea of genetics knowledge parks held out enormous and hopeful promise for finding ways to deal with this mix, with much of the promise lying in their collaborative structure and the synergy this would generate. Fostering "new research initiatives and collaborations" and "working synergistically towards a common goal" were twinned in the park's aims as stated in the grant proposal.

This chapter is based on an anthropological study of this emergent institution that resulted in an (unanticipated) invitation from the consortium's staff to the anthropologist to make a contribution to the institution's own efforts. Anthropologist Elena Khlinovskaya Rockhill became a participant social scientist in the Genetics Knowledge Park (GKP for short), and the following account draws on her findings (Khlinovskaya Rockhill 2007; Khlinovskaya Rockhill and Strathern 2005; Strathern and Khlinovskaya Rockhill 2007). She describes how this mixed academic and nonacademic enterprise[4] existed as a series of disparate subenterprises brought together under one umbrella. The "umbrella" was an early idiom under which the GKP saw itself as facilitating communication and promoting partnership.[5] While the GKP was a largely virtual organization, existing online and through various activities such as workshops and papers, it was

4. Structurally, the GKP was both part of and outside a major research university and the local National Health Service hospital trust. The result was a multidisciplinary mix of conventional university disciplines and the kind of multidisciplinarity to be found in medical teams and health programs. "Interdisciplinarity" was adopted as the GKP's principal term, and I retain it in this chapter as a generic shorthand for what one might otherwise wish to differentiate as multi- or interdisciplinarity.

5. Khlinovskaya Rockhill points to the promise that the GKP would "take on a leadership role and establish shared values, building on the twin concepts of partnership and interdisciplinarity." Its working style was to be "collaborating by mutual agreement" and "responding to needs of partners" (2007, 125–26).

run by a core public health facility (an already existing Genetics Unit) with staff members and offices.

In Khlinovskaya Rockhill's view, the GKP's institutional practices gave rise to certain paradoxes. Indeed, in the end, her analysis questions the very usefulness of the term "interdisciplinarity." Yet this was one of the GKP's two platform concepts, partnership being the other. The GKP aspired to bring different sources of knowledge together, as evinced in the social form of its workshops and symposia. They followed a standardized pattern,[6] with presentations from diverse specialists drawn from within or outside the GKP and never confined to a single area of expertise. The GKP regarded itself as adding value to preexisting fields of expertise precisely by "bringing together" different experts, and in its eyes these occasions not only performed interdisciplinarity but enacted it. These *were* the moments when disciplines came together. What was rhetorical about the ensuing interchanges was their promissory nature—because although there was discussion of the papers, typically there was no attempt to "bring together" the material or arguments or viewpoints being aired. How the intellectual presumptions and conclusions were to relate to one another was not part of the master plan. To the contrary, the consortium's principal architect—here called the Founder—was clear that synergy was *not* to be managed: its fruits would ripen in the future. Accordingly, as Khlinovskaya Rockhill emphases, GKP policy embraced open-endedness and was radically nonprescriptive; the idea was that participants would take away from workshop occasions whatever was helpful or useful.

In referring to partnership, the GKP's rhetoric was also overtly collaborative. Yet, as the consortium gave almost no epistemic investment to determining what it meant for making knowledge that academic and nonacademic interests were being brought together, the academic/nonacademic distinction itself became an ideological fault line. It was a division to which the GKP directorate constantly referred, stressing a contrast between research and management modes in the handling of knowledge. Research modes were left to the academics and their careers; it was the creative brokering and filtering of academic knowledge that the GKP directorate wanted

6. This pattern is well established in science and society conferences of all kinds. Sunder Rajan (2006, 39) gives an iconic example; see also the discussion in Konrad 2007b. This is the hallmark of "interdisciplinary" engagement, whether or not the public in some form or other is also present. On GKP occasions, speakers would be labeled through institutional affiliations that revealed their disciplinary background. May (2006, 518) offers a description of being brought in as a sociological expert at government-level meetings concerned with the evaluation of "telehealthcare."

to implement. What the GKP believed that it could offer was expertise in turning research findings into other kinds of information, which would be useful, for example, to government or public bodies; indeed, its publications borrowed the format of government or public body consultation papers. Across the academic/nonacademic divide, what partnership meant was thus relative to management goals.

Khlinovskaya Rockhill points to the paradox here. The very open-endedness that characterized the GKP's approach to the independent flowering of everyone's enterprises—namely, its horizon-scanning trajectory—gave the consortium a particular cast: it offered "a research model of a management enterprise" (Khlinovskaya Rockhill 2007, 139). The charismatic Founder had a diffuse vision of the transformative effects of bringing experts together but a precise one of how his diverse (personal) networks could yield patterns. Khlinovskaya Rockhill describes networking as his forte; tremendous work went into securing collaborators, getting people to contribute to different parts of the enterprise, enrolling all manner of expertise. And time was spent in patterning itself. Producing paper and screen diagrams of how the different parts of the overall enterprise flowed into other parts—via arrows and the arrangement of boxes—was an exercise frequently undertaken. Still, the diagrams were less a modeling of existing relationships than the *promise* of how everything would tie in once the GKP was mobilized to its fullest extent. There was a sense, one might say, in which the looked-for synergy took a particular management form. Synergy was all in the planning, and planning, whether immediate or remote, was about future dividends that one could not, it was said, necessarily foresee.

This context sets the scene for understanding the fate of social science in particular. Sociology was one of three academic disciplines brought on board to give the GKP the distinctive "ELSI" dimension that loomed large in its funding proposal, which spoke of considering the "Ethical, Legal, and Social Implications" of various issues, especially as applied to biomedical research.[7] Prepared to be open to diverse concerns, the Founder had embraced ELSI aspirations in an experimental mode because "ethical, legal, and social implications" were beyond his own particular interests or expertise. However, he was prepared to experiment, so judgment regarding these disciplines was thus initially suspended. The Founder was in effect waiting to be convinced.

7. ELSI, which began in the United States as a research program attached to the Human Genome Project and now is under the umbrella of the U.S. National Institutes of Health and the National Human Genome Research Institute, has been adopted as an acronym for social impact studies more generally and is applied more or less literally elsewhere.

As it turned out, the legal and ethical components of the consortium endured within the GKP longer than sociology did, no doubt due to the normative—and thus inherently practical—purchase that law and ethics provided, in contrast to the social sciences, where both sociology and anthropology operate as largely nonnormative disciplines. But the contrasting fate of sociology versus the legal and ethical elements of the project may also have been the cumulative outcome of the academic/nonacademic fault line in the whole enterprise. For the GKP directorate evoked this distinction time and again—in a manner that recalls the clinical project described by May and Ellis, where similar internal divisions went "not only unresolved, but [were] made afresh at almost every pause in the story" (2001, 1000). In the GKP case, there was a further cascade effect from the general disparagement of research that was "too academic" to a genuine query about the value of ELSI activities and to a sense of perplexity as to what a discipline such as sociology (or anthropology) could offer. At base, this sequence resulted from an instrumental approach to knowledge that put social science into what Barry, Born, and Weszkalnys (2008, 28–29) describe as a subordinate-service mode in relation to the GKP's interests in translating and disseminating genetic knowledge. Sociology was not going to change this underlying approach.

Indeed, this instrumentalism held for academic work in general: anything was tolerated but only if it could also be turned to "useful" ends (Khlinovskaya Rockhill 2007, 131). It has to be said that many of the core GKP participants, including those on the ELSI side of the consortium, shared with one another a generalized anxiety about the value of their work and about the difference their own efforts would make. These concerns merged with the anxiety that some felt on behalf of the whole GKP: what did the GKP have to offer the world, and what difference did its efforts make to anyone? (I read these feelings as "interdisciplinary anxieties," which arise at the moment when one's own enterprise extends into those of other people [Strathern 2006b].) From the Founder's own perspective, it was the specific usefulness of certain areas of social science—and, here, anthropology initially came to be bracketed with sociology—that was not obvious.

Eventually, however, the anthropologist-ethnographer became assimilated into the GKP's imagined networks. From the perspective of the GKP's directorate, what the anthropologist could do, in accord with the stereotype of the exotic outsider, was to tell people about themselves. Hereby, in management parlance, anthropology could offer evaluative feedback. In return, the GKP was generous in allowing the anthropologist access to its materials and records. Still, if the anthropologist was tolerated as an evaluator who could assist management, then it was precisely in her role as ethnographer, where ethnographer meant observer. On the assumption of management, observations could be relayed through iterative feedback, understood as a kind of interactive monitoring process; and observations could be relayed more or less at once, without reflection or analysis. (Reflection and analysis belonged to the "academic" side of things, in which the GKP management was not interested.) However, although the ethnographer in question contributed a great deal (as did the sociologist before his departure), she was never going to meet the expectations of this evaluative standard.

Evaluation dogged the fortunes of the GKP itself. The GKP was well aware that its funders would subject it to review by an advisory group on genetics research (Khlinovskaya Rockhill 2007, 134). However, its ethic of open-endedness meant that it regarded itself as having goals beyond what could be audited (this was part of the "research" side of its management practices), and the GKP disputed the criteria that could be applied to it. Thus, its business plan sheered away from impact assessment toward developmental goals such as establishing trust between partners or "adding value" to the activities of other organizations (Khlinovskaya Rockhill 2007, 134). These goals set the frame for a work program that took the GKP's outreach activities, publications, and so on as the enterprise's outputs but did not develop means of assessing either the audience for or the influence of these activities. Management did not think it necessary to evaluate the social dimensions of the GKP's activities in terms of, say, the networks that the consortium activated or how its communications competed with numerous others. The constituencies imagined to be in need of information from the GKP remained distant and unidentified consumers.[8] Moreover, GKP personnel could themselves (they believed) judge what was useful for dissemination. This assumption was epitomized in the Founder's patience: waiting to be convinced by ELSI—and above all by sociology and anthropology. His own opinion was sufficient to judge what would be useful; he would or would not be convinced himself. In other words, the rhetoric of "usefulness" took the place of other standards of evaluation.[9] What was

8. In relation to academic research proposals, Rip and Shove (2000) have suggested that proposals often lead applicants to make unspecific claims about their audience, sketching in undefined but self-evidently significant goals such as greater well-being or better knowledge. Researchers imply, they say, unbounded opportunities for potential use.

9. Khlinovskaya Rockhill (2007) emphasizes the instrumentalism that governed the management's outlook. The limit to which such an approach can be generalized to other interdisciplinary ventures is investigated by Barry, Born, and Weszkalnys (2008), who uncover equally deep-rooted strands of a noninstrumental nature.

more, usefulness could discriminate between the success of different parts of the GKP operation. Seemingly very practical, here was a criterion that management could apply both externally (to what was going to be communicated to the outside world) and internally (to how different organizational elements were tied in to, were useful to, the overall goals of the GKP). Management of the GKP would be "change management" for the world.[10]

However, while the GKP offered its various activities as "outputs," its funders regarded them as "inputs," since they were looking for what the GKP had accomplished by way of impact. No doubt the funders assumed from the GKP's grant proposal that assessment of impact would correspond to the statement of aims and objectives. Lack of clarity on this issue eventually became one of the reasons that funding was not continued beyond the initial five years for any of the knowledge parks. (Insofar as some of the programs survived, they were diverted into other channels.) Yet, at the outset, the funders, being government departments, had not just been persuaded to set the fifteen-million-pound project into motion but had specified what they wanted, and it was in the light of their own aims and objectives that they had lobbied for the GKPs. The GKP proposals were, so to speak, proposals within a proposal: interdisciplinarity, partnership, and communication were all top-down requirements laid out in the government departments' tender document (Department of Health 2002; Khlinovskaya Rockhill 2007, 125).

Again, however, what is particularly noteworthy is how evaluation of success in terms of usefulness was managed such that sociology emerged, in the view of the directorate, as the least useful contributor to the interdisciplinary project. Of course, the kind of knowledge that specialists at the GKP were making had to be translatable into other people's agendas, yet for sociologists—as for anthropologists—this requirement was not in itself new to their working practices; it was a routine expectation of communication. Neither was there anything novel in having to work to demonstrate relevance to other people's goals, although the chance to establish this point to the GKP directorate on the basis of research was cut short. For sociology, a stronger disadvantaging factor that perhaps would not have been so evident a couple of decades ago, however, was the new *promissory atmo-*

---

10. This was a creative orientation toward management practices that fits the ethos that Osborne describes: "creative individuals are not those who simply innovate . . . but those who can change the domain within which they work. . . . Whereas once it was the case that creativity would allow you, as the saying went, 'to get to the future first,' contemporary creativity enables you, as it were, to invent the future itself" (2003, 508, 509).

sphere in which grant proposals were created—a state of affairs in which government departments were as much caught up as anyone by the lure of a hopeful horizon. (When setting up the GKPs and at the time of the mid-term review two years later, the Department of Health was "still unclear what the GKPs should be doing" [Khlinovskaya Rockhill 2007, 125].)

At all events, the kind of social knowledge that the GKP sought to create was continually dominated by these paired issues: the problem of evalua-tion (including performance evaluation relative to goals coming from the top down) and the promissory atmosphere that laid so much emphasis on objectives articulated in advance in the originating grant proposal and was underlined in the consortium's interdisciplinary aims. It was this novel kind of future-oriented practice, I suggest, that rendered the distinctive pre-sentism of much of sociology (and anthropology) a decided disadvantage in the GKP's interdisciplinary context.

Speculative Synergy

To better understand this institutional context, it is helpful to bring in one of anthropology's own knowledge practices and look to the wider milieu. In so doing, the purpose of this section is to furnish some quizzical dis-tance from the GKP's negative assessment of social science by relating the preceding observations on the promissory atmosphere of grant proposals to anthropological work on hope in quite another arena of social life. The point of departure for this analysis is the prevalent emphasis in interdisci-plinary contexts on that kind of creativity—often called synergy—that is generated through interaction and specifically through collaboration and partnership.

In the immediate background here again is the grant proposal—and at this point we might reflect on the tremendous emphasis that is placed these days on its preparation, indicative as this is of a more general ap-proach to knowledge making in contemporary academia. For preparation of the research proposal lends itself to prospective rhetoric, to grant appli-cants finding justifications for their plans and putting a positive value on all aspects of method and protocol. To raise a proposal's chances of receiv-ing funding, every item within it must be seen to contribute an advantage to a product that funders will buy. Funders, in turn, have to gamble on the standing of the researcher, his or her past success, and the general plausi-bility of the ideas found in the proposal, while at the same time respond-ing to the promise based on the as-yet-unproven value of the applicant's expertise with regard to this or that new line of research. Not surprisingly in this circumstance, funders may well stipulate what they want, as we have seen in the GKP tendering process and in the U.K. Research Councils' endorsement of interdisciplinary collaboration as a methodological goal.

Almost inevitably, collaboration invites another prospect: that of the synergy that active partnership is bound to generate. We may see collaboration here as akin to the romanticization of dialogue in the promotion of international encounters, in how dialogue "is believed to facilitate not only the idea of a common world, but a good common world—namely a world comprised of ameliorative imagination" (Konrad 2007a, 334, italics removed). Certainly the present policy direction in U.K. government-sponsored research takes as self-evident the inherent creativeness of synergy, a common good that is also a condition for innovation (Leach 2004). So synergy is not left to unfold unaided. It is frequently written into the aims and objectives of a project as a driver, which will bring a return straightaway. This is what collaboration appears to promise: for, in the present rhetorical moment of the proposal, institutional and funding expectations focus on the future moment of getting the mix of expertises together. The advantages and benefits of assembling people from diverse backgrounds anticipate an outcome that is brought forward as an aim.[11] After all, synergy is otherwise an odd virtue to plan for. It either does or does not happen. Yet there has emerged a widely shared expectation that interaction as such is an achievement that will have spin-off effects.[12] Perhaps this is the optimism of the managerial approach to knowledge making (Deem, Hillyard, and Reed 2007, 24; see also Strathern 2006a) or, more generally, of the "politics of protention [i.e., projections or anticipations]" found in commercial fields (Born 2007). Bringing together different kinds of expertise—or of whatever other forms the partnership takes—holds a *promise* of synergy. Here, then, is *speculative synergy*. Question marks (about the outputs of an interdisciplinary project) at once turn into plus signs.

I borrow the epithet "speculative" from anthropologist Sunder Rajan (2006), who has used it to characterize the contemporary fields of biotechnology and genomics as offering a "strategic promissory horizon" in

11. Outcomes become aims the way measures become targets (Hoskin 1996). Rip (2000, 467) analyzes the problems for potential funders in assessing what has not yet been done, for which he depicts various scenarios. The difficulties of specifying social encounters in advance come to a head in ethics protocols; see Lederman et al. 2006 on working practices borrowed here from disciplines outside social science.

12. Interaction thereby participates in the cultural nexus of communication for its own sake, networking for its own sake, and so forth (e.g., Agar, Green, and Harvey 2002). It is also well embedded in a management ethos that puts social relations to the fore (e.g., Wheatley 2002, 7).

which biocapital fuels a twenty-first-century speculative form of capitalism (Sunder Rajan, 2006, 113; on biocapital, see, e.g., Franklin 2003, 2007).[13] In the sphere of biocapital, value is created in the promise of things to come: in a market that literally consists in promissory statements from firms against which investment is raised. Sunder Rajan writes that promissory marketing generates "value in the present to make a certain kind of future possible, [for] a vision of that future has to be sold, even if it is a vision that will never be realized" (2006, 115–16). It is as though the speculative marketplace were one huge funding proposal! In the marketplace of biocapital, what matters is how things are described and how elements are put into place to realize the promise. Similarly, in academia, the very securing of collaborators to work together on a project enacts the hope for a future outcome, a hope pinned to the temporality of combination. Here will be the moment of mixing that, although designated as no more than a prelude to the actual research subsequently to be undertaken, looms large in a project's promissory value.[14]

For Sunder Rajan, promissory biocapital futures constitute a speculative marketplace that is tied (in ways that he considers shifting and variable) both to exchange values and to normative or ethical values (2006, 41). Even so, in his view, there is an accounting. For biotechnology enterprises, successful returns on investment are evident (or otherwise) both in the immediate finance market and in marketable goods downstream from the point of manufacture. Further, futuristic discourse, colloquially known as "hype," serves "as a discursive mode of calling on the future to account for the present" (Sunder Rajan 2006, 116). In this sense, hype is about credibility, and where marketplace credibility is concerned, investor relations and public relations are crucial. In academia, however, where investors are research councils or government agencies, one deals not only with demonstrating immediate value for money in terms of accountability to the taxpayer (Miller 2003, 2005)—as well as of downstream publica-

---

13. There is a large literature on speculation in the critical study of financial markets, into which anthropology has begun to make inroads (Miyazaki 2007). Franklin (2007, 47; see also 2003, 7, 9–10) notes Thompson's use of "promissory capital" in relation to "bio-futures markets in health, regenerative medicine and stem cell manufacture"; she refers both to Thompson's 2005 monograph and to an unpublished 2000 paper, "Biotech Mode of Reproduction." Helmreich (2008) situates these usages within a wider intellectual history of "biocapital."

14. Not only does the very open-endedness that characterized the GKP's approach to the independent flowering of everyone's enterprises offer a research model of a management enterprise, but, I might add, it also affords us an example of a management model of speculative synergy. For academia, Deem, Hillyard, and Reed (2007) sketch out the terrain of manager-academics.

tions or reports—but also with credibility as evidenced by the engagement or endorsement of other researchers or by the interest of the public (Hirsch 2004).[15]

There have been strong statements about how hard interdisciplinary knowledge making in particular is to evaluate after the event as well as before. Perhaps we can now understand some of this difficulty as due to the fact that what is under assessment is not simply the outcome of collaborative projects but the peculiar power associated with interdisciplinarity itself. Because what is to be judged in retrospect was laid out in prospect, it is almost as though synergy itself, and not just the objective to which the collaborative enterprise was directed, should show a return. Speculative synergy indeed! But from whence comes the measure of that result? The answer is not at all clear.

I will leave altogether aside here two sets of factors that bear on the evaluation of synergy: first, normative concerns about the possible degree of epistemic impact that relate to the difficulties of measuring the "amount" of interdisciplinary engagement discernible in a project (e.g., Mansilla and Gardner 2003; Rhoten 2003); and, second, the logical inhibition against evaluating a narrative that cannot be rendered singular (Strathern 2006a). A third set of factors can also militate against measuring synergy: these arise when synergy itself is used as a measure. This problem emerges when interdisciplinary collaboration becomes a criterion for the evaluation of other things, notably the appropriate management of knowledge (Strathern 2004, 79). Indeed, I have elsewhere suggested that involvement in interdisciplinary partnerships can be used—in a judgmental view—as evidence of the ability of researchers in particular disciplines to communicate with researchers in other disciplines and, by extension, with the public. That a judgment of this type will occur may regularly be anticipated, enhancing the prospective value of interdisciplinary collaboration. However, the prospective orientation of the rhetoric of synergy itself points to a fourth problem with taking synergy as a yardstick. An evaluation of yet another kind may well have already occurred at the outset of an interdisciplinary project, even if elided from the ledger of the project's apparent promissory capital. Let me spell out this fourth point in some detail.

Because there is very little interest from outside bodies in the promulgation of the actual research itself, colleagues' experiences of externally funded research projects in social science have been that much measure-

---

15. Rip 2000 examines European and U.S. funding bodies and sketches different scenarios of evaluation.

ment takes place downstream in terms of publication or similar outputs. Notable exceptions are public presentations during the course of a project, in the genre of the interdisciplinary seminar, conference, or workshop, such as those that the GKP mounted. These are moments of performance, whether for an internal or an external audience, and what is being performed is, if not exactly collaboration, interaction. Such interaction is generally presented in a stylized way, with individual contributions reflecting the involvement of individuals in the project, often under the rhetoric of papers "speaking to one another." Behind the papers may or may not lie other collaborative work. To be sure, persons giving public presentations are normally under scrutiny; yet when they are also contributors to an interdisciplinary exercise, there may well be questions that they are asking *of themselves* in this role because they may well imagine that others—including other presenters—are asking the same questions too. Not the question, *Is this work really interdisciplinary?* That is, will its arguments persuade this or that camp; will its originality be recognized; will its intellectual genealogy be evident?—all questions one can ask of disciplines. But, *Will this work fit in?*—what difference or contribution will it make; will it be understood at all? Success during the day of the performance can provide some indication of the answer.

In these situations, the attitude of the presenters is as likely to take the form of anxiety as it is of a readiness to be open to stimulus and information from unexpected quarters. Either affective stance entails an evaluation of what it means to be engaging with and thus partnering with others under an explicit interdisciplinary umbrella. Perhaps the day of the performance will *not* bring success. Does facing this personal predicament point to one of the consequences of speculating in the promise of synergy? *Is disappointment not a counterpart to hope?*

Germane here is Miyazaki's thesis about hope as "a methodological problem for knowledge" (2004, 2).[16] The problem, very simply, is that the after-the-fact acknowledgment of hope in scholarly descriptions of people's expectations prevents or occludes conveying its prospective momentum.

---

16. Miyazaki's argument is that the anthropologist, when studying social practices predicated on hope, requires a method that resists viewing those practices retrospectively, as finished results, because this perspective effaces the temporality of these practices—"the prospective momentum entailed in anticipation of what has not-yet become" (2004, 14). Drawing on Ernst Bloch and Walter Benjamin, Miyazaki writes: "moments of hope can only be apprehended as other moments of hope; any attempts to objectify these moments and turn them into outcomes of some process, as both philosophy and history tend to do, are destined to fail to capture the temporality of these moments" (2004, 23).

Hope is thus a problem "for the retrospective character of contemplative knowledge" (2004, 10). The problem is as acute with regard to feelings of disappointment. Hope can be deferred, reinvented; disappointment, in being overtly retrospective, conceals the preemptive nature of any judgment that anticipated how expectations would *not* be fulfilled. The problem for knowledge would be how to know what effect such (concealed) anticipation might have had on the outcome. Empirical evidence suggests that interdisciplinary projects are particularly prone to being regarded as only patchily successful and that, in some cases, *negative evaluations appear in play from the outset.* Researchers may embark on a collaborative enterprise while being skeptical about the likely impact of some of the contributions in a disciplinary sense.

If so, how would one know that such a prospective negative evaluation had been made? Miyazaki and Riles (2005, 325) speak of an "endpoint" as the moment when a project becomes apprehended, retrospectively, as an epoch closed. At an endpoint, failure of knowledge—with regard to financial markets, in the cases that Miyazaki and Riles study—can be made known and acknowledged. Yet in academia, explicitly interdisciplinary projects allow for closure that is only patchy. At the outset of a project, researchers and their managers are hardly in a position to declare that they are more confident about some parts of an enterprise than others. However, during the course of a project quite as much as at its formal end, an identifiable shortfall may turn into a tool for public evaluation, becoming a mark of internal criticism to the benefit of the rest of a project. That is, disappointment in some elements of the project can work to reinforce hope in other elements. It could be, for instance, that in a project that brings together researchers from different disciplinary backgrounds, some contributors are a priori thought to be more useful than others, whereas other researchers become gradually marginalized or themselves fall prey to doubts about what they thought they had to offer since their contributions appear to have been dismissed in advance. Indeed, these researchers might think it was only for rhetorical reasons—for the comprehensiveness of a project or the importance of its being seen to take this or that added dimension into account—that they were included at all. But how would one know? The temporality of prospective judgment is what I referred to above as the fourth principal difficulty for evaluating the success of synergy.

I am brought to this last set of observations here by reflecting on the "marginalization" of social science in interdisciplinary endeavors that has been reported by some observers[17]—and perhaps "marginalization" is not too strong a word to use for the fate of sociology in the GKP. Suppose that we now situate this outcome in the larger context I have described in this section. In examining knowledge making in the contemporary era, we should take into account projects where hope for interdisciplinary engagement lies ahead as well as those where the value of interdisciplinarity, or the value of some component of the interdisciplinary enterprise, is questioned from the outset in a covert judgment that is recoverable only in retrospect.[18] To understand the outcomes of interdisciplinary projects, I suspect, it is essential to view these two enactments in tandem—to acknowledge hope and disappointment as two sides of the same promissory coin. For the question marks that such projects raise may turn, as it were, to minus as well as plus signs.[19]

Further Difficulties for Social Science:
The Future and the Social

The prospective negative evaluation of social science at the GKP would appear to be part and parcel of a more general tendency for certain social science disciplines to disappoint nonpractitioners of these disciplines. To understand why this is so, it is instructive to consider some of the epistemological and logical difficulties that may be involved in creating social knowledge and that some of the social science disciplines encounter particularly acutely in interdisciplinary ventures.

While hope and disappointment necessarily accompany proposals and plans for any kind of future enterprise, there are areas of social science that

17. Somekh (2007) writes about the marginalization of social science researchers in the political context of current U.K. government policy formation, where a discourse of common sense discredits knowledge making through research as such. More general is the purported (and to Osborne's mind much exaggerated) eclipse of the social in postmodern knowledge making (Osborne 2002, 177).

18. This is where the model of speculative synergy (in interdisciplinary endeavor) breaks with the speculative marketplace of biocapital. I am not talking about particular calculations of risk, for the risks of an interdisciplinary enterprise need be no different from those entailed in any collaborative research venture. Rather, it is a question of doubt already in place that later comes to the fore (cf. Miyazaki 2007).

19. Value oscillation is discernible in other contexts, for example, when ethical objections to innovations are anticipated, and promissory value is shadowed by likely (public) impact. Further innovations may try to take this into account to bypass the earlier ethical problem. Whether or not this is explicit strategy, the social scientist can see the strategic effect. That technology can "build a degree of management of public opinion into its product" is seemingly part of "seeding a corporate plan for the production of biocapital" (Franklin 2001, 342, 343).

appear to provoke more than their fair share of anticipated disappointment, such as, for example, in the advance evaluation of these disciplines
that is seemingly inscribed into certain institutional programs. If this kind
of temporality raises Miyazaki's general "methodological problem for
knowledge," however, there is a parallel problem specific to the usefulness of much social science. This is the problem that practitioners of other
disciplines voice when they assume (much like government funders) that
present-time studies of social conditions not only must inform and provide
information about the future but can also be extrapolated into the future.
Given these lofty expectations, disappointment seems built into the typically already skeptical attitude—of funders and of knowledge brokers—as
to what nonpredictive social science descriptions have to offer the real
world. After all, much social science research is notoriously a reluctant pre-
dictor of future trends. Arguably, the strength of social science lies precisely
in retrospective reflection; social science illuminates *after* the fact. Indeed,
sociologists and anthropologists might contend, rather strongly, that it is
not futuristic knowledge that will help us in the future but knowledge that
does *not* look future oriented at all and consists, instead, in the ability to
inform about the present (an ability mediated or trained by specific knowledge practices, including practices of observation, interpretation, model
building, and so forth). That is an ability that those in the future are certainly going to need.

So where does this leave social science speculation about the future?
Somekh (2007) supplies the phrase "speculative knowledge" to give social
scientists some encouragement. The phrase evokes the "engaged, oppor-
tunistic and political" means through which researchers in social science,
by building "scenarios of possibility," can have a greater impact on policy
formation and social change than they do at the current time. "Speculative
knowledge creates best guesses for possible futures on the basis of research
into current social practices" (Somekh 2007, 204). The prospect for knowledge of this kind finds a realization of sorts in what Dumit depicts as marketable "venture science" as it presently exists in the United States in regard
to the natural sciences: for here is research that is "promissory, risk-laden
and steeped in the ideology of innovation" (Sunder Rajan 2006, 114, citing
an unpublished essay by Joseph Dumit). Or speculative knowledge may
find realization in the assets that are created by families' expectations for
biological material (see Lepinay's [2007, 547] comment on Thompson's
(2005) discussion of promissory capital). The ways in which the future can
be brought into the present have long been a source of optimism as well as
apprehension, and this is a source that biotechnology nowadays fuels quite

directly (see, e.g., Konrad 2005). Expectations for (technological) development in general create prospective structures that lack nothing but activation (see van Lente and Rip 1998). Likewise, the emplacement of future risk scenarios within the present functions as a prudent exercise of the political imagination (see Mallard and Lakoff, chap. 11, this volume). Protentions (as Born [2007] calls them)—that is, projections or anticipations—enable the future to be lived more knowledgeably in the present, imparting a closeness that is not necessarily achieved by predictions as such, since predictions can construe alien worlds from which the present, for the moment, saves us. With speakers on their behalf, with the invitation to act on them, protentions become promises.

If social science demonstrates its capacity to bring forth future-oriented speculative knowledge when researchers imagine what societal developments might turn out to be important or interesting, however, social scientists' dominant methodological commitment to producing knowledge of the present nevertheless appears rhetorically at odds with that form of continuous speculation that seeks to realize value now by making future visions present. I have used synergy in collaborative practices as an example of this form of speculation: the future is made present at the moment when the collaboration is secured, standing as an icon for the promise of interdisciplinary engagement. Indeed, one might say that an emphasis on interdisciplinarity overdetermines the value put not only on collaboration but also on the affects—promise/hope, anxiety/disappointment—that accompany concerns about the outcome of future synergistic interactions. Given this context, what is striking is the way in which social science, when it is brought into interdisciplinary ventures, sometimes appears to dissipate the power of such synergy.

Exacerbating this situation are two further factors that appear to plague present-day efforts to make social science a partner in interdisciplinary endeavors. One is the sheer range of dimensions covered by the possibility of bringing a "social" element into a project. Anyone can have a view on what counts as "social." At the GKP, this problem was encapsulated in the very notion of ELSI—the notion that particular topics have ethical, legal, and social implications. In this setting, "social" covered all kinds of relational and institutional issues that were not included in the GKP's "ethical" and "legal" components, while at the same time the whole ELSI configuration could be interpreted as taking society into account by addressing "social impact." Depending on the context, society may be valorized as an arbiter, an audience, a public needing enlightenment, or an eager policy maker. DuGay (2007, 109, 112) refers to the contemporary obsession in (U.K.)

government circles with society rather than with the state as the source of public policy, as well as to the increasing accountability on the part of public sector institutions to users' groups. (With regard to the United States, DuGay refers to the 1993 National Performance Review, which, in introducing an entrepreneurial management regime, stipulated that primary accountability would not be to the president but to the customer.) Even so, the social scientist in an interdisciplinary forum might well ask, What is or is not referenced as "social"? Is "society" as such herein signaled or not signaled?

These questions lead to the second factor that confounds attempts to bring social science into interdisciplinary ventures. This is the assumption that "society," rather than inherently present as context or background, can be included as an add-on.[20] There is "a sort of in-built redundancy," to use Edwards's phrase,[21] when disciplines are added on to provide a perspective that is thereby rendered extrinsic to the undertaking at hand. Yet this idea of adding on is a widely mobilized construction in present-day discourse on knowledge making. The point is likely to be most irksome for scholars whose home disciplines (sociology, social anthropology) take society as their object of knowledge. (I imagine that this idea does not bother economists, political philosophers, or social psychologists to the same extent.) Indeed, the marginalization that some researchers report in interdisciplinary projects refers principally to practitioners of sociology and social anthropology, where what is meant is "marginalization in advance."[22] For addition also allows subtraction. Built into "adding on" is the implication that the social dimension is an optional extra that can equally well be ignored or discarded—an implication that, when it appears in settings like the GKP, signals a prior evaluation as to the (dispensable) kind of contribution social science practitioners can make. Here are further grounds for anticipated disappointment about social science.

Side by side with these observations about settings such as the GKP, however, it is only right to acknowledge other interdisciplinary contexts that are characterized by less instrumental forms of social knowledge (a

20. The supposition has long been a target of science studies. Franklin (2003, 104–5) summarizes a set of sociological critiques arising from "public understanding of science" programs that are quite explicit on the point that "the social" cannot be considered a realm apart that emerges only at the point of application (of the benefits of science).

21. Jeanette Edwards, University of Manchester, pers. comm., August 23, 2007.

22. I am conscious that the relationship between sociology and anthropology is, or was, very differently placed in the United States than in the United Kingdom—for instance, along the axis of radicalism and conservatism. My understanding of U.S. anthropology has much benefited from Lederman 2005; Segal and Yanagisako 2005.

strong point made by Barry, Born, and Weszkalnys 2008). Here, indeed, are reasons for hope as well as disappointment for the social scientist. Hope comes unexpectedly, for example, from a Japanese financial trader searching for new forms of market knowledge in human relations and then coming "to see social relations as its own object of knowledge" (Miyazaki and Riles 2005, 326; see also Riles 2004). Disappointment, on the other hand, follows recent reports on the de-instrumentalization of "socially robust" knowledge in U.K. government policy thinking, reflected in National Health Service managers lauding "practice-based evidence" over "evidence-based practice," as they increasingly evaluate programs in light of pragmatic experience and local situations that make "sense to people on the ground" (May 2006, 524–25).[23] Requiring no interpretation, such immediately accessible evidence dispenses with the mediation of the social science specialist since, it would seem, one person's experience can speak directly to another's.[24]

Sociologists and anthropologists are all too aware that in studying society they may also be cast as society's spokesmen—as somehow representing society's interests—in interdisciplinary settings, inasmuch as bringing in social science implies "taking society into account." This was true of the GKP, with the promise—laid out in the grant proposal—to "transform information from scientific studies on genetics into knowledge through its validation by critical appraisal, by seeking a patient and public perspective, and by placing it in its ethical, legal and social context." In this kind of situation, social scientists may also be cast in the role of evaluators, their evocation of society holding out promise of an internal audit of the project's activities. At the same time, the social scientist may be regarded as lumbered with or impeded by his or her disciplinary association, so that the discipline finds itself on the line. The case on behalf of the discipline is already prejudged, because in the view of management, project evaluation ought to be a matter of iterative feedback that contributes in an unmediated fashion to ongoing managerial practice—and, accordingly, disappoints when it does not. I have been suggesting that such a prejudging

23. May (2006) studied how policy makers in the United Kingdom assessed the effectiveness of heath and social care delivery systems in the emerging area of "telemedicine" and "telecare." May documents policy makers' growing preference for firsthand evidence from community-based service providers ("practice-based evidence") rather than for the clinical trials that academic researchers developed for use as models for service provision ("evidence-based practice").

24. Coterminously, the production of "socially robust" knowledge itself "has been delegated to university based researchers rather than retained within the apparatus of the state itself" (May 2006, 514).

takes on a special force in the present climate, which encourages a constant orientation to future horizons.

What Kind of Social Knowledge Have These Practices Created?

The introduction to this volume speaks of social knowledge practice sites as locations where "different genres of social knowledge are co-present" and commingle. What is telling, however, about the GKP discussed in this chapter is that, although one of its principal purposes was exactly to provide an arena where this kind of genre cross-fertilization might happen, its day-to-day working practices and assumptions resisted commingling. Still further, the resistance appeared specifically to target social science disciplines, with the "social" in social knowledge reduced simply to a matter of public presentation. Covert and not-so-covert processes of internal evaluation prejudged the probable contributions of the different disciplines involved in the interdisciplinary experiment. These practices sprang from what turned out to be a less-than-experimental situation after all: the GKP management's advance (presumed) knowledge as to how useful certain results were likely to be. This situation led to a double exclusion of social science and its practitioners, at once epistemologically and organizationally. In striving to produce social knowledge, the GKP also produced knowledge socially—albeit without the involvement of some of its social scientists.

This exclusion may have been largely an institutional effect, which might or might not be replicated elsewhere, but a more general conclusion about contemporary knowledge practices comes from the implementation and management of the GKP's proposal to government funding bodies. This effort to manage change in the knowledge production process operated with all the future hype of a grant proposal itself: everything had to succeed. And one could say as well that in academic research, too, the grant proposal appears with all the future hype of change management. Still, however rhetorical the uses that academics and others make of interdisciplinarity, that does not lessen the importance of the practice as a feature of current knowledge production. In this way, the routine and ubiquitous practice of writing funding proposals showcases certain current issues in knowledge making as they involve social scientists. There have been proposals since project grants began, to say nothing of the stating of ideas that served as trial balloons for other initiatives. Yet the early granters of industrial patents knew what they were doing when they licensed, not the idea for an invention, but the idea already embodied in a working artifact, an invention accomplished. In contrast, in academia today, promissory capital and the resulting practices of speculation do not require anything to have been made yet. Proposals have to show enough preliminary substance for funders to trust the promise (Rip and Shove 2000), but ample promise there must also be. What is more, while the example of a genetics knowledge park may seem to overlap the biotechnology field where Sunder Rajan observed the workings of speculative synergy, my impression is that a similar kind of future orientation affects contemporary knowledge practices more broadly and that the promise of biocapital has a general academic counterpart, and that is the promise of interdisciplinarity.

References

Abbott, Andrew. 2001. *Chaos of Disciplines*. Chicago: University of Chicago Press.

Agar, Jon, Sarah Green, and Penny Harvey. 2002. "Cotton to Computers: From Industrial to Information Revolutions." In *Virtual Society? Technology, Cyberbole, Reality*, edited by S. Woolgar, 264–85. Oxford: Oxford University Press.

Barry, Andrew, Georgina Born, and Gisa Weszkalnys. 2008. "Logics of Interdisciplinarity." *Economy and Society* 37:20–49.

Born, Georgina. 2007. "Future-Making: Corporate Performativity and the Temporal Politics of Markets." In *Cultural Politics in a Global Age: Uncertainty, Solidarity and Innovation*, edited by D. Held and H. Moore, 288–95. London: Oneworld.

Brenneis, Don. 2006. "Reforming Promise." In *Documents: Artifacts of Modern Knowledge*, edited by A. Riles, 41–70. Ann Arbor: University of Michigan Press.

Cohen-Cole, Jamie. 2003. "Thinking about Thinking in Cold War America." PhD diss., Princeton University.

Deem, Rosemary, Sam Hillyard, and Mike Reed. 2007. *Knowledge, Higher Education, and the New Managerialism*. Oxford: Oxford University Press.

Department of Health. 2002. *The Genetics Knowledge Parks Network—Overview*. London: Department of Health.

DuGay, Paul. 2007. *Organising Identity*. London: Sage Publications.

Franklin, Sarah. 2001. "Culturing Biology: Cell Lines for the Second Millennium." *Health* 5:335–54.

———. 2003. "Ethical Biocapital: New Strategies of Cell Culture." In *Remaking Life and Death: Towards an Anthropology of the Biosciences*, edited by S. Franklin and M. Lock, 97–127. Santa Fe, NM: School of American Research Press.

———. 2007. *Dolly Mixtures: The Remaking of Genealogy*. Durham, NC: Duke University Press.

Helmreich, Stefan. 2008. "Species of Biocapital." *Science as Culture* 17:463–78.

Hirsch, Eric. 2004. "Boundaries of Creation: The Work of Credibility in Science and Ceremony." In *Transactions and Creations: Property Debates and the Stimulus of Melanesia*, edited by E. Hirsch and M. Strathern, 176–92. Oxford: Berghahn Books.

Hoskin, Keith. 1996. "The 'Awful Idea of Accountability': Inscribing People into the Measurement of Objects." In *Accountability: Power, Ethos and the Technologies of Managing*, edited by R. Munro and J. Mouritsen, 263–82. London: International Thomson Business Press.

Khlinovskaya Rockhill, Elena. 2007. "On Interdisciplinarity and Models of Knowledge Production." *Social Analysis* 51:121–47.

Khlinovskaya Rockhill, Elena, and Marilyn Strathern. 2005. "Interdisciplinarity and the Cambridge Genetics Knowledge Park." Paper presented to CGKP Annual Symposium, Hinxton, U.K.

Konrad, Monica. 2005. *Narrating the New Predictive Genetics: Ethics, Ethnography and Science*. Cambridge: Cambridge University Press.

———. 2007a. "International Biodiplomacy and Global Ethical Forms: Relations of Critique between Public Anthropology and Science in Society." *Anthropological Quarterly* 80:313–53.

———. 2007b. "Placebo Politics: On Comparability, Interdisciplinarity and International Collaborative Research." *Monash Bioethics Review* 25:67–84.

Leach, James. 2004. "Modes of Creativity." In *Transactions and Creations: Property Debates and the Stimulus of Melanesia*, edited by E. Hirsch and M. Strathern, 151–75. Oxford: Berghahn Books.

Lederman, Rena. 2005. "Unchosen Grounds: Cultivating Cross-Subfield Accents for a Public Voice." In *Unwrapping the Sacred Bundle: Reflections on the Disciplining of Anthropology*, edited by D. Segal and S. Yanagisako, 49–77. Durham, NC: Duke University Press.

Lederman, Rena, et al. 2006. "IRBs, Bureaucratic Regulation, and Academic Freedom." *American Ethnologist* 33:477–548.

Lepinay, Vincent-Antonin. 2007. "Economy of the Germ: Capital, Accumulation and Vibration." *Economy and Society* 36:526–48.

Mansilla, Veronica Boix, and Howard Gardner. 2003. "Assessing Interdisciplinary Work at the Frontier: An Empirical Exploration of 'Symptoms of Quality.'" In *Rethinking Interdisciplinarity*, moderated by C. Heintz and G. Origgi. http://www.interdisciplines.org. Accessed April 11, 2011.

May, Carl. 2006. "Mobilising Modern Facts: Health Technology Assessment and the Politics of Evidence." *Sociology of Health and Illness* 5:513–32.

May, Carl, and Nicola Ellis. 2001. "When Protocols Fail: Technical Evaluation, Biomedical Knowledge, and the Social Production of 'Facts' about a Telemedicine Clinic." *Social Science and Medicine* 53:989–1002.

Miller, Daniel. 2003. "The Virtual Moment." *Journal of the Royal Anthropological Institute*, n.s., 9:57–75.

———. 2005. "What Is Best 'Value'? Bureaucracy, Virtualism and Local Governance." In *The Values of Bureaucracy*, edited by P. Du Gay, 233–54. Oxford: Oxford University Press.

Miyazaki, Hirokazu. 2004. *The Method of Hope: Anthropology, Philosophy, and Fijian Knowledge*. Stanford, CA: Stanford University Press.

———. 2007. "Between Arbitrage and Speculation: An Economy of Belief and Doubt." *Economy and Society* 36:396–415.

Miyazaki, Hirokazu, and Annelise Riles. 2005. "Failure as an Endpoint." In *Global Assemblages: Technology, Politics, and Ethics as Anthropological Problems*, edited by A. Ong and S. Collier, 320–31. Oxford: Blackwell.

Osborne, Thomas. 2002. "History, Theory, Disciplinarity." In *The Social in Question: New Bearings in History and the Social Sciences*, edited by P. Joyce, 175–90. London: Routledge.

———. 2003. "'Against Creativity': A Philistine Rant." *Economy and Society* 32:507–25.

Rhoten, Diana. 2003. "A Multi-method Analysis of the Social and Technical Conditions for Interdisciplinary Collaboration." Abstract. *Hybrid vigor*. Final Report. National Science Foundation. Cited with permission. http://www.hybridvigor.net/interdis/pubs/hv_pub_interdis-2003.09.29.pdf. Accessed May 24, 2011.

Riles, Annelise. 2004. "Real Time: Unwinding Technocratic and Anthropological Knowledge." *American Ethnologist* 31:392–405.

———. 2006. "[Deadlines]: Removing the Brackets on Politics in Bureaucratic and Anthropological Analysis." In *Documents: Artifacts of Modern Knowledge*, edited by A. Riles, 71–92. Ann Arbor: University of Michigan Press.

Rip, Arie. 2000. "Higher Forms of Nonsense." *European Review* 8:467–86.

Rip, Arie, and Elizabeth Shove. 2000. "Users and Unicorns: A Discussion of Mythical Beasts." *Science and Public Policy* 27:175–82.

Segal, Daniel, and Sylvia Yanagisako, eds. 2005. *Unwrapping the Sacred Bundle: Reflections on the Disciplining of Anthropology*. Durham, NC: Duke University Press.

Somekh, Bridget. 2007. "Last Words: Speculative Knowledge." In *Knowledge Production: Research Work in Interesting Times*, edited by B. Somekh and T. Schwandt, 197–207. London: Routledge.

Strathern, Marilyn. 2004. *Commons and Borderlands: Working Papers on Interdisciplinarity, Accountability and the Flow of Knowledge*. Wantage: Sean Kingston.

———. 2006a. "A Community of Critics: Thoughts on New Knowledge." *Journal of the Royal Anthropological Institute*, n.s., 12:191–209.

———. 2006b. "Useful Knowledge." Isaiah Berlin Lecture, British Academy. *Proceedings of the British Academy* 139:73–109.

Strathern, Marilyn, and Elena Khlinovskaya Rockhill. 2007. "Cascade Effect: Unexpected Consequences and an Unanticipated Outcome." Paper presented to symposium "Interdisciplinarity and Society," convened by Andrew Barry, Georgina Born, Gisa Weszkalnys, University of Oxford.

Sunder Rajan, Kaushik. 2006. *Biocapital: The Constitution of Postgenomic life*. Durham, NC: Duke University Press.

THES. 2007. *The Times Higher Education Supplement*. London: Times Newspapers.

Thompson, Charis. 2005. *Making Parents: The Ontological Choreography of Reproductive Technologies*. Cambridge, MA: MIT Press.

van Lente, Harro, and Arie Rip. 1998. "Expectations in Technological Developments: An Example of Prospective Structures to Be Filled in by Agency." In *Getting New Technologies Together: Studies in Making Sociotechnical Order*, edited by C. Disco and B. van der Meulen, 203–29. Berlin: Walter de Gruyter.

Wheatley, Margaret. 2002. "Can Knowledge Management Succeed Where Other Efforts Have Failed?" In *Knowledge Management: Classic and Contemporary Works*, edited by D. Morey, M. Maybury, and B. Thuraisingham, 3–8. Cambridge, MA: MIT Press.

Wilsdon, James, and Rebecca Willis. 2004. *See-through Science: Why Public Engagement Needs to Move Upstream*. London: Demos.

PART THREE

Social Knowledge beyond the Academy

NINE

Subjects of Persuasion

Survey Research as a Solicitous Science;
or, The Public Relations of the Polls

SARAH E. IGO

"To know America, tell America." "You can know your country only if your country knows you." With these words, crafted by a newly established Public Relations Division, the Bureau of the Census set out in 1940 to tally the U.S. population. That the oldest official survey in the nation required a public relations drive is itself striking. But still more intriguing are the terms in which the bureau attempted to persuade a hesitant citizenry to take part in its work. Sounding the notes of trust, representation, and social benefit, the census campaign suggested that there was something to gain from divulging personal information: that answering surveyors' questions was a necessary and even virtuous path toward collective self-knowledge. The data that resulted could aid in national planning and inform public policy. Just as importantly, they could help citizens to see their country better, their composite answers providing a "photograph of important phases of national and local life." Pamphlets urging "This is *your* 1940 census" showcased the effort's democratic purpose, one that afforded "an opportunity for almost everyone to participate in a national enterprise" (Thomson 1940, 315, 313).

The slogans of the Census Bureau portrayed official data collection as individual acts of voluntarism and equated standardized responses with civic participation.[1] As such, the publicity campaign hints at some of the unique problems entailed in gathering data from human respondents. It also gestures to some of the tactics that social scientists have employed to solve those problems. Taking survey research as a particularly illuminating case of a larger social scientific dilemma, this chapter inquires into the

---

1. Indeed, the bureau acknowledged that "emphasis on the cooperative, publicly approved character of the census required minimizing emphasis on the compulsory aspects of census procedures" (Thomson 1940, 313).

ways social investigation is marked by its dependence on the consent and cooperation of its research specimens.

My questions are straightforward: By what methods have social researchers attempted to procure data from their subjects? And with what ramifications for their craft? I will argue that *persuasion* is one crucial, if nearly always unspoken and invisible, practice that social investigators rely on in gaining access to relevant research materials, making theirs a solicitous science. When thinking about the human sciences especially, if not uniquely, we must therefore take an expansive view of what counts as a knowledge-making practice. We must pay attention not simply to experimental or statistical design but to how investigators get individuals to walk into a laboratory, submit to a survey, or even grant that the research at stake is worthwhile. After all, for the interview, experiment, and questionnaire to operate as successful knowledge-making instruments, first there must be willing subjects.

Long gone are the days when it was plausible to imagine that scientists simply "happen upon" the raw materials from which they produce their findings. Several generations of scholars in science studies have demonstrated, often in intricate detail, how physicists, biologists, astronomers, and geologists help summon their research materials into being in order to extract new knowledge. At the most literal, this process can involve the creation of the research object itself: biologists' model organisms (Creager, Lunbeck, and Wise 2007)—genetically standardized specimens such as the JAX mouse or *Drosophila* fly (Rader 2004; Kohler 1994)—or nuclear physicists' elaboration of the quark (Pickering 1984).[2] The titles of key works, such as Karen Rader's *Making Mice* and Andrew Pickering's *Constructing Quarks*, pointedly emphasize the artificiality of these entities, which would not exist without scientific intervention. Similar processes are at work in the "alignment" of scientific instruments, techniques, conditions, and materials that together make, for example, the branch of cancer research based on oncogenes "doable" (Fujimura 1987; see also Knorr Cetina 1999).

Scientists, we have learned, not only shape the materials they work on and with. Their science is also shaped by the material culture in which they are embedded, and especially the limitations that certain materials

2. Kohler writes: "experimental creatures are a special kind of technology in that they are altered environmentally or physically to do things that humans value but that they might not have done in nature. Some are dramatically designed and constructed: the 'standard' organisms . . . that most resemble spectrophotometers, bubble chambers, ultracentrifuges, and other physical instruments" (1994, 6).

place on scientists' practices and theories. The very "thingness" of worms and mountains, light beams and electrons, microbes and microscopes, helps to constrain and resist scientific prerogatives (e.g., see Kohler 2002 on the constraints posed by field science). A fertile middle ground—where the natural world is conceived of as neither a blank slate acted upon by investigators nor littered with intact, unpliable stuff—has opened up for sociological, ethnographic, and historical excavations into how scientific knowledge is made, illuminating complex, recursive negotiations between researcher and researched.

Surprisingly, much less attention has been paid to this deeply symbiotic relationship in the social and human sciences. This is so even though it is a relationship that has vexed the U.S. Census Bureau and in fact any undertaking that necessarily relies on its peculiar sort of raw material. In other words, although the challenge of dealing with human subjects is absolutely central to practitioners' concerns in the fields of social psychology, anthropology, sociology, and survey research, it has until recently merited little sustained discussion by those interested in the production of social knowledge.[3]

It is not only *access* to individuals that concerns social researchers, although ensuring that respondents actually respond and that those under investigation agree to be investigated is a key, underappreciated aspect of social knowledge making. Subject pools in psychology departments, cash or other sorts of payment for participation, and the creation of "focus groups" all point to this fragile dependence on volunteered data. It is also the problematic *nature* of human beings as research material that prompts recurring doubts as to whether social scientific work is "real" science, always threatening to undercut its bids for scholarly respectability and its claims to resemble the harder sciences (see Solovey 2004). Compared with the objects of natural science, human subjects seem especially unstable as a resource for making knowledge because of their abilities to lie, withdraw, exaggerate, hide, forget, and otherwise taint the data that are sought from them. To take just one example, social psychological experiments have long provoked concerns about the self-selection bias introduced by volunteers, the failure of experimental deception to dupe supposedly naïve subjects, and the distorting effects of researcher-subject rapport (see Rosenthal and Rosnow 1975; Morawski 2005, 2010).

Indeed, at first glance, the college sophomores who are the research ma-

3. Emblematic are major histories of survey research such as Converse 1987 and Platt 1996, which provide thorough accounts of the development of statistical techniques and questionnaire methods but make almost no mention of the methods employed to recruit subjects—making clear, in fact, that they do not consider these to be research methods at all.

terial of choice for many social psychological experiments and the rural villagers subject to anthropologists' observations may seem utterly unlike particles, genomes, or even mice. Philosopher Ian Hacking has made just such a claim, arguing that the "human kinds" (such as child abusers, multiple personalities, or the unemployed) studied by sociologists or psychologists are fundamentally different from the "natural kinds" (gold, electrons, or tigers) investigated by the hard sciences. Because people are conscious of the ways they are described, he reasons, the very act of classification leads to feedback that can create or alter the object under investigation (Hacking 1986, 1995; for a similar, earlier argument, see Adorno [1957] 1976). As one of Hacking's interpreters puts it, "in a nutshell, homosexuals respond to being studied, spiders and copper do not" (Cooper 2004, 74). That human subjects could confound researchers' experimental designs—altering their behavior simply as a consequence of being studied—was a social scientific truism by the mid-twentieth century, so much so that the phenomenon had its own name: the "Hawthorne effect" (Gillespie 1991). For different reasons, of course, special research ethics and federal regulations emerged for the treatment of human subjects, first in medical and then in social scientific settings (see Lederer 1997; Rothman 1991; Schrag 2010; Stark, forthcoming; Weindling 2004).

Even if one concedes the basic point, one ought not overstate the divergence between the natural and social sciences with respect to the sorts of entities they probe. One of the broad areas of agreement in science studies is that investigators of all stripes actively work on the resources they investigate, transforming them in dramatic or subtle ways in the process. The raw materials of sociology may be more or less tractable than those of physics, but in this one aspect, at least, they have something in common. It is also worth noting that, not unlike laboratory mice, participants in interviews, experiments, or questionnaire studies must be standardized, up to a point, to be usable. Whether in political polling or economic modeling, the data taken from one individual need to be made equivalent to, or at least commensurable with, those taken from another. And, as in the natural sciences, the social and behavioral sciences must convincingly generalize: the views of "representative" individuals measured in an attitude scale are meant to stand in for those of a larger group (sometimes even "human beings" in general), just as one electron's behavior is usually considered able to stand in for all.

My interest, then, is not in demonstrating that a reliance on human subjects makes the "softer" sciences a qualitatively different enterprise than the natural sciences. What I do want to point out is that gaining access to the raw materials from which much social knowledge is made—individual people's words, actions, beliefs, and behaviors—poses special challenges that have not been adequately attended to in science studies or standard accounts of the sociology of knowledge. These are in the first instance problems of participation and trust, issues that in the main do not affect quarks or flies. A related problem is that, in some cases, the subjects of social scientific research themselves can cast doubt on the validity of the data they are instrumental in providing and even the overall research project in which they are enlisted. Again, it is difficult to conceive of an analogous situation in the natural sciences.

These characteristic dilemmas of working with human subjects must be managed in order for social research to proceed. This is where public relations tactics like those of the 1940 Census Bureau come into play. Of all the possible means of procuring social data, I will emphasize just these strategies of persuasion. I do so primarily because of the chasm between the centrality of these techniques to workaday social investigation and their absence from scholarly accounts of it.[4]

Certainly, builders of supercolliders and advocates for cancer therapies also engage in campaigns to garner public or government support for their research. The difference is that they do not generally aim these efforts at their potential research subjects. What is worth underscoring is the solicitous attitude social researchers must often adopt toward their own "raw materials." (Even the quotation marks with which I have surrounded those words point to the delicate concern with which social investigators treat their specimens. It is no longer considered good practice to address human subjects as research objects; rather, the terms "participants" and "volunteers" are employed.) This solicitousness, necessary to compile data, not only inflects social scientific rhetoric but also consumes a good deal of practitioners' time and energy. And the results of such cajoling are mixed, inviting both wanted and unwanted engagement of laypeople with the research process.

Because of the high degree of consent it entails, survey research offers one of the clearest examples of the solicitous interplay of researcher and subject in

4. A major exception is in studies of the biomedical sciences, which lie somewhere between scholarship on the natural and the human sciences. Scholars have begun to examine recruitment tactics for clinical trials (especially for "hard-to-recruit" populations) as well as to probe the ethics and effects of the regime of "informed consent." For excellent examples, see Epstein 2007, 2008; Fisher 2007; Reardon 2006.

the human sciences. It is also worth considering because the sample survey has become one of the most familiar—and protean—routes for producing empirical social knowledge. Defined by the statistical relationship between a selected sample and the entire universe of possible subjects, it has been hailed as "arguably the single most important methodological development and contribution of twentieth-century social science" (House et al. 2004, 453). The sample survey is one of the "new technologies of mass feedback," or systems for monitoring the population's wants and desires, that emerged during the early twentieth century (Beniger 1986, 376; see also Converse 1987). In the ensuing decades survey techniques were seized upon by governments as well as demographers, political campaign strategists, public policy institutes, economists, activists, and advertisers. Survey-based social science has been brought to bear on an almost bewildering array of problems, from financial expectations to pedagogical effectiveness, and from sexual habits to military morale. As such, it—and the corresponding imperative to extract reliable data from human respondents—is critical to the normal operating procedures of all manner of social and political institutions.

Let us now return briefly to the 1940 U.S. census campaign, because it begins to suggest what is peculiar about much survey research: that "the public," the ostensible object of data collectors, functions also as a participant in, and sometimes audience for, that same research. Knowledge of the citizenry was the central goal of the Census Bureau, but citizens were also billed as helpful volunteers and as parties interested in its findings. In the words of its rather wishful publicists, not only were census results "universally accepted as accurate," but they were also "universally demanded for the purposes of the people." The census queries "were the people's questions, selected because of popular demand, and useful to throw light on the people's business" (Thomson 1940, 313, 317).

This imagined horizontal relationship between researchers and their objects—and between subjects and their own scientific representation (here, the citizenry and its statistical portrait)—is rather unusual in the history of scientific investigation. At least rhetorically, it alters the hierarchical terms of investigator and investigated, scientist and subject. And it begins to blur the clear line between the producers and consumers of social knowledge. These moves are characteristic, I will argue, of knowledge-making practices that require the robust consent of their research materials.

To secure human data, survey research enterprises have often presented themselves as inclusive, responsive, and even "democratic." First, participation in surveys is voluntary, it is stressed, their primary purpose not governance or control but objective knowledge "about ourselves." Second, survey data are described as representing the public and clarifying its desires—and, as a corollary, making government officials or corporations responsive to them. Implicit in the measurement of mass opinion, that is, is an argument for heeding it. Third, unlike many types of scientific knowledge, the results of surveys are regularly intended, not simply for their social scientific creators or policy makers, but for the public at large. Accordingly, survey techniques (and their results) are broadcast to the very individuals who are also their putative subjects.[5] Fourth, surveys, which create knowledge out of the aggregated responses of anonymous individuals, treat the attitudes of all respondents as equivalent, bestowing each citizen's preferences—at least in the abstract—with identical weight.

In the middle decades of the twentieth century, such democratic arguments and related public relations work were crucial in legitimizing the best-known sort of sample survey: the modern opinion poll. Judging by the strenuous efforts of its inventors, persuasion was at the very core of this novel form of social knowledge. Potential respondents had to be coaxed not only to take part in doorstep interviews conducted by strangers but also to believe in techniques such as statistical sampling and to place their trust in the larger social good of the surveying project. Looking back at the public relations campaigns surrounding the opinion poll at the moment of its introduction reveals that "the people" were conceived of not just as the subject of research but as subjects of persuasion—and perhaps the most intractable problem for a new and ambitious social scientific field.

Pioneered in the United States by George Gallup, Elmo Roper, and Archibald Crossley, "scientific" opinion polls were a key episode—in fact, by some lights, *the* key episode—in the use and popularization of the modern sample survey (Frankel and Frankel 1987).[6] The three pollsters, and opinion polling itself, made their entrance onto the national stage in 1936. Publicly challenging conventional wisdom and the famous straw poll conducted by the *Literary Digest*, each employed new statistical methods that permitted a small sample of carefully selected respondents to stand in for the entire U.S. electorate. And each correctly predicted Franklin Roosevelt

---

5. Of course, this particular characteristic of much public survey research is absent from private survey research such as marketing studies.

6. The remaining sections of this chapter draw some of their analysis and illustrative evidence from Igo 2007.

as the victor over the favored Alfred Landon in the presidential contest of that year.

Gallup's American Institute for Public Opinion and Roper's *Fortune* Survey quickly moved beyond the electoral field, discovering a ready market for syndicated opinion polls on a broad range of topics: labor unions and wartime mobilization, taxation policies and working women. Their goal was tallying not simply the external characteristics but rather "the subjective propensities of collectivities of citizens" (Osborne and Rose 1999, 373). To accomplish this, they peered more deeply into the population than had earlier surveyors, a practice both unfamiliar and unsettling to their potential respondents. The questions put to scattered, anonymous individuals would disclose, in the words of George Gallup, a "week-by-week picture of what Americans are thinking" (Gallup 1940a, 23).

In their 1940 public relations tract for polling, *The Pulse of Democracy*, Gallup and his collaborator, Saul Forbes Rae, laid out the rationale for and techniques underwriting their new science. Asking "What is the common man thinking?" they boldly asserted: "The following pages provide a modern answer on the basis, not of guesswork, but of facts. They tell the story of a new instrument—the public opinion poll—and describe how it works to provide a continuous chart of the opinions of the man in the street" (Gallup and Rae 1940, v). Gallup proudly announced that the new polls applied "scientific methods to the old problem of finding out what the people of this free-thinking, free-speaking democracy wish to do with their society" (Gallup 1940a, 23; see also Hogan 1997). From the beginning, the polls were sold—literally, to corporate sponsors and, rhetorically, to the American public—not just as a scientific technology but as a public service.

Gallup's confident pronouncements notwithstanding, public opinion polling posed nettlesome problems for its practitioners. This was because the polls' subjects were also, in large part, the polls' consumers: the fabled "man in the street." To Gallup's disappointment, in 1936 and throughout the next two decades, many Americans proved suspicious of polling's methods and refused to grant truth status to the statistics that resulted, challenging surveyors' carefully built claims to speak for "public opinion." The self-proclaimed scientists of democracy in turn worked continually to shore up laypeople's confidence in their methods, Gallup and Roper both attempting throughout their careers to convince the public of the validity and value of the polls. This turned out to be an uphill battle.

Pollsters depended on the public they surveyed in at least three senses. Americans' views on a broad range of social and political issues were of course the essential raw materials for the new science of opinion. So pollsters first and foremost relied on individuals' release of private data. Second, surveyors' authority as a channel for public opinion flowed from a generalized faith in their techniques, a willingness among their audiences to accept the polls' descriptions of themselves. The public opinion profession, commercially based and not sheltered by an academic establishment, in fact could not exist without a certain amount of public credibility. Finally, because Roper and Gallup relied for their very livelihood on sustained interest in their findings from the corporate buyers of their polls and by extension the people they studied, they depended on the public embrace of their novel queries and data as a worthwhile endeavor. For the same reason, opinion polling was accessible to wide audiences and extremely vulnerable to popular scrutiny. Thus, the public needed not just to be counted. It needed to be courted.

Most obviously, a vital component of surveyors' practice—although less visible than designing questionnaires or devising representative samples—was ensuring that individual citizens were willing to become respondents. This meant fostering participation in actual, as well as potential, subjects. Given that the subject pool of opinion surveys shifted with each new poll and that respondents were, at least in theory, randomly chosen from the entire population, Gallup and Roper needed continually to persuade individuals to submit to their questioning. The foundation for individuals' willingness to answer pollsters' queries was, in Gallup's public statements anyway, "the average American's belief that what he thinks is important; that expressing himself is part of his birthright" (Gallup 1941, 3). Gallup claimed that "nine people in every ten" were willing to talk to pollsters and, moreover, were eager to furnish their opinions (1941, 3). According to him, instances of suspicion or refusal to answer were infrequent. Instead, "the anonymity of the surveys, their fact-finding objectives, and the natural though often shy curiosity which most people feel in their own and in their neighbor's opinions—all these factors dispose the public to cooperate with the surveys" (Gallup and Rae 1940, 158).

The pollster's optimistic view of people's desire to talk to his corps of interviewers was certainly inaccurate, however, in the case of some segments of the public. Nonresponse, a contemporary researcher reported, was "most frequent among poor people, women, and in large cities" (Harding 1944, 119). The problem was familiar enough that pollsters invented new categories of people in order to discuss it: the nonrespondent and the "hard to reach individual" (Rugg 1944, 90–91). Gallup's characterization of eager, voluble volunteers was further undercut by scholarly articles that plumbed the topic of breaking down survey respondents' resistance. An entire literature was spawned by the problem of "refusal," which dwelled on coercing respondents to talk, and to talk truthfully. The "interesting research problem," observed market researcher Alfred Politz, was obtaining honest answers: "Why should a respondent tell the truth to a stranger?" What was needed was research into "how to treat a respondent, how to question him in order to make him tell the truth" (Politz [1948] 1990, 54). Alfred Kinsey, lead investigator of the famous midcentury Sexual Behavior surveys and a party to the same problem as the pollsters, put it this way: "The gathering of the human data would involve the learning of new techniques in which human personalities would be the obstacles to overcome and human memories would be the instruments whose use we would have to master" (Kinsey, Pomeroy, and Martin 1948, 9–10). The element of force implied here was not uncommon. As a 1949 report on electoral polls by the Social Science Research Council explained, "evidence suggests that undecided responses are evasions which can be broken through by persistent questioning" (Mosteller 1949, 287).

As these commentaries suggest, overcoming barriers to obtaining data was not a challenge pollsters alone faced. Many enterprises—social scientific, commercial, and bureaucratic—were coming to depend upon ordinary people's feedback for their functioning. For its part, the 1940 census, hoping to overcome "citizen resistance" to its probing questions, offered individuals "assurances about their personal safety in dealing fairly and frankly with census enumerators" (Thomson 1940, 311, 312). Similarly, opinion pollsters worked assiduously to engender public trust in their doorstep interviews. One Gallup interviewer explained that individual "resistance can be overcome, usually, by understanding the reason for it." Those who were afraid—which accounted for most cases, she noted—could be reassured by the skillful questioner who promised anonymity, explained why the opinion was requested, and "removed" from the respondent "any feeling he may have that what he is going to say may be the wrong thing. He must be made to think that what he is saying is important" (London 1940, 9). Cajoling wary respondents, making them believe their views were both wanted and valuable, was thus as much a part of the interviewer's job as was recording their answers.

Gallup's public relations campaign did not end there. Pollsters' task was not only to gain consent and extract honesty from the respondents they selected but also to explain why some people's views were *not* solicited in their surveys. For their methods to appear legitimate in the public eye, pollsters had to convince those citizens who were not questioned that they too were accounted for in majority and minority percentages.

Even once responses were gathered and tallied, that is, the public could be an uncooperative partner in the survey enterprise. A novel practice at midcentury, opinion surveying did not necessarily fit popular conceptions of what was scientific, leading to countless charges of hocus-pocus and hucksterism from pollsters' presumptive subjects and audiences. In particular, the logic of sampling—the idea that the nation's spectrum of beliefs could be divined from questions put to as few as one thousand people— was never intuitive to many citizens, who saw it not just as implausible but as fundamentally unrepresentative and undemocratic. Charged one political campaigner, "Dr. Gallup's findings are the ouija board variety. Gallup freely admits his poll is based on what he calls 'cross-section sampling' of somewhere between 1,500 and 3,000 people . . . so even at the maximum Gallup polls on the average less than one voter in each county."[7] This method's fundamental dubiousness, it was implied, was so obvious as to require no further rebuttal. Such critics resisted the pollsters' conflation of *some* people—their respondents—with "the people." As one woman wrote to Gallup, "I notice you always say 'The Public' in the headline, but further down in very small print you say the question was put to a carefully selected sample of 1,536 persons. Now, how in the world, by any stretch of the imagination can 1,536 people be termed '*the public*'?"[8] Another writer borrowed the language of the U.S. Constitution to make the case: "obviously, you haven't asked the majority of 'We The People.'"[9]

A related reaction came from those who had never been interviewed by Gallup or Roper and believed that this fact alone gave lie to the polls' claims to representativeness. The pollsters had in fact invited such critique. Given pollsters' many statements extolling the democratic function of their surveys, many Americans found it surprising or even inappropriate that they had never been polled. "I am 48 years old—Have lived in Calif., N.Y., Colo., and Massachusetts and *never* in my long life have I ever known anyone who was quizzed by you or even approached! *Who* do you quizz [*sic*]

7. Quoted in Gallup, "Public Opinion and Depth Materials," speech to the American Association of Public Opinion Research, June 15, 1952, George H. Gallup Papers, Gallup Organization, Princeton, NJ (hereafter GGP).

8. Elinor Nevins to Gallup, undated, GGP.

9. Anonymous to Gallup, 1956, George H. Gallup Papers, University of Iowa Libraries, Iowa City (hereafter GGI).

and where and when??" inquired a woman of Gallup.[10] One man wrote to Elmo Roper after hearing one of his radio broadcasts to ask: "Where do you get your information? I am 44 yrs old and have never been interviewed by a poll taker." He went on to challenge Roper's figures, reasoning that the pollster had not queried anyone like him.[11] The frequency of this complaint makes plain that many citizens did not buy the conceit that a handful of respondents could stand in for their views, much less "public opinion."

In such responses, commonsense understandings of what constituted accurate representation of public opinion clashed with the pollsters' scientific one. The letters that poured into Roper and Gallup's offices testify to individuals' anger at and disbelief in the techniques that produced official-looking majority and minority percentages. One such critic was a Connecticut woman who complained in 1951 that Elmo Roper was "98 per cent wrong" regarding American support for universal military training. He might speak for "a certain group" (she suspected New Yorkers), but certainly not "the American people."[12] That same year, a man from Southern California heard and promptly dismissed Roper's statistics on majority support for the Truman administration versus General MacArthur during the Korean War. "In Los Angeles county," he asserted, "it is 10 to 1 against the administration." He continued: "You will learn that the public is still for [MacArthur]. . . . Your statement tonight about the *People* being of majority opinion on Adm[inistration] policy is your opinion and you should say so."[13] Some lay critics even conducted their own local surveys to challenge poll results. A factory worker who accused Gallup of a bias favoring Republican incumbent Dwight Eisenhower urged him to "clamp your eyes on something true right from our plant. This straw vote was taken yesterday: Ike 3—Democrat 24. . . . Ike *can not get elected*."[14]

Pollsters worried about widespread distrust of their central methodology. "It is exceedingly difficult to convince the public that a sample or a cross-section of the general population can be selected in such a way as to represent with a high degree of accuracy the entire population," Gallup wrote in frustration as early as 1936. "Tell [the average man] that it is possible to select a few hundred or a few thousand persons in his state who rep-

10. Mrs. Robert W.(?) to Gallup, November 11, 1955, GGI.

11. D. J. Stoner to Roper, September 12, 1952, Elmo Roper Papers, Archives and Special Collections, Thomas J. Dodd Research Center, University of Connecticut Libraries, Storrs (hereafter ERP).

12. Eleanor Holmes to Roper, June 6, 1951, ERP.

13. W. C. Hollingworth to Roper, June 3, 1951, ERP.

14. Anonymous to Gallup, 1956, GGI.

resent the divergencies in point of view of the entire voting population of that state, and he will laugh, if he does not swear" (1936, 39). Gallup later confirmed the regularity of this vein of criticism, remarking that the most common query he received was "Why haven't I been interviewed?" (1940a, 24), and this continued to be the case all the way through the late 1950s.

The sheer volume of lay critics forced Gallup and Roper into a defensive position. More significantly, it prompted them to respond publicly and regularly to such skepticism. Polling was a solicitous science not simply because pollsters needed to secure participants for their ongoing surveys. Surveyors also sought public trust in their techniques, a more abstract and complicated form of consent. Through their correspondence, Gallup and Roper were well aware of their problem with the public. Believing that their own careers and profession depended on correcting it, they engaged laypeople, attempted to assuage their concerns, and mounted arduous efforts to educate their consumers and potential subjects about sampling techniques.

Pollsters responded to those dismayed by their exclusion from the polls by emphasizing how rare it was, statistically, to be selected for one of their surveys. A typical reply from Roper's office emphasized "how small are any one individual's chances of being interviewed." To one man who inquired as to why neither he nor any of his professional colleagues had yet been polled, for instance, Roper wrote, "the question you raise is one that often comes up in connection with surveys." He gently explained that the chance of a particular person twenty-one years of age being interviewed by either the *Fortune* Survey or the Gallup Poll by the time that individual turned seventy-seven years old was only one in twenty-seven. Roper went on to assure his correspondent that although he himself had not been interviewed, his "counterpart has been."[15] In such replies by Gallup and Roper alike, pollsters emphasized the interchangeability of respondents and the well-oiled statistical process that chose them. Roper's personal note, however, signaled a respect for laypeople's concerns as well as his need for individuals like this one not just to serve as respondents but also to believe in the resulting statistics.

The pollsters' leading solution to the constant stream of complaints from their consumers, however, was to peddle their trade to the public directly. They laid out in straightforward prose how the polls were constructed in the hope of allaying doubts about their new science. In a real sense, justifying their sampling methods and reassuring their audiences

15. Roper to R. D. Keim, July 19, 1946, ERP. Gallup had a similar stock reply.

became part of Gallup's and Roper's social scientific practice. In his very
first weekly radio broadcast in 1948, an analysis of Americans' views on
food aid to Europe, Roper mused to his audience: "Perhaps you're asking
yourself on what basis we can make such claims." He explained that the
conclusions were drawn from his *Fortune* Survey and based on his polling experience of fifteen years. Tracking public opinion entailed asking
"representative cross-sections of the American people how they feel about
this or that question, and what they'd like to do about this or that proposal. That's exactly what we have done on this aid to Europe question.
We've placed it before a representative sample of the American people."[16]
In another broadcast, he noted that while election sampling "sounds
like a very technical subject," he believed it could "be made clear to the
layman."[17]

Indeed, in seeming contradiction to their talk of the opinion poll as
a technical scientific instrument, surveyors frequently portrayed sampling
as a rather elementary human practice. Gallup nearly always described the
polling process in folksy language that personalized the science behind it.
Rather than intimidate through complicated statistical analysis, he borrowed the simplest images possible from everyday experience. A housewife
tasting a spoonful of soup, a doctor drawing a sample of blood, and a boy
eating in one bite the meringue, filling, and crust of a lemon meringue pie
were all illustrations the pollster used to explain the relation between a
small segment of a mass and the whole—or why sampling "worked" (Gallup and Rae 1940, 56; Gallup 1940b, 13). One of Roper's favorite tactics
was using personal icons to stand in for impersonal percentages. The working man and the farmer were prominent among his examples of individuals the pollsters queried in their search for "representative Americans."
Roper aired majority opinions on his radio broadcasts using "a doctor who
lives in the corn belt" or "a prosperous businessman in Detroit" to articulate those views.[18] Humanizing the statistics and appealing to their audiences directly, pollsters used a common touch to help make less alien and
more familiar the sampling methods that were the tools of their trade.

Opinion surveyors were not immune to scientific-sounding jargon; for
example, Gallup invented the "quintamensional plan of question design"
(which examined five different aspects of opinion) in 1947 (Gallup 1947).
But unlike many of their scientific colleagues, they found little to gain in

---

16. Roper, CBS broadcast, "Where the People Stand," February 15, 1948, ERP.
17. Roper, CBS broadcast, "Where the People Stand," January 2, 1949, ERP.
18. Roper, CBS broadcast, "Where the People Stand," February 22, 1948, ERP.

cloaking their basic methods in a shroud of technical language. Observed Gallup, "we know that the more the public knows about the whole polling process, the greater their reliance is on it."[19] This is not to say that every aspect of pollsters' methods was equally visible to their audiences. Some problems that plagued the polls, such as "cheating" interviewers and the difficulty of establishing rapport across economic and racial lines, were discussed in specialized journals rather than public forums (see Mosteller 1949, 141–42; Cantril and Research Associates 1944, 146, 148). Others that the general public was aware of, such as the bandwagon effect, were breezily written off. But broadly speaking, rather than targeting other social scientists or government agencies, Gallup and his colleagues deliberately made a popular case for polling. This publicity campaign should properly be seen not as peripheral to the survey enterprise but as a practice integral to making and legitimating pollsters' brand of social knowledge.

What becomes clear in looking more closely at Gallup's and Roper's interchanges with the public is that, beyond gaining access to respondents' opinions and justifying polling methods to lay critics, surveyors also believed that they needed to establish the larger cultural validity of their science. Based on the sheer number of words they spent on the topic, pollsters appear to have deemed this a vitally important aspect of their public relations effort. In venues like *Good Housekeeping* and *Newsweek*, in radio broadcasts and syndicated newspaper columns, surveyors portrayed opinion polls not just as a scientific instrument but as a tool for civic betterment—and themselves as populist servants and men of the people. This involved a delicate balancing act between the stance of the technical expert, on the one hand, and the humble democratic channeler, on the other.

Pollsters made extravagant claims regarding the social benefits that would flow from their profession, from more transparent governance to enriched civic dialogue. Regular public opinion surveys would cure many of the ills of the modern polity, combating the deleterious influence of unresponsive legislatures, political machines, and pressure groups, all of whom Gallup described as "minorities representing themselves as the majority" (Gallup and Rae 1940, 144). For his part, Roper billed polling techniques as the "greatest contribution to democracy since the introduction of the secret ballot." "Certainly we will have a constantly improving

19. Gallup, "Polling Experiences, 1936–1948," speech to World Association for Public Opinion Research meeting, Paris, France, September 7, 1949, GGP.

electorate," he declared, "now that good newspapers, good magazines and good radio stations bring to the man in the street the news of events and the views of other men" (Roper 1944). Both Gallup and Roper contended that polls were *more* representative, *more* democratic, even than elections since they ascertained the views of those who never made it to the voting booth (Roper and Woodward 1948). In their telling of it, the representative scientific survey could perfect, if not quite replace, representative government.

Precisely because they touted their science as democratic, however, pollsters were careful not to bestow too much power on the new technology or its creators. Emphasizing instead that their surveying was subservient to "the people," they positioned the polls as neutral vessels for transmitting Americans' opinions. "As vital issues emerge from the fast-flowing stream of modern life," pledged Gallup, public opinion polls would "enable the American people to speak for themselves." Polling would permit "the 'people's own story,' as told in their own words, [to] be more fully understood" (Gallup and Rae 1940, 4, 117). By these lights, collecting information about the public was neither intrusive nor manipulative (here, pollsters fended off still other critiques) but democratic and empowering.

Distinguishing themselves from those who pretended to know the public mind—newspaper editors, political commentators, and "so-called 'thought leaders'"—pollsters in this way aligned themselves with "the people," right or wrong.[20] They were not above flattering their respondents: a key dimension of their public relations pitch was that their subjects were, in fact, rarely wrong. Gallup argued again and again for the "aggregate intelligence" of the public, and against those who would castigate "the people" (Gallup 1936, 36–37)· The people were almost always ahead of their leaders, he argued, and he was able to prove it scientifically (Gallup 1942).[21] Roper agreed that polls on a broad range of political and social issues demonstrated "the soundness of majority opinion."[22] Placing power with the people rather than the polling profession, Roper and Gallup made their statistics democratic, and thus more difficult to dispute without at the same time challenging the presumed will of the majority.

20. Roper, CBS broadcast, "Who Is Complacent?" May 3, 1942, ERP.
21. Gallup's most common pieces of evidence for this were that Americans were more eager than Congress had been, and earlier on, to build up the military before World War II; were in favor of conscription before any leader had suggested it; and were in favor of lower and more "equitable" tax rates on all income brackets.
22. Roper, CBS broadcast, "Where the People Stand," May 28, 1950, ERP.

In a final bid for public support, surveyors contended that polling did not simply further but was *itself* a democratic practice. Writing against the backdrop of fascism and dictatorship abroad, Gallup celebrated the free exercise of choice reflected in the very existence of opinion surveys. Whereas totalitarian nations ruled through the "artificial creation of an apparent majority," democratic ones listened to their publics; and the neutral pollster, as opposed to the dictator, could know "the real mind of [the] people" (Gallup and Rae 1940, 6–8, 10). There are parallels here to the 1940 census campaign, which posed a contrast between government actions in authoritarian countries and the U.S. census, which was "a democratic undertaking, done in a cooperative and free manner. . . . To participate in the census is to break a lance in the cause of freedom, since, through the census, democracy is made stronger" (Thomson 1940, 313). Gallup and Roper went so far as to equate voicing opinions—directly to surveyors and indirectly to government leaders and corporations—with political participation itself. Submitting to surveys constituted active participation in national affairs, helping to create rational citizens. As one of Gallup's interviewers put it, "for many," being polled was "a first lesson in being articulate" (London 1940, 9). Pollsters thus worked to make their technology not a cause of passive spectatorship, as some might have feared, but a tool for heightening democratic participation and improving citizenship. It was in these terms that they enlisted individuals in their surveying project.

The founders of modern polling were practitioners of a solicitous science: one that produced knowledge about the public but also sought to recruit, educate, and persuade it. Pollsters deliberately engaged volunteers and consumers by arguing that public opinion surveys were positive tools of social knowledge, exemplars of *both* scientific progress and democratic responsiveness. "Participation," through voicing opinions to a pollster, was the key to both.

There is some evidence to suggest that pollsters were successful in their campaign to win over their subjects, actual and potential. Some Americans, as we have seen, wrote to Gallup and Roper to protest their lack of inclusion in the polls. Others were moved to tell the pollsters how they *would* have spoken on the issues had they been asked—in one woman's words, to add her "penny's worth to the discussion."[23] They wrote in unbidden,

23. Alice W. Baker to Roper, June 3, 1951, ERP.

as did "A Contented Ford Employee" in 1947, to say to Roper: "I did not happen to be one of those selected to answer questions on your recent [poll], but I would like to express my views."[24] Others responded not to any particular survey but to a more open invitation, which had been implied by the pollsters, to offer their opinions. Thus did a woman, one of many such correspondents, write to Gallup with detailed views on the political climate—her conversations with other shoppers in the grocery store, she explained, revealed great discontent with prices, the national budget, and taxes.[25] Sharing their insights with the pollsters, and even placing themselves on an equal footing, such individuals seemed convinced that polling was a genuinely participatory, inclusive social interaction. They did not need to be solicited directly in order to proffer their views.

Pollsters had taken great pains to present their new scientific tool as a democratic instrument, and at least some of their readers and listeners treated it that way. One man mused in a letter to Gallup in 1956, "I do not know where you get your figures." Nevertheless, he wanted the pollster to "add all four votes from my family" against the proposition of a visit by Soviet premier Nikita Khrushchev to the United States.[26] This equation between votes and poll responses was adopted by others as well. A man who had viewed a Gallup Poll in the *Los Angeles Times* in the mid-1950s fired off a missive to the pollster, explaining, "I want to get my vote in against the U.N. and all foreign entanglements."[27] Still another reader, this one anonymous, sent a brief note to Gallup on behalf of his household regarding a survey on daylight saving time: "Sir, you may add 3 more *no[s]*" to the tally.[28] Such writers, it seems clear, had adopted the pollsters' quantitative version of public opinion and wanted to make their voices heard in it. Polling in this way was becoming an accepted, unremarkable technology as well as a proxy for other sorts of political representation.

Pollsters' dialogue with their respondents thus engendered two contradictory developments: a perhaps unprecedented level of public scrutiny and challenge from individuals who were in the first instance research subjects, but also a profound conversion in some of those same subjects to the very terms of the pollsters' project. This sort of investment—by the doubters and the persuaded alike—may too be the mark of a solicitous science. Those fields that rely most heavily on the consent and cooperation of their

24. Contented Ford Employee to Roper, September 19, 1947, ERP.
25. Anonymous to Gallup, undated, GGI.
26. R. F. Holmes to Gallup, October 24, 1956, GGI.
27. Charles E. Moore to Gallup, May 7, 1956, GGI.
28. Anonymous to Gallup, undated, GGI.

"raw materials" can tell us much about processes inherent to all the sciences. But the heavy public relations work and the intense solicitation of subjects that defined Gallup's and Roper's polling operations speak also to the distinctiveness of survey research and of social knowledge making more generally. It is not simply that human subjects, unlike rocks, respond to being studied. At times, to secure their participation, they are also made to feel that they are attended to, and might even be coequal producers of scientific knowledge.

The fact that survey respondents could, and did, talk back colored surveyors' techniques for obtaining data as well as the ways they framed their efforts. This ongoing exchange between researchers and subjects, I have argued, moved *persuasion* to the center of pollsters' battery of methods, even if it has rarely surfaced in scholars' accounts of survey research. More broadly, Gallup's and Roper's dilemma—as well as the way they went about solving it—helps us recognize that public cooperation and popular support can determine the very feasibility of social investigation. If we are serious about rethinking social knowledge–making practices, we will need to consider carefully the role of human subjects as obstacles and allies in the making of that knowledge.

That said, as the example of early scientific polling in the United States suggests, the linking of "democratic" survey techniques to "the people" had equally significant ramifications in the other direction: for the subjects of surveys themselves. The participatory inflection of the sample survey ensured that it was quite easy for individuals to challenge specific poll findings. Yet it would be difficult once such surveys were firmly established for lay critics to launch effective critiques of an inclusive, not to mention scientific, technique for conjuring the public's preferences. How to argue with a social scientific instrument that (theoretically) permitted each citizen a say and allowed majority views to become visible? Even if Gallup and Roper were never able fully to overcome popular resistance to their prying or public doubts about the merits of statistical sampling,[29] they achieved a larger goal: installing the opinion survey as a permanent technology of American democracy.

---

29. Recent arguments for employing statistical sampling in the census, for example, have not fared well. In a lawsuit against the U.S. Department of Commerce, it was charged that by "using statistical methods commonly referred to as sampling" the proposed 2000 census would "include millions and millions of people who are simply deemed to exist based upon computations of statisticians" (Anderson and Fienberg 1999, 200).

References

Adorno, Theodor W. [1957] 1976. "Sociology and Empirical Research." In *Critical Sociology: Selected Readings*, edited by Paul Connerton, 237–57. New York: Penguin Books.

Anderson, Margo J., and Stephen E. Fienberg. 1999. *Who Counts? The Politics of Census-Taking in Contemporary America*. New York: Russell Sage.

Beniger, James R. 1986. *The Control Revolution: Technological and Economic Origins of the Information Society*. Cambridge, MA: Harvard University Press.

Cantril, Hadley, and Research Associates in the Office of Public Opinion Research. 1944. *Gauging Public Opinion*. Princeton, NJ: Princeton University Press.

Converse, Jean. 1987. *Survey Research in the United States: Roots and Emergence, 1890–1960*. Berkeley and Los Angeles: University of California Press.

Cooper, Rachel. 2004. "Why Hacking Is Wrong about Human Kinds." *British Journal for the Philosophy of Science* 55:73–85.

Creager, Angela N. H., Elizabeth Lunbeck, and M. Norton Wise, eds. 2007. *Science without Laws: Model Systems, Cases, Exemplary Narratives*. Durham, NC: Duke University Press.

Epstein, Steven. 2007. *Inclusion: The Politics of Difference in Medical Research*. Chicago: University of Chicago Press.

———. 2008. "The Rise of 'Recruitmentology': Clinical Research, Racial Knowledge, and the Politics of Inclusion and Difference." *Social Studies of Science* 38:739–70.

Fisher, Jill A. 2007. "'Ready-to-Recruit' or 'Ready-to-Consent' Populations? Informed Consent and the Limits of Subject Autonomy." *Qualitative Inquiry* 13:875–94.

Frankel, Martin R., and Lester R. Frankel. 1987. "Fifty Years of Survey Sampling in the United States." *Public Opinion Quarterly* 51, pt. 2 (Supplement: 50th Anniversary Issue): S127–S138.

Fujimura, Joan H. 1987. "Constructing 'Do-able' Problems in Cancer Research: Articulating Alignment." *Social Studies of Science* 17:257–93.

Gallup, George. 1936. "Putting Public Opinion to Work." *Scribner's* 100:36–39, 73–74.

———. 1940a. "Polling Public Opinion." *Current History and Forum* 51:23–26, 57.

———. 1940b. "Polls and Prophets." *Current History and Forum* 52:12–14.

———. 1941. "We, The People, Are Like This—a Report on How and What We Think." *New York Times Magazine*, June 8, 3, 24.

———. 1942. "The People Are Ahead of Congress." *New York Times Magazine*, March 29, 16, 35.

———. 1947. "The Quintamensional Plan of Question Design." *Public Opinion Quarterly* 11:385–93.

———. 1948. *A Guide to Public Opinion Polls*. Princeton, NJ: Princeton University Press.

Gallup, George, and Saul Forbes Rae. 1940. *The Pulse of Democracy: The Public-Opinion Poll and How It Works*. New York: Simon and Schuster.

Gillespie, Richard. 1991. *Manufacturing Knowledge: A History of the Hawthorne Experiments*. New York: Cambridge University Press.

Hacking, Ian. 1986. "Making Up People." In *Reconstructing Individualism*, edited by Thomas C. Heller, Morton Sosna, and David E. Wellbery, 222–36. Stanford, CA: Stanford University Press.

———. 1995. "The Looping Effects of Human Kinds." In *Causal Cognition: A Multidisciplinary Debate*, edited by Dan Sperber, David Premack, and Ann James Premack, 351–94. New York: Oxford University Press.

Harding, John. 1944. "Refusals as a Source of Bias." In *Gauging Public Opinion*, by Hadley

Cantril and Research Associates in the Office of Public Opinion Research, 119–23. Princeton, NJ: Princeton University Press.

Hogan, J. Michael. 1997. "George Gallup and the Rhetoric of Scientific Democracy." *Communication Monographs* 64:61–79.

House, James S., F. Thomas Juster, Robert L. Kahn, Howard Schuman, and Eleanor Singer, eds. 2004. *A Telescope on Society: Survey Research and Social Science at the University of Michigan and Beyond.* Ann Arbor: University of Michigan Press.

Igo, Sarah E. 2007. *The Averaged American: Surveys, Citizens, and the Making of a Mass Public.* Cambridge, MA: Harvard University Press.

Kinsey, Alfred C., Wardell B. Pomeroy, and Clyde E. Martin. 1948. *Sexual Behavior in the Human Male.* Philadelphia: W. B. Saunders.

Knorr Cetina, Karin. 1999. *Epistemic Cultures: How the Sciences Make Knowledge.* Cambridge, MA: Harvard University Press.

Kohler, Robert E. 1994. *Lords of the Fly: Drosophila Genetics and the Experimental Life.* Chicago: University of Chicago Press.

———. 2002. *Landscapes and Labscapes: Exploring the Lab-Field Border in Biology.* Chicago: University of Chicago Press.

Lederer, Susan. 1997. *Subjected to Science: Human Experimentation in America before the Second World War.* Baltimore, MD: Johns Hopkins University Press.

London, Pearl. 1940. "Ringing Doorbells with a Gallup Reporter." *New York Times Magazine,* September 1, 9, 15.

Morawski, Jill. 2005. "Reflexivity and the Psychologist." *History of the Human Sciences* 18:77–105.

———. 2010. "Querying the Ontological Status of Subjects: The Psychology Laboratory and the Cold War." Paper presented at "Human Science, Human Subjects" conference, University of Chicago–Max Planck Workshop, April 2–3.

Mosteller, Frederick. 1949. *The Pre-election Polls of 1948: Report to the Committee on Analysis of Pre-election Polls and Forecasts.* New York: Social Science Research Council.

Osborne, Thomas, and Nikolas Rose. 1999. "Do Social Sciences Create Phenomena? The Example of Public Opinion Research." *British Journal of Sociology* 50:367–96.

Pickering, Andrew. 1984. *Constructing Quarks: A Sociological History of Particle Physics.* Chicago: University of Chicago Press.

Platt, Jennifer. 1996. *A History of Sociological Research Methods in America: 1920–1960.* New York: Cambridge University Press.

Politz, Alfred. [1948] 1990. "Validity and Reliability of Marketing Studies." In *The Politz Papers: Science and Truth in Marketing Research,* edited by Hugh S. Hardy, 46–55. Chicago: American Marketing Association.

Rader, Karen A. 2004. *Making Mice: Standardizing Animals for American Biomedical Research, 1900–1955.* Princeton, NJ: Princeton University Press.

Reardon, Jenny. 2006. "Creating Participatory Subjects: Race, Science and Democracy in a Genomic Age." In *The New Political Sociology of Science: Institutions, Networks, and Power,* edited by Scott Frickel and Kelly Moore, 351–77. Madison: University of Wisconsin Press.

Roper, Elmo. 1944. "What People Are Thinking." *New York Herald-Tribune,* November 30.

Roper, Elmo, and Julian L. Woodward. 1948. "Democracy's Auxiliary Ballot Box." *New York Herald-Tribune,* April 4.

Rosenthal, Robert, and Ralph L. Rosnow. 1975. *The Volunteer Subject.* New York: Wiley.

Rothman, David J. 1991. *Strangers at the Bedside: A History of How Law and Bioethics Transformed Medical Decision Making.* New York: Basic Books.

Rugg, Donald. 1944. "'Trained' vs. 'Untrained' Interviewers." In *Gauging Public Opinion*, by Hadley Cantril and Research Associates in the Office of Public Opinion Research, 83–97. Princeton, NJ: Princeton University Press.

Schrag, Zachary M. 2010. *Ethical Imperialism: Institutional Review Boards and the Social Sciences, 1965–2009*. Baltimore, MD: Johns Hopkins Press.

Solovey, Mark. 2004. "Riding Natural Scientists' Coattails onto the Endless Frontier: The SSRC and the Quest for Scientific Legitimacy." *Journal of the History of the Behavioral Sciences* 40:393–422.

Stark, Laura. Forthcoming. *Behind Closed Doors: IRBs and the Making of Ethical Research*. Chicago: University of Chicago Press.

Thomson, Charles A. H. 1940. "Public Relations of the 1940 Census." *Public Opinion Quarterly* 4:311–18.

Weindling, Paul Julian. 2004. *Nazi Medicine and the Nuremberg Trials: From Medical War Crimes to Informed Consent*. New York: Palgrave Macmillan.

ARCHIVAL SOURCES

George H. Gallup Papers (GGP). Gallup Organization. Princeton, New Jersey.

George H. Gallup Papers (GGI). University of Iowa Libraries. Iowa City, Iowa.

Elmo Roper Papers (ERP). Archives and Special Collections, Thomas J. Dodd Research Center. University of Connecticut Libraries. Storrs, Connecticut.

TEN

The Practices of Objectivity in Regulatory Science

SHEILA JASANOFF

Objectivity and Public Reason

Of all the noteworthy features of modernity, one of the most remarkable, yet least remarked, is our reliance on policy makers to know what is good for us. "We," after all, are not children or persons who through age, infirmity, or accident of heredity have lost the ability to think for ourselves. It is "we the people" of mature democracies who have delegated the task of public knowledge making to policy makers who serve us, in this regard, almost in loco parentis. These anonymous guardians know, as we do not, when our air is safe to breathe, what speeds are tolerable on our roadways, where to install our fire alarms and light switches, which drugs to take without intolerable side effects, and what counts as malpractice in medicine or stock trading. Not only do we, as adult citizens of democratic societies, not know the answers to such questions, but for the most part, we do not even know how answers are produced or why we should rely on them. Citizens delegate such issues to unelected policy makers and trust the policy system on the whole to make the right choices.

But why do modern societies rely on policy makers' epistemic expertise and good sense? What makes policy knowledge credible? That question deserves a great deal more attention than it has received in the social sciences. Even the field of science and technology studies (STS), which takes as its problematic all aspects of knowledge production and use, has devoted less energy to studying knowledge making in policy environments than in laboratories or other scientific workplaces. It is well established that knowledge created to serve policy needs—especially regulatory science—is sociologically distinct from other forms of knowledge. Knowledge for policy is produced in institutional settings and under criteria of validity that differ from those of "basic" or "research" science (Jasanoff 1990). It is equally well understood that such knowledge is contingent, vulnerable to criticism, and tends to unravel under adversarial challenge (Collins 1985; see also Nelkin 1992). The puzzle is how such weakly institutionalized knowledge withstands partisan attacks and manages to keep the engines of policy humming without paralyzing conflict or stifling dissent.

That problem becomes even thornier when we look at policy making above the level of the nation-state. Unlike national governments, which certify their knowledge claims through relatively well-established administrative processes, global policy making unfolds in a zone of tacit knowledge and inexplicit rules. Norms, including the epistemic norms that underpin all public knowledge, are constituted at the global scale through practices that are rarely exposed to critical scrutiny from citizens or social scientists. As a result, it is not known, for instance, whether global policy systems manufacture autonomous rules of reasoning, superseding those of nation-states and substate entities, or whether particular national ways of knowledge making become hegemonic in global institutions at the expense of other possible approaches.

In this chapter, I address both sets of puzzles: how policy-relevant knowledge attains stability at all and how global knowledge transcends national particularities. I argue that the authority of such knowledge rests on a highly sought-after and hard-won epistemic achievement, namely, objectivity. The term "objective" means, in its dictionary definition, "not influenced by personal feelings, interpretations, or prejudice; based on facts; unbiased."[1] Objectivity, in other words, partakes of the neutrality and impartiality of science itself, and demonstrations of objectivity can insulate the claimant against charges of arbitrariness or self-interest. In the skeptical modern world, objectivity is therefore a priceless adjunct to governmental power. But how are objectivity claims sustained when arguments for any significant policy position can be (and often are) opposed by strong counterarguments, and huge stakes ride on the resolution? The short answer is that making objectivity takes hard work. That work, as described in this chapter, is culturally situated, contested, and enacted at multiple sites and organizational levels. In other words, the ideal of policy objectivity is differently articulated in disparate political cultures and is performed and reproduced by diverse actors operating only in loose concert with one another. Objectivity reflects, in this sense, locally powerful ideologies of public reason.

To elaborate this argument, I review the institutionalized practices of

---

1. See definition 5 of "objective" (adjective) online at http://dictionary.reference.com/browse/objective (accessed April 11, 2011).

policy making from three angles to show how the objectivity of policy knowledge is operationally constructed. My first analytic lens is comparative, across national policy cultures. Here, I draw on the literature of comparative regulatory policy, including my own prior work, to illustrate how national styles of epistemic legitimation constitute the objectivity of policy-relevant knowledge. Focusing on risk regulation, I show that American law and policy have favored a type of objectivity that I call (borrowing a phrase from the philosopher Thomas Nagel) the "view from nowhere."[2] This approach to claims making achieves power by ostensibly detaching knowledge from potentially biased standpoints and from the distortions that any perspective or viewpoint necessarily entails. Regulatory objectivity in America, in short, rests on the kind of purification that scientists have historically aimed for in making representations of nature (Daston and Galison 2007; Latour 1993).

My second lens is procedural. I examine in microdetail three U.S. administrative practices—quantitative risk assessment, expert peer review, and judicial review of administrative decisions—that have worked in tandem to produce what passes as objective knowledge for purposes of risk management. This analysis directly confronts the problem of stability in the contested environment of high-stakes policy making. It illustrates deeply institutionalized modes of achieving pragmatic closures around epistemic claims and controversies that science alone could not have settled.

My third analytic tool is a mini–case study through which I look at the construction and maintenance of objectivity in one global regulatory body, the World Trade Organization (WTO). Here, in a first-person narrative voice, I analyze the WTO as a knowledge-producing institution through a proceeding in which I played a substantial personal role. This was a procedurally successful attempt to present an *amicus curiae* (friend of the court) brief to the WTO to expand that body's use of social science knowledge. The shift of voice and method in this section underscores one of my prime

2. Thomas Nagel (1986) uses the phrase the "view from nowhere" to characterize objective scientific knowledge, which he distinguishes from standpoint-based subjective perceptions of reality. While he concedes that these two standpoints are in tension, he does not denigrate or deny the possibility of constructing more and more objective representations of the world as it is. Donna Haraway (1988, 589) rejects the idea of a view-from-nowhere objectivity in favor of "situated knowledges," which she equates with the objectivity of an embodied, feminist perspective: "I am arguing for the view from a body, always a complex, contradictory, structuring, and structured body, versus the view from above, from nowhere, from simplicity." While my essay is broadly sympathetic toward Haraway's position that all objectivities are situated and embodied, my analytic focus is not on objectivity per se, nor on the relationship between subjectivity and objectivity, but on the role of objectivity as a cultural resource in collective knowledge making, institutional legitimation, and the construction of public reason.

theoretical arguments about the robustness of policy-relevant knowledge. It is constituted, in my view, by a cluster of highly specialized, routinized, opaque, and unreflexive micropractices, which may add up to hegemonic formations at the national and global levels because no one is studying (let alone intervening in) them. There is little analytic literature on the ways in which global policy knowledge—for example, what the WTO accepts as good science about risk—gets formed or articulated. By narrating this story, I show how the American understanding of objectivity, itself not universal but situated, has become embedded in the WTO to the point where it is difficult for new perspectives to find a way in or for critique to make a difference.

Through these sequenced moves across national, international, and global institutional scales, I not only display the complex and contested practices that produce and certify the objectivity of policy-relevant knowledge but also suggest that a multisited, indeed multivocal, approach is best suited to the sociological exploration of knowledge-power dynamics in a globalizing world.

Objectivity in Science and Policy

Objectivity in itself is not a new topic for students of science. Historians and sociologists of science have long contended that the most taken-for-granted features of scientific knowledge, such as objectivity, intelligibility, and truth itself, are social achievements that can be documented through careful inquiry (Dear 2006; Shapin 1994; Shapin and Schaffer 1985). In their social history of objectivity, Lorraine Daston and Peter Galison (2007) trace the concept's evolution through the production of scientific atlases in the nineteenth century. They discern three stages in the formation of what they evocatively call the "blind sight" of objectivity: truth to nature, in which the experienced observer represents an ideal of reality; mechanical objectivity, in which recording instruments remove the bias of the observer; and trained judgment, for which the observer's eye is disciplined by shared professional norms.

The periodicity of this development has been questioned (Porter 2007), and the three modalities of objectivity identified by Daston and Galison are more interdependent, both temporally and in practice, than the authors acknowledge. More constraining for our purposes, however, is their narrow focus on scientific atlases, which cannot do justice to the wide circulation of objectivity as an ordering concept in society. Histories of scientific practices, concentrating as they do on representations of nature, overlook the dual role that objectivity plays whenever knowledge is invoked as a rationale for power—as a legitimator of knowledge and also of the knowledge maker. Once scientific claims reach past conversations among scientists into contexts of use and empowerment, what matters is not only how truly the scientific observers have rendered nature but also how objectively decision makers have resolved the interpretive flexibility of available knowledge. This double hermeneutics of objectivity is always on the line in policy conflicts: questions center not only on the right way to read nature's manifestations but also on the right ways to translate ambiguous observations into policy.

Contemporary studies of regulatory politics thus provide essential inputs to my analysis of objectivity, supplementing historical and philosophical accounts. According to one well-documented body of research, science produced for policy commands respect because—though deeply enmeshed in politics—it successfully invokes the wider cultural authority of pure science. During regulatory controversies, varied credibility-enhancing mechanisms, such as expert peer review, are used to pull contested claims back into the preserves of certified knowledge. The most common strategy for distinguishing valid policy-relevant knowledge from mere politics is epistemic boundary work: the demarcation process through which official interpretations of relevant evidence are placed on the "good science" side of the margin that separates objective knowledge from illegitimate, politically tainted, or subjective preferences (Gieryn 1995; Jasanoff 1987, 1990).

Another approach to explaining the authority of policy-relevant science stresses the performative dimension of claims making in public fora. Here, the concern is not primarily with how policy actors sort out authority problems when challenged by interested parties but more with how they communicate their decisions to wider audiences. Thus, experts speaking for the National Academy of Sciences tend to present their findings through carefully orchestrated performances, in which certainty and reliability command the action on the frontstage while doubt and uncertainty, even if privately acknowledged, are relegated to the relative obscurity of the backstage (Hilgartner 2000). Performance builds authority even more plainly in the courtroom, that most skeptical of all the spaces in which we see public knowledge making in action. Advocates establish the credibility of their expert witnesses through a series of ritualized moves, as if manipulating pieces on a game board, so that expert testimony carries the ring of objective truth (Jasanoff 1998).

These approaches to analyzing scientific authority reflect the turn toward practice in the social studies of science in recent decades. In contrast to historical accounts that link scientific success to scientists' styles of work, sociological approaches stress the added work of representation and persuasion that actors must do to project credibility, objectivity, and truth to nonscientific audiences. In this chapter, I follow this line of scholarship by describing the specialized legal and political practices of reasoning that establish the objectivity of policy-relevant knowledge. Much of the "knowledge work" done in policy settings is abstract, nonmaterial, and manifested in habitual forms of argument. Just as a pianist knows without thinking how to dramatize a crescendo or modulate a diminuendo, so habits of reasoning are inculcated into policy actors until they become almost automatic, built into their forms of life or, in Bourdieu's term, their habitus. Uncovering the epistemic habits that enter into the making of objectivity calls for the ethnographer's eye, the literary critic's sensitivity to text and discourse, and the sociologist's awareness of organizational structures and dynamics. It also requires sensitivity to the political contexts in which the coin of objectivity is minted.

Objectivity, American Style

Speaking at the National Academy of Sciences in 1990, George Herbert Walker Bush, forty-first president of the United States, neatly summed up the dual role of objectivity as a legitimator of both science and politics:

> Science, like any field of endeavor, relies on freedom of inquiry; and one of the hallmarks of that freedom is objectivity.
>
> Now more than ever, on issues ranging from climate change to AIDS research to genetic engineering to food additives, government relies on the impartial perspective of science for guidance. And as the frontiers of knowledge are increasingly distant from the understanding of the many, it is ever more important that we can turn to the few for sound, straightforward advice. (Bush 1990)

This statement from a man not known for eloquence articulates a political philosophy for modern times. Here, Bush acknowledges the specialization of science, the distancing and possible alienation of citizens from technical decision making, and society's reliance on experts. Recognizing the tension for democracy when the uncomprehending many must depend on the knowledgeable few, the president offers a simple remedy—objectivity, secured through "sound, straightforward advice." In different words, but expressing a similar faith in objectivity, presidential candidate Hillary Clinton (2007) spoke at another respected forum, the Carnegie Institution for Science, on the fiftieth anniversary of the Soviet Union's launch of *Sputnik*: "Less than two weeks after news of Sputnik swept the globe, President Eisenhower called a meeting of his Science Advisory Committee and asked for recommendations. He would come to rely on that panel for unvarnished, evidence-based scientific advice."

A striking feature of both comments, too often echoed in American policy discourse to be dismissed as chance or irony, is the distancing of the advice that policy makers need from the persons charged with providing it. Bush and Clinton both assume that scientific advice, like science itself, can be impartial, sound, straightforward, unvarnished, and evidence based—all terms that depend on impersonal, exogenous standards of validity. Both political leaders take for granted that expert judgments, even in contested policy domains, can be driven by "science" and "evidence," words that effectively erase the stamps of agency and subjectivity. Even evidence relevant to policy, in Bush's and Clinton's telling, can be located in a world in which facts speak for themselves, unmediated by biased and fallible human actors. The personalities and viewpoints of the knowledge producers become irrelevant if they do their job right. It is their objective, evidence-based findings that carry weight, as the best approximations to the facts of the matter.

The cultural particularity of this U.S. insistence on standpoint independence has been persuasively documented through cross-national comparison. Studies of science-based regulation over the past few decades display the persistent strategies of depersonalization that distinguish U.S. policy making from other regulatory cultures (Brickman, Jasanoff, and Ilgen 1985; Jasanoff 2005a; Porter 1995; Vogel 1986). U.S. policy processes include greater reliance on scientific evidence to justify governmental decisions, significantly more polarized debate about the quality of scientific and technical assessments, and a marked preference for quantitative analysis and formal models to manage both what is known and what remains uncertain. The very fact that policy controversies so often play out in a scientific idiom draws attention away from human decision makers, while modeling and quantification hide professional judgment behind the seeming objectivity of formal simulations and mathematical representations.

The contrast between the United States and Britain is especially stark on all these dimensions. For example, far from dissociating policy expertise from personal affiliations, British investigative and advisory commissions are routinely identified with an eminent chairperson, as if the legitimacy of advice depends on the virtue of the orchestrator of the advisory process. In return, successful handling of such proceedings serves as a stepping stone to higher office and honors for those who, in Othello's words, "have done the state some service." Thus, the 1998–2000 inquiry following Britain's economically and politically wrenching "mad cow" crisis took its name from Lord (Nicholas) Phillips of Worth Matravers, who became a Law Lord during his conduct of the inquiry and subsequently rose to the position of Lord Chief Justice. The Warnock report, possibly the most significant bioethics report produced for a national government in the twentieth century, was named for Mary Warnock, an Oxford philosopher who later became Mistress of Girton College at the University of Cambridge and a peeress in the House of Lords (Warnock 1984; see also Jasanoff 2005a).

Britain's predilection for entrusting the credibility of public knowledge to elite figures, a practice that historians have traced to the gentlemanly culture of the Scientific Revolution in Restoration England (Shapin and Schaffer 1985), does not, however, mean that expert claims are accepted solely on the basis of social capital. As I showed in detail in *Designs on Nature* (Jasanoff 2005a), key to the epistemic authority of men and women like Lord Phillips and Baroness Warnock is that they articulate a plain, commonsense vision: knowledge whose truthfulness anyone in society, from the highest to the lowest, can in theory review and attest to. The result, when successful, is objectivity based on a truly communal viewpoint, a "view from everywhere" that can be contrasted with the impersonal purity and social detachment of America's view from nowhere. For example, the famous distinction that the Warnock report drew between the embryo before and after fourteen days—permitting research before but not after that cutoff date—was founded on the observation of developmental biologists that significant changes in embryonic structure and the formation of the nervous system happen around that time (Jasanoff 2005a, 152–55). It was not elite scientific consensus alone that caused the fourteen-day rule to gain acceptance. Both the Warnock Committee and the British public accepted this line of demarcation as one that made sense, given that some line drawing was essential;[3] this one, by virtue of its simplicity, seemed to guard against the slippery slope toward experimentation at later, more con-

---

3. Baroness Warnock told me in a personal interview that all the committee members were aware of the need to draw a bright line, allowing some embryo research to continue but preventing unregulated intervention. Where exactly to fix the line was less important than that there should be an enforceable line. The fourteen-day solution was proposed by Anne McLaren, a distinguished developmental biologist and herself a peer's daughter. McLaren extrapolated the idea of a fourteen-day limit from her work with nonhuman animals, and it struck the majority of the committee as reasonable.

troversial stages of embryonic development (McLaren 1989). There was no need in Britain's pragmatic policy culture to invoke transcendental concepts such as human dignity, enshrined in article 1 of the postwar German Basic Law.[4] Nor did the attempt to define a workable rule provoke, as in the United States, a quest for unambiguous scientific answers to the question of when human life begins.

German practices of knowledge making also produce an objectivity that could be called a "view from everywhere," but its political underpinnings are different from those in Britain. Whereas public knowledge in the British empiricist tradition tends to draw its credibility from collective witnessing of demonstrable facts (Ezrahi 1990; Jasanoff 2005a; Shapin and Schaffer 1985), German expert bodies create common knowledge through a process of group reasoning explicitly based on principles of political representation. In effect, German knowledge practices enact the Habermasian model of the public sphere, with its emphasis on neutral deliberative spaces and perfect communication. There is no assumption, as in the United States, that objectivity exists in an impersonal space, divorced from social standpoints. Rather, epistemic authority comes about through the inclusion of all legitimate points of view. Thus, German parliamentary inquiry commissions (*Enquête-Kommission*), appointed by the Bundestag to explore solutions to long-range problems, are formed of legislators, proportionally represented by party, as well as subject-matter experts nominated by the parties and associated in this sense with party positions.[5] Similarly, advisory committees serving regulatory agencies are broadly representative of all interested constituencies, and procedural rules generally require each member to be represented by an alternate. It is as if the validity of the expert consensus would be weakened by the loss of a single recognizable standpoint, a problem that is not confronted in Britain's epistemic culture of common witnessing or in America's construction of standpoint-free knowledge.

A telling illustration of Germany's inclusive approach to knowledge making comes from the rich history of biotechnology regulation (Jasanoff 2005a). A parliamentary inquiry commission formed to consider the risks and opportunities of the new technology in the late 1980s included rep-

---

4. Article 1.1 of the Basic Law (*Grundgesetz*) states: "Human dignity shall be inviolable. To respect and protect it shall be the duty of all state authority."

5. The German Wikipedia entry for *Enquête-Kommission* states (in my translation): "In the Inquiry Commission a common position is supposed to be worked out. The goal is to come to a solution to problems of this sort that can be tolerated by the overwhelming majority of the people (even by that portion which does not consider itself represented by the current ruling majority)."

resentatives of the Green Party, then enjoying its first election to the Bundestag.[6] Against the normally consensual approach followed by such commissions, the Greens insisted on producing a long, strident indictment of biotechnology, which they saw (together with nuclear power) as a suspect project enlisting state power to control both nature and citizens. This fifty-page dissent was published as part of the commission report. It ensured that Green concerns, however far-fetched they appeared to other commission members, remained alive in the political debate. One effect was to frame biotechnology as a programmatic undertaking of the German state instead of merely as a new industrial process, as in Britain, or a series of new commercial products, as in the United States (Jasanoff 2005a, 45–61; see also Gottweis 1998).

These necessarily brief comparative sketches, extracted from the voluminous literature on risk regulation, underline this chapter's first argument that the objectivity of policy-relevant knowledge is itself a cultural product. It is related to but more encompassing than objectivity in science pure and simple. Objectivity in policy necessarily confronts and accommodates cultural conceptions of what counts as proper representation not only of nature but also of public interests. This double objectivity, scientific and political, is achieved through institutionalized practices whose tacit epistemological implications remain largely unrecognized by the participants in public knowledge making. We turn now to the epistemic practices through which the U.S. regulatory system produces its "view from nowhere" and, to some degree, exports it beyond the borders of the United States.

Objectivity in Regulatory Science

Objectivity became a talisman for American policy makers well before the middle of the twentieth century. Theodore Porter's (1995) history of quantitative policy analysis in Britain, France, and the United States relates how numbers warded off the appearance of political bias in the cost-benefit analyses carried out by the U.S. Army Corps of Engineers to justify its huge water management projects. British actuaries and French railroad engineers come across in Porter's study as significantly more prepared to admit the influence of professional judgment on their calculations. Quantification,

6. There is no precise analogue to the German inquiry commission in the American policy process, reflecting structural differences between parliamentary and presidential political systems. In the United States, the congressional Office of Technology Assessment, which adopted a bipartisan approach to technical advice giving, was dissolved in 1995 by a resurgent Republican Congress.

Porter suggests, is most likely to be represented as impartial science when other means of producing credibility, such as elite status or professional solidarity, are missing in a policy culture: the strength of quantitative analysis is that "it can permit administrative decisions to be made quietly, discouraging public activism. In a suspicious democratic order, even truth claims depend on the appearance of objectivity in the sense of impartiality" (Porter 1995, 47).

Quantitative Risk Assessment

U.S. regulators extended the use of quantification to new problems in the mid-1970s, particularly to assessing the risk of human cancer from growing numbers of chemical products and pollutants in the environment. The earliest efforts to regulate carcinogens were based on qualitative judgments derived from testing such compounds on nonhuman species. A well-known example was the so-called Delaney Clause of the Federal Food, Drug, and Cosmetic Act, which in 1958 mandated a ban on food additives found to induce cancer in humans or animals. This cut-and-dried rule precluded for a time any need for mathematical extrapolation from test animals to humans. It was enough to demonstrate that a substance had tested positive for cancer in an animal bioassay. That qualitative finding was sufficient to keep the product out of the food supply.

A massive expansion of environmental controls during the 1970s, along with improved technologies for detecting toxic pollutants and residues, drew a much larger array of chemical products into the regulatory net. Impatient with the Delaney standard, now seen as a recipe for over-regulation, Congress increasingly asked for regulatory costs to be balanced against benefits to health and the environment. Federal agencies came under pressure to develop a nuanced, yet still objective, basis for imposing burdensome controls on the chemical industry. Gradually and somewhat reluctantly, under mounting legal and political scrutiny, U.S. regulators turned to quantitative risk assessment and the relative safety of numbers (Rushefsky 1986). Numerical estimates of probable cancer deaths offered a kind of legitimation that agency officials could no longer claim solely on the basis of institutional expertise and legal authority. The turn from informed, experiential judgment to impersonal objectivity was especially pronounced at the Environmental Protection Agency (EPA), which faced formidable challenges to its competence and credibility from the moment it was created by presidential executive order in 1970.

As we know from the social studies of science, it takes work to detach judgment from fact, or the knower from the known. Massive forces must be brought into play, and long networks constructed, to make nature speak for itself, whether in science or for policy (Callon 1986; Latour 1988). Risk assessment was no exception. This analytic strategy could not achieve the look of objectivity without enrolling a heterogeneous network of social and nonhuman actors into the project. Federal funds created extensive programs for testing and assessing environmental carcinogens to justify federal policies. Again, comparison sheds light on the cultural uniqueness of these objectivity-building practices. No other national government focused so heavily on cancer risk, which in the United States marginalized almost all other risks to humans and the environment; nowhere else were so many public resources invested in developing animal tests for carcinogens or mathematical models for extrapolating human risk estimates from animal data. Economic analysis of regulation also took on a significantly more elaborate and professional character than in other countries, spurred by legislative mandates, court decisions, and presidential executive orders all calling for explicit balancing of costs and benefits. Put differently, the expert networks created to justify environmental regulatory policies in Europe were thinner and shorter, requiring fewer mathematical modelers, fewer animals, fewer economists, and much less paper. Yet—somewhat paradoxically—in no other regulatory system was the scientific basis for policy decisions subjected to such sustained testing, or taken apart and reexamined so thoroughly, as in the adversarial, legalistic culture of the United States (Brickman, Jasanoff, and Ilgen 1985; Hoberg and Harrison 1994).

Once a distinctive analytic approach to risk assessment was in place, knowledge evolved within that framework along complex pathways. Both government (through the National Toxicology Program) and industry (through, inter alia, the Chemical Industry Institute of Toxicology) devoted substantial resources to the systematic conduct and refinement of bioassays, especially with rodents. Like any technical tests, these tests for carcinogenicity had to overcome doubt and contention (Pinch 1993; MacKenzie 1990). Controversies arose and persisted about the suitability of animal models as predictors of risk to humans, and regulators were called upon to identify and differentiate, chemical by chemical, the precise mechanisms of cancer induction in animals and humans. Through this dialectic of epistemic challenge and policy response, the principles and techniques of risk assessment evolved from early, almost intuitive judgments, validated by the experiential knowledge of regulators, to more complex, technically sophisticated, and rule-governed—in short, "objective"—methods of uncertainty assessment (National Research Council 1994).

The changes needed to represent risk assessment as impartial and objective entailed far-reaching shifts in academic and private-sector scientific practices as well. A new market opened up for risk analysis, influencing the agendas of epidemiologists and toxicologists and spurring the creation of specialized institutions such as the Center for Risk Analysis at Harvard University's School of Public Health and the Cambridge-based Health Effects Institute.[7] Other impacts included a boom in industrial testing laboratories, the formation of professional societies for risk analysis, and, more subtly, the emergence of new scientific subspecialties, such as the mathematical technique of meta-analysis, which sought to draw reliable and objective conclusions from studies that were inconclusive when taken on their own. But bridges were still needed to connect these dispersed knowledge-generating activities to regulatory decisions, and regulatory peer review supplied a crucial component. Unlike advances in testing and modeling, peer review directly addressed the second prong of the paradox of representation in regulatory science: whose claims count as objective? Designed to remove subjectivity from policy knowledge, peer review, as we shall see, proved to be another lightning rod for controversy.

Peer Review: Everybody Wants It

The term "sound science" has acquired sufficient standing to merit its own Wikipedia entry, where its use in policy is helpfully distinguished from its use in acoustic physics. Although some trace the term's first use to the tobacco industry's efforts to discredit the evidence for smoking-linked cancer (Michaels 2008), policy critics of the Left and the Right equally invoked the sound-science label to support their positions by the late 1990s. It has been dismissed as "doublespeak for trouble" (Mooney 2004); yet it endures as a term that confers respectability. Correspondingly, legitimacy is drained from claims whose soundness is successfully questioned. "Sound science" operates in U.S. policy discourse as a powerful signifier that detaches scientific claims from their messy human origins. One practice more than any other serves to distinguish sound science from its unsound and unreliable alternatives. That practice is peer review.

Review by qualified experts has been part of the apparatus of fact making and credibility building from the early years of the Scientific Revolution

---

7. The Health Effects Institute was jointly funded by the EPA and the automobile industry to sponsor credible scientific research for use in assessing the health risks of air pollutants. In this case, standpoint independence was ensured by making adversaries collaborate in knowledge production. For more on the institute's organization and operations, see Jasanoff 1990.

(Shapin and Schaffer 1985; Zuckerman and Merton 1971). Criticism of scientists' work by knowledgeable others helped validate claims and allowed them to circulate more freely. By the middle of the twentieth century, the "organized skepticism" that Robert Merton ([1942] 1973) named as one of the four constitutive norms of science was thoroughly institutionalized as peer review. Any scientific claim had to pass the screen of more then one pair of observant eyes to be certified as fact. To be sure, the conduct of peer review remained inconsistent, and the doorkeepers of science—journal editors, grant-making agencies, and regulatory authorities—tailored their review procedures to the exigencies of particular situations (Jasanoff 1990). Yet passing through a process called peer review usually sufficed to translate subjective observation into objective knowledge; by the same token, to undermine a study's soundness, it was generally enough to show that it had not undergone peer review.

A controversy during the early years of the George W. Bush presidency illustrates the centrality of peer review in maintaining the view-from-nowhere objectivity of U.S. policy-relevant science. In this case, the process of peer review became intensely political, and yet the power of peer review to deliver objectivity remained unchallenged. The episode did not call into question whether the imagination of impersonal objectivity is philosophically or practically sustainable in political settings; instead, conflict centered on who should manage the review process so as to achieve the desired standard of objectivity. What the controversy threw into relief was not the right representation of nature but the right representation, and resolution, of interpretive plurality.

Historically, the events of the Bush era recapitulated an almost identical controversy in the early Reagan years, though with a different cast of characters. On the earlier occasion, debate centered on the EPA's peer review practices, and pitted agency experts against those of the chemical industry (Jasanoff 1987, 2005b). The later episode positioned one part of the executive branch (the economically minded and deregulatory White House) against others (the health and safety regulatory agencies). In both cases, however, the adversaries understood the political, as well as the epistemic, work done by so-called peers. Whoever controlled the peer position, they saw, would ipso facto control the standpoint from which regulatory science would be declared free of bias. In other words, actors saw that the choice of peer reviewers, and therefore the right to make those choices, would define the coordinates of the "nowhere" position.

On August 29, 2003, the Office of Information and Regulatory Affairs (OIRA), an obscure but influential unit within the Office of Management and Budget (OMB), issued a *Proposed Bulletin on Peer Review and Information Quality* (OMB 2003; hereafter, the *Bulletin*). Its purpose was to ensure "meaningful peer review" of science pertaining to regulation, as part of an "ongoing effort to improve the quality, objectivity, utility, and integrity of information disseminated by the federal government" (OMB 2003, Summary). The *Bulletin* singled out the category of "significant regulatory information," which was defined as information that could have "a clear and substantial impact on important public policies or important private sector decisions with a possible impact of more than $100 million in any year." Any process for reviewing such information, according to the *Bulletin*, would have to be approved by the OMB. According to one estimate, this proposal would potentially have subjected two hundred or more draft technical documents each year to OMB-certified "formal, independent, external" peer review (Anderson 2003).

To take the reins of regulatory peer review into OMB's antiregulatory hands was a highly political move. To neutralize the appearance of a political power grab, OIRA sheathed itself in the language of objectivity, taking its cues from science itself: "Independent, objective peer review has long been regarded as a critical element in ensuring the reliability of scientific analyses. For decades, the American academic and scientific communities have withheld acknowledgment of scientific studies that have not been subject to rigorous independent peer review" (OMB 2003, 54024). If the objectivity of regulatory science was now in doubt, OIRA concluded, the reason must be an erosion of the independence of the review process through capture by pro-regulation interests.

The *Bulletin* described numerous alleged defects in agency practices that kept peer review from functioning as an effective check on the subjectivity of regulatory knowledge:[8]

· "Existing agency peer review mechanisms have not always been sufficient to ensure the reliability of regulatory information disseminated or relied upon by federal agencies." (54024)
· "Even when agencies do conduct timely peer reviews, such reviews are sometimes undertaken by people who are not independent of the agencies." (54024)
· "When an agency does initiate a program to select outside peer reviewers for regulatory science, it sometimes selects the same reviewers for all or nearly all of its peer reviews on a particular topic." (54025)

8. All page citations are to OMB 2003.

- "It is also essential to grant the peer reviewers access to sufficient information." (54025)
- "The results are not always available for public scrutiny or comment." (54025)
- "Experience has shown that they are not always followed by all of the federal agencies, and that actual practice has not always lived up to the ideals underlying the various agencies' manuals." (54025)

These problems, in OIRA's judgment, justified the creation of a new point of authority within OMB from which the integrity of peer review could be restored. By implication, the result would be the elimination of the agencies' standpoint-induced bias.

Even in a period of harmony between science and the state, such a sweeping realignment in knowledge-validating practices might not have passed unchallenged. In a climate of high tension between the Bush administration and the nation's scientific leadership (see, e.g., National Academy of Sciences 2003), OIRA's move raised eyebrows and temperatures. Prominent scientific and professional societies, including the American Association for the Advancement of Science and the National Academy of Sciences, dismissed OMB's position as unfounded and as introducing biases of its own. In response, OMB issued a revised document, considerably toning down its prior claims to objectivity but not altogether relinquishing its watchdog role. OIRA's Web site as of mid-2008 described that role as follows:

> Peer review is an important procedure used by the scientific community to ensure the quality of information prior to publication. It involves critical review of a draft report by qualified scientists not involved in developing the report. Peer review includes an exchange of judgments about the appropriateness of methods and the strength of the author's inferences. The "Information Quality Bulletin for Peer Review," issued on December 16, 2004, establishes government-wide guidance aimed at enhancing the practice of peer review of government science.[9]

Though represented as a "practice," and not as a silver bullet, peer review was still advanced as a procedure for aligning "government science" with the judgments of the scientific community. By claiming both the right and

9. Office of Information and Regulatory Affairs (OIRA), http://www.whitehouse.gov/omb/inforeg/qa_062205.html (accessed August 2008). This language was removed from the OIRA Web site during the Obama administration, but peer review continues to be governed by OMB's "Final Information Quality Bulletin for Peer Review" issued in December 2004.

the capacity to enhance regulatory peer review, OIRA implicitly claimed a position of objectivity that it did not concede to regulators themselves.

Objectivity in Judicial Review

Like any robust cultural property, policy objectivity is produced by multiple actors at multiple sites, or "fields of practice" (Bourdieu 1987), whose logics and modes of operation reinforce one another. Thus, while performances of objectivity may be situated and contingent, such as OIRA's attempt to hijack regulatory peer review in 2003, the concept's cultural meaning in a given political system tends to remain durable over time. Through repeat performances of practices such as regulatory peer review, a political culture's commitment to a specific form of objectivity is continually reaffirmed, until it operates in effect as a binding norm.

In the United States, such performances occur not only in expert committees and regulatory agencies but also in the courts, which through review of administrative rule making often enjoy the last word on the adequacy of policy makers' knowledge and reasoning. In this section, I show how two Supreme Court justices, Antonin Scalia and Stephen Breyer, representing opposite poles of the liberal-conservative spectrum, have nevertheless reinforced the construction of regulatory objectivity as a view from nowhere. This requires, at the core, strategies for preserving the objectivity of judicial review itself. Both jurists, I will show, operate with similar, role-conditioned discourses of reticence and the need for closure, but where Breyer draws his sense of limits from dominant cultural notions of expertise and objectivity, Scalia takes his cues from interpretations of the law. Despite some local perturbations and disagreements, neither approach fundamentally challenges the possibility of objective judgment.

My analysis of judicial reasoning here parallels the study of judicial discourse and practice proposed by Robert Brisbin, drawing on the sociology of Pierre Bourdieu. Judges, Brisbin argues, employ shared linguistic repertoires that can nevertheless be tailored to reinforce a consistent set of political or ideological commitments within a single jurist's practices: "The field of practice is a partially autonomous political space relatively independent of external pressures and determinations. It has its own languages for defining political institutional roles and rights and its own methods for addressing problems. The legal struggles about the language of the law within a field of judicial practice represent a political struggle about the construction of the state" (Brisbin 1991, 1006). Going beyond Brisbin, however, I show that American judicial reasoning, regardless of its orientation toward state power, reinforces the basic epistemic commitments of the U.S. policy culture. Of particular interest are ways in which shared ideas of deference and restraint, key to the legitimacy of an unelected judiciary, reinforce enduring cultural understandings of objectivity and reason.

Justices Scalia and Breyer have led, in many respects, parallel lives, despite their allegiances, respectively, to the conservative and liberal ends of the American political spectrum. Scalia joined the Supreme Court as a Reagan appointee following a distinguished career in government and academia, including a professorship at Chicago Law School. Breyer, a Clinton appointee, was a Harvard law professor and federal appellate judge before joining the Supreme Court. Articulate and opinionated, they share a longstanding interest in administrative law, the branch of jurisprudence that directly addresses the adequacy of policy makers' knowledge claims. I trace below their roles in sustaining a view-from-nowhere objectivity: from their comments on a landmark administrative law decision before they joined the Supreme Court to their part in one of the most important cases to come before the Court in the first decade of the twenty-first century—a suit against the EPA successfully challenging the agency's failure to regulate greenhouse gas emissions from motor vehicles under the Clean Air Act.

First, some legal background. The most important U.S. law addressing the quality of administrative knowledge and reasoning is a piece of late New Deal legislation dating from just after World War II. The 1946 Administrative Procedure Act (APA) required all federal agencies to open up their reasoning to public review. Under the APA, persons dissatisfied with administrative decisions may sue the decision maker for failure to offer substantial evidence or for arbitrary and capricious action not adequately grounded in the decision-making record. In contested cases, a reviewing court decides whether the challenge is merited and whether the agency must go back and strengthen its arguments. Litigation under the APA serves as a powerful instrument for testing an agency's construction of objectivity. Knowledge claims that do not stand up to legal scrutiny clearly fail the test. Judicial review allows the window of skepticism to open wide, revealing bias and subjectivity, and yet the process leaves agencies room to defend their knowledge claims as views from nowhere. But how? The strategies used by Scalia and Breyer to effect closure offer some insights.

A strict constructionist of legal texts and an accomplished legal technician, Scalia invokes the alleged clarity of legal principles to justify his conclusions. He takes seriously the judge's duty to interpret—not make—the law; for him legal texts and their histories provide all the guidance needed to formulate unambiguous decisions.[10] As a law professor before he was appointed an appellate judge, Scalia instructively commented on one of the noted administrative law decisions of the late 1970s, *Vermont Yankee Nuclear Power Corporation v. Natural Resources Defense Council*, 435 U.S. 519 (1978). The case involved a challenge to an Atomic Energy Commission (AEC) license to a nuclear power plant operated by Vermont Yankee. The petitioning environmental organization contended that the AEC had not sufficiently considered the technical issues relevant to high-level nuclear-waste disposal; the AEC had relied primarily on a twenty-page report by a member of its own staff, supplemented by an inadequate hearing record, hardly a picture of objectivity. The D.C. Circuit Court of Appeals agreed and asked the agency to adopt additional procedures so as to air its assessment of an exceptionally risky technology more thoroughly. On appeal, the Supreme Court resoundingly upheld the AEC's position. The agency, the Court unanimously concluded, had no obligation to adopt procedures over and above those required by law, that is, the APA and the agency's governing statute. It was not a court's job to "impose upon the agency its own notion of which procedures are 'best' or most likely to further some vague, undefined public good" (435 U.S. at 549). The holding reaffirmed the classical conception of the separation of powers endorsed by both Scalia (Brisbin 1991) and Breyer (1978): Congress makes the law; executive agencies implement it; courts second-guess agencies only if they have deviated from the law's explicit requirements.

Breyer, also a professor at the time, warmly endorsed *Vermont Yankee*, but his defense rested as much on deference to impersonal expertise (view from nowhere) as deference to the executive's discretionary power. He accepted that the gravity of the interests at stake might sometimes demand more rigorous judicial scrutiny of knowledge claims, possibly requiring more procedures. But that was just his starting point. In a rehearsal sounding remarkably like an expert brief for the nuclear industry, Breyer took apart the argument that nuclear energy deserved such heightened scrutiny. His text was sprinkled with statistics, a persistent marker of U.S. regulators' preference for numerical objectivity:

10. I personally witnessed an interesting demonstration of Scalia's modus operandi on September 28, 2004, when he delivered the Edwin L. Godkin Lecture at Harvard University's John F. Kennedy School of Government. At a dinner following his lecture, one of my colleagues mentioned that the late Justice Harry Blackmun used to walk to the Lincoln Memorial at night to reflect on what to do with particularly agonizing cases. He asked what Justice Scalia did when faced with similarly agonizing choices. Matter-of-factly and without a moment's hesitation, Scalia answered that he never faced agonizing choices because his role was to be a good lawyer, and as a lawyer, he needed only to carry out what the law and the Constitution said.

- "coal plants are likely to cause seven to twelve times as many deaths as nuclear plants and four to six times as much sickness and injury";
- "few additional power plants are likely to be built. The number of new nuclear plants ordered has fallen from 38 in 1973 to 5 in 1975, 3 in 1976, and 4 in 1977";
- "the average nuclear plant takes ten to twelve years to bring from initial plan to operation—four to six years longer than a comparable coal plant." (Breyer 1978, 1835, 1838)

On the basis of such comparisons, Breyer concluded that the proponents of more process were seeking, not the legitimate goal of better analysis, but rather the untenable political goal of a shift from nuclear power to coal. This move Breyer dismissed as unreasonable on the (numerical) merits.

Breyer reiterated his faith in expert risk analysis, and the disembodied objectivity it confers, in his 1992 Oliver Wendell Holmes Lectures at Harvard Law School, delivered while he was chief judge in the First Circuit Court of Appeals. There, he addressed a problem that had exercised segments of the risk assessment and administrative law communities, as well as American industry, since the early 1980s, namely, the gap between expert and public risk perceptions. Social psychologists have documented that public appraisals of risk are swayed by cognitive biases, such as a tendency to overvalue unfamiliar and feared events (Slovic 1991). In turn, critics of regulation have argued that such skewed perceptions produce a vicious cycle of irrational regulatory responses, such as the 1980 Superfund Act, which mandates cleanup of abandoned toxic dump sites at unwarranted expense. In his Harvard lectures, Breyer uncritically accepted these arguments and proposed greater centralization of risk analysis as the best antidote to inefficient, fear-driven regulation. He advocated delegating technical decision making to good experts, experienced in rendering sound analytic judgments and avoiding the traps of emotion and fear (Breyer 1993). With this vigorous defense of expertise, Judge Breyer served as both producer and consumer of his policy culture's preferred style of detached objectivity.

Scalia's (1978) article on *Vermont Yankee* in the *Supreme Court Review* also endorsed the decision's formal correctness, but there the similarity with Breyer ended. Where Breyer offered a twelve-page comment, Scalia produced a densely argued sixty-four-page article; where Breyer reached out to technical experts to justify his position, Scalia remained within the four corners of legal analysis; and while Breyer expressed wholehearted support for the Supreme Court, Scalia tempered his approval with grudging admiration for the D.C. Circuit, which in his view had more clearly understood the politics of procedural choice. Scalia deplored the lower court's renegade tendency to take administrative law into its own hands, flouting the Supreme Court's disciplinary authority, and its attempt to create a common law of hybrid administrative procedures that undermined the "proper functioning of a court of appeals in a hierarchical legal system" (Scalia 1978, 371). Yet, unlike Breyer, he rejected the proposition that agencies should be expected to resolve complex regulatory issues "solely on the basis of science and reason" (Scalia 1978, 403). Administrators need a political space in which to strike the compromises and craft the adjustments required to placate powerful political interests. Under these circumstances, procedural choices are bound to serve as political instruments, constraining the agencies' freedom to strike bargains. Congress, Scalia noted, had recognized this method of asserting control over the executive and had enacted multiple statutory procedures that fractured the APA's streamlined approach to rule making. But this unruliness, he wistfully concluded, was how things should be, because it was ultimately up to Congress—not courts or agencies—to determine how the politics of process should play out in diverse regulatory settings. Backhandedly, but no less decisively than Breyer, Scalia too relinquished to regulators the power to craft their knowledges and reasons, including their preferred modes of objectivity, so long as they complied with the (in his view) unambiguous legal constraints imposed by Congress.

Nearly thirty years later, in *Massachusetts v. EPA*, 549 U.S. 497 (2007), Breyer and Scalia, as justices of the Supreme Court, again had the opportunity to articulate their respective views of the right relations between scientific knowledge, regulatory objectivity, and administrative law. Substantively, the issue before the Court was whether the EPA could justifiably refuse to treat greenhouse gases as air pollutants under the Clean Air Act. The two justices differed in their conclusions but, without violating shared canons of judicial practice, reaffirmed their longstanding ideological positions about where objectivity comes from: science or law.

Scalia insisted that the law protects the EPA's reasoning against challenge by the petitioning states. For this conclusion he relied on both his sense of the plain meaning of the statute and the agency's constitutional right to interpret the law within acceptable limits. In oral argument on the case, Scalia tried to draw a distinction between "air pollution"—plainly regulated by the Clean Air Act—and global warming, which he suggested was an effect on an atmospheric system not synonymous with "air." The following exchange with James R. Milkey, assistant attorney general of Massachusetts, captures Scalia's thinking:

JUSTICE SCALIA: Mr. Milkey, I had—my problem is precisely on the impermissible grounds. To be sure, carbon dioxide is a pollutant, and it can be an air pollutant. If we fill this room with carbon dioxide, it could be an air pollutant that endangers health. But I always thought an air pollutant was something different from a stratospheric pollutant, and your claim here is not that the pollution of what we normally call "air" is endangering health. That isn't, that isn't—your assertion is that after the pollutant leaves the air and goes up into the stratosphere it is contributing to global warming.

MR. MILKEY: Respectfully, Your Honor, it is not the stratosphere. It's the troposphere.

JUSTICE SCALIA: Troposphere, whatever. I told you before I'm not a scientist. (Laughter.)[11]

When the Supreme Court rendered its 5–4 split decision against the EPA, Scalia filed a separate dissent, even though he agreed with Chief Justice John G. Roberts on the dissenters' argument that the petitioners lacked standing to pursue the case in the first instance. Clearly, he felt that a defense of the EPA's administrative discretion was important enough to merit a separate statement concerning the right way to interpret the law. He again insisted on the plain meaning of the act, which in his view reasonably puts global warming outside the domain of "air pollution." Understandably, neither his mistake about the meaning of "troposphere" nor his admission of scientific illiteracy made an appearance in the official text. Instead, Scalia turned to the dictionary for its communally endorsed monopoly on establishing the "natural" (and hence objective) meaning of language:

We need look no further than the dictionary for confirmation that this interpretation of "air pollution" is eminently reasonable. The definition of "pollute," of course, is "[t]o make or render impure or unclean." Webster's New International Dictionary 1910 (2d ed. 1949). And the first three definitions of "air" are as follows: (1) "[t]he invisible, odorless, and tasteless mixture of gases which surrounds the earth"; (2) "[t]he body of the earth's atmosphere; esp., the part of it near the earth, as distinguished from the upper rarefied part"; (3) "[a] portion of air or of the air considered with respect to physical

11. The full text of the oral argument can be found at the following link: http://www.supremecourtus.gov/oral_arguments/argument_transcripts/05-1120.pdf (accessed July 2010).

characteristics or as affecting the senses." Id., at 54. EPA's conception of "air pollution"—focusing on impurities in the "ambient air" "at ground level or near the surface of the earth"—is perfectly consistent with the natural meaning of that term.[12]

Breyer sided with the majority in rejecting the EPA's legal interpretation, but he filed no separate opinion and his views are less well documented than Scalia's. Yet even in his relatively limited interventions during oral argument, he displayed his tendency to conceptualize risk in quantitative terms. An exchange with Gregory C. Garre, deputy solicitor general representing the EPA, illustrates the point:

JUSTICE BREYER: Suppose it is not greenhouse gas. Suppose it was Agent Orange. Suppose there [sic] a car is coming down the street and it sprays out Agent Orange. And I come into the Court and I say, you know, I think that Agent Orange is going to kill me with cancer. And the reply is, well, we have some scientists here who say your chance of dying of cancer from Agent Orange is only 1 in 30. Maybe 1 in 50. Maybe 1 in a thousand. Maybe 1 in 10,000. And therefore, you have no standing to require the EPA to regulate this pollutant, Agent Orange, which is in a green cloud all over the city.

Now, would you say that the person who's made that claim has no standing?

MR. GARRE: Your Honor, I think that that is a fundamentally different case, for the simple reason that global climate change is a global phenomenon. I mean one—

JUSTICE BREYER: I was only addressing, using that to—to address your problem that the chances are too small that, in fact, any one individual will be affected by the 7 percent or 6 percent of the material that comes out of the truck—the CO_2.[13]

In disparate styles, and often reaching different conclusions, Scalia and Breyer agree on a point fundamental to their field of practice: that there is a foundation of shared understanding for judges to fall back on in resolving regulatory controversies. Each justice seamlessly integrates the two aspects of policy objectivity: which is the right representation of nature and which the right representation of political authority. For Breyer, it is nature's text that takes precedence, and his reasoning repeatedly draws affirmation from

---

12. *Massachusetts v. Environmental Protection Agency*, 549 U.S. 497 (2007), at 559–60.
13. Oral argument in *Massachusetts v. EPA*, http://www.supremecourtus.gov/oral_arguments/argument_transcripts/05–1120.pdf (accessed April 2011).

expert accounts of reality. For Scalia, legal texts provide the unambiguous baseline on which reason is built; the law prescribes who can speak, who can challenge, and, in contested cases, whose reason prevails. Either way, the objectivity of judicial review itself remains beyond question.

Globalizing Objectivity

The proliferation of international treaties for such matters as trade, environment, human rights, and nuclear security ensures that knowledge making for policy no longer lies wholly within the sovereign control of nation-states. Indeed, varied global recognition systems have come into place to certify policy-relevant expert knowledge as competent and trustworthy. Producing epistemic credibility is an evolving field of practice for international institutions. How do such bodies deal with differences among nationally or culturally specific norms of knowledge making? Do they craft their own practices, including distinctive definitions of objectivity, or do they incorporate and reproduce practices drawn from particular national traditions? In this section, I briefly discuss a dispute at the World Trade Organization (WTO) to show how this powerful global body has in effect adopted the U.S. culture of objectivity. In this case, a handful of close colleagues and I presented an *amicus* brief to the WTO and thus experienced in practice some of the techniques by which this agency, in decisions involving risk, guards itself against radical challenges to its notions of objectivity.

On May 13, 2003, the United States, Canada, and Argentina filed an action against the European Union (EU) for maintaining an illegal moratorium against American-made genetically modified organisms (hereafter *Biotech Products* case). That summer, five of us, all scholars of risk and regulatory science, met together for a week to draft our *amicus* brief. Our aim was to introduce into a policy dispute of global significance a body of social science knowledge on risk assessment that we believed was highly relevant to the case and yet in danger of being ignored. In particular, we wanted to make the WTO aware of the socially constructed character of risk assessment and to adjust its dispute resolution practices accordingly. The fate of our effort sheds light on the high entry barriers against voices questioning established epistemic norms in the world of global policy.

The *Biotech Products* dispute arose under the Agreement on Technical Barriers to Trade (TBT Agreement) and the Agreement on the Application of Sanitary and Phytosanitary Standards (SPS Agreement). Both agreements acknowledge that national governments may legitimately restrict the import of products from other countries if those products threaten their citizens' health and safety. Both provisions, however, also stipulate that exceptions must be justified through risk assessment. The relevant treaty language represents risk assessment as impersonal and judgment free, and hence as an objective basis for policy.[14] This is consistent with the U.S. understanding of risk assessment as sound science, capable of producing a universal, translocal form of objectivity.

Statements by high-level U.S. politicians left no doubt that what was at stake for the United States went beyond the economic consequences of the EU's reluctance to import genetically modified crops. Centrally implicated as well was the American approach to decision making, a threat to the concept of sound (regulatory) science that underwrote the safety of products made in the United States. American officials intuitively grasped that genetically modified crops would circulate freely in world trade only if the scientific assessments that supported them also enjoyed universal acceptance; these had to be placed, as it were, *hors de combat*. At the 2000 annual meeting of the American Association for the Advancement of Science, Secretary of State Madeleine Albright asserted that Europeans were rejecting not only genetically modified imports but also science: "But science does not support the Frankenfood fears of some, particularly outside the United States, that biotech foods or other products will harm human health."[15]

---

14. The relevant sections of the two agreements read as follows:

TBT Agreement, article 2.2: "Members shall ensure that technical regulations are not prepared, adopted or applied with a view to or with the effect of creating unnecessary obstacles to international trade. For this purpose, technical regulations shall not be more trade-restrictive than necessary to fulfil a legitimate objective, taking account of the risks non-fulfilment would create. Such legitimate objectives are, inter alia: national security requirements; the prevention of deceptive practices; protection of human health or safety, animal or plant life or health, or the environment. In assessing such risks, relevant elements of consideration are, inter alia: available scientific and technical information, related processing technology or intended end-uses of products."

SPS Agreement, article 2.2: "Members shall ensure that any sanitary or phytosanitary measure is applied only to the extent necessary to protect human, animal or plant life or health, is based on scientific principles and is not maintained without sufficient scientific evidence, except as provided for in paragraph 7 of Article 5."

SPS Agreement, article 5.7: "In cases where relevant scientific evidence is insufficient, a Member may provisionally adopt sanitary or phytosanitary measures on the basis of available pertinent information, including that from the relevant international organizations as well as from sanitary or phytosanitary measures applied by other Members. In such circumstances, Members shall seek to obtain the additional information necessary for a more objective assessment of risk and review the sanitary or phytosanitary measure accordingly within a reasonable period of time."

15. Madeleine K. Albright, plenary address, AAAS annual meeting, "Science in an Uncertain Millennium," Washington, DC, February 21, 2000, http://secretary.state.gov/www/statements/2000/000221.html (accessed July 2010).

In 2003, press releases from the U.S. Trade Representative's office declared that the moratorium was not only illegal but "non-science-based."[16]

Procedurally, a controversy of this kind goes before the WTO's Dispute Settlement Body (DSB); this is the WTO's General Council, consisting of ambassadorial representatives of member state governments, meeting together as the DSB. After required attempts at consultation and mediation, the DSB, through a closed process, appoints an ad hoc Dispute Settlement Panel to review the case, consult with appropriate experts, and prepare a preliminary report.[17] Unless an appeal is filed, the DSB adopts the report, which then becomes final. If an appeal is filed, it is heard by the seven-member Appellate Body, which again files a report that the DSB finalizes. The process, as imagined, is supposed to consume no more than a year without appeal and fifteen months with appeal. In the *Biotech Products* case, that period extended to nearly three years. The Dispute Settlement Panel issued its 1,050-page interim report on February 7, 2006, and the DSB adopted the final panel reports on November 21, 2006.

There is no process for allowing parties other than the disputing national governments into the dispute settlement process. The WTO Web site indicates that *amicus* briefs by third parties remain a deeply contested issue and there is no formal procedure for filing these.[18] In part, the lack of agreement reflects the multiplicity of legal cultures represented at the WTO: *amicus* briefs are recognized forms of intervention in common-law systems such as that of the United States but they have no comparable status in civil law. Accordingly, the WTO does not officially sanction the practice but leaves it up to each panel to decide in a given case whether or not to accept *amicus* submissions.

My colleagues and I were convinced that the U.S. position on sound science did not stand up to scholarly scrutiny. As contributors to the social studies of risk, we were in a strong position to communicate the deeply judgmental and culturally situated character of the "science" of risk analysis, but we lacked the practical know-how to make our views known in a forum where clear procedural channels are unavailable. Our team consisted of two trained lawyers, myself and David Winickoff, then a postdoctoral

16. Press release, U.S. Trade Representative, Executive Office of the President, Washington, DC, May 13, 2003, http://www.ustr.gov/releases/2003/05/03-31.htm (accessed October 2003).

17. In the *Biotech Products* case, the Dispute Settlement Panel consisted of Christian Haeberli (chair, Switzerland), Mohan Kumar (India), and Akio Shimizo (Japan).

18. See Dispute Settlement System Training Module at the WTO Gate's Interactive Course link, which leads to a statement on "*amicus curiae* submissions": http://www.wto.org/english/tratop_e/dispu_e/disp_settlement_cbt_e/c9s3p1_e.htm (accessed July 2010).

fellow in my program at the Harvard Kennedy School; two sociologists, Lawrence Busch, a noted expert on food and agriculture from Michigan State University, and Brian Wynne, a leading sociologist of science at Lancaster University; and a prominent British environmentalist and policy adviser, Robin Grove White, also of Lancaster University. We had no material resources other than our modest research budgets, and so we met at Lancaster, the Americans traveling on their own means and the British team members offering hospitality and a room rented at almost no cost from the Lancaster Friends' Meeting House for us to work in.

Our problem was twofold. In a field without transparent practices, especially for non-state actors, how could we nevertheless intervene as if we were acting in a procedurally legitimate manner? And how could we hope to gain recognition as knowledge bearers who should be heard in a domain where social science expertise seemed profoundly at odds with policy decisions, political interests, and the language of the international agreements—in short, with the governing law? On the first point, we found invaluable allies among a shadow network of nongovernmental practitioners united by a common desire to open up the WTO's much-criticized and nontransparent modes of operation.[19] On the second point, we had to compromise, translating our expertise and epistemic concerns into terms that the Dispute Settlement Panel might accept as sufficiently "legal" and thus allow into its deliberations.

The detailed story of how to insert an *amicus* brief into a system that does not officially tolerate such interventions will have to be told elsewhere. Within the constraints of this chapter, however, it is important to note that our record was one of mixed (and limited) success and failure: success in inserting a new text into the body of materials that the panel and, to some extent, the parties accepted and officially acknowledged; failure in disrupting the dominant global discourse around the objectivity of policy-relevant science. On the advice of experienced trade lawyers, environmental nongovernmental organizations (who submitted a separate *amicus* brief), and knowledgeable individuals at the Center for International Environmental Law, we notified the parties in advance of our desire to submit a brief, and we eventually sent the brief to the WTO with the support of the EU. Privately, persons working in the EU's legal and policy offices

19. The first public meeting of the WTO Appellate Body was held on July 28 and 29, 2008, in the controversial and long-running *Hormones* case, involving trade in meat treated with growth hormones. The public could observe the proceedings on closed-circuit television in a designated observation room. See CIEL report, http://www.ciel.org/Tae/WTO_Hormones.html (accessed July 2010).

assured us that our brief had been read and noticed and made an impression; publicly, the panel report made only the most glancing references, as follows, to our brief (that of "a group of university professors") in all of its thousand plus pages:[20]

> 7.10 In the course of these proceedings, we received three unsolicited *amicus curiae* briefs: on 6 May 2004 we received an *amicus curiae* brief from a group of university professors; on 27 May 2004 we received an *amicus curiae* brief from a group of non-governmental organizations represented by the Foundation for International Environmental Law and Development (FIELD); and on 1 June 2004 we received an *amicus curiae* brief from a group of non-governmental organizations represented by the Center for International Environmental Law (CIEL). These briefs were submitted to us prior to the first substantive meeting of the Panel with the Parties, and the Parties and Third Parties were given an opportunity to comment on these *amicus curiae* briefs.
>
> 7.11 We note that a panel has the discretionary authority either to accept and consider or to reject any information submitted to it, whether requested by a panel or not, or to make some other appropriate disposition thereof. In this case, we accepted the information submitted by the amici curiae into the record. However, in rendering our decision, we did not find it necessary to take the *amicus curiae* briefs into account.

The panel concluded, in summary, that the EU had violated the SPS Agreement by failing to complete approval procedures without undue delay. In addition, several individual member states had violated the agreement by adopting discriminatory measures that, in defiance of article 2, were not based on scientific principles of risk assessment and thus were maintained without sufficient scientific evidence.[21] The panel's logic had more to do with its construal of its legal responsibilities as a reviewing body than with upholding a particular norm of scientific objectivity. The result, however, left standing treaty language that, on its face, runs counter to significant bodies of social science scholarship on the nature of risk assessment.

Did our intervention make a difference to global policy-relevant knowledge or practice? Formally, it was accepted by the panel, receiving a docket

20. The numbers refer to paragraphs 7.10 and 7.11 in the panel's Interim Report. Footnotes are omitted, including one listing us by name.

21. For a summary of the panel's own preliminary summary report, see the International Economic Law and Policy Blog, http://worldtradelaw.typepad.com/ielpblog/2006/02/from_800_pages_.html (accessed July 2010).

number that gave it official status. Informally, it began circulating as part of the material culture of knowledge making, in which individual items may eventually join up with others to produce unexpected effects. It was published as an article in the *Yale Journal of International Law* and thus achieved academic recognition (Winickoff et al. 2005). In a more personal display of the power of networking, Lawrence Busch in 2008 accepted a professorship at Lancaster University, continuing the collaboration with Brian Wynne begun in 2003. As an attempt to reshape global policy discourse on risk assessment, however, our brief was at best a drop in a bucket of slowly accumulating scholarship contesting the U.S. narrative of regulatory science and its decontextualized objectivity.[22]

Conclusion

Policy makers earn our trust through demonstrations of epistemic virtue, which include in the modern world the capacity to produce and act on objective knowledge. I have argued in this chapter that the practices of knowledge production for public policy are culturally inflected, institutionally dispersed, distributed across time and space, and involve the making of epistemic norms that are not given in logic or nature. Nevertheless, through entrenched institutional practices, such norms become naturalized and taken for granted. Objectivity is an especially powerful norm, a claim of authority that commands respect in Enlightenment societies because it mirrors reality without distortion and hence is not contestable, even in the conflict-ridden territory of political judgments. By claiming objectivity, decision makers also claim reason, transcending standpoints and interests. There can be no higher form of rationality than acting on the strength of objective knowledge.

Objectivity is easy to claim but hard to accomplish "in practice," and that is the entry point for the analysis undertaken in this chapter. Policy objectivity, like all social norms, is painstakingly constructed, contested, reaffirmed, and performed in routine practices of social actors and institutions. As research in science and technology studies has repeatedly shown, these modes of construction and affirmation become most visible at moments of controversy, when opposing actors challenge each other's assumptions and so reveal the interpretive flexibility of concepts such as

22. On July 13, 2010, the European Commission announced that it would hand greater freedom to member nations to decide whether or not to grow genetically modified plants (Kanter 2010). This move is consistent with the tenor of our argument.

objectivity. To controversy studies I add *comparison*—across space, time, actors, and decisions—as another potent method for revealing the cultural specificity of seemingly universal epistemic norms such as objectivity. Through cross-national comparisons of regulatory practice, historical studies of peer review, divergent practices of judicial reasoning, and a case study of global policy, I have tried to show how the view-from-nowhere objectivity prized by the American policy process is achieved, held in place, and internationally disseminated by one of the modern world's most contentious policy cultures.

The WTO case strikingly illustrates the importance of looking at epistemic practices in close detail. Here is a global body with power to determine the fates of nations and industries but whose ways of gathering facts and accumulating knowledge have fallen almost entirely outside the scope of social analysis. Our group's attempt to inject current social science knowledge into the WTO's thinking failed in many respects, but even the small wedge of an academic *amicus* brief may have done its bit to demonstrate that the objectivity of policy judgments on the world stage is anything but a standpoint-neutral achievement. Our experience highlighted yet again the inseparable connections between speaking for nature and speaking for institutional positions (e.g., nation-state, nongovernmental organization, academic) in the manufacture of policy-relevant objectivity.

I would like to end by stressing the need for greater institutional breadth as well as ethnographic thickness in our analyses of epistemic practices. It is not, after all, a single expert body or court decision or legislative enactment that determines how U.S. policy makers go about making their knowledge claims seem objective. Instead, we see through decades of history how diverse actors in disparate institutional settings strategically deploy the resources of reason and argument, observation and evidence, models and materiality, as well as divergent discursive forms—from academic articles to laws and judicial opinions—to open up some aspects of knowledge making while keeping others under wraps. We see how locally specific disagreements, such as that between two levels of the U.S. court system, are ironed out in practice so as to reinforce dominant epistemic norms. Analyses of single actors, institutions, or events can provide micro-insights into particular knowledge controversies and exercises of epistemic power. But to understand something as pervasive and of *longue durée* as the norms of objectivity in a regulatory culture, we need to adopt a sidelong gaze from alternative temporal and spatial worlds. Others' practices offer in the end the clearest windows on the strangeness that so often hides behind the familiarity of our own present.

References

Anderson, Frederick R. 2003. "Peer Review of Data." *National Law Journal*, September 29.

Bourdieu, Pierre. 1987. "The Force of Law: Toward a Sociology of the Juridical Field." Translated by Richard Terdiman. *Hastings Law Journal* 38:814–53.

Breyer, Stephen. 1978. "*Vermont Yankee* and the Courts' Role in the Nuclear Energy Controversy." *Harvard Law Review* 91:1833–45.

———. 1993. *Breaking the Vicious Circle: Toward Effective Risk Regulation*. Cambridge, MA: Harvard University Press.

Brickman, Ronald, Sheila Jasanoff, and Thomas Ilgen. 1985. *Controlling Chemicals: The Politics of Regulation in Europe and the United States*. Ithaca, NY: Cornell University Press.

Brisbin, Robert A. 1991. "Justice Antonin Scalia, Constitutional Discourse, and the Legalistic State." *Political Research Quarterly* 44:1005–38.

Bush, George H. W. 1990. Remarks at the National Academy of Sciences, Washington, DC, April 23.

Callon, Michel. 1986. "Some Elements of a Sociology of Translation: Domestication of the Scallops and the Fishermen of St. Brieuc Bay." In *Power, Action, and Belief: A New Sociology of Knowledge?* edited by John Law, 196–233. London: Routledge and Kegan Paul.

Clinton, Hillary. 2007. "Scientific Integrity and Innovation." Remarks at the Carnegie Institution for Science, Washington, DC, October 4.

Collins, H. M. 1985. *Changing Order: Replication and Induction in Scientific Practice*. London: Sage Publications.

Daston, Lorraine, and Peter Galison. 2007. *Objectivity*. New York: Zone Books.

Dear, Peter. 2006. *The Intelligibility of Nature: How Science Makes Sense of the World*. Chicago: University of Chicago Press.

Ezrahi, Yaron. 1990. *The Descent of Icarus*. Cambridge, MA: Harvard University Press.

Gieryn, Thomas F. 1995. "Boundaries of Science." In *The Handbook of Science and Technology Studies*, edited by Sheila Jasanoff et al., 393–443. Thousand Oaks, CA: Sage Publications.

Gottweis, Herbert. 1998. *Governing Molecules: The Discursive Politics of Genetic Engineering in Europe and the United States*. Cambridge, MA: MIT Press.

Haraway, Donna. 1988. "Situated Knowledges: The Science Question in Feminism and the Privilege of Partial Perspective." *Feminist Studies* 14:575–99.

Hilgartner, Stephen. 2000. *Science on Stage: Expert Advice as Public Drama*. Stanford, CA: Stanford University Press.

Hoberg, George, and Kathryn Harrison. 1994. *Risk, Science and Politics: Regulating Toxic Substances in Canada and the United States*. Montreal: McGill-Queen's University Press.

Jasanoff, Sheila. 1987. "Contested Boundaries in Policy-Relevant Science." *Social Studies of Science* 17:195–230.

———. 1990. *The Fifth Branch: Science Advisers as Policymakers*. Cambridge, MA: Harvard University Press.

———. 1998. "Expert Games in Silicone Gel Breast Implant Litigation." In *Science in Court*, edited by Michael Freeman and Helen Reece, 83–107. London: Dartmouth.

———. 2005a. *Designs on Nature: Science and Democracy in Europe and the United States*. Princeton, NJ: Princeton University Press.

———. 2005b. "Judgment under Siege: The Three-Body Problem of Expert Legitimacy."

In *Democratization of Expertise? Exploring Novel Forms of Scientific Advice in Political Decision-Making*, edited by Peter Weingart and Sabine Maasen, 209–24. Dordrecht: Kluwer.

Kanter, James. 2010. "Europe's New Approach to Biotech Food." *New York Times*, July 7.

Latour, Bruno. 1988. *The Pasteurization of France*. Cambridge, MA: Harvard University Press.

———. 1993. *We Have Never Been Modern*. Cambridge, MA: Harvard University Press.

MacKenzie, Donald. 1990. *Inventing Accuracy: A Historical Sociology of Nuclear Missile Guidance*. Cambridge, MA: MIT Press.

McLaren, Anne. 1989. "IVF: Regulation or Prohibition?" *Nature* 342:469–70.

Merton, Robert K. [1942] 1973. "The Normative Structure of Science." In *The Sociology of Science: Theoretical and Empirical Investigations*, edited by Robert K. Merton and Norman W. Storer, 267–78. Chicago: University of Chicago Press.

Michaels, David. 2008. *Doubt Is Their Product: How Industry's Assault on Science Threatens Your Health*. New York: Oxford University Press.

Mooney, Chris. 2004. "Beware 'Sound Science.' It's Doublespeak for Trouble." *Washington Post*, February 29, B2.

Nagel, Thomas. 1986. *The View from Nowhere*. Oxford: Oxford University Press.

National Academy of Sciences. 2003. *Ensuring the Quality of Data Disseminated by the Federal Government: Workshop Report*. Washington, DC: National Academies Press.

National Research Council. 1994. *Science and Judgment in Risk Assessment*. Washington, DC: National Academy Press.

Nelkin, Dorothy, ed. 1992. *Controversy*. 3d ed. Newbury Park, CA: Sage Publications.

OMB (Office of Management and Budget). 2003. *Proposed Bulletin on Peer Review and Information Quality*. *Federal Register* 68 (September 15): 54023–29.

Pinch, Trevor. 1993. "'Testing—One, Two, Three . . . Testing': Toward a Sociology of Testing." *Science, Technology, and Human Values* 18:25–41.

Porter, Theodore M. 1995. *Trust in Numbers: The Pursuit of Objectivity in Science and Public Life*. Princeton, NJ: Princeton University Press.

———. 2007. "Eras of Judgment." *Nature* 449:985–87.

Rushefsky, Mark. 1986. *Making Cancer Policy*. New York: State University of New York Press.

Scalia, Antonin. 1978. "Vermont Yankee: The A.P.A., the D.C. Circuit, and the Supreme Court." *Supreme Court Review*, 345–409.

Shapin, Steven. 1994. *A Social History of Truth*. Chicago: University of Chicago Press.

Shapin, Steven, and Simon Schaffer. 1985. *Leviathan and the Air-Pump: Hobbes, Boyle, and the Experimental Life*. Princeton, NJ: Princeton University Press.

Slovic, Paul. 1991. "Beyond Numbers: A Broader Perspective on Risk Perception and Risk Communication." In *Acceptable Evidence: Science and Values in Risk Management*, edited by Deborah G. Mayo and Rachelle Hollander, 48–65. New York: Oxford University Press.

Vogel, David. 1986. *National Styles of Regulation*. Ithaca, NY: Cornell University Press.

Warnock, Mary. 1984. *Report of the Committee of Enquiry into Human Fertilisation and Embryology*. London: HMSO.

Winickoff, David, et al. 2005. "Adjudicating the GM Food Wars: Science, Risk, and Democracy in World Trade Law." *Yale Journal of International Law* 30:81–123.

Zuckerman, Harriet, and Robert K. Merton. 1971. "Patterns of Evaluation in Science: Institutionalization, Structure and Functions of the Referee System. *Minerva* 9:66–100.

ELEVEN

How Claims to Know the Future Are Used to Understand the Present

Techniques of Prospection in the Field of National Security

GRÉGOIRE MALLARD AND ANDREW LAKOFF

It might be assumed that when political officials and experts try to envision the future, they do so in order to predict the outcomes of their actions in the present. And indeed this is often the case. For instance, in a press briefing given in the aftermath of the 2002 U.S. invasion of Afghanistan, U.S. Defense Secretary Donald Rumsfeld said about the results of the American military action: "There are known knowns. These are things we know that we know. There are known unknowns. That is to say, there are things that we now know we don't know. But there are also unknown unknowns. These are things we do not know we don't know."[1] In this sense, imagining the future helps national leaders not only find out how "known unknowns" might play out but also perhaps discover some "unknown unknowns." It can help them transform unknown uncertainty into known risk. When national leaders seek to anticipate the likely consequences of their actions in the face of identifiable threats, imagining the future serves a "predictive" purpose.

But there are other purposes served by what we call "techniques of prospection," by which we mean a set of practices for envisioning an unknown future. In this chapter, we analyze techniques of prospection when they are used in the field of national security for a second purpose, which can be termed "constitutive" rather than predictive. Techniques of prospection are used for a constitutive purpose when national leaders develop scenarios of the future to help them understand whether or not ambiguous

---

1. Donald Rumsfeld, Department of Defense press briefing, February 12, 2002, http://www.defense.gov/transcripts/transcript.aspx?transcriptid=2636 (accessed December 14, 2010).

events should be seen as present security threats.[2] In this case, social scientific knowledge is used to create plausible futures in order to enlighten the present rather than to predict the future based on the present. In this chapter, we focus on this second—constitutive—use of techniques of prospection, which, we argue, helps policy makers recognize a threat when they see one or, conversely, helps policy makers deconstruct the characterization of a given threat.

Our analysis of techniques of prospection builds on an existing literature in the sociology of knowledge and science studies that looks at the significance of knowledge practices designed to envision the future, such as modeling, forecasting, and scenario planning. Much of this literature has emphasized the predictive use of these practices: their use by policy makers to foresee the consequences of their action in a world of uncertainties (Dahan Dalmedico and Guillemot 2008; Jasanoff 2005; Stinchcombe 2001) or their use by politicians to provide a veneer of rationality to justify controversial decisions (Kuklick 2006). For instance, historians of the Cold War have examined the use of war-gaming techniques as part of the development of predictive thinking and nuclear strategy in think tanks such as the RAND Corporation (Kaplan 1983; Kuklick 2006). Other authors have shown how the techniques of prospection pioneered at RAND diffused beyond nuclear strategy to fields such as economics and urban policy, where they were used to predict the likely consequences of policy decisions (Amadae 2003; Light 2003; Mirowski 2002).[3] However, for the most part, these studies have not been concerned with how this knowledge production technique constitutes certain events as salient problems for policy makers and specialists. Only recently have studies by sociologists of knowledge and science studies scholars begun to focus on the constitutive use of state-of-the-art techniques of prospection in the fields of banking and high finance (Callon 2007; MacKenzie 2007; Muniesa and Callon 2007).

Our focus here on the constitutive use of techniques of prospection in

2. Security planning is conducted in a heterogeneous institutional field that includes think tanks, policy institutes, government agencies, and advisory commissions. It is not surprising that policy makers can use a large number of techniques of knowing, including techniques of prospection, to assess whether their characterizations of certain events as constituting national security threats are credible.

3. These studies share with analyses of the use of forecasting methods in fields such as environmental and industrial policy a concern for describing how new techniques of prospection empower competing groups of bureaucrats and experts in various fields of knowledge to claim a monopoly over "rationality" (Espeland 1998; Hecht 1998; Jasper 1990; Stinchcombe and Heimer 1985).

the field of national security allows us to expand the range of questions asked by scholars of knowledge practices about the role of social scientific knowledge in the public arena. Like other scholars who focus on the question of how truth claims attain cultural authority (Camic and Gross 2001), we ask: How do specialists and policy makers assess the validity of representations of the future? And how do such techniques help truth claims attain credibility in charged political settings?[4] Our focus on the constitutive purpose of techniques of prospection builds upon pioneering studies by Reinhart Koselleck (2004) and François Hartog (2003), who define various macrohistorical *"régimes d'historicité"* (i.e., articulations between past, present, and future). But in contrast to them, and like previous scholars of knowledge practices, we place emphasis on the specific contexts and situated actions in which these techniques of prospection are used, without making any claim about their historical generality.

We also suggest that the study of this relatively uncharted territory—the constitutive uses of techniques of prospection—provides analysts of knowledge practices in the social sciences with an opportunity to pose new questions. Such questions include: How do policy makers and security specialists constitute potential events as being relevant to the field of national security through reference to their likely consequences? How, conversely, are they led to ignore certain events based on their plausible future consequences? What methods of representing plausible future events do security specialists use to lead national leaders to focus on certain events and ignore others? And finally, when techniques of prospection are used with a constitutive purpose, what kinds of knowledge do they leave aside?

In what follows, we examine how policy makers and security experts come to the conclusion that they can ignore certain potential events while focusing their attention on others.[5] Our emphasis is therefore on the articulation between knowledge and ignorance (Proctor 2008). Techniques of prospection, we argue, play an essential part in constituting events as relevant to the field of national security. In this chapter, we analyze two constitutive techniques of prospection, each of which brings potential future events into the present as objects of knowledge and intervention: first,

4. See Shapin 1995 on the articulation between rationality and credibility in other scientific fields.

5. But we are not concerned with making normative judgments about policy makers' conclusions. We do not assess whether or not they should have considered the events we study as constituting threats to the national security of their country. Indeed, we analyze the role of techniques of prospection in security experts' decision-making process, but we do not assign a specific value to the outcome in each case under study.

economic forecasting, which is based on econometric predictions about future supply and demand functions of a given good in a given market; and second, the scenario-based exercise, which is based on the imaginative enactment of an uncertain but potentially catastrophic future event in a given territory. Our two cases show that techniques of prospection can be used to convince national leaders that either (1) events that are a priori relevant to national security (such as the signing of an international nuclear deal) can be legitimately ignored by national leaders, who come to believe that they do not constitute security threats; or (2) events that are a priori not relevant to national security (such as the spread of a disease) need to receive the full attention of public officials in charge of national security.

The first case is based on the study of debates over European nuclear strategy in the Cold War, while the second concerns scenario-based exercises that have only recently been extended into new domains such as health by U.S. national security experts concerned with decision making in crisis situations. While the strategic issues involved in these cases are historically specific to these contexts, the reasons why such techniques are used by security specialists are more general. In the field of national security, experts must make decisions in the face of limited knowledge, as other countries' motives may be hidden or data about weapons programs may be classified.[6] When knowledge of the present is limited, it is understandable that the construction of plausible scenarios of the future might be used to enlighten understanding of the present. Even today, security specialists use techniques of econometric prospection to help them decide whether or not certain events constitute security threats—for instance, when nuclear nonproliferation specialists try to assess whether it makes economic sense for Iran to enrich uranium or whether such a decision can make sense only from the military point of view.[7] Techniques of prospection are also central to a number of contemporary areas of security strategy, such as the use of scenarios ranging from nuclear terrorism to a major hurricane by the Department of Homeland Security in its major planning documents (Lakoff 2007).

6. Regarding the last point, it is well known that the level of security clearance often signals the level of credibility and power one has in the national security administration.

7. Just after the Second World War, econometric predictions were also used by American economists to assess whether there existed economic justification for the worldwide construction of nuclear power plants that produced so-called dual-use materials, like plutonium (Mallard 2008b).

Techniques of Prospection and Diplomatic Negotiations

It is of prime importance for national leaders to know the intentions of other states, both friendly and hostile. To gain knowledge about the exact meaning of a geopolitical event and to learn about states' intentions and motivations, the best way is often to make inferences from a large set of clues and signals sent by other states in the near past. This form of interpretive knowledge is akin to that of diplomatic historians, who infer states' motivations from their knowledge of the past (acquired through the gathering of public declarations to the press by foreign national leaders or by the legal analysis of pacts and treaties signed by foreign countries) and their continually updated knowledge of the present (acquired by intelligence work, by inspectors working on foreign ground on behalf of an international organization or a national government and/or spies working under cover). But do national security specialists also use knowledge of the future to understand present geopolitical events?

Techniques of prospection such as simulations and war gaming have sometimes been used to re-create the world in laboratory conditions to infer how enemies would react when confronted with a specific geopolitical event. When one uses laboratory methods to decide the nature of future events, controversy often ensues. Envisioning worst-case scenarios in the laboratory has been criticized as either useless or immoral. For instance, as Kaplan (1983) and Kuklick (2006), among others, have shown, when members of the RAND Corporation started to design war-gaming techniques to aid in formulating U.S. nuclear military strategy, the American military hierarchy objected that laboratory conditions could not reflect the chaos of war, and their allies (the West Germans, in particular) objected that whether real or fictional, the simulation of Germany being wiped out by Soviet nuclear weapons was shocking. Such criticisms might explain why such cases as those presented in the next section, where techniques of prospection are used in laboratory-like conditions to determine the nature of an event, are relatively new knowledge practices that constitute the exception rather than the norm in the field of national security—even though their importance is growing.

But techniques of prospection that are used for constitutive purposes are not always experimental: they do not always seek to re-create the world with all its complexity in laboratory conditions. In this section, we will describe other techniques of prospection that are used in real-life negotiations by national leaders to reduce the complexity and multifaceted character of a geopolitical event to a single aspect of it. These techniques test whether a complex event, with potential ramifications in many adjacent sectors (both military and civilian), can be reduced to one dimension in a way that still makes sense.

We present a case in which these techniques of prospection were used to see whether Europe's projected nuclear development in the late 1950s could be reduced to serving a single (and peaceful) economic purpose: the development of electricity production.[8] These techniques were used by Americans and Europeans to give credibility to the claim that Europeans' present decision to sign a major treaty of nuclear cooperation did not hide military motivations on their part but that Europeans wanted to optimize electricity production in the long term. We first show that Americans could not infer from the analysis of European past legal history whether Europeans' present intentions were peaceful-economic or military-strategic when Europeans signed such a treaty. Second, we show how Europeans, when confronted with a real-life test by American policy makers, responded by using classic economic techniques of prospection that helped them convince the Americans that their intentions were purely peaceful. Third, we show that these techniques were used as techniques of suggestion: they concentrated American policy makers' attention on the bright technological representation of the future and away from the legal uncertainties and opacities that existed in the treaty itself. In that sense, these techniques actually succeeded in concealing Europeans' secret intentions, which included military ambitions as well as peaceful ones.

Two Groups Eager to Know Europeans' Intentions

The signing of treaties is a major cause of concern for states and their leaders. Treaties are one of the general forms through which states commit to a future course of action based on a shared geopolitical diagnosis of the intentions of their allies and enemies. In this section, we analyze how the 1957 treaty creating the European Community of Atomic Energy (hereafter called Euratom) was understood by U.S. national leaders when they were discussing whether they wanted to sign an agreement of nuclear

---

8. Such techniques are used regularly to plan not only the development of one sector but also the development of a firm, for instance, by corporate managers who justify their decisions before shareholders by projecting expected growth levels; or the development of a national economy, by governmental officials who assess expected changes in unemployment or inflation rates to justify their yearly budget.

cooperation with this new Western European organization.[9] At the time, those American leaders who were called to decide on the desirability of signing such a treaty of cooperation with Euratom could be divided into two groups holding competing normative ideals and strategic goals: the "European federalists" and the "nationalists."

If a treaty of cooperation between Euratom and the United States were to be signed, it was clear that the decision lay to a great extent in the hands of the U.S. president, Dwight Eisenhower, and his secretary of state, John Foster Dulles, and the men who worked with them in the State Department. These men were "European federalists" in the sense that they wanted to help Europeans develop nuclear technologies within a European integrated framework, such as that provided by Euratom, whatever their uses by Europeans and whatever the complexity and ambiguity of Europeans' motivations. Although they believed that an integrated Europe should first concentrate on developing peaceful technologies for the purpose of producing electricity, they also believed that a stronger and more independent Europe producing its own nuclear weapons would be good for U.S. national security in the long term (Trachtenberg 1999, 149). That meant that they wanted to sign a treaty of cooperation with Euratom even if the Europeans planned to use American technological help in developing dual-use technologies (technologies used for both peaceful and military goals). For instance, they were in favor of helping Europeans acquire the technologies by which one can enrich uranium, either at low levels of enrichment to produce fuel for their power plants (peaceful use) or at high levels of enrichment to produce weapons-grade materials for future European bombs (military use). Key politicians in this first group had long-term ties with the leading figure behind the European treaties being proposed in dual-use sectors (like coal, steel, and nuclear development): Jean Monnet, who founded the Action Committee for the United States of Europe (hereafter Action Committee) in the mid-1950s. They helped Monnet gather the funds necessary to hire engineers and economists (such as the Frenchman Louis Armand) who had the technical knowledge needed to answer questions about the rationality of Europeans' decisions when evaluated from the perspective of electricity development.

For a future treaty of cooperation between Euratom and the United States to be signed, the U.S. Congress also needed to ratify it, as required

---

9. Most Cold War historians (e.g., Gaddis 2005) and analysts of European integration (e.g., Moravcsik 1998) ignore the role that the Euratom Treaty played in the U.S. Cold War foreign policy in Europe.

by the U.S. Constitution. Among those people whose opinion was decisive in the U.S. Congress were the senators sitting on the powerful Joint Committee on Atomic Energy (JCAE) and the members of the Atomic Energy Commission (AEC), particularly its chairman, Lewis Strauss, who reported his activities to the JCAE. Indeed, Strauss's opinion was highly sought after by members of the Republican Party. Eisenhower, when he became president, had appointed Strauss, whose nationalist views were known to the Republican Party, to balance the nomination of John Foster Dulles to the post of secretary of state, as the internationalist and pro-European views of the latter were also known (and disliked) by the Republican Party (Greene 2007). American nationalists were not in favor of helping an integrated Europe develop dual-use nuclear technologies. They wanted to keep the Western nuclear deterrent in U.S. hands, and they believed that European governments on the Continent were too unreliable to be entrusted with the possession of dual-use technologies.[10] Therefore, they wanted to make sure that the future treaty of cooperation with Euratom did not open the door to helping Europeans develop military applications of nuclear energy.[11] For them, it was essential to know what the intentions of the Europeans led by Jean Monnet and his Action Committee were, and to make sure that Europeans would be able to use the nuclear technologies bought from the United States for only peaceful purposes. Selling U.S. power plants and the fuel for these plants to Europeans was the simplest way to ensure that Europeans would not be able to divert any nuclear materials for military purposes, as these plants were the safest from the perspective of nonproliferation.

The Mixed Signals Sent by Europeans

There were different ways through which the AEC and U.S. Congress could find out about Europeans' intentions when they created Euratom, with which the U.S. government was asked to sign a treaty of cooperation.

First, they could read the legal documents that emerged from the Conference of European Foreign Ministers, who negotiated the Euratom Treaty.

---

10. The fact that some of these European countries still had strong Communist Parties was also relevant for nationalists.

11. Among nationalists, of course, there were some differences of opinion on many topics, as some of them were in favor of a strict protectionism on nuclear trade, while others were closer to "international liberals," like Senator Pastore, who argued in favor of increased international trade of purely peaceful nuclear technologies. But the issue of whether the United States should help Europeans acquire military nuclear technologies clearly separated these nationalists from European federalists.

The drafters of the Euratom Treaty, Jean Monnet and the Action Committee, claimed that Euratom concerned only peaceful activities (Action Committee 1955). Still, even though Europeans claimed that the Euratom Treaty ruled out cooperation in purely military research like the assembly of nuclear warheads, it left open cooperation in dual-use nuclear applications of nuclear energy, including those that the U.S. Congress considered to be "military" by nature, like the enrichment of uranium.

American nationalists could also read the treaty against the recent legal history of European treaties in the field of nuclear energy to decide whether there was a risk that Euratom could be used to channel American help to a weapons program.[12] Such an analysis of the recent legal and diplomatic history was also inconclusive, however. The Euratom Treaty was the successor of the failed European Defense Community (EDC) Treaty, whose ratification was defeated in the French parliament in 1954. The creation of the EDC would have been a clearly military event of strategic consequences. Had it been ratified by the French parliament, the EDC Treaty would have created a European Defense Commission in charge of administering all nuclear activities in Europe, most of which were considered by the treaty as "military" activities (Winand 1993). The Euratom Treaty proposed a cosmetic change compared with the nuclear provisions of the EDC Treaty, since the Euratom Commission planned to develop nuclear technologies that it now called "peaceful" but that had been framed as "military" by the EDC Treaty; the enrichment of uranium and many other nuclear activities that could serve the purpose of producing electricity were characterized as military in the EDC Treaty.

Furthermore, it was also unclear whether future Euratom member states were legally prohibited from producing nuclear weapons on their own (rather than within the Euratom Treaty framework). The former Axis powers (Germany and Italy) were supposed to have renounced the military benefits of nuclear energy. When West Germany was given back its international legal sovereignty, the West German chancellor had pledged in 1954 that West Germany would not "produce" nuclear weapons on its soil. But the promise was ambiguous. The chancellor added the clause *sic rebus stantibus* (everything held constant), and he did not say whether West Germans could produce nuclear weapons on the soil of one of its allies, such as France. France's intentions to acquire nuclear weapons became more

12. Here, we do not mean that senators sat in a subcommittee examining recent legal European history. Instead, we reconstruct what they were likely to know, based upon what every contemporary who was at least vaguely informed of the European situation at the time knew.

clearly expressed during the EDC Treaty ratification debate (the limitations put on France's nuclear military ambitions were one of the main reasons why parliamentarians rejected it), but in the mid-1950s France still denied that it sought to acquire nuclear weapons on its own (Skogmar 2004).

Considering these legal uncertainties, knowledge of Euratom's technological program, for which the Europeans planned to ask for American aid, was another great source of information to deduce what Europeans' intentions were when they signed the Euratom Treaty. This technological program was not described in the Euratom Treaty itself, but the experts in the Conference of Foreign Ministers of the six countries who negotiated the Euratom Treaty made official statements arguing that Euratom should acquire dual-use nuclear technologies—specifically a uranium enrichment plant, which was too costly for European nation-states like France to develop on their own. In fact, a leading French nuclear specialist, Louis Armand, initially defended Euratom for the precise reason that France would receive financial help for its enrichment program from future Euratom partners and technical help from the United States through the future United States–Euratom treaty (Perrin 1956; Armand 1956).

This choice to develop dual-use technologies sent mixed signals—to say the least—about Europeans' intentions, which did not reassure Lewis Strauss and other nationalists. Indeed, if the Europeans built an enrichment plant, nothing would prevent them from enriching uranium at higher levels to build weapons-grade materials. One way to confirm that suspicion was to see if it made sense for Europeans to build an enrichment plant to produce fuel for the purpose of electricity development in Europe. The mobilization of engineering knowledge to infer foreign nations' intentions is quite common in the field of nonproliferation. Today, nuclear experts infer that Iran's intentions must be military from the fact that Iran is producing enriched uranium in large quantities when no power plant that can use this fuel *presently* exists in Iran. In our case, simple engineering knowledge could also be used as proof in a similar way. In the mid-1950s, France had no *present* civilian use for such an enrichment plant since its power plants used natural (rather than enriched) uranium as a combustible. As Jules Guéron (1983), another French nuclear specialist who participated in the Euratom Treaty negotiations, wrote: "France's European partners entertained no illusion about the military ambitions of such a project" because of the "simultaneous pressures by the French to build nuclear power plants using natural uranium as well as a uranium enrichment plant." For this reason, some Europeans, like Guéron himself, believed that Euratom should invest in R&D with the Americans to produce prototypes of new power plants using low-enriched uranium and buy cheap British power plants to cover *immediate* electricity needs.

If European partners "entertained no illusion" about France's military goals, why would the U.S. nationalists hesitate to reach the same conclusion? The technological program proposed by nuclear experts was only one clue, in a sea of other, contradictory signals. Louis Armand himself argued that the construction of a Euratom enrichment plant responded to a *future* technological need, if not a *present* one—just as Iranians argue today when justifying the construction of their enrichment plant. Indeed, Armand believed that France and other European nations would soon switch from power plants using natural uranium to power plants using low-enriched uranium. But as the price of low-enriched uranium was high, the operational costs of these power plants would be too great for the Europeans to continue buying it on the international market. Therefore, it was prudent for the Europeans themselves to produce low-enriched uranium (but not the highly enriched uranium used for nuclear weapons). Armand mobilized economic techniques to argue his case. An engineer by training who presided over the reorganization of the French postwar scientific and industrial landscape, Armand had released various reports (e.g., Armand 1955) that had all been noted for the emphasis he placed on the economic principle of cost efficiency for defining the future of Europe's nuclear joint program with the United States.[13]

One last simple way for U.S. senators to insure themselves against the risk that future American technological aid to Euratom could be used by Europeans to develop military applications was to maintain their system of controls and inspections in Europe. Since the end of World War II, inspectors from the AEC directly controlled European activities in which United States–made sensitive fissile materials and technologies were used, and they prohibited their usage by Europeans for military purposes. If the AEC maintained its control, the United States could monitor in real time how the Europeans used the technologies sold to them by the Americans. Such a real-time knowledge of the *present* provided the Americans with some robust guarantees against risks of undetected diversion. However, it was extremely costly, especially if Europeans were going to build many new nuclear power plants, as they now claimed they would.

---

13. Armand was not an expert in nuclear military strategy or armaments, so his point was not that Europeans could buy a cheaper defense if they developed their own H-bombs.

Furthermore, maintaining that form of intelligence on the ground raised a legal problem because of the Euratom Treaty. It was not only against the wish of European federalists, both in the United States in the Eisenhower administration and in Europe in Monnet's Action Committee, but it was also in contradiction with the treaty itself. Indeed, the innovation represented by the Euratom Treaty was that it created a European-wide system of controls, in which all the activities of not only West Germany but also France, Italy, and other signatories of the Euratom Treaty would be controlled exclusively by the Euratom Commission. The treaty of cooperation with Euratom that arrived on the desks of U.S. senators required that, should they sign a treaty with Euratom, they recognize the Euratom system of control as the only valid one in most of continental Europe. Americans would thus be deprived of an important source of knowledge about Europeans' intentions. It was unlikely that American nationalists would accept such a clause if they were not convinced that Europeans' present intentions were exclusively peaceful.

Testing the Credibility of the Europeans' Peaceful Intentions

When access to information is limited or unclear, one can complement the inferences made by observing the past and present with some form of hypothetic-deductive reasoning and predictions of future outcomes that may derive from the present. States can manipulate some real-life variables up (or down) to a certain threshold, after which they are better able to predict another state's intentions. In particular, states can easily manipulate the price of the goods controlled by state industries to test hypotheses about behavioral changes among the buyers of these products. These predictions can take the following form: "*If* the price of that type of good goes down past that threshold, and *if* a state still seeks to produce it even though it makes more economic sense to buy it directly from the international market rather than produce it, *then* it means that this state wants it for reasons that are external to the economy of the sector in question [here electricity production], and *then* the real reasons might be military." Typically, nuclear exporters will manipulate the price of enriched uranium to test the nature of the intentions of states that declare that their acquisition of an enrichment plant follows a purely economic rationale. In this case, the United States manipulated one variable (the price of enriched uranium) to test the seriousness and credibility of the Europeans' claims that the only reason they wanted an enrichment plant *now* was due to the economic characteristics of the electricity production sector. So they were testing whether the Europeans were really acting according to an economic—rather than a "national security"—form of reasoning, and whether the Euratom Treaty constituted an event with relevance for U.S. national security.

The decision to manipulate the price of enriched uranium was taken after a long series of cabinet meetings in 1956, in which Lewis Strauss wanted to convince Europeans to buy low-enriched uranium and power plants using low-enriched uranium from the United States, and John Foster Dulles wanted to see how the AEC could commit to collaborating with Euratom to build a Euratom uranium enrichment plant (if that was what Europeans wished), independent of the kind of power plants Europeans would choose to build (Dulles 1956a, 1956b). Strauss finally convinced President Eisenhower to reduce the price of low-enriched uranium in November 1956, because President Eisenhower knew that the senators agreed with the AEC chairman that he "should propose cheap nuclear fuels [low-enriched uranium] to the Europeans in order to avoid that they produce these fuels by themselves" (Duchêne n.d.).[14] Therefore, at the end of 1956, when Euratom Treaty negotiations were coming to an end, the future price of the low-enriched uranium to be sold by the United States on the international market was decreased to a third of the projected price of the nuclear fuel to be produced by the future European enrichment plant.

By conducting such a real-world experiment, the Americans made an economic justification for a European enrichment plant less credible. If Europeans insisted on building their own plant, rather than buying purely peaceful power plants and the fuel for them from the United States, their military motivations would be proven. After the price reduction of the U.S. enriched uranium, Jean Monnet and the Action Committee wanted to make it clear that they wished to devote Euratom to acquiring the most efficient peaceful technologies for the single purpose of producing the cheapest electricity—even if that meant buying no dual-use technology from the United States. With funds provided to his think tank by the Ford Foundation, Monnet hired three nuclear experts—the so-called Three Wise Men (one of whom was Louis Armand)—and made them responsible for reassessing Euratom's technological program. The choice of Armand as chairman of the Three Wise Men sent a signal to the AEC and U.S. senators that

14. If Lewis Strauss wanted to reveal the Europeans' true intentions, Eisenhower's reasons for reducing the price were more complex, as he also wanted to make a gesture toward Europeans after the Suez Crisis, which had strained transatlantic relations (on this episode, see Mallard 2008a, 199–203; Sokolski 2001).

the European response to the American offer to sell fuel would be evaluated from the purely economic perspective of the electricity sector.[15]

The Three Wise Men responded to the American test by including the new projected prices in their economic models, which predicted the future prices of electricity in Europe based upon standard economic factors (prices of raw materials, labor wages, depreciation of capital, etc.). After calculating the effect of the new price reduction of enriched uranium on the operating costs of the future power plants that the Europeans could buy (based on either American or British designs), Armand claimed that the construction of the Euratom enrichment plant was no longer desirable from the purely economic point of view and that the energy-starved Europeans should buy the power plants and their nuclear fuel from the United States. Even though these plants were relatively too expensive for oil-rich Americans to develop on their own soil, Armand claimed they were more cost efficient for Europeans than alternatives, including British plants.

To compare the cost efficiency of American and British plants (the latter used natural uranium for fuel, so their cost was unaffected by the price reduction of low-enriched uranium), Armand used classic econometric techniques of prospection, which were commonly used by French engineers, especially at the French planning commission (Muniesa and Callon 2007, 175), where Armand had worked under Monnet. From his computations, Armand concluded that the price reduction of low-enriched uranium not only made the construction of the Euratom enrichment plant no longer of interest but also made the operating costs of U.S. plants cheaper than those of Britain, and the overall cost of electricity produced by American plants cheaper in the long term. This conclusion was debatable, as it made sense if, and only if, Europeans adopted a long-term approach to solving the energy crisis in Europe. Indeed, it would take years for these cheaper operating costs to make the price of the electricity produced by American plants lower than that produced by British plants, whose capital costs were much lower (Krige 2008, 35).

The choice of horizon for the computations was therefore key for Armand to justify a European preference for American plants over British plants fueled with natural uranium. Armand believed that Europeans should consider the problem of energy in the long term (more than thirty

15. The other two Wise Men were Franz Etzel, a fifty-five-year-old West German parliamentarian, who served as vice president of the first European Community (the ECSC) under the presidency of Jean Monnet, and Francesco Giordani, a fifty-nine-year-old chemist who had authored the first postwar bill organizing Italian nuclear research and then presided over the Italian Nuclear Research Council.

years) rather than in the short term. This was not a self-evident claim, as much of the European willingness to complete Euratom Treaty negotiations was due to the expected short-term shortage of oil that resulted from the Suez Crisis, which had happened only a few months earlier. If Europeans had wanted to find a quick solution to the short-term energy shortage, then, it would have made more sense for them to buy British plants. But that was not Armand's solution.

Questioning the Credibility of the Europeans' Economic Scenarios

To appear plausible, the new projected technological program for Euratom to which techniques of prospection gave credibility needed to be backed up by hard economic facts. This is why the Three Wise Men decided to visit the United States shortly after the price reduction announced by Eisenhower. As Armand (1957) wrote to Dulles, "Tackling our problems as Europeans, we can and must think of embarking immediately on a massive atomic power program amounting to 15 million KW in the first five years," which could be achieved through the ratification of a bilateral treaty between the United States and Euratom planning for "1) the sale of five to six US nuclear power plants to Euratom member-states; 2) the organization of a joint US-Euratom R&D program in nuclear technologies; 3) the sale of fissile materials (enriched uranium and plutonium) to Euratom member-states; 4) and the substitution of the control that the AEC exercised over these materials to the Euratom Control Agency" (Kohnstamm 1957c). The credibility of Armand's representations of the future of the electricity sector in Europe depended upon whether the Americans were serious about the sale of low enriched uranium to Euratom at the reduced price of November 1956.

Armand took the opportunity of his fact-finding mission in the United States to ask the AEC chairman to confirm the price of the low-enriched uranium, which was particularly key to assessing the realism of Europeans' projections of long-term operating costs. Armand and the other two Wise Men asked Dulles "whether the U.S. would ensure some part of the supply of fissile materials and some of the industrial resources essential for our rapid development" (Armand 1957). When they met with Strauss, the latter agreed with the soundness of their plan and assured them that "the United States will be able to guarantee nuclear fuel procurement for Europe for the goal considered by the Three Wise Men of producing 3 million KW/h/year" (Kohnstamm 1957b) at the expected price announced a few months before.

The techniques of prospection were used by the Three Wise Men to give internal credibility (i.e., whether there were any errors in the calculations) to a peaceful representation of the future of Euratom that assuaged American concerns. The European federalists in the State Department were instrumental in helping Armand challenge those experts who questioned the internal validity of some of his assumptions. For instance, the RAND expert Arnold Kramish suggested that the Three Wise Men's report made no economic sense; according to him, the Europeans needed to buy cheap nuclear power plants from the British to cover their immediate energy needs, and they should start a Euratom program of R&D on prototype reactor plants based on U.S. designs rather than buy six first-generation U.S. power plants (Guéron 1983; Kramish 1957). Then, the State Department warned Monnet that the Three Wise Men needed to address these criticisms, which they did (Schaetzel 1957a, 1957b; Kohnstamm 1957e). Thanks to this help, the internal logic of Armand's scenarios seemed impeccable.

The external validity of Armand's scenarios (whether the scenarios reflected Europeans' real intentions) was also believed to be credible by the U.S. senators of the JCAE. Armand and other European experts were able to avoid a reality test because the credibility of their scenarios depended on Europe's political will rather than on a "natural" external geopolitical reality against which one could judge the validity of their models. The fact that the Three Wise Men were nominated to represent Euratom abroad by the parliamentary leaders of Europe represented in Monnet's Action Committee lent their scenarios credibility that other experts lacked (Guéron 1957). Indeed, the Action Committee had quasi-legislative authority in Europe, since it was composed of all the noncommunist parliamentary leaders of the six European nations, who, when they voted for Monnet's resolutions within the Action Committee, committed their respective parties to vote the same resolutions should they be presented in the form of a treaty to their national parliament. When Armand claimed that buying six U.S. power plants and the fuel was the most rational solution to solve Europe's energy problem, he spoke for the European political leaders.

Furthermore, when they visited the United States, the Three Wise Men were welcomed by President Eisenhower and Secretary Dulles like heads of state, as if they were the officials of the future European institutions and not just technical experts coming to the United States to compare numbers with their American counterparts (Dulles 1956b). So it is easy to understand, as Guéron (1957) noted after his visit to the United States, "among all the Americans whom I met, these false ideas are shared by everyone: the report of the Three Wise Men is the official program of Euratom; and the

Euratom Commission is composed of the Three Wise Men." Monnet's emissaries in the United States had succeeded in convincing both the senators and the members of the AEC that they "represented" Euratom in the sense of being its *"porte-parole"* (Latour 1987).[16]

In this sense, the techniques of prospection used by Armand gave a strong credibility to the claim that the *future* of Europe's nuclear development was purely peaceful. It convinced American senators that they did not need to rely on other sources of information to gauge Europeans' intentions with Euratom (and to clarify whether Europeans had military intentions as well). Their knowledge of the future, made credible by Armand's models, convinced them that they should no longer insist on inspectors having a continued knowledge of the Europeans' present nuclear activities, since Europeans would not seek to produce dual-use nuclear technologies (such as enrichment technologies). The sheer size of the future Euratom program of electricity production (the sale of not just one but six power plants for an astronomical 350 million dollars) made it both unjustified from the strategic viewpoint and impractical for the United States to monitor Europe's nuclear activities. A few weeks before the ratification of the agreement between Euratom and the United States, Europeans were assured by the powerful chairman of the JCAE, Senator Pastore, that "he did not expect difficulties for the program in the respect of safeguards" insofar as the Europeans remained committed to the Three Wise Men's program (Kohnstamm 1958). As Senator Pastore told members of the Action Committee, the AEC could not pretend to control European nuclear activities, especially in light of the fact that, as planned by Armand's scenarios, "the US will sell 30,000 Kg of enriched uranium and plutonium [necessary to fuel the future power plants to be bought from the United States] to Euratom," with "ownership and responsibility transferred to the [European] Community" (Kohnstamm 1958). Furthermore, since all the technologies that the Three Wise Men promised to buy from the United States could not be diverted for military purposes, there was little point in keeping these American inspectors on the ground.

The economic scenarios produced by the Three Wise Men were used in a quasi-hypnotic way, as techniques of suggestion, that fixed U.S. leaders' attention on a certain economic reality that existed only in the European

16. In February 1957, when the Soviets denounced the Franco-German military "Junktim" that made up the core of the Euratom Community (Soutou 1994), the Eisenhower administration also rebuked the Soviet claims that Euratom was a nuclear military organization and had objectives that were not revealed in the Three Wise Men's report (Euratom Commission 1958a, 1958b).

experts' economic scenarios, rather than on the legal aspects of Euratom's controls. Indeed, it was a deliberate tactic designed by Monnet, the Action Committee (Kohnstamm 1957b, 1957d), and European federalists in the State Department (Schaetzel 1958a, 1958b), which consisted of preventing "this issue of security control [from being] raised and discussed as an independent issue," but rather ensuring that it was discussed "as a subordinate point and as part of the joint U.S.-Euratom program planned by the Three Wise Men" (Schaetzel 1958b). Rather than explaining to U.S. senators how the Euratom system of control was supposed to work, the Three Wise Men told them that "Euratom provides the essential system of control on lines closely analogous to those of the United States' AEC" (Armand 1957). This was largely a misrepresentation, since European foreign ministers decided that Euratom would have the responsibility only to verify conformity between the real and declared uses of nuclear activities (be they civil or military uses) within Euratom territory (it did not control whether the use of nuclear technologies would be purely peaceful, as the Americans had done).[17] When they recognized the Euratom system of controls by signing the treaty of cooperation with Euratom, the U.S. senators overlooked the fact that it legalized for the first time Europeans' use of American technologies and materials (such as highly enriched uranium or plutonium) for military purposes as long as the importing state declared to the Euratom Commission that its materials would be of American origin.[18] The focus on the future technological program of Euratom, and the use of techniques of prospection, helped Europeans relegate this most important aspect of the comprehensive United States–Euratom Treaty to a minor technicality, which did not deserve the senators' attention.[19]

The idea that the Americans would become disillusioned after they signed a bilateral treaty with Euratom mattered less to Monnet and the Three Wise Men than the possibility that the U.S. Congress would refuse to ratify the bilateral United States–Euratom Treaty and that the AEC would retain its right of inspection in Europe. Once the U.S. Congress ratified the

17. Here again, when attacked, the Three Wise Men's tactic benefited from the unfailing support of President Eisenhower, who, in the last few weeks before the ratification of the United States–Euratom Treaty (Mallard 2009), fired Strauss from the AEC chairmanship after Strauss asked for more consultation over the desirability of Euratom controls (*New York Times* 1958).

18. After the signing of the United States–Euratom Treaty, the U.S. president would no longer need the approval of Congress to sell sensitive materials (like plutonium) to Euratom if the Euratom Commission asked for them.

19. As in the case, studied by Rosental (2003), of expert negotiations over the credibility of a theorem in logic, European experts were "more involved in dramatic than in communicative acting."

treaty in August 1958, the Euratom Commission freely abandoned the Three Wise Men's plan. Of the six power plants that the Three Wise Men had promised to buy from the United States and to bring into operation by 1963, Euratom sponsored only one bid, by Italy, and as the French expert Bertrand Goldschmidt wrote, "the target of 15,000 MW(e) by 1967," which was fixed "in the report of the Three Wise Men, seemed completely out of step with the developing situation" (1982, 308). All along, the European federalists concealed from the AEC and the U.S. Congress (but not from the European federalists in the White House and State Department)[20] that they had not renounced their project of building a joint enrichment plant, for which they intended to commit most of their scarce financial resources, and which they intended to use to fabricate material for military purposes (highly enriched uranium). Indeed, the French, West German, and Italian governments signed treaties planning military cooperation in the nuclear field, first between France and West Germany in February 1957 (a month before the signing of the Euratom Treaty), and later extended to Italy in November 1957 (a month before the Euratom Treaty came into force) (MAEF 1957). Then, in May 1958 (as the United States–Euratom Treaty negotiations came to an end), the French government secretly agreed to open participation in the production of enriched uranium in the French plant to the West Germans and Italians, in order to produce nuclear warheads owned by the three countries (Soutou 1996, 113).

This example shows that the real-world experiment that Americans made when they decided to reduce the price of enriched uranium led to unintended consequences: initiated by nationalist skeptics to reveal Europeans' present true intentions, the experiment focused the debate on the future of Euratom's technological program rather than on the legal uncertainties and opacities that existed in the Euratom Treaty itself. Once they hired Louis Armand, a talented planner, it became easy for European federalists to reduce the perception of Euratom to the economic representation that national leaders gave of it, rather than delve into the legal complexities which showed the ramifications that Euratom had for European nations' defense purposes. The internal and external validity of the scenarios proposed by Armand convinced U.S. national leaders that the creation of Euratom constituted an event with no relevance to the field of national security. This example shows that assessing the nature of a geopolitical event

---

20. The fact that Europeans were still planning to jointly build an enrichment plant despite the Three Wise Men's assurances to the contrary was carefully hidden from the U.S. senators and the AEC. In the United States, only Dwight Eisenhower and John Foster Dulles were kept privy to these secret agreements.

based on the plausibility of possible futures that might derive from it is a risky strategy that can backfire, as it can draw attention away from the diplomatic and legal complexity of states' past and present intentions.

Controlled Contingency: The Scenario-Based Exercise as a Knowledge Practice

This section describes another constitutive technique of prospection involved in security planning and policy making: the work of designers of scenario-based exercises.[21] In this case, the problem of design is central to the constitution of a potential future event as a security threat. The scenario-based exercise is a tightly structured narrative in which decision makers are presented with an urgent crisis, must take action to intervene, and then watch the results of their decisions play out. This technique of prospection assumes the disruptive, potentially catastrophic nature of certain events. Insofar as the event's occurrence cannot be prevented, from the vantage of security planners the only way to avert disaster is to have plans to address it already in place and to have practiced a response. Although the probability and severity of the event are not known, one must behave as if the worst-case scenario were going to occur.[22]

Scenario-based exercises aim to make policy makers aware of existing security vulnerabilities and to thereby shape new policy interventions. The scenarios do not predict the future; rather, they narrate plausible events whose repercussions have lessons for the present. A crucial element in the design of such exercises is to structure a deeply affecting experience for participants: while participants know that the event is fictional, they must nonetheless engage with it as though it were real. In their reflections on how to generate this sense of realism, exercise planners focus on design—on the proper narrative construction of the event. The first part of this section looks at the introduction of the scenario-based exercise in U.S. national security planning, analyzing experts' design methods; specifically, it focuses on the role of the "exercise controller" in shaping the experience of contingency among participants. The second part illustrates the use of these methods in contemporary scenario-based exercises. It describes a 2001 national security exercise, "Dark Winter," which is often cited as a

21. The section draws on Lakoff's 2007 and 2008 interviews with designers of scenario-based exercises.

22. A common admonition from this vantage point, heard often during discussions of bioterrorism in the 1990s, is that "it is not a question of if, but when" (Wright 2007). For the contrast between preparedness and risk calculation as forms of security rationality, see Lakoff 2007.

significant event—before the attacks of 9/11 and the anthrax letters—in gal-vanizing support for large increases in civilian biodefense spending in the early 2000s.[23] The section analyzes how the assumptions of scenario-based exercises transformed in the post–Cold War period, as exercise designers no longer included a rational enemy to take on the role of the opponent in their games. Exercise design changed in tandem with a changing security problem: from a potentially knowable enemy to a catastrophic and un-foreseeable contingency. This can be seen as a shift from understanding and anticipating an opponent's actions to becoming aware of one's own internal vulnerabilities to an unpredictable outside world. Along with im-parting such knowledge, a crucial function of the technique of prospection described here was to constitute a certain kind of event—an outbreak of infectious disease—as a problem of national security.

"Nature" and Contingency: The Control Group

Designers of scenario-based exercises face the challenge of convincing par-ticipants of the seriousness of the threat the exercise depicts even while everyone knows that the event is a fictional depiction. As one group of designers put it: "One of the greatest challenges for game designers is to induce players to take their actions seriously without having any actual ability to force them to accept responsibility for their actions the way the president, Congress, or the Soviet Union might" (Goldberg et al. 1987, 15). Early developers of these exercises reflected explicitly on how to gener-ate a sense of serious engagement among participants despite their aware-ness that the exercise was only a game. They argued that it was necessary to create an environment of "controlled contingency" through which partici-pants would be able to experience a charged combination of uncertainty and vulnerability—what one exercise developer called a "twilight zone" between reality and nonreality. The verisimilitude of the exercise was criti-cal to its success in making participants feel responsible for its outcome.[24] Controlled contingency meant that participants could experience uncer-tainty about the outcomes of their decisions—and the attendant anxiety this implied.

23. Total U.S. government spending on civilian biodefense increased markedly between 2001 and 2005, from $294.8 million in fiscal year 2001 to $7.6 billion in fiscal year 2005 (Lam, Franco, and Schuler 2006).

24. Sharon Ghamari-Tabrizi (2000) has shown that verisimilitude was both a goal of game designers and a source of some anxiety: too much realism could give participants more confi-dence in the results of the game than were justified by its methodology.

Scenario-based political exercises were initially developed in the Cold War United States by social scientists working in national security think tanks and academic policy institutes. These exercises differed from classical war games in that they involved the strategic thought of political decision makers rather than military planners. In the context of Cold War nuclear escalation and the catastrophic consequences of actual military confrontation, a key issue for political strategists was how to *avoid* going to war with the Soviet Union. The focus of this early type of exercise was thus political decision making in crisis situations—and specifically, the problem of understanding the motivations and likely behavior of the enemy. From the vantage point of their designers, these exercises could substitute for actual experience in the conduct of nuclear war—since, fortunately, no leaders had actual experience of a nuclear war.

The leaders of the RAND Corporation's social science division in the early 1950s, Herbert Goldhamer and Hans Speier, are credited with the invention of this type of exercise.[25] The RAND Corporation was a national security–oriented think tank in which a number of important Cold War era developments in social science took place (Amadae 2003; Kaplan 1983; Light 2003). The events depicted in the RAND political exercises were typically diplomatic crises, in which a "blue team" representing the United States and its allies faced off against a "red team," representing the Soviet Union. Goldhamer and Speier (1959) emphasized the importance of incorporating qualitative social scientific knowledge into the design of these exercises. In this respect their exercises were very different from the formal, mathematical games for which RAND was better known. Indeed, Goldhamer and Speier were skeptical of the ability of formal models of human behavior—as used in game-theoretic approaches—to provide insight into the complex realities of political decision making. They abandoned their initial attempts to formalize decision-making processes in crisis, they wrote, "when it became clear that the simplification imposed in order to permit quantification made the game of doubtful value for the assessment of political strategies and tactics in the real world." In contrast to formal models' simplification of the international situation, the political exercise made it possible "to simulate as faithfully as possible much of its complexity" (Goldhamer and Speier 1959, 72–73). As opposed to the RAND

25. Over the next decade, the political exercise methodology was disseminated broadly in academic and policy arenas, as the field of "strategic and international studies" became institutionalized. Goldhamer and colleagues collaborated with scholars of international relations at the Social Science Research Council, Stanford's Center for Advanced Study in the Behavioral Science, Yale, the Brookings Institution, Northwestern, and elsewhere (Kuklick 2006).

mathematicians' abstract simulations of nuclear confrontation, the social scientists argued, these exercises required concrete political and historical knowledge and so were able to replicate the chance and contingency characteristic of real-life political crises (Kaplan 1983, 201; Ghamari-Tabrizi 2000, 197).[26] Realism was central to the success of the political exercise as a technique of prospection.

The RAND social scientists pointed to the need for players to invest themselves in the exercise in order for it to generate the feeling of anxious uncertainty characteristic of actual crisis situations. Insofar as the exercise provided players with "new insight into the pressures, the uncertainties, and the moral and intellectual difficulties under which foreign policy decisions are made," they wrote, this was "a tribute to the earnestness and sense of responsibility with which the participants played their roles, since otherwise these pressures and perplexities would not have made themselves felt" (Goldhamer and Speier 1959, 79). How then to ensure that participants played their roles earnestly and thereby took on responsibility for the consequences of their actions?

A key requirement of the exercise's success in producing a sense of realism was the "simulation of contingent factors"—that is, the incorporation of the unexpected. Unplanned events should be designed into the exercise. This was the role of what Goldhamer and Speier called "Nature." As they wrote: "In political life many events are beyond the control of the most powerful actors, a fact designated in political theories by such terms as *fortuna*, 'chance,' 'God's will,' 'changes in the natural environment,' etc. We tried to simulate this by the moves of 'Nature.'" Designated referees played the role of Nature, evaluating and intervening in the "state of affairs" that had been reached at a given point in the game. Referees exercised control over the players' ostensibly contingent experiences through the introduction of developments from the world outside: "the referees could introduce such evaluations in the form of press roundups, trade union resolutions, intelligence reports, speeches made in the United Nations, etc." (Goldhamer and Speier 1959, 73–74).

Interventions coming from "Nature" pointed to the limits of the players' capacity to shape the course of events. As Goldhamer and Speier summarized: "The role of 'Nature' was to provide for events of the type that happen in the real world but are not under the control of any government:

26. Goldhamer, it is worth noting, was a pioneer in the social scientific analysis of the unconscious motivations behind leaders' actions. A former student of Harold Lasswell's at Chicago, he had applied "psychocultural" analysis to North Korean leaders as a U.S. adviser to the Korean War armistice talks (Robin 2001, 125).

certain technological developments, the death of important people, non-governmental political action, famines, popular disturbances, etc." (1959, 73). In later iterations of the scenario-based political exercise, the role of Nature was taken up by the "control group." The behind-the-scenes actions of the control group during the enactment of the exercise were central to participants' experience of responsibility for their actions. As two prominent exercise designers put it in 1965, the control group "represents 'nature,' introducing unexpected events; it is umpire, ruling on the plausibility and outcomes of moves; it is, as it were, 'god,' requiring the players to live with the implications of their chosen strategies" (Bloomfield and Whaley 1965, 858).

Generating Knowledge about Vulnerability

In ensuing years, the use of the scenario-based exercise as a technique of prospection expanded from diplomatic confrontation to more general crisis situations. The Center for Strategic and International Studies (CSIS), a foreign policy think tank in Washington, DC, was one setting for this expansion. In the 1980s a national security expert there, Robert H. Kupperman, initiated a series of high-profile exercises. Kupperman had become concerned about government readiness for unanticipated crises during his tenure in the Nixon administration's Office of Emergency Preparedness, which was forced to respond to a series of unexpected national crises: natural disasters such as Hurricane Camille in 1969, economic crises such as the 1972 wage price freeze, terrorist attacks such as the 1972 Munich massacre, and the 1973 oil crisis. In this context, Kupperman developed an interest in the common structure of crisis situations and in the development of techniques that could be used to prepare for them in advance. "As we begin to recognize the complex problems that threaten every nation with disaster," he and two colleagues from the Office of Emergency Preparedness asked in 1975, "can we continue to trust the ad hoc processes of instant reaction to muddle through?" (Kupperman, Wilcox, and Smith 1975, 406). The design and exercise of crisis simulations would, they argued, help in responding adequately to such disasters by demonstrating vulnerabilities in response systems that needed to be addressed in advance of a crisis.

In the early 1980s, after a stint as head of the U.S. Arms Control and Disarmament Agency, Kupperman joined CSIS, known at the time as a bastion of conservative strategic thought. There he was coauthor, with future CIA director R. James Woolsey, of a report on "crisis management in a society of networks" called *America's Hidden Vulnerabilities*. The report built on

Kupperman's earlier experiences in the Office of Emergency Preparedness. Its authors argued that the United States relied for its well-being on a sophisticated and intricate set of systems, or networks, for energy distribution, communication, and transportation. They noted recent disruptions of these systems and warned: "A serious potential exists . . . for much more serious disabling of networks crucial to life support, economic stability, and national defense" (Woolsey and Kupperman 1984, 2). What Woolsey and Kupperman called the "emergency exercise" was a tool for demonstrating to leaders the vulnerabilities of these critical systems. As they wrote: "If planning has involved the operating teams and managers (as it always should) these critical personnel gain an increased understanding of how the system works and, particularly valuable, how it is likely to behave under abnormal conditions. Training with crisis games and emergency exercises will augment this benefit significantly" (1984, 16).

At CSIS, Kupperman and his colleagues held a series of scenario-based simulations of crisis situations to persuade national security officials of the problem of system vulnerability and the need to implement contingency planning. They cited the RAND political exercises of the 1950s and 1960s as the forerunners of these simulations. The CSIS group's emphasis in designing such exercises was not on preventing future crises but rather on improving leaders' decision-making process once a crisis was under way.[27] Thus, the technique did not seek to predict the future but rather to constitute potential events as problems for thought in the present. The goal of such exercises was to expose current gaps in readiness—to generate awareness of what had to be considered before an event in order for response to be adequate. In a 1987 interview, Kupperman explained that a successful exercise had four key elements: first, a plausible scenario; second, a rapid sequence of events, leading to a feeling of intense pressure; third, experienced participants; and fourth, a "control staff" to simulate the real world.[28] Like Goldhamer and Speier, he noted that participants' absorption in the game depended on its realism: "We try to make the players feel personally

---

27. In his foreword to a volume summarizing the exercises, Admiral Thomas Moorer wrote: "The CSIS crisis simulations are not designed to be predictive. Rather, they are intended to provide insight into policy dilemmas likely to plague national leaders during real crises and to identify key decision-making pathologies that could lead to unwanted escalation" (Goldberg et al. 1987, vii).

28. The article noted the widespread use of simulations: "today, simulations have gone beyond military strategy to include politics, diplomacy, economic leverage, public opinion and the psychology of decision makers under the pressures of time, confusion and demands from every direction" (Halloran 1987).

responsible," he said. "We create a twilight zone; they know it's not real, but they're not quite sure" (Halloran 1987).

Echoing Speier and Goldhamer's simulation of "Nature" through the moves of referees, the exercise designers at CSIS emphasized the central role of the "control strategy" in creating a realistic feeling of crisis in which unpredictable events unfolded in real time and demanded immediate response. As they noted: "In formulating control strategy, the research group sought to pose to the team a number of functional problems, which would reflect key dimensions of crisis dynamics. This was done by simulating organizational impediments, domestic political impediments, problems of allies and regional actors and, finally, issues invoking U.S.-Soviet coercive diplomacy" (Goldberg et al. 1987, 12). The reality effect of the exercise depended on the interventions, during the event itself, of the "control group"—that is, the behind-the-scenes figures who supplied the real-world results of the official players' interventions. "Team players, therefore, bore the consequences of their acts in the domestic or global arena. NSC players experienced the threats, penalties, and opportunities posed by environmental factors through the control of informational input" (Goldberg et al. 1987, 12). It was the control group that decided how the external world would respond to players' decisions and so structured the experience of contingency that fostered players' sense of real-world responsibility. For example, in a CSIS exercise simulating a crisis on the Korean peninsula, "the control group deliberately structured a leaky news environment to heighten the tension, as well as the realism, of the exercise" (Goldberg et al. 1987, 18). Such outside forces demonstrated the inability of players to fully control the outcome of a crisis situation, generating the anxiety and sense of responsibility crucial to an effective exercise.

Simulating the New Biological Threat

Over the course of the 1990s, the techniques of prospection that had initially been developed to create realistic depictions of political crisis during the Cold War were applied to new threats such as "asymmetric warfare." For example, in the wake of the Cold War, a small but vocal group of scientists and security experts began to issue dire warnings about a new threat to U.S. national security: a massive bioterrorist attack (Wright 2007). On the one hand, these experts argued, the increasing accessibility of biological knowledge and the global proliferation of bioweapons made an eventual attack highly plausible. On the other hand, the disrepair of the country's public health system and a lack of investment in biodefense measures meant that the United States was woefully unprepared for such an attack. Prominent among this group were scientists such as epidemiologist D. A. Henderson of the Johns Hopkins Center for Civilian Biodefense Strategies, as well as national security experts such as Richard Clarke (Miller, Engelberg, and Broad 2001; Alibek 1999). These experts pointed not only to the problem but also to its solution: adequate preparation for such an attack would require a massive infusion of resources into biodefense research and public health response capacity; more broadly, it would be necessary to incorporate the agencies and institutions of the life sciences and public health into the national security establishment.

Biological security advocates' claims about the urgency of the threat had to compete in a crowded terrain of emerging security problems, each vying to fill in what Senator Sam Nunn called the "threat blank" left by the end of the Cold War: prospective new security threats included rogue nations and nuclear proliferation, asymmetric warfare, "netwar," the Y2K bug, and rising powers such as China.[29] It was difficult for advocates of new biosecurity measures to convince government leaders of the urgency and severity of the biological threat for at least two reasons. First, national security officials were not accustomed to thinking about issues of public health and medicine. And second, security officials were not convinced that the threat was credible: a mass biological attack was an event that had never occurred, and its likelihood was difficult to assess. Expert claims about the characteristics of the biological threat typically took the form of the conditional—of what *would* happen in the event of an attack.[30] For example, as Henderson wrote of the aerosol release of a biological agent: "No one would know until days or weeks later that anyone had been infected (depending on the microbe). Then patients would begin appearing in emergency rooms and physicians' offices with symptoms of a strange disease that few physicians had ever seen" (Henderson 1999, 1279). But such statements did not by themselves transmit to national security and public health policy makers the sense of urgency felt by authorities such as Henderson to deal with the possibility of a biological attack.

Biosecurity advocates thus had to constitute a potential bioweapons at-

29. In 1991, General Colin Powell said, "We no longer have the luxury of having a threat to plan for" (cited in Mann 2004). Over the following years, a number of new candidates emerged, including a biological attack.

30. For the distinction between "possibilistic" and "probabilistic" approaches to threats, see Clarke 2005. In his discussions of "risk society," Ulrich Beck focuses on the rise of dire hazards that are the products of modern technology and that cannot be managed through the calculative methods of technocratic planning (Beck 1992).

tack as a recognized national security problem. As part of this effort, they decided to develop an exercise that could serve as a pedagogical tool for public authorities charged with thinking about and anticipating security threats. On June 22–23, 2001, the Johns Hopkins Center for Biosecurity, in collaboration with the CSIS and the ANSER Institute for Homeland Security, held a scenario-based exercise called Dark Winter. The exercise simulated a large-scale smallpox attack on the United States. Although the Dark Winter exercise inherited much of its structure from its Cold War era precursors, there was at least one significant difference. In Dark Winter, there was no "red" team against which the U.S. leaders played: in the case of a bioterrorist attack, there was no longer a rational adversary whose actions would have to be understood and managed in a crisis situation. Whereas the strategizing foreign enemy had been a central factor in the RAND and the earlier CSIS exercises, "Nature" was now the only opponent against which the United States was playing. Indeed, the key problem for players in the exercise had shifted: from anticipating and managing enemy motivations and intentions to understanding the nation's internal vulnerabilities to an ostensibly unmanageable external threat. As former CIA director and coauthor of *America's Hidden Vulnerabilities* James Woolsey later said, this was a new type of enemy: "we are used to thinking about health problems as naturally occurring problems outside the framework of a malicious actor." With disease as tool of attack, he continued, "we are in a world we haven't ever really been in before" (O'Toole, Mair, and Inglesby 2002, 980).

The explicit aim of Dark Winter was "to increase awareness of the scope and character of the threat posed by biological weapons among senior national security experts and to catalyze actions that would improve prevention and response strategies" (O'Toole, Mair, and Inglesby 2002, 972). In other words, the exercise sought to constitute the possibility of a biological attack as a significant national security threat.[31] The organizers of the exercise recruited twelve prominent public figures as role players—these were "accomplished individual(s) who serve or have served in high level government or military positions," including eminent national security authority Sam Nunn (former chairman of the Senate Committee on Armed Services and chairman of the Board of Trustees of CSIS) as the president, veteran presidential adviser David Gergen as national security adviser, and James Woolsey (former CIA director and longtime national security analyst) as director of the CIA. These government leaders were chosen both because of their firsthand knowledge of how officials would react to the events in

31. Tom Inglesby, phone interview, June 6, 2008.

question and because their later descriptions of the lessons of the experience would be credible to a wide range of current officials.

In interviews, Dark Winter's designers described some of the reasons for holding such an exercise. One argued that exercises like Dark Winter teach participants lessons that cannot be understood in other ways, such as narrative prose. Without enacting the event, he elaborated, "they can't feel it." This designer added that successful exercises have a dimension of unpredictability—and therefore allow for unexpected insights to come to light from people with significant experience. Indeed, it was important to design such unpredictability into the scenario. Dark Winter's planners described the design process, which began six months before the exercise. You begin with the specific objectives of the exercise, said one designer: an exercise to test the capabilities of an existing agency is a totally different thing than Dark Winter, which sought to clarify the problem posed by biological threats—to learn about how certain choices would change outcomes. Distinctive elements of the exercise were built in to explore specific problem areas, said another. For example, they chose to use smallpox as the pathogen—rather than anthrax, widely considered a more likely bioweapon—because it was contagious and therefore would generate uncertainties among participants, such as whether new reports of outbreaks were the result of another attack or of the spread of the disease.

The actual exercise took place in three segments over two days, depicting a time span of two weeks after the initial biological attack. It was held before an audience of over one hundred observers, including national security analysts and members of the press. While the scenario's designers used historical data on the patterns of smallpox outbreaks to structure the exercise, the point of using these epidemiological data was not so much to accurately model how such an event would unfold as to create a plausible scenario—one that had a poor outcome.[32] The designers structured the exercise to focus participants on certain pre-identified critical issues, including the amount of vaccine available, information systems for tracking disease, and plans for coordinating response to an outbreak. For example, the fact that according to the scenario there were only fifteen million doses of smallpox vaccine available helped to demonstrate the lack of existing plans on how government should coordinate its response. To shape the

---

32. A critical question, for example, was the transmission rate assumed. The smallpox transmission rate fluctuates widely based on multiple contextual factors. To determine the rate for the exercise, the developers analyzed thirty-four European cases of smallpox between 1958 and 1973 and chose the example of an outbreak in Yugoslavia as their model (O'Toole, Mair, and Inglesby 2002, 972–83). For a critique, see Barrett 2006.

unfolding of events, "exercise controllers played the roles of deputies or special assistants, providing briefings of facts and policy options to participants throughout the meeting as needed" (O'Toole, Mair, and Inglesby 2002, 973).

The first National Security Council meeting laid out the situation for Security Council members. There were reports of an outbreak of smallpox in Oklahoma City, assumed to be the result of a terrorist attack. Initial questions for the council were technical—but did not lend themselves to obvious solutions: "With only 12 million doses of vaccine available, what is the best strategy to contain the outbreak? Should there be a national or a state vaccination policy? Is ring vaccination or mass immunization the best policy?" This sense of uncertainty about appropriate action had been built into the exercise: part of the point, as one of the exercise designers put it in a later interview, was that there was no decision that could avert disaster. The participants found that they did not have enough information about the scale of the attack to come up with a solution, especially given limited vaccine stocks. By the second meeting of the National Security Council, the situation looked grim. "Only 1.25 million doses of vaccine remain, and public unrest grows as the vaccine supply dwindles," read the scenario. "Vaccine distribution efforts vary from state to state, are often chaotic, and lead to violence in some areas." International borders were closed, leading to trade disruption and food shortages. Meanwhile, simulated twenty-four-hour news coverage, shown to participants as ongoing video clips, sharply criticized the government's response to the outbreak. These news clips also included graphic photographs of dying American smallpox victims.

As vaccine stock dwindled further, the prospect of using the National Guard to enforce disease containment was broached. But who had the authority to make such emergency decisions? In one sequence, a National Security Council member advised the president to federalize the National Guard, as states had begun to seal their borders. "That's not your function," objected the governor of Oklahoma, defending states' rights. The attorney general responded, "Mr. President, this question got settled at Appomattox. You need to federalize the National Guard." President Nunn then interjected: "We're going to have absolute chaos if we start having war between the federal government and the state government." The exchange illustrates the structured improvisation built into the exercise to help authorities formulate for themselves the vulnerabilities presented by the threat of a biological attack.

Meanwhile, civil unrest intensified as the exercise unfolded. "With vaccine in short supply, increasingly anxious crowds mob vaccination clinics," reported the simulated news. "Riots around a vaccination site in Philadelphia left two dead. At another vaccination site, angry citizens overwhelmed vaccinators."[33] By the third meeting, there had been hundreds of deaths and the situation was growing still worse. The exercise ended as the disaster continued to escalate: there was no smallpox vaccine remaining and none was expected for four weeks.

Realism and Affect

A significant effect of Dark Winter was to give political leaders a *feeling* of how a biological attack would play out—and how little prepared they were for such an event. Its circle of influence extended outward through a series of briefings featuring a realistic video portraying the events as they unfolded. Vice President Dick Cheney, Homeland Security Secretary Tom Ridge, and key congressional leaders were among those briefed. At a congressional hearing where the video was about to be shown, Representative Christopher Shays asked John Hamre, director of the CSIS, about its affective qualities: "I'm told that some of it is not pleasant." Hamre answered with reference to the felt sense of realism of the exercise: "It is not pleasant. Let me also emphasize, sir, this is a simulation. This had frightening qualities of being real, as a matter of fact too real. And because we have television cameras here broadcasting, we want to tell everyone, this did not happen, it was a simulation. But, it had such realism, and we are going to try to show you the sense of realism that came from that today" (U.S. Congress 2001, 3).

And indeed, Representative Shays did react strongly to the video, noting afterward how nervous he had felt while watching it: "I felt like I've been in the middle of a movie, and maybe that's why I was anxious. I wanted to know how it turned out. And so I asked my staff how did we finally get a handle on it, you know, 12 million vaccines out, the disease spreading? And the response was we did not get a handle on it. They stopped the exercise before resolution. Kind of scary, huh?" (U.S. Congress 2001, 74). The dire outcome of the attack was built into the exercise design, given the designers' assumptions about the scale of the attack and the disease transmission rate (Barrett 2006). CSIS director John Hamre later narrated the final stage of the video simulation in testimony before Congress: "In the last

33. For quotations from the exercise, see *Dark Winter Exercise*, Final Script, UPMC Center for Biosecurity, http://www.upmc-biosecurity.org/website/events/2001_darkwinter/dark_winter .pdf (accessed June 12, 2008).

48 hours there were 14,000 cases. We now have over 1,000 dead, another 5,000 that we expected to be dead within weeks. There are 200 people who died from the vaccination, because there is a small percentage [of risk], and we have administered 12 million doses. . . . At this stage the medical system is overwhelmed completely" (U.S. Congress 2001, 13).

Dark Winter's designers described how such exercises work to create a sense of responsibility among participants. If participants are given an assigned role, and are made to stay in it, they begin to see themselves as responsible for the outcomes of their decisions, said one. In an interview, another scenario designer, a former air force pilot, made an analogy to a flight simulator in his description of the importance of generating tension. It should not be like an academic debate, he said: "I want drama, I want to put it under pressure." As an illustration he cited the staging of the event: in the enactment of Dark Winter, the lights were dimmed, with spotlights trained on the participants before the audience.

At the congressional hearing, participants reported on their own experiences of the exercise. For example, Sam Nunn reflected on the debate over whether to use the National Guard to enforce quarantine: "It is a terrible dilemma. Because you know that your vaccine is going to give out, and you know the only other strategy is isolation, but you don't know who to isolate. That is the horror of this situation" (U.S. Congress 2001, 8–9). Key lessons included the political vulnerabilities such an event would reveal. As Hamre said, "We thought that we were going to be spending our time with the mechanisms of government. We ended up spending our time saying, how do we save democracy in America? Because it is that serious, and it is that big" (U.S. Congress 2001, 3–4). Dark Winter was successful in that it convinced participants—and later briefing audiences—of the urgent need for advanced planning in order to be able to govern in the event of a biological emergency. Governor Keating of Oklahoma was stunned at the lack of preparedness demonstrated by the exercise: "We think an enemy of the United States could attack us with smallpox or with anthrax . . . and we really don't prepare for it, we have no vaccines for it—that's astonishing" (O'Toole, Mair, and Inglesby 2002, 982).

The exercise achieved its effect by generating among participants an "experiential" knowledge of vulnerability—that is, a visceral sense of their own incapacity to deal with this type of event. It targeted this experience at the moment of political decision—what Nunn called "the horror of this situation" (U.S. Congress 2001, 9). To produce such affect, exercise designers had to constitute a plausible future in the present in which the affect and judgment of decision makers were invested. Hamre referred to this as a feeling of "realism": the way in which events that were seemingly out of the players' control—such as the rapid spread of the disease in the absence of countermeasures—shaped the scenario's outcome.

Dark Winter imparted knowledge about such vulnerabilities through its verisimilitude. First, officials did not have real-time "situational awareness" of the various aspects of the crisis while it unfolded.[34] Second, without adequate stockpiles of medical countermeasures, leaders could not properly manage the crisis. Third, there was a gulf between public health and national security expertise: "It isn't just [a matter of] buying more vaccine," said Woolsey. "It's a question of how we integrate these public health and national security communities in ways that allow us to deal with various facets of the problem" (O'Toole, Mair, and Inglesby 2002, 982).

Participants had concrete suggestions for improvement. Nunn argued for vaccination of first responders in advance of an attack: "every one of those people you are trying to mobilize is going to have to be vaccinated. You can't expect them to go in there and expose themselves and their family to smallpox or any other deadly disease without vaccinations" (U.S. Congress 2001, 12). Hauer, a former New York City emergency manager, spoke of the problem of distributing vaccines in cities: "The logistical infrastructure necessary to vaccinate the people of New York City, Los Angeles, Chicago is just—would be mind-boggling" (U.S. Congress 2001, 54). But the broader lesson was the need to imaginatively enact the event in order to plan for it. As Hamre said, "We didn't have the strategy at the table on how to deal with this, because we have never thought our way through it before, and systematically thinking our way through this kind of a crisis is now going to become a key imperative. It clearly is going to require many more exercises" (U.S. Congress 2001, 14). And indeed, among the programs funded during the rapid increase in support for civilian biodefense of the early 2000s was a nationwide program of public health preparedness exercises, to be run by the RAND Corporation under contract from the Centers for Disease Control (Lurie, Wasserman, and Nelson 2006). In these events, as well, participants' investment in their experience would depend on the off-screen practices of exercise controllers. As a technique of prospection, the significance of Dark Winter lay not in its predictive capacity but rather in its ability to constitute a biological attack as a national security problem and to generate knowledge about current vulnerabilities to such an attack.

34. As the scenario designers wrote, "this lack of information, critical for leaders' situational awareness in Dark Winter, reflects the fact that few systems exist that can provide a rapid flow of the medical and public health information needed in a public health emergency" (O'Toole, Mair, and Inglesby 2002, 980).

Conclusion

This chapter shows that techniques of prospection can be used for constitutive purposes in different ways. The techniques of prospection that we have described in this chapter differed in the extent to which they elicited a response to a pressing real-life diplomatic problem or prepared national leaders for unlikely but possible contingencies.

In the first example, security specialists used techniques of prospection to convince U.S. leaders that the reasons behind a nuclear deal between Americans and Europeans were primarily economic rather than strategic. The economic scenarios produced by diplomats and experts were used in quasi-hypnotic way, as techniques of suggestion, which fixed U.S. attention on a bright economic reality rather than on legal opacities that might have betrayed darker intentions. We showed that in this case, security experts used economic forecasting techniques to provide U.S. national leaders with a credible representation of the future of Europeans' nuclear program that gave them little incentive to seek further knowledge about Europeans' present intentions. Techniques of prospection were used not just to produce knowledge but also to produce ignorance, conceived as "a deliberately engineered and strategic ploy" rather than "a kind of natural absence or void where knowledge has not yet spread" (Proctor 2008, 2).[35]

In contrast, in the case of the scenario-based simulation of a bioterrorist attack, representations of the future were very much things in the making in which direct participation by national leaders became a reflexive object of knowledge per se. Exercise designers who created the "events" that structured the experience of contingency central to their games' success encouraged public authorities to turn the simulated policy process of emergency resolution into an open object of questioning, to be known through practices of self-reflection. Designers of scenario-based exercises created a sense of uncertainty among participants, provoking leaders to inquire more deeply into the threat of an outbreak of infectious disease and to plan for its eventuality. In this second case, techniques of prospection were used to induce in national leaders who participated in the exercise the disquieting feeling of their own lack of preparedness for an unlikely but possible event. They brought the future's uncertain-seeming quality into the pres-

---

35. Sociologists of knowledge and academics are the least likely to accept the view that ignorance is not necessarily bad (Proctor 2008). Still, even in the field of national security, ignorance is sometimes beneficial, although it can be catastrophic.

ent, in order to instigate in national leaders' minds the need to demand more knowledge about this uncertain future by reflecting upon the simulation in which they had participated. Through a controlled simulation, exercise designers sought to represent events as realistically as possible, not for the sake of forecasting an actual future whose advent is almost certain, as the economic planners in the first case did, but for the practical lessons it could teach policy makers in the present.

The two cases that we have presented here therefore illustrate two different ways in which projections of the future can be granted credibility through the use of expert knowledge and can be used to shape how questions of public accountability will be understood in the present. Just as Karin Knorr Cetina (1999) has shown that in academic fields scientists do not always advance knowledge by turning their interpretations into factual black boxes but also produce knowledge by taking their own practices as objects of reflection, here we find that techniques of prospection are used by security specialists either to turn the future into an unquestioned black box or, on the contrary, to turn the present into an object of concern and care. Thus, we suggest, techniques and practices of prospection should be studied not only as instruments for producing predictive truths about the future but also as methods for delimiting what issues are salient for policy makers' intervention in the present. We therefore believe that the study of the multiple uses of techniques of prospection can become a promising field of inquiry for scholars of knowledge practices interested in understanding the articulation between knowledge claims and forms of public accountability.

References

Action Committee for the United States of Europe. 1955. "Joint Declaration, October 15." JMDS-000117. Archives of the European Communities, Florence.

Alibek, Ken. 1999. *Biohazard: The Chilling True Story of the Largest Covert Biological Weapons Program in the World—Told from Inside by the Man Who Ran It.* New York: Random House.

Amadae, S. M. 2003. *Rationalizing Capitalist Democracy: The Cold War Origins of Rational Choice Liberalism.* Chicago: University of Chicago Press.

Armand, Louis. 1955. "Some Aspects of the European Energy Problem, May." MK-000026. Archives of the European Communities, Florence.

———. 1956. "Exposé sur l'Euratom fait a la tribune de l'Assemblée nationale le 5 juillet." BAC 118/1986 1452. Archives of the European Communities, Florence.

———. 1957. Letter of the Three Wise Men to John Foster Dulles. January 31. JMAS-000033. Archives of the European Communities, Florence.

Aron, Raymond, and Daniel Lerner, eds. 1956. *La querelle de la CED: Essais d'analyse sociologique.* Paris: Armand Collin.

Barrett, Ronald. 2006. "Dark Winter and the Spring of 1972: Deflecting the Social Lessons of Smallpox." *Medical Anthropology* 25:171–91.

Beck, Ulrich. 1992. *Risk Society: Towards a New Modernity*. London: Sage.

Bloomfield, Lincoln P., and Barton Whaley. 1965. "The Political-Military Exercise: A Progress Report." *Orbis* 8:854–70.

Callon, Michel. 2007. "What Does It Mean to Say That Economics Is Performative?" In *Do Economists Make Markets? On the Performativity of Economics*, edited by Donald MacKenzie, Fabian Muniesa, and Lucia Siu, 311–57. Princeton, NJ: Princeton University Press.

Camic, Charles, and Neil Gross. 2001. "The New Sociology of Ideas." In *The Blackwell Companion to Sociology*, edited by Judith R. Blau, 236–50. Oxford: Blackwell.

Clarke, Lee. 2005. *Worst Cases: Terror and Catastrophe in Popular Imagination*. Chicago: University of Chicago Press.

Collier, Stephen, Andrew Lakoff, and Paul Rabinow. 2004. "Biosecurity: Towards an Anthropology of the Contemporary." *Anthropology Today* 20:3–7.

Dahan Dalmedico, Amy, and Hélène Guillemot. 2008. "Climate Change: Scientific Dynamics, Expertise and Geopolitical Challenges." In *Global Science and National Sovereignty: Studies in Historical Sociology of Science*, edited by Grégoire Mallard, Catherine Paradeise, and Ashveen Peerbaye, 195–221. New York: Routledge.

Dark Winter Exercise. Final Script. UPMC Center for Biosecurity. http://www.upmc-biosecurity.org/website/events/2001_darkwinter/dark_winter.pdf. Accessed June 12, 2008.

Duchêne, François. n.d. Memo on moratorium on French nuclear tests. JMDS 000235. Archives of the European Communities, Florence.

Dulles, John Foster. 1956a. Memorandum for the President. January 9. JMAS-000033. Archives of the European Communities, Florence.

———. 1956b. Letter to Paul Henri Spaak. December 21. JMAS-000014. Archives of the European Communities, Florence.

Espeland, Wendy N. 1998. *The Struggle for Water: Politics, Rationality, and Identity in the American Southwest*. Chicago: University of Chicago Press.

Euratom Commission. 1958a. Memo prepared for the Second Session of General Assembly of the IAEA to oppose Eastern arguments. September 26. BAC059/1980–481. Archives of the European Communities, Florence.

———. 1958b. "Report of the Second General Assembly, October 4." BAC059/1980–481. Archives of the European Communities, Florence.

Foucault, Michel. 1980. *Power/Knowledge: Selected Interviews and Other Writings, 1972–1977*. Edited by Colin Gordon. London: Harvester.

———. 1988. *Technologies of the Self: A Seminar with Michel Foucault*. Edited by Luther H. Martin, Huck Gutman, and Patrick H. Hutton. Amherst: University of Massachusetts Press.

Gaddis, John Lewis. 2005. *The Cold War: A New History*. New York: Penguin Press.

Ghamari-Tabrizi, Sharon. 2000. "Simulating the Unthinkable: Gaming Future War in the 1950s and 1960s." *Social Studies of Science* 30:163–223.

Goldberg, Andrew, C. Debra van Opstal, Michael E. Brown, and James H. Barkley. 1987. *Leaders and Crisis: The CSIS Crisis Simulations; A Report of the Arms Control and Crisis Management Program*. Washington, DC: Center for Strategic and International Studies.

Goldhamer, Herbert, and Hans Speier. 1959. "Some Observations on Political Gaming." *World Politics* 12:71–83.

Goldschmidt, Bertrand. 1982. *The Atomic Complex: A Worldwide Political History of Nuclear Energy*. LaGrange, IL: American Nuclear Society Press.

Greene, Benjamin P. 2007. *Eisenhower, Science Advice, and the Nuclear Test-Ban Debate (1945–1963)*. Stanford, CA: Stanford University Press.

Guéron, Jules. 1957. "Note sur ma visite aux Etats-Unis en juillet." JG-000212. Archives of the European Communities, Florence.

———. 1983. Lettre à Renou, note sur le livre de Renou du 3 janvier. JG-000194. Archives of the European Communities, Florence.

Halloran, Richard. 1987. "The Game Is War, and It's for Keeps." *New York Times*, June 1.

Hartog, François. 2003. *Régimes d'historicité: Présentisme et expériences du temps*. Paris: Seuil/La librairie du XXIe siècle.

Hecht, Gabrielle. 1998. *The Radiance of France: Nuclear Power and National Identity after World War II*. Cambridge, MA: MIT Press.

Henderson, Donald A. 1999. "The Looming Threat of Bioterrorism." *Science* 283: 1279–82.

Jasanoff, Sheila. 2005. *Designs on Nature: Science and Democracy in Europe and the United States*. Princeton, NJ: Princeton University Press.

Jasper, James M. 1990. *Nuclear Politics: Energy and the State in the United States, Sweden, and France*. Princeton, NJ: Princeton University Press.

Kaplan, Fred. 1983. *The Wizards of Armageddon*. New York: Simon and Schuster.

Knorr Cetina, Karin. 1999. *Epistemic Cultures: How the Sciences Make Knowledge*. Cambridge, MA: Harvard University Press.

Kohnstamm, Max. 1957a. "Note du 20 janvier sur le régime de contrôle et les pouvoirs de la Commission en matière d'exportation et de propriété des matières fissiles en préparation de la tournée des Trois Sages." CEAB1–79/DOC539/57f. Archives of the European Communities, Florence.

———. 1957b. "Compte-rendu des réunions du comite des trois sages, février." MK-000007. Archives of the European Communities, Florence.

———. 1957c. February memorandum on background of Euratom negotiations in Brussels. JMDS-000102. Archives of the European Communities, Florence.

———. 1957d. Letter to Jean Monnet. February 10. MK-000007. Archives of the European Communities, Florence.

———. 1957e. Memorandum. July 26. MK-000046. Archives of the European Communities, Florence.

———. 1958. Letter to Admiral Strauss. May 7. JMDS-000120. Archives of the European Communities, Florence.

Koselleck, Reinhart. 2004. *Futures Past: On the Semantics of Historical Time*. New York: Columbia University Press.

Kramish, Arnold. 1957. "Euratom: First Phase: Financial Evaluation of Costs, November 18." MK-000014. Archives of the European Communities, Florence.

Krige, John. 2008. "The Peaceful Atom as Political Weapon: Euratom and American Foreign Policy." *Historical Studies in the Natural Sciences* 38:9–48.

Kuklick, Bruce. 2006. *Blind Oracles: Intellectuals and War from Kennan to Kissinger*. Princeton, NJ: Princeton University Press.

Kupperman, Robert H., Richard H. Wilcox, and Harvey A. Smith. 1975. "Crisis Management: Some Opportunities." *Science* 187:404–10.

Lakoff, Andrew. 2007. "Preparing for the Next Emergency." *Public Culture* 19:247–71.

Lam, Clarence, Crystal Franco, and Ari Schuler. 2006. "Billions for Biodefense: Federal

Agency Biodefense Funding, FY2006-FY2007." *Biosecurity and Bioterrorism: Biodefense Strategy, Practice, and Science* 4:113–27.

Latour, Bruno. 1987. *Science in Action: How to Follow Scientists and Engineers through Society.* Cambridge, MA: Harvard University Press

Light, Jennifer S. 2003. *From Warfare to Welfare: Defense Intellectuals and Urban Problems in Cold War America.* Baltimore, MD: Johns Hopkins University Press.

Lurie, Nicole, Jeffrey Wasserman, and Christopher D. Nelson. 2006. "Public Health Preparedness: Evolution or Revolution." *Health Affairs* 25:935–45.

MacKenzie, Donald. 2007. "Is Economics Performative? Option Theory and the Construction of Derivatives Market." In *Do Economists Make Markets? On the Performativity of Economics*, edited by Donald MacKenzie, Fabian Muniesa, and Lucia Siu, 20–54. Princeton, NJ: Princeton University Press.

MAEF (Ministère des affaires étrangères français). 1957. "Protocole secret entre les Ministres Français, Allemand, Italien de la défense du 25 Novembre." MAEF 000019–21. Archives of the European Communities, Florence.

Mallard, Grégoire. 2008a. "The Atomic Confederacy: Europe's Quest for Nuclear Weapons and the Making of the New World Order." PhD diss., Princeton University.

———. 2008b. "Who Shall Keep Humanity's 'Sacred Trust': International Liberals, Cosmopolitans, and the Problem of Nuclear Nonproliferation." In *Global Science and National Sovereignty*, edited by Grégoire Mallard, Catherine Paradeise, and Ashveen Peerbaye, 82–119. New York: Routledge.

———. 2009. "L'Europe puissance nucléaire, cet obscur objet du désir: Vers une sociologie des stratégies d'énonciations du projet européen." *Critique internationale* 42:141–63.

Mann, James. 2004. *Rise of the Vulcans: The History of Bush's War Cabinet.* New York: Penguin.

Merton, Robert K. [1942] 1973. "The Normative Structure of Science." In *The Sociology of Science: Theoretical and Empirical Investigations*, edited by Robert K. Merton and Norman W. Storer, 267–78. Chicago: University of Chicago Press.

Miller, Judith, Stephen Engelberg, and William Broad. 2001. *Germs: Biological Weapons and America's Secret War.* New York: Simon and Schuster.

Mirowski, Philip. 2002. *Machine Dreams: How Economics Became a Cyborg Science.* Cambridge: Cambridge University Press.

Monnet, Jean. 1976. *Mémoires.* Paris: Fayard.

Moravcsik, Andrew. 1998. *The Choice for Europe: Social Purpose and State Power from Messina to Maastricht.* Ithaca, NY: Cornell University Press.

Muniesa, Fabian, and Michel Callon. 2007. "Economic Experiments and the Construction of Markets." In *Do Economists Make Markets? On the Performativity of Economics*, edited by Donald MacKenzie, Fabian Muniesa, and Lucia Siu, 163–89. Princeton, NJ: Princeton University Press.

Neustadt, Richard, and Ernest R. May. 1986. *Thinking in Time: The Uses of History for Decision-Makers.* New York: Free Press.

New York Times. 1958. "Euratom Resists Inspection by US of Future Plants." April 13.

O'Toole, Tara, Michael Mair, and Thomas Inglesby. 2002. "Shining Light on Dark Winter." *Clinical Infectious Diseases* 34:972–83.

Perrin, Francis. 1956. "Exposé sur l'Euratom fait à la tribune de l'Assemblée nationale le 5 juillet." BAC 118/1986 1452. Archives of the European Communities, Florence.

Proctor, Robert N. 2008. "Agnotology: A Missing Term to Describe the Cultural Production of Ignorance (and Its Study)." In *Agnotology: The Making and Unmaking of Igno-*

rance, edited by Robert N. Proctor and Londa Schiebinger, 1–37. Stanford, CA: Stanford University Press.

Robin, Ron. 2001. *The Making of the Cold War Enemy: Culture and Politics in the Military-Intellectual Complex.* Princeton, NJ: Princeton University Press.

Rosental, Claude. 2003. "Certifying Knowledge: The Sociology of a Logical Theorem in Artificial Intelligence." *American Sociological Review* 68:623–44.

Schaetzel, Robert. 1957a. Letter to Max Kohnstamm. November 19. MK-000014. Archives of the European Communities, Florence.

———. 1957b. Letter to Max Kohnstamm. December 17. MK-000014. Archives of the European Communities, Florence.

———. 1958a. January memo to Max Kohnstamm. JMDS-000120. Archives of the European Communities, Florence.

———. 1958b. Letter to Max Kohnstamm. January 28. JMDS-000120. Archives of the European Communities, Florence.

Shapin, Steven. 1995. "Cordelia's Love: Credibility and the Social Studies of Science." *Perspectives on Science* 3:255–75.

Skogmar, Gunnar. 2004. *The United States and the Nuclear Dimension of European Integration.* London: Palgrave Macmillan.

Sokolski, Henry D. 2001. *Best of Intentions: America's Campaign against Strategic Weapons Proliferation.* Westport, CT: Praeger.

Soutou, Georges Henri. 1994. "Les accords de 1957–1958: Vers une communauté stratégique et nucléaire entre la France, l'Allemagne et l'Italie." In *La France et l'atome: Etudes d'histoire nucléaire*, edited by Maurice Vaïsse, 123–63. Brussels: Bruylant.

———. 1996. *L'alliance incertaine: Les rapports politico-stratégiques franco-allemands, 1954–1996.* Paris: Fayard.

Stinchcombe, Arthur L. 2001. *When Formality Works: Authority and Abstraction in Law and Organizations.* Chicago: University of Chicago Press.

Stinchcombe, Arthur L., and Carol A. Heimer. 1985. *Organization Theory and Project Management: Administering Uncertainty in Norwegian Offshore Oil.* Oxford: Oxford University Press.

Trachtenberg, Marc. 1999. *A Constructed Peace: The Making of the European Settlement.* Princeton, NJ: Princeton University Press.

U.S. Congress. House of Representatives. 2001. *Combating Terrorism: Federal Response to a Biological Weapons Attack; Hearing before the Subcommittee on National Security, Veterans Affairs and International Relations of the Committee on Government Reform.* July 23.

Winand, Pascaline. 1993. *Eisenhower, Kennedy, and the United States of Europe.* New York: St. Martin's Press.

Woolsey, R. James, and Robert H. Kupperman. 1984. *America's Hidden Vulnerabilities: Crisis Management in a Society of Networks.* Washington, DC: Center for Strategic and International Studies, Georgetown University.

Wright, Susan. 2007. "Terrorists and Biological Weapons: Forging the Linkage in the Clinton Administration." *Politics and the Life Sciences* 25:57–115.

TWELVE

What Do Market Designers Do When They Design Markets?

Economists as Consultants to the Redesign of Wholesale Electricity Markets in the United States

DANIEL BRESLAU

Reforms in the governance of social provision in the late twentieth century, global in scope, have been accompanied by the emergence of new professional roles—among them, the market designer. Mostly trained economists working outside academe, market designers aspire to treat markets as the objects of a design intention and are consultants to public administrators, political officials, and private stakeholders. Appropriating design as a metaphor from the professions with which the term is usually associated, the field of market design implies that these markets can be rationally constructed to maximize desired properties and effects. Extending the metaphor, the rules and administrative infrastructure of market exchanges are routinely referred to as the "architecture" of the market (Wilson 2002). Economists have been involved in the design of auctions for Federal Communications Commission licenses, in professional labor markets, kidney exchanges, emissions trading, and markets for electricity, among other new and newly redesigned markets (Cramton and Kerr 2002; Klemperer 2004; Roth 2002; Roth, Sönmez, and Ünver 2007). Recognition of this new role for economists has come in the form of the 2007 Nobel Prize in economics to three key figures in developing the formal theory behind market design. And other social scientific specialties, notably economic sociology and sci-

This chapter is based upon work supported by the National Science Foundation under grant no. 0620900. Any opinions, findings, and conclusions or recommendations expressed in this material are those of the author and do not necessarily reflect the views of the National Science Foundation. I would also like to thank the editors of this volume for their careful reading and constructive advice on earlier drafts. The work could not have been carried out without valuable research assistance from Sunita Raina and Jin Yu.

ence studies, have recognized the intensified involvement of economists and economics in the constitution of markets in the form of a new but already extensive literature, to which this chapter belongs (see, e.g., MacKenzie, Muniesa, and Siu 2007; Pinch and Swedberg 2008, 3).

What kind of activity is market design? This chapter aims to characterize the work of these economists in terms of a distinct epistemic stance and set of practices. While the expertise of market designers is grounded in the discipline of economics, the political and technological realities of their work rule out a straightforward application of economic theory or research results. But as the analysis of those involved in the redesign of wholesale electricity markets will show, they nonetheless make extensive use of economic models in reconciling their designs to political forces and technological constraints. Their distinctive repertoire of practices is dedicated largely to this task.

Economists and the Politics of Markets: Two Views

"Market design" evokes an image of economists as engineers or architects, who draw blueprints for markets that are then materialized, with the support of powerful clients. And it implies a relationship of experts to clients that conforms to a familiar model of professional work. It suggests that the configuration of these markets can be detached from local and historically variable cultural traditions and made the object of an instrumental rationality based in scientific knowledge. The metaphor of design also holds out the promise of an apolitical application of science, with the potential of transforming a contentious process tending toward zero-sum struggles to a rational harmonization of opposed interests in the form of an optimal design. This is precisely the kind of imagery offered in works proclaiming the successes of designed markets (McMillan 2002; Milgrom 2004).

But anyone familiar with the voluminous social historical literature on markets has reason to be skeptical of the design imagery. Markets, wherever they have been studied, are formed neither spontaneously nor without power struggles (Fligstein 1996; Polanyi 1944). Those with a stake in the rules of the market can be counted on to attempt to influence those rules to their advantage. Markets are generally the result of a project carried out, in conjunction with state powers, by those who hope to extract new streams of revenue from a relatively orderly and protected exchange (MacKenzie 2006). It would be a very special set of circumstances indeed that would permit stakeholders in the formation of a market to delegate their ability to shape the market to technical experts.

Recent discussions of market design and market designers in a social science vein have confronted exactly this set of issues, recapitulating the internalist/externalist divide that is familiar to historians of science and technology. Is market design, true to the metaphor, an application of expert knowledge to the rational development of real institutions? Or does economic knowledge lend a scientific veneer to what is essentially the outcome of political struggle? Looking at the case of the Federal Communications Commission's auctions of the electromagnetic spectrum, Guala describes an iterative process, in which market designers, based in the game theory subspecialty of auction theory, first proposed a set of design options (Guala 2001). To be fair, Guala did not suggest that the game theorists who consulted on the design of the spectrum auctions derived their designs from economic theory in any straightforward way. Indeed, he points out that the practical problem at hand was complex beyond the limits of existing formalizations in the field of mechanism design. The design work was therefore supplemented by testing using the methods of experimental economics. But even in the laboratory, there was no possibility of determining if the designed institutions allowed the determination of efficient prices. Market designers supplemented their disciplinary knowledge with accumulated firsthand experience of markets in the laboratory and as implemented in real institutions. But Guala's analysis did treat the market design process as an autonomous one, allowed to follow its internal logic and motivated by a purely technical aim of producing an efficient market.

Guala's narrative reconstruction strikes Mirowski and Nik-Khah as irreparably internalist, basically adopting the market designers' own narrative, which characterizes the design process as scientific inquiry, guided by experience and theory (Mirowski and Nik-Khah 2007; Nik-Khah 2008). Mirowski and Nik-Khah shift the analytical context, locating the market designers in terms of the political economy of market design. They note that the game theorists who worked on the Federal Communications Commission spectrum auctions were in the employ of major players in the telecommunications industry. They offered their design ideas as advocates for the interests of their clients. For instance, game theorists who worked for national telecom companies who wanted to consolidate many regional licenses into national coverage promoted auction rules that would facilitate such packaging of licenses. Where it was impossible to simply read an efficient market design off of economic theory, differences tended to correspond to the structure of the industry and the divergent interests of the major firms. With irony, Mirowski and Nik-Khah note that the economists, in this case specialists in game theory, who provided consulting services for specific corporations were the same ones who proclaimed the spectrum auctions to be the fullest realization of scientific market design. Finally, their analysis concludes that the market designers succeeded only in helping their clients obtain licenses at bargain prices. The eventual design did not produce the optimum distribution of licenses (Nik-Khah 2008).

As important as it has proven to be to locate the work of market designers in the political struggles over the configuration of markets, we should not be too eager to reduce their work to the interests of their clients. Granted, in the final analysis neither economists nor purely scientific criteria determine the market rules that are proffered or those that are ultimately adopted. But this does not mean that economics is an empty vessel to be filled with economic interests. Indeed, economists would have little to offer in the way of authoritative advice if not for the relative autonomy secured by their disciplinary credentials and theoretical knowledge (Breslau 1998). And as the sociological literature on professions would lead us to expect, the market designers have interests of their own in a classic jurisdictional competition (Abbott 1988).

In the remainder of this chapter, I will describe some features of this collective project as found in the work of economists who serve as consultants in the design of wholesale electricity markets in the United States. The designs that they advance are neither the result of a scientific search for a design that works nor simply the embodiment of the interests of the designers' powerful clients. Instead, the work of the market designers can best be described as a kind of mediation. Sometimes posing their recommendations in opposition to "political" proposals of stakeholders in the design process, they continually mediate between an abstract object, the competitive market, and the technological and political realities of the electricity industry. As with the securities analysts discussed by Knorr Cetina (chap. 13, this volume), they embody a specific epistemic stance and a characteristic set of knowledge-making practices. It is this stance, which I will describe as "applied Platonism," that allows them to produce design recommendations that incorporate those realities in market mechanisms. In the course of their mediation, the economists "educate" the professionals that populate the market design process, redefining the features of existing markets in terms that correspond to economic theory. The terms of economic theory are progressively incorporated into the markets and into the politics of market design, and increasingly provide the terms by which market rules must be formulated and justified.

Data for this study are drawn from dockets at the Federal Energy Regulatory Commission (FERC), where changes to market rules are considered.

Any market rules that will affect prices of electricity in interstate trade fall into the jurisdiction of the FERC. The commission initiates a legal process by opening a docket into which are gathered all filings of any parties with an interest in the rules under consideration. These include generating companies, utilities that sell power to customers, investors, state agencies, and groups representing both residential and industrial consumers. Many of these "stakeholders" hire consulting economists, or employ them in-house, to submit testimony or affidavits proposing specific design elements and providing a scientific assessment of proposed rules. Analysis of the docket materials allowed for the mapping of the scientific positions on market design onto the positions of the major stakeholders in the politics of market design. The materials in the docket were used to identify the subjects of sixteen open-ended interviews that I conducted. These were supplemented by interviews with six additional economists, selected on the basis of their published work on the design of electricity markets.

Capacity Markets

The empirical focus of this chapter is the redesign of the capacity markets in the largest regional wholesale market in the United States, operated by an independent system operator (ISO) known as PJM Interconnection.[1] Capacity markets are a response adopted by some power systems in order to assure a reliable supply of power under the peculiar physical, technological, and legal constraints of the electricity industry. In the capacity markets, generators sell, not power, but rather the rights to their generating capacity over a specified period of time. The purpose of these markets is to secure adequate generating capacity to ensure a reliable supply of power, even during times of peak demand. Commodity markets in general do not have separate markets for productive capacity. When buyers pay for a commodity, they do not pay a separate price for the capacity to produce the commodity. The capacity cost is included in the price of the commodity itself; it is simply the portion of the price that covers fixed, as opposed to variable, inputs. And incentives to build more productive capacity, or to halt new construction of capacity, are communicated by price signals. Ideally, when there are shortages of supply, prices and profits increase, sending a signal to investors to build more capacity. But in wholesale electricity markets in

1. PJM stands for Pennsylvania, New Jersey, and Maryland, although this ISO now includes Delaware, West Virginia, most of Virginia, and parts of North Carolina, Ohio, Kentucky, Indiana, Michigan, and Illinois. It is the largest system in the United States in terms of sheer megawattage served.

the U.S., there is a legal mandate for regulatory bodies to ensure a reliable supply. And regulators have not been willing to rely on electricity prices alone to "incent" investment in power generation that will be adequate to achieve the required level of reliability. As a consequence, wholesale markets for power are often supplemented by a separate capacity market.

Capacity markets work by imposing a requirement on load-serving entities (LSEs)—these are the organizations, mostly private electric companies, that buy power wholesale and sell it to consumers—to procure capacity contracts sufficient to meet their projected load reliably. Engineers have developed criteria for determining the amount of capacity needed to ensure adequacy. In general, this consists of calculating an installed reserve margin of capacity beyond projected peak demand, which yields an acceptable reliability scenario. The installed reserve margin is a percentage margin above the peak demand, usually around 15–20 percent, that is estimated to provide a "one-in-ten" standard of reliability, meaning a level of reliability allowing only one day of loss of load (blackout) in ten years. The capacity markets are established to centralize trade in capacity contracts, offering a central clearing house for LSEs to meet their capacity obligations. In the case that will be discussed here, the system operator determines the total amount of capacity that must be procured to ensure the required level of reliability and then bids on behalf of all the LSEs, passing the cost of capacity on to them. LSEs can offset these costs through bilateral contracts with generation owners or by "self-supplying" their capacity requirement with generators that they own. The capacity market consists of a periodic auction at which generator owners bid their capacity at a specific asking price and the ISO buys it, starting with the lowest-priced bids, until it has acquired the amount needed for reliability purposes.

By 2005, the capacity market in PJM was fraught with problems and was met with dissatisfaction from LSEs, owners of generation, and consumers. PJM's market had been plagued by noncompetitive practices on the part of generators who benefited from the high concentration of generating resources in a small number of companies (PJM Interconnection 2006). Owners of generation could exercise "market power" by withholding capacity from the market and thereby inducing high prices. And when market power was kept under control, owners of generation complained that the revenues from the capacity market were insufficient to cover their investments in peaking generators. Representatives of the financial sector reported that investment capital for new generation was drying up because of the low return and high risk in what had become an unpredictable market. Meanwhile, reliability shortfalls were looming for areas where bottlenecks in the transmission system prevented importing sufficient power. The next section will discuss the practices of economists in diagnosing this failure and prescribing solutions.

Applied Platonism

Economists involved in electricity market design are not "free-market fundamentalists" (Kozul-Wright and Rayment 2007). They are pragmatic in their orientation and do not have a doctrinaire vision of a perfect market that they then try to realize in their design. Rather, they are very willing to adapt their design proposals to the constraints presented by the technology and politics of electricity (Cramton 2003). This is particularly true of the nonacademic consultants who are closest to the market participants and to the authorities that make market design decisions (Stoft 2002). The standard of good design is not the closest possible approximation to the ideal market but the integration of existing features of the power system with a market mechanism. These are the terms of evaluation embedded in one economist's discussion of a particular market design:

> I think it makes a lot of sense because it really does integrate the market, the solution to the market prices and quantities with the physical attributes of the network, and I always thought that was the biggest technical challenge for creating competitive electricity markets. How do you put the engineering and physical attributes of electricity, which are quite unusual, together with a market system? And this does it by integrating the two in a market framework; so I like it.

As will be elaborated below, what these comments say about the "physical attributes of the network" can be extended to the political constraints on market rules.

While economic idealizations of competitive markets are not treated as blueprints that should be fully realized in the electricity markets, the economic model of competitive markets is nonetheless central to the practices of the economic consultants. It will help to characterize their approach, which is based on mainstream neoclassical economic techniques, as applied Platonism. The orienting reality of their work is the abstract object called the competitive market, and throughout this chapter, I will use this term to denote the abstract object rather than any actual market. It furnishes the horizon against which features of existing markets can be described, thus providing the terms of perception of real markets. Existing markets, true to Platonism, are viewed by market designers as flawed approximations of the ideal competitive market. In a way that will be described and documented below, the competitive market guides the economic consultant's work of mediating the political conflict over the rules of the market. In practical terms, applied Platonism therefore refers to the array of formal and informal techniques for characterizing existing markets as departures from the competitive market. It involves translating market rules into terms that are directly comparable to representations of the competitive market, in graphical, numeric, or conceptual form.

This Platonism structures textbook treatments of the subject, which begin by describing the functioning of this abstract object before proceeding to the imperfect world of real markets (Hunt 2002; Stoft 2002). The competitive market has none of the problems that are endemic to actual electricity markets. It is competitive in the sense that no participant is big enough to influence the price, so buyers and sellers alike are "price takers." The use, or abuse, of market power by large players in the market that has plagued some of the deregulated markets in the United States does not exist in the competitive market. It is a complete market, in which all relevant information is realized in the bids of participants and there are no structured constraints on what exchanges can take place. It provides the precise price signals to optimize investment in generation. It will consistently set equilibrium prices at the marginal cost of production while simultaneously providing an incentive to producers to reduce costs. It will therefore outperform any kind of regulation, which can keep prices low or offer strong incentives but never both. The competitive market finds the price that maximizes the overall surplus to producers and consumers. And most importantly for the discussion in this chapter, reliability problems simply do not arise in the competitive market. With both supply and demand responsive to the price signals that they mutually generate, the market will always clear with no unmet demand.

Steven Stoft's *Power System Economics* (2002), the most widely used textbook devoted to power markets, thus begins by describing the competitive market and its advantages, and then characterizes existing markets in terms of their departures from the ideal case. Real markets are described as systems of flaws, which can then be traced to features of the institutional or technological boundaries in which the market operates. Journal articles that propose market designs follow the same logic and justify their proposals as mechanisms to compensate for or eliminate market flaws. Like textbook accounts, discussions of suggested designs for capacity markets are introduced by first characterizing the market as a system of departures from the competitive case (Bidwell and Henney 2004; Cramton and Stoft 2005). Any departure from the competitive market realizes a suboptimal level of efficiency and deprives participants of the maximum surplus they could otherwise realize. Testimony and affidavits filed with the FERC in the capacity market proceedings adopt the same analytic/rhetorical strategy, justifying specifics of market design in terms of market flaws that the capacity "constructs" are supposed to correct. And indeed, when interviewed on their work in this area, economists often begin by noting the ways that the logic of the ideal competitive market does not obtain in this case:

> Anyhow, let's try the recent incarnations of this "can competitive prices pay for investment?" And the answer is that if you really had a normal competitive market in electricity then the answer would be yes. It would work just like other normal competitive markets. And so, at the theoretical level there's no dispute. I take the same side as all standard economists do, which is that if you have a normal competitive market, then the spot prices will do the job. And I take also the standard economic view that if you don't have a normal market, that's got something really weird going on with the pricing, it probably won't do the job. And so it's not like I'm trying to overturn the economics here. I'm just trying to apply—I do apply—just standard, straightforward economic theory and get the standard answer.

Most of what is "really weird" about pricing in electricity markets derives from one major flaw: namely, the absence of a responsive demand side. Retail markets for electricity have not been deregulated in most areas, except for offering consumers the possibility, in some states of the United States, of choosing from a selection of retailers. Economic analysts will describe this flaw in terms of a market failure that is actually a failure of communicating effective price signals. "The customer does not see the real-time price." Retail rates are negotiated and subject to long-term contracts and restrictions. They are allowed to change annually, or every six months, but wholesale prices change hourly, sometimes fluctuating by factors of ten or more over the course of a day. Because the price to consumers does not follow these fluctuations, and because electricity metering does not yet take price into account, demand cannot adjust to shortages. At moments of scarcity, consumers will not reduce their consumption, even as the wholesale price spikes to many times its average level.

The absence of a responsive demand side provides the diagnosis for many of the other ways that the electricity markets depart from the competitive one (Hirst 2001). The gap in functioning between the existing market and the competitive market can be attributed to flaws in market rules, and the absence of an active demand is the most important of these. Because demand does not adjust to high prices in times of shortage, prices can continue to spike. In the extreme case, incidents of blackouts or "load shedding," the supply and demand curves economists use to describe price formation simply fail to intersect (Stoft 2002). This produces a cascade of further deviations from a competitive market. As prices spike, price caps are imposed, further removing the market from the behavior of the ideal competitive model and, in the Platonic view, further distorting the price signals. As we will see below, this distorts the incentives that in a competitive market ensure the right level of investment in generation. The reliability problems faced by existing markets, but not the nonexistent competitive market, would be sharply mitigated, or even disappear entirely, if consumers of electricity were able to vary their consumption in response to real-time variation in prices. Virtually every general treatment of market design begins by pointing out the absence of an active demand side, and as we shall see below, capacity markets are designed and justified as a mechanism to compensate for this flaw.

Identification of the market's flaws is rarely straightforward, however, as existing markets do not present themselves in a form that allows for a direct comparison to the competitive market. The administrative terms in which the market rules are couched are the product of a complex history, involving a range of actors and cognitive terms more likely to be drawn from engineering, public administration, and law. The preliminary work of market design therefore consists of a translation of the features of the market into the terms of economic theory. Such terms will permit an explicit identification of the market's flaws. The most common technique of translation is the redescription of the market rules in terms of their effect on the familiar supply and demand graphs, the "scissors" developed in the nineteenth century and given a privileged place in the analysis of price formation in markets by Alfred Marshall. The market rules are given economic meaning through their effects on the shape of these curves and the characteristics of their intersection. For instance, the lack of an active demand side to the market yields a demand curve that is very close to vertical, having a minimum of elasticity in response to changes in price. Other market flaws, such as market power and price caps, are rendered graphically in terms of the way that they divert prices from the efficient equilibrium of the competitive market.

Reconstructing Capacity Markets

As I have mentioned already, typical commodity markets do not feature separate markets for capacity. And the competitive market of economic theory provides no rationale for such a feature. In the abstract world of perfect competition, the price signals generated in the competitive market are the most efficient possible way to "incent" investment in capacity and ensure the optimal level of production for the market. Moreover, the price mechanisms of the market are the best way to return a market to the optimal equilibrium level of capacity after an external shock has created either a shortage or a surplus. And indeed, many economists have argued for an "energy only" market, where electricity prices alone would be relied on to induce the hoped-for level of investment in generation, or have advocated a design that would allow for a capacity market to be eventually phased out (Hogan 2005; Oren 2005). The Midwest ISO today operates without a separate market for capacity.

But economists who have consulted the ISOs that already have capacity markets in place, particularly those whose clients are the ISOs themselves, have not advocated abolishing the capacity markets. Rather than simply arguing for the closest possible approximation to the competitive market, these market designers have translated the features of the existing markets into the terms of economic theory. Rather than rejecting an obvious deviation from an ideal market, the economists redefined the capacity markets, incorporating them in a comprehensive economic interpretation of the wholesale markets in general.

And it is by applying the same Platonist apparatus to markets that economists have produced a rationale for capacity markets. They noted that all wholesale electricity markets deviate from the competitive market by including rules that cap prices during periods of scarcity. Occasional periods of scarcity and price spikes are an inevitable feature of electricity markets, due to the inability to store electricity on a large scale and the consequence that power must be generated at the same moment that it is consumed. And even blackouts are inevitable, although at a tolerably low probability for most systems in the United States. Without exception, regulators or system operators find ways to keep prices during these periods within a tolerable maximum. Uncapped prices during these spikes can be more than a hundred times the average price. Most of the ISOs in the United States cap wholesale prices at $1,000 per megawatt hour, compared to an average price between $50 and $100. In addition, all ISOs contain rules for mitigating market power and are required to have their markets reviewed by independent "market monitors." Economists also suspected that these measures, in their zeal to crack down on market power, were in effect suppressing the price below the competitive equilibrium.

Placing the capped prices in an economic framework, directly juxtaposing the capped market with the unregulated competitive market, reveals a new object or, more accurately, a void known as the "missing money." The abstract competitive market spontaneously realizes the precise price signals for optimal investment. It is the "scarcity rents," profits realized during price spikes, that allow generators to cover the costs of their investments, and if high enough, encourage new entry into the market. But these peaks are cut off in the capped market, and the area of those peaks represents a nonnegligible quantity of money that fails to materialize. Although price caps are invoked infrequently, keeping prices at $500 per megawatt-hour when an uncapped market would allow prices to rise to ten times that price means that the total amount of missing money can be a significant percentage of the revenues earned by generators. Some have estimated that the missing money amounts to 15 percent of the total revenues in the wholesale power markets. The lore among market designers, both in print and in interviews for this study, credits Roy Shanker, an independent consultant who has advised both PJM and the New England ISO, with introducing the term "missing money" into the market design discussion as recently as 2003, in a filing with the FERC.

Figure 12.1, from a document filed at a FERC technical conference, illustrates the missing money by comparing the revenues actually paid in the power market with what would have been paid in the absence of a price cap. The figure is a "price-duration curve," representing the number of hours over the course of one year that the wholesale price for one megawatt-hour of power is at a particular level. The shape of the curve is derived from theoretical assumptions about the behavior of prices in a competitive market, and the area under the curve represents the total revenues generators would receive under competitive conditions. The shaded peak of the curve is therefore the result of comparing the actual, capped, market with the abstract competitive market.

Accepting the missing money as inevitable, now the economic consultants are able to provide an economic rationale for capacity markets—namely, to restore the missing money that would provide the proper signals for investment. The capacity markets had been instituted as a reliability assurance mechanism, to allow LSEs to purchase their required capacity contracts in a centralized auction. With the penetration of the term "miss-

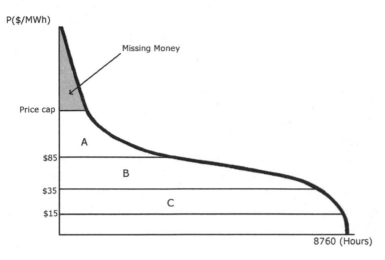

Figure 12.1. Constructing the "missing money" (Hogan 2005)

ing money" and the framework that gives it meaning, the engineering rationale for capacity markets has been replaced. They are now reconstructed with an economic rationale. Recent deliberations over market design in the PJM, New England, Midwest, and California ISOs have all been explicitly couched in these terms. The capacity markets are now understood as an answer to an economic problem of providing price signals, as the market Platonism of the economic consultants becomes built into the horizon of those who establish and administer market rules, as well as those subject to them. When the Midwest ISO was considering a capacity market, the discussion was entirely devoted to mechanisms for solving the problem of the missing money (Federal Energy Regulatory Commission 2008). The missing money, in turn, owes its existence to a permanent comparison of the existing market with an abstract competitive market.

In the first five years of the twenty-first century, when dissatisfaction with PJMs capacity market led to calls for a redesign, economic consultants proceeded by characterizing this compensating market in terms of economic theory—in other words, as a structure of deviations from a competitive market. When the capacity market that was then in use in PJM was submitted to this kind of analysis, the economic consultants found something interesting. The demand curve did not assume a familiar downward-sloping shape, determined by typical utility functions of consumers. Instead, it was almost completely specified by the rules of the market. LSEs were required to procure a predetermined quantity of capacity and, if they failed to meet their reserve requirement, had to pay a fixed penalty for every megawatt-day they were under. This means that an LSE that has not met its requirement will be willing to pay up to the penalty for every unit they need, until the requirement is met. Once they have obtained an adequate number of capacity contracts, an additional contract is worthless. On the familiar price-quantity graph, this means that the price paid for capacity will be zero when there is more than enough capacity to meet the system's requirement. But when the quantity of capacity is below the requirement, the price immediately jumps to a level equal to the penalty. The curve, over most of the price range, is vertical, meaning that a fixed quantity is demanded regardless of price. The capacity market had a vertical demand curve! Here is how two leading figures in capacity market design described this market, once it is re-represented in standard economic terms:

> Thus, the competitive outcome is determined from the intersection of the true supply curve (near zero up to the system capacity and then infinite) and the demand curve (vertical at the capacity requirement), as shown in Figure 1 [not reproduced here]. This yields a competitive price near zero, whenever the system capacity is sufficient to satisfy the requirement, which through planning should be all the time. (Cramton and Stoft 2005, 45)

Once this deviation from the competitive market is identified, it becomes the diagnosis for problems in the functioning of the market. The capacity markets in PJM had been prone to market power. This was partly due to the concentrated ownership of generating resources, allowing specific companies to be "price makers," elevating prices by withholding resources from the market or bidding in necessary resources at elevated prices. But a competitive market, with many buyers and a demand determined by their separate valuations of the commodity on offer, will typically have a downward-sloping demand curve. This is a curve that is responsive to prices, but responsive in a continuous and gradual fashion. Opportunities for market power are thus limited, since a withholding of small amounts of output can have only a small effect on prices. The vertical demand curve was also blamed for the volatility occasionally exhibited in capacity market prices. This could be easily blamed on the way that prices immediately jump from near zero to the insufficiency penalty as soon as the quantity of capacity dips below the resource requirement. The behavior of prices, and even a predicted tendency of the market toward boom and bust cycles, could be directly linked to the market's design features, which were visible only against the horizon of the competitive market.

Again, an "orthodox" approach would consist of eliminating every feature of existing markets that constitutes a flaw when juxtaposed with the competitive market. This would mean, at the least, eliminating price caps and capacity markets and subjecting all buyers to real-time prices. But rather than using the competitive market as an ideal to be actualized, the economic consultants use it as a guide to compensate for market flaws that cannot be simply eliminated. They develop a compensating mechanism that corresponds as precisely as possible to the nature and extent of the market flaw.

For the design of the capacity market, with its vertical demand curve, a number of economists, working with several of the ISOs, proposed a simple solution. There is no active demand in the capacity market, and no demand at all without the ISO requiring LSEs to buy an adequate quantity of capacity. The effective demand is shaped entirely by the reserve requirement, yielded by engineering criteria for system reliability. Since that fixed requirement is set administratively, it would be just as simple to set a variable requirement that allows the price paid for capacity to increase when capacity is scarce and decrease when capacity approaches and exceeds the reserve requirement. The result would be a gradually downward-sloping demand curve, with a shape much like one would expect in a competitive market. Such a curve was proposed, according to the informal network of market designers, by an economist named Mark Reeder, who worked for the New York Public Service Commission. The curve would mimic the equilibrating effect of market demand by setting the price for capacity, when quantity is at the desired reserve level, equal to the "cost of new entry" of a peaking generator. If the quantity of capacity offered drops below this level, the elevated price will provide an incentive for investors to build new power plants. If there is excessive capacity, the price signal will discourage new entry. Figure 12.2 illustrates what came to be referred to within PJM as the "Variable Resource Requirement," or VRR, curve. The new capacity market proposed by PJM was named the Reliability Pricing Model, or RPM (PJM Interconnection 2005).

The Battle over the RPM

From its introduction in meetings of PJM stakeholders in 2005, the RPM was the object of heated contention. An analysis of this contention helps to illustrate the political effects of the reconceptualization promoted by the market design consultants. Though the RPM was supported by PJM, the large generating companies, utilities that included generation businesses,

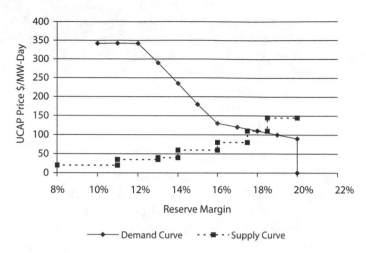

Figure 12.2. Clearing the capacity market with a downward-sloping demand curve

and financial corporations, it was opposed by most of the other stakeholders in PJM. These consisted primarily of "load side" interests, meaning the LSEs themselves, industrial and residential consumer groups, and state regulatory agencies. Despite the opposition, PJM went ahead and submitted a slightly modified RPM proposal for the approval by the FERC in August 2005.

As is its normal procedure in response to such filings, the FERC opened a docket for RPM, an action that automatically initiates a quasi-judicial proceeding. Over fifty distinct corporations, government agencies, and industry and consumer groups filed motions to intervene in order to be heard in the FERC proceedings. While the filings are legal documents, noting the interest and position of the parties, most of them included economic analyses. Attached to many of the filings are reports by hired consultants.

Those opposed to the RPM were exclusively parties who would be liable for the immediate increase in capacity prices. Many of these formed associations for the purpose of opposing the RPM. One of the larger groups was the Coalition of Consumers for Reliability (CCR). It included the consumer advocacy agencies of the states of Pennsylvania, Maryland, Ohio, Illinois, Virginia, and Indiana, as well as the District of Columbia. These were joined by a number of electricity cooperatives, which are actually associations of smaller, consumer-owned cooperatives for buying electricity, generally for industrial and residential consumers in rural areas. The CCR had contracted with a consulting firm, Synapse Economics, of Cambridge,

Massachusetts, to conduct an analysis of the RPM and to devise an alternative design for the PJM capacity market.

The Synapse study, which was incorporated into the coalition's ninety-seven-page FERC filing, rejected not only the RPM but the Platonic framework of the economic market designers. The latter interpreted a capacity shortage, even a local one that is confined to the transmission-constrained load pockets, as a failure of price signals to "incent" adequate investment. The Coalition of Consumers for Reliability filing, however, argued that there was no failure of price signals in PJM. The system as a whole had a reserve margin near 25 percent, indicating that installed capacity was 25 percent above the projected peak load. The required installed reserve margin was only 15 percent. This should be taken as a sign of overwhelming success of the capacity market to provide the right price signals (PJM Interconnection 2005). The impending violation of reliability criteria in New Jersey, according to the coalition, was due to the problem that creates the load pocket in the first place—namely, inadequate transmission. The coalition, as well as most of the other "load side" opponents of the RPM, argued that this local problem should have a local solution. The impending reliability crisis in New Jersey was not an economic problem at all but a problem of planning transmission and capacity.

For market designers, such solutions are termed "out-of-market" fixes, or what one of my interviewees pejoratively labeled the "engineering approach": "And if the market doesn't stimulate that amount, the system operator starts doing various outside, special contracts and other deals to comply with the engineering reliability criteria. And the system operator's behavior ends up . . . screwing up the market even more." The system operator "screws up" the market by contracting outside the market for needed generation, either for the construction of new plants or to forestall the retirement of existing and unprofitable plants. Such contracts, including what are known as RMR, or "reliability must-run," contracts, further distort the market by preventing the shortage of capacity to be manifested in a price signal consisting of higher prices throughout the market. Market design seeks to establish market rules that, when instituted, will render prices that will spontaneously stimulate the right level of investment. The same interviewee went on to describe the virtues of the capacity market design in terms of the way it realizes reliability criteria through a market mechanism rather than through administrative intervention. The new design "tries to integrate the reliability rules, the capacity obligations into a market mechanism that reflects, into a market mechanism."

The moral valence of the out-of-market fixes, such as the RMR contracts, is reversed when these arrangements are compared with the competitive market. What was initially an orderly administrative process of making sure that needed generating capacity remained available within load pockets is now revealed to be a stark instance of price discrimination. These opposed framings were placed in particularly high relief at a 2005 technical conference convened by the FERC to hear a range of views on the current capacity market design in PJM. Technical conferences are also used by the FERC to establish a record of these views that can be used in justifying subsequent decisions. This particular conference featured representatives of all the major stakeholder groups in PJM, as well as academics, a representative of Citicorp, and others. Here a number of representatives of load-side interests opposed the proposed RPM on the grounds that capacity shortfalls are local, while investment in capacity for the system as a whole is robust. They opposed a market system that would force higher capacity prices and higher payments throughout the system to remedy local shortages of capacity. These proposals were met with stern disapproval from consultants to generator interests, but in the name of economic rationality. Roy Shanker's comments illustrate the new meaning of RMR contracts when they are placed in relation to the competitive market:

> I'm sorry. Something that I'm sort of uncomfortable letting stand is the notion that RMR is sort of beneficial when it has to occur; it's least cost, and we shouldn't have windfalls to other people in a clearing situation. Let's take them a piece at a time. I think Joe alluded to this about the inefficiency of RMR. First off, if you're going to essentially seize assets and price discriminate, RMR is cheaper. I thought we were here to talk about markets. So, let's pull that off the table. (Federal Energy Regulatory Commission 2005, 57)

The Politics of Simulation

To test the effects of alternate shapes of the new demand curve, PJM contracted with an economic analyst from Johns Hopkins University to run a simulated market. Benjamin Hobbs, an environmental engineer who has specialized in modeling electricity markets, was hired to conduct an analysis that would simulate the response of markets to a range of possible demand curves. Using Microsoft Excel, Hobbs set up a simulated electricity market, consisting of the market for power and a capacity market. The analysis considers a range of different shapes of the demand curve, examining how the simulated market responds to the structure of incentives presented by each curve. The model is dynamic, because the incentives for investment are themselves influenced by previous investment decisions. For instance, new investment in one period will increase reserve margins and reduce capacity payments (and incentives to invest) in subsequent periods.

Hobbs's model is reported in an affidavit submitted by PJM to the FERC, along with its filing of the new capacity market design. True to the logic and genre of economic analysis, Hobbs's exposition begins by describing the competitive market, in which the optimal level of reliability is achieved through the price signals spontaneously generated by competition. The features of electricity markets are then characterized as departures from the competitive market. The market lacks a responsive demand side; prices are capped well before reaching their equilibrium level during a price spike. The model is calibrated using the assumptions of perfect information and risk-neutral investors. At this setting, it yields a constant reserve margin, determined entirely by the location of the demand curve. The cost of the reserve margin is almost identical across all the curve shapes. Structural features of the market are then added to the model. It is therefore not quite accurate to describe the model as a simplification of the actual market. It is an articulation or specification of the competitive market. For instance, in determining the supply curve for capacity, it is assumed that the market is competitive, and that therefore capacity owners will bid their capacity into the market at its cost, including a fixed return (Hobbs 2005).

Most of the variation in results of Hobbs's analysis is due to the relationship between volatility and cost of investment, given risk-averse investors. Since steeper demand curves will generate greater price volatility, they will, of necessity, require higher prices to "incent" adequate investment. This effect, which means that the cost of reliability will increase as the downward slope of the demand curve becomes steeper, dwarfed the other effects examined. This led to the conclusion that a sloping demand curve will achieve the target level of reliability more efficiently. Hobbs identified one curve among those tested as the superior one.

Hobbs's analysis, however, was not simply a technical one. It was designed to mediate the political contention that PJM correctly anticipated would surround its new capacity market design. The alternate demand curves that were tested were also alternate politically charged policies. Each shape traces out transfers of huge sums from electricity consumers to generators and exposes all parties to widely varying risks. Against the backdrop of very low capacity prices in recent years, and the excess installed capacity in most of the PJM system, all the demand curves, except for the vertical one that modeled the existing market, would immediately levy large payments on the buyers of electricity and would award large capacity revenues to generators throughout the system. Hobbs's analysis embodies the bargain that is offered in exchange for the new capacity payments. His conclusion is that the reduced volatility in the capacity market would mean that the buyers of electricity would save money over the long run, compared with what they would pay to achieve the same level of reliability under the current market rules. Within the PJM stakeholder discussions, the simulation was used to dissolve the concerns of the "load side" objectors to the RPM design. With the preferred curve, which approximated competitive market conditions, the load side would initially pay more for capacity, but in the longer run, the new design would give them the benefits of greater reliability and lower electricity prices. It also allowed the marginalization of out-of-market remedies recommended by the Coalition of Consumers for Reliability, which would introduce further distortions.

The simulation continued to play this mediating role in the subsequent negotiations over the RPM. The shape of the demand curve itself became the focus of political bargaining during the settlement process before an administrative law judge in late 2006 (Doucet and Littlechild 2006). The buyers' caucus in the settlement process, which had begun with fairly basic objections to the model, ended up conceding that there would be a downward-sloping demand curve and sought alterations in its shape that would reduce the capacity payments when the reserves were either greater or less than the installed reserve margin. Figure 12.3 illustrates the adjustments the buyers requested. The two curves intersect at the inflection point, which represents capacity 1 percent above the required margin (101 percent on the horizontal axis) at a price equal to the estimated cost of new entry for a peaking generator. But to the left and to the right of this point, the new curve is markedly below the original one proposed by PJM. The highest capacity price would now be only one and a half times the cost of new entry rather than three times. The financial interest of the sellers' caucus was expressed in euphemistic terms, as a concern that the new curve would provide too weak of a price signal to "incent" investment. When the new curve was plugged into Hobbs's simulation, it was found to provide reliability at a cost that was not significantly different from that generated by the PJM-proposed curve.

Participants in this process noted a certain irony in this outcome. Both sides to the settlement adopted the terms of the economic theory but by their positions indicated that they did not believe that very theory. The buy-

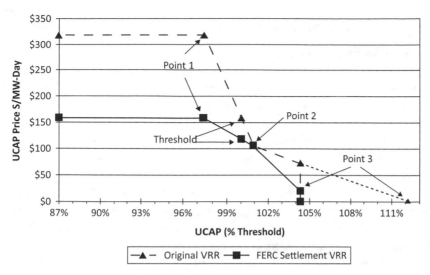

Figure 12.3. Adjustments to the VRR curve during the negotiated settlement proceedings

ers showed a strong preference for the new demand curve, yet that curve was ultimately justified by an analysis that said that it would not cost them more than the one that they opposed so strenuously. The incumbent sellers, for their part, strongly advocated a design that, given the analysis they used to promote it, would lead to an erosion of energy prices and competition from new entries to the market. As an interviewee commented:

> And the sellers also apparently don't believe the dynamic equilibrium view. If they did, they wouldn't want a demand curve that pulls capacity to a high level, which will crush what they can earn in the short-term markets. It kills energy and ancillary services prices. If they believe, if sellers believe, the dynamics, they wouldn't be pushing for a demand curve that's way out there. So the fact that they are suggests that they also don't believe in the dynamics. They're also thinking in terms of a fixed supply curve.

The implication is that the generating firms did not believe that the RPM would encourage new investment and ultimately a reduction in energy prices. This observation was even used as an argument against the RPM, suggesting that those promoting it, and claiming it would lower costs to consumers, were the parties who would benefit most when those lower costs failed to materialize (Hausman et al. 2006, 2005).

Conclusions: Economics Mediating the Politics of Markets

The economists involved in the reforms of the wholesale electricity markets, usually as consultants to participants in the markets, engage in a characteristic set of practices that I have termed "applied Platonism." This consists, first, of the characterization of existing markets as a configuration of departures from a competitive market. Market rules, "physical" or technological constraints, and political realities are translated into terms that allow the existing market to be compared directly with the competitive case. The economists define their design problems in terms of these departures: the absence of a responsive consumer demand, the vertical demand curve in the capacity market, and the "missing money." But their design proposals do not attempt to achieve a perfectly competitive market in practice. Instead, they offer mechanisms to accommodate physical constraints and political interests, including those of their clients. Their designs are formulated and justified as compensating mechanisms for the market flaws, which realize in practice the behavior of prices that would be the outcome of a competitive market.

But in opposition to the metaphor, market design is a distributed process. Although the FERC oversees any rules that impact the wholesale pricing of electricity, it is not empowered to design markets. Instead, it is the regional transmission organizations, which can also serve as ISOs, which voluntarily establish market rules. The rules must be approved by the FERC, but the latter can at best order the ISOs to change rules that are determined to be, according to the commission's legal mandate, "unjust and unreasonable." The ISO itself must determine the rules that will satisfy the FERC that they comply with the FERC's legislated task of ensuring that all wholesale electricity rates are "just and reasonable."

But the design process is further decentralized and distributed due to the nature of the ISOs themselves. These are nonprofits and membership organizations composed of the parties that use the transmission grid: electricity generators, LSEs, industrial customers, and residential customers, with their government representatives and interest-group organizations. Although the ISOs have boards of directors that are independent of the stakeholders, the design work is carried out in a committee structure.

Like the analysts discussed by Knorr Cetina in this volume, their work contains a specific epistemic stance, but it is a stance with which they work to colonize the markets themselves, embedding economic Platonism in the rules by which the market operates and is evaluated. Thus the collective interest of economists themselves is served by introducing the terms of their professional discourse into the terms by which market designs are developed, debated, and justified. They view this as a process of educating the engineers and administrators in the industry. In interviews with some of these economists, they classified personnel in the ISO and the FERC in terms of whether they "understood" the economics. Understanding can be safely interpreted here as an orientation to the markets in economic terms, for instance, treating the issue of reliability as the problem of replacing the "missing money" rather than primarily one of planning generating and transmission resources. The same economists consistently remark that the level of understanding, the penetration of the economic outlook into the design and administration of markets, has improved significantly since the early 1990s, when electricity restructuring was initiated.

As we saw in the case of the struggle over the RPM for the PJM capacity market, it would be a mistake to see this transformation as the replacement of politics by science. A transformation, however incomplete, of the institutional framework has accompanied the transformation of the terms by which market rules are formulated and legitimated. The political conflicts over the pricing of electricity have not vanished, but they are no longer mediated by the regulatory process. Instead, they are now a politics of market design, mediated by an abstract and technical object, the competitive market. The competitive market is not realized in the actual markets but remains inscribed in its rules and practices as a potentiality, the potentiality of the market to efficiently aggregate individual transactions into a socially valued aggregate outcome. Political positions in the struggle over market rules, what some economists refer to as "rent-seeking" behavior, are couched in and mediated by this object. Thus, the desire of large generating firms to extract additional revenues was effective only when articulated as a call for a redesign of the capacity market, which would provide higher revenues on the basis of a mechanism that mimicked the competitive market, namely, the VRR demand curve. And subsequent dispute over the redesign took the form of a negotiation over the shape of that curve, ultimately framed in terms of its market-like efficiency-enhancing features.

But as a mediator of market politics, the competitive market is by no means politically neutral. The perspective of the Coalition of Consumers for Reliability, and similar arguments raised by other participants in the FERC proceedings, were effectively marginalized, not only by the advocates of RPM, who represented the generating firms and financial interests, but by the economic analysts in the FERC and the ISO as well. In interviews with economic consultants, and even analysts within the FERC, I was repeatedly told that the opponents of the RPM, who would indeed have to

pay millions of dollars more for capacity in the short term, were irrationally disregarding their long-term interests. In the FERC technical conference in June 2005, every consumer or LSE advocate who argued for out-of-
market remedies and transmission planning as solutions was dismissively
countered as calling for further distortions that threatened to "overturn"
the market. For the logic of the competitive market to be preserved, and
along with it the promised benefits, reliability could be understood only
as a matter of market design, of setting up the market to provide the right
price signals.

References

Abbott, Andrew. 1988. *The System of Professions: An Essay on the Division of Expert Labor.*
Chicago: University of Chicago Press.

Bidwell, Miles, and Alex Henney. 2004. "Will the New Electricity Trading Arrangements
Ensure Generation Adequacy?" *Electricity Journal* 17:15–38.

Breslau, Daniel. 1998. *In Search of the Unequivocal: The Political Economy of Measurement in
U.S. Labor Market Policy.* Westport, CT: Praeger.

Coalition of Consumers for Reliability. 2005. "Protest and Request for Rejection of Filing."
Docket EL05–148. Washington, DC: U.S. Federal Energy Regulatory Commission.

Cramton, Peter. 2003. "Electricity Market Design: The Good, the Bad, and the Ugly." In
Proceedings of the 36th Annual Hawaii International Conference on System Sciences. Hawaii: IEEE Computer Society.

Cramton, Peter, and Suzi Kerr. 2002. "Tradeable Carbon Permit Auctions: How and Why
to Auction, Not Grandfather." *Energy Policy* 30:333–45.

Cramton, Peter, and Steven Stoft. 2005. "A Capacity Market That Makes Sense." *Electricity
Journal* 18:43–54.

Doucet, Joseph, and Stephen Littlechild. 2006. "Negotiated Settlements: The Development of Legal and Economic Thinking." *Utilities Policy* 14:266–77.

Federal Energy Regulatory Commission. 2005. "Transcript of Technical Conference in
the Matter of: Capacity Markets in the PJM Region, June 16, 2005." Docket PL05–7.
Washington, DC: U.S. Federal Energy Regulatory Commission.

———. 2008. "Midwest Independent Transmission System Operator, Inc., Order on Resource Adequacy Proposal." 122 FERC ¶ 61,283.

Fligstein, Neil. 1996. "Markets as Politics: A Political-Cultural Approach to Market Institutions." *American Sociological Review* 61:656–73.

Guala, Francesco. 2001. "Building Economic Machines: The FCC Auctions." *Studies in
History and Philosophy of Science* 32:453–77.

Hausman, Ezra, Paul Peterson, David White, and Bruce Biewald. 2005. "An RPM Case
Study: Higher Costs for Consumers, Windfall Profits for Exelon." Cambridge, MA:
Synapse Energy Economics.

———. 2006. "RPM 2006: Windfall Profits for Existing Base Load Units in PJM, an Up-
date of Two Case Studies." Cambridge, MA: Synapse Energy Economics.

Hirst, Eric. 2001. "Price-Responsive Demand in Wholesale Markets: Why Is So Little Happening?" *Electricity Journal* 14:25–37.

Hobbs, Benjamin F. 2005. "Affidavit of Benjamin F. Hobbs on Behalf of PJM Interconnection, L.L.C." Docket ER05–1440. Washington, DC: U.S. Federal Energy Regulatory Commission.

Hogan, William W. 2005. "On an 'Energy Only' Electricity Market Design for Resource Adequacy." Cambridge, MA: John F. Kennedy School of Government.

Hunt, Sally. 2002. *Making Competition Work in Electricity*. New York: J. Wiley.

Klemperer, Paul. 2004. *Auctions: Theory and Practice*. Princeton, NJ: Princeton University Press.

Kozul-Wright, Richard, and P. B. W. Rayment. 2007. *The Resistible Rise of Market Fundamentalism: Rethinking Development Policy in an Unbalanced World*. London: Zed.

MacKenzie, Donald A. 2006. *An Engine, Not a Camera: How Financial Models Shape Markets*. Cambridge, MA: MIT Press.

MacKenzie, Donald A., Fabian Muniesa, and Lucia Siu. 2007. *Do Economists Make Markets? On the Performativity of Economics*. Princeton, NJ: Princeton University Press.

McMillan, John. 2002. *Reinventing the Bazaar: A Natural History of Markets*. New York: Norton.

Milgrom, Paul R. 2004. *Putting Auction Theory to Work*. New York: Cambridge University Press.

Mirowski, Philip, and Edward Nik-Khah. 2007. "Markets Made Flesh: Performativity, and a Problem in Science Studies, Augmented with Consideration of the FCC Auctions." In *Do Economists Make Markets? On the Performativity of Economics*, edited by Donald A. MacKenzie, Fabian Muniesa, and Lucia Siu, 190–224. Princeton, NJ: Princeton University Press.

Nik-Khah, Edward. 2008. "A Tale of Two Auctions." *Journal of Institutional Economics* 4:73–97.

Oren, Shmuel S. 2005. "Generation Adequacy via Call Options Obligations: Safe Passage to the Promised Land." *Electricity Journal* 18:28–42.

Pinch, Trevor, and Richard Swedberg, eds. 2008. *Living in a Material World: Economic Sociology Meets Science and Technology Studies*. Cambridge, MA: MIT Press.

PJM Interconnection, Inc. 2005. "Reliability Pricing Model Filing." Docket ER05–1440. Washington, DC: U.S. Federal Energy Regulatory Commission.

———. 2006. "2005 State of the Market Report." Norristown, PA: PJM.

Polanyi, Karl. 1944. *The Great Transformation*. New York: Holt, Rinehart.

Roth, Alvin E. 2002. "The Economist as Engineer: Game Theory, Experimental Economics, and Computation as Tools of Design Economics." *Econometrica* 70:1341–78.

Roth, Alvin E., Tayfun Sönmez, and M. Utku Ünver. 2007. "Efficient Kidney Exchange: Coincidence of Wants in Markets with Compatibility-Based Preferences." *American Economic Review* 97:828–51.

Stoft, Steven. 2002. *Power System Economics: Designing Markets for Electricity*. Piscataway, NJ: IEEE Press; New York: Wiley-Interscience.

Wilson, Robert B. 2002. "Architecture of Power Markets." *Econometrica* 70:1299–1340.

THIRTEEN

Financial Analysis

Epistemic Profile of an Evaluative Science

KARIN KNORR CETINA

Fortunes are made and lost on Wall Street based on advice from security analysts.
They evaluate the prospects of companies issuing common stocks and provide
"buy" and "sell" recommendations. (Hooke 1998, 1)

In this chapter, I begin to develop an analysis of "analysis"—a form of research and inquiry prevalent in finance and financial markets. Financial
analysis is an area of some importance to contemporary, finance-oriented
societies. It researches macro- and microeconomic conditions along with
company fundamentals to make business, sector, and industry recommendations.[1] Professional analysts guide investors and asset managers in their
investment choices. They are central to investment banking, providing expertise on initial public offerings, mergers, and acquisitions; they assess
and manage financial risks in a variety of settings; and they help create new
investment instruments. Analysts are on the trading floors of large global
banks. They work in hedge funds, asset management units, rating agencies,
information provider firms, and commercial lending and in the specialized
press and other media. They often aspire to become asset and fund managers themselves, and they move into chief financial officer and expert accounting positions. In terms of the amounts of money involved, the areas
researched and overseen by financial analysts are huge. For example, investment funds alone had assets worth 18 trillion euros under management in

---

1. This definition is taken from Investopedia.com, a comprehensive dictionary for investing
and finance terms; http://www.investopedia.com/articles/financialcareers/06/FinancialAnalyst
.asp (accessed October 7, 2007). More detailed definitions can be found on the Web pages of
analysts' professional associations indicated here.

2007 worldwide.[2] In 2007 there were over 93,000 professional analysts in 134 countries, of whom 79,000 were certified by the Financial Analysts' Association. More than 64,000 of these worked in the United States and Canada (CFA Institute 2007; see fig. 13.1 for an overview of this development). The Chartered Financial Analysts Institute's CFA designation[3] requires passing three levels of exams (the first level is passed by roughly a third of the applicants) and is usually awarded only after four years of work experience. Additionally, a bachelor's degree in economics, business administration, or commerce is usually expected, and a master's degree in finance or an MBA with a concentration in finance may also be required for employment. Analysts' training and certification evolve continually. For example, designations for alternative investment vehicles (such as hedge funds) and for mutual funds, as well as for institutional portfolios, emerged in 2003 and 2006, and for some time large business schools in the United States and elsewhere have incorporated elements of the CFA into their curricula, sometimes offering concentrations and degrees in the area.[4]

Financial analysis is a core area of information knowledge production and information use. As participants view things, financial markets are markets in information, and analysts are the professional experts in charge of the information component of markets. In fact, several of the characteristics of financial analysis that I will propose in this chapter are tied to the fact that the knowledge involved is information knowledge. An epistemics of financial analysis is, accordingly, an epistemics of information. Information

2. See EFAMA—The European Funds and Asset Management Association, "Worldwide Investment Fund Assets and Flows: Trends in the Second Quarter 2007," http://www.alfi .lu/file admin/files/Statistics/World/6_International_Statistical_Release_2007_Q2.pdf (accessed April 15, 2008).

3. The Chartered Financial Analysts Institute (CFA Institute), inaugurated in 1963, is a global nonprofit association of investment professionals that awards the Chartered Financial Analyst® (CFA®) and Certificate in Investment Performance Measurement (CIPM) designations (see http://www.cfainstitute.org/aboutus/index.html). The pass rate for the first level of the three-level exam is low; it was only 34 percent in 2005 (Butcher 2005). Butcher calls the CFA the world's most gargantuan financial services qualification: over 100,000 applicants sit for the three qualification levels annually, in locations as distant as Dubai and Shanghai.

4. At the moment, the MBA and the CFA can be seen as competing qualifications in the United States. According to the managing director of the CFA Institute, CFA charter holders with ten years' experience out-earn MBAs by 18 percent (Butcher 2005). On an international level, two associations compete directly with the CFA designation, according to the CFA Institute (www.cfainstitute.org): in Europe the Certified International Investment Analyst (CIIA; 3,000 designees in 2007; www.aciia.org) and in India the Institute of Chartered Financial Analysts of India (ICFAI), which split off from the CFA (2,482 members in 2006; www.icfai.org). In affiliation with the University of India, the ICFAI appears to offer master's degrees in finance, which lead to the Indian CFA Charter issued by the Council for Indian CFAs (see http:// en.wikipedia.org/wiki/Chartered_Financial_Analyst; accessed April 11, 2011).

	1995	2006	2007	2010
Institute Members	29,600	81,400	90,900	106,800
CFA Candidates	24,800	116,200	139,700	200,000

Figure 13.1. Number of financial analysts (CFA Institute 2007, 2010)

has been widely discussed and explored by social scientists. However, what has attracted most authors is the grounding of information concepts in the history of cybernetics and the relevance of this paradigm to the emergence of the computer, to notions of both human intelligence and human and posthuman existence, and to related topics (see, e.g., Hayles 1999; Heintz 1993; Lafontaine 2004; Mirowski 2002; Turkle [1984] 2005). Sociologists have mainly been interested in information in relation to social transformation through the advent of information and communication technologies and the digital age—the computer is here a focus once again, but as a postmodernist, networking, and global technology that transmits information (see, e.g., Castells 1996; Lash 2002; Lyotard [1979] 1984; Webster [1995] 2006, 2004). Writers and artists have also been preoccupied with such topics (consider the film *The Matrix*; Gibson 1984). To be sure, electronic information technologies and systems are implicated in finance and financial markets. They enable the organization of these markets, assume certain automated functions, and in some areas have brought forth global electronic markets, an innovation developing in the last part of the twentieth century (Knorr Cetina 2003). Yet these electronic systems tend to be taken as given and "transparent" by participants, who are oriented to their information content rather than to the technologies themselves. Trading floors, for example, are expensive, complex, hardwired technological facilities at the intersection of worldwide cable and satellite connections. The issue for floor traders, however, is the information and deals they find on-screen; the technologies are left to the care of specialists and often remain opaque to their users. Financial analysts focus on information as content—as analysis material that lies at the center of their knowledge practices. The point of this chapter, then, is to follow practitioners in their focus on information knowledge. In contrast to the ongoing work on information technologies, I look here at information as the core of a form of scientific practice.

In the eyes of its founders, the analyst's profession emerged to help accomplish a turn to science: its widely publicized purpose was to turn investment into more of a "scientific procedure." Benjamin Graham, the acknowledged founder of the discipline, saw his own work as exploring the "scientific possibilities" of financial analysis and gave a famous review article that he wrote in 1952 the title "Toward a Science of Security Analysis" (Graham [1952] 1995, 25–26; see also Wolfe 1952). But what science are we in fact talking about? Financial analysis is simply not "like" research in physics or like other natural science fields, even though some physicists and other scientists work as investment analysts. The question "what science are we pursuing?" also bothered early analysts, who furnished a variety of answers, situating their field, for example, somewhere between psychoanalysis and engineering (Graham [1952] 1995, 25). But these answers glossed over the question that interests us here: what principles and mechanisms, if any, characterize this research as an information science and as "analysis," a specific form of inquiry? The few social scientists who have looked at analysis do not consider either the question of its epistemics or that of information; implicit in their work is a generalist stance treating all knowledge areas as alike. The work provides important insights on the intermediary status of analysts as market critics and their company coverage (Zuckerman 1999, 2004; Zuckerman and Rao 2004) as well as on their interpretations and storytelling (Beunza and Garud 2006; Mars 1998). Economists' extended and substantive research on analysis tends to focus on yet other questions: for example, on forecasting bias, career constraints, and analysts' under- and overresponse to new data (e.g., Bildersee, Radhakrishnan, and Ronen 1996; Bolliger 2003; Clement and Tse 2005; Hong and Kubik 2003).

To characterize the epistemic features of financial analysis, I will suggest three concepts: the concept of the flow character of the observational ground data of the discipline; that of an affective discipline based on "visceral" numbers that targets and implicates inclinations and desire, on the one hand, and rational actorhood, on the other; and that of the proxy character of the epistemic procedures of financial analysis. I will trace these concepts historically to show how some of their aspects were implicated in the beginning of the discipline and have defined it since. I will also discuss each concept systematically, based on contemporary research. I will draw on observations and interviews conducted between 1996 and 2006 on the trading floors of several large global banks in Zurich, New York, London, and Sydney, as well as on interviews with traders, asset managers, analysts, and strategists in these locations. Much of this research focuses on global trading microstructures and is described in detail elsewhere (e.g., Knorr

Cetina and Bruegger 2002; Knorr Cetina and Preda 2007). The interviews with analysts, economists, and strategists relevant here resulted in thirty hours of taped and transcribed material; I also draw on newspaper articles on analysts that have appeared in the *Financial Times*, the *Wall Street Journal*, and the financial sections of the *New York Times* and *Herald Tribune* between 2000 and 2007. The historical material includes the reflections, comments, columns, and articles written by early analysts and commentators as the profession developed in the United States in the first half of the last century. My historical research also includes records of the Financial Analysts' Federation.

The present effort is not a full analysis of an epistemic culture. Rather, I am interested here in what one might call epistemic profiling—I specify broad characteristics of the field's data and context and of the analysis strategy it has adopted. These characteristics are not exclusive (other fields may share them) and do not rule out further internal differentiation or the blending of information knowledge strategies with other epistemic practices in some areas of analysis. But they nonetheless tell us something about what analysis means in finance. They are also intended to substantiate the claim that the information knowledge sciences warrant an analysis in their own right. Such fields are not well served if we simply extend concepts developed on laboratory science to their epistemic projects.

Information Flow: The Temporal Character of Financial Information

The Informational Reality of Finance

Analysis starts from processes and produces not just information but information knowledge. I choose this combinatorial term to emphasize from the start that information in this area cannot simply be contrasted with knowledge in the sense sometimes found in the literature—where information may be treated as uninterpreted data and knowledge as having the properties of interpretation, accounts, and explanation. Information processes in financial analysis include such components; I have yet to see ground data in this area that are not already interpreted—as, for example, an earnings figure or an index indicating consumer confidence. The very point I wish to make about the proxy character of many of this field's epistemic practices also means that the field does not normally start with (or, worse, end with) "raw data." Nevertheless, I would argue that information knowledge needs to be differentiated from the major branches of the natural sciences along other lines, and one distinguishing characteristic concerns the data that analysts use and their characteristic temporality. Two points are important here. First, the information that analysts use almost always represents temporal series and, second, it is itself "periodicized" in a variety of ways: it arrives at analysts' desks at predetermined or moving intervals. An earning figure, for example, tends to be a monthly, quarterly, or annual aggregate of daily or hourly transaction data. The Consumer Confidence Index that the University of Michigan has prepared since 1952 is based on a nationally representative monthly survey and poses five questions about consumer sentiment.[5] Market data have a much higher frequency, scrolling down analysts' screens at split-second rates, thus reflecting the frequency of market transactions. One of the tasks analysts perform is to combine and cross-analyze different series when new input arrives. This may include bringing them onto a temporal par, "collapsing" their different underlying patterns of temporal activity into an array of significant features.

Technically, then, analysts deal with time-series data that are a temporal aggregate of underlying event and action sequences. This brings me to my second point, which regards the decay of this information. Data arrive, and are expected to arrive, both continually (market data, news) and serially at predetermined intervals (all other data) on the analyst's desk. As the data arrive, they may supplement earlier information, but they may also replace earlier series. In fact, after certain periods (usually not more than a year) all data are replaced by the arrival of new information. To be sure, some of this information may become incorporated into long-term trends, calculated and delivered by information provider firms. But these, too, represent a series and are subject to updating, revision, and replacement. What this suggests is that in financial analysis (and financial markets), reality has the character of a continually decaying and recomposing information flow. It streams steadily, following certain pathways, but not like a river that swells up as more water trickles into it. Rather, the flow's internal composition changes continually as new particles enter and old ones disappear. The image of the river neglects these compositional changes and the persistent undertow of decay—the regular, structural dissipation and elimination of information. In finance and financial analysis, reality thus has no preexisting materiality that continues to be available for inspection, awaits scientific representation, and serves as the baseline for the creation of a final

5. See http://www.sca.isr.umich.edu/main.php for more information (accessed April 11, 2011).

truth. As an informational reality, it is itself never finished but rather is perpetually under construction. Within this construction process, information speeds outward from its points of emission in sharply periodicized form; it is "present" only long enough to be analyzed, incorporated into period reports, and supplanted by fresher information. The reports that emerge from this process also come in series matching the sequential and periodical character of the ground flow of information. To be sure, there are material and symbolic structures of an enduring nature involved in the production of this flow—for example, government regulations or a firm's material infrastructure, equipment, and machines. However, the information that analysts work with tends to capture the transactions, events, and productive processes arising within these structures. When illiquid assets are counted and factored into analysts' equations, they tend to become temporalized themselves—for example, they may be represented as depreciations, deductions, or fluctuating asset prices. The notion of "economic fundamentals" that analysts use for factors that drive and explain output does not refer to stable features of the world but to the micro- and macroeconomic performance indicators to which causal efficacy is attributed. The main distinction here is between fundamentals indicating the soundness of an economy or production process and market quotations that may depart significantly from such actual "worth." For example, in 2007 the euro thus counted as overvalued—that is, as stronger than the European economies to which it is tied.

Consequences of Information Flow: Decay and Temporalized Truth

The discussion thus far already points beyond ground data to what I take to be a basic characteristic of financial analysis as an information knowledge field: its logic of decay, dissipation, and temporary truth. This contrasts with the intended production of stable findings and permanent truth that we find in the natural sciences. Financial analysis does not lead to such truths but to temporalized, time-indexed facts that become dissipated and absorbed in a process of information consumption. In the empirical study of the natural sciences over the past thirty years, researchers have implicitly or explicitly adopted a production framework: they have looked at how knowledge is created or constructed in different sciences and how a consensus emerges among scientists that determines which of the relevant products count as "true" (Collins 1985; Knorr Cetina 1981, 1999; Latour and Woolgar 1979; Lynch 1985; Traweek 1987). Natural scientific research centers on the creation of knowledge claims, the published and publishable products of scientific work. The laboratory is the "fact factory"[6] in which this work is located. Many natural sciences are laboratory sciences, even when they are not experimental sciences. Astronomers, for example, cannot conduct experiments with distant stars and planets, but they measure these objects, processing the measurements into findings in laboratory contexts. The production metaphor serves as an adequate theoretical framework for analyzing this situation. It suggests that as modern scientific fields arose during the period of industrialization, they became organized in ways corresponding to industrial production. The metaphor is also in line with the distinctive role production has played in the social sciences' understanding of capitalism and the focus early sociologists placed on the internal workings of organizations. But within the natural sciences, the metaphor also implies that over time, production results in finished products of an enduring nature. And this characterization is not in line, I would argue, with what we observe in finance analysis as an information science.

To make this clearer let us look at what is commonly considered the opposite side of production: consumption. With respect to natural scientific knowledge, consumption is something of an oxymoron; knowledge is not "consumed" in these sciences but survives its implementation. Economists refer to this phenomenon as the character of knowledge as a public commodity that can be used repeatedly and transferred at marginal costs (e.g., Kogut and Zander 1993, 628). The idea of knowledge being consumed also runs counter to a broadly accepted understanding of theoretical knowledge. Daniel Bell, for example, built his argument about the coming of a post-industrial society (1973) upon the idea that the axial principle of such a society was theoretical knowledge, which he defined as applicable to many areas *without* loss of significance or value. The epistemic equivalent of this idea of the nonconsumability of natural scientific knowledge can be taken to be the timelessness of truth: true knowledge is a specific commodity in that it does not decay. One is not committed here to a concept of truth as objective, factual, or corresponding to reality. All we need to grant is that in the natural sciences, true knowledge has an afterlife: scientific objects that count as true may be lastingly applied and endowed with significance as actively usable background knowledge in laboratories, textbooks, science education, and so on. Now the problem is that information knowledge in the area under discussion does not appear to have this afterlife. Rather, it lives on for a relatively short time, passing through various stages of diges-

---

6. I owe the expression to Ian Hacking, oral communication.

tion and use, then being replaced by new information, new analysis, new information knowledge. In other words, such knowledge does not become more stable as it is developed and used but decays into past, outdated, or simply no longer available information.

Processes of elimination do of course also exist in the natural sciences, but there they are tied to consensus formation: a process of implicit or explicit decision making about the soundness, usefulness, and so forth of a knowledge claim. If knowledge is found wanting in this critical examination, it may become labeled as false or problematic and be discarded—it may, for example, no longer be published; be withdrawn, contradicted, or challenged by other claims; be ignored; or be forgotten. To be sure, consensus formation is not always a judiciously corroborated process. It is historically situated, involves perspective, and is likely to rely on the use of epistemic proxies. For example, scientists may place their bets on knowledge that comes from a trusted source rather than actually assess the evidence, which is often not possible short of replicating the research. (As Collins [1985] has shown, replication itself is not a straightforward process and remains problematic in contested research areas.) Yet some sort of debate or critical examination is likely to ensue when the knowledge involved counts—if only because scientists defend their own interests, because science is a distributed process and different viewpoints compete, and because institutions have been created to assess knowledge, for example, by means of expert panels (e.g., Guetzkow, Lamont, and Mallard 2004). Information knowledge decay, in contrast, does not result from critical examination, disproof, or any other form of evaluation. It is not a process of discarding a piece of knowledge that for some reason is found wanting. It is not based on the deconstruction of its premises and hidden assumptions or the disclosure of inconsistencies in, perhaps, Derrida's sense. It is rather that the information loses its clout after some time and is then considered to be no longer informative.

What History Tells Us

Before turning to the next characteristic of financial analysis I would like to contextualize these considerations through a brief look at the history of the field; this will also introduce new aspects of analysis relevant to our discussion. An initial distinction between what the founders of the discipline called "security analysis" and "market analysis" may be useful here. The former is what I have discussed so far here. It is the branch of analysis that aims to become scientific and includes the analysis of fundamental or underlying processes driving financial instruments' "intrinsic" value and their potential for future growth. Security analysis has long since grown into "financial analysis"; it has been extended to many asset classes and investment activities that now indicate the specific specialization of an analyst. For example, an analyst specializing in foreign exchange may be called a "foreign exchange analyst." In contrast, market analysis typically focuses on market prices or quotations. This branch of analysis can be traced back to the introduction of the ticker in 1886, a technology that for the first time made sequential price and volume data reflecting past market transactions available in convenient form (Preda 2006). Analysis of such data began shortly after the ticker was introduced, focused on discernible patterns and trends, and led over time to what was later called technical and chart analysis: the attempt to categorize these patterns and predict likely price directions as well as market turns solely on the basis of the shape of trends themselves. The distinction between the two kinds of analysis had already been established at the beginnings of security analysis. In fact, in their foundational work on security analysis, Graham and Dodd (1934), and Graham in later articles, explicitly distinguish their effort from that of "technical market analysis." Graham even denies, against what he calls a widely held belief, that technical market analysis could be a "useful adjunct" to security analysis that would somehow belong in the analysts' toolkit (Graham 1965, 20).

Technical, or market, analysis is not the focus of this chapter, but I want to consider it briefly to shed light on an interesting similarity in the initial phase of the two analytic branches: in both cases, the *release of information* appears to drive the emergence of a profession. Let us begin with the ticker (see Knorr Cetina and Preda 2007). Its price and volume data were printed on a narrow running tape visible to all sharing access to the ticker (fig. 13.2 shows a contemporary reproduction of such a ticker).

Previously, use had been made of handwritten slips of paper, carried back and forth between brokerage houses and the stock exchange; these were subject to error and loss and were accessible only to the extent that they were collected within particular firms.[7] (Although charts of securities

7. The transatlantic telegraph had been inaugurated in 1865, replacing the transfer of information by messenger boys and messenger pigeons. But due to costs, among other factors, it was used only rarely and did not reduce previous information uncertainties. Some of these resulted from the repeated coding and decoding of messages that the telegraph necessitated. At the transmitting end, a Morse operator coded the message; at the receiving end, another Morse operator decoded it. This took time and required two skilled, well-paid mediators between the machine and its observers. It also included the risk of misinterpretation: one or two dots

Figure 13.2. Reproduction of stock ticker (courtesy of
Klaus Berner, Berner Machine Labs, Pontiac, MI)

traded had existed since the early nineteenth century, they at best displayed
monthly variations.) The new tickers provided a material and itemized
market memory. The tape differed from previous price lists, which provided
mainly opening and closing prices, in that it itemized past transaction
prices and volumes.[8] These could be scrolled through, prices at different
times could be compared, and inferences about market movements could
be formed. In other words, the data on tape were no longer considered
merely a confirmation of orders that had been sent to the exchange but
were considered information in their own right, to be mined for market
trends. Brokerage houses began to produce new data sequences from the
tapes. They employed specialized clerks who sat by the machines, picking
out prices of individual securities and tabulating their prices and transaction volumes at different times. The original ticker tape provided strictly
temporal sequences: securities were listed in the sequence in which they
were traded, with the tape indicating, for example, price x and quantity y,
at $t = 1, 2, 3, \ldots, n$, for a sequence of securities A, B, C, $\ldots$, N. Brokers'
security-specific new sequences had the form $N_1 x_1 y_1, N_2 x_2 y_2, \ldots, N_n x_n y_n$—
meaning security N was transacted at price x and quantity y at time 1, then
at price and quantity 2 at time 2, and so on. Security-specific sequences
could then be further tabulated in the form of daily, weekly, and monthly

---

missed by the decoding operator, and the message could become a completely different one
(see Knorr Cetina and Preda 2007).

8. Even after the introduction of the stock ticker, better price lists included only opening,
closing, and highest and lowest prices during a trading day. The tabulation of these prices required the kind of scrolling memory provided by the tape: while it was relatively easy to find out
the opening and closing prices (situated at the ends of the tape), highest and lowest prices could
be identified only by scrolling down the tape and comparing prices at different times of the day.

charts of price variations. (Although security price charts had existed since the early nineteenth century, they at best presented monthly variations; chart production was a specialized activity requiring statistical knowledge, drawing accuracy, and data-gathering skills—for example, through archival research.) Around 1900, which is to say relatively soon after the introduction of the stock ticker, several mutually acquainted brokers from the East Coast switched from trading securities to interpreting price charts, claiming that this special knowledge could not be properly gained from brokers. Technical analysis would emerge as a full-fledged profession only in the 1960s and 1970s. But the discipline's beginnings were marked by the tape-reading clerks who helped chart prices into systematic information.

A similar supply-driven argument can be made in regard to the second branch of analysis, security analysis, to which I now return. However, the decisive event in this case was not the arrival of a recording, transmitting, and printing instrument like the ticker, used—until the computer's arrival in the 1970s—to record market data and later some news and not providing the information security analysis needed. Rather, it was a historical event of a momentous nature, the market crash starting in October 1929 and continuing until February 1933. The crash put an end to a period of self-regulation that had governed security trading. In the wake of the crash, founding legislation for the security-analysis profession was established: the Securities Act of 1933 required disclosure of financial information about security issuers and registration of securities offerings with the Federal Trade Commission; the Glass-Steagall Act of 1933 separated investment and commercial banking functions; and the Securities Exchange Act of 1934 established the Securities and Exchange Commission, requiring companies to provide detailed financial information and stock exchanges to get approval for their rules. Jacobson has described this legislative impetus as the emergence of "cornerstone laws that burned the imperative of 'disclosure' onto the psyche of American business" (1997, 25). There was precedent for such a development in the wake of calamity. After earlier speculation scandals, the New York Stock Exchange (NYSE) and the then-existing Open Board (another exchange) required registration of securities and thirty days' notice of new issues from 1868 onward; in the 1880s, the NYSE (with which the Open Board had by then merged) began to require listed companies to produce annual reports. These appear, however, to not have had much substance on which analysis could be based (Poitras 2005, 92, 97). In England, the British Company Act of 1900 had the explicit goal of providing more and better information important to stockholders about the financial performance of companies. It stipulated annual reports to stockholders and required prospectuses covering thirteen items, extending an older disclosure philosophy. But in the United States, what information there was seems to have been trapped in "back offices" and stuck with "statisticians"; company leaders felt that shareholders had no right to the disclosure of information (Jacobson 1997, 14). In fact, Gray relates that Raymond Sidney, the force behind the formation of the first analysts' society in Chicago in 1925, "started gathering a group of individuals from the bond houses, rating agencies and underwriting banks to discuss securities over lunch" *because* the information then available was so limited—balance sheets provided "no more than a comparison of current assets and current liabilities and were often outdated" (cited in Graham 2004, 31). In an article on the evolution of the analyst, Randell confirms that the necessary information became generally available for study only in the 1940s, that is *after* the Security and Exchange Acts of 1933 and 1934: "The tools which it [financial analysis] employs are new because the raw materials with which it works—business statistics, corporation records and the like—have only in the past couple of decades become available for study" (1961, 68).

There was another source of earlier information that should not be ignored. As Poitras points out, early in the twentieth century the financial press spearheaded a number of innovations, especially indexes to measure stock market performance. For example, Charles Dow, a newspaper journalist, joined with fellow reporter Edward Jones to form the Dow Jones and Company, which started its work next door to the NYSE by collecting flimsies and slips containing the market news of the day (Poitras 2005, 97). However, these data pertained to questions of market analysis rather than to a more fundamental way of evaluating securities and their potential. One of the problems cited in the historical literature is that World War I, leading to the great war bond drives of 1917 and 1918, actually stimulated investment in the United States by directing previous savings-bank depositors to financial markets. The postwar boom of the 1920s "fed on this rush to riches," increasing considerably the activities of unsophisticated speculators and their numbers (Randell 1961, 67). Implied here is a double limitation of any potential for professional analysis. On the one hand, as Graham and Dodd argue, prior to the crash there was a "persistence of imaginary values"—values unchecked by the availability of data that could have provided a basis for a "real" security evaluation. In addition, what analytical approach there had been appears to have been abandoned altogether beginning in 1927 and continuing through the disappearance of real value during the Great Depression (Graham and Dodd 1934, 14).

What, then, have we learned from this brief historical overview? Perhaps, first and foremost, that financial analysis as it emerged after 1933 was founded on a major shift in attitude and policy that brought about the release of information. While a mentality of *privileged access* to information appears to have prevailed up to the 1930s, the legislation and its impact provoked a policy of *disclosure* of information. Second, it appears to have taken a historical crisis of epic proportions and the distrust and revulsion with which a population reacted to the finance and business community to bring about this shift. What the ticker accomplished more "innocently" and silently for its community of users since 1867—to reiterate, replacing the embodied technology and information fragments of earlier times with a connecting and recording technology that streamed continued information to participants—governmental legislation accomplished through a radical break with previous ground rules. But it did so only after a terrifying drama began to unfold on the world stage, a drama that began to dictate such a move (a fact that may tell us something about the performance and effectiveness of technological and political action under specific circumstances). Third, the information that was disclosed had the same character that it has now—that of a periodically released time-series set to be replaced by the arrival of new information. Financial performance data, then as now, consisted of running, periodicized records of ongoing economic capacity on a firm or state level; the data were intrinsically processual. Market data streamed at an even faster rate and were equally processual, though not periodicized (except through secondary analysis). Reality always flowed, so to speak, once it became available for inspection.

An Affective Science: A Cool Logic with Visceral Dimensions

The Analyst's Advisory Role

For a time, I would like to continue this historical look at financial analysis before explaining in analytic terms what I mean by an "affective" discipline. The point I want to focus on is that the discipline both involves and evolved from financial advising. In other words, analysis was geared to identifying and recommending attractive investments. It developed from "mere" advising based on personal experience or belief into a discipline meant to found such advice upon the study and understanding of past performance.

Early proponents of financial analysis all refer in one way or another to the advisory role of security analysis. Graham, for example, suggests that the end product of such analysis is the selection of securities: safe securities of the bond type, undervalued securities, growth securities, that is, "common stocks that are expected to increase their earning power at considerably better than the average rate"; and "'near-term opportunities,' that is, common stocks that have better-than-average prospects of price advance, within, say, the next 12 months" ([1952] 1995, 25). While these categories involve different types of risks and are more or less scientifically developed—Graham thus observing that "growth stock investment is still in the pre-scientific stage" ([1952] 1995, 27)—it is plain that he sees analysts as in the business of making choice recommendations. Marmer, in an article about investment management on a large, pension fund scale, sees a late takeoff of financial consultation in this area: of "planners" who provide "unbiased" recommendations and supply "unique value added information insights." He states that this sort of money management did not really exist until the 1960s[9] and complains somewhat vaguely about the dark ages of the distant past in which "the investment world of the individual was ruled by an ancient monster, the dinosaur, also known as the stockbroker. Your savings were best invested in the hot stock of the week" (1996, 9–10).

In those dark ages, Marmer adds, pension managers left it to their treasurers to oversee their funds, and the role of the consultant on the investment side was trivial. Thus, he too emphasizes the advisory function of analysis and its evolution from the time of broker-advisers and trustees to whom money was committed. On the first pages of the first chapter of Graham and Dodd's foundational 1934 volume on security analysis, they list three functions of security analysis (Graham and Dodd 1934, 15–26). First there is "descriptive analysis," to which the authors devote one paragraph. It means "marshalling the important facts" relating to a (stock) issue, revealing its strong and weak points, comparing it with others, and appraising factors that are likely to influence future performance. Then there is the "selective function," discussed over the next ten-odd pages and tied to the concept of intrinsic value, together with the principal obstacles to determining it: inadequate data, uncertainties involving the future, and the irrational behavior of the market. Third, there is a "critical function" (again, just one paragraph). This refers to the analyst's right and obligation to oversee and criticize accounting methods, the presentation of stocks and bonds issued, and so on. This is the function Zuckerman (1999, 2004) recently put forward as a defining component of the status of

9. That is, until pension fund fiduciary responsibilities were formalized by the Employee Retirement Income Security Act of 1974, microprocessors were invented, and portfolio theory was implemented.

analysts as intermediaries. Clearly, the pioneering authors in the field gave most weight to the selective function that "seeks to determine whether a given issue should be bought, sold, retained, or exchanged for some other" (Graham and Dodd 1934, 15). To date, many others have provided definitions of security analysis that emphasize its selective and advisory function. For example, a 1998 comprehensive guide to such security analysis starts out by stating: "Fortunes are made and lost on Wall Street based on advice from security analysts. They evaluate the prospects of companies issuing common stocks and provide 'buy' and 'sell' recommendations" (Hooke 1998, 1).

It is plain, then, that the financial analyst's profession has defined itself since the start as in the business of creating investment advice based on systematic methods and scientific evidence. It explicitly established itself as an alternative to the sort of intuitive, experiential knowledge participants developed and transmitted as advice—often through autobiographical accounts, of which Henry Clews's *Fifty Years in Wall Street* (1908) or Edwin Lefèvre's *Reminiscences of a Stock Operator* (1923) are famous examples. In economic language, the original experience-based advisers were "principals" investing their own money or "agents" acting as caretakers (e.g., brokers or treasurers) of principals' money. Analysts, on the other hand, are professional advisers—they have developed a third role for themselves, that of the legitimated Other.[10] In other words, they took on the role of disinterested outsiders and observers, qualified by scientific training and an upholding of a "line of separation" between principals, agents, and their own function.

Affectedness and Affectivity

Are analysts purely legitimated Others? While those writing in the profession's first stage articulated precisely such a distanced role for the discipline, today analysis often seems to join and blend scientific concerns and market needs. A main question that emerges is what we are to make of the various hybridizations. My general idea here is that analysts are in a kind of epistemic bind: like psychoanalysts who must work with their clients' passions through transference and countertransference, analysts must work with the passions inherent in their object world—for example, the levels of affectivity that characterize interested financial actors. This affectivity is information, and information routinely evokes affectivity. Analysts cannot

---

10. See Meyer and Jepperson 2000 for a discussion of this sort of Otherhood.

simply stand back and calculate neutral equations; to know the market they have to engage it along with its affectedness; to advise investors they have to engage their passions. More generally speaking, the particular object relations that markets involve come to be reflected in the financial analyst's work. I choose to term this form of analysis an "affective" discipline in order to suggest that it may not be enough to understand it as compromised by conflicts of interest, though these clearly occur (see below). I will suggest that this particular kind of information science not only developed into the rationalizing discipline envisaged by its founders but also accrued incentivizing functions responding to and playing with the affectivities inherent in markets.

To clarify: any kind of financial market participation implies a sort of existential "thrownness" into concerns resulting from the fact that participants are putting their money on the line. With their money, they naturally risk their identities and financial futures. Entering a market implies a shift in a previous structure of existence. It brings with it an affectedness that entails affectivity, an emotional involvement underpinning market activities. Participants and observers have long noticed and commented on this emotional underpinning of market activities when it reaches a certain level of intensity. Alan Greenspan, the longtime chairman of the Federal Reserve Bank, has commented on the "irrational exuberance" stamping an overconfident American bull market before the turn of the twenty-first century (Shiller 2000). Much earlier, Mackay ([1841] 1932) refers to Holland's tulip bubble in terms of "extraordinary popular delusions," and in the beginning of the eighteenth century, both Jonathan Swift and Daniel Defoe use similar phrases in denouncing the "fancies wild" and "most unaccountable emotions" operating in the stock market's "exotick projects" (cited in Nicholson 1994, 76, 48). Participants themselves repeatedly refer to life in the market as a back-and-forth between "greed" and "fear." Drawing on psychological theory, researchers in the field of behavioral finance (De Bondt and Thaler 1985, 1987; Thaler 1993) have described such greed and fear, distinguishing, for example, between *ego*, defined here as self-worth tied to financial worth; *overconfidence*, a mind-set resulting from too much ego, operating late into long rallies and the final stages of financial bubble building; and *vividness*, an impulse to act based on the vividness of the information one receives (Shefrin 1999). It should be noted that financial markets breed such mind-sets even when they are not "exuberant." They generate emotional energy, or what Durkheim called "electricity" (Collins 2004, 38–39), and this energy appears to be constitutive of financial markets. The emotional energy affects not only investors but also traders and other mediators, the whole spectrum of principals and agents. For example, in the study of foreign exchange trading that I conducted with Urs Bruegger (see Knorr Cetina and Bruegger 2002), traders expressed their reaction to the market in a vocabulary resounding with visceral emotion. As an experienced proprietary trader in Zurich summarized it, the terms traders use refer "basically to sex and violence and a lot of them seem to have to do with anal penetration." The list of terms we accumulated included "I got shafted," "I got bent over," "I got blown up," "I got raped," "I got stuffed," "the guy stuffed me," "I got fucked," "I got hammered," and "I got killed."

When emotional energy is intense, it is often denounced as "irrational," and investors and traders are advised to exercise "discipline" to counteract their affect. For example, they are told to conduct their transactions according to predetermined strategies rather than to react on the spur of the moment to market swings. But while discipline may reign in ego responses, it does not eliminate participants' personal affectedness in response to market moves. On the one hand, a market's emotional energy reflects something like the sum total of participants' personal affectedness. It becomes visible through price movements, market trends, and "runs" that reflect buyers, and sellers, affect-driven decisions. On the other hand, emotional energy is also generated directly in these markets in the context of their "information events": the scheduled announcement and release of information—for instance, the speeches of the chairman of the Federal Reserve—but also rumors and information fragments of uncertain origin that run through markets at high speed. Technological media play an important role here, not only enabling the fast diffusion of information but also reflexively mirroring or "scoping" market states, a process that has been detailed elsewhere (Knorr Cetina 2003). This mirroring feeds market moods by providing feedback about its aggregate state, as do the information runs that flow through informal channels. Emotional energy, one assumes, is channeled through individual and group participants who may reinforce it or try to cool it. Their affectedness surely lies at the root of this energy. But as an identifying detail of financial markets, the phenomenon has many facets, some deriving from the institutional structures and conventions of finance.

To do this topic full justice, we would need a more differentiated picture distinguishing between invested participants who do not even observe their investments and those who do, between fully electronic, fully scoped and mirrored markets and those relying, like some bond markets, on rumors on "the street" (e.g., by brokers). But for present purposes, it is enough to emphasize the existence of structures of feeling (Williams 1977, chap. 9) as something analysts have to contend with—a reality that signifies the demand for information. I would argue that they contend with it in two ways (see fig. 13.3). On the one hand, they assuage the affectedness of market participants by transforming market uncertainties into promising futures substantiated by data and argument. They propose promising investments, predict future growth and outcomes, rate the prospects of bond and stock issuers, and reason out both the intrinsic tendencies of financial instruments and contextual economies and sociologies. They suggest ways to pursue these promises; these are the normative models that help discipline emotions by providing investors and traders with a "view" upon which they can act. In this sense, analysis rationalizes investment and speculation by providing concrete, believable, promissory goals. This is the goal of professional financial analysis that its founders had in mind when they argued for the need to put investment advice on a scientific basis. It is also the foundation of the role of legitimated Otherhood as a disinterested mode of behavior.

But there is a second way in which analysts contend with structures of feeling, one no less important than the first. This project was not explicitly scripted into the beginnings of the discipline by its early promoters, but it was there from the start, sometimes addressed by worries and admonitions: analysts also contribute significantly to refueling the emotional energy spent on investments and speculation. This happens with or without analysts' intention and has to do with several factors, to which I now turn.

The first has recently been much commented on in the financial press and other public media (after the ENRON scandal). It has to do with the fact that analysts, particularly those working on the sell side of the financial service industry that underwrites large numbers of public offerings (launching firms' stocks and bonds and municipal and government bonds on the market), develop conflicts of interest that are "wide ranging" according to

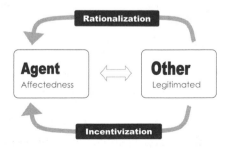

Figure 13.3. Rationalization and incentivization in financial analysts' work

the Securities and Exchange Commission (SEC) and others. Since analysts tend to be paid by the firms that underwrite such offerings, they help the investment departments of their firms win underwriting deals by "drumming up" investor interest with their analyses and by initiating research coverage in prospective client firms with buy recommendations. After 2001, the SEC conducted many investigations into such conflicts of interest, finding among other things that analysts hold private opinions differing from their public statements; that they may execute trades for their own accounts that are contrary to their recommendations; that they acquire shares at start-up companies at a fraction of their later costs before the shares are offered to the public; and so forth (e.g., McGeehan 2002; Morgenson 2001). The most direct statement of this tendency has been attributed to the then chairman of Citigroup, Sanford I. Weill, who reportedly already advised in the mid-1980s that research "has no value except of course to get banking fees" (McGeehan 2002). On a more general level, analysts have been found to have a preference for positive evaluations—to issue significantly more buy or hold recommendations for stocks than sell recommendations. As one of our interviewees in the above-mentioned study put it, "research has been exceptionally weighted on the positive side." Accounts of this tendency are readily available. For example, Hooke (1998, 21–22), in his guide to security analysts' evaluation methods, reports how Peter Oakes, a top-ranked analyst at Merrill Lynch, issued a favorable report on McDonald's, which had experienced a "tough introduction" for its Arch Deluxe sandwich. The report refuted the critics, reaffirming a buy recommendation on McDonald's stock. "Coincidentally," Hooke reports, "Merrill Lynch investment bankers managed a $200 million preferred stock financing for McDonald's 10 days later." Hooke also comments on the "Chinese Wall" separating analysts from investment banking to assure investment clients that analysts' reports are unbiased. In practice, Hooke says:

> This ideal is unworkable and an analyst's opinions are frequently compromised. Many earn more money by bringing in investment banking deals than by writing research reports; thus, they are reluctant to annoy corporate banking clients by issuing sell reports on their respective shares. As a result, most analysts' recommendations are buys. . . . Companies that generate a lot of investment banking often have 20 buy recommendations for every sell, despite the inherent uncertainties regarding corporate performance. (1998, 22)

He then cites a Columbia business school report that "proved the obvious," based on a review of eight thousand stock evaluations: 93% of analysts working for investment banks doing work for issuers rated the stock higher than analysts at firms not doing such work. Sociologists have taken this situation as a starting point for further investigation of conflicts of interest and their legal aspects (Swedberg 2005), as have economists, who have investigated many aspects of such positive weightings (Bolliger 2003).

The prevalence of advertising in contemporary Western societies clearly suggests that wants are as much aroused and instilled as simply pre-given. If we apply this to financial markets, it means that the interest of investors and speculators in securities, their hopes and confidence, while surely subject to motives and desires that are individual, will also be subject to externally induced incentivization. Analysts provide this incentivization— precisely when they serve a sell-side firm's purpose of boosting investor confidence and hopes. As evidence from SEC investigations and other sources, including comments by those concerned, has shown, analysts may be pressured into such services, experiencing sanctions when they fail to comply.[11] But analysts' ratings, we may assume, affect investors' emotional energy whether or not investors try to guard against such influence—to those already interested in and affected by markets, the numbers and ratings analysts turn out take on a visceral meaning. Incentivization may also flow from analysts' epistemic procedures, their laying out of investment objects through which they continually construct new ground for further investment. The work of natural scientists with objects tends to "explode" and mutate those objects into new ones by unfolding their previously unknown components and complexities. Analysts' work, as I will argue, is limited on a fundamental level by the proxy character of measurement. Yet it augments the investment landscape in other ways—for example, by forging new links between elements, disclosing hidden assets, mapping detailed areas of development, or proposing new investment instruments. Presumably, even analysts in buy-side institutions, in asset management units, pension funds, and the like, will help motivate financial market activities through this work of enhancement and elaboration. In the natural sciences, epistemic extension is a motivating force for scientists; it affects insiders' structure of wanting, their passion to carry on and pursue the emerging opportunities of scientific work. In financial markets, epistemic extension affects those outside the profession, those to whom analysts direct their advice. We might say that it runs from the Other to the Agent, impacting market participants' interests and passions.

---

11. The first book-length qualitative study of the activities of financial analysts that I am aware of, Mars 1998, provides evidence for this.

I would like to propose one additional dimension of the analysts' linkage to the emotional energy of markets. As indicated, analysts are often themselves invested in markets. Moreover, while they are not likely to leave their profession to become spot traders or brokers, they are likely to move into asset management, opening their own investment firm, starting a hedge fund, and so forth. Among the analysts I talked to, this seemed to be not only a career possibility but a career goal. They argued that those dealing in money had higher status and higher earnings than those dealing in technical advice and that such a move would allow them to profit directly from their knowledge. The point here is that in making or even just envisaging such moves, analysts buy into the structure of wanting that characterizes financial markets—the order of acceptable ends, and the projects and tasks to be pursued for the sake of these ends.[12] They switch between legitimated Otherness and agency in these markets—sometimes only in their imagination, when thinking about becoming asset managers, but often also in parallel to their activities as analysts. In Meadian terminology: in their role as part-time participants and envisaged future full-time members, they take the perspective of market agents. What this means, it appears, is that the emotional undertow of all market activities is not foreign to analysts. Unlike physicists, who will not share the emotional tone of the physical world (if there is any such tone), since it will be entirely foreign to them, the emotional attraction of investment and speculation cannot be foreign to analysts. Put otherwise, both to accomplish their work of selection and advising and to manage their own investments, analysts will take positions in structures of wanting (e.g., those of the investors and speculators they advise). They will also develop object relations—with the market and with particular firms or countries whose bonds and stocks they rate.

In all these senses, then, financial analysis is an affective science. As argued, research in this area offers a rationalizing and stabilizing antidote against the "wild fancies" and "irrational exuberance" of speculative activities. Furthermore, through their promissory character, research and analysis build emotional energy for continued market activities. They work out sequences of development to which emotions can bind; here not only numbers but the quality and semantics of the "stories" analysts produce become important. The stories must be logically coherent, but they should also be designed to be innovative, surprising, and challenging to the imagination. Good plots, interesting heroes, and surprising but plausible turns (against the background of previous or other market stories) provide

12. For a discussion of such ends, see Schatzki 1996, 99, 123–25.

"binding sites" for desires. They afford both hope and these desires and set in motion the processes through which cognitive promise is translated into financial borrowing and commitment. The result is a self-sustaining, autoaffective system[13] in which research and analysis play a crucial incentivizing role (see fig. 13.3).

Analysis as a Proxy Science

Scientific procedure is itself a process of cultural invention, differentiation, and extinction that speeds forward together with the process of knowledge production. High-energy physics provides an example. It developed a negative epistemics—a tendency to elaborate the limits of knowing, the errors and mistakes one made in knowing, and the universe of enemy processes that mask those one is interested in and interfere with a gain in knowledge. High-energy collider physics defines the perturbations of positive knowledge in terms of the limitations of its own apparatus and approach. But it does not do this just to put the blame on these components and to lament their existence. Rather, it teases these fiends of empirical research out of their liminal existence; it draws distinctions between them, elaborates on them, and creates a discourse about them. It puts the components under a magnifying glass and presents enlarged versions of them to the public. In a sense, high-energy experimental physics has thus forged a coalition with the evil that bars knowledge, by turning such barriers into a principle of knowing.

Financial analysis, too, has developed preferences for approaching empirical reality, but these are not akin to such a liminal epistemics. Instead, it likes epistemic proxies, stand-ins and substitutes for what other fields (and to some degree analysis itself) consider desirable. The use of epistemic proxies is not limited to analysis. When social scientists rely on secondary data drawn from data banks that have gathered the data for purposes at best obliquely related to their own interests, they are using proxy measurements. Economists routinely forgo original data collection. If they use empirical data, the data will often be in the form of economic indica-

---

13. A similar notion is Schatzki's (1996, 99, 123–25) idea of "teleoaffective" structures, which he defines as orders of acceptable ends (that include the projects and tasks to pursue for the sake of these ends) and acceptable, even correct, emotions, feelings, and passions that, together with other ingredients such as explicit rules, organize complex social practices. I use the notion of "autoaffective" to point not only to the unified goal structure and exhibited and prescribed affectivities that govern financial market activities but also to the fact that this tends to be a self-sustaining and self-replicating autoaffective system that builds goals and replenishes emotional energy from information knowledge.

tors prepared for them by statistical offices; they may also survey data from which they then extract information (see the studies collected in Levitt and Dubner 2005). However, economists have adapted their questions to the character of their data—they have long studied variables that refer to indicators rather than to economic reality (consider forecasts of economic growth or of earning ratios). Economics has also often been considered as more of a modeling science interested in formalizing theoretical arguments than as an empirical discipline. These formalizations serve more as models for thinking about a particular empirical reality than as models of that reality. Financial analysis finds itself in more of a predicament, since its task is intrinsically empirical and often centered on individual entities such as companies. The point of analysis is to get at the fundamental or intrinsic value of a business, defined, for example, by its earning power. But as Graham and Dodd already argue in their early treatise, for this it is not sufficient to extrapolate past earnings. "There must be plausible grounds," they indicate, "for believing that this average or this trend is a dependable guide to the future" (1934, 17). What constitutes a plausible ground? The future value of a business should be determined by a number of factors, several of which are laid out by these authors: the "management and reputation" of a firm; its "competitive conditions and prospects"; "possible and probable changes in volume, price and cost"; together with earnings, assets, capital structure, and so forth. The attitude of the public also matters, its sentiments and decisions. The public is seen here as a "voting machine whereon countless individuals register choices" (1934, 23). If it fails to buy a product, earning power goes down, and this should be registered by the market price of shares and bonds.

Later treatments of the work of security analysts reaffirm these propositions. For example, Johnson declares management the most important variable, since it "is the clue to the probable success or failure of an enterprise" and "holds the key to whether the securities of that company may represent a real investment or not" (1960, 72). What would analysts have to do to unlock fundamental values and prospects with such keys? Students of business (who often follow the Harvard case study approach), organizational sociologists, and anthropologists may have a ready answer. They might say: "Immerse yourself in the organization and find out what's really going on there. Pick up any reports and statistics you can, but don't avoid looking behind the scenes since we know such reports are edited for specific accounting purposes and may hide as much information as they disclose. Also, we know that there tend to be multiple and conflicting goals and an informal organization that may thwart and redefine them. And we know that organizational culture can influence (and may be constitutive of) organizational success. Find out about all these factors and how they may jeopardize or aid in accomplishing official management strategies." Such a strategy would yield firsthand, primary data that can only be acquired by "going there," distilling ground information into assessments of future prospects. Of course, the strategy would have to include some of the other variables mentioned: information about the competition, consumer sentiment, and so on.

There are various ways analysts approach their task, but none involves following their business school colleagues' or social scientists' advice. Instead, they will start out with a quantitative analysis of, for example, published annual reports or investment material, using a spreadsheet noting sales figures, pre-tax income, net income, earnings per share, the price/earnings ratio, and so forth over several years. As Hooke describes it in his handbook, such an analysis should be done comparatively across several companies, leading to relational values. On the basis of spreadsheet analysis, a research report on, for example, Campbell Soup may thus include information on the whole packaged-food industry, addressing the question of how many competitors are entering the industry or that of whether more people prefer eating out than cooking at home. The report should include information on general capital market conditions and on macroeconomic prospects (Hooke 1998, 67–69). The analysis should also involve what Johnson (1960, 72–77) calls qualitative considerations, which he suggests will be based on company visits and answers to questions and impressions the analyst receives. Hooke (1998, 68) notes that this methodology of security analysis has changed little since the 1960s.

What kind of proxies are involved in this procedure? Figure 13.4 gives an overview.

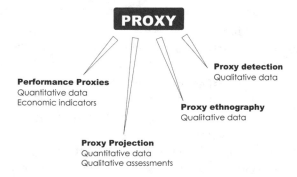

Figure 13.4. Kinds of proxy measurements in financial analysis

Proxy Quantitative Data

Analysts do not as a rule have access to a firm's or a government's internal accounting data, the primary data in this area. Rather, they have to make do with company and government reports that depend on (professional) accounting, accounting regulation, and oversight. For Graham and Dodd, "inadequate or incorrect data" constituted the first serious obstacle to a scientific security analysis, besides the "uncertainty of the future" and the "irrational behavior of the market." These authors thought that "deliberate falsification of the data" was rare, that concealment was more common than misstatement, and that misrepresentations flowed "from the use of accounting artifices" that capable analysts were expected to detect—though they sometimes might not (1934, 20–21). We have seen that the American regulations introduced in the 1930s were meant to implement a policy of "full disclosure" for publicly traded corporations. Nonetheless, the continued concerns of the SEC and the scandals unfolding since the year 2000 suggest that "full disclosure" translates at best into required disclosure under legal provisions and that input manipulation for accounting, shareholder persuasion, and tax evasion purposes cannot be ruled out. Disclosure matters in relation to the quality of the analysts' findings. In a study of the forecast performance of analysts in forty-seven countries, Chang, Khanna, and Palepu (2000) report that the quality of accounting disclosures and legal and institutional environments enabling or preventing disclosure are important factors in determining the quality of that performance. The analysts' own initiative also matters. The editor of the *Financial Analysts Journal* has thus complained in an editorial that the analysts' industry may have become "intellectually lazy" since it fails to critically investigate accepted assumptions and practices in order to improve them. Among the various examples he lists, some concern data. He asks, for example, "When various 'earnings' figures diverge, why not ask why? When reported earnings, operating earnings, tax earnings, and earnings before interest, taxes, depreciation, and amortization . . . diverge, we should want to know the reason. . . . analysts should more closely examine earnings measurements discrepancies in order to better understand their root causes" (Arnott 2004, 7). The concern suggests that while there is presently a torrent of data on which analysts can rely, it is not simply filtered through the lens and the legitimate scientific interests of researchers, which is often the case for secondary social science data. Rather, it is also strategically generated with respect to stakeholders' concerns, and it incorporates rhetorical strategies of persuasion. It may also be withheld from view altogether, as

Chang, Khanna, and Palepu (2000) suggest. The question of course is how analysts can overcome such structural data problems.

Proxy Ethnography

Analysts are naturally aware of the limitations of their data. In fact, they adopt the qualitative analysis mentioned above to counteract such tendencies—and to answer questions and contradictions that may emerge from the quantitative approach. As described by Johnson (1960), qualitative analysis involves site visits, or what we may call mini-ethnographies. And as the prefix "mini" suggests, such visits usually last no more than a few hours and cannot yield the sort of primary data and insights we associate with ethnography. In fact, as described by Johnson, the methodological yield of analysts' site visits constitutes "impressions," a notion that connotes superficiality and suggests a substituting of such perceptions for real answers.

The following vignettes that Johnson presents to illustrate the kind of information analysts gain through mini-ethnographies can serve as an example:

> Even before planning his trip an analyst will receive a preliminary impression of a company when he telephones to arrange an appointment. This is a trivial point, it's true; but it's just one of a series of smaller points upon which an analyst bases his inferences as to the relative attractiveness of a company. The impression I am talking about is, of course, that made by a telephone operator. There can be all the differences in the world in the voices of two different people on a telephone switchboard. (1960, 71)

Johnson later provides another example, repeating that analysts (should) draw a great many inferences from observations and impressions made while visiting a company and touring its plant:

> On one occasion when I was traveling on a Midwest itinerary the first stop that I made was at a large industrial concern in St. Paul. As I approached the group of buildings which comprised the company's offices and plants I was impressed by the beauty of the landscaping surrounding the entire area.
>
> While not all of the buildings were new, the overall architectural plan was one of simplicity and function; the buildings were all clean, well-painted; and the grounds surrounding them were unusually well-kept. As I entered the main gate a member of the company's security force approached, and as

soon as I gave him my name he affected instant recognition and said, "Oh, yes, Mr. Johnson, we're expecting you." (1960, 74)

It should be emphasized here that from the beginning of financial analysis to the present, an interest in, even fervor for, conducting site visits has been apparent. Several analysts who have commented on their careers at the profession's beginnings appear to have seen such visits as a highlight of their work—though most also seem aware of the visits' limitations. For example, in Graham's much cited and reprinted address to the analysts' convention of 1952, "Toward a Science of Security Analysis," he refers to the "40 or more plant inspections" that were on the scheduled field trips for the convention week, suggesting the chief emphasis would be on new products and process developments and that these would strongly influence analysts' conclusions about "the long pull prospects of the various companies." But he also emphasized that "dependable measurements such as projections of future earnings would be preferable"—while also wondering whether "a definite price could be put on future growth" (Graham [1952] 1995, 27), given the risk that an expected growth would materialize. Others have appeared to both simply treasure this process of site visits for its own sake and be intrigued by its extension to other countries. In his 1961 review of the evolution of financial analysis, Randell highlights the New York Society's "maiden voyage to Europe in 1959, when a large group of analysts traveled through England, France, Germany, and Holland interviewing top-level financial and business leaders." He adds that representative company and industrial complexes were visited en route, that another trip was scheduled for April 1961,[14] and that a Far Eastern visit was under study (1961, 74). That latter trip must have taken place in 1966, since Kahn—a founding member of the New York Society of Security Analysts who wrote a column for the *Financial Analysts Digest* between 1964 and 1971—reports in a letter to the *Financial Analysts Journal* on its sixtieth anniversary that one of his most memorable trips was that in 1966 to Japan. "We flew," he recounts, "from New York to Anchorage and Anchorage to Tokyo. The Japanese were so anxious to show how they were climbing out of the disaster of World War II that *they let us see everything*. We went to a small two story building to see a poor little company that was trying to enter into the radio business by copying U.S. technology. It was Sony, and today, its huge building is right across the street from me in Manhattan" (2005, 7, emphasis added).

14. The year is gleaned from the publication date of October 1961.

The analyst's interest in "plant inspections," "train rides," and "seeing everything" suggests the recognition of the importance of site visits. Accordingly, I have certainly not cited the above material on impressionist data collection procedures to denigrate the recommended ethnographic experience; I think such experiences are telling, and full-fledged ethnographers also take their cue from such impressions. And yet, what such harvesting of first impressions suggests, when we combine it with the shortness of analysts' visits, is again the substitute character of such observations. Impressions must fill in for nonobtainable information since the observation period is too short and the visitor has time only for talking to one or a few selected corporation officers. Any site visit, one assumes, must be better than none in terms of the opportunity it provides for evidence collection. Yet anthropological methodology suggests that first impressions may be misleading when they substitute for the whole of a qualitative case study. It is surely not possible to achieve the empirical saturation that inductive approaches recommend.

Proxy Projection

A third major area subject to proxy measurement is that of forecasting. To make the claim that analysts' forecasts are proxy projections may seem unwarranted, since all predictions, within whatever discipline, can only be approximations. However, the proxy claim is not about the element of intrinsic uncertainty in any projection but about the data that analysts use when they approach uncertainty probabilistically, as a kind of risk. Knight's often-quoted distinction between risk and uncertainty (1921, chaps. 7 and 20) suggests that uncertainty refers to future situations to which we cannot assign probabilities, while risk refers to situations where we take the position that we can make such assignments. Analysts, we may say, are in the business of transforming uncertainty into risk—into future scenarios to which probabilities can be assigned. Financial projection appears almost impossible according to some of the academic literature on the subject. A firm's performance, or a country's exchange rate, is affected by so many variables at different levels, it is subject to so much uncertainty, that analysts should in fact have a great deal of trouble getting things right. And they do, as empirical studies show (e.g., Chang, Khanna, and Palepu 2000; Tyszka and Zielonka 2002). This literature suggests that financial analysts' efforts at future measurement are often inaccurate, and the profession might be better off, at least with regard to some problems, avoiding projections. But at the same time, the basis for prices in financial markets today is "almost

100% forward looking," and earnings forecasts have become increasingly popular in and important to an efficient functioning of capital markets (Riahi-Belkaoui 1998, 20).

This, we should note, was not always the case. Interestingly, Graham ([1952] 1995) and Graham and Dodd in their foundational volume (1934) recommended the selection of "safe" bonds and undervalued securities based on a comparison between the "intrinsic" value of a security and its market price. The intrinsic value was the value justified by what the authors call "the facts," for example, assets, earnings, dividends paid, and definitive prospects (e.g., orders) in relation to debt. The authors emphasize the elusiveness of this concept compared with the definiteness of the market price. But that price does not simply reflect intrinsic value, since it tends to be distorted by artificial manipulation, psychological excesses, and so on. The work of the financial analyst is to identify intrinsic worth that is clearly higher than market prices. It is not to forecast future value. In fact, Graham and Dodd explicitly differentiate between "intrinsic value" and the "earning power" of a business, which points to the future. They see the latter as fraught with the problem of uncertainty that adheres to extending past earnings into the future and therefore reject it as a "general premise of security analysis" (1934, 17). Almost twenty years later, in his 1952 article on the rising science of security analysis, Graham continues to warn against the pitfalls of future-oriented analysis, though he also acknowledges its relevance for the selection of "growth stocks": "Can your work in this field be truly scientific unless it is solidly based on dependable *measurements*, that is, specific minimum projections of future earnings . . . ? Can a definite *price* be put on future growth, below which the stock is a sound purchase, above which it is dear, or in any event speculative? What is the risk that the expected growth will fail to materialize? What is the risk of an important downward change in the market's evaluation of favourable prospects?" ([1952] 1995, 27, emphasis in original). Graham adds the following: "A great deal of study in this field is necessary before dependable answers to such questions will be forthcoming. . . . In the meantime, I cannot help but feel that growth stock investment is still in the prescientific stage. It is at the same time more fascinating and less precise than the selection of safe bonds or undervalued securities."

Thus, what we find in these early discussions is a differentiation between forecasting attempts based on the extension of past data (see below), on the one hand, and the sound activity of identifying undervalued securities, on the other. The former may be "fascinating" but they are also "prescientific." The question raised earlier by Graham and Dodd of "how far it is the function of security analysis to anticipate changed conditions" still lingers. It is evident, the authors indicate, "that future changes are largely unpredictable, and that security analysis must ordinarily proceed on the assumption that the past record affords at least a rough guide to the future. The more questionable this assumption, the less valuable is the analysis" (1934, 21).

The foundational writings, then, remained largely hesitant in regard to future projections, seeing the future in terms of Knight's notion of uncertainty. They denounced rather than embraced the method that is now the main tool of financial analysts' forecasts: trending the past. How then do today's analysts make their projections, and on what data are they based? It is interesting that here again, quantitative and qualitative methods are distinguished (see Hooke 1998, chap. 11, particularly 200–204). The vast majority of financial forecasts are trend analyses or time-series analyses that project the future as a reflection of the past. Analysts prepare a sales forecast, for example, by examining historical results and then bring them forward through the use of trend lines and various moving-average techniques.[15] The acknowledged weakness of these techniques remains that they cannot capture unexpected events (from natural disasters and terrorist attacks to product innovations and new competition). Additional problems occur with business cycles. In general, cyclical events, such as seasonal weather conditions, appear to be easier to forecast because of their periodical nature (Tyszka and Zielonka 2002, 156). Yet unlike climatological cycles, business cycles are longer-term episodes, and they vary considerably in duration and magnitude.

In addition to the "rearview-mirror" approach, analysts may engage in "causal" analysis by identifying external, broadly economic, demographic, and other factors that shape the environment and prospects of a particular financial instrument or business product. For example, economic and population growth and savings patterns in countries like China or India may influence the prospects of aircraft producers and of the financial service industries in the United States and in Europe. These factors are quantified in econometric and regression analyses, and they may be complemented by customer surveys that quantify presumed demand.

The qualitative version of future projection will be applied when, for example, trending is impossible because a start-up company has no history.

---

15. A moving average is a weighted mean of the previous n data points. It "moves" in that when successive values are calculated, a new value comes into the sum of values from which the average is calculated and an old value drops out.

Hooke (1998) notes that the results of such projections are sometimes not more than educated guesswork, since the market reaction to truly new products is hard to gauge. The data for qualitative assessments come from four sources: experts, historical analogy, visionaries who may be consulted about long-term future developments, and consumer studies or market research. With the exception, perhaps, of the latter, all these data involve proxy measurements. Experts in many areas are not particularly good at predicting the future, as empirical studies show. Historical analogy is subject to problems similar to trend lines; it is clear, for example, that the historical contexts change, and unclear to what degree old experiences can be extended to the future. The judgments of "futurists" are presumably more speculative than those of experts.

What, then, can we conclude from this survey? For the present purpose the main conclusion surely is that financial projection is an area in which proxy measurements dominate. Quantitative forecasts work with the same type of proxy measurements as quantitative analysis but have to contend with the additional problem of future uncertainty. Qualitative forecasts resort mostly to professional judgments as surrogates for the impossibility of accurate measurement.

Proxy Detection

There is another set of strategies I wish to discuss briefly. These are not proxy versions of classical quantitative or qualitative measurement techniques but rather strategies of detection based on the assumption that things have been dressed up, or at least are not being disclosed to the degree necessary for a correct assessment and representation. While analysts may not embrace the full process of investigating the internal environment of their knowledge objects, they forage into that environment, using their own proxy strategies. Fully aware of the preconstructed character of the information they get, and the possible spin those issuing the information may have put on it, analysts seek to look behind the figures and accounts they receive. What defines strategies of detection is precisely this assumption: that there is something nondisclosed, nontransparent, and perhaps purposefully hidden about the reality they get to see. The strategies of detection attempt to remedy this situation by tricks of the trade. Here is a list of the tricks that I have collected:

· Reading the appendix of company reports
· Reading old company reports (and comparing them with new ones)

- Going to analysts' conferences
- Developing a personal relationship with the "investor relator," the person responsible for communicating with stockholders and investors
- Visiting the company
- Conducting mini-ethnographies

Some of these strategies, for example, site visits and mini-ethnographies, are part of analysts' repertoire of qualitative methods that are also used for purposes of detection. Others are simply heuristics developed in practice to open ways to the backstage of an investment unit. A number of strategies work through examining the consistency of the information provided. These include looking at:

- Employee turnover
- Number of defective products
- Company executives' criminal convictions
- Details of disagreements with auditors, bankers, and lawyers

By and large, sociologists and other social scientists can count on the neutral attitude, if not cooperation, of the human subjects and institutions they investigate. Once these subjects are convinced that the project is worth their time, and confidentiality is guaranteed, there would appear to be little reason for them to withhold or misrepresent information (cf. chapter 9 of this volume). Analysts are in quite a different situation. Their objects of study cannot remain anonymous, since they are to be individually evaluated and recommended for investment. Moreover, these entities have strategic goals related to their finances and will represent themselves accordingly, within and sometimes without existing regulations. Proxy strategies that rely on such actors' self-reports are confronted with an epistemic complication that analysts attempt to alleviate by the strategies listed but cannot easily resolve, short of abandoning the proxies.

Let me conclude this discussion and the chapter with a comment that outlines another epistemic complication for analysis, one potentially more fundamental than the previous. For many natural sciences, particularly laboratory sciences, measurement lies at the core of research. Measurements give access to epistemic objects (objects of investigation and knowledge), and these have peculiar characteristics when they are compared with our notion of everyday objects. The defining characteristic of an epistemic object is its changing, unfolding character—or its lack of "objectivity" and completeness of being and its nonidentity with itself. The lack of completeness of being is crucial: objects of knowledge in many fields have material instantiations, but they must simultaneously be conceived as unfolding structures of absences: as things that continually "explode" and "mutate" into something else, and that are as much defined by what they are not (but will, at some point, have become) as by what they are. The idea that "every component of an organism is as much of an organism as every other part," expressed by a scientist who had seen a particular factory explode in that way, offers an example of the experience of an unfolding ontology.

My point is that when fields work with epistemic proxies, they are also likely to forgo much of the complex question-generating opportunities that objects of knowledge provide. For example, a company analyst looking at an earning figure sees a long-term aggregate outcome of management practices and decisions but cannot unfold the actual decision processes and the variables that have contributed to them. Yet management practices, as analysts are well aware, may be highly relevant to performance outcomes. In the natural sciences, the unfolding ontology of initial knowledge objects leads over time to new objects, new realities, and scientific innovation. Access to and work with epistemic objects generates new understandings and leads to the change and development of scientific fields. Cutting off the measurement part of representation or delegating it to outside sources thus does not just add an element of indirection to the working practices of a science. When it is done on a massive scale (many sciences use some proxy measurements), it changes the character of inquiry. In the case of financial analysis, I propose that cutting off measurement processes is a defining characteristic of what that activity means: a form of research at a distance, conducted from exteriorized viewpoints. Such analysis, we might say, is what remains to be done when one of the major engines of unfolding reality and of fueling scientific change is turned off. To be sure, some of the unfolding questions will be taken on by other fields. For example, behavioral economics and rational-choice approaches now aggressively investigate decision-making processes with results of interest to many areas. But in the proxy science affected by the cutoff, research takes on characteristics of a process of information consumption outlined in the beginning of this chapter. The consumption stance I have postulated as a feature of financial analysis is clarified, I maintain, if we take account of the loss of an unfolding dynamic defining representation in other areas.

References

Arnott, Robert. 2004. "Is Our Industry Intellectually Lazy?" *Financial Analysts* 60:6–8.

Bell, Daniel. 1973. *The Coming of Post-industrial Society: A Venture in Social Forecasting*. New York: Basic Books.

Beunza, Daniel, and Raghu Garud. 2006. "Frame-Making: An Interpretive Approach to Valuation under Knightian Uncertainty." Working Paper. Columbia University, Business School.

Bildersee, John, Suresh Radhakrishnan, and Joshua Ronen. 1996. "Dispersion of Analysts' Forecasts, Precision of Earnings, and Trading Volume Reaction." *International Review of Financial Analysis* 5:99–111.

Bolliger, Guido. 2003. "On the Properties of Financial Analysts' Earning Forecasts: Some New Evidence." PhD diss., University of Neuchatel.

Butcher, Sarah. 2005. "Almost Everything You've Ever Wanted to Know about . . . the CFA Charter." http://news.efinancialcareers.co.uk/JOB_MARKET_ITEM/newsItemId-4085. Accessed October 7, 2007.

Castells, Manuel. 1996. *The Rise of the Network Society*. New York: Blackwell.

CFA Institute. 2007. CFA Facts Sheet 2007. http://www.cfainstitute.org/aboutus/pdf/CFAInstituteFactSheet.pdf. Accessed October 10, 2007.

———. 2010. CFA Facts Sheet 2010. http://www.cfainstitute.org/about/Documents/cfa_institute_factsheet.pdf. Accessed October 10, 2007.

Chang, James, Tarun Khanna, and Krishna Palepu. 2000. "Analyst Activity around the World." Working Paper. Harvard Business School.

Clement, Michael B., and Senyo Y. Tse. 2005. "Financial Analyst Characteristics and Herding Behavior in Forecasting." *Journal of Finance* 60:307–41.

Clews, Henry. 1908. *Fifty Years in Wall Street*. New York: Irving Publishing Co.

Collins, Harry M. 1985. *Changing Order: Replication and Induction in Scientific Practice*. London: Sage.

Collins, Randall. 2004. *Interaction Ritual Chains*. Princeton, NJ: Princeton University Press.

De Bondt, Werner, and Richard Thaler. 1985. "Does the Stock Market Overreact?" *Journal of Finance* 40:793–805.

———. 1987. "Further Evidence on Investor Overreaction and Stock Market Seasonality." *Journal of Finance* 42:557–81.

Gibson, William. 1984. *Neuromancer*. New York: Ace Books.

Graham, Benjamin. 1965. *The Intelligent Investor: A Book of Practical Counsel*. New York: Harper and Row.

———. [1952] 1995. "Toward a Science of Security Analysis." *Financial Analysts Journal* 51:25–28.

Graham, Benjamin, and David L. Dodd. 1934. *Security Analysis*. New York: McGraw-Hill.

Graham, Kathleen A. 2004. "The History of Investment Analysts' Societies." *Financial History Magazine* (Spring): 30–33.

Guetzkow, Joshua, Michèle Lamont, and Grégoire Mallard. 2004. "What Is Originality in the Social Sciences and the Humanities?" *American Sociological Review* 69:190–212.

Hayles, Katherine. 1999. *How We Became Posthuman: Virtual Bodies in Cybernetics, Literature and Informatics*. Chicago: University of Chicago Press.

Heintz, Bettina. 1993. *Die Herrschaft der Regel: Zur Grundlagengeschichte des Computers*. Frankfurt: Campus.

Hong, Harrison, and Jeffrey D. Kubik. 2003. "Analyzing the Analysts: Career Concerns and Biased Earnings Forecasts." *Journal of Finance* 58:313–51.

Hooke, Jeffrey C. 1998. *Security Analysis on Wall Street: A Comprehensive Guide to Today's Valuation Methods*. New York: John Wiley.

Jacobson, Timothy C. 1997. *From Practice to Profession: A History of the Financial Analysis Federation and the Investment Profession*. Charlottesville, VA: AIMR.

Johnson, Robert B. 1960. "What a Security Analyst Wants to Know." *Financial Analysts Journal* 16:71–77.

Kahn, Irving. 2005. "Early Days at the *Financial Analysts Journal*." *Financial Analysts Journal* 61:6–7.

Knight, Frank H. 1921. *Risk, Uncertainty and Profit*. Boston: Houghton Mifflin.

Knorr Cetina, Karin. 1981. *The Manufacture of Knowledge: An Essay on the Constructivist and Contextual Nature of Science*. Oxford: Pergamon Press.

———. 1999. *Epistemic Cultures: How the Sciences Make Knowledge*. Cambridge, MA: Harvard University Press.

———. 2003. "From Pipes to Scopes: The Flow Architecture of Financial Markets." *Distinktion* 7:7–23.

Knorr Cetina, Karin, and Urs Bruegger. 2002. "Global Microstructures: The Virtual Societies of Financial Markets." *American Journal of Sociology* 107:905–50.

Knorr Cetina, Karin, and Alex Preda. 2007. "The Temporalization of Financial Markets." *Annual Review of Theory, Culture, and Society* 24:116–38.

Kogut, Bruce, and Udo Zander. 1993. "Knowledge of the Firm and the Evolutionary Theory of the Multinational Corporation." *Journal of Business Studies* 24:625–45.

Lafontaine, Celine. 2004. *L'empire cybernétique: Des machines à penser à la pensée machine*. Paris: Editions du Seuil.

Lash, Scott. 2002. *Critique of Information*. New York: W. W. Norton.

Latour, Bruno, and Steve Woolgar. 1979. *Laboratory Life: The Social Construction of Scientific Facts*. Beverly Hills, CA: Sage.

Lefèvre, Edwin. 1923. *Reminiscences of a Stock Operator*. New York: G. H. Doran.

Levitt, Steven D., and Stephen J. Dubner. 2005. *Freakonomics: A Rogue Economist Explores the Hidden Side of Everything*. New York: William Morrow.

Lynch, Michael. 1985. *Art and Artifact in Laboratory Science: A Study of Shop Work and Shop Talk in a Research Laboratory*. London: Routledge and Kegan Paul.

Lyotard, Jean-François. [1979] 1984. *The Postmodern Condition*. Manchester: Manchester University Press.

Mackay, Charles. [1841] 1932. *Extraordinary Popular Delusions and the Madness of Crowds*. Boston: L. C. Page.

Marmer, Harry S. 1996. "Visions of the Future: The Distant Past, Yesterday, Today, and Tomorrow." *Financial Analysts Journal* 52:9–12.

Mars, Frank. 1998. "Wir sind alle Seher: Die Praxis der Aktienanalyse." PhD diss., University of Bielefeld.

McGeehan, Patrick. 2002. "The Crux of Reform: Autonomous Stock Rating." *New York Times*, October 7, C1, C6.

Meyer, John W., and Ronald Jepperson. 2000. "The 'Actors' of Modern Society." *Sociological Theory* 18:100–20.

Mirowski, Philip. 2002. *Machine Dreams: Economics Becomes a Cyborg Science*. Cambridge: Cambridge University Press.

Morgenson, Gretchen. 2001. "S.E.C. Leader Cites Conflicts of Analysts at Large Firms." *New York Times*, August 1, C1–2.

Nicholson, Colin. 1994. *Writing and the Rise of Finance*. Cambridge: Cambridge University Press.

Poitras, Geoffrey. 2005. *Security Analysis and Investment Strategy*. Oxford: Blackwell Publishing.

Preda, Alex. 2006. "Socio-technical Agency in Financial Markets: The Case of the Stock Ticker." *Social Studies of Science* 36:753–82.

Randell, Donald. 1961. "Evolution of the Analyst." *Financial Analysts Journal* 17:67–75.

Riahi-Belkaoui, Ahmed. 1998. "Financial Analysis and the Predictive Approach." In *Financial Analysis and the Predictability of Important Economic Events*, 1–32. Westport, CT: Quorum Books.

Schatzki, Theodore R. 1996. *Social Practices: A Wittgensteinian Approach to Human Activity and the Social*. New York: Cambridge University Press.

Shefrin, Hersh. 1999. *Beyond Greed and Fear*. Boston: Harvard Business School Publishing.

Shiller, Robert. 2000. *Irrational Exuberance*. Princeton, NJ: Princeton University Press.

Swedberg, Richard. 2005. "Conflicts of Interests in the US Brokerage Industry." In *The Sociology of Financial Markets*, ed. Karin Knorr Cetina and Alex Preda, 187–203. Oxford: Oxford University Press.

Thaler, Richard, ed. 1993. *Advances in Behavioral Finance*. New York: Russell Sage Foundation.

Traweek, Sharon. 1987. "Discovering Machines: Nature in the Age of Its Mechanical Reproduction." In *Making Time: Anthropologies of Time in Science and High Technology Organizations*, ed. Frank A. Dubinskas, 39–91. Philadelphia: Temple University Press.

Turkle, Sherry. [1984] 2005. *The Second Self: Computers and the Human Spirit*. New York: Simon and Schuster.

Tyszka, Tadeusz, and Piotr Zielonka. 2002. "Expert Judgments: Financial Analysts versus Weather Forecasters." *Journal of Psychology and Financial Markets* 3:152–60.

Webster, Frank, ed. 2004. *The Information Society Reader*. London: Routledge.

———. [1995] 2006. *Theories of the Information Society*. London: Routledge.

Williams, Raymond. 1977. *Marxism and Literature*. Oxford: Oxford University Press.

Wolfe, Harry D. 1952. "Science as a Trustworthy Tool." *Financial Analysts Journal* 8: 45–50.

Zuckerman, Ezra W. 1999. "The Categorical Imperative: Securities Analysts and the Illegitimacy Discount." *American Journal of Sociology* 104:1398–438.

———. 2004. "Structural Incoherence and Stock Market Activity." *American Sociological Review* 69:405–32.

Zuckerman, Ezra W., and Hayagreeva Rao. 2004. "Shrewd, Crude, or Simply Deluded? Comovement and the Internet Stock Phenomenon." *Industrial and Corporate Change* 13:171–213.

CONTRIBUTORS

ANDREW ABBOTT is the Gustavus F. and Ann M. Swift Distinguished Service Professor in the Department of Sociology of the University of Chicago. His substantive work has focused on professions, occupations, and knowledge. He has also written widely on methodology and the philosophy of social science, as well as on general issues in social theory.

DANIEL BRESLAU is associate professor in the Department of Science and Technology in Society at Virginia Tech. His work involves the role of social sciences in the construction of modern institutions, with an emphasis on economics, sociology, and statistics. He is currently preparing a book on economics and the politics of electricity market design in the United States.

CHARLES CAMIC is John Evans Professor of Sociology and a member of the Science in Human Culture Program at Northwestern University. He has published extensively in the history of the social sciences and is completing a book on the social origins of Thorstein Veblen's economics. Recently, he has coedited *Essential Writings of Thorstein Veblen* (2011).

CRYSTAL FLEMING is a PhD candidate in sociology and a fellow at the Weatherhead Center for International Affairs at Harvard University. Her research examines practices of meaning making and knowledge production in diverse settings, as well as perceptions of inequality and strategies for responding to racism and discrimination across a range of national contexts. Her dissertation bridges these agendas by analyzing boundary work and antiracist discourse in contemporary depictions of French colonial slavery.

ANTHONY T. GRAFTON is Henry Putnam University Professor of History at Princeton University. He studied history, classics, and history of science at the University of Chicago and University College London and received his PhD at Chicago in 1975. His books include *Joseph Scaliger* (1983–93), *The Footnote: A Curious History* (1999), and *Worlds Made by Words* (2009).

NEIL GROSS is associate professor of sociology at the University of British Columbia. He is the author of *Richard Rorty: The Making of an American Philosopher* (2008) and the editor of *Sociological Theory*. His next book will be about professors and politics.

JOHAN HEILBRON is a sociologist at Erasmus University Rotterdam and at the Centre de sociologie européenne (CSE-CNRS) in Paris. Among his research interests are the historical sociology of the social sciences, economic sociology, and the sociology of transnational exchange. Recent books include *The Rise of Social Theory* (1995), *The Rise of the Social Sciences and the Formation of Modernity* (with L. Magnusson and B. Wittrock; 1998), and *Pour une histoire des sciences sociales: Hommage à Pierre Bourdieu* (with R. Lenoir and G. Sapiro; 2004).

KATRI HUUTONIEMI is a doctoral candidate in environmental policy at the University of Helsinki. Her doctoral thesis investigates the concepts and conventions of evaluating interdisciplinary research. Her publications include the report "Promoting Interdisciplinary Research: The Case of the Academy of Finland" (2005), "Analyzing Interdisciplinarity: Typology and Indicators" (*Research Policy*, 2010), and "Evaluating Interdisciplinary Research" (*Oxford Handbook of Interdisciplinarity*, 2010).

SARAH E. IGO is associate professor of history at Vanderbilt University and the author of *The Averaged American: Surveys, Citizens, and the Making of a Mass Public* (2007). She is currently writing a book on the history of privacy in the twentieth century.

SHEILA JASANOFF is Pforzheimer Professor of Science and Technology Studies at Harvard University's John F. Kennedy School of Government. Her work explores the role of science and technology in the law, politics, and policy of modern democracies. Among her books are *Controlling Chemicals* (1985), *The Fifth Branch* (1990), and *Designs on Nature* (1990). She was founding chair of the Department of Science and Technology Studies at Cornell University and has held distinguished visiting appointments at numerous institutions, including MIT, Cambridge University, Kyoto University, the University of Vienna, and the Wissenschaftskolleg Berlin.

KARIN KNORR CETINA is professor of sociology at the University of Chicago. Most of her work is based on observational studies of complex expert settings—for example, of high-energy physics and molecular biology and of global financial markets in Zurich, New York, London, and Sidney. Her recent publications include *Epistemic Cultures: How the Sciences Make Knowledge* (1999), *The Sociology of Financial Markets* (edited with A. Preda; 2005), and *Maverick Markets: Financial Markets as Global Social Forms* (forthcoming).

ANDREW LAKOFF is associate professor of sociology, anthropology, and communication at the University of Southern California. He is the author of *Pharmaceutical Reason: Knowledge and Value in Global Psychiatry* (2006) and editor of *Disaster and the Politics of Intervention* (2010). His current research concerns the contemporary intersection of public health and national security expertise in response to the problem of emerging infectious disease.

MICHÈLE LAMONT is the Robert I. Goldman Professor of European Studies and professor of sociology and African and African American studies at Harvard University. Her most recent books are *How Professors Think* (2009) and *Successful Societies* (with Peter A. Hall, 2009). Previous books include *Money, Morals, and Manners* (1992) and *The Cultural Territories of Race* (1999). Ongoing projects concern interdisciplinary collaboration, responses to stigmatization, valuation processes, and social resilience as a dimension of successful societies.

REBECCA LEMOV is the author of *World as Laboratory: Experiments with Mice, Mazes, and Men* (2005). An assistant professor in the Department of the History of Science, Harvard University, she is currently writing a book about mid-twentieth-century experiments in gathering subjective data, including dreams.

GRÉGOIRE MALLARD is assistant professor of sociology at Northwestern University. He is completing a book on the role of interpretation in the development of international treaties in the field of nuclear nonproliferation. He coedited *Global Science and National Sovereignty: Studies in Historical Sociology of Science* (2009). His articles have appeared in the *American Sociological Review*, *Critique Internationale*, *The Nonproliferation Review*, and *Sociologie du travail*.

LAURA STARK is assistant professor in the Program in Science in Society and the Department of Sociology at Wesleyan University. She works on the cultural history of science and moral sensibilities. Her forthcoming book is titled *Behind Closed Doors: IRBs and the Making of Ethical Research*.

MARILYN STRATHERN is the William Wyse Professor of Social Anthropology at the University of Cambridge. Her most recent book is *Kinship, Law, and the Unexpected: Relatives Are Always a Surprise* (2005).